COMPUTER FUNDAMENTALS AND PROGRAMMING IN C

Second Edition

A K Sharma

Professor
Department of Computer Engineering
B S Anangpuria Institute of Technology and Management
Faridabad

Universities Press

COMPUTER FUNDAMENTALS AND PROGRAMMING IN C

UNIVERSITIES PRESS (INDIA) PRIVATE LIMITED

Registered office
3-6-747/1/A & 3-6-754/1, Himayatnagar, Hyderabad 500 029, Telangana, India
info@universitiespress.com; www.universitiespress.com

Distributed by
Orient Blackswan Private Limited

Registered office
3-6-752 Himayatnagar, Hyderabad 500 029, Telangana, India

Other offices
Bengaluru, Bhopal, Chennai, Guwahati, Hyderabad, Jaipur, Kolkata, Lucknow, Mumbai, New Delhi, Noida, Patna, Vijayawada

First edition published by Dhanpat Rai Publications 2005
Second edition published by Universities Press 2018

ISBN: 978-93-86235-29-9

501352

11072017

Typeset in Palatino 11/13 by
MacroTex Solutions, Chennai 600 091, Tamil Nadu, India

Printed in India at Rajiv Book Binding House, Delhi

Published by
Universities Press (India) Private Limited
3-6-747/1/A & 3-6-754/1, Himayatnagar, Hyderabad 500 029, Telangana, India

Dedicated to

Dr J P Gupta, my Guru

PREFACE TO THE SECOND EDITION

This second edition of *Computer Fundamentals and Programming in C* has been revised to include key topics that are often covered at the undergraduate level. The book continues to follow the precedent set by the first edition in its lucid treatment of concepts, maintaining a student-friendly approach. The contents have been revised in accordance with the feedback and suggestions received from teachers who handle the subject as well as those from the publisher. First edition topics that are no longer relevant have been removed, while several new ones have been included to enable the student keep abreast of emergent technologies in computers and communication. Distinctive features of the second edition include:

1. A detailed discussion on cache memory
2. An exclusive chapter on microprocessors with an introduction to multicore microprocessors
3. New sections on binary arithmetic operations and the concept of interpretation
4. A new chapter on Boolean algebra and logic gates
5. A new section on System Vulnerabilities and Application Study in the chapter on Operating Systems
6. An expansive introduction to searching and sorting techniques in the chapter on Arrays
7. A new chapter on preprocessor for C programming language
8. More examples in each chapter of the section on C programming.

I hope that the readers will like this revised edition and, as before, provide me their much-needed feedback and comments for improving the book further.

PREFACE TO THE FIRST EDITION

Encouraged by the overwhelming appreciation and encouragement I received for my books on Computer Science with C++, I now present this book, *Fundamentals of Computers and Programming with C*, which is designed to serve as a first course on Fundamentals of Computers and C Programming for students with or without programming knowledge. The book can be useful as a first course for students pursuing Diploma, B.Tech., MCA, B.Sc. (Computer Science), BCA, BBA, BBS and 'A' and 'B' level syllabus prescribed by DOEACC. The various topics of the book have been explained in clear and simple language.

The book is divided into **two** parts: **Computer Fundamentals** and **Programming with C**. The **first part** discusses the basics of computer hardware, computer networks and operating systems. Recent trends in microprocessors and their related technologies have been discussed. Keeping the engineers and working professionals in mind, a special chapter on I/O ports and Connectors has been provided.

The **second part** introduces C as a programming language. The programs have been designed in such a way that simple programs are presented initially, touching upon more difficult programs towards the later part of the book.

For serious programmers, **graded problems** have been included at the end of each chapter. Although the solutions to these problems have been given, it is expected that the students would solve them on their own before comparing their programs with the solutions provided in the book.

All the programs in this book have been practically executed and tested on the computers.

At the end of each programming chapter, a section called **Test your Skills** has been given. This will definitely help the students towards preparing for **Campus Interviews.** At the end of the book, a **glossary of computer terms** is also available.

During the preparation of this book, I have talked, listened, discussed and argued with many people, all of whom deserve my thanks. To name a few and mention some of their contributions, I am thankful to Dr Ashok Kumar, Director YMCA for his encouragement and Prof. R K Gaur for suggestions and guidance. I also owe my thanks to my well wishers Prof. C K Nagpal, Prof. Rajiv Kapoor, Prof. S K Gupta, Prof. Amit Goel and Prof. Aushutosh, Prof. Rajender, Prof. Savita, Prof. Jyoti and Prof. Kavita Kapur.

Dr J P Gupta, Dr Moinuddin, and Dr D P Agarwal, my research guides, have a special place in my heart. I have tremendous regards for these scholars of eminence. I am thankful to them for their encouragement throughout. I am also thankful to my wife Suman and my daughter Sagun who gave me their precious time to write this book

My special thanks go to Sh. Ish Kapur of Dhanpat Rai Publications (P) Ltd. His vision and planning make beautiful books happen. His suggestions and comments remain very valuable to me.

It is possible that some errors might have inadvertently crept in. I shall be grateful if the same are brought to my notice. Suggestions for further improvement of the book will be thankfully acknowledged. I wish the readers success and many accomplishments.

A K Sharma

CONTENTS

Preface to the second edition *v*

PART I Computer Fundamentals 1

1 Fundamentals of Computers 3

1.1 Data and information 3
1.2 Introduction to computation and computers 4
1.3 Components of computer hardware 6
1.4 Types of computers 24
Exercises 26

2 Introduction to Microprocessors 27

2.1 History 27
2.2 Microprocessor fundamentals 28
2.3 Motherboards 37
Exercises 40

3 Input/Output Devices 41

3.1 Input devices 41
3.2 Graphic input devices – Pointing devices 44
3.3 Output devices 48
Exercises 57

4 Data Representation 58

4.1 Introduction 58
4.2 Number systems 58
4.3 Octal number notation 67
4.4 Hexadecimal notation 70
4.5 Data representation 73
4.6 Internal storage encoding of characters 79
4.7 Binary arithmetic operations 84
Exercises 90

5 Boolean Algebra and Logic Gates 92

5.1 Boolean algebra 92
5.2 Logic gates 104
Exercises 108

6 Introduction to Programming Languages 110
6.1 Introduction 110
6.2 Low-level languages 110
6.3 High-level languages 113
6.4 Generations of programming languages 120
Exercises *123*

7 Operating Systems: An Introduction 124
7.1 Introduction 124
7.2 Evolution of operating systems 126
7.3 Multiprocessor operating systems 132
7.4 Networking operating systems 134
7.5 System vulnerabilities and application security 134
7.6 Functions of operating systems 142
7.7 Unix kernel architecture 143
7.8 Linux kernel architecture 144
7.9 Windows architecture 145
7.10 Mach system architecture 147
Exercises *148*

8 Computer Networks and Internet 149
8.1 Introduction 149
8.2 Data communication 149
8.3 Modulation 161
8.4 Network devices 161
8.5 Local area networks 164
8.6 Wide area network (WAN) 170
8.7 Switching techniques 171
8.8 Indian networks 173
8.9 Internet and protocols 174
8.10 Backbone network 177
8.11 Network connecting devices 178
8.12 Client server model 181
8.13 Mobile phone communication 181
8.14 Home page 186
8.15 Network security 191
Exercises *197*

PART II Programming in C **199**

9 Introduction to C 201
9.1 The history 201
9.2 Characters used in C 202

9.3 Data types 202
9.4 C tokens 205
9.5 Structure of a C program 210
9.6 The `printf ()` and `scanf ()` Functions 212
9.7 Comments 215
9.8 Escape sequence (Backslash character constants) 217
9.10 Use of an editor 220
Frequently asked questions *220*
Test your skills *221*
Exercises *223*

10 Operators and Expressions **226**
10.1 Operators 226
10.2 Arithmetic operators 226
10.3 Relational and logical operators 232
10.4 Order of evaluation of expressions 236
10.5 Some special operators 242
10.6 Assignment statement 243
10.7 Bitwise operators 245
Frequently asked questions *251*
Test your skills *252*
Exercises *256*

11 Flow of Control **258**
11.1 Introduction 258
11.2 The compound statement 259
11.3 Selective execution (Conditional statements) 259
11.4 Repetitive execution (Iterative statements) 276
11.5 Nested loops 290
11.6 The `goto` statement (unconditional branching) 294
11.7 Graded problems 298
Frequently asked questions *301*
Test your skills *302*
Exercises *306*

12 Input–Output Functions **310**
12.1 Introduction 310
12.2 Buffered I/O 311
12.3 Single character functions 312
12.4 String based functions 319
12.5 More on `scanf ()` and `printf ()` functions 324
Test your skills *328*
Exercises *329*

13 Arrays 331
13.1 Introduction 331
13.2 One-dimensional arrays 332
13.3 Strings 363
13.4 Multidimensional arrays 368
13.5 Array of strings 373
13.6 Array initialization 375
13.7 Representation of arrays in physical memory 378
13.8 Applications of arrays 383
13.9 Graded problems 387
Frequently asked questions *394*
Test your skills *395*
Exercises *398*

14 Structures 400
14.1 Introduction 400
14.2 Defining a structure in C 401
14.3 Initializing structures 407
14.4 Assignment of complete structures 407
14.5 Nested structures 408
14.6 User defined data types 410
14.7 Enumerated data types 412
14.8 Unions 418
14.9 Graded problems 421
Frequently asked questions *428*
Test your skills *428*
Exercises *432*

15 Pointers 434
15.1 Introduction 434
15.2 Pointer variables 436
15.3 Pointers and arrays 442
15.4 Array of pointers 448
15.5 Pointers and structures 450
15.6 Dynamic allocation 452
Frequently asked questions *459*
Test your skills *460*
Exercises *462*

16 Functions 465
16.1 Introduction 465
16.2 Function declaration 466
16.3 Function prototypes 468

16.4 Calling a function 469
16.5 Parameter passing in functions 472
16.6 Returning values from functions 487
16.7 Passing structures to functions 488
16.8 Scope rules of variables 492
16.9 Storage class specifiers 495
16.10 Recursion 498
16.11 Libraries 504
16.12 Graded problems 516
Frequently asked questions *529*
Test your skills *529*
Exercises *535*

17 Files **538**

17.1 Data and information 538
17.2 File concepts 539
17.3 File organization 542
17.4 Files in C 542
17.5 Files and streams 543
17.6 Working with files using stream I/O 545
17.7 Sequential file organization 560
17.8 Direct file organization 576
17.9 Graded problems 579
Exercises *587*

18 Preprocessor **589**

18.1 Introduction 589
18.2 The # define directive 589
18.3 Conditional compilation 596
18.4 File inclusion 598
Frequently asked questions *599*
Test your skills *600*

Index *603*

Part I

Computer Fundamentals

CHAPTER

1 Fundamentals of Computers

1.1 DATA AND INFORMATION

The terms data and information are often used interchangeably. Let us now put them in perspective and define them as follows:

Data: It is the plural form of *datum* meaning fact. It can be defined as a collection of incoherent symbols and observations. For example: a collection of meaningless numbers, words, quantities etc. are data, such as those given in Fig. 1.1. The random display of numbers in this figure does not convey any meaning and therefore we can term this collection as data items.

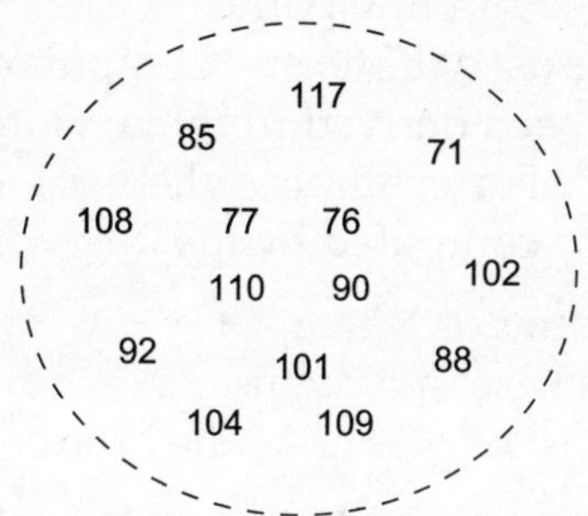

Fig. 1.1 Collection of incoherent numbers – data items

Information: When a data item is placed in context with another data item or items so that this arranged data becomes meaningful, then it is termed as information. For instance, the data items of Fig. 1.1 have been rearranged in a tabular in Table 1.1.

Now this table provides the meaning that students with roll nos. 101, 102, … , 117 secured the marks 71, 88, …, and 76 respectively, which is nothing but information.

Information is one of the most important resources available to humankind. It is growing at such a fast rate that humans have difficulty in keeping pace with it. Every day, the radio, television, newspapers, books, journals, satellite channels, and cinema are pouring data and information at a fast, almost unmanageable rate.

It may be noted from Table. 1.1, that some data items listed under the column 'Roll' have been tabulated in the context of related data items under the column 'Marks'. In this Information age, computers are being used very widely to manage information. The computer is used to generate, process, store, and transmit information.

Table. 1.1 Arranged data - information

Roll	Marks
101	71
102	88
104	85
108	92
109	90
110	77
117	76

1.2 INTRODUCTION TO COMPUTATION AND COMPUTERS

The philosophers and saints of the past were adept at recording information and performing computations. For instance, consider the following facts:

- The 90ft tall *Samrat Yantra* built by King Jai Singh of Jaipur measures the time with a precision of two seconds per day.
- A French astronomer validated that – "the movement of stars calculated by Vedic scholars 4500 years ago, does not differ by a minute from the tables of today.
- Most of the Indian scriptures were written on thin sheets of the bark of a tree called Bhojpatra and also on palm-tree leaves.

The computations were done manually and the information was recorded on clay tablets, walls of caves, and sheets of Bhojpatra.

It may be noted that we have used the term –'Computation' instead of 'Calculation'. The word 'Computation' has been derived from the word '**Compute**' which means - "to determine by calculation". For example, whether a company that sells N items has made a profit or not can be computed by the following steps:

1. Calculate the selling amount of N items.
2. Calculate the cost of purchase of N items.
3. If the selling amount > cost of purchase, then the company has earned a profit.

In the first two steps we have made mathematical calculations. In step three, we have determined that the company has made profit, based on the calculations done in steps one and two. Now, we can say that *the device that can compute is called a* ***computer***. The above given three steps indicate that a computer must have at least the following components:

1. **Arithmetic Unit:** that can do arithmetic calculations
2. **Logical Unit:** that can take logical decisions based on the arithmetic calculations performed by the Arithmetic Unit
3. **Control Unit:** that can control the actions of the arithmetic and logical units.

In a present day computer, the above components are encased in one unit called processor, as shown in Fig. 1.2. The processor consists of: ALU (arithmetic and logical unit) and CU (control unit). It may be noted that the arithmetic and logical units have been fabricated as one unit called ALU. The ALU also has one more component called registers which are sets of memory locations used for storing temporary and intermediate results.

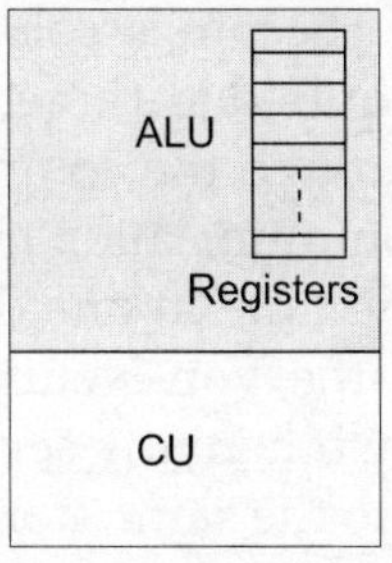

Fig. 1.2 The processor

The processor is capable of performing arithmetic and logical operations under the control of the control unit. However, it is a passive device, in the sense that it cannot work on its own. The processor needs to be instructed as to what operation is to be performed on what data. The set of instruction that are provided to the computer to accomplish a task is called a 'program'. A sample program is given below:

```
1. Input N                /* read n umber of items*/
2. Input itemCost              /* read cost price of one »tem */
3. input salePrice             /* read sale price of one item */
4. tot_temCost = itemCost * N  /* Calculate cost price of N
                                  items */
5. tot_salePrice= salePrice * N/* Calculate sale price of N
                                  items */
6. if (tot_salePrice> totj_temCost)
   profit = tot_salePrice- tot_temCost      /* compute profit*/
7. Output profit               /* print the profit*/
```

A program such as that given above needs to be stored in some storage device called **store**. Thus, the computer system needs two devices: the processor and the store. Therefore the essential architecture of a computer as proposed by Von-Neumann consisted of two components – a processor and a store connected through a communication channel, as shown in Fig. 1.3.

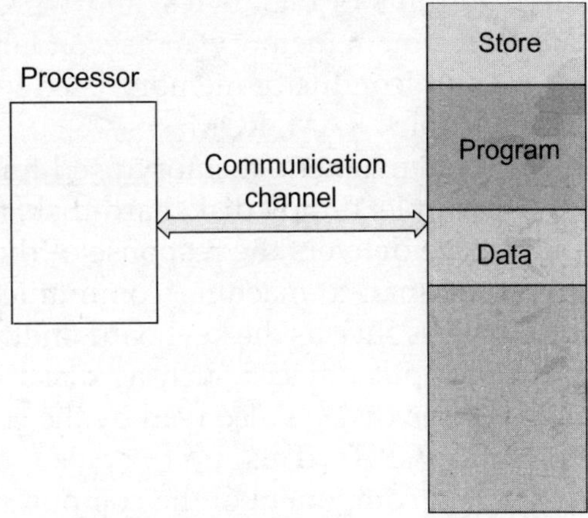

Fig.1.3 Von Neumann architecture

The processor reads the program instructions, executes them, and performs the required arithmetic and logic operations on the data. The instruction and data travel through the communication channel to and from the processor and store. Since the communication channel is only one, only one item (instruction or data) can travel at one time in one direction on the communication channel. This restriction is known as the **Von-Neumann bottleneck**. Therefore, computers based on this architecture are inherently serial and sequential. The program and its associated data are loaded into the same store. Therefore, it is also called a **stored program computer.** A precise definition of a computer is given below:

Computer: It is an electronic device which processes data under the control of a set of instructions called a program. It accepts data, performs mathematical and logical operations on the data as per the instructions of the program.

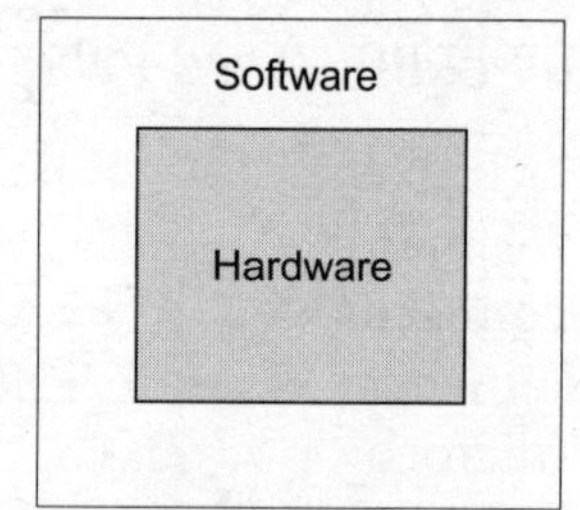

Fig. 1.4 Computer system

In fact, a computer is a complete system in itself. The computer system has two components – hardware and software, as shown in Fig. 1.4. The **hardware** is a programmable digital machine capable of performing computations. It consists of electronic circuits, integrated circuits (ICs), memories, cables, keyboard etc. **Software** is a collection of all the programs that run on the hardware .

1.3 COMPONENTS OF COMPUTER HARDWARE

A present day computer has the following four main components:

1. **Memory**: This part of the computer is used as storage for programs as well as data. It is measured in units of bits, bytes, and words. Memory is broadly divided into two categories: main memory and secondary memory.
   a. The main memory is a semiconductor memory, used for temporary storage of program and data. Example : RAM, ROM
   b. The secondary memory is magnetic memory used for permanent storage of programs and data. Example: floppy disk, hard-disk, flash drive etc.
2. **Input Unit**: An input device delivers the response of the user to the computer system thereby providing man-to-machine communication. The input unit comprises a variety of devices such as the keyboard, mouse, optical mark reader (OMR), disk etc. Certain input devices such as disks are inherently storage devices. The data recorded on disks is also read by the computer system.
3. **Central Processing Unit** (CPU): This unit is also called the 'processor' indicating that it is the main component of the computer system that processes the instruction as well as data. It performs the following tasks:
   a. Fetches instructions from the memory.

b. Interprets (understands) the fetched instruction to determine what action is to be performed and on what data.
c. Fetches data, if required, from the main memory or an input device.
d. Performs arithmetic or logic operations on the data.
e. Writes data to the target location in memory or a device.

4. **Output Unit**: An output device delivers the results of a program to the user thereby providing a way of machine-to-man communication. The output unit comprises a variety of devices such the computer screen, printer, plotter, disks. The output of a computation is generally permanently stored on a disk. The disks are used both for input and output purposes.

It may be noted that input and output devices act as an interface of the computer for man–machine communication. The components of the computer system can be connected to each other in many ways to a give a variety of computer architectures. However, bus based computer architecture is more popular, especially at microcomputer level. A 'bus based' computer architecture is shown in Fig. 1.5.

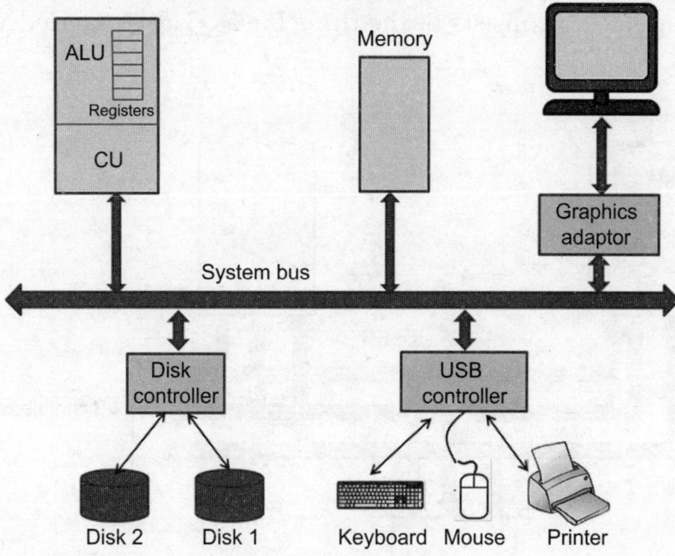

Fig.1.5 A bus based computer

We must view the computer as a system because it is an interrelated group of multiple components that accepts input, processes it and produces output. The necessary communication among the various components takes place through a system bus, where the **bus** is a group of electrically conducting wires over which data or information is transferred from one device to another. In computer systems, buses are classified into three categories: data, address, and control buses. A brief discussion on these buses is given overleaf.

1. **Data bus:** This bus transfers data between two devices such as the CPU and main memory. The size of the data bus is generally in proportion to the power of the CPU. For example, a 64bit microprocessor shall have a data bus of size 64bits. This bus is generally bidirectional in nature.
2. **Address bus:** Every device connected to a computer system is identified by a unique address. The address bus carries the address of a device with which another device desire to interact. For example, when the CPU wants to read an instruction from the main memory then it places the address of the instruction on the address bus. The address is precisely mapped to the location within the main memory from where the instruction is loaded onto the data bus, which carries it to the CPU.
3. **Control bus:** This bus carries control signals to connected devices on the computer system. For instance, when the address of an instruction is mapped onto a specified location of the main memory, the CPU sends a 'read' signal to the main memory over the control bus. On receiving the signal, the main memory loads the instruction on the data bus.

These three buses are collectively called a system bus. This means that the system bus as shown in Fig. 1.5 consists of the three buses. The expanded view is given in Fig. 1.6.

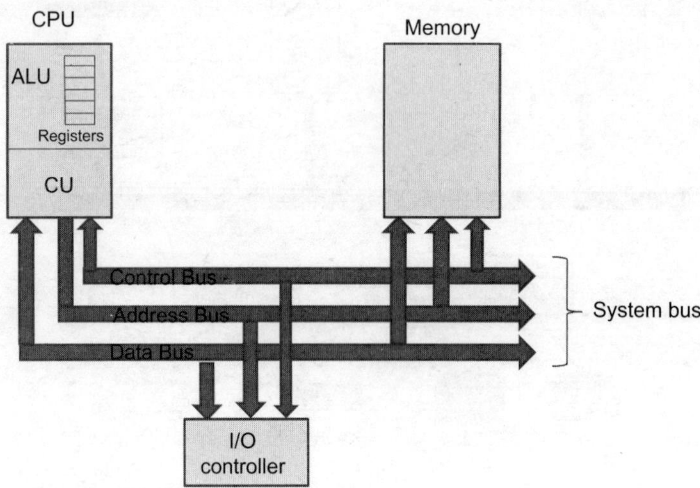

Fig. 1.6 Three groups of lines comprising the system bus

1.3.1 Components of the CPU

The main components of the CPU are: control unit (CU), arithmetic and logical unit (ALU) and a set of registers.

1. **Control Unit** (CU): This component is responsible for controlling the movement of data and instructions in and out of the memory and CPU. It decodes the fetched instruction and initiates the desired operation to be performed by the ALU. This activity is called instruction execution.

2. **Arithmetic and logical unit** (ALU): During instruction execution, it receives the signal from the CU and accordingly it performs the desired arithmetic and logical operations on the data.
3. **Registers:** These are sets of temporary memory locations in the CPU. Depending upon the power of the CPU, the size of the registers varies in the power of 2 i.e., 8 bits, 16 bits, 32 bits, 64 bits, 128 bits etc. The registers are of two types: general purpose registers and special purpose registers.
   a. General Purpose registers: These registers are also called user registers. The programmer can use them for storing, operands, temporary results etc.
   b. Special registers: These registers are used for special purpose. Some of them are:
      i. Program counter(PC): It contains the address of the next instruction to be executed.
      ii. Instruction register (IR): It contains the instruction currently being executed.
      iii. Memory address register (MAR): Contains the address of a location in the memory.
      iv. Memory data register (MDR): This register is a buffer between the CPU and main memory. The data is temporarily held in MDR before it is transferred from source to destination.
      v. Accumulator (ACC): This is the main register of the ALU. It contains one of the operands of an operation to be performed in the ALU. The other operand is held in a temporary register. The result of the operation is accumulated in the ACC.

In addition to the above, a CPU also contains a clock, as shown in Fig. 1.7. The purpose of the clock is to accurately control the speed and operations of the computer in general and the CPU in particular. Its speed is measured in Hz. A modern day microprocessor such as Intel -i3 has a clock speed of 3.33GHz.

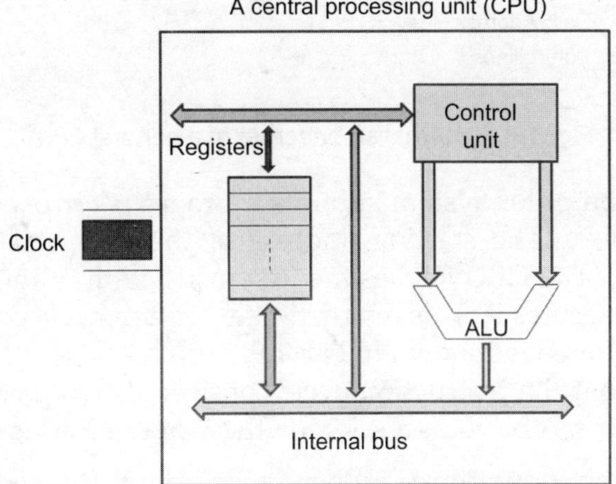

Fig. 1.7 A CPU

1.3.2 Internal Architecture of the CPU

The internal architecture of a CPU is given in Fig. 1.8. The CPU executes instructions stored in the main memory of the computer. An instruction usually consists of two parts: **op-code** and **operands.** The operation code specifies what operation is to be done (add, multiply, compare etc.). The operands specify the address of the data. The address may be a main memory address, or a CPU register number, or device address from where the data is to be accessed. The CPU clock controls the timing of each basic operation. The length of time required to go through one machine operation is called a *machine cycle.* The number of machine cycles required to execute one program instruction is called an instruction cycle.

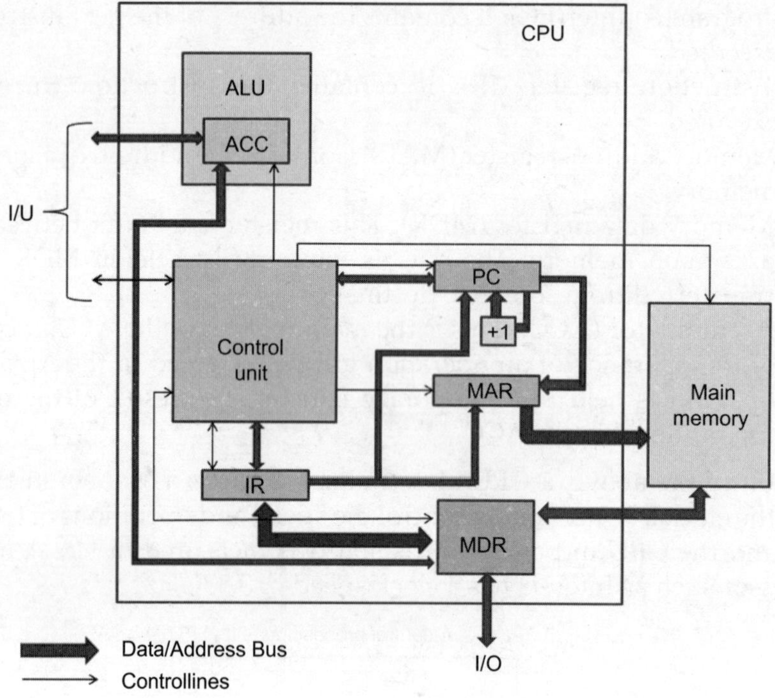

Fig. 1.8 Internal architecture of a general CPU

The user of the computer system submits a program for execution. It is loaded into the main memory. The starting address of the program is loaded into the program counter PC. The CPU fetches the first instruction of the program from the main memory and executes it. This instruction execution cycle continues till a 'Halt' instruction is encountered, as shown in Fig. 1.9.

It may be noted that the instruction cycle consists of two parts: fetch operations and execute operations. A brief discussion on these operations is given below:

1. **Instruction fetch operation**: When a program is executed, the address of its first executable instruction is loaded into the program counter (PC).

The address is then transferred to the memory address register (MAR). The address stored in the MAR is the address of a location in main memory. It is placed on the address bus. The CU issues a 'read' signal to main memory. From the specified address, the main memory places the instruction onto the data bus that transfers it to the memory data register (MDR). From the MDR, the instruction is transferred to the instruction register (IR). The IR has two parts: IR(opcode) and IR(address), as shown in Fig. 1.10

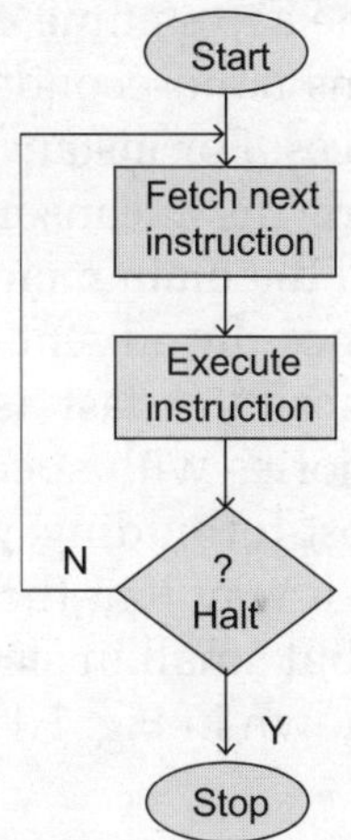

Fig. 1.9 Instruction cycle

2. **Instruction execution operation**: The IR decodes the opcode part of the instruction to determine what operation is desired. The operand part of the instruction is loaded into the MAR or an internal CPU register, depending upon the operand being an address or data. If the operand is an address then the data is brought from the main memory in a similar manner but this time the data is taken from the MDR to the accumulator (ACC). However, if the operand is data then it is loaded into a designated register of the CPU. Now the CU issues signals to the ALU to perform the required operation. The result of the operation is stored in the target location which can again be main memory or an internal CPU register or a device, depending upon the type of instruction being executed.
Now the contents of the PC are incremented so that it points to the next instruction to be fetched. However, if the previous instruction was a branch instruction or a jump instruction then the address of the next instruction is loaded into both MAR and PC.

Fig. 1.10 Instruction register

It may be noted that the time taken by the CPU to execute an instruction is called the CPU cycle. The time taken by the CPU to access the memory is called the memory cycle.

1.3.3 Memory

As discussed earlier, the memory is used to hold the program and its associated data. It is of two types: primary memory and secondary memory. The secondary memory is magnetic memory whereas the primary memory is semiconductor memory. The primary memory, also called main memory, is directly accessible to the CPU. The time taken by the CPU to access the primary memory is called a memory cycle. The secondary memory permanently stores the program and data files. If the CPU requires some data which is not available in main memory, then it is brought from the secondary memory into the main memory from where it is supplied to the CPU. The time taken to access the secondary memory or a similar device is called an input/output cycle.

The access time of semiconductor memory is to the tune of 50-150 ns, where 'ns' means nanoseconds. Comparatively, secondary memories such as disks are slower devices. For instance the access speed of a fast hard disk is to the tune of 10-100ms, where 'ms' means milliseconds. Thus, there is a drastic speed mismatch between the CPU, the main memory, and the secondary memory.

Since the advent of computer systems, designers have been trying to create main memories as fast as the processor (CPU) itself. Though it is possible to create fast memories with speed closer to those of the CPU, the cost becomes extremely high, almost forbidding. Therefore, a compromise between the speed and size is made in such a way that the memory units that are directly accessible to the CPU are made fast but small in size. In fact, there is a hierarchy of memory in a computer system, as shown in Fig. 1.11.

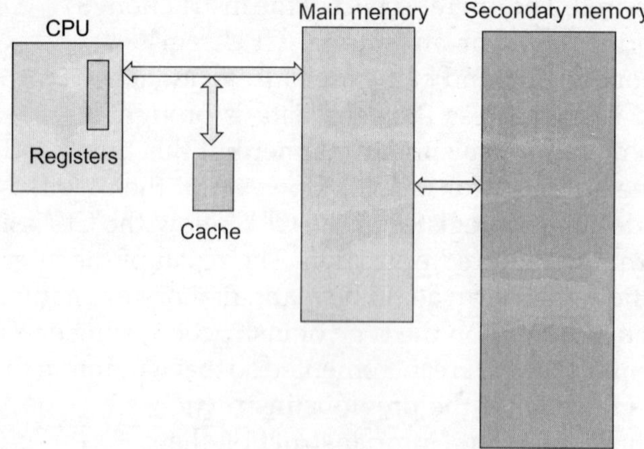

Fig. 1.11 Hierarchy of memory

From Fig. 1.11, it may be noted that the logical memory can be grouped into the following four groups:

1. CPU registers
2. Cache memory
3. Main memory
4. Secondary memory

The CPU registers are part of the CPU and therefore the speed of registers is as high as the processor itself. The cache memory is very fast semiconductor memory built from static RAM i.e., SRAM. It is placed between the CPU and main memory. It is directly accessible to the CPU. The size of cache is of the order of 256Kb to 512 Kb.

The main memory is also semiconductor memory but slower than the cache memory. It is built from dynamic RAM i.e., DRAM. It is used to store active programs and data. This memory is also directly accessible to the CPU. The size of main memory is to the tune of 1GB to 2GB. It is also called primary memory.

The secondary memory is the largest memory. It is the slowest memory in the memory hierarchy. It is built using a variety of technologies. For instance, floppy disks, hard disks are magnetic disks whereas CD-ROM/DVD disks are optical disks. This memory is not directly accessible to the CPU. The size of a hard disk is in the range of 512MB to 1 TB (Terra byte).

1.3.3.1 Primary Memory (Main Memory)

It is a semiconductor memory consisting of thousands of memory cells. A cell is the smallest part of the memory accessible to the CPU. Each cell can store a word comprising data in multiples of 8 bits. The common computer words sizes are: 8, 16, 32, 64 bits, where a group of 8 bits is called a byte. Each cell has a unique physical address. The addressing system is so designed that the address generated by CPU is uniquely mapped to the designated cell in the memory. The total number of memory cells that can be addressed by the CPU depends upon the number of address lines in the address bus. For instance, an address bus of n lines can address 2^n memory locations, as shown in Table1.2.

Table 1.2 Addressing scheme

Number of lines	Addressable locations	
	Address	Cell
$n = 1 \Rightarrow 2^1 = 2$	0	
	1	
	00	
$n = 2 \Rightarrow 2^2 = 4$	01	
	10	
	11	
	000	
	001	
	010	
$n = 3 \Rightarrow 2^3 = 8$	011	
	100	
	101	
	110	
	111	

Generally, the number of data lines in the data bus of a CPU is equal to or in multiples of the word size of the memory. For example, the memory unit shown in Fig. 1.12 is a '**1024** × **8** memory' indicating that it has 1024 cells and each cell is of size 8 bits.

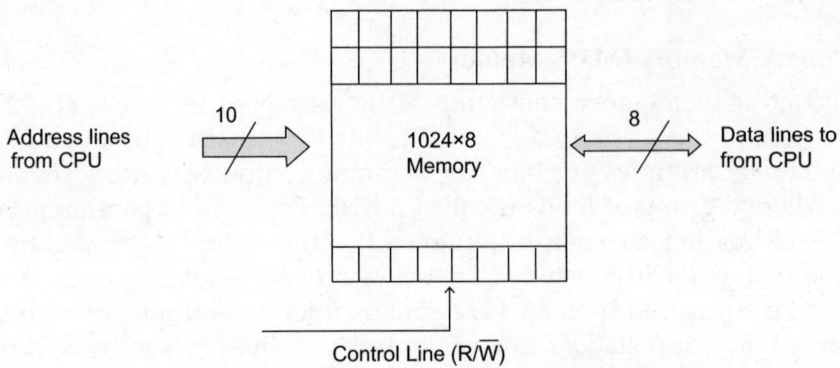

Fig. 1.12 Block diagram of a typical memory

It may be noted that the memory unit (1024 X 8) is addressed by a 10-bit (1024 = 2^{10}) address bus. It communicates its word (8 bits) through a data bus of 8 bit size. The read/write operation on the memory is controlled by the signal being 1 and 0 respectively.

The data from a cell in the memory can be accessed in the same length of time irrespective of its address within the memory. Therefore, the memory is called 'Random Access Memory' (RAM). In fact the main memory or semiconductor memory can be of two types: RAM and ROM, as discussed in the following text.

A. **Random Access Memory** (RAM): This memory is a random access memory because any of its cells can be accessed in the same amount of time irrespective of their address within the memory. It is also called a R/W (Read/Write) memory because the data can be both written to and read from the memory as per the requirement of the executing program in the computer system. During the write (R/$\overline{W}$) operation the data present on the data bus is (R/$\overline{W}$) stored in the memory at the address presented by the address bus from the CPU and the low signal i.e., 0 on the control line. Similarly, during the read operation, the CPU issues an address and the high signal i.e., 1 on the control line. Accordingly, the memory loads the data from its addressed location on the data bus.

With the changing technology of RAMs, the size of memory has also increased from 1MB RAM to 4GB RAM where MB means mega bytes and GB means Giga bytes of storage size of the memory chip. Nowadays, a regular personal computer has a RAM ranging from 1GB to 4GB capacity.

A RAM is generally made from Dynamic random access memory (DRAM) technology. DRAM has following **advantages**:

- Smaller in physical size. Therefore, large sized RAMs can be produced.
- Generates less heat.

The data stored in a DRAM has to be continously refereshed. Therefore, DRAM is a slower memory. As soon as the computer is switched off, the contents of the RAM are lost and that is why the RAM is also called volatile memory.

A RAM is packaged either as SIMMs (Single In-Line Memory Modules) Chip or DIMMs (Dual In-Line Memory Modules) Chip. A 72 pin 8 RAM SIMM is shown in Fig. 1.13.

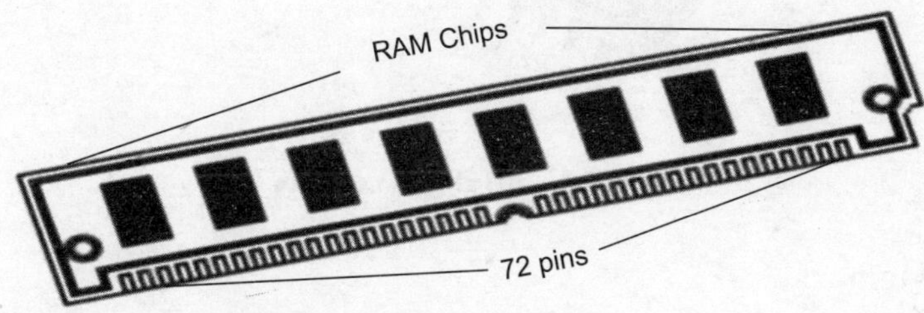

Fig. 1.13 A SIMM chip

B. **Read Only Memory (ROM)**: This is a non-volatile random access memory which retains its contents even if power is switched off. It is called read-only memory because the data once stored in this memory is generally not changed thereafter. The ROM is used to store permanent data of the computer system such as BIOS (Basic Input Output System), interrupt service routines, diagnostic routines etc.

Note: **ROM is also a random access memory and therefore we can say that 'ROM is also a RAM'**

There are the following popular variations of ROMs :

a. Programmable Read-Only Memory (PROM): This is a programmable ROM. Each bit of this memory can be individually programmed to a 1 or 0 by burning out a fusible link using electrical impulses. The programming is done by a device called PROM programmer. However, PROM cannot be reprogrammed i.e., a link once fused becomes permanent and the data stored therein cannot be changed.
b. Erasable Programmable Read-Only Memory (EPROM): It is a reprogrammable ROM. A programmed ROM is exposed to ultra-violet light to erase the data

stored in the ROM. Once erased, EPROM can be reprogrammed by the PROM programmer. An EPROM chip is shown in Fig. 1.14.

c. Electrically Erasable Programmable Read-Only Memory (EEPROM): This ROM can be erased and programmed by electrical signals.

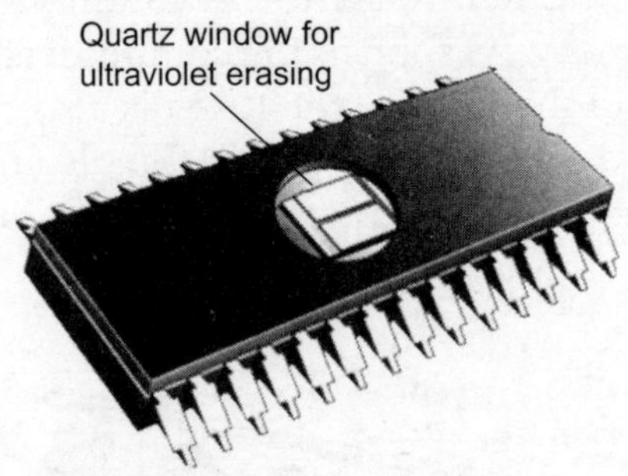

Fig. 1.14 An EPROM chip

1.3.3.2 Cache Memory

The access time of main memory is about 60 ns. The clock cycle of a 100 Mhz processor is 10 ns and therefore it will execute one instruction in 10 ns. Obviously, the time taken to bring an instruction (or piece of data) into the processor is 60 ns which is very high compared to the time taken to execute the instruction. Therefore, Cache memory, with access time of 15 ns, is introduced between main memory and the CPU with a view to bridge the mismatch of speeds between the CPU and the main memory. The arrangement works on the principle of 'locality of reference'. This principle suggests that at any given time the CPU will be accessing memory in a localized region of memory.

When an instruction is fetched by the CPU from the main memory, a block containing the required instruction is copied into the cache. The block may contain 128–256 instructions. Now the next instruction is supplied to the CPU from the cache which is a comparatively faster memory than the main memory. In fact all subsequent instructions are supplied from the cache memory till either the block is exhausted or the CPU requests for an instruction which is not present in the cache.

When the instruction is found in the cache then it is considered a hit, otherwise it is called a miss. If the program is structured and program control remains local to the block kept in the cache then more than 90% hits are encountered. On the other hand, if the program is unstructured then the number of misses is more. Thus, system performance increases only when hits are more than the misses.

It may be noted from Fig. 1.11 that the cache unit is sitting in parallel with main memory. This architecture of cache is called 'look aside cache architecture'. In this arrangement, both main memory and cache can see the bus cycle at the same time. Now when the CPU starts a read cycle, the cache monitors the bus. This activity of cache is called the **snoop** operation. If it finds that the address is present in the cache then it responds by supplying the required instruction or data. In case of a miss, the main memory responds by supplying the required instruction or data. The instruction or data supplied by main memory is copied by the cache. This operation is called the **Snarf** operation. So the cache remains updated.

If the required data is available in the cache, the CPU performs operations on the data and stores the data back into the cache. Now the cache contains data which has been modified whereas the copy of the data in main memory remains unmodified. The modified data of cache is also called 'dirty data'. On the other hand, if data is modified in main memory and not in cache then the data present in cache is called 'stale' data.

During a write cycle, two policies are used: write back and write through. In the 'write back' policy, the CPU writes the data into the cache and thereafter the cache writes the data back to the main memory as soon as the bus becomes available. In the 'write through' policy, the CPU writes through the cache into the main memory. The former policy is faster than the latter policy of writing the data.

In order to further increase the access time, cache memories have been introduced at several levels. For example, all latest microprocessors contain an on-chip cache. The on-chip cache operates at the speed of the processor. For example, if the processor operates at 100 MHz, the on-chip cache also works at 100 MHz. The external cache works at the speed of the system bus which is generally of 66 MHz for a processor of 100 Mz. Moreover the data transfer from external cache is limited by the size of the data bus. If the data bus size is 32 or 64 bits then the data transfer from external cache is also in terms of 32 or 64 bits. In case of on-chip cache, the data is transferred as per the size of internal registers and the bus of the processor which is generally of the order of 64 to 256 bits.

The on-chip cache is further divided into two parts: instruction and data cache. For instance, on a Pentium chip, there are two caches: instruction cache and data cache. The on-chip cache is called the **L1 cache** and the external cache which is present on the motherboard of the computer system is called the **L2 cache**, where L1 and L2 mean levels 1 and 2 respectively.

With the advancements in technology, cache memory has been moved into the chip from the motherboard. For instance, the Intel 80386 had an external cache on the motherboard and no on-chip cache. In the 80486, both on-chip and external caches in the form of L1 and L2 were provided. In Pentium II, L2 was moved into the processor chip. L1 was divided into separate L1 instruction and L1 data caches. In Pentium III, an external cache called L3 was provided on the motherboard in addition to L1 and L2 on-chip caches. From Pentium IV onward, even the L3 has been moved to processor chip.

1.3.5 Secondary Memory (Storage Devices)

Magnetic disks, optical disks, and PenRams are principal storage devices in a computer system. Magnetic tapes, though old technology, are still in use in some organizations. A detailed discussion on these devices is given on the next page.

A. Magnetic disks: Magnetic disks are the most important and common secondary storage devices in a computer system. A magnetic disk is a circular disk with a coating of γ-ferrite on both its surfaces. The γ–ferrite can be locally magnetized in the form of magnetic spots. The direction of magnetization of the spot is used to represent binary data in '0' or '1'.

During a write operation, the binary data from the computer is supplied in the form of electric pulses. The electric pulses are converted into magnetized spots on the disk surface. On the other hand, while reading data from the disk the magnetized spots are converted into equivalent electric pulses. The electric pulses are then converted into binary data.

The data is stored on a disk on a number of invisible concentric circles called tracks. A disk can have from 40 to more than 6000 tracks on the surface. These tracks begin from the outer edge of the disk and continue towards the centre. Each track has a designated number starting from 0. The tracks are divided into sectors. The number of sectors per track varies from system to system. For example, the disk shown in Fig. 10.1 has 8 sectors per track. It may be noted that all tracks, outer as well as inner, have the same number of sectors i.e., 8 sectors per track (Fig 1.15). Thus, the density of information is more in the sectors of the inner tracks as compared to the outer tracks. This configuration was popular in old technology disks leading to wastage of storage space in outer tracks. In modern disks, **multiple zone recording** is used, wherein the tracks are divided into zones, as shown in Fig. 1.16. The number of sectors per track is increased in the outer zones. The disk shown in Fig. 1.14 has two zones, and while the inner zone has 16 sectors per track, the outer zone has 32 sectors per track. This technique helps in storing more data on the disk. Generally, the number of sectors per track varies from manufacturer to manufacturer. In earlier hard disks, the range was 16 to 63 sectors per track and 40 to 400 tracks per inch. In modern hard disks, the range is 232 to 792 sectors per track and 10000 to 1 lakh tracks per inch.

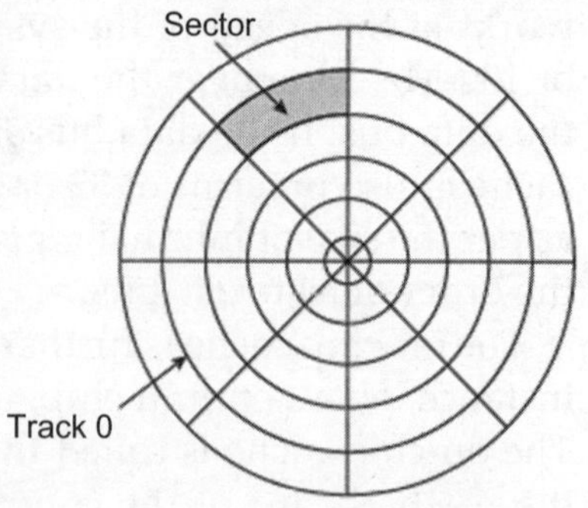

Fig. 1.15 A disk with 8 sectors per track

Magnetic disks are of two types: hard disks and floppy disks. The disks in which the number of sectors/tracks is fixed by the manufacturer are called **hard disks**. In a **floppy disk**, the number sectors/tracks can be changed by a software controlled formatting operation. Accordingly the hard disks and floppy disks are named hard-sectored disks and soft-sectored disks respectively.

Hard Disk: A hard disk consists of a stack of disks, called platters, mounted on a common spindle. Each surface of the platter is coated with magnetic material. Therefore, both surfaces of the platter are used for recording data. However, in the case of top and bottom platters, only the inner surfaces are used. For each recording surface, a separate read/write head is used. The set of read/write heads is joined to a common arm in a comb like structure. It moves over the surfaces of the spinning platters to access data from the concentric tracks. The arrangement is as shown in Fig. 1.17.The disk pack is rotated at a high speed, to the tune of 7600 rpm (rotations per minute). The high speed of rotation causes the read/write (R/W) head to float above the surface of the platter.

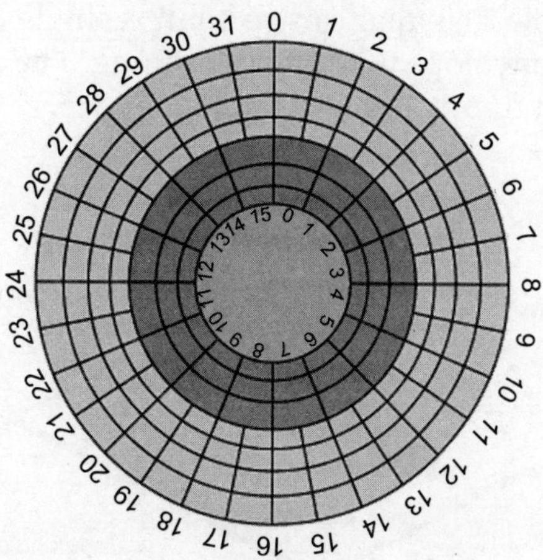

Fig. 1.16 Multiple zone recording

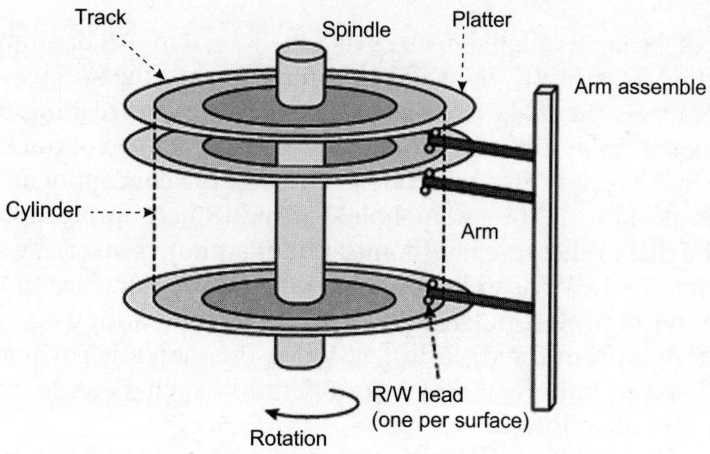

Fig. 1.17 Components of a hard disk

When a constant speed is reached, all arms move together to position the R/W heads on the required track on all surfaces. However, only one head is selected at a time by the system, to access the data from its corresponding track. In a sound record player, the pickup arm can move directly to a specific song without having to play other in-between songs. Similarly, the access arm assembly of the hard disk can move the R/W heads directly to a desired track without accessing the in-between tracks. Therefore, disks are called direct access storage devices (DASD).

Floppy Disk: A floppy disk consists of a flexible disk. It is called floppy because it is physically pliable disk that can be bent. A single disk is packaged inside a square hard plastic envelope with an inner lining. The disk can be accessed from both sides. A typical floppy is shown in Fig. 1.18.

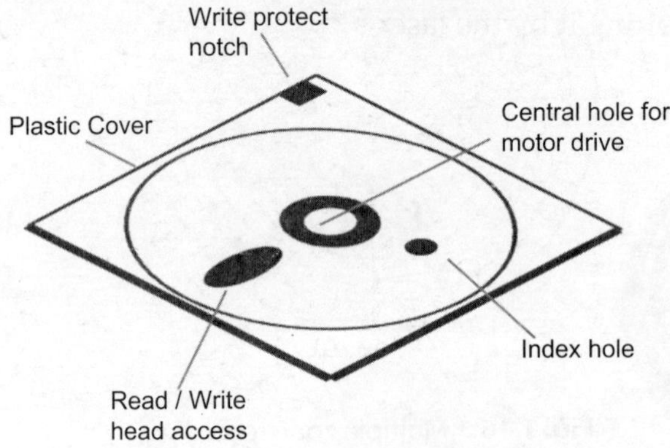

Fig. 1.18 Components of a floppy disk

Floppy disks are available in sizes of 8 in, 5 in, 3 in. An opening in the cover allows the read/write (R/W) head to come closer to the surface of the disk so that it can access the disk. However the recording and reading of data on the floppy disk is similar to that in a hard disk i.e., in the form of tracks and sectors. Since the disk has only two recordable surfaces, the concept of a cylinder is not of much importance. The 'index hole' is used to help in positioning the R/W head on the disk. When the hole comes under a photo sensor, the system comes to know that the R/W head is now positioned on the first sector of the current track. The 'write protect notch' is used to protect the floppy against accidental deletion of data from the disk. In fact when this notch is covered by a sticker then the disk can only read and other operation such as write, modify, delete, format etc. are not allowed.

After the advent of CD/DVD ROM disks and PenRams, floppies have become outdated and are not in vogue.

B. **Optical Disks**: These disks are called optical disks because data is both recorded and read using a laser light-beam. These disks are plastic disks with a thin layer of aluminium stamped on both the surfaces. As the name suggests, a laser is projected on the surface of the disk by a focusing coil. While writing, the heat produced by the laser creates a pit on the surface of the disk. The laser is turned on and off to create pits and lands, where the space left between two pits is termed as a land. Therefore, the disk surface contains data recorded in the form of a continuous spiral (see Fig. 1.19) having pits and lands representing 0 and 1 respectively. The data is grouped into blocks. Each block contains 2352 bytes consisting of 2048 bytes for data, 16 bytes for header of the block and 288 bytes for advanced error control.

Kindly note that a pit scatters the light and the land reflects the light. Some optical disks are re-writable in nature. In that case, the surface of the disk is 'repaired' by re-melting it by the laser and writing again.

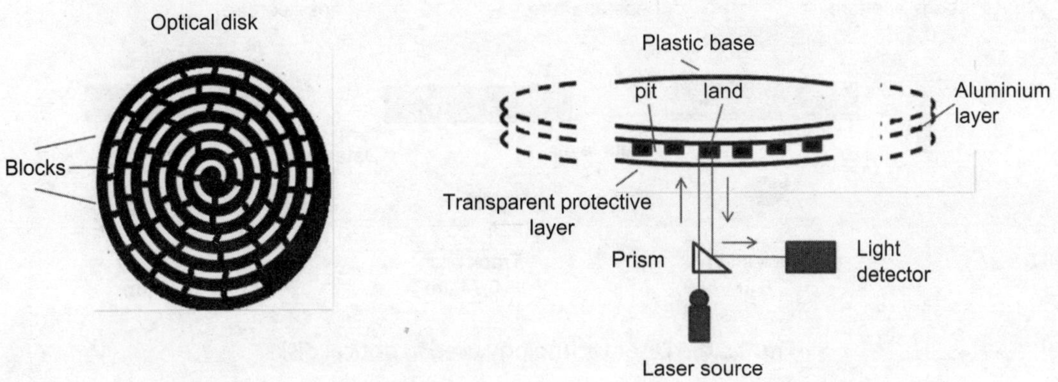

Fig. 1.19 Optical disks

The data from the disk is read as follows:

1. A laser is projected on the surface of the disk by a focusing coil.
2. If the beam strikes a land then it is reflected back.
3. The reflected light is diverted through a prism to strike a light detector, as shown in Fig. 1.17.
4. If the beam strikes a pit then it gets scattered.

Thus the reading process senses the presence of pits and lands on the disk.

The optical disks (5.25 inch in diameter) are primarily of three types: CD (Compact disk), DVD (Digital Video Disk), and BD (Blue-Ray Disk). The CD and DVD technology uses red laser to read/write data on the disk. On the other hand the BD technology uses blue laser to read/write data on the disk. A comparison between the type of laser and the wave length used by various optical disk technologies is given in Table 1.3.

Table 1.3 Comparison between optical disks

Type of disk	Type of laser	Wave length	Capacity of disk
CD	Red laser	780nm	680MB
DVD	Red Laser	650nm	4.7GB (single layer)

In fact, by shortening the wave length and increasing the aperture of the lens, the laser can be focused to create a smaller spot on the disk surface, as shown in Fig. 1.20. The smaller spot size results in more data storage on the disk surface.

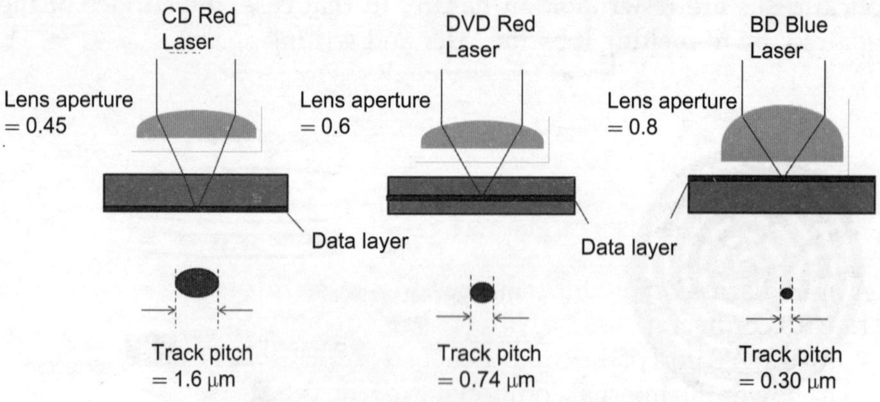

Fig. 1.20 Laser technology used in optical disks

It may be further noted that the data layer, in case of a BD, is much nearer to the surface of the disk. Therefore, a BD is more prone to corruption of data due to scratches as compared to DVD and CD.

As far as recording of data is concerned, optical disks are labelled as: R, RW. The disk marked as 'R' means that it can be written once and read many times whereas 'RW' means that the disk can written, erased, and rewritten many times.

C. **Pen Drive**: It is also known as 'PenRam' or a 'USB flash drive' because of its size and shape like a pen. It is an 'EEPROM' based flash memory. It can be repeatedly erased and rewritten by electric signals. It has the following four major components:

1. USB connector
2. USB mass storage controller
3. Flash memory
4. Crystal oscillator

Besides the major components, a Pen Drive has also an LED that indicates the data transfer operation taking place on the drive. A write protect switch (See Fig. 1.21) on the drive can be used to set the drive to read-only or read/write mode.

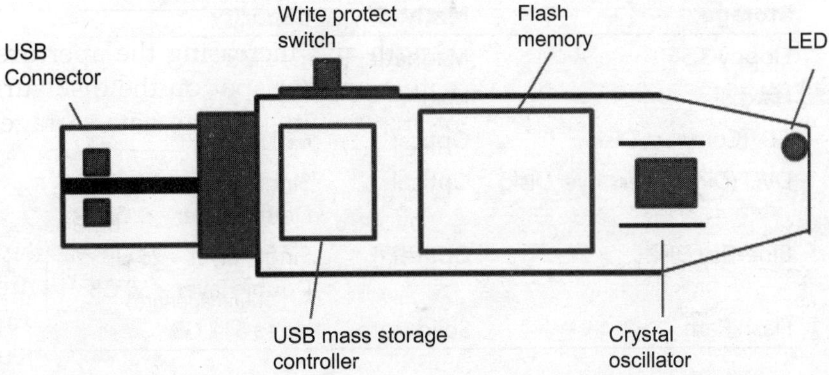

Fig. 1.21 Pen drive

A brief discussion on the major components of a pen drive is given below:

1. **USB connector**: A male Universal Serial Bus (USB) connector that connects to the USB port of the computer. It also utilizes the power from the computer to power the internal components of the pen drive.
2. **USB mass storage controller**: This component controls the operations of the other components of the pen drive such flash memory, crystal oscillator, and the USB connector.
3. **Flash memory**: The basic storage element of the flash memory is based on NAND gates. The address supplied by the computer to the pen drive is decoded by its controller. The controller then issues the necessary control signal for random access of the desired memory location. The size of memory varies from 128 KB to more than 256 GB.
4. **Crystal oscillator**: It produces a 12 MHz clock signal for synchronizing the activities of the various components of the pen drive.

The pen drive can be formatted for a particular file system such as FAT16, FAT32, NTFS etc. Modern operating systems allow themselves to be booted from a pen drive. In fact, a bootable pen drive is also called a 'Live' USB.

The application areas of a pen drive are:

1. Data transport from one digital device to another.
2. Allowing users to secure their data on a personal pen drive.
3. Is widely used as a Backup drive.
4. It is a popular medium for storing and sharing audio and video files.

1.3.5.1 Comparison of Secondary Storage Devices

A comparison of different types of secondary storage devices is given in Table 1. 4

Table 1.4 Storage device comparison table

Storage	Method	Capacity
Floppy 3.5"	Magnetic	1.44 MB
Hard disk	Magnetic	Up to 4 TB
CD (Compact Disk)	Optical	650 MB
DVD (Digital Versatile Disk)	Optical	Single layer – 4.7 GB Double layer - 9 GB
Blue-Ray Disk	Optical	Single layer – 25 GB Double layer - 50 GB
Flash Ram	Solid state	Up to 512 GB

1.4 TYPES OF COMPUTERS

Computers can broadly be classified into three broad groups: **analog, digital**, and **hybrid** computers (see Fig. 1.22). Analog and hybrid computers are not in vogue and are therefore be considered to be extinct. In fact the word computer has become a synonym of digital computers. A digital computer essentially works on discrete digits or numbers i.e., 0 and 1, called binary digits. Each data item (numeric or non-numeric) is represented by a binary number consisting of 0s and 1s.

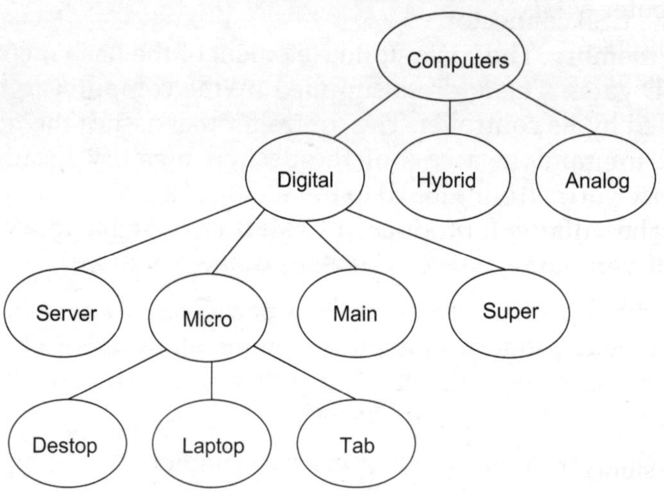

Fig. 1.22 Types of computers

A digital computer computes by counting and adding operations. The accuracy of digital computers is very high and is only limited by the size of the internal registers of its CPU. Digital computers can be classified according to their computing capabilities, physical size, applications etc. The various classes of digital computers are discussed below:

A. **Microcomputers** (Personal computers): A microcomputer is a digital computer built around a microprocessor. A microprocessor is a complete CPU fabricated on a single chip. Examples of microprocessors are: Intel Pentium i3, i5, AMD Athlon 64, 64*2 etc. Microcomputers are used as personal computers, popularly called PCs. Personal computers are available in many variants such as desktops, laptops, notebooks, tablets etc.

B. **Servers**: A server is a computer program that is used to provide services to other programs or users. The computers on which such programs are deployed are also called servers. Examples of servers are: Network servers, application servers, printer servers, database servers, web servers etc.

C. **Mainframe computers**: The term mainframe is used for large and very powerful computer systems. These systems have a very high capacity of storage and can process huge databases at an extremely fast rate. A mainframe can support more than 100 users at a time on time sharing basis. Owing to their large size and high computing capacity, these expensive machines are used by government institutions or organizations that need to process data of complex nature.

The application areas for mainframes are those that require bulk data processing such as census data management, market consumer statistics processing, enterprise resource planning and transaction processing etc.

Examples of mainframe computers are: IBM 9375, IBM z Systems, Honeywell 6000, ICL superdual 2988 etc.

Note: Computer systems smaller than mainframe computers and larger than microcomputers are known as mini-computers. These computers are suitable for small organizations with a support for 10-20 users. However, these systems are not in vogue.

D. **Super Computers**: A super computer is an extremely fast computing machine that can perform of the order of terra floating point operations per second (TFlop/s). The super high speed is achieved by designing an architecture consisting of very large numbers of coordinating processors. For instance the OSC **Orac** system has the following configuration:

- **Processors** :256 Itanium2 cores
- **Speed:** 1.6 TFlop peak
- **Main Memory**: 1024 GB
- **Secondary storage**: 5.5 TB.

Other examples of supercomputers are: CRAY XMP -24 , PARAM 10000, OSC HAL etc.

Note: The PARAM series of computers have been produced by the Centre for Development of Advanced Computing (C-DAC) of India.

Exercises

1. Differentiate between data and information with the help of suitable examples.
2. Define the term 'compute'.
3. List the three essential components of a computer.
4. What is a processor? Describe briefly the capabilities of a processor with the help of a block diagram.
5. Draw the block diagram of a Von-Neumann architecture and explain why it is inherently a serial computing device?
6. Define the term computer.
7. What is purpose of a store in the Von-Neumann architecture?
8. Explain Von-Neumann bottleneck in brief.
9. Define the terms: hardware and software.
10. What are the four main components of a computer?
11. Why are modern digital computers often referred to as stored program computers?
12. Draw the block diagram of a bus based computer explain it in brief.
13. What is a bus? Explain the purpose of data bus, address bus, and control bus.
14. What are the components of a CPU? Explain with the help of a diagram.
15. Draw the internal architecture of a CPU. Explain in brief the working of its main components.
16. Differentiate between op-code and operand.
17. Define the terms: machine cycle and instruction cycle.
18. What is the purpose of memory in a computer system? Differentiate between primary and secondary memory.
19. What is the trade-off between size and speed of a memory?
20. Draw the block diagram of memory hierarchy prevalent in a typical digital computer.
21. Differentiate between SRAM and DRAM.
22. Given a primary memory: 2048 × 16 RAM. What will be the size of address bus and data bus?
23. Define the terms: RAM and ROM.
24. Give your comments on the statement: "A ROM is also a RAM".
25. Write an explanatory note on popular variations of ROMs.
26. What is a cache memory? What is need of this memory in computer system?
27. Explain the term: Look aside cache architecture.
28. Differentiate between snoop and snarf operation of a cache.
29. Differentiate between dirty data and stale data.
30. Explain in brief the 'write through policy.
31. Differentiate between L1 and L2 caches.
32. Give the working of a Hard disk with the help of a diagram.
33. What is the need of 'multiple zone recording' on a hard disk?
34. Define the terms: sector, track, and cylinder in context of a hard disk.
35. What is an optical disk?
36. Define the terms: CD, DVD, and BD.
37. Write an explanatory note on various types of lasers used in optical disks.
38. Explain the working of a USB flash drive and its components with the help of block diagram.
39. Give the classification computers.
40. What are various classes of a digital computer on the basis of their size and configuration?

CHAPTER

2 Introduction to Microprocessors

2.1 HISTORY

With the advancements in semiconductor technology, it became possible in the 1970s, to integrate a complete CPU on a single integrated chip (IC). The CPU on a single chip was named a **microprocessor (μP).** The first 4-bit μP was fabricated by Intel Corporation using Metal Oxide Semiconductor technology (MOS) and it was termed as '4004'. Later, 8-bit μPs were built using NMOS (N-Type MOS) technology. For example, Intel 8085, Zilog Z80, Motorola 6800 were NMOS technology based 8-bit microprocessors. Similarly, in 1978, HMOS (high density MOS) technology was used to develop 16-bit μPs such as the Intel 8086, 80186, 80286 and Motorola 68000/68010 microprocessors.

An IC's component size is measured in terms of micrometres called microns. For instance, Intel 4004 and 8008 μPs were fabricated on 10 microns technology. Similarly Intel 8085 and 8088 were fabricated using 3 micron technology.

Over the years, the microprocessor process technology has evolved significantly from 10 microns (10μm) to 14 nanometres (14nm). For instance the 'Intel core i7' is a 14nm microprocessor. A list of various microprocessors and their process size is given in Table 2.1

Table 2.1 Microprocessor process technologies

Microprocessor	Process technology	Year
Intel 4004	10 μm	1971
Intel 8085	03 μm	1975
Intel 80286	1.5 μm	1982
Intel 80386	1.0 μm	1985
Intel 80486	0.8 μm	1989
Intel Pentium Pro AMD K5	350 nm	1995

(contd)

Table 2.1 Continued

Microprocessor	Process technology	Year
Intel Pentium IV AMD Athelon XP	130 nm	2002
Intel Xeon AMD Athelon 64	90nm	2004
Intel Core 2 IBM Z10	65nm	2006
Intel i3, i5 AMD FX	32nm	2010
Intel Core i7	14nm	2015

2.2 MICROPROCESSOR FUNDAMENTALS

As mentioned earlier, a complete CPU fabricated on a single chip is called a **microprocessor (μP).** The IC chip and block diagram for a typical microprocessor is shown in Fig. 2.1. It may be noted from Fig.2.1 (a) that a large number of metal pins protrude from the chip. These pins are used to connect to other components of the computer system such as memory, input/output ports etc. The pins are connected to other devices through metal tracks. A group of metal tracks is called a bus. Depending upon the utility of pins, the pins of a microprocessor are divided into three broad groups: Address pins, data pins, and control pins, which connect to the address bus, data bus, and control bus respectively, as shown in Fig. 1.2(b). A detailed discussion on the internal components of a CPU is given in Section 1.3.1.

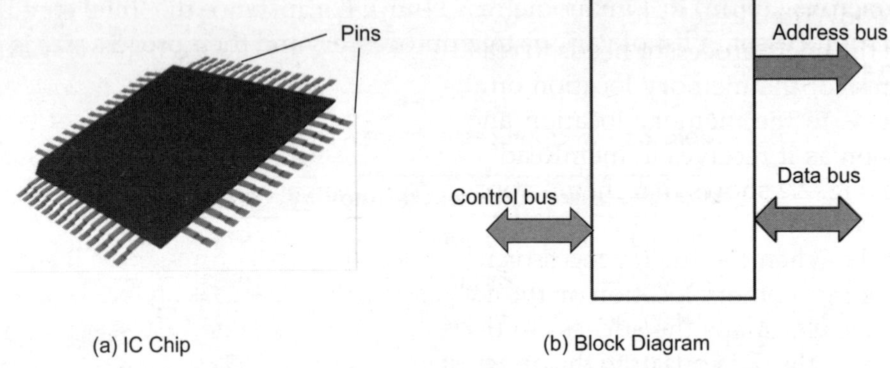

Fig. 2.1 A typical microprocessor

The processing power of a microprocessor depends upon its word size. The word size is measured in terms of the number of bits, in multiples of 2, as shown in Table 2.2. Accordingly the microprocessors are called 8-bit µP, 16-bit µP, 64-bit µP etc.

Table 2.2 word length of microprocessors

Microprocessor	Word length (bit)
Intel 8085	8
8086	16
80386	32
80486	32
Pentium	64

Generally, the size of internal registers (see Fig. 1.8) of a microprocessor is same as or is in multiples of the word size. Therefore, an 8-bit microprocessor can process 8-bit data at a time and the 64-bit microprocessor can process 64-bit data at a time. Obviously, the 64-bit microprocessor is almost four times faster than an 8-bit microprocessor. Since the data is transported to and from memory through a data bus, the size of the data bus is also the same as or is in multiples of word length. For example, a Power PC microprocessor has a word size of 32 bits with a data bus of size 64 bits.

From Section 1.3, we know that the **data bus** is a bidirectional group of lines on which the data can travel both ways i.e., from a microprocessor to a device and vice versa. The **address bus** is a unidirectional group of lines on which address of a memory location or a device is sent by the microprocessor. The **control bus** is a group of lines on which control signals flow from the microprocessor to the connected devices and vice versa. Examples of control signals are 'memRead', 'memWrite', 'ioRead', 'ioWrite', 'reset' etc.

When the microprocessor needs to read data or instructions from memory, it sends the address of the memory location on the address bus. An address decoder maps the address to the memory location and the memory places the data on the data bus as soon as it receives a 'memRead' control signal from the microprocessor. For example, Fig. 2.2 shows that the microprocessor has read data (780) from a memory location 345.

Similarly, when the microprocessor needs to write data to memory, it sends the address of the memory location on the address bus and the data on the data bus. An address decoder maps the address to the memory location and the memory writes the data from the data bus onto the designated memory location as soon as it receives a 'memWrite' signal from the microprocessor. For example, Fig. 2.3 shows that the microprocessor has written data (984) to a memory location (517). It may be noted that the previous contents of memory location 517 have been overwritten by the new contents i.e., 240 has been overwritten by 984.

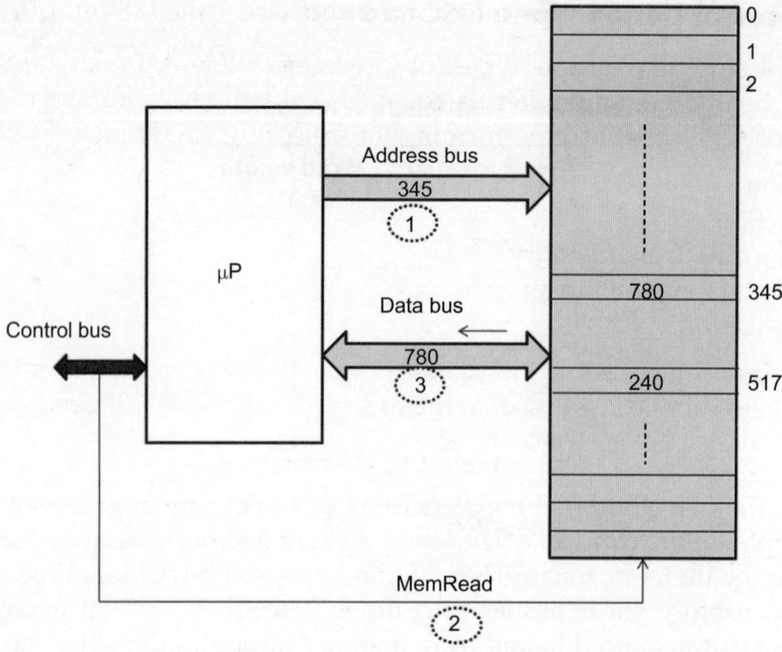

Fig. 2.2 Memory read operation

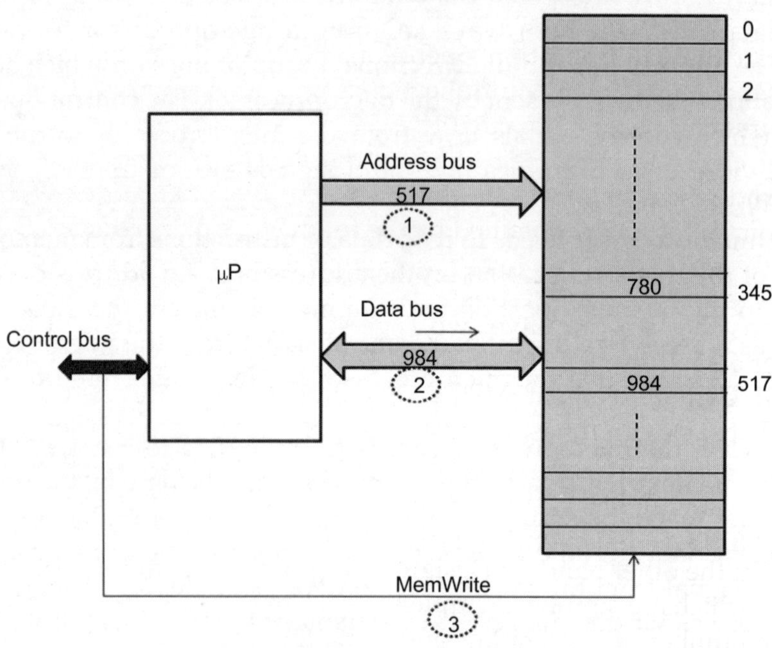

Fig. 2.3 Memory write operation

2.2.1 Processor Design Types: CISC and RISC

Before discussing the design types of processors, let us understand the basic philosophy behind the same. Let us consider a situation where one is required to design a processor capable of performing the following operations:

1. Addition
2. Subtraction
3. Loading data from memory
4. Storing data into memory
5. Multiplication

One obvious choice would be to assign operation codes called op-codes to the operations listed above. Assume that the codes given in Table 2.3 have been assigned:

Table 2.3 Op-codes

S.No.	Operation	Op-Codes
1	Addition	ADD
2	Subtraction	SUB
3	Loading data from memory	LOAD
4	Storing data into memory	STORE
5	Multiplication	MULT

Other than the Multiplication operation, the rest of the operations are easily implemented at digital level. Multiplication is implemented using Booth's algorithm which requires complex digital circuitry.

The other choice to implement the multiplication operations is to avoid Booth's algorithm and instead perform multiplication by repetitive addition. For example, the operation 'A * 5' can be obtained by the following expression:

$$A * 5 = A + A + A + A + A$$

This means that we can have two types of designs, Processor I and Processor II. Processor I shall implement the MULT operation using Booth's algorithm and Processor II shall implement MULT operation by repetitively calling the ADD operation. Thus, Design II has one instruction less to implement. In fact, most of the complex operations can be carried out as a sequence of simpler operations.

In Design I, the emphasis is on having an op-code for every possible operation and implementing the same using complex digital circuitry that performs the required operation. On the other hand, in Design II, the emphasis is to have lesser number of instructions which are simpler to implement. Therefore, the first approach results in a very large number of instructions and some them are designed to perform rather complex tasks. Therefore, the processor designed with this approach is called a 'Complex Instruction Set Computer' (CISC). The second approach results in having a reduced number of instructions and most of the instructions are designed to perform simple operations. Therefore, the processor designed with the second approach is called a 'Reduced Instruction Set Computer' (**RISC**). A comparison of CISC and RISC is given in Table 2.4.

Table 2.4 CISC versus RISC

S. No.	CISC	RISC
1	Large number Instructions	Reduced number Instructions
2	Lesser number of general purpose registers i.e. 8–10 registers	Large number of general purpose registers i.e. 32–35 registers
3	Variable instruction length	Uniform instruction length
4	Compilers are hard to write	Compilers are simple to write
5	Program size is small	Program size is large
6	Processor is difficult to design	Processor is easier to design
7	High cost	Low cost

The major advantage of a CISC design is that complex instructions make the program smaller in size i.e., less instructions are required to perform a task. The reduction in the number of instructions leads to faster execution of the program.

RISC based processors use a reduced number of simple instructions. Therefore to perform a task, a higher number of instructions are required resulting in a large sized program. The increase in the number of instructions leads to slower execution of the program. However, in order to increase the performance, a large number of general purpose registers are used in RISC to retain necessary data in the processor itself so as to reduce the memory cycles. The reduction in memory cycles obviously results in faster execution of a program.

Examples of CISC machines: Intel 8086, Dec VAX ML80X0 etc.

Examples of RISC machines: IBM RS/6000, PowerPC etc.

Note: The CISC/RISC dividing lines have blurred over the years. Nowadays, there is a trend to include more instructions in RISC architectures and have uniform instruction length in CISC architectures. Though Pentium chips are inherently CISC processors, Pentium III and IV onwards, more and more RISC features have been incorporated.

2.2.2 Generations of Microprocessors

Microprocessors can also be categorized according to their generations. A brief discussion about various generations of microprocessors is given below:

1. **First Generation Microprocessors**: After Intel 8085, Intel developed the 8086 chip with a clock speed of 4.77MHz. This 1st generation microprocessor had a 16-bit data bus and 20-bit address bus, capable of addressing 1 MB of RAM.

In order to increase the computational efficiency of the 8085 microprocessor, Intel developed the 8087, another chip called Maths processor. It was a specially designed processor to carry out floating point calculations at a much faster rate than the 8086 chip. Therefore, the instructions involving floating point were handed over by 8086 to 8087 and that is why 8087 was also named the co-processor. In fact, microcomputers were built using both 8086 and 8087 chips on the motherboard of the computer. Thereafter, applications such as word processors, spreadsheets, animation software etc. became faster.

2. **Second Generation Microprocessors**: Intel produced the 80286 chip as a 2nd generation microprocessor with a 16-bit data bus, 24-bit address bus, and 6-20 Mz clock speed. Therefore, it was capable of addressing 16 MB of RAM. Similar to the 8087, the 80287 was developed as a co-processor. It was very widely used for multitasking applications.

3. **Third Generation Microprocessors**: As the name suggests, Intel 80386, and 80387 were developed as 3rd generation microprocessor and coprocessor respectively. The 80386 had 32-bit data as well as address bus, capable of addressing 4 GB of RAM. The clock speed varied from 16–33MHz. In the meantime, Microsoft developed the Windows operating system which was designed to harness the complete power of a 32-bit microprocessor such as 80386.

4. **Fourth Generation Microprocessors**: Intel 80486 was the 4th generation microprocessor with a 32-bit data bus as well as address bus. The clock speed varied from 25 MHz to 33 MHz. No separate co-processor was developed; the maths processor was integrated onto the 80486 chip itself. The second important feature was that a small cache memory of 8 KB was also included on the 80486 chip with a view to increase the performance of the chip. The third important development was that in the fourth generation microprocessors, Intel provided an internal clock multiplier that could enhance the clock speed of the processor by 2X and 4X and accordingly the chips were named as 484DX2 and 486DX4 respectively. In fact, the 486DX4 had a wide variety of clock speeds: 25, 33, 50, 66, 75, and 100 MHz.

   It was a pipelined processor wherein the operations like instruction fetching, decoding, execution, memory access, and writing back the results were performed in parallel, of course, for different instructions.

5. **Fifth Generation Microprocessors**: Till the 3rd and 4th generation microprocessors, Intel shared its μP technology with companies like AMD and IBM. Due to copyright problems, Intel named its 5th generation microprocessor Pentium instead of the conventional 80586, though Pentium also means five. The Pentium was designed by Vinod Dham, an electronics engineer from India.

   Pentium, a CISC processor, had data and address buses of size 64 and 32 bits respectively. The initial versions of Pentium had clock speed 33 Mz, 60 Mz, 66 Mz. With the help of internal 1.5 multipliers, the speed was increased to 90 and 100 Mz. Later on, Pentium with 133, 166, and 200M z were also introduced.

In 1997, Intel added 72 new instructions to enhance multi-media computing and the chip was accordingly called Pentium MMX.

6. **Sixth generation Microprocessors:** Intel produced the Pentium Pro as a 6th generation microprocessor. This processor was designed to have a RISC core. An internal circuit was used to convert CISC instructions to RISC instructions, as shown in Fig. 2.4.

CISC instructions
Conversion circuit
RISC instructions

Fig. 2.4

The secondary cache 'L2' of size 256 K was also taken into the Pentium Pro Chip. Thus, Pentium Pro contained the CPU and L2 Cache on the same chip, connected by a 64-bit wide backside bus, as shown in Fig. 2.5.

Since the chip became larger in size, a new socket called 'Socket 8' was provided on the motherboards that supported the Pentium Pro microprocessors. The clock speed of Pentium Pro ranged from 166-200 MHz.

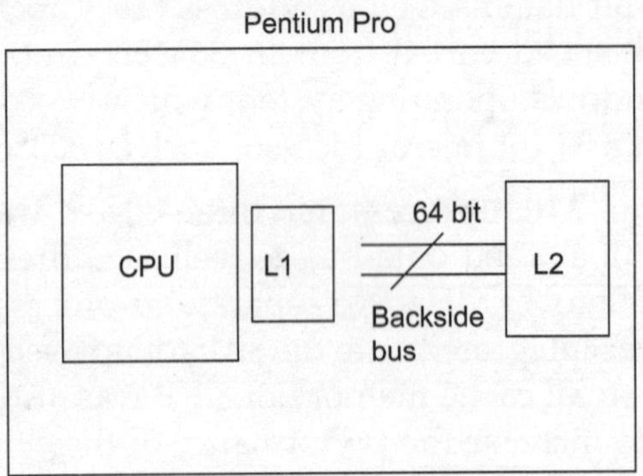

Fig. 2.5 Pentium Pro microprocessor

Later, Pentium II and Pentium III with improved CISC to RISC translation were produced. L1 was moved into the CPU. The CPU and L2 were connected through a 64-bit backside bus, as shown in Fig. 2.6. A new socket called Slot 1 connector was designed to house these processors on the motherboard. The clock speed ranged from 650 Mz – 1.4 GHz.

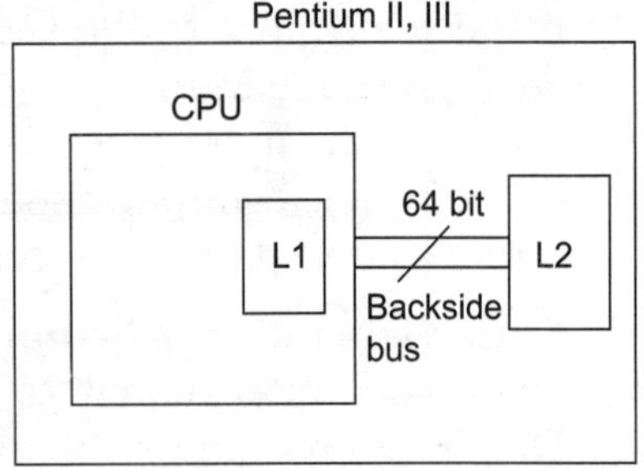

Fig. 2.6 Pentium II, III

7. **Seventh generation Microprocessor:** AMD Athelon K7, Intel Pentium IV, and Alpha 21264 are the 7th generation microprocessors.

Pentium PIV onwards, Intel used the concept of **hyper threading** where it allows parallel parts of a process to execute in parallel on the microprocessor. Since the parallel parts of a process are called threads, the process is called a threaded process and the phenomenon is called multithreading. It is highly suitable for multitasking applications. The clock speed ranges from 2.4 Ghz to 3.2 Ghz. The AMD FX is also a hyper threading microprocessor.

8. **Eighth generation Microprocessors:** Intel Itanium, Itanium -2 and AMD Athelon 64 are 8th generation 64-bit microprocessors. Intel Itanium 2 has a 1.4 GHz clock speed and 1.5 MB L3 cache.

   Besides Itanium, Intel has also produced other very powerful microprocessors called the Intel Xeon 3.20 GHz processor with 1 MB integrated cache. Xeon processors are intelligent server processors. These are being used for high end workstations and enterprise servers.

2.2.3 Recent Trends in Microprocessor Architecture

A typical microprocessor consists of following components:

1. Control Unit (CU)
2. Arithmetic and Logic Unit (ALU)
3. Register Array
4. System Bus

The arrangement is shown in Fig. 2.7.

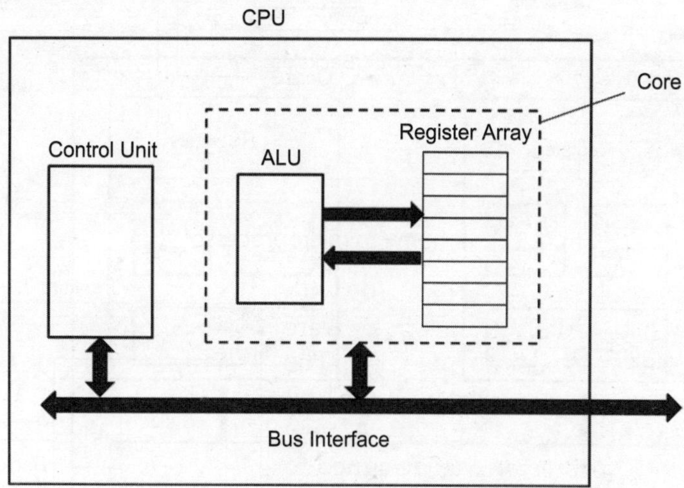

Fig. 2.7 A single core CPU

It may be noted that the computational unit on a CPU is the 'ALU and register array'. It is called a core (see Fig. 2.6). Now, to increase the performance of the CPU, the trend is to include more than one core on the chip. The microprocessors based on such CPUs are called multicore microprocessors, as shown in Fig.2.8. For instance, the Core 2 Duo 64-bit processor from Intel has two cores.

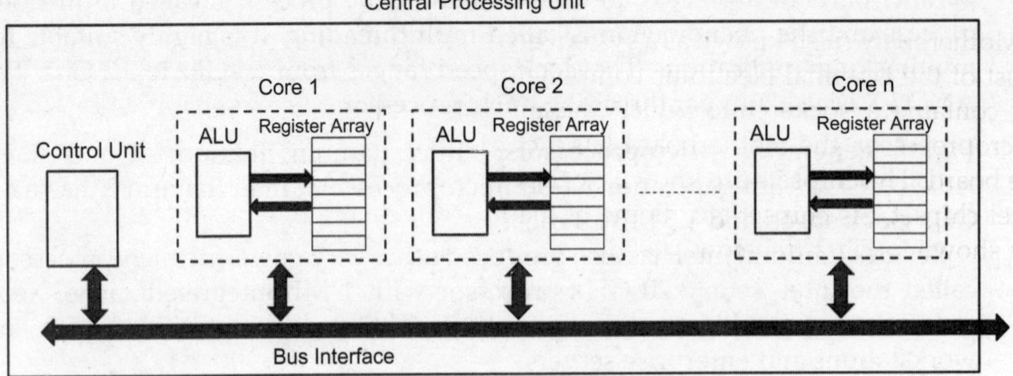

Fig. 2.8 Multicore microprocessor

The latest microprocessors from Intel have as many sets of L1 and L2 caches as there are cores on the chip.

The Intel Core I7 cache hierarchy is shown in Fig. 1.9. It may be noted that the CPU shown in Fig. 2.9 has four cores. Each core has its own L1 and L2 caches. The L1 cache has two parts, L1 data cache and L1 instruction cache. The L2 cache is shared by both L1 data and instruction caches. There is also an L3 cache on the chip, which is shared by the four cores. The L3 cache interacts with the main memory.

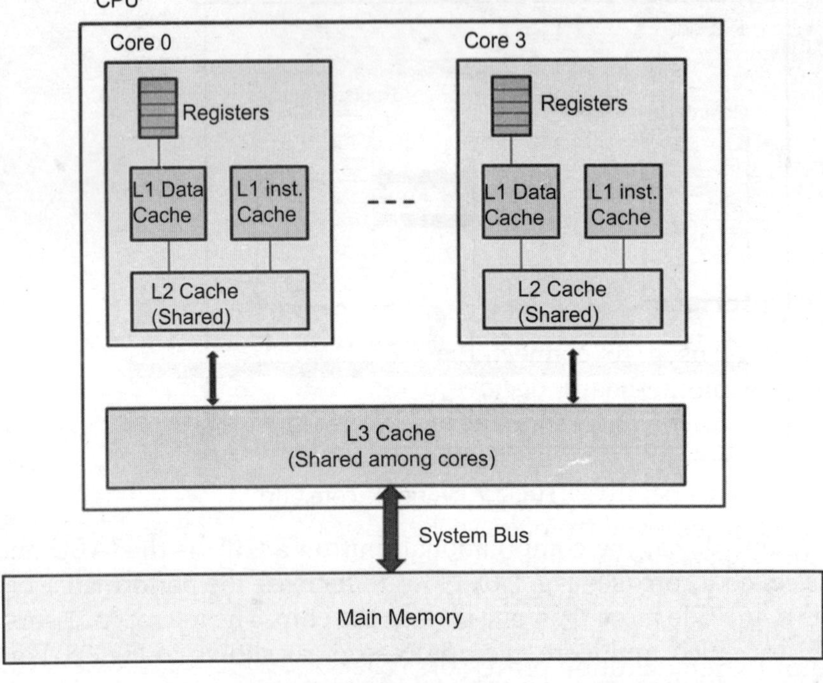

Fig. 2.9 Intel Core I7 cache hierarchy

2.3 MOTHERBOARDS

A Motherboard, also known as a system board, is a printed circuit board that contains most of the essential electronic components of the computer system (see Fig. 2.10). It contains a socket into which the microprocessor is plugged in. Besides the microprocessor, the motherboard has a cluster of chips called a chipset, present on the board. The chipsets are known by the names of their vendor i.e., the VIA chipset, Intel chipset, Sis chipset etc. Some of the functional components of a motherboard are shown in Fig 2.10 below.

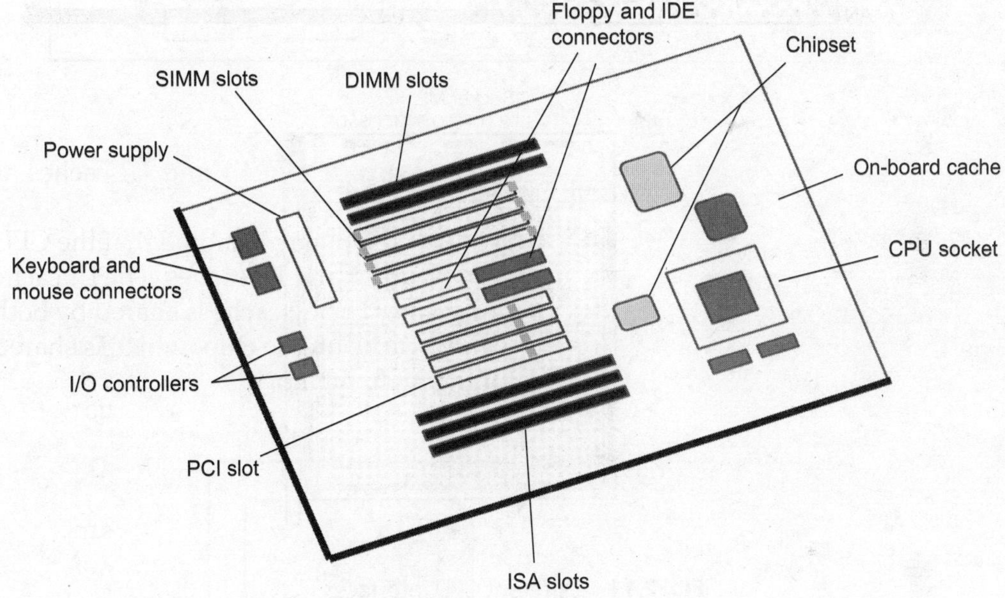

Fig. 2.10 A typical motherboard

2.3.1 CPU Interface

This interface is used to connect the CPU to the motherboard. The interface present on the motherboard decides as to which microprocessor or family of microprocessors can be plugged to the motherboard. For instance, Socket A connects Duron microprocessors whereas Socket 7 connects AMD K6, and Intel MMX microprocessors. Generally, a socket is so designed that the microprocessor can be easily inserted or removed from the socket. Accordingly, the sockets are called Zero In Force (ZIF) sockets. Some typical sockets are shown in Fig. 2.11.

Socket 7 is a 321 pin interface for Pentium, Pentium MMX and their AMD equivalent chips. Socket T is used by Pentium 4 Prescott processor, Pentium D and Pentium Extreme Edition processors. The socket M2 is used for AMD Athelon processors.

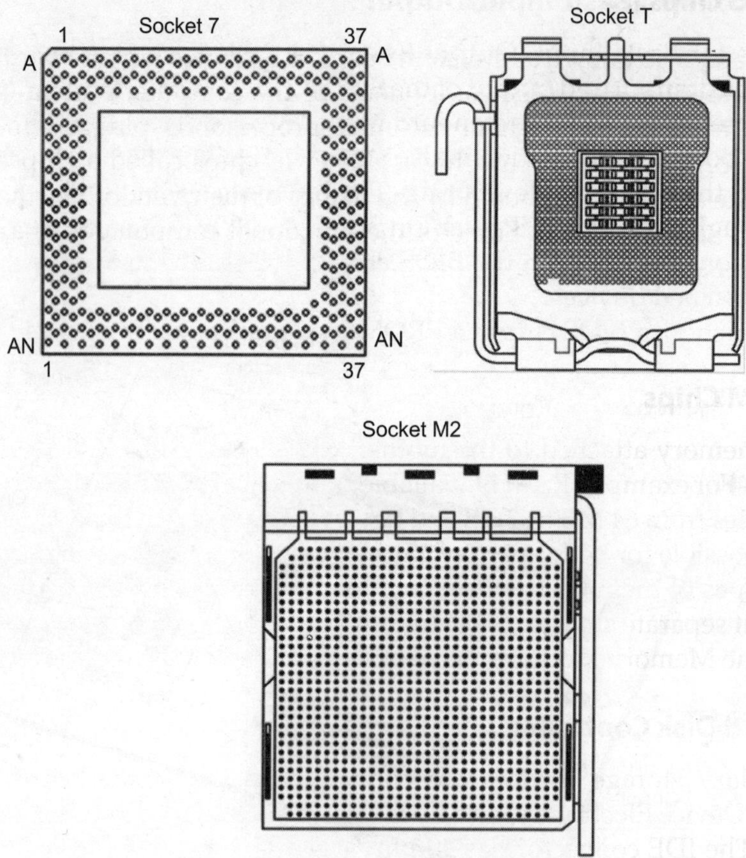

Fig. 2.11 Different CPU interfaces

2.3.2 Front Side Bus

A front side bus (FSB) connects the CPU with the motherboard chipset and the main memory. The commonly available speed of the FSB is in the range of 66-800 Mz. The speed of the FSB is very important because the maximum speed at which the main memory can interact with CPU is the FSB speed. If the FSB transfers 64 bits of data (8 bytes) at 800 MHz then the data transfer rate is (800 * 8) 6400MBps.

2.3.3 Chipset

A chipset is a cluster of IC chips present on the motherboard to control basic devices such as hard disks, floppy disks, serial/parallel ports etc. The chipset also controls the information flow from one component of the motherboard to another. A chipset is specific to a processor and therefore, the motherboard with a specific chipset can support only a compatible processor on board.

2.3.4 BIOS chips (Basic Input/Output System)

BIOS stands for Basic Input/Output System. As the name suggests these IC chips contain the basic input and output of the System. BIOS is a set of program instructions capable of interacting with the standard input output devices attached to a computer system. The boot-up information is also stored in the BIOS chips. When the system is switched on, the BIOS starts executing. The BIOS checks the status of the connected devices through a test called 'Power-On Self-Test' (POST). Thereafter, based on boot-up information contained on the BIOS chip, BIOS loads the operating system from one of the attached devices.

By construction, a BIOS chip is a PROM (programmable Read-Only Memory).

2.3.5 RAM Chips

The main memory attached to the motherboard is called the RAM, which comes in many types. For example, RAM is available as SDRAM, EDRAM, RDRAM etc. The size of RAM varies from 64 MB to 4 GB and beyond. The speed of the RAM chip should be as high as possible for better performance of the computer system. A brief discussion on many types of memory has been included in Section 1.3.3. It may be noted from Fig. 2.10 that separate slots for SIMMs (Single In-Line Memory Modules) and DIMMs (Dual In-Line Memory Modules)have been provided on the motherboard.

2.3.6 Hard Disk Controller

The secondary storage devices are connected to the motherboard through IDE (Intelligent Device Electronics) and FDD (Floppy Disk Drive) connectors provided on the board. The IDE connector has 40 pins through which the following IDE devices can be attached

1. Hard disk drives
2. High density disk drives
3. CD-ROM/DVD drives

Similarly, Floppy drives are connected to the motherboard through a 34-pin connector.

2.3.7 Expansion Slots

Peripheral devices are connected to the motherboard through expansion slots called PCI (Peripheral Connect Interface) slots. For instance, sound cards and graphic cards, gaming cards, network cards are plugged to the motherboard's available standard 32-bit PCI slots.

2.3.8 USB Ports

Universal Serial Bus (USB) has become an industry standard to connect peripheral devices to the computer system. Therefore, a motherboard supports more than one

USB port to which devices such as keyboard, printers, scanners, PenRam, mouse etc. are connected in 'plug-n-play' mode. A USB port is a 5 pin connector. The operating system detects a device as soon as it is plugged to the USB port of the computer system.

EXERCISES

1. Define the term: microprocessor? Why it is called a 'micro'?
2. Name the first microprocessor developed by Intel. On which semiconductor technology was it built?
3. Name some 8-bit microprocessors.
4. Name some 16-bit microprocessors.
5. Draw the broad level block diagram of a typical microprocessor.
6. Explain memory read operation by a CPU through memRead instruction.
7. Explain memory write operation by a CPU through memWrite operation.
8. Differentiate between CISC and RISC processor design types.
9. Name some CISC microprocessor.
10. Name some RISC microprocessors.
11. Write short notes on the following:
    a. First generation microprocessors
    b. Second generation microprocessors
    c. Third generation microprocessors
    d. Fourth generation microprocessors
    e. Fifth generation microprocessors
12. Write short notes on the following
    a. Sixth generation microprocessors.
    b. Seventh generation microprocessors
    c. Eighth generation microprocessors
13. Define the term: hyperthreading.
14. Why fifth generation microprocessor was named Pentium by Intel instead of 80586.
15. What is meant by a core in a microprocessor?
16. Draw the block diagram of a multicore microprocessor.
17. Draw the block diagram of Intel Core i7 microprocessor.
18. Comment on the utility of a motherboard in a microcomputer.
19. Draw a line diagram of a typical motherboard and label the various components present on such a system board.
20. What is a CPU interface? Name some popular CPU interfaces.
21. Explain in brief the following components of a motherboard:
    a. Front side bus
    b. Chipset
    c. BIOS chips
    d. RAM chips
    e. Expansion slots
22. How many pins are there in a USB port?

CHAPTER

3 Input/Output Devices

3.1 INPUT DEVICES

An input device is connected to the computer system to provide data to the computer system. A wide variety of input devices are available and some of the popular devices are discussed in brief in the following sections.

3.1.1 Keyboard

This is the most essential input device which is connected to the computer system. The user can issue commands and provide data to the computer system by pressing a sequence of keys present on the keyboard. As the name suggests, the keyboard has a large number of keys. The layout of the keys on the keyboard is similar to that of a typewriter, as shown in Fig. 3.1. A standard computer keyboard is called a QWERTY keyboard because of the type of layout of the keys in its typing area.

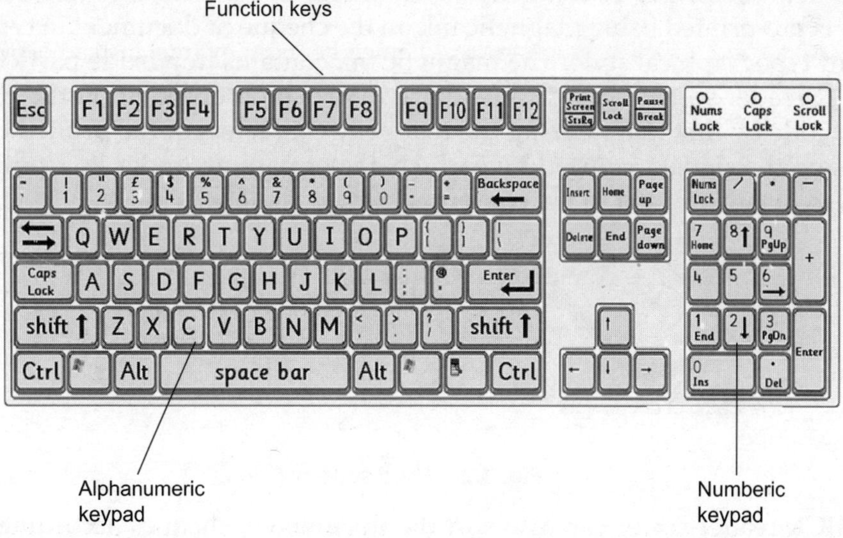

Fig.3.1 Keyboard

The IBM PC AT enhanced keyboard has 101 keys. As far as layout is concerned, a keyboard can be divided into three parts: Alphanumeric keypad, Numeric keypad, and Function keys.

The Alphanumeric Keypad: This is the central part of the keyboard. It contains all the alphanumeric keys i.e., letters, numbers, punctuation keys, and some special purpose keys such as 'shift', 'space bar', 'enter', 'back space', 'tab', 'ctrl', 'esc', and 'Alt' keys.

The Numeric Keypad: This is a group of seventeen keys consisting of nine numeric keys, four of which are also marked with directional arrows.

The Function Keys: On a typical keyboard, there are 10–12 function keys labelled F1 to F12. These keys perform functions or provide shortcuts to commands such as invocation of on-screen menus, assignment of commands, system settings etc.

Thus, there are separate keys for each letter, digit, and symbol. When a key is pressed, the keyboard encoder generates the corresponding 8-bitcode which is thereafter submitted to the computer system. If a key is pressed for more than 0.5 sec then the keyboard repeatedly generates and sends the character code to the computer system. Therefore, the character is repeatedly displayed on the VDU (Visual Display Unit) of the computer. This action is called **typematic** and the typematic rate is 10 times per second. The keyboard supports typematic action for all keys except the shift key.

It may be noted that for some characters such as '#', '%', '&' etc., one must press and hold more than one key at the same time.

3.1.2 Magnetic Ink Character Recognition (MICR)

MICR is primarily used in banks for capturing information from cheques. The MICR coding system consists of 14 characters (four special symbols and 10 decimal digits). The code is pre-printed using magnetic ink on the cheque or document in type E-13B, a standard typographical style. The magnetic ink contains iron oxide particles.

A MICR reader-sorter is used to read the information encoded on the cheque. It reads the code by first magnetizing the magnetic characters of the printed code and then sensing the signals induced by each character passing under its reading head. The data so obtained is fed to the computer system, as shown in Fig. 3.2

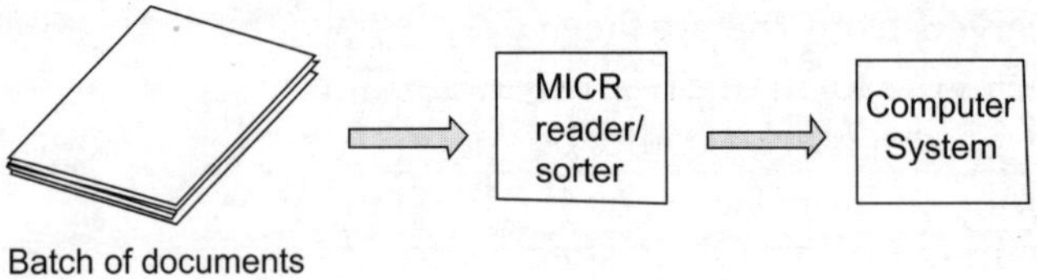

Fig. 3.2 MICR system

The MICR reader-sorter can also sort the documents/cheques according to their identification code numbers.

The advantages of MICR are:

1. The identification codes can be read by both MICR and human beings.
2. Error detection and correction becomes easier.
3. Extremely useful for the banking industry.

However, the strength of the magnetic ink of the printed characters decreases in due course of time.

3.1.3 Optical Character Recognition (OCR)

Optical character recognition (OCR) is a process of recognizing pre-printed characters. An OCR system distinguishes one character from another provided the characters meet OCR standards. OCR-A, and OCR-B are two popular OCR standards.

OCR - A

ABCDEFGHIJKLMNOPQRSTUVWXYZ

abcdefghikl;mnopqrstuvwxyz

1234567890

Fig. 3.3 Optical font OCR-A

An OCR reader can read alphabetic, numeric and special characters which are printed or typed on a paper. The OCR reader uses photoelectric devices to scan the characters. It converts the reflected light patterns of data into binary data suitable for computer processing. The normal speed of an OCR reader is 1500–3000 characters per second.

3.1.4 Optical Mark Reader (OMR)

An optical mark reader detects the presence or absence of a pencil/pen mark on a paper. Light is shone onto the marked paper and reflected light is observed by the OCR. The mark reflects less light as compared to a white space. When an OCR scans the document, it confirms the presence or absence of a mark from the intensity of the reflected light received from the surface of the paper. The only limitation is that the document must be in the form of pre-printed cards, sheets, or forms having specified portions or boxes where marks could be made. A sample OMR sheet is shown in Fig. 3.4.

The major advantage of an OMR sheet with pre-printed boxes is that it is very widely used for objective type tests. The questionnaires are designed accordingly with multiple choice entries. The examinee selects an appropriate box out of the option boxes and fills it using a soft pencil. The OMR easily reads such sheets at a considerable speed of 300–500 documents per minute.

Answer Sheet

For each answer, please fill in marks like this: ● not like this ⊠ ⊘ ⊘

1	Ⓐ	Ⓑ	Ⓒ	Ⓓ	Ⓔ	31	Ⓐ	Ⓑ	Ⓒ	Ⓓ	Ⓔ
2	Ⓐ	Ⓑ	Ⓒ	Ⓓ	Ⓔ	32	Ⓐ	Ⓑ	Ⓒ	Ⓓ	Ⓔ
3	Ⓐ	Ⓑ	Ⓒ	Ⓓ	Ⓔ	33	Ⓐ	Ⓑ	Ⓒ	Ⓓ	Ⓔ
4	Ⓐ	Ⓑ	Ⓒ	Ⓓ	Ⓔ	34	Ⓐ	Ⓑ	Ⓒ	Ⓓ	Ⓔ
5	Ⓐ	Ⓑ	Ⓒ	Ⓓ	Ⓔ	35	Ⓐ	Ⓑ	Ⓒ	Ⓓ	Ⓔ
6	Ⓐ	Ⓑ	Ⓒ	Ⓓ	Ⓔ	36	Ⓐ	Ⓑ	Ⓒ	Ⓓ	Ⓔ
7	Ⓐ	Ⓑ	Ⓒ	Ⓓ	Ⓔ	37	Ⓐ	Ⓑ	Ⓒ	Ⓓ	Ⓔ
8	Ⓐ	Ⓑ	Ⓒ	Ⓓ	Ⓔ	38	Ⓐ	Ⓑ	Ⓒ	Ⓓ	Ⓔ
9	Ⓐ	Ⓑ	Ⓒ	Ⓓ	Ⓔ	39	Ⓐ	Ⓑ	Ⓒ	Ⓓ	Ⓔ
10	Ⓐ	Ⓑ	Ⓒ	Ⓓ	Ⓔ	40	Ⓐ	Ⓑ	Ⓒ	Ⓓ	Ⓔ
11	Ⓐ	Ⓑ	Ⓒ	Ⓓ	Ⓔ	41	Ⓐ	Ⓑ	Ⓒ	Ⓓ	Ⓔ
12	Ⓐ	Ⓑ	Ⓒ	Ⓓ	Ⓔ	42	Ⓐ	Ⓑ	Ⓒ	Ⓓ	Ⓔ
13	Ⓐ	Ⓑ	Ⓒ	Ⓓ	Ⓔ	43	Ⓐ	Ⓑ	Ⓒ	Ⓓ	Ⓔ
14	Ⓐ	Ⓑ	Ⓒ	Ⓓ	Ⓔ	44	Ⓐ	Ⓑ	Ⓒ	Ⓓ	Ⓔ
15	Ⓐ	Ⓑ	Ⓒ	Ⓓ	Ⓔ	45	Ⓐ	Ⓑ	Ⓒ	Ⓓ	Ⓔ
16	Ⓐ	Ⓑ	Ⓒ	Ⓓ	Ⓔ	46	Ⓐ	Ⓑ	Ⓒ	Ⓓ	Ⓔ
17	Ⓐ	Ⓑ	Ⓒ	Ⓓ	Ⓔ	47	Ⓐ	Ⓑ	Ⓒ	Ⓓ	Ⓔ
18	Ⓐ	Ⓑ	Ⓒ	Ⓓ	Ⓔ	48	Ⓐ	Ⓑ	Ⓒ	Ⓓ	Ⓔ
19	Ⓐ	Ⓑ	Ⓒ	Ⓓ	Ⓔ	49	Ⓐ	Ⓑ	Ⓒ	Ⓓ	Ⓔ
20	Ⓐ	Ⓑ	Ⓒ	Ⓓ	Ⓔ	50	Ⓐ	Ⓑ	Ⓒ	Ⓓ	Ⓔ
21	Ⓐ	Ⓑ	Ⓒ	Ⓓ	Ⓔ	51	Ⓐ	Ⓑ	Ⓒ	Ⓓ	Ⓔ
22	Ⓐ	Ⓑ	Ⓒ	Ⓓ	Ⓔ	52	Ⓐ	Ⓑ	Ⓒ	Ⓓ	Ⓔ
23	Ⓐ	Ⓑ	Ⓒ	Ⓓ	Ⓔ	53	Ⓐ	Ⓑ	Ⓒ	Ⓓ	Ⓔ
24	Ⓐ	Ⓑ	Ⓒ	Ⓓ	Ⓔ	54	Ⓐ	Ⓑ	Ⓒ	Ⓓ	Ⓔ
25	Ⓐ	Ⓑ	Ⓒ	Ⓓ	Ⓔ	55	Ⓐ	Ⓑ	Ⓒ	Ⓓ	Ⓔ
26	Ⓐ	Ⓑ	Ⓒ	Ⓓ	Ⓔ	56	Ⓐ	Ⓑ	Ⓒ	Ⓓ	Ⓔ
27	Ⓐ	Ⓑ	Ⓒ	Ⓓ	Ⓔ	57	Ⓐ	Ⓑ	Ⓒ	Ⓓ	Ⓔ
28	Ⓐ	Ⓑ	Ⓒ	Ⓓ	Ⓔ	58	Ⓐ	Ⓑ	Ⓒ	Ⓓ	Ⓔ
29	Ⓐ	Ⓑ	Ⓒ	Ⓓ	Ⓔ	59	Ⓐ	Ⓑ	Ⓒ	Ⓓ	Ⓔ
30	Ⓐ	Ⓑ	Ⓒ	Ⓓ	Ⓔ	60	Ⓐ	Ⓑ	Ⓒ	Ⓓ	Ⓔ

Fig. 3.4 A sample OMR sheet

Note: In some cases, the OMR senses the conductivity of the graphic marking for recognizing the presence or absence of a mark. This activity is called 'mark sensing'. Accordingly, the sheets or forms are filled by the examinees by soft pencils so as to deposit adequate graphite in the box.

3.2 GRAPHIC INPUT DEVICES – POINTING DEVICES

Some input devices are used to show a moving pointer on the screen. The pointer can be moved to any location on the screen by moving the pointing device. Therefore, such input devices are called pointing devices. They are useful in working with menu-driven applications on a computer system. Pointing devices are also useful for computer graphics applications. Some popular pointing devices are discussed in the following sections.

3.2.1 Mouse

A mouse is a hand held pointing device (see Fig. 3.5). It is moved on a flat surface and the changing position of the mouse in terms of x and y coordinates is captured. The x, y coordinates are conveyed to the computer system. The computer system accordingly controls the direction and magnitude of a pointer's movement on the screen, in the form of a graphic shape called the **cursor**.

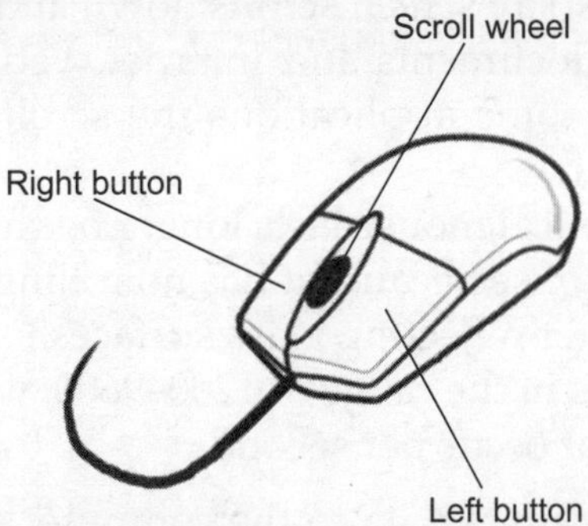

Fig. 3.5 A computer mouse

The movement of the mouse is captured by two methods: roller based and optical based methods and accordingly the mouse is termed as an electromechanical mouse or an optical mouse.

Electromechanical mouse: This mouse has a rubber ball at its bottom that rolls on the flat surface. The rolling ball is coupled with potentiometers that sense the relative movement of the mouse in the orthogonal directions. The motion is converted to digital values which when fed to the computer system are used to determine the direction and magnitude of the mouse's movement. For the sake of convenience, the user can pick up the mouse and move it in the air and then place it at a suitable place without causing any change in the apparent position of the cursor on the screen.

Optical mouse: An optical mouse, as the name suggests, uses light emitting diodes (LED) to transmit a red coloured light on the lower surface. The light gets bounced back onto a complementary metal-oxide semiconductor (CMOS) sensor in the form an image. A digital signal processor (DSP) detects patterns in the images. In fact 1500 images are generated per second and the change in patterns observed by the DSP in a sequence of images help in deciding how far the mouse has moved. DSP sends the changed coordinates to the computer which in turn displays the cursor on the screen.

Generally, a mouse has 2 buttons and a scroll wheel which are used to provide input signals to the computer system by the user.

The mouse is moved in such a manner that the cursor on the screen gets positioned on a desired item or icon present on the screen. To select the item, the left button is pushed and the action is called left-clicking or single-clicking. To open or execute the file/command associated with the icon/item, the left button is clicked twice in quick succession. On the other hand, a right-click (right button pushed) displays a list of optional operations available for the item at the time. For example, the operations such as 'cut', 'copy', 'paste', open' etc. are displayed after a right-click on an item.

The scroll wheel is a small plastic disk located between the left and right buttons. It is rolled by using the index finger in the forward and backward direction and accordingly the computer display screen scrolls down and up respectively. It is very useful in scrolling through documents and internet web pages. It can be pushed down also and therefore in some applications the scroll wheel is used as a third button.

It may be noted that the optical mouse lasts longer because it has no moving parts. It is also lighter than a ball mouse because it has no rolling ball. However, an optical mouse should not be used over reflecting glass surfaces.

The baud rate of a mouse is in the range of 1200–9600, where, baud rate means the number of signal changes that occur per second.

Note: A **wireless mouse** transmits data to the computer using wireless technology such as radio waves or infrared light waves.

3.2.2 Digitizer (Graphic Tablet)

A digitizer is a flat surface device (see Fig. 3.6). A hand-held stylus is moved over the flat surface in the form of a pencil. The movement of the stylus is displayed on the screen as a continuous line on the computer screen. The current position of the stylus is represented by a graphic cursor on the screen.

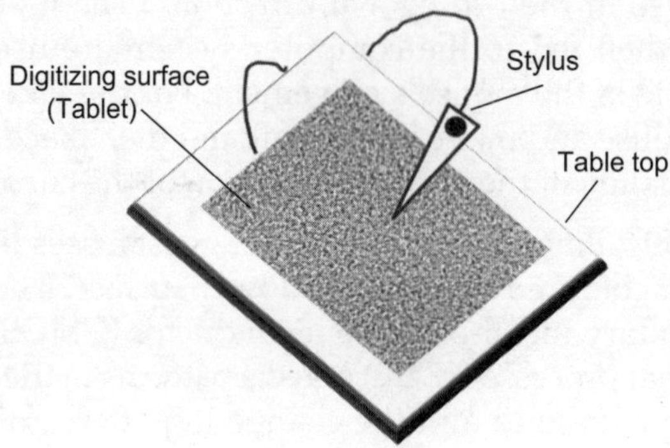

Fig. 3.6 A digitizer

With a little practice, curves and drawings can be drawn easily on the screen by carefully manoeuvring the stylus on the digitizer. It is also very widely used by the transport department to capture the signature of persons who apply to them for a driving licence. The internal working of a digitizer is explained below:

A mesh of wires is embedded on the surface of a digitizer. Each cross-section point on the digitizer represents an absolute point on the display screen. Generally, a digitizer has more than or equal to 1024 such points, also called pressure points. The movement of the stylus is captured through a transducer (pressure sensitive switch). Electromagnetic coupling between the electrical signals in the mesh and the stylus induces an electrical signal in a coil of wire in the stylus. The value of electrical signal conveyed to the computer system is used to determine roughly how far the stylus is from the digitizer surface (far, near, on).

The information is obtained by a computer from a digitizer in one of the following ways:

1. The computer makes a request after every t units of time. This time interval sampling is useful for displaying the screen cursor corresponding to the position of the stylus on the surface.
2. Each time the stylus is moved for more than a specified distance d. The distance–interval sampling is appropriate for digitizing drawings in order to avoid recording of an excessive number of points.

A digitizer is also known as a 'digitizing tablet' or simply a 'tablet'.

Note: A mouse reports relative movement only, whereas a tablet reports absolute positions moved by a stylus. The important parameters of a digitizer are: resolution, linearity, repeatability, range etc.

3.2.3 Joystick

A joystick is an input pointing device. It is a stick that pivots on a base through a ball and socket arrangement. Therefore, the stick can be moved in any direction. A potentiometer senses the movement of the stick in terms of its angle and direction. Very often, sets of springs are used to return the joystick to its home centre position.

A joystick contains many buttons (see Fig. 3.7) which when pressed activate some events. Some of the buttons are called triggers.

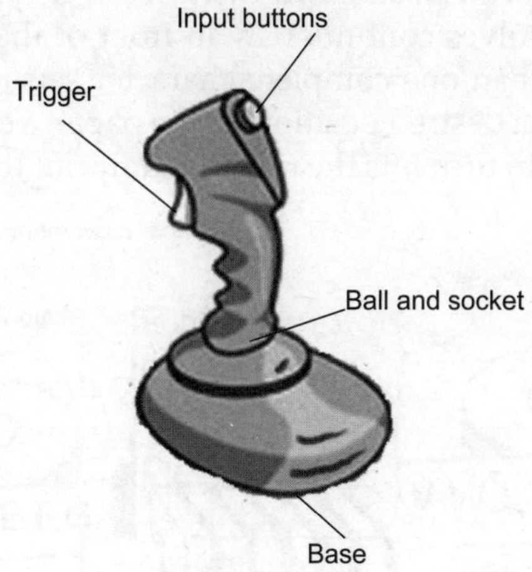

Fig. 3.7 Joystick

Generally, a joystick is used to control the velocity of the screen cursor's movement. It is very widely used to play games and control its components especially games wherein fast interactions are required.

3.3 OUTPUT DEVICES

The data input to the computer is processed to produce some output, also called results. The results are presented in the form of information that can be of four types: text, graphics, sound (audio) and video. An **output device** delivers the information to the user of the computer system. The main online output device is the computer screen, also called a visual display unit (VDU). The other output devices are printers, plotters, storage devices etc.

3.3.1 Printers

A printer is an output device. It is used to produce text and graphics on a physical medium such as paper. The output so obtained is called a **hard copy**. Printers can be broadly divided into the following two classes:

1. Impact printers
2. Non-impact printers

3.3.1.1 Impact Printers

Impact printers produce the output by striking a print element against an ink ribbon that is pressed against a paper. In fact the working is similar to that of a typewriter. These types of printers can be further divided into two categories: line printers and character printers. A brief discussion on both types of impact printers is given below:

Line Printers: A line printer produces a line-at-a-time printed output. A chain or drum of letters and symbols pass at a very high speed in front of a row of hammers. There is one hammer for every print position in the printer. In the case of chain printers, a closed circular chain revolves continuously in front of the print line (see Fig. 3.8). The chain contains more than one complete character sets on its periphery. When a character comes in front of a desired position on the paper, a corresponding hammer is made to hit the paper that in turn hits the ribbon to imprint the character on the paper.

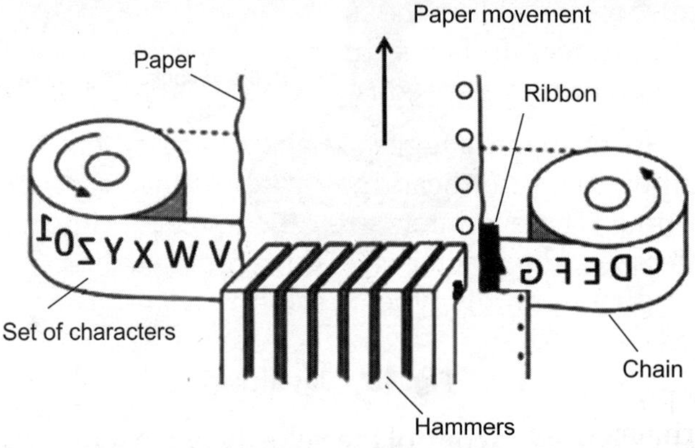

Fig. 3.8 A chain printer

Since the chain is continuously revolving, a stage arrives when the required character on the chain comes on its print position. The printing mechanism activates the corresponding hammer to strike against the ribbon. Moreover, in one complete revolution of the chain, a complete line gets printed. The paper is thereafter moved up by a line.

In case of a drum line printer, a complete character set is embossed around the circumference of a solid cylindrical drum at every print position. The number of print positions depends upon the size of the printer. For instance, a 132 column printer shall have 132 print positions, where each print position contains a complete character set (see Fig. 3.9). The drum continuously rotates at a high speed. Similar to chain printers, there is one hammer for every print position in the drum printer. A hammer is activated when the required character passes under it.

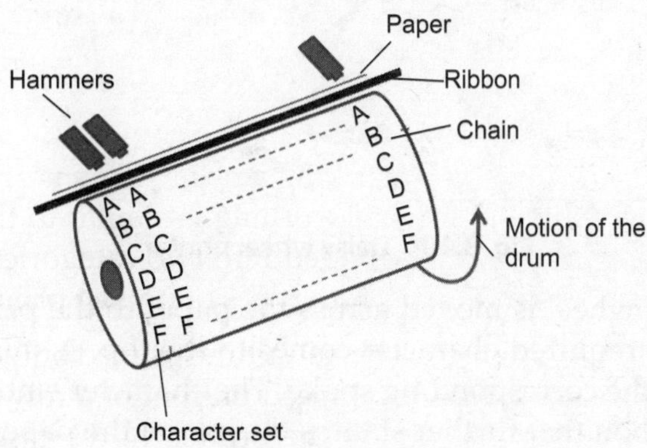

Fig. 3.9 A drum printer

Similar to a chain printer, one complete revolution of the drum is required to print each line.

Note: Line printers are available in the size range of 80–132 columns. Drum printers are faster than chain printers. In fact a drum printer works at 300 to 2000 lines per minute whereas a chain printer's speed is 400 to 2500 characters per minute.

Character Printers: As the name suggests, a character printer prints a **character-at-a time** of printed output. The print head moves across the page line by line, printing one character at a time. These printers are called smart printers because these are bi-directional printers i.e., the printer can print in either direction forward as well as backward. Depending upon the type of printing head, the character printers are broadly classified as:

1. Letter quality printers
2. Dot matrix printers.

A letter quality printer uses high quality, solid font characters. The print head is in the form of a wheel consisting of spokes radiating out of the central hub in the form of a 'daisy' flower. The printer is called daisy wheel printer, as shown in Fig. 3.10. The characters are embossed near the tip of the spokes.

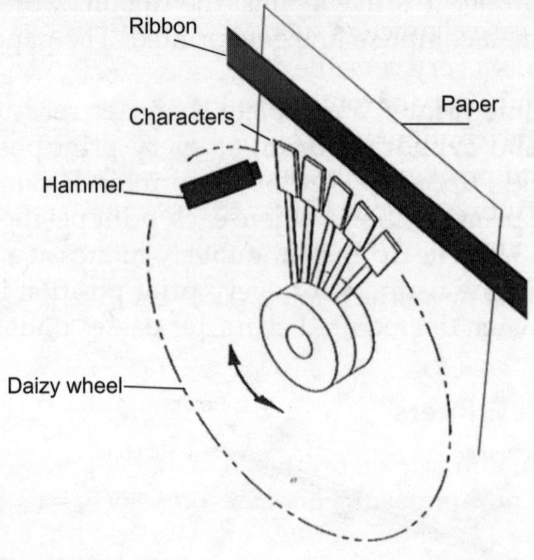

Fig. 3.10 Daisy wheel printer

While printing, the wheel is moved across the paper to the printing position and then rotated until the required character comes to the top. A small hammer is then activated to strike on the corresponding spoke. The character embossed on the spoke strikes against the ribbon that further stamps the ink on the paper.

Since a lot of mechanical movement is involved in this printing method, daisy wheel printers are very slow and therefore not in vogue.

A dot matrix printer creates a character from a set of dots. The print head contains a vertical array of pins. Fig. 3.11 illustrates a typical dot matrix print head.

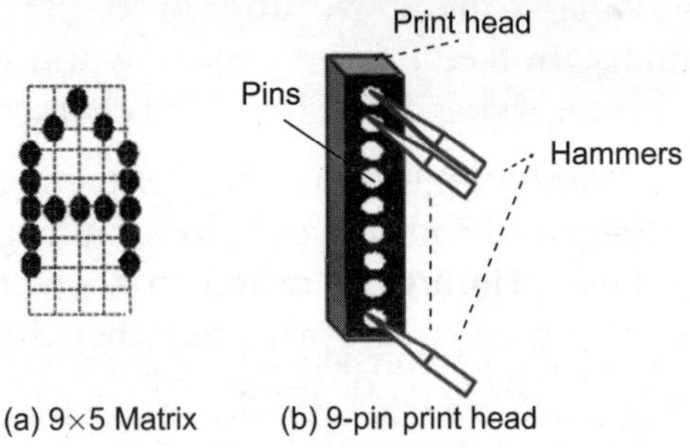

Fig. 3.11 Dot matrix print head

While printing, the head moves across the paper to the printing position and selected pins are made to strike against an inked ribbon to form a pattern of the character on the paper. To print the full character, the print head moves a predetermined number of column positions to complete the matrix. The matrix contains 7 rows and 5 columns. Since the number of pins in the print head is 9, the remaining 2 pin are used form descendants of lower case characters such as p, g, q and y.

A dot matrix printer is a very versatile device because by changing the order of pins that strike the paper, a variety of fonts of different sizes and types can be produced on the paper. In fact, the configuration of pins can easily be changed to print data in different languages and print graphics as well.

For high quality printing, 24-pin dot matrix printers are used wherein the print head contains 24 pins instead of the usual 9 pins.

Note: With the advent of newer technology printers, these printers are also not very popular anymore.

3.3.1.2 Non-impact Printers

The technology used in non-impact printers is just the opposite of that used in impact printers. The popular non-impact technology printers are: ink-jet printers and laser printers.

Ink-jet Printers: An ink-jet printer produces a character by shooting small ink droplets onto the paper. There are many ways of shooting or spraying the droplets onto the paper. One simple technique is the thermal heating of ink called **bubble inkjet technology**. In this method, ink is heated from one end to more than 300^{0}C and the vaporized ink forms a bubble (see Fig. 3.12). When the bubble expands, a drop of ink is forced out of an orifice.

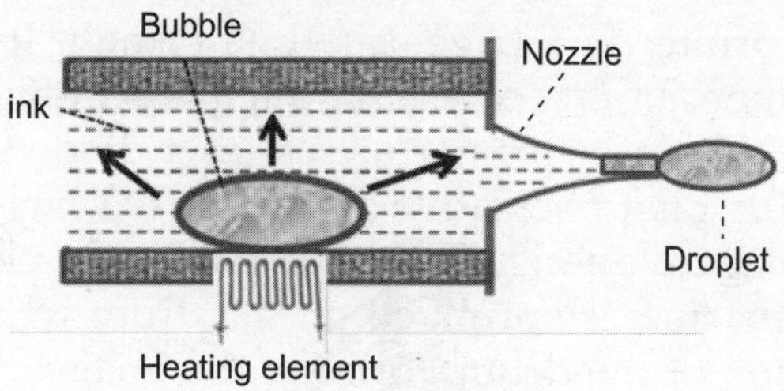

Fig. 3.12 Bubble jet

Now, the cartridge of a bubble jet consists of a reservoir of ink and a set of fine nozzles, 64–128 in number. Each nozzle contains a heating element. The heating element creates heat at one end of the nozzle filled with ink. The localized heating causes ink to vaporize in the form of a bubble (see Fig. 3.12). The bubble expands to eject a droplet from the nozzle onto the paper. It may be noted that all nozzle can eject droplets simultaneously. By selectively controlling the nozzles, a required pattern is obtained on the paper.

The other method is **piezoelectric inkjet technology**. We know that when charge is applied on a piezo crystal, it changes its shape. A cone shaped piezoelectric crystal is fixed at one end of an ink reservoir connected to a nozzle, as shown in Fig. 3.13. The crystal changes its shape as and when electric current is passed through it. The flexing action of the crystal ejects a droplet from the nozzle onto the paper.

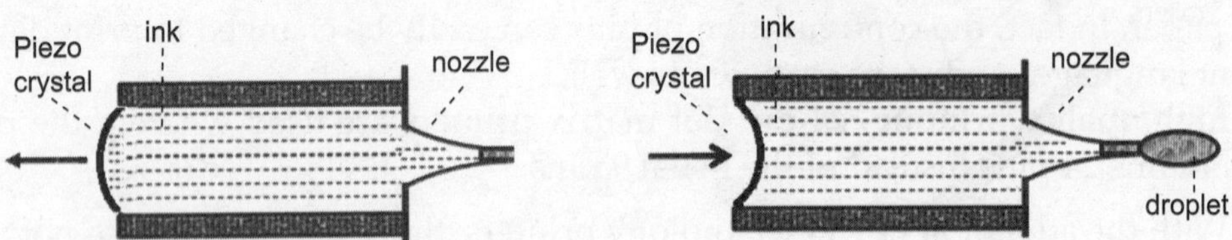

(a) Before charge is applied on the crystal (b) After charge is applied on the crystal

Fig. 3.13 Piezoelectric inkjet

Similar to a bubble jet, the cartridge of a piezoelectric inkjet also consists of a reservoir of ink and a set of fine nozzles, 128–192 in number. Each nozzle contains a piezoelectric crystal and all nozzles can eject droplets simultaneously. By selectively controlling the nozzles, a required pattern is obtained on the paper.

It may be noted that piezoelectric inkjet technology is faster than the bubble jet technology because the thermal technology inherently wastes some time waiting in each heating and cooling cycle. Moreover much smaller droplets can be produced by piezoelectric method as compared to thermal technology. Thus, the piezoelectric inkjet printers have a higher resolution of graphic output i.e., in the range of 1440 X 720 dpi (dots per inch).

Laser Printers: A laser printer is a page-at-a-time printer. It works in a fashion similar to a Xerox machine. In fact a laser printer is an offshoot of electrostatic photocopier technology. The laser printer uses a laser diode to write information onto a drum coated with photo sensitive material (see Fig. 3.14). The drum is initially charged with negative ions. The laser positively charges the drum on selected areas. Special ink dust is sprinkled on the drum which gets stuck to the positively charged portion of the drum, forming the image. As the drum rotates, the paper is wrapped around it and the image is transferred onto the paper. Rollers and heaters are used to fuse the ink on the paper. Finally a flange scrapes the residual toner from the drum.

The printed paper is rolled out on an output tray by 'paper exit rollers'. In the meantime, the drum passes under the 'erase lamp', also called the 'discharge lamp'. The bright light of the discharge lamp erases the electric image. Now the drum is ready for the next cycle of printing.

Laser printers are very high quality printers. The standard speed of a laser printer is to the tune of 12–24 ppm (pages per minute).

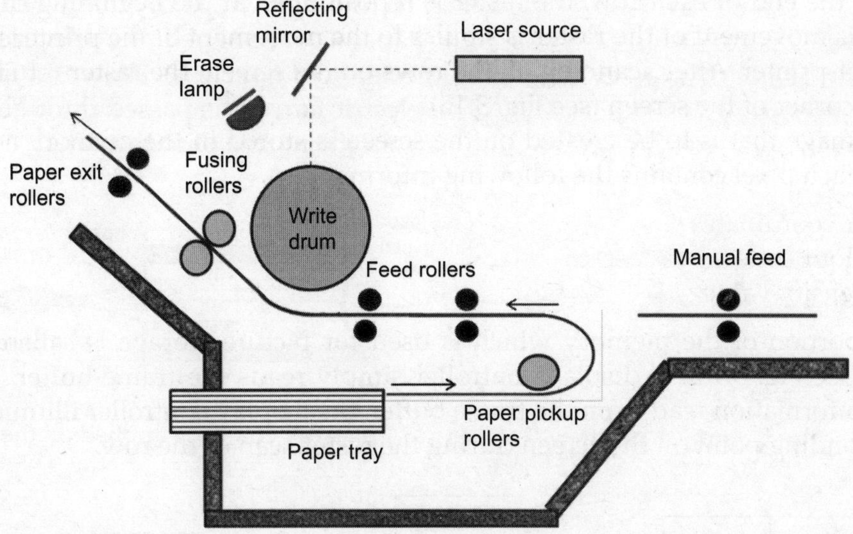

Fig. 3.14 A laser printer

3.3.2 Display Devices

A computer display unit, also called a screen, is the primary man-machine interface. The screen consists of a grid of points in the form rows and columns. The grid point is called a **pixel** (picture element). Each pixel can be illuminated. An image can be formed by selectively illuminating specified pixels on the screen. The image is created on the screen by two methods: raster scan display and vector scan display.

Raster Scan Display: In this method the various pixels are continuously scanned row by row. Within the row, the pixels are scanned column by column, as shown in Fig. 3.15. The scanning process starts from the upper left corner of the screen and travels in a horizontal direction along a row. If a pixel at a column in the row needs to be illuminated then that pixel is excited to illumination; otherwise, the pixels remain off and is skipped. This pattern of scanning is called **raster**.

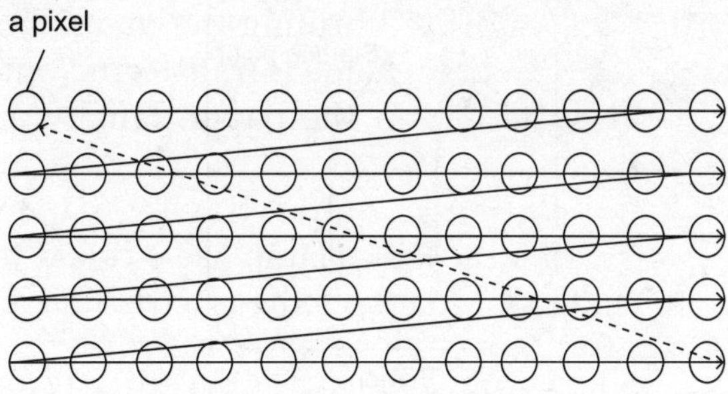

Fig. 3.15 Raster scan

After the end of each row, the raster is repositioned at the beginning of the next row. This movement of the raster is similar to the movement of the printer head of a character printer. After scanning all the rows on the screen, the raster returns to the top left corner of the screen (see Fig. 3.15).

The image that is to be created on the screen is stored in the memory as a set of pixels. Each pixel contains the following information:

1. X-Y coordinates
2. Colour code
3. Intensity value

The portion of the memory which is used for picture storage is called a frame buffer (See Fig. 3.16). A display controller simply reads the frame buffer. For each pixel's information read from the frame buffer, the display controller illuminates the corresponding point on the screen during the raster scan of the row.

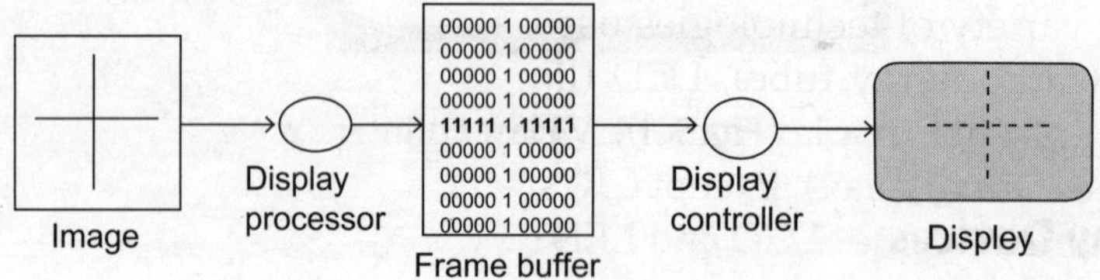

Fig. 3.16 Raster graphic display

Since the raster continuously moves from line to line, it becomes necessary for the raster to retrace each and every point on the screen at regular intervals. The activity of retracing is called refresh cycle. Generally the refresh frequency is equal to or more than 60 Hz i.e., 60 cycles per second.

Vector Display (Random Scan): The display system directly moves to the starting point of the picture and illuminates it. Thereafter, the display system traces the image like a pen by moving on the screen between successive points and lines of the outline of the picture (see Fig. 3.17). In fact the vector scan moves in a pen-plotter fashion.

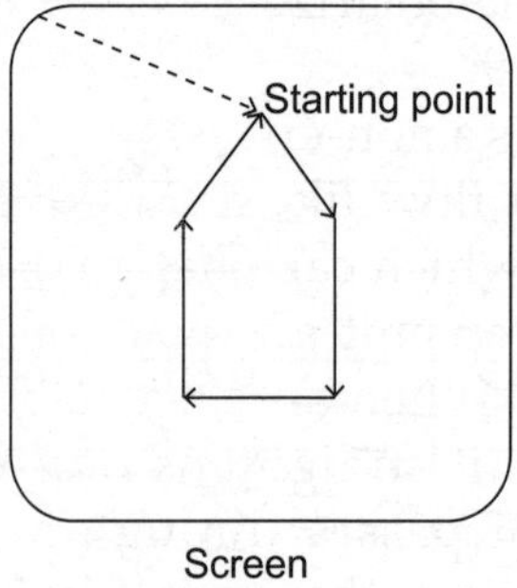

Fig. 3.17 Vector scan

In this method, the picture is converted to a set of line-drawing commands by a display file translator. The set of line-drawing commands, called **vectors**, are written into an area of memory referred to as the (refresh) display file. These commands are interpreted by a Display processor which in turn illuminates the corresponding lines on the screen, as shown in Fig. 3.18.

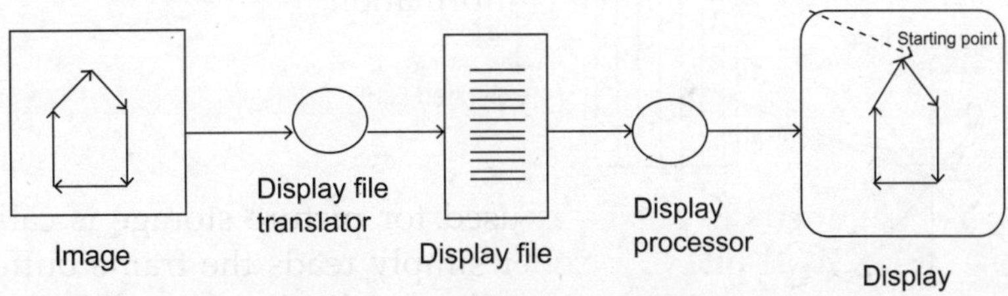

File 3.18 Vector scan display system

There are a variety of technologies used for the construction of computer screens namely CRT (cathode ray tube), LCD (liquid crystal display), LED (light emitting diodes), PDP (plasma display panel), VFD (vacuum florescent display), and ELD (electro luminescent display). Except CRTs, all display screens are flat panel displays. CRTs are no more in vogue. LCD and LED displays are very widely used as computer screens.

Cathode Ray Tube (CRT) display: In this method an image is created on the face of a cathode ray tube. The CRT face is coated with phosphor coating. An electron gun, guided by horizontal and vertical voltages, is focused on the desired point at the face of the CRT. When the beam strikes at the phosphor coating of the point, a short duration glow is produced. Since the refresh rate is to the tune of 60 refresh cycles per second (60 Hz), the image produced on the CRT face looks unceasing. However, the emissions emanated from the face of the CRT are hazardous in nature.

LCD (Liquid crystal display): We know that light waves vibrate in all possible directions. When the light passes through a polarizer, only the light waves that vibrate along the grid lines of the polarizer are allowed to pass and all other waves are blocked, as shown in Fig. 3.19.

Compared to a CRT, an LCD is a non-emissive device. The liquid crystal material has rod shaped molecules that flow like a liquid. It uses special liquid crystals, called nematic liquid crystals, which can change orientation by an electric charge so that they either block or transmit an incident light ray. Normally, a crystal adopts a twisted-up structure. When an electric current is applied to the liquid crystal, it tends to untwist i.e., it straightens out. When there is no current, the crystal is twisted and the light passes through it. However as soon as electric current passes through the crystal, the crystal untwists and blocks the incident light.

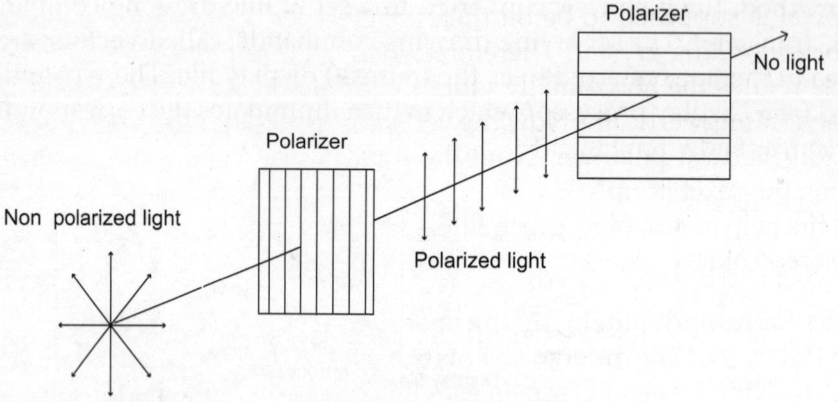

Fig. 3.19 Polarized light

The liquid crystal material is sandwiched between two glass plates. Each glass plate contains a light polarizer positioned at right angle to the other plate. A light source is placed at the back of a plate which has a horizontal polarizing filter. It uses CCFL(Cold Cathode Fluorescent Lamp) fluorescent tube as the source for the backlight, as shown in Fig. 3.20.

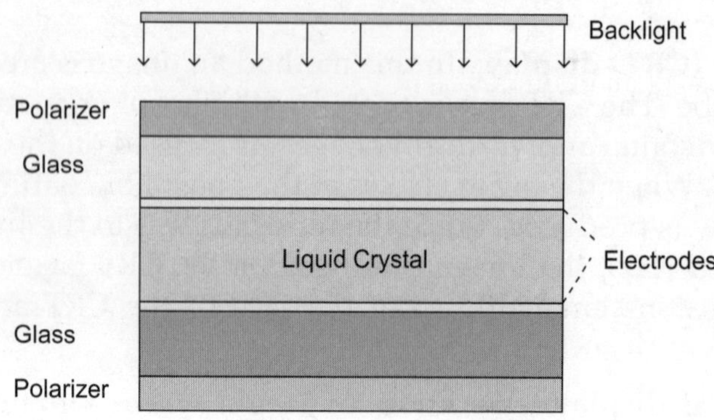

Fig. 3.20 LCD display

The arrangement works as given below:

1. The plate with the vertical polarizer faces the user and the plate with the horizontal polarizer is towards the back of the screen. A large bright light is placed at the back of the screen.
2. The light travels from the back of the screen towards the front.
3. A horizontal polarizer allows only the horizontally vibrating light waves and blocks the rest of them.
4. If a pixel is supposed to be switched off then the current is passed through its corresponding crystal, making it straight. The horizontally vibrating light passes through it which gets blocked by the vertical polarizer. No light is seen on the screen on this point thereby making the pixel dark.

5. If a pixel is supposed to be on then the electric current is not passed through its corresponding crystal. Therefore, the crystal remains twisted. The twisted crystal rotates the horizontally vibrating light waves to 90 degrees such that it starts vibrating vertically. Now the vertically vibrating light waves pass through the front vertical polarizer. Now the light is seen on the screen on this point making the pixel lit up.
6. With the help of red, blue, green filters, the lit up pixels are appropriately shown in desired colors.

LED (Light Emitting Diode): LED primarily uses the LCD technology to display images on the screen. The difference, however, lies in the type of backlighting used to illuminate the screen. The LED screen uses light emitting diodes to illuminate its LCD panel providing more illumination as compared to LCD panels. The LCD screen uses the 'Cold Cathode Fluorescent Lamp' (CCFL). The LED is much thinner than the CCFL technology and therefore LED screens are comparatively lighter and thinner than LCP panels. Moreover, LED technology consumes less power and generates low heat as compared to CCFLs.

Thus we can say that "All LEDs use LCD technology but not all LCDs use LEDs."

Exercises

1. What is the purpose of an input device in a computer system?
2. Draw the layout of a keyboard. Label its three components: Alphanumeric keypad, Numeric keypad, and Function keys
3. Why a keyboard is called QWERTY keyboard?
4. Define the term typematic in context of keyboards.
5. Which device is used for reading information coded on Bank cheques?
6. How many characters are used code MICR coding system and in what typographic style?
7. Write a short note on Magnetic Ink Character Recognition system.
8. Write a short note on Optical Character Recognition.
9. Name an input pointing device.
10. Write a short note on a computer mouse.
11. Discuss the types of computer mouse popularly used by the users.
12. Write a short note on digitizers.
13. Write a short note on joysticks.
14. Discuss the following impact printers:
    a. Line printers
    b. Character printers
15. Discuss the working of a bubble inkjet printer with the help of a block diagram.
16. Discuss the working of a piezoelectric inkjet printer with the help of a block diagram.
17. Discuss the working of a laser printer with the help of a block diagram.
18. Differentiate between raster scan and vector scan display systems.
19. Discuss the working of a raster scan display system with the help of a block diagram.
20. Discuss the working of a vector scan display system with the help of a block diagram.
21. Discuss the working of a liquid crystal diode display with the help of a block diagram.
22. How LED is different from LCD display?

CHAPTER

4 Data Representation

4.1 INTRODUCTION

The computer hardware is a digital machine that can work at an extremely fast rate. The main component of a digital device is a transistor. The transistor is a bi-stable device i.e., it can operate only in two states: fully conducting and non-conducting states. Therefore, it is used as a switch. The switch is **on** or **off** when it is in the fully conducting and non-conducting states respectively.

Since the basic component of a computer is a two state device, the data is accordingly represented in a computer by way of the presence or absence of electronic signals. This is called a binary or two state representation of data in terms of two numbers 0 and 1. Consequently, the number system is called a **binary number system**.

A brief discussion on number systems is given in following section.

4.2 NUMBER SYSTEMS

In our day to day life, we work with the decimal number system having 10 digit values 0 through 9 as ten symbols. Therefore, it is a base-10 counting number system. This system was given by ancient Indian mathematicians. A digit of a number written in the decimal system derives its meaning from its following two values:

1. **Symbol value**: It is the digit's value ranging from 0 to 9.
2. **Positional value**: it is determined by the position of the digit in the number, counting from the right hand side to the left i.e., units ($10^0 = 1$), tens ($10^1 = 10$), hundreds ($10^2 = 100$), thousands ($10^3 = 1000$) etc.

For example, the decimal number 108 derives its meanings in the manner shown in Table 4.1

Table 4.1

Number	Symbol value	Position from the right one	Positional value	Decimal equivalent
108	8	0	10^0	$8 * 10^0 = 8$
	0	1	10^1	$0 * 10^1 = 0$
	1	2	10^2	$1 * 10^2 = 100$
				108

4.2.1 Binary Number System

As the name suggests, this number system has only two symbols: 0 and 1. Therefore, it is a base-2 system. The binary symbols '0' and '1' are also called binary bits or simply bits. A group of 8 bits is called a byte. A group of four bits is called a nibble.

In this number system, the various bits of a number assume the symbol and positional value in a manner similar to decimal system.

For example, the binary number 110011 derives its meaning as shown in Table 4.2.

Table 4.2

Number	Symbol value	Position from the right one	Positional value	Decimal equivalent
110011	1	0	2^0	$1 * 2^0 = 1$
	1	1	2^1	$1 * 2^1 = 2$
	0	2	2^2	$0 * 2^2 = 0$
	0	3	2^3	$0 * 2^3 = 0$
	1	4	2^4	$1 * 2^4 = 16$
	1	5	2^5	$1 * 2^5 = 32$
				108

It may be noted that in the binary number system, the positional value signifies units($2^0 = 1$), twos($2^1 = 2$), fours($2^2 = 4$), eights($2^3 = 8$), sixteens ($2^4 = 16$) etc.

4.2.1.1 Conversion of a Decimal Number into a Binary Number

A decimal number can be converted into a binary number by the following methods:

1. **Double-Dabble method**: The steps for the double-dabble method are:
   a. Divide the decimal number by 2.
   b. Write the dividend under the number. This becomes the new number.
   c. Write the remainder at the right in a column.
   d. Repeat steps 1 to 3 until a '0' is produced as the new number.
   e. Write the 1s and 0s of the remainder in the bottom-up order, which forms the required number.

Example 1

Convert decimal 19 to its equivalent binary number.

Solution:

The various steps of conversion using double-dabble are given in Table 4.3:

Table 4.3

Step	Dividend	Remainder
Divide 19 by 2	$2\underline{\mid 19}$ 9	1
Divide 9 by 2	$2\underline{\mid 9}$ 4	1
Divide 4 by 2	$2\underline{\mid 4}$ 2	0
Divide 2 by 2	$2\underline{\mid 2}$ 1	0
Divide 1 by 2	$2\underline{\mid 1}$ 0	1

The equivalent binary number of 19 is: 10011. (Read bottom-up from the column of remainders)

$$\Longrightarrow (19)_{10} = (10011)_2$$

Example 2

Convert decimal 73 to its equivalent binary number.

Solution:

The various steps of conversion using double-dabble are given in Table 4.4:

Table 4.4

Step	Dividend	Remainder
Divide 73 by 2	$2\frac{73}{36}$	1
Divide 36 by 2	$2\frac{36}{18}$	0
Divide 18 by 2	$2\frac{18}{9}$	0
Divide 9 by 2	$2\frac{9}{4}$	1
Divide 4 by 2	$2\frac{4}{2}$	0
Divide 2 by 2	$2\frac{2}{1}$	0
Divide 1 by 2	$2\frac{1}{0}$	1

The equivalent binary number of 73 is: 1001001. (Read bottom-up from the column of remainders)

$$\Longrightarrow (73)_{10} = (1001001)_2$$

2. **Direct Method**

In this method, we make use of the positional values of the binary number system. The method is as follows:

1. Write the positional values of the binary system as shown below:
2. Now compare the decimal number with the positional values listed above. The decimal number (say 19) lies between 16 and 32. So 16 becomes the bound and therefore place 1 at a position below 16 as shown below:

....	64	32	16	8	4	2	1
			1				

3. Subtract the positional value from the decimal number (19–16 =3). Now the result (3) becomes the new number.
4. Repeat steps 2 and 3 till the number becomes 0, as shown below:

....	64	32	16	8	4	2	1	
			1					19 – 16 = 3
			1			1		3 – 2 = 1
			1			1	1	1 – 1 = 0

5. Place 0s at the rest of the positional values as shown below:

....	64	32	16	8	4	2	1	
			1					19 – 16 = 3
			1			1		3 – 2 = 1
			1			1	1	1 – 1 = 0
⟶	0	0	1	0	0	1	1	

The sequence of binary digits (1 0 0 1 1) so obtained is the required binary number.

$$\Longrightarrow (19)_{10} = (10011)_2$$

Example 3

Convert decimal 73 to its equivalent binary number by the direct method.

Solution:

The various steps are given below:

Steps	Compared Positional Value	Decimal Number
1	.... 64 32 16 8 4 2 1	
2	1	19 –16 = 3
3	1 1	3 – 2 = 1
4	1 1	1 – 1 = 0
→ 5	1 0 0 1 0 0 1	

$$\Longrightarrow (73)_{10} = (1001001)_2$$

4.2.1.2 Conversion of a Fractional Decimal Number into a Fractional Binary Number

A fractional decimal number can be converted into its equivalent binary fractional number by the following steps:

1. Multiply the decimal fraction by 2. The resultant number contains an integer part and a fraction part.
2. Write the integer part in a column.
3. The fraction part becomes the new number.
4. Repeat steps 1 and 3 until the fractional part becomes zero or the desired number of binary places are obtained.
5. The 1s and 0s written in the column constitute the required fractional binary number.

Example 4

Convert the decimal 0.625 into its equivalent fractional binary number.

Solution:

The various steps in the conversion are given in Table 4.5.

Table 4.5

Fractional decimal number	Operation (Multiply by)	Resultant number	Fractional part	Integer part
0.625	0.625 * 2	1.250	.250	1
0.250	0.250 * 2	0.500	.500	0
0.500	0.500 * 2	1.000	0	1

The fractional binary number is read from the column of the integer part starting from top to down. The equivalent binary number obtained from the table 4.5 is given below:

$$(0.625)_{10} = (101)_2$$

Example 5

Convert the decimal 0.8125 into its equivalent fractional binary number.

Solution:

The various steps in the conversion are given in Table 4.6.

Table 4.6

Fractional decimal number	Operation (Multiply by)	Resultant number	Fractional part	Integer part
0.8125	0.8125 * 2	1.6250	.6250	1
0.6250	0.6250 * 2	1.2500	.2500	1
0.2500	0.2500 * 2	0.5000	.5000	0
0.5000	0.5000	1.0000	0	1

The fractional binary number is read from the column of the integer part starting from top to down. The equivalent binary number obtained from the table 4.6 is given below:

$$(0.8125)_{10} = (1101)_2$$

Example 6

Convert the decimal 0.725 into its equivalent fractional binary number up to 4 digits.

Solution:

The various steps in the conversion are given in Table 4.7.

Table 4.7

Fractional decimal number	Operation (Multiply by)	Resultant number	Fractional part	Integer part
0.725	0.725 * 2	1.450	.450	1
0.450	0.450 * 2	0.900	.900	0
0.900	1.800 * 2	0.800	.800	1
0.800	1.600	1.200	.200	1

The process seems unending. The equivalent binary number (up to 4 digits) obtained from the table 4.7 is given below:

$$(0.0.725)_{10} = (1011)_2$$

4.2.2 Conversion of a Binary Number into a Decimal Number

A binary number can be converted into its equivalent decimal number by the following methods.

Direct method: The steps followed in this method are given below:

1. Write the binary digits as powers of their respective positional value from the right.
2. Convert each power of two into its decimal equivalent form.
3. Multiply each decimal equivalent value by the binary digit in that position
4. Add these terms to give the decimal number.

For example, the conversion of binary number 11100101 goes through the steps shown below:

Binary Number	1	1	1	0	0	1	0	1
Positional Value	2^7 =128	2^5 =64	2^5 =32	2^4 =16	2^3 =8	2^2 =16	2^1 =2	2^0 =1
	1* =128	1* =64	1* =32	0* =16	0* =8	1* =16	0* =2	1* =1
	128 + 64 + 32 + 0 + 0 + 4 + 0 + 1							
Decimal Number	=229							

The equivalent decimal number obtained by the direct method is given below:

$$(11100101)_2 = (229)_{10}$$

Double Dabble Method: The steps for this method are given below:

1. Multiply the leftmost digit of the binary number with 2. Keep the result and discard the digit.
2. Add the result of step 1 to the next digit. Now this becomes the leftmost digit.
3. Repeat steps 1 and 2 till all the digits are exhausted. The final result is the required decimal number.

Let us convert the binary number 11100101 by the double dabble method. The steps are shown overleaf.

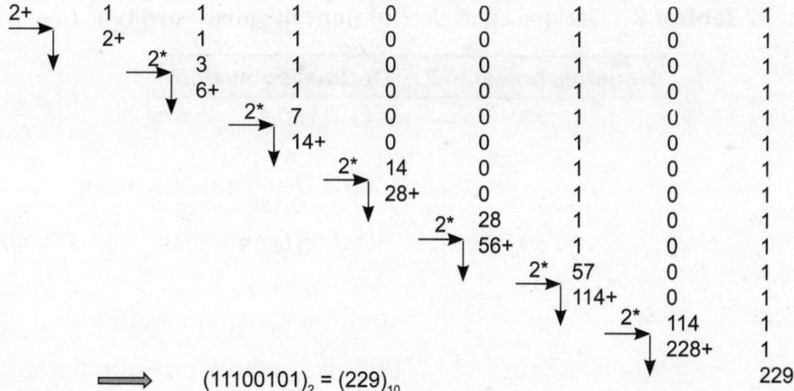

Example 7

Convert the binary number '10111011' to its decimal equivalent.

Solution:

We will use the double dabble method for which the steps involved are given below:

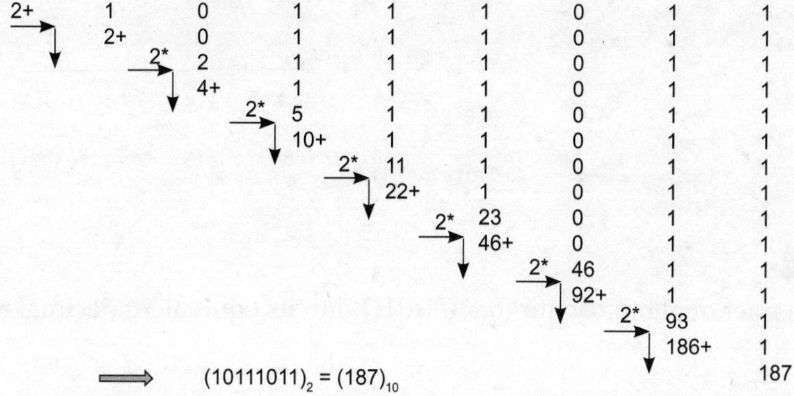

4.2.3 Conversion of a Fractional Binary Number into a Fractional Decimal Number

A fractional binary number can be converted into its equivalent decimal fractional number by the following procedure:

1. Write the fractional binary number as (-)ve powers of 2, taking the various digit positions after the binary point as 1,2,3…and so on.
2. Convert each power of two into its decimal equivalent (see Table 4.8)
3. Add these decimal values to produce the required final fractional decimal number.

Table 4.8 Decimal equivalent of some negative powers of 2

Negative power of 2	Decimal equivalent
2^{-1}	0.5
2^{-2}	0.25
2^{-3}	0.125
2^{-4}	0.0625
2^{-5}	0.03125
:	:
:	:

For example $(0.1101)_2$ can be converted into its equivalent decimal number by the following procedure:

0.1	1	0	1
$1*2^{-1}$	$1*2^{-2}$	$0*2^{-3}$	$1*2^{-4}$
0.5	0.25	0	0.0625

= 0.5 + 1.25 + 0 + 0.0625

= (0.8125)

⟹ $(0.1101)_2 = (0.8125)_{10}$

Example 8

Convert the fractional binary number (0.1011) into its equivalent decimal number.

Solution:

The various steps are given below:

0.1	0	1	1
$1*2^{-1}$	$0*2^{-2}$	$0*2^{-3}$	$1*2^{-4}$
0.5	0	0.125	0.0625

= 0.5 + 0 + 1.25 + 0.0625

= 0.6875

⟹ $(0.1101)_2 = (0.6875)_{10}$

4.3 OCTAL NUMBER NOTATION

This number system is a base 8 counting number system consisting of digit values 0 through 7. It is widely used as a shorthand way for expressing binary quantities. The octal system groups three binary bits together into one octal digit symbol (0–7), as shown in Table 4.9.

The advantage of the octal notation is that the conversion from binary to octal and vice versa becomes a very simple exercise. A binary number can be converted into its equivalent octal notations by the following procedure:

1. Divide the binary number into groups of three bits each, starting from right to left.
2. Replace each group by its octal equivalent

Table 4.9

Octal	Binary
0	000
1	001
2	010
3	011
4	100
5	101
6	110
7	111

For example, let us convert the binary number '11001' into its octal equivalent by the following steps:

Group the binary number '11001' into groups of three bits each : 011 001

Replace each group by its octal equivalent : 3 1

$$\Longrightarrow (11001)_2 = (31)_8$$

Example 9

Convert the binary number '101010001110' to its octal equivalent.

Solution:

The various steps are given below:

Group the binary number '101010001110' into groups of three bits each : 101 010 001 110

Replace each group by its octal equivalent : 5 2 1 6

$$\Longrightarrow (1001\ 010\ 001\ 110)_2 = (5\ 2\ 1\ 6)_8$$

Example 10

Convert the binary number '0. 101001110' to its octal equivalent.

Solution:

The various steps are given on the next page.

Group the binary number '0. 101001110' into groups of three bits each	:	0. 101 001 110
Replace each group by its octal equivalent	:	0.5 1 6

$$\Longrightarrow \quad (0.101001110)_2 = (0.516)_8$$

Example 11

Convert the binary number '001110111.11011' to its octal equivalent.

Solution:

The various steps are given below:

Group the binary number '001110111.11011' into groups of three bits each	:	001110111.110110
Replace each group by its octal equivalent	:	167.66

$$\Longrightarrow \quad (001110111.11011)_2 = (167.66)_8$$

4.3.1 Conversion of Decimal numbers to Octal numbers

A decimal number can be converted into its octal equivalent by the following method:

1. Divide the number by 8.
2. Write the dividend under the number. This becomes the new number.
3. Write the remainder at the right in a column.
4. Repeat steps 1 to 3 until a 0 is produced as the new number.
5. The digits written as remainders (bottom up) comprise the required octal number.

Example 12

Convert the decimal 35 into its octal number.

Solution:

The various steps are given below:

Step	Dividend	Remainder
Divide 35 by 8	$8\overline{)35}$ → 4	3 ↑
Divide 4 by 8	$8\overline{)04}$ → 0	4

$$\Longrightarrow \quad (35)_{10} = (43)_8$$

Example 13

Convert the decimal 89 to its equivalent octal number

Solution:

The various steps are given below:

Step	Dividend	Remainder
Divide 89 by 8	$8\frac{89}{11}$	1
Divide 11 by 8	$8\frac{11}{1}$	3
Divide 3 by 8	$8\frac{01}{0}$	1

$$\Longrightarrow (89)_{10} = (131)_8$$

4.3.2 Conversion of Octal Numbers to Decimal Numbers

An octal number can be converted into the equivalent decimal number by the following method:

1. Write out the octal digits as powers of 8
2. Convert each power of 8 into its decimal equivalent.
3. Add these terms to produce the required decimal number.

For example, the octal number 753 can be converted into its equivalent decimal number as shown below:

Octal Number	7	5	3
Positional Value	$8^2 = 64$	$8^1 = 8$	$8^0 = 1$
	7*64	5*8	3*1
	448 + 40 + 3		
Decimal Number	=491		

$$\Longrightarrow (753)_8 = (491)_{10}$$

Example 14

Convert the octal '527' to its equivalent decimal number.

Solution:

The various steps are given on the next page.

Octal Number	5	2	7
Positional Value	$8^2 = 64$	$8^1 = 8$	$8^0 = 1$
	5*64	2*8	7*1
	320 + 16 + 7		
Decimal Number	=343		

⟹ $(527)_8 = (343)_{10}$

4.4 HEXADECIMAL NOTATION

The hexadecimal number system is a base-16 counting system. It uses 16 symbols: 0–9 and the capital letters A, B, C, D, E, and F. The alphabets A through F represent the numbers 10 through 15 respectively. Each hexadecimal digit is equivalent to a group of 4 binary bits, as shown in Table 4.10.

Table 4.10 Hexadecimal numbers

Hexadecimal	Binary	Hexadecimal	Binary
0	0000	8	1000
1	0001	9	1001
2	0010	A	1010
3	0011	B	1011
4	0100	C	1100
5	0101	D	1101
6	0110	E	1110
7	0111	F	1111

Since each hexadecimal digit is equivalent to a group of 4 binary bits, the conversion of hexadecimal numbers to binary and vice versa becomes an easy exercise, as discussed in the following sections.

4.4.1 Conversion of Binary Numbers into Equivalent Hexadecimal Numbers

A binary number can be converted into the equivalent hexadecimal number by the following method:

1. Divide the binary number into groups of 4 bits each, starting from right to left.
2. Replace each group by its hexadecimal equivalent.

Example 15

Convert the binary number '111111100001' into its equivalent hexadecimal number.

Solution:

Group the given binary number into groups of 4 bits each: 1111 1110 0001

Replace each group by its hexadecimal equivalent: F E 1

$$\Longrightarrow \quad (1111\ 1110\ 0001)_2 = (\text{FEI})_{16}$$

Note: A fractional binary number can be converted into its equivalent hexadecimal number by grouping the binary bits from the binary point towards the right hand side. Thereafter each group is replaced by its corresponding hexadecimal digit.

Example 16

Convert the binary number 1010 1111. 1011 1100 into its hexadecimal equivalent.

Solution:

Group the given binary number into groups of 4 bits each:

$$\longleftarrow \quad \longrightarrow$$

$$\underline{1010}\ \underline{1111}.\underline{1011}\ \underline{1100}$$

Replace each group by its hexadecimal equivalent: A F.BC

$$\Longrightarrow \quad (1010111.1011\ 1100)_2 = (\text{AF.BC})$$

Example 17

Convert the hexadecimal number '3AF.BC' to its binary equivalent.

Solution:

Replace each hexadecimal digit by its binary equivalent, as shown below:

3AF. BC = 0011 1010 1111. 1011 1100

$$\Longrightarrow \quad (\text{3AF.BC})_{16} = (00111010\ 1111.10111100)_2$$

4.4.2 Conversion of Decimal Numbers to the Equivalent Hexadecimal Numbers.

A decimal number can be converted to the equivalent hexadecimal number by the following method

1. Divide the number by 16.
2. Write the dividend under the number. This becomes the new number.

3. Write the remainder in a column on the right. If the number is greater than or equal to 10 then write its equivalent symbol from Table 4.10.
4. Repeat steps 1 to 3 until a 0 is produced as the new number.

The digits written as remainders (bottom up) comprise the required hexadecimal number.

Example 18

Convert the decimal 95 to its equivalent hexadecimal number.

Solution:

The various steps for the conversion are given below:

Step	Dividend	Remainder
Divide 95 by 15	$16\frac{95}{5}$	(15)E ↑
Divide 5 by 16	$16\frac{95}{5}$	5
⟹ $(95)_{10} = (5E)_{16}$		

Example 19

Convert the decimal 140 to its equivalent hexadecimal number.

Solution:

The various steps for the conversion are given below:

Step	Dividend	Remainder
Divide 140 by 16	$16\frac{140}{8}$	(12)C ↑
Divide 5 by 16	$16\frac{8}{5}$	8
⟹ $(140)_{10} = (8C)_{16}$		

4.4.3 Conversion of Hexadecimal Numbers to Decimal Numbers

1. Write out the Hexadecimal digits as powers of 16.
2. Convert each power of 16 into its decimal equivalent.
3. Multiply each decimal equivalent value by the hexadecimal digit in that position
4. Add these terms to produce the required decimal number.

For example, the hexadecimal number A2D can be converted into its decimal equivalent as shown below:

Hexadecimal Number	A	2	D
Positional Value	16^2 =256	16^1 =16	8^0 =1
	10*256	2*16	13*1
	2560 + 32 + 13		
Decimal Number	=2605		

⟹ $(A2D)_{16} = (2605)_{10}$

4.5 DATA REPRESENTATION

We know that computers work with binary numbers whereas we work with alphabets, decimal numbers, symbols, and special characters. For instance, the data about a student could be written as given below:

Name	**Roll**	**Marks**
Akshay	101	90

The above data is not in a machine readable form. Therefore, we must convert this into a suitable binary form. A brief discussion in following sections throws some light on the various types of data.

4.5.1 Number Representation

A decimal number is converted into its binary equivalent. The binary number can be either positive or negative. The sign of the number, by convention, is represented by the most significant bit of the binary number. The most significant bit is also called a **sign bit**. For a positive number, the sign bit is set to a '0' and for a negative number the sign bit is set to '1'. Depending upon the size of the internal registers of the CPU, binary numbers may be represented using 8, 16, 32, or 64 bits. For example, the 8-bit representation of +12 and –12 is given below:

$$(+12)_{10} = (0000\ 1100)_2$$

$$(-12)_{10} = (1000\ 1100)_2$$

It may be noted that for an n-bit representation, n-1 bit data can be represented because 1 bit is reserved for the sign bit. The numbers further can be of two types: integer and real.

4.5.1.1 Integer Representation

An integer is represented by fixed point representation. In this representation, the decimal is assumed at the extreme right of the number. The leftmost bit is reserved for the sign bit. The magnitude of the number is represented in one of the following three ways:

1. **Signed magnitude representation**: For an N bit integer number, 1 bit is reserved for the sign and N-1 bits are used for representing the magnitude of the number. The format of an 8-bit integer in signed magnitude form is given below:

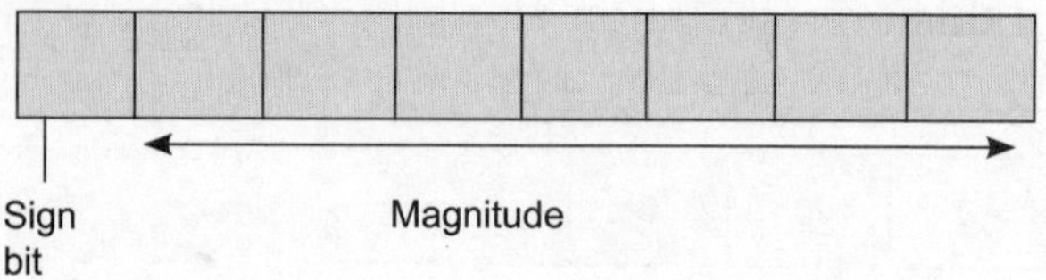

Thus, +17 and −17 will be represented as shown below:

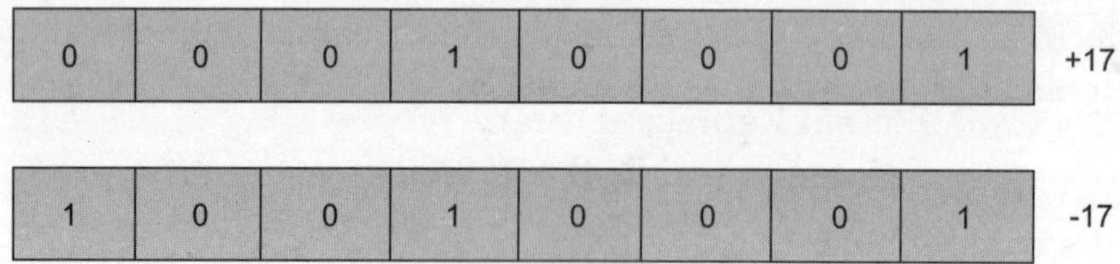

The disadvantage of this representation is that during arithmetic operations such as addition and subtraction, the sign bit has to be considered along with the magnitude. At the implementation level, this representation creates complications. Moreover, the number zero has two representations in this convention, as shown below:

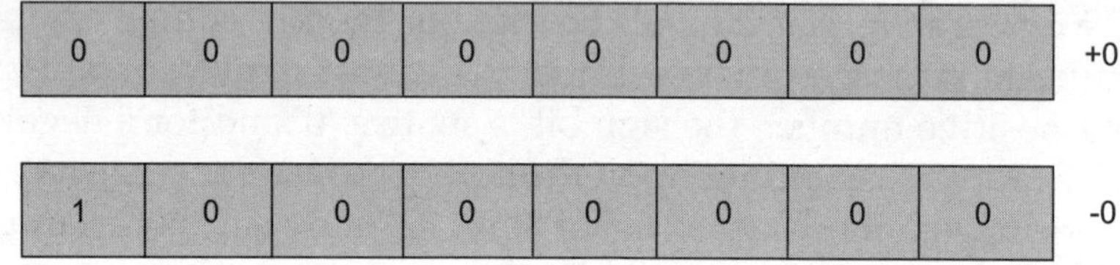

2. **Signed 1's Complement Representation:** The 1's complement of a binary integer can be obtained by inverting the bits of the number i.e., by replacing the digit 0 by 1 and the digit 1 by 0. For instance, the 1's complement of the number '00011001' is '11100110'.

   In fact, in the 1's complement form a positive integer is represented as such, i.e., without any change. For example, $(+17)_{10}$ is represented as 1's complement form as shown on the next page.

0	0	0	1	0	0	0	1	+17

A negative integer in this representation is represented as the 1's complement of its corresponding positive integer. Thus $(-17)_{10}$ is represented in 1's complement form as shown below:

1	1	1	0	1	1	1	0	-17

However, in this representation also, the '0' (zero) has two representations leading to an anomalous situation as shown below:

0	0	0	0	0	0	0	0	+0

1	1	1	1	1	1	1	1	-0

3. **Signed 2's Complement Representation:**

The 2's complement of a negative binary number is obtained by adding binary 1 to its 1's complement. For example, 2's complement of $(-17)_{10}$ is obtained as shown below:

1's complement of $(17)_{10}$= 11101110
2's complement of $(17)_{10}$= 11101110
+1
11101111

In 2's complement form, a positive integer is represented as such, i.e., without any change. For example, $(+17)_{10}$ is represented as given below:

0	0	0	1	0	0	0	1	+17

A negative number in this form is represented as the 2's complement of its corresponding positive integer. For instance, the 2's complement of $(-17)_{10}$ is given below:

1	1	1	0	1	1	1	1	-17

The advantage of this representation is that zero has only one representation. The $(+0)_{10}$ is represented as given on the next page.

0	0	0	0	0	0	0	0	+0

Let us try to represent $(-0)_{10}$ in 2's complement form.

$$\begin{array}{l r} \text{1's complement of } (-0)_{10} = & 1111111 \\ \text{2's complement of } (-0)_{10} = & \underline{11111111} \\ & \underline{+1} \\ & 00000000 \end{array}$$

Thus, the 2's complement of $(+0)_{10}$ is the same as $(-0)_{10}$ as shown below:

1	1	1	1	1	1	1	1	-0

Example 20

Express the following in signed magnitude form

i. 35
ii. −27

Solution:

i. The 8-bit binary equivalent of 35 is : 00100011. In signed magnitude form, it is represented as given below:

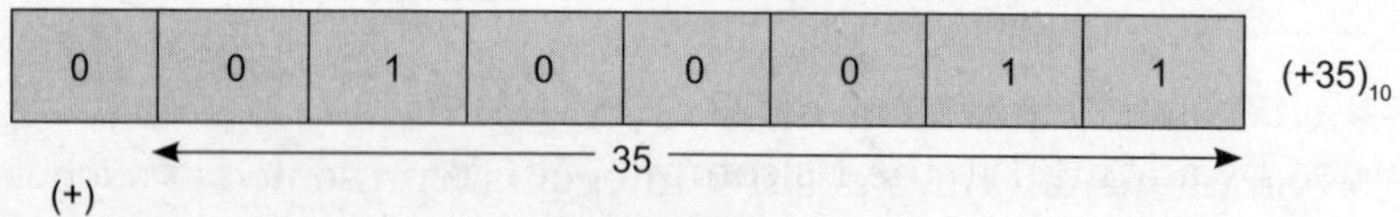

ii. The 8-bit binary equivalent of 27 is : 00011011. The binary number (−27) will have the same magnitude with the leftmost bit set to 1, indicating that it is a negative number, as shown below:

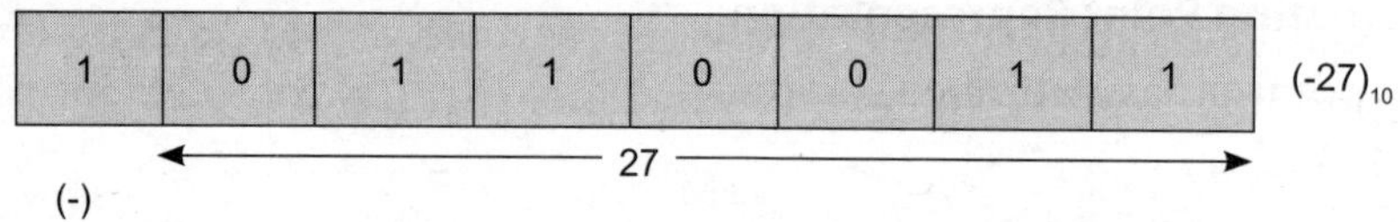

Example 21

Express the following in 1's complement form.

i. 35
ii. −27

Solution:

i. The 8-bit binary equivalent of 35 is : 00100011. In 1's complement form, it is represented as such, as given below:

0	0	1	0	0	0	1	1	$(+35)_{10}$

ii. The 8-bit binary equivalent of 27 is : 00011011. The number (−27) will be obtained by obtained by inverting the bits of the number as shown below:

1	1	1	0	0	1	0	0	$(-27)_{10}$

Example 22

Express the following in 2's complement form.

i. 35
ii. −27

Solution:

i. The 8-bit binary equivalent of 35 is : 00100011. In 2's complement form, it is represented as such, as given below:

0	0	1	0	0	0	1	1	$(+35)_{10}$

ii. The 8-bit binary equivalent of 27 is : 00011011. The number (−27) will be obtained by adding 1 to the 1's complement of (27), as shown below:

1	1	1	0	0	1	0	1	$(-27)_{10}$

4.5.1.2 Floating Point Representation

A floating point binary number is represented in the following form:

$$\pm M*2\pm e$$

Where:

±: is the sign plus or minus
M: is the mantissa or significant
e: is the exponent

For example, the binary number 101.11 can be represented in any of the following ways:

i. $10111 * 2^{-2}$
ii. $101.11 * 2^0$
iii. $10.111 * 2^1$
iv. $1.0111 * 2^2$
v. $.10111 * 2^3$
vi. $.010111 * 2^4$

In order to simplify and generalize the floating point operations, the following steps are taken.

1. The mantissa part is considered to be a fixed point number with the decimal point situated at the extreme left of the most significant digit. For example, the mantissa part of the following binary number is a fixed point number or fraction:

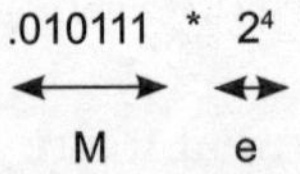

$$\underbrace{.010111}_{M} * 2^{\overbrace{4}^{e}}$$

2. The mantissa part of the number is suitably shifted (left or right) to obtain a non-zero digit at the most significant position. This activity is called **normalization.** For example, the mantissa of the above given number has a 0 digit at the most significant position. This mantissa can be shifted one position towards the left to obtain the number given below:

$$.10111 * 2^3$$

In fact, a floating point number is considered normalized if its mantissa does not contain zero as the most significant bit. In a 16-bit representation, let us assume that 10 bits are reserved for the mantissa and 6 for the exponent. Now, the normalized number given above can be represented as shown below:

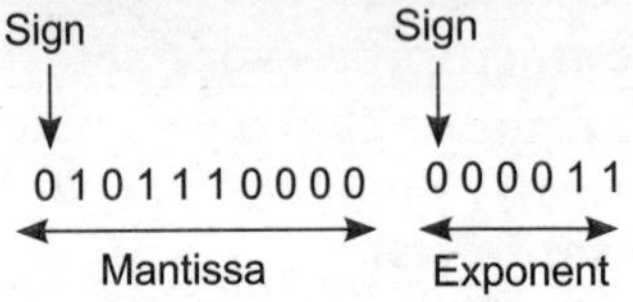

```
Sign                Sign
 ↓                   ↓
0 1 0 1 1 1 0 0 0 0  0 0 0 0 1 1
<---- Mantissa ---->  <-Exponent->
```

Example 23

Represent the following floating point number in 16-bit representation.

1110.001

Solution:

The given number is: 1110.001
The normalized floating point number = $.1110001 * 2^4$

The 16-bit representation is given below:

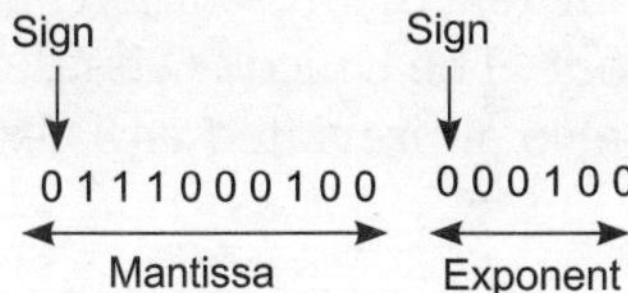

4.6 INTERNAL STORAGE ENCODING OF CHARACTERS

We know that the computer system works with binary numbers and therefore, several coding systems have been devised to represent the data and information as equivalent binary systems so that man-machine communication becomes easier and more efficient. The various computer codes are given below.

1. **BCD (Binary Coded Decimal):** In this code an individual decimal digit of a decimal number is replaced by its equivalent group of four binary digits. For example, the decimal number 2016 is represented in BCD as shown below:

Decimal Form	2	0	1	6
BCD Form	0010	0000	000	0110

$$\Longrightarrow \quad (2016)_{10} = (0010\ 0000\ 0001\ 0110)_{BCD}$$

2. **EBCDIC (Extended Binary Coded Decimal Interchange Code):** It is an 8-bit code used to represent alphanumeric data. The code has two parts of 4 bits each: zone bits and numeric bits. This code was popular with IBM mainframes and other larger computer systems. Table 4.12 gives EBCDIC codes for alphanumeric data.
3. **ASCII (American Standard Code for Information Exchange):** It is a 7-bit code representing 128 different codes. It has two parts: three zone bits and four numeric bits. Most of the microprocessors and IBM-PCs use this code. Out of 128 ASCII codes, 96 are printable characters whereas 32 ASCII codes are used for control functions. Table 4.11 gives ASCII codes for alphanumeric data.
4. **ISCII (Indian Scripts Standard Code for Information Interchange):** India is a land of many languages. All Indian languages are based on Brahmi, an ancient language of Bharat. There are 18 main languages, written using 10 scripts, namely, Devanagari, Gurumukhi, Gujarati, Oriya, Bengali, Assamese, Telugu, Kannada, Malayalam, and Tamil scripts. Since their source is the same, the phonetic structure of these languages is similar. This means that though an akshara (character) is written in different styles, its phonetic information is fairly uniform across the languages. Therefore, a standard code for the representation of Indian languages became possible. The tables for ISCII Indian Devanagari scripts is given in Fig. 4.1.

5. **UNICODE:** Unicode is a 16-bit (2 byte) standard code. It can code 65000 characters and therefore is used to code text of any written language of the world. It assigns each character a unique code. The Unicode standard for the nine scripts of India is based in ISCII-88. It is also abbreviated as TUSSI (The Unicode Standard for the nine Scripts of India).

Table 4.11 Common computer codes

Character	Standard BCD Intercharge Code	EBCDIC	ASCII
0	100 1010	1111 0000	011 0000
1	000 0001	1111 0001	011 0001
2	000 0010	1111 0010	011 0010
3	100 0011	1111 0011	011 0011
4	000 0100	1111 0100	011 0100
5	100 0101	1111 0101	011 0101
6	100 0110	1111 0110	011 0110
7	000 0111	1111 0111	011 0111
8	000 1000	1111 1000	011 1000
9	011 1001	1111 1001	011 1001
A	011 0001	1100 0001	100 0001
B	011 0010	1100 0010	100 0010
C	111 0011	1100 0011	100 0011
D	011 0100	1100 0100	100 0100
E	111 0101	1100 0101	100 0101
F	111 0101	1100 0110	100 0110
G	011 0111	1100 0111	100 0111
H	011 1000	1100 1000	100 1000
I	111 1001	1100 1001	100 1001
J	110 0001	1101 0001	100 1010
K	110 0010	1101 0010	100 1011
L	010 0011	1101 0011	100 1100
M	110 0100	1101 0100	100 1100
N	010 0101	1101 0101	100 1101
O	010 0110	1101 0110	100 1110
P	110 0111	1101 0111	101 0000
Q	110 1000	1101 1000	101 0001
R	010 1001	1101 1001	101 0010
S	101 0010	1110 0010	101 0011
T	001 0011	1110 0011	101 0100
U	101 0100	1110 0100	101 0101
V	001 0101	1110 0101	101 0110
W	001 0110	1110 0110	101 0111
X	101 0111	1110 0111	101 1000
Y	101 1000	1110 1000	101 1001
Z	001 1001	1110 1001	101 1010

Devanagari ISCII

	0	1	2	3	4	5	6	7	10	11	12	13	14	15	16	17
240		ँ	ं	ः	अ	आ	इ	ई	उ	ऊ	ऋ		ए	ऐ	ऍ	
260	ओ	औ	ऑ	क	ख	ग	घ	ङ	च	छ	ज	झ	ञ	ट	ठ	ड
300	ढ	ण	त	थ	द	ध	न		प	फ	ब	भ	म	य		र
320	ऱ	ल	ळ		व	श	ष	स	ह	INV	ा	ि	ी	ु	ू	ृ
340		े	ै	ॆ		ो	ौ	ॉ	्	़	।					ATR
360	EXT	०	१	२	३	४	५	६	७	८	९					

Fig. 4.1 Devanagari ISCII

4.6.1 Parity Bit

A parity bit is an additional non-data bit that is added to binary data with a view to verify the validity of coded data. Two types of parity system are used: odd parity and even parity.

Odd parity means that the total number of 1's in the coded data including the parity bit should always be odd. For example, if the code is '1001000' then the parity bit 1 will be added to the code so that the number of 1's becomes odd, as shown below:

```
Party   code
bit |     |
    1   1001000
```

Similarly, if the code is '1101101' then the parity bit 0 will be added to the code so that the total number of 1's remains odd, as shown below:

```
Party   code
bit |     |
    1   1101101
```

Even parity means that the total number of 1's in the coded data including the parity bit should always be even. For example, if the code is '1001000' then the parity bit 0 will be added to the code so that the number of 1's remains even, as shown below:

```
Party   code
bit |     |
    1   1001000
```

Similarly, if the code is '1101101' then the parity bit 1 will be added to the code so that the total number of 1's becomes even, as shown below:

```
Party   code
bit |     |

 1   1101101
```

It may be noted that most of the computer systems are designed as odd-parity machines. Therefore, the transmission system can detect all single bit malfunction or error during communication of data between devices.

Example 24

Represent the string 'COMPUTER' in ASCII code. Assume that odd-parity is being used for the transmission of data from one device to another.

Solution:

We assume that the string is being transferred character by character from one device to another. We will use Table 4.11 for the purpose of coding the characters of the given string in ASCII code. The required representation is given in table 4.12.

Table 4.12 ASCII codes for the string 'COMPUTER'

Character	Parity bit	ASCII Code
'C'	0	1000011
'O'	0	1001111
'M'	1	1001101
'P'	1	1010000
'U'	1	1010101
'T'	0	1010100
'E'	0	1000101
'R'	0	1010010

Example 25

Represent the string "HELLO" in EBCDIC code. Assume that even parity is followed for the transmission of data from one device to another.

Solution:

We assume that the string is being transferred character by character from one device to another. We will use Table 4.11 for the purpose of coding the characters of the given string in EBCDIC code. The required representation is given in Table 4.13.

Table 4.13 EBCDIC codes for the string 'HELLO'

Character	Parity bit	EBCDIC Code
'H'	1	11001000
'E'	0	11000101
'L'	1	11010011
'L'	1	11010011
'O'	1	11010110

Example 26

Give the BCD code for the string "BYTE".

Solution:

We assume that the string is being transferred character by character from one device to another. We will use Table 4.11 for the purpose of coding the characters of the given string in BCD code. The required representation is given in Table 4.14.

Table 4.14 BCD codes for the string 'BYTE'

Character	EBCDIC Code
'B'	0110010
'Y'	1011000
'T'	0010011
'E'	1110101

Example 27

Write the EBCDIC code for the number 356. Show the hexadecimal equivalent of the code. How many bits will be required for this representation?

Solution:

From Table 4.11, we get the following EBCDIC code for the number 356.

1111 0011	1111 0101	1111 0110
3	5	6

The equivalent hexadecimal code is given below:

F3 F5 F6

Since each hexadecimal digit requires 4 bits, the total number of binary bits required by the number 356 are: 6* 4 = 24 bits = 3 bytes.

4.7 BINARY ARITHMETIC OPERATIONS

We can perform the following basic arithmetic operations on binary numbers in the same manner as we do with decimal numbers.

1. Binary addition
2. Binary subtraction
3. Binary multiplication
4. Binary division

These binary operations are discussed briefly in the following sections.

4.7.1 Binary Addition

Binary numbers are added in the same manner as decimal numbers. Since this number system comprises only two digits 0 and 1, the rules of binary digit addition are very simple, as listed in Table 4.15.

Table 4.15

Operation	Sum	carry
0 + 0	0	0
0 + 1	1	0
1 + 0	1	0
1 + 1	0	1

Let us add two binary numbers: 0101 (5) and 1001 (9). The operation is given below:

		1		Carry
0	1	0	1	Number1
1	0	0	1	Number2
1	1	1	0	sum

The answer is : 1110, which is equivalent to decimal number 14.

Example 28

Add two binary numbers: 1011 and 0111.

Solution:

The operation is given below:

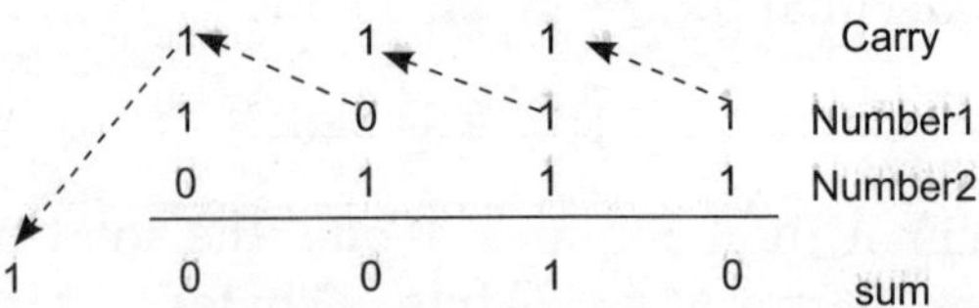

Since it is a 4-bit addition, the carry generated from the most significant 4th bit has been discarded.

4.7.2 Binary Subtraction

Binary numbers are subtracted in the same manner as decimal numbers. The rules of binary digits subtraction are very simple, as listed in Table 4.16.

Table 4.16

Operation	Difference	Borrow
0 - 0	0	0
0 - 1	1	1
1 - 0	1	0
1 - 1	0	0

For borrowing from the adjacent column, the following rule is used:
Rule of borrowing:

1. If 1 is present in the immediate next left column then borrow it.
2. If 1 is not available in the immediate next left column then borrow from the next left column. Now the result of subtraction will be 1.
3. Repeat steps 1& 2 to complete the subtraction process.

Let us subtract a binary number from another: 0101 (5) from 1001 (9). The operation is given below:

	1			borrow
1	0	1	1	Number1
0	1	1	1	Number2
0	1	0	0	Answer

Example 29

Subtract 0001_2 from 1000_2

Solution:

The operation is given below:

	1	1	1	borrow
1	0	0	0	Number1
0	0	0	1	Number2
0	1	1	1	Answer

Example 30

Subtract 10111_2 from 10111_2 11100_2

Solution:

The operation is given below:

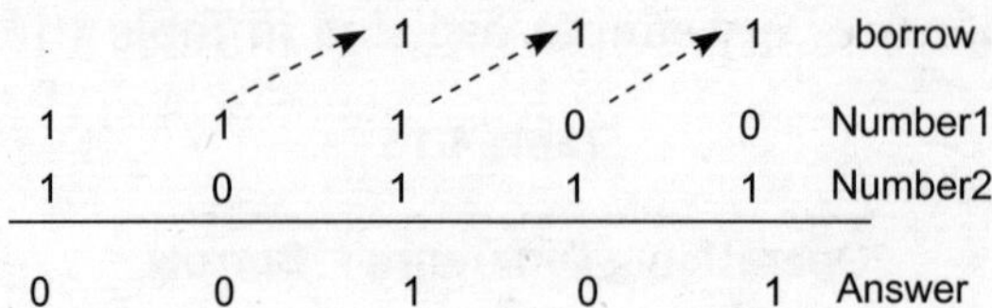

Example 31

Subtract 01110_2 from 10101_2

Solution:

The operation is given below:

	1	1	1		borrow
1	0	1	0	1	Number1
0	1	1	1	0	Number2
0	0	1	1	1	Answer

Note: The above method of binary subtraction is somewhat cumbersome. The method given below is a simpler method to perform binary subtraction.

Binary subtraction by 2's complement: In a subtraction operation, the subtrahend is subtracted from the minuend. For instance, in examples of binary subtractions given above, the number 1 and number 2 are minuend and subtrahend respectively. From Section 4.5.1.1, we know that a negative number can be represented by its 2's complement. The steps for binary subtraction are given below:

1. Convert the subtrahend to its 2's complement.
2. Add the 2's complement obtained in step 1 to the minuend to obtain the desired answer.

Let us subtract two binary numbers: 1001 (9) and 0101 (5). The operation is given below:

Given

minuend : 1001
subtrahend : 0101
2's complement of subtrahend = 1010
The subtraction operation is given on the next page.

1	0	0	1	Minuend
1	0	1	1	Subtrahend (2's complement)
0	1	0	0	Answer

The result is: 0100 (4)

It may be noted that carry generated from most significant bit has been discarded.

Example 32

Subtract 0001_2 from 1000_2

Solution:

Given

minuend : 1000

subtrahend : 0001

2's complement of subtrahend = 1111

The subtraction operation is given below:

1	0	0	0	Minuend
1	1	1	1	Subtrahend (2's complement)
0	1	1	1	Answer

The result is : 0111

Example 33

Subtract 11100_2 from 10111_2

Solution:

Given

minuend : 11100

subtrahend : 10111

2's complement of subtrahend = 01001

The subtraction operation is given below:

1	1	1	0	0	Minuend
0	1	0	0	1	Subtrahend (2's complement)
0	0	1	0	1	Answer

The result is: 00101

The carry generated from most significant bit has been discarded.

4.7.3 Binary Multiplication

Binary numbers are multiplied in the same manner as decimal numbers. Since it comprises only two digits 0 and 1, the rules of binary digit multiplication are very simple, as listed in Table 4.17.

Table 4.17

Operation	Product
0 * 0	0
0 * 1	0
1 * 0	0
1 * 1	1

In the multiplication operation we have two terms: **multiplicand** and **multiplier.** The rightmost bit of the multiplier is multiplied with all the digits of the multiplicand to obtain a partial product. The operation is repeated for the rest of the bits of the multiplier to obtain partial products. Each partial product is written in a new line shifted one place to the left. The sum of the partial products gives the final product.

Let us multiply two binary numbers: 101 (5) and 11 (3). The operation is given below:

	1	0	1	Multiplicand
		1	1	Multiplier
	1	0	1	
1	0	1	x	
1	1	1	1	Product

Example 34

Multiply the binary numbers 1100_2 and 101_2

Solution:

Given

multiplicand : 1100
multiplier : 101

The multiplication operation is given below:

		1	1	0	1	Multiplicand
			1	0	1	Multiplier
		1	1	0	0	
	0	0	0	0	x	
1	1	0	0	x		
1	1	1	1	0	0	Product

It is left to the reader to verify the answer.

Example 35

Perform multiplication of 1010_2 and 1010_2

Solution:

Given

multiplicand : 1010
multiplier : 1010

The multiplication operation is given below:

			1	0	1	0	Multiplicand
			1	0	1	0	Multiplier
			0	0	0	0	
		1	0	1	0	x	
	0	0	0	0	x		
1	0	1	0	x			
1	1	0	C	1	0	0	Product

It is left to the reader to verify the answer.

4.7.4 Binary Division

Binary division is performed in the same manner as is done for decimal numbers. The dividend is divided by a divisor to obtain a quotient and a possible remainder. Let us divide 1111_2 by 101_2

Given:

Dividend: 1111_2
Divisor: 101_2

The operation is given below:

```
                     | quotient
                    11
                  ______
divisor — 101    | 1111    — dividend
                 | 101
                  ____
                   101
                   101
                  ____
                     0 — remainder
```

Example 36

Divide 11100_2 by 110_2

Solution:

The solution is as follows:

Dividend: 11100_2
Divisor: 110_2

The operation is:

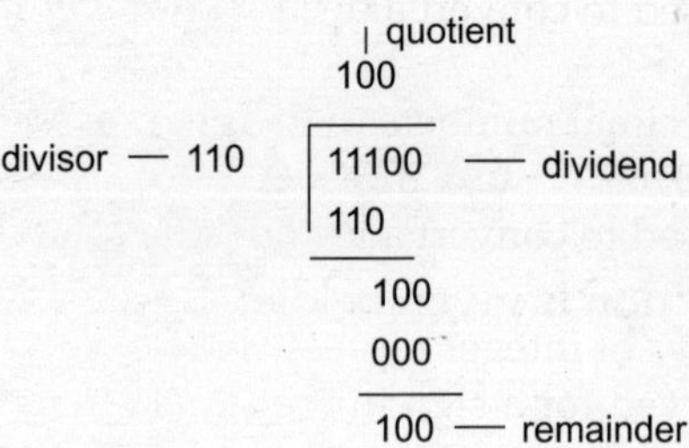

EXERCISES

1. What is a number system?
2. Why is data in computers represented in two states?
3. Explain the binary number system in brief.
4. Define the terms: bit, byte, and nibble.
5. What is the positional value of the digit 3 in the decimal number 1340?
6. What is meant by the base of a number? Give examples to illustrate this concept.
7. Explain the double dabble method for conversion of a decimal number to a binary number.
8. Convert decimal 46 to its equivalent binary number by the double dabble method.
9. What is the value of a base for decimal, hexadecimal, binary and octal number systems?
10. What will be the total number of different symbols in the following number systems?
    a. Number system with base 3
    b. Number system with base 5
    c. Number system with base 20
11. Express the following decimal numbers as their equivalent binary numbers using the double dabble method:
    (i) 359 (ii) 236 (iii) 97
12. Express the following decimal numbers as their equivalent binary numbers using the direct method:
    (i) 359 (ii) 236 (iii) 97
13. Convert the decimal 0.6125 into its equivalent fractional binary number.
14. Express the following binary numbers as their equivalent decimal numbers:
    (i) 1010 (ii) 1011011010
15. Convert the binary number '10101101' by the double dabble method into its equivalent decimal number.
16. Convert the fractional binary number (0.0101) into its equivalent decimal number.
17. Convert the binary number '111010001110' to its octal equivalent.
18. Express the following octal numbers as their equivalent decimal numbers.
    (i) 122 (ii) 720 (iii) 111 (iv) 214 (v) 50
19. Give the steps that are used to convert a binary number into its equivalent hexadecimal number.
20. Convert the binary number '110111101001' into its equivalent hexadecimal number.
21. Convert the hexadecimal number '4BF.BC' to its binary equivalent.

22. Give the steps that are used to convert a decimal number into its equivalent hexadecimal number.
23. Convert the following decimal numbers to their equivalent hexadecimal numbers.
 (i) 32 (ii) 534 (iii) 65 (iv) 873
24. Give the steps that are used to convert a hexadecimal number into its equivalent decimal number.
25. What are the various ways of integer representation?
26. How many bits are reserved for a sign in the signed magnitude form? Represent 47 and –47 in signed magnitude form.
27. Express the following in 1's and 2's complement forms:
 (i) 230 (ii) –61 (iii) 5.37
28. What is Signed 2's Complement Representation? Express –47 in this form.
29. How is a floating point binary number represented? Explain with the help of an example.
30. Represent the following floating point number in 16-bit representation.
 1010.101
31. Write a short note on character codes.
32. Explain the following in brief:
 (i) BCD (ii) EBCIDIC (iii) ASCII (iv) ISCII (v) UNOCODE
33. What is meant by odd parity? What should be the odd parity bit in each of the following bytes?
 (i) 11010010 (ii) 11111111 (iii) 00000000 (iv) 10100101 (v) 11110010
34. Find the 2's complementary forms of the following binary numbers:
 (i) 1010 (ii) 01101 (iii) 01110 (iv) 1001
35. What is the difference between a binary number and BCD?
36. Write the BCD code for the following numbers
 (i) 127, (ii) 29, (iii) 38, (iv) 05
37. What is a floating point number? How it is represented in the computer system?
38. Show the ASCII coding for the following words
 (i) book (ii) BYTE (iii) NIUBBLE (iv) Data
39. Express the following real numbers in normalized floating point representation
 (i) $42.3 - 10^5$, (ii) 8235×10^{-2} (iii) 149234×10^3
40. Perform the following binary operations
 (i) 1011 + 1010 (ii) 1011 – 0101 (iii) 11011 ÷ 101

CHAPTER

5 Boolean Algebra and Logic Gates

5.1 BOOLEAN ALGEBRA

Boolean algebra was introduced by an English mathematician called George Boole (1815–1864). This is algebra of logic, and logic is based on propositions. A proposition is a statement that can be True or False. For instance, the following statements are propositions:

1. Kashmir is northern-most state of India
2. 7 is less than 6
3. Boolean is a propositional algebra

The propositions 1 and 3 are true and proposition 2 is false. The two logical values 'True' and 'False' are called logical constants.

5.1.1 Boolean Variables and Expressions

A variable is a symbol used to represent a logical quantity. It can have only two values: true or false. The terms True or False can also be expressed by binary bits 1 or 0 respectively. The inverse of a variable is called its complement. The complement of a variable is represented by a dash or bar over the variable. For instance, the variable A′ is a complement of variable A.

Boolean algebra uses the following Boolean (logical) operators:

Operator	Symbol
AND	'.' or ∧
OR	'+' or V
NOT	′ or –

In this text, we will use 1 for True, 0 for False, a dot ('.') for AND, a plus ('+') for OR and dash (′) for NOT operators. A truth table represents the operational definitions of important logical operators. By using the truth table, the truth value of a Boolean formula can be calculated.

The truth tables of the three basic operators are as follows:

AND ·

P	Q	R
0	0	0
0	1	0
1	0	0
1	1	1

OR +

P	Q	R
0	0	0
0	1	1
1	0	1
1	1	1

NOT ′

P	R
0	1
1	0

It may be noted that the Boolean operators AND and OR are binary infix operators and the Logical NOT operator is a unary operator. The summary of these operators is given below:

1. P . Q = 1 if and only if both P and Q are 1
   = 0 otherwise
2. P + Q = 0 if and only if both P and Q are 0
   = 1 otherwise
3. P′ = 1 if P is 0
   = 0 if P is 1

Using any of the Boolean operators, a Boolean expression can be written in the form given below:

E = P < Boolean operator> Q

Where: P and Q are Boolean variables
Examples of valid Boolean expressions are:

I. E1 = A + B′ + C . D
II. E2 = a + b + c′ . d′ + b′ . e

If a complex Boolean expression such as (ii) given above is to be evaluated, then there is some confusion regarding which Boolean operator is to be applied first. This problem can be solved by following the order of precedence of Boolean operators as given below:

NOT (′)	Highest
AND(.)	↓
OR (+)	Lowest

However, the parenthesis can be suitably used to enclose a sub-expression that needs to be evaluated first. The evaluation of a Boolean expression is done by the following steps:

1. Evaluate from left to right
2. Evaluate the expression in parenthesis

3. Perform all NOT operations
4. Perform all AND operations
5. Perform all OR operations

Consider the expression: $a + b' . (c + d') + b' .d$
The order of evaluation for the above expression is given below:

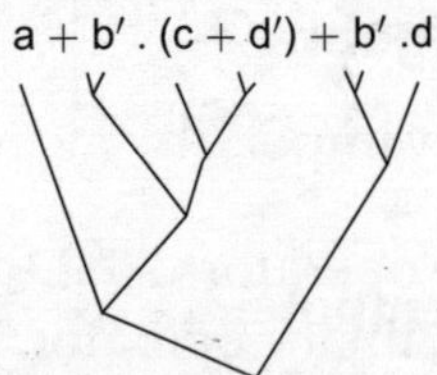

5.1.2 Basic Postulates of Boolean Algebra

Boolean algebra deals with only binary values (True / False). It has a set of postulates and theorems with the help of which a complex Boolean expression can be simplified. The basic postulates and theorems are discussed below:

Let B be a set of elements of Boolean algebra such that a, b, c, 0, 1, ∈ B.

Postulate 1. The elements 0 and 1 are unique identity elements such that:

$a + 0 = a$ (additive identity)
$a . 1 = 1$ (multiplicative identity)

Postulate 2. The binary algebra is complete. For every element a ∈ B, there is an element a′ such that

$a + a' = 1$
$a . a' = 0$
where a′ is known as the complement of a.

Postulate 3. The logical AND and logical OR operators are commutative

$a . b = b . a$
$a + b = b + a$

Postulate 4. The logical AND and logical OR operators are distributive

$a . (b + c) = a . b + a . c$
$a + (b . c) = (a + b) . (a + c)$

Postulate 5. The logical AND and logical OR operators obey the principle of substitution in such a way that if a = b then b can be substituted for a, and vice versa.

$a + c = b + c$
$a . c = b . c$

Postulate 6. The logical AND and logical OR operators obey the principle of associative laws

$a + (b + c) = (a + b) + c$
$a . (b . c) = (a. b) . c$

Postulate 7. The logical AND and logical OR operators obey the closure property such that

$a + b \in B$
$a . b \in B$
$a' \in B$

5.1.3 Theorems of Boolean Algebra

The theorems, given below, are very important and form the basis for the manipulation of Boolean expressions.

Theorem 1: Boolean algebra is **idempotent.**

$a + a = a$
$a . a = a$
The above stated laws are called **idempotent** laws

Theorem 2: Boolean algebra allows dominance of truth values 0 and 1 such that

$a + 1 = 1$
$a . 0 = 0$

Theorem 3: Boolean algebra is absorptive

$a + (a . b) = a$
$a . (a + b) = a$
The above stated laws are called **absorptive** laws

Theorem 4: Boolean algebra is involute

$(a')' = a$
Note: The following two theorems are called **De Morgan's theorems.**

Theorem 5: The complement of a sum equals the product of the complements

$(a + b)' = a' . b'$

Theorem 6: The complement of a product equals the sum of the complements

$(a . b)' = a' + b'$

Example 1

Prove the following by the deduction method:

(i) $a + a = a$
(ii) $a. a = a$

Solution:

By successive application of various postulates of Boolean algebra, we get:

(i) $a + a = (a + a) .1$
$= (a + a) . (a + a')$
$= a + (a. a')$

$= a + 0$

$= a$

(ii) $a . a = a. a + 0$

$= a. a + a. a'$

$= a . (a + a')$

$= a. 1$

A

5.1.4 The Duality Principle

It may be observed from Boolean theorems that the theorems are symmetric with respect to operators and truth values AND, OR, 1 and 0. In fact, we can produce a dual identity by the following steps:

1. Change . sign to + sign and vice versa
2. Complement all 0's and 1's
3. Do not touch NOT (′) operator

For example the expression: <u>a + a′ = 1</u> has the dual <u>a . a′ = 0</u>
Similarly, the dual of the expression: <u>a . (a + b) = a</u> is <u>a + (a . b) = a</u>

Example 2

Write the dual for the Boolean expression:

(i) a + a′ . b
(ii) a.b + a.b′ + a′b
(iii) x.y + x.y.z + x′.y + x.y.′z
(iv) (x + 0). (y. 1. x′)

Solution:

By changing '.' to '+' and vice versa and complementing 0's and 1's, we get

(i) a + a′ . b	dual = a. (a′+ b)
(ii) a.b + a.b′ + a′b	dual = (a + b) . (a + b′) + (a′ + b)
(iii) x.y + x.y.z + x′.y + x.y.′z	dual = (x +y) .(x+y+z) . (x′+y) . (x+y′+z)
(iv) (x + 0) . (y. 1. x′)	dual = (x . 1) + (y + 0 + x′)

5.1.5 Terminology and Standard Forms

A Boolean expression can be described by the following terms:

1. **Product term**: A product term contains one or more variables connected by AND operators. For instance <u>a. b. c</u> is a product term.
2. **Sum term**: A sum term contains one or more variables connected by OR operators. For instance, <u>a+ b + c</u> is a sum term.

3. **Sum of products**: This is a Boolean expression that contains product terms connected by OR operators. For instance, a'.c + b . c is a sum of products.
4. **Product of sums**: This is a boolean expression that contains sum terms connected by AND operators. For instance, (a' + c) . (b + c) is a product of sums.
5. If a Boolean expression has *n* variables, then in a truth table we can identify and associate the following two terms:
   a. Minterm: A product term of all entries in a row of a truth table. The variables that are 0 for the row are complemented and the variables which are 1 for the row are not disturbed.
   b. Maxterm: A sum term of all entries in a row of a truth table. The variables that are 1 for the row are complemented and the variables which are 0 for the row are not disturbed.

For the variables x, y, all the possible minterms and maxterms are given in Table 5.1

Table 5.1 Minterms and Maxterms

Row	X	Y	Minterm	Maxterm
0	0	0	X'.Y'	X+Y
1	0	1	X'.Y	X+Y'
2	1	0	X.Y'	X'+Y
3	1	1	X.Y	X'+Y'

A minterm or maxterm is also called a **canonical** term

5.1.6 Canonical Forms of Boolean Expressions

A. **Conversion of a truth table to a Boolean expression:** This can be done by two methods.

Method1: The following steps are used to write a boolean expression in a **sum of products** form for a given truth table.

1. Find all the rows of the truth table with a 1 in the output column.
2. Write minterms for the rows found in Step 1.
3. OR all the minterms.

Consider the following truth table:

	A	B	Y
→	0	0	1
	0	1	0
→	1	0	1
→	1	1	1

It may be noted that row numbers 0, 2, and 3 have the output as 1. Therefore the minterms are : A′. B′, A . B′, and A . B.

Thu\s, the final Boolean expression is:

E = A′ . B′ + A . B′ + A . B

The above expression is called **a canonical sum of products.** This is also called an AND-OR form. It is also expressed as : indicating that the minterms of rows 0,2, and 3 are to be ORed together.

Method 2: The following steps are used to write a Boolean expression in a **products of sums** form for a given truth table

1. Find all the rows of the truth table with a 0 in the output column.
2. Write maxterms for the rows found in Step 1.
3. AND all the maxterms

Consider the following truth table:

	A	B	Y
	0	0	1
→	0	1	0
	1	0	1
→	1	1	0

It may be noted that row numbers 1 and 3 are have output as 0. Therefore the maxterms are A + B′ and A′ + B′.

Thus, the final Boolean expression is :

E = (A + B′) . (A′ + B′)

The above expression is called **a canonical product of sums.** This is also called an OR-AND form. It is also expressed as : ndicating that the minterms of row 1 and 3 are to be ANDed together.

Example 3

Given the following truth table, derive the sum of products and product of sums forms of a Boolean expression from it.

X	Y	Z	G
0	0	0	0
0	0	1	1
0	1	0	1
0	1	1	0
1	0	0	0
1	0	1	1
1	1	0	0
1	1	1	1

Solution:

The minterms and maxterms of the truth table are given below:

X	Y	Z	G	Mintrem	Maxterm
0	0	0	0		$x + y + z$
0	0	1	1	$x' . y' . z'$	
0	1	0	1	$x' . y . z'$	
0	1	1	0		$x + y' + z'$
1	0	0	0		$x + y + z$
1	0	1	1	$x . y' . z$	
1	1	0	0		$x' + y' + z$
1	1	1	1	$x + y + z$	

(i) Sum of products: The canonical sum products is produced by ORing all minterms as given below:

$$\mathbf{P = x'.y'.z + x'.y.z' + x.y'.z + x.y.z}$$

(i) Product of sums: The canonical product of sums is produced by ANDing all maxterms as given below:

$$\mathbf{P = (x + y + z) . (x + y' + z') . (x' + y + z) . (x' + y' + z)}$$

B. **Conversion of a Boolean expression to a truth table:**

The following steps are used to draw a truth table for a given Boolean expression:

1. Draw a column for each separate variable/proposition of the expression.
2. Fill the first row with all 0's for the input variables.
3. Fill the rest of the row by counting in binary until all 1s appear in a row.
4. Identify all separate ANDed sections of the expression. Consider all True propositions to be 1s and all False propositions to be 0s.
5. Find the horizontal rows in the truth table corresponding to the combinations of 1s and 0s of each part of the expression. In the final column mark 1s.
6. Place 0s in the rest of the places in the final column.

Let us apply the above steps on the following expression:

$$Y = AB' + AB$$

1. Draw columns for each variable.

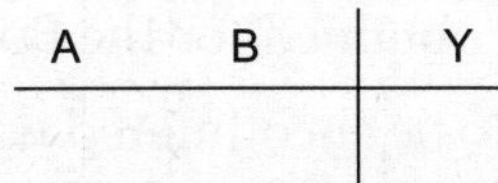

2. Fill in the first row with 0s for input variables A and B.

A	B	Y
0	0	

3. Fill in the remaining rows by counting in binary until all 1s appear.

A	B	Y
0	0	
0	1	
1	0	
1	1	

4. Identify each ANDed part of the expression.

AB′	the row is	1	0
AB	the row is	1	1

5. Find the horizontal rows for each part of the expression

	A	B	Y
	0	0	
	0	1	
AB′ ←	1	0	
AB ←	1	1	

6. Place all 1s in the final column corresponding to these rows.

A	B	Y
0	0	
0	1	
1	0	1
1	1	1

7. Place 0s in the remaining places in the final column.

A	B	Y
0	0	0
0	1	0
1	0	1
1	1	1

The above truth table has been obtained for the Boolean expression: y = AB′ + AB

Note: A problem is most likely to be encountered when an expression has a variable or so missing in a term. Consider the following expression:

$$Y = AB + B'C' + A'BC'$$

↑ C ↑ A
is missing

This situation can be handled easily. The term AB has the variable/ proposition C missing. Now C is introduced in both True and False form i.e., AB becomes **ABC + ABC′**. Similarly, the term B′C′ in which A is missing, is modified to **AB′C′ +A′B′C′.** Thus, the final expression becomes:

$$Y = ABC + ABC' + AB'C' + A'B'C' + A'BC$$

The above expression is ready to put in the truth table form. The procedure is exactly as in the previous case. The generated truth table is given below:

A	B	C	Y
0	0	0	1
0	0	1	0
0	1	0	0
0	1	1	1
1	0	0	1
1	0	1	0
1	1	0	1
1	1	1	1

Example 4

Prove the following by the truth table method:

(i) $a + b = b + a$

(ii) $a .b = b. a$

Solution:

(i) The required truth table is given below:

a	b	a + b	b + a
0	0	0	0
0	1	1	1
1	0	1	1
1	1	1	1

It may be noted that LHS is equal to RHS
It is left to the reader to prove part (ii) in a similar way.

Example 5

Prove the following (i) by the truth table (ii) by the deduction method:

$$a + a'b = a + b$$

Solution:

(i) Truth table method: The required truth table is given below:

a	b	a′b	a + a′b	a + b
0	0	0	0	0
0	1	1	1	1
1	0	0	1	1
1	1	0	1	1

It may be noted that LHS is equal to RHS

(ii) LHS $= a + a'b$
$= (a + a') . (a + b)$
$= 1. (a + b)$
$= a + b$
= R. H. S

Example 6

Prove the following (i) by the truth table (ii) by the deduction method:
$a + ab = a$

Solution:

(i) Truth table method: The required truth table is given below:

a	b	a . b	a + a . b
0	0	0	0
0	1	0	0
1	0	0	1
1	1	1	1

Kindly note that the column of a and a + a . b has the same entries. Hence LHS is equal to RHS.

(ii) By the deduction method
LHS $= a + a.b$
$= a\,(1 + b)$
$= a.\,1$
$= a$
= RHS

Example 7

Prove De Morgan theorems given below:

(i) $(a + b)' = a' . b'$

(ii) $(a . b)' = a' + b'$

Solution:

(i) By close observation of the expression $(a + b)' = a' . b'$, it may be observed that this theorem states that the complement of term $(a +b)$ is equal to the term $a' . b'$. Therefore, we can write the following:

$(a + b)' . (a' . b') = 0$

LHS $= (a + b)' . (a' . b')$

$=((a + b)''. a') . b'$ (Law of association)

$= ((a.a') + (a'.b) . b'$ (Law of distribution)

$= (0 + a'.b) . b'$

$= a'.b .b'$

$= a'.0$

$= 0$

= RHS

(ii) As in the previous example, we can write

$(a .b) . (a' + b') = 0$

LHS $= (a .b) . (a' + b')$

$= (a.b)'. a' + (a.b)). b'$ (law of distribution)

$= a.b.a' + a.b.b'$

$= 0.b + 0.a$

$= 0 + 0$

$= 0$

= RHS

Example 8

Evaluate the following Boolean expression

$$f (w,x,y,z) = (wx + (x'y)') z + y$$

for w =1, x = 1, y = 0,, and z = 1

Solution:

Evaluate the following terms:

$(x'y)' = (1'. 0)' 0' = 1$

$wx = 1 . 1 = 1$

$(wx + (x'y)') z + y = (1 +1) .1 + 0 = 1.1 + 0 = 1 + 0 = 1$

5.2 LOGIC GATES

Boolean operators are implemented in electronic circuits as logic gates. A logic gate performs a basic logic function and accordingly the gates are named as AND gate, OR gate, NOT gate etc.

The Boolean AND operator is implemented as an AND gate and its symbol is shown in Fig. 5.1(a). Similarly, OR and NOT gates are shown Fig. 5.1(b) and Fig.5.1 (c) respectively.

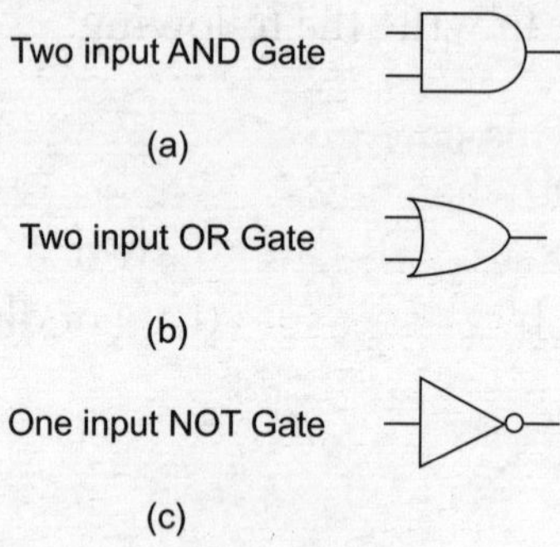

Fig. 5.1 Basic gates

The basic gates are connected together to obtain the following important gates

a
c
b

(a) Circuit realization

(b) Symbol

Fig. 5.2 NAND gate

NAND Gate: It is a combination of AND and NOT gates, as shown in Fig. 5.2

The output of a NAND gate is high if **any** of the inputs is low. The symbol is an AND gate with a small circle on the output. The small circle represents inversion. The truth table of a NAND gate is given below:

a	b	c
0	0	1
0	1	1
1	0	1
1	1	0

NOR Gate: It is a combination of OR and NOT gates, as shown in Fig. 5.3.

a
c
b

(a) Circuit realization

(b) Symbol

Fig. 5.3 NOR gate

The output of a NOR gate is high if all of the inputs are low. The symbol is an OR gate with a small circle on the output. The small circle represents inversion. The truth table of a NOR gate is given below

a	b	c
0	0	1
0	1	1
1	0	1
1	1	0

Exclusive OR gate (XOR): This gate gives 'True' as output if either of its input is true. It gives 'False' as output when all of its inputs are the same. The combination of simple gates that produces an XOR gate is given in Fig. 5.4 (a) and its symbol is given in Fig. 5.4 (b).

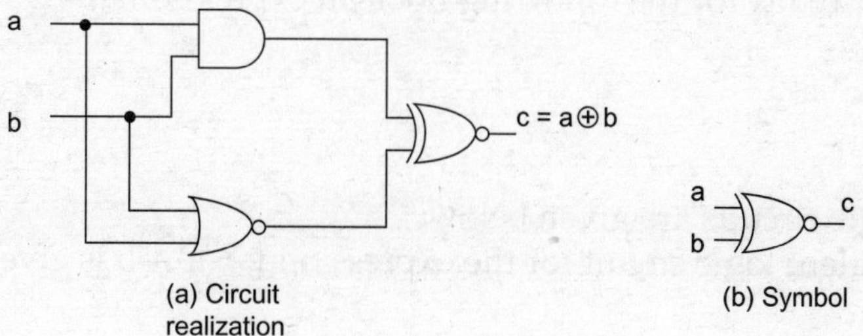

Fig. 5.4 XOR gate

It may be noted that an encircled plus sign (⊕) is used to show the XOR operation. The truth table of an XOR gate is given below:

a	b	c
0	0	1
0	1	0
1	0	0
1	1	1

Exclusive NOR gate (XNOR): This gate is inverse of XOR. It gives 'False' as the output if either of its inputs is True. It gives 'True' as the output when all of its inputs are the same. The combination of simple gates that produces an XOR gate is given in Fig. 5.5 (a) and its symbol is given in Fig. 5.5 (b).

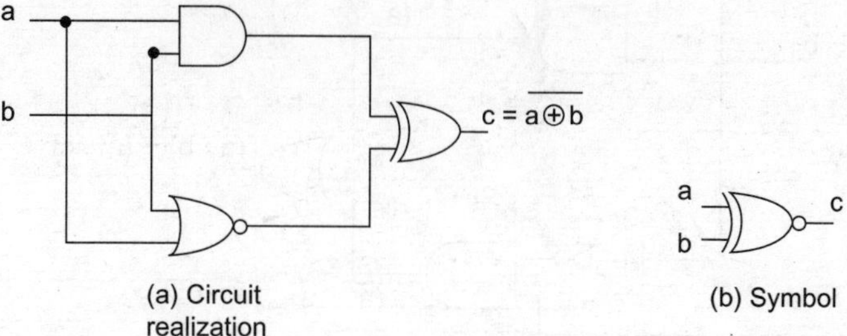

Fig. 5.5 XNOR gate

The output of XNOR is represented by $(a \oplus b)'$. The truth table of an XNOR gate is given below:

a	b	c
0	0	1
0	1	0
1	0	0
1	1	1

Note: ALL the logic gates given above have two inputs. However, we can have more than two inputs to a gate. For instance, a gate may have three or four inputs as per the requirements of a logic circuit.

Example 9

Draw the Logic circuits for the following Boolean expressions:

(i) y = a′ + b

(ii) y = a . b + c . a′

Solution:

The required logic circuits are given below:

(i) The equivalent logic circuit for the expression y = a′ + b is given in Fig. 5.6.

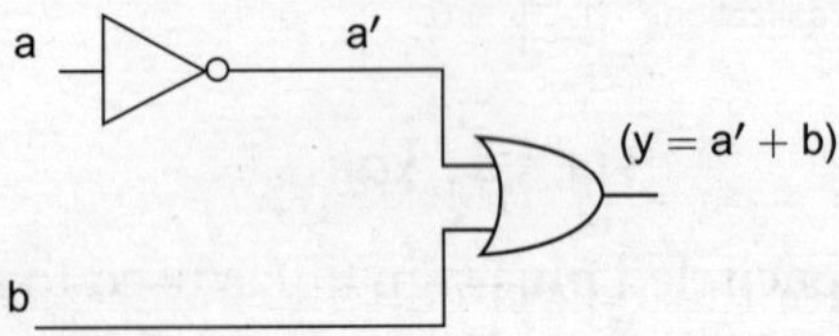

Fig. 5.6

(ii) The equivalent logic circuit for the expression y = a . b + c . a′ is given in Fig. 5.7.

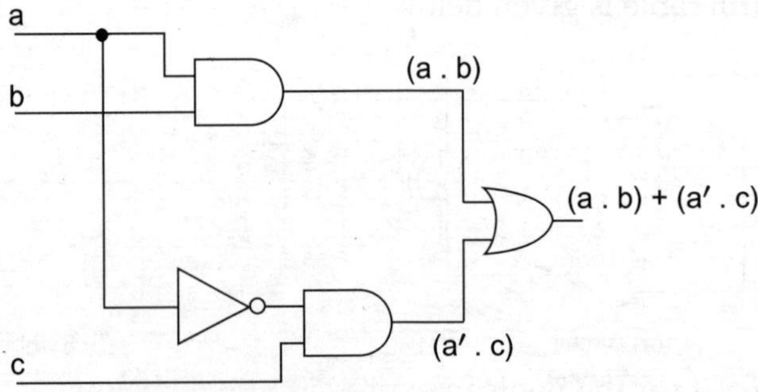

Fig. 5.7

Example 10

Construct the truth table for the logic circuit given in Fig. 5.8

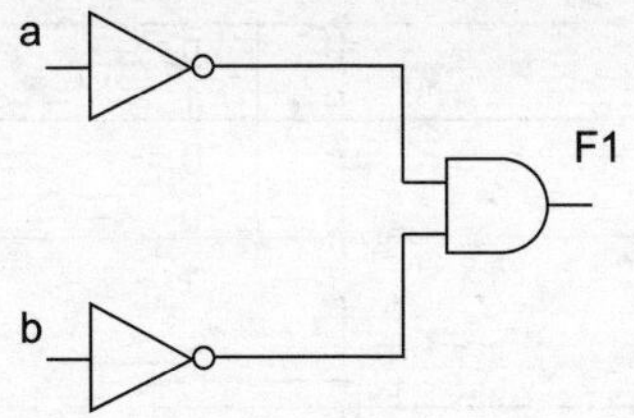

Fig. 5.8

Solution:

The Boolean expression for the logic circuit is given below:

$$F1 = a' . b'$$

The equivalent truth table is given below:

a	b	a′	b′	F1
0	0	1	1	1
0	1	1	0	0
1	0	0	1	0
1	1	0	0	0

Example 11

Construct the truth table for the logic circuit given in Fig. 5.9

Fig. 5.9

Solution:

The Boolean expression for the logic circuit is given below:

$$F1 = (a + b) '$$

The equivalent truth table is given below:

a	b	a+b	f2
0	0	0	1
0	1	1	0
1	0	1	0
1	1	1	0

Example 12

Draw the logic circuit for the Boolean expression given below:

$$p = xyz + xy'z + xyz'$$

Solution:

The required logic circuit is shown in Fig. 5.10.

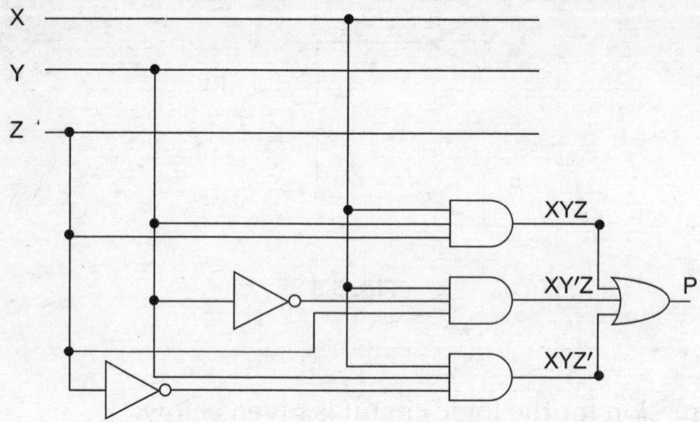

Fig. 5.10

EXERCISES

1. What do you mean by the logical operators: NOT, AND, and OR? Explain in brief with the help of truth tables.
2. Explain the commutative and distributive laws of AND and OR operators.
3. Prove that the Boolean algebra is idempotent.
4. What do you understand by the duality principle? Explain in brief.
5. Define the following terms:
   a. Boolean variables b. product term c. sum terms
6. Define the following terms:
   a. sum of products b. product of sums c. minterm and maxterm
7. Write the truth table for the following Boolean expressions:
   a. y = a . b. + a′ . c + c′ .b
   b. a . b . c + a′ . b . c′ + a . b′ .c′
   c. y = ac + ab
   d. y = a (a′ + b) c
   e. y = ab′ + a′b + ab + a′b′
8. Evaluate The following expressions for a= 0, b= 1, c = 1, d = 0:
   a. y = a . b . d′ + a′ . c . d + c′ .b
   b. a . b′ . c + a′ . b + c′ + a . b′ .c′
   c. y = acd′ + ab
   d. y = a (a′ + b + d) c
   e. y = ab′ + a′bc + ab + a′b′d′
9. What are De Morgan's theorems? Explain with the help of suitable examples. Convert the following into a sum of products form:
   (i) (a + b) (c + d)
   (ii) (ab′ + a′b + ac′) (a′b′ + ab′+ ac′)

10. Write the boolean expression for the following truth table:

x	y	z	f
0	0	0	0
0	0	1	0
0	1	0	0
0	1	1	0
1	0	0	1
1	0	1	0
	1	0	1
1	1	1	1

11. Prove the De Morgan's theorems.
12. Prove the following with the help of truth tables.
    (i) x + y = y + x
    (ii) x . y = y . x
13. Write the dual for the following:
    (i) a . c + a . 1 + b. c
    (ii) ab + ab′
    (iii) a′b′ + b′c + bc′
    (iv) a′ (b′ + c′) + a′ (b + c)
14. Draw the circuit diagram for the following boolean expressions:
    (i) y = x′z + xyz′
    (ii) y = ab + ab′c
    (iii) y = (a′+ b) c + cd
    (iv) y = a.b.c + (a.b.c) ′ + a.b.c.d
15. Express the following digital circuit (Fig. 5.11) as its equivalent Boolean expression.

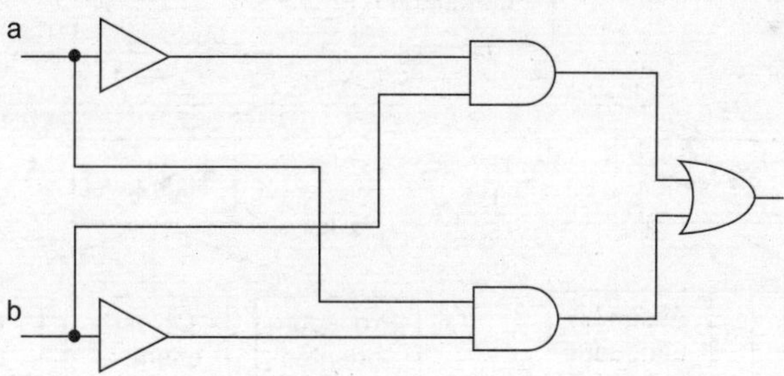

Fig. 5.11

CHAPTER

6 Introduction to Programming Languages

6.1 INTRODUCTION

From our earlier discussions on computer systems, we know that the computer hardware can work at an extremely fast rate. However, it cannot work on its own in the sense that every operation of a computer has to be expressed in the form of an instruction written in a programing language.

A programming language can be defined as "The language used for expressing a set of instructions that can be executed by the computer". Programming languages can be divided into two major categories: **low-level** and **high-level** languages. Low level languages can be further divided into machine and assembly languages. The high-level languages can be, however, categorized into many types, as shown in Fig. 6.1.

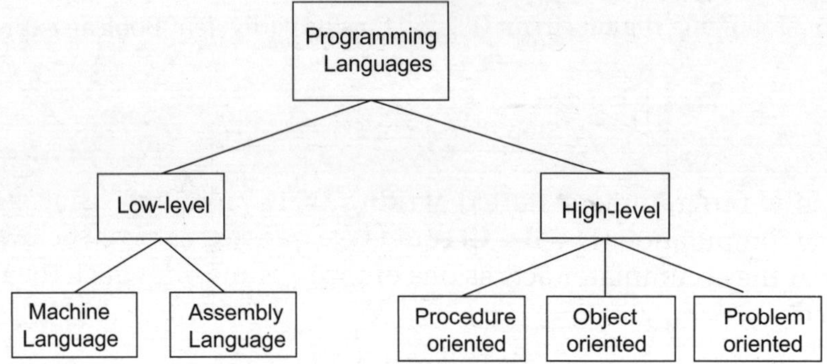

Fig. 6.1 Programming languages

A brief discussion on each type of programming languages is given in the following sections.

6.2 LOW-LEVEL LANGUAGES

We know that the computer hardware is a digital machine that can work at an extremely fast rate. It works on binary electronic pulses – 0s and 1s. However, the

CPU is a passive device. It cannot work on its own, in the sense that every operation has to be expressed as a binary instruction. The binary instructions are also called machine instructions. The programmers of earlier machines of the 1940s used to write their programs using machine instructions. A machine instruction consists of two parts: op-code and operand, as shown in Fig. 6.2.

op-code	operand
01101011	11100011

Fig. 6.2 Format of a simple machine instruction

It may be noted that a machine instruction is simply a string of binary digits. It is incomprehensible to human beings and very difficult to work with. Further on, with a view to increase readability, programmers assigned appropriate symbols to the op-codes on the basis of the operation performed by the instructions. The symbols of a hypothetical machine are given in Table 6.1.

Table 6.1 Binary op-codes and their equivalent symbols

Symbol (mnemonic)	Binary code
Load	0000 0000
Add	0000 0001
Sub	0000 0010
:	:
Stop	1111 1111

Accordingly, programmers started writing their programs using symbols. For example, the computation **(D = B + C)** could be expressed as given below. It has been assumed that the accumulator acts as one of the operands in which the result is also accumulated.

Load B

Add C

Store D

This symbolic language for writing programs was termed assembly language and the instructions were called assembly instructions. The major difference between machine language and assembly language lies in the manner in which both the languages refer to memory locations. Machine language refers to absolute addresses of the memory whereas assembly language gives symbolic names to memory locations. There is a one-to-one correspondence between the assembly and machine language, in the sense that for every binary code, there is an equivalent symbol (mnemonic) in assembly language (see Table 6.1).

However, an assembly language program cannot be directly executed on a computer as such, because the computer can only run machine language programs. Therefore, some mechanism is required to convert symbolic instructions of assembly language into binary machine instructions. An assembler does this job for the programmer. It converts the assembly language program into an equivalent machine executable program, as shown in Fig. 6.3.

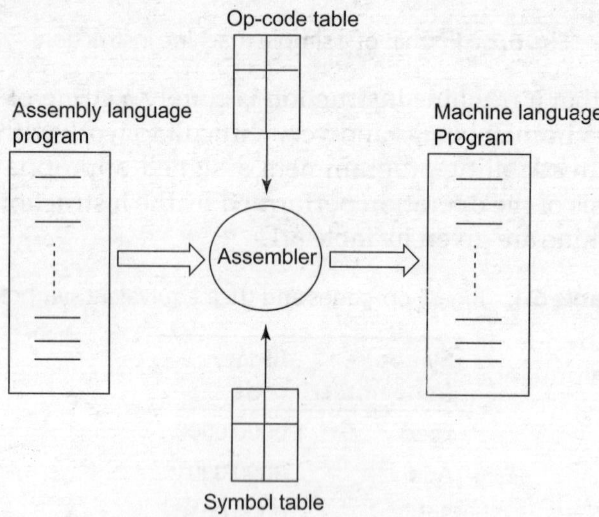

Fig. 6.3 The assembler

The assembler is quite a simple program because for the purpose of conversion, it uses primarily two tables: op-code table and symbol table. The op-code table contains the machine code equivalent op-codes whereas the symbol table contains the binary equivalent values of symbolic addresses. For a given assembly language instruction, it picks up the binary equivalent machine code for the op-code from the op-code table and the binary equivalent value of the symbol from the symbol table and assembles the machine code instruction.

It may be noted that the assembler does not translate but assembles the target instruction by picking values from tables and writing them in a pre-defined order. Therefore, the assembler can also be called a 'transcriptor'.

Nevertheless, both machine and assembly languages are machine dependent. Owing to their one-to-one correspondence with machine architecture, these languages are also called low-level languages. Therefore, only a specialist who knows the architecture of the machine can write program in assembly language. In fact assembly language programming is a slow and tedious process.

6.3 HIGH-LEVEL LANGUAGES

In order to overcome the drawbacks of low-level languages, more easily understandable computer languages were developed in the 1950s. These languages were English-like, having their own architecture. Therefore, these languages were termed high-level languages (HLL). FORTRAN and COBOL were two popular languages among scientists and commerce professionals respectively. For example, the computation **(D = B + C)** could be expressed in an English-like expression, as given below:

FORTRAN: **D = B + C**

COBOL: **Add B to C giving D**

It may be noted that the statements given above in HLL are not only understandable and elegant but are also machine independent i.e., the program written in HLL can be made to run on different hardware platforms.

Since HLL is English-like, a statement written in this language is not understandable to the machine. Therefore, a translator is needed that could translate a program written in HLL to machine language. The HLL program is called the 'source code' and the machine language program is called the 'target code'. The translator is also a program. A high-level language translator is called a compiler. The compiler takes the source code as input and translates it line by line into machine code, as shown in Fig. 6.4.

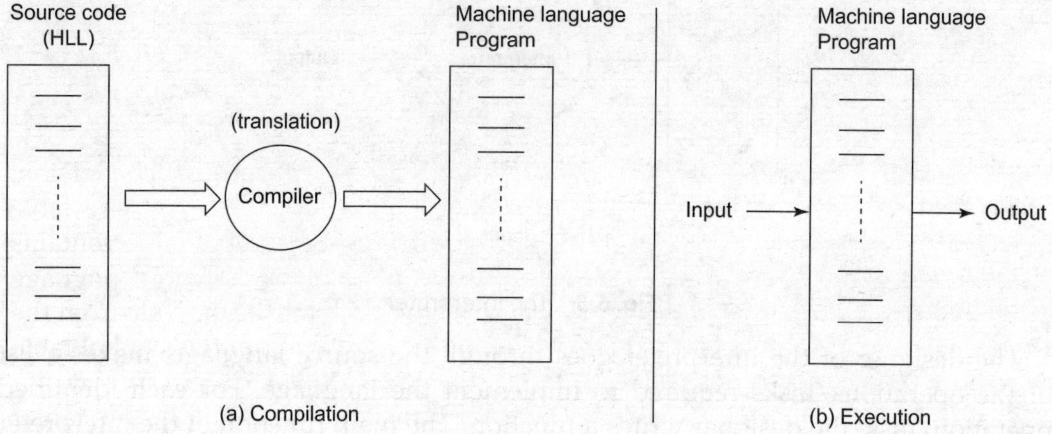

Fig.6.4 The compiler

A compiler is a much more complex program than an assembler. It not only translates the source code instructions into machine code but also maps the data structures of the HLL program onto the linear memory of the underlying hardware. At machine code level, there are no data structures such as arrays, stacks, queues, pointers, trees etc. A data structure is a logical representation of the data as visualized by the programmer. For instance, the programmer may view his data as a list or as a tree of nodes whereas the underlying memory at the hardware level is a linear memory. Therefore the compiler has to map the list or tree of nodes into the addresses of a linear flat memory. A **compiler** can be precisely defined as *a program that translates a program written in high-level language into machine language.*

The source code and executable code are two different forms of the same computational entity. Thus, after the translation process neither, the source code nor the compiler is needed. In fact it is the executable code and not the source code that runs on the machine.

Examples: Turbo 'C', Borland 'C', Aztec 'C' are popular compilers for 'C' programming language.

6.3.1 The Concept of Interpretation

An **interpreter** is a simple program. It does not translate the source code into machine code. In fact it reads the source code program line by line and executes it (see Fig. 6.5). Therefore, an **interpreter is also called a program execution environment.**

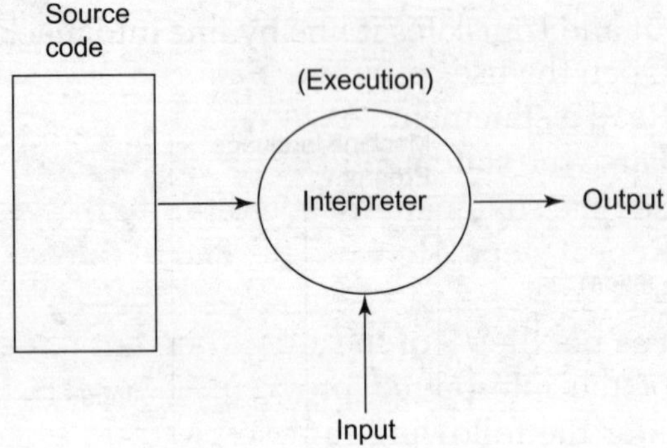

Fig. 6.5 The interpreter

The designer of the interpreter goes through the source language, makes a list of the operations/tasks required to implement the language. For each identified operation/task, the designer writes a function. The main function of the interpreter reads the source program line by line, checks its syntax/semantics. The parsed statement is executed through an appropriate function.

Let us take a very small set of a language that supports three operations:

1. Read a variable
2. Print a variable
3. Add two variables.

The above operations can be executed through the functions given below:

```
int Read ( )    /* Function to read a variable */
{
   int val;
   cin >> val;
   return val;
}
void Print ( int val)   /* Function to print a variable */
{
   cout << val;
}

int Add ( int op1, int op2)  /* Function add two variables */
{
   return op1 + op2;
}
```

Having written the above functions, the designer of the interpreter uses the following algorithm to execute the user programs.

Algorithm **interpreter** ()

{

Step 1. Open the user program file.
2. Read a statement.
3. Parse the statement. If error, then report.
4. Get the statement executed through corresponding function.
5. Repeat steps 2 to 4 till the end of the file.

}

It may be noted that as per Step 3 of the algorithm, if it finds a syntax or semantic error in a statement of the interpreted program, it reports the error and further execution stops. Consider the following sample program segment that needs to be executed by a user:

Read A
Read B
C= A + B
Print C

The program statements of the sample program get executed by the interpreter as given below:

Statement	**Function called**
Read A	A = Read();
Read B	B = Read();
C= A + B	C = add (A, B);
Print C	Print (C);

It may be noted that the program statements of the user program are executed by the interpreter and no translation takes place. Therefore the interpreter is required whenever the program needs to be executed. Since every statement is interpreted again on every execution of the program, the overall execution of the program becomes slow. Additionally, this arrangement consumes more memory space as compared to a compiled program, because along with the interpreted program, the interpreter also needs to be loaded into the main memory.

When a new language is designed, generally an interpreter is built and offered to the users so that they can experiment and give comments/feedback. A compiler for the language is developed later, if the language becomes popular. In fact interpreters are popular in program development environments.

Example: GW Basic was a very popular interpreter for the programming language BASIC. Java Virtual Machine interprets the byte code.

6.3.2 Types of High Level Languages

High level languages are generally subdivided into the following categories:

1. **Procedure-Oriented Languages**: A procedure-oriented language is normally a machine independent language. It is designed to help the programmer in the accurate description of the logic of how to solve the problem at hand. The logic is coded as a high-level program comprising procedures.

   Importance is given to the procedure that can solve a given problem with the following view in mind.

   "What do we have to do to solve the problem?"

   The problem at hand is divided into sub-problems. Then each sub-problem is divided into sub-sub-problems and so on, till each of them can be solved separately. Each sub-problem is coded as a procedure or function. The arrangement is shown in Fig. 6.6.

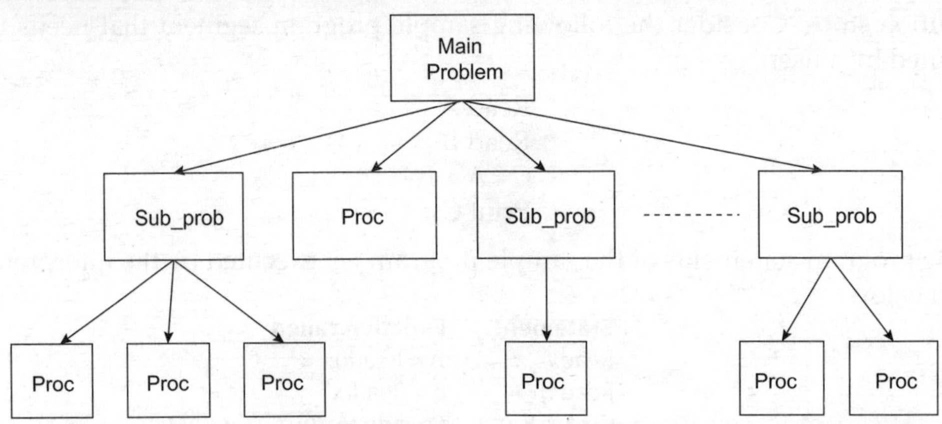

Fig. 6.6 Hierarchy of procedures

The advantage of a procedure is that if it is correct then on every call it produces correct results.

Examples of procedure-oriented languages are: BASIC, FORTRAN, 'C', PASCAL etc.

Some characteristics of procedure oriented programming are:

- Emphasis is on how to solve the problem.
- The program is divided into procedures.
- The procedures share global data.
- The code is generally not reusable.

2. **Object Oriented Programming Languages:** Object oriented programming creates programs consisting of interacting objects. An object is a software entity that mimics any real life entity which is capable of providing services. For instance, a software agent can provide the same services through a program to a user that are provided manually by a clerk in a bank.

An object is divided into two parts: interface and implementation (see Fig. 6.7). In this arrangement, the data and implementation can be changed without changing the interface, resulting in reusable software objects. A programmer can very quickly assemble software by interconnecting such reusable objects, as shown in Fig. 6.8.

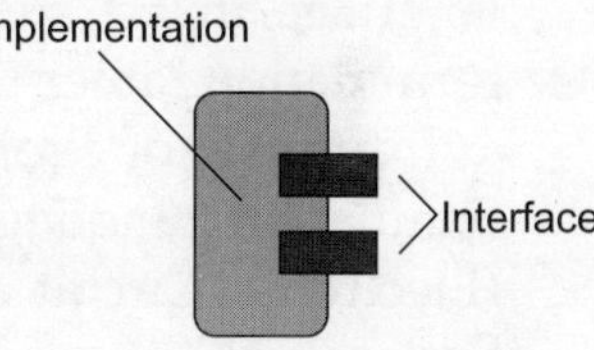

Fig. 6.7 Software object

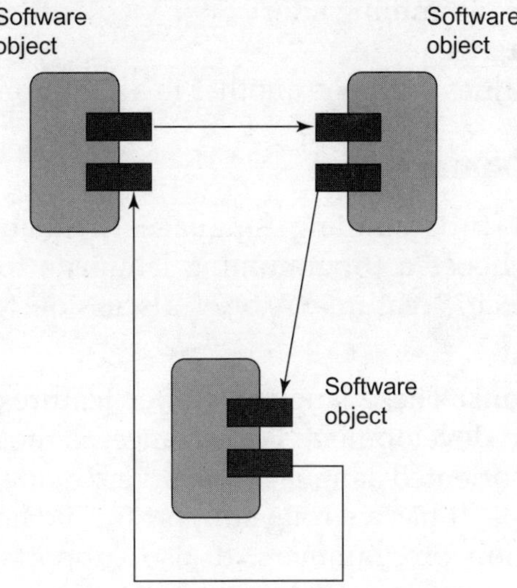

Fig. 6.8 Interacting software objects

Object Oriented Programming has three prominent aspects: encapsulation, inheritance and polymorphism.

Some **characteristics** of object oriented programming are:

- More emphasis is placed on data and information.
- A program is a collection of objects.
- Objects are usable entities.
- Objects interact with each other through interfaces.

Examples of object oriented languages are: C++, java, python etc.

3. **Problem-Oriented Programming Languages:** A problem-oriented language is designed to help the programmer in the accurate description of problems belonging to specific sets of problem types. This type of language is very useful in a situation where the user cannot, normally, solve the problem himself or herself or the solution to the problem is too complex. The programmer does not provide the procedure for solving the problem but only describes the input-output requirements and other necessary parameters. The method is generally built into the software that interprets the instructions of the problem-oriented language. In fact, such languages allow the users to concentrate more on problem formulation rather than numerical computations and computer programming.

   Examples of Problem Oriented Languages: **ACSL** (Advanced Continuous Simulation Language), **CSMP** (Continuous System Modeling Program), **ECAP** (Electronic Circuit Analysis Program), **GPSS** (General Purpose Simulation System) etc.

   Some **characteristics** of problem-oriented programming are:

   - Reduction in programming effort
   - Flexibility of change
   - Relating the entities with one another in a common environment

6.3.3 Programming Domains

There are hundreds of programming languages available to programmers. A programmer is free to choose a programming language for a specific application domain based on its specific features. A brief discussion follows, on the different programming domains.

1. **Business applications**: These languages offer features which are suitable for business application development. For instance, as the name suggests, COBOL (common business-oriented language**)** was very widely used for developing business applications. It has a strong support for file handling, a much needed feature by application programmers. It also supports long variable and file names resulting in an easily readable program. RPG is another language used for business application development. Nowadays this language is not in vogue.
2. **Scientific applications**: These languages support a wide variety of data types i.e. very large and very small numbers can be easily represented. However,

such languages support few built in data structures. Example ALGOL 60and FORTRAN programming languages are very widely used to develop scientific applications. Even 'C' and C++ can also be used for this purpose.

3. **Programming languages for artificial intelligence**: These languages are used to represent logical statements and their manipulation to arrive at a particular inference. LISP and PROLOG languages are widely used languages for this purpose.
4. **Parallel Programming languages**: These languages are designed to program algorithms and applications that can run on parallel computers. The program is written as a set of concurrent tasks. The tasks are mapped onto different parallel computing elements of a multiprocessing environment. These languages are also called concurrent programming languages. Concurrent Pascal, Occam, Parallel Fortran, and Hope are some parallel programming languages.

6.3.4 Popular High-level Languages

Several hundred programming languages are available to present day programmers. However, a few of them are very widely used for programming purposes. Salient features of popular programming languages are discussed here.

1. **'C' Programming language**: 'C' Was developed by Dennis Ritchie around 1970 as a general purpose language. He implemented the UNIX operating system in C. It is a block structured language wherein a construct enclosed between a pair of curly braces '{ }'is considered a block. A block has one entry and one exit. Examples of blocks are: compound statements, loops, functions etc. The salient features of C are:
   - It is an imperative language i.e., imperative to Von –Neumann architecture.
   - C programs are elegant and precise.
   - A 'C' program is a collection of functions, with one of them named as **main** (). The execution of the program always starts with the execution of the **main** () function.
   - Highly suitable for development of system software
   - It has been standardized by the American National Standard Institute (ANSI C)
   - It is a compiled language.
2. **'C++' Programming Language**: C++ (cee plus plus) is an object oriented programming language developed by Bjarne Stroustrup in 1980. It is a superset of the C language, and therefore shares most of the strengths and weaknesses of C. The additional strengths of C++ are listed below:
   - It supports function prototyping
   - It supports encapsulation
   - It assists inheritance

- It provides reusable code
- It allows code sharing
- It is a compiled language.

3. **Java Programming Language**: Java is also an object oriented programming language, developed by James Gosling at Sun Microsystems. The language is designed to be platform independent i.e., the compiled java code can run on all platforms. In fact, the java code is compiled into a file consisting of bytecode instructions. The bytecode is a machine independent code. Each platform is loaded with a java virtual machine (JVM) capable of interpreting bytecode instructions. The salient features of Java are:
    - Most of the object oriented concepts have been drawn from C++
    - Portable programs: Java programs can be executed on any platforms (Linux, Window, Mac), loaded with a JVM.
    - Highly suitable for multithreaded applications
    - It supports cross-platform code
    - Highly suitable for internet programming
    - It is both a compiled and an interpreted language.
4. **Python Programming Language**: Python supports multiple programming paradigms: structured, object oriented, and functional programming paradigms. It has built-in data structures that help increase the productivity of the programmer. Therefore, it is highly suitable for 'Rapid Application Development (RAD)'. The salient features of Python are:
    - Supports dynamic typing and dynamic binding.
    - Supports the construction of reusable modules.
    - Has an extensive standard library available as free distribution.
    - The built-in data structures increase productivity.
    - Its syntax promotes readability thereby reducing the cost of maintenance.
    - It is also used as a scripting language.
    - Program size is small compared to Java and C++ programs.
    - It is an interpreted language.

6.4 GENERATIONS OF PROGRAMMING LANGUAGES

Since the advent of computers, programming languages have evolved from unstructured, difficult-to-read languages to object oriented, easy-to-read programming languages. In fact, at every increase in the power of a programming style, we have moved one step away from the machine. Based on different styles of programming, the programming languages can be classified into five generations of programming languages.

1. **First generation Languages** (1GL): The machine language comprising 0s and 1s is termed a 1st generation computer language. It is a machine dependent

language designed to program as per the architecture of the processor of the machine.

Example machine instruction: 11010111 10011011

Since it is a machine language, no translation is required and the program runs very fast and efficiently on the machine

2. **Second generation Languages** (2GL): Assembly languages are called 2nd generation programming languages. An assembly language is a sugared form of the machine language. It uses symbols, called **mnemonics**, to write the programming code. The symbolic codes are easier to comprehend as compared to the code written using binary language.

   Example assembly instruction: Load Val

   The assembly instructions have one-to-one correspondence with their equivalent machine instructions and therefore both machine and assembly languages are also called low-level languages.

3. **Third generation Languages** (3GL): These languages are also called high-level languages. The architecture of a 3GL is different from that of the underlying machine. As discussed earlier, 3GL (high-level languages) are further divided into procedural, object oriented, and problem oriented languages.

   Examples of 3GL are: 'C', 'C++', Java, Python etc.

4. **Fourth generation Languages** (4GL): Fourth generation languages (4GL) are one level above the third generation languages. 4GL have been developed keeping in view the following observation:

   "The number of lines of documented, delivered code produced per programmer per day is constant, regardless of the language "

   4GL offer non-procedural constructs such as 'sort', 'index', 'search', 'create table' etc. A non-procedural construct performs a task for which the programmer need not provide the programming logic. The language has built-in logic for the construct. Thus, the programming effort is drastically reduced. For instance, a programmer can issue a statement such as that given below:

   'Search all records where Marks > 70'

   It may be noted that the programmer has not supplied the procedure for searching into the file or data base. In an equivalent 3GL program, the programmer would have had to provide some lines of code for this task.

   In fact, the number of statements in a 4GL program is much less compared to an equivalent 3GL program, resulting in increased programmer productivity.

   Examples of 4GL are: FoxPro, SQL, MATLAB, Oracle Reports etc.

5. **Fifth generation languages** (5GL): The fifth generation languages have been designed to develop machines that behave like humans. These machines

respond to input provided in a natural language such as English. The machines are still in development stage. If developed, these machines would be capable of learning and self-organization. Therefore, the machines are also called artificially intelligent machines. Artificial Intelligence is branch of computer science concerned with making computers behave like humans.

Examples of fifth generation computing devices are: Game playing computers, voice recognition devices, intelligent robots that autonomously accomplish a given job based on the surroundings.

Examples of 5GL are: LISP and Prolog.

Table 6.2 shows the timeline of the development of some popular programming languages.

Table 6.2 Chronology of development of programming languages

Year	Language	Remarks
1950-56	Assembly languages	Low level languages
1957	FORTRAN	High level language for Sc. applications
1958	ALGOL	Algorithmic language supporting block structures
1960	COBOL, LISP	Business programming and List processing
1962	Simula	Simulation programming, first OOP language
1964	BASIC	General purpose, easy to program language
1970	PROLOG, Hope	Logic programming language suitable for AI applications Hope was a functional programming language
1972	'C'	High level language suitable for system programming
1973	PASCAL	Block structured language
1983	Smalltalk, Ada	OOP languages
1984	ML	Functional programming
1986	C++, Eiffel	OOP languages
1990	Haskell	Functional programming
1990–1995	Perl, Python, JavaScript, PHP	Scripting languages
1995	Java	OOP language suitable for Internet programming
2000	C#	A multi-paradigm programming language
2005–2006	Ruby on Rails	Web application framework
2010	(Standard) PHP	Scripting language
2014	Ios/swift	Programming language for iOS and OS X developers

EXERCISES

1. What is a programming language? Name the various categories of computer languages.
2. What is a machine language? Why it is required?
3. What is meant by a mnemonic? What is an assembly language? What are its advantages over machine language?
4. What is an assembler?
5. Give your comments on the following statement –
   "An assembler is not a translator"
6. Why is assembly language called a machine dependent language?
7. What are the components of an assembly language instruction? Identify these parts and discuss the functions of each.
8. What are the advantages of an assembly language over its machine language equivalent?
9. What is a high-level language?
10. Discuss the following statement:
    "low-level languages are machine dependent and high-level languages are machine independent"
11. What is the difference between a source program and an object program?
12. What are the merits and limitations of a high-level languages?
13. Define the terms compiler and interpreter.
14. Explain the concept of interpretation with the help of an example.
15. Differentiate between problem-oriented and procedure oriented languages?
16. Write a short note on "Object oriented programming languages"
17. What is meant by a software object?
18. What are the characteristics of object oriented programming?
19. What are the characteristics of problem-oriented programming?
20. Write an explanatory note on programming domains
21. Describe what is meant by a 4GL and discuss its importance.
22. Compare the various generations of computer programming languages.
23. Briefly discuss the salient features of the C programming language.
24. Briefly discuss the salient features of the C++ programming language.
25. Briefly discuss the salient features of the programming language Java.
26. Briefly discuss the salient features of , the programming language Python.

CHAPTER

7 Operating Systems: An Introduction

7.1 INTRODUCTION

A computer system is a composition of two main components: hardware and software. The hardware is a programmable digital machine capable of performing computations and taking logical decisions. Since this is a digital machine, it provides a binary interface to interact with its users, as shown in Fig. 7.1

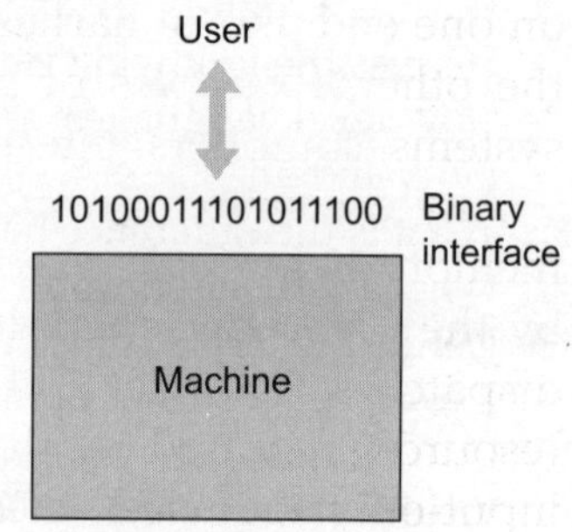

Fig. 7.1 The binary interface offered by the machine

We know that binary code is difficult to work with. So we need to have *an intermediate* layer of software that can interact with the binary interface on one hand and the user on the other. In fact, this layer of software takes the user away from the hardware, as shown in Fig. 7.2.

It may be noted that the software interacts with the user in English-like language that the user is good at and gets the required work done from the machine through the binary interface. The most important software is the operating system (OS). When the system is switched on, the **operating system (OS)** gets loaded into the main memory and takes control of the computer system. It provides an interface to the user for interaction. Now the user can submit commands at the interface for managing files or execution of a program, printing of a job etc. In fact, the user does not work with the actual machine but with a *virtual machine* that is offered by the operating system. Examples of operating systems are: Windows XP, Windows 10, Mac OS, Unix, Linux etc. Thus, we work with a Windows machine or a UNIX machine depending upon which operating system has been loaded on the machine.

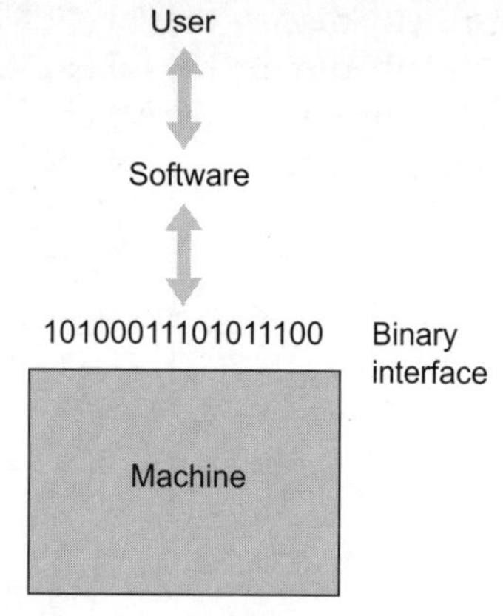

Fig. 7.2 The layer of software between the user and the machine

Software can be divided into two major categories: Application software and System software, as shown in Fig. 7.3. Application software is third party software. It is generally brought by the user and loaded on the computer system for his/her application needs. For example, an astrologer might use the 'Kundli software' for forecasting horoscopes of his clients. An engineer might use 'AutoCAD' or 'ORCAD' for design applications. Therefore, the software like 'Kundli', 'AutoCAD', 'mysin' etc. are called application software.

User
Application Software
System Software
10100011101011100 Binary Interface
Machine

Fig. 7.3 Types of software

The system software is a layer between application software and the machine. The purpose of this software is to provide services and resources to application software on one end and to harness the power of the machine on the other. Examples of system software are: operating systems, compilers, interpreters, assemblers etc.

Any executable program must get space in the main memory before it is executed instruction by instruction by the CPU. The operating system loads the program into the main memory and dispatches it to the CPU for execution. Additionally, it also provides the other resources required by the program. For example, CPU time, memory space, files, input-output devices, messages, interrupts etc., are all instances of resources.

Note: In a single CPU system, only one program entity can run at a time on the machine i.e., the CPU execution is interleaved between executable programs including the OS, as shown in Fig. 7.4. For example, the OS runs for t1, t3, and t5 instants of time. Programs P1, P2, and P3 run for t2, t6, and t4 instants of time respectively.

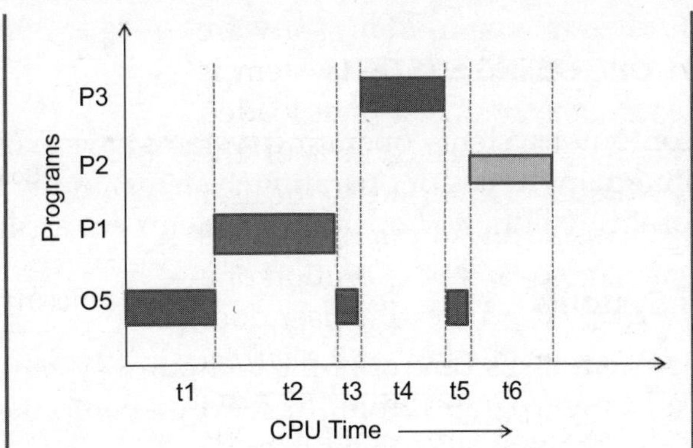

Fig. 7.4 Interleaved executions of programs

Let us precisely define the operating system as: "The operating system is a set of programs. It acts as an interface between user and machine. It manages and allocates the resources available in the computer system". Therefore, an operating system is also called **a resource manager**.

So, **the basic objectives of an operating system** are to:

1. Provide a 'user-friendly' interface to the user so that the user need not bother about the underlying hardware. The commands given by the user in English-like language are interpreted by the operating system, which in turn uses the hardware to get the required task done.
2. Create an environment for other programs to execute on the CPU and allocate resources to the executing programs as and when required.
3. Harness the full powers of the machine so that users can make best possible use of the hardware for their application needs.

From the above discussion we can say that a machine has no value without an operating system because it is the operating system that transforms the machine into a manageable device that can be easily used by the user. The user works on the virtual machine offered by the operating system namely, a 'Windows machine', a 'UNIX machine', or a 'Mac machine'.

This situation is similar to the situation of a television (TV), which cannot, on its own, show any programmes unless it connected to any of the following.

1. DTH
2. Cable TV
3. DVD player (or other media input)

So, we watch the virtual TV offered by various channels provided by the above service providers. Thus TV, the hardware, is valueless without the software being supplied by the Cable or DTH connection. Similarly, the computer hardware is valueless without software, especially the operating system.

7.2 EVOLUTION OF OPERATING SYSTEMS

Since the advent of computer systems, operating systems have evolved through many stages and phases into many types of operating systems. In the following sections, the various phases of the evolution of operating systems are explained.

7.2.1 Single User Systems

Once the operating system takes control of the computer system, on a user request it loads a program (say myProgram) from the hard disk into the main memory, as shown in Fig. 7.5.

Kindly note that the program called 'myProgram' has been loaded from the hard disk to the main memory by the operating system. This action involves an input/output (I/O) operation from the I/O device i.e., the hard disk in this case. Since I/O devices are slower by nature of their construction, this movement of a program from hard disk to main memory is extremely slow, relative to the speed of other CPU operations.

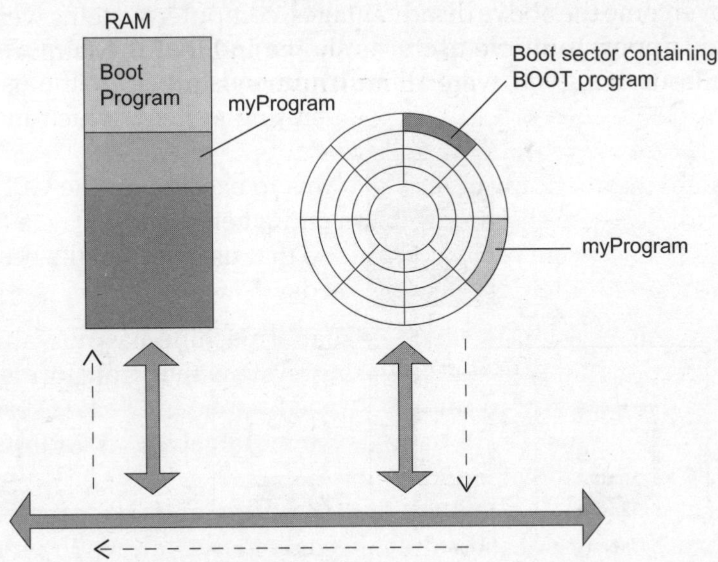

Fig. 7.5 MyProgram loaded into main memory

Now the operating system hands over the control to 'myProgram' by loading the address of its first instruction onto the program counter (PC), a register of the control unit. Since the PC points to the next instruction to be executed, the execution of 'myProgram' starts.

In this type of arrangement, there is only one user and his/her program called 'myProgram' is executing in the system. Since there is only one user, the operating system can make all resources available to the user and his/her program. 'myProgram' can read from or write to any location in the user area of the memory. There are no serious security issues because the user is the sole user of the system. This type of operating system is called a **single user mono programming** system. Operating systems of the 1950s were of this type and the I/O device was a magnetic tape instead of a hard disk.

Example: DOS (Disk Operating System) was a single user mono programming system. Modern-day handheld palmtops also fall in this category.

7.2.2 Multi-user Operating Systems

The major disadvantage of single user systems was that most of time the CPU remained idle because of following two reasons:

1. After completion of a job, the loading of new program required an I/O operation from the secondary storage devices.

2. If the currently executing program asked for an I/O operation, the CPU had to wait till the I/O device provided the required service to the program.

In order to overcome the above disadvantages, computer systems were so designed that they could support multiple users, as shown in Fig. 7.6. Mainframe computers like IBM 360, Elbrus, ICL 2900, were all **multiuser** systems.

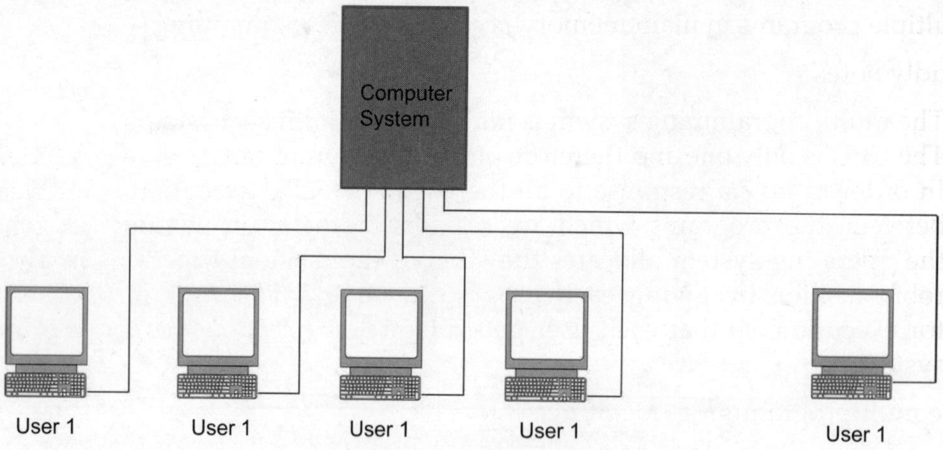

Fig. 7.6 Multiuser computer systems

It may be noted that the computer system is only one. It is connected with N number of dumb terminals. Thus, N users can simultaneously sit on this type of system. The operating system loads one program per user into the main memory, as shown in Fig. 7.7.

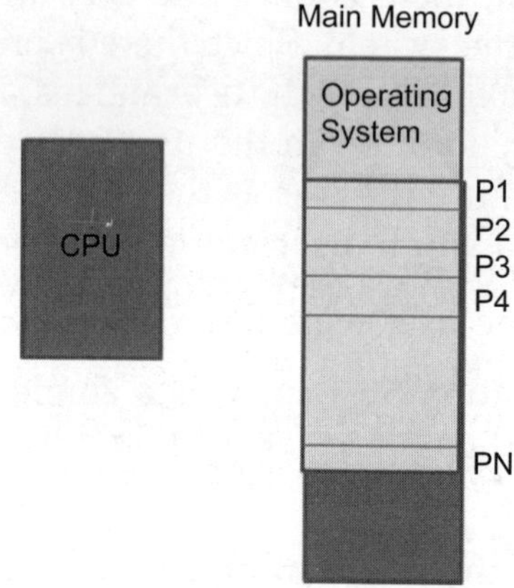

Fig. 7.7 Programs belonging to all users loaded into the main memory

Since multiple programs are resident in the main memory, as soon as the currently executing program completes its execution the operating system dispatches another program to the CPU for execution. Similarly, if the currently executing program asks for an I/O operation, the operating system suspends the execution of the program and makes it wait till its I/O is complete. Meanwhile the operating system dispatches another program to the CPU for execution. Thus, the CPU never remains idle. This type of operating system is called a **multiprogramming** system.

The term multiprogramming can be precisely defined as: "simultaneous residency of multiple programs in main memory is called **multiprogramming**".

Kindly note:

1. The multiprogramming system is inherently a multiuser system.
2. The CPU is only one and therefore only one program can execute at a time.
3. In order to give a response to all the users, the CPU execution is interleaved between the programs which are resident in the main memory. In general, the operating system allocates the CPU to the resident programs in a round robin fashion by giving each program a quantum of time in nanoseconds for execution, so that each user gets adequate continuous response from the system.

The multiprogramming operating system has the following objectives:

1. Maximum utilization of CPU time
2. Efficient management of main memory

To achieve the above objectives it has to answer the following two questions:

1. Which program is to be brought into the main memory?
2. Out of the resident programs, which program is to execute next?

The operating system uses many loading and scheduling strategies to answer the above questions.

Examples of Multi-user Multiprogramming operating systems are: VAX-11, IBM z/OS, UNIX etc.

In earlier multiprogramming systems, a user was allowed to submit one job at a time. Later on when processors with high speed were available, the operating systems were designed to accept more than one job per user, as shown in Fig. 7.8. The jobs submitted by the same user were termed as tasks. For example, the tasks submitted by user 1 are T11, T12, and T13. A **task** can be defined as: The user or system job that needs to be performed is called as a task.

The ability of an operating system to accept more than one job from a single user is called ***multitasking.***

It may be noted that with the addition of a multitasking facility, an operating system became complex in the sense that it had to cater not only to the various users of the system but also to the multiple tasks submitted by each user.

Example: UNIX is a multiuser, multiprogramming, and multitasking operating system.

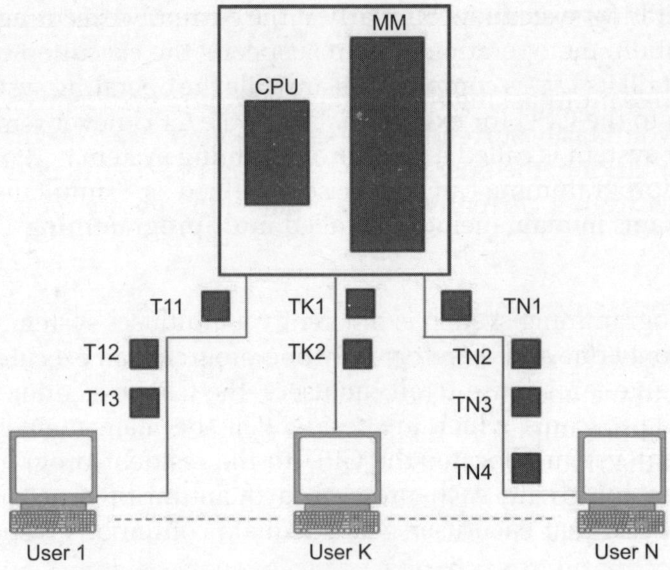

Fig. 7.8 Multitasking system

7.2.3 Single User Multitasking Operating Systems

With the advent of microprocessors in the 1970s, the computing scenario changed drastically. Since, a microprocessor was a complete CPU fabricated on a single chip, it became possible to design low cost computers based on microprocessors. Owing to their small size, these computers were termed **desktop computers**.

The performance/price ratio of desktop computers was found to be better than that of mainframe computers. Therefore, in the mid 1980s, desktop computers became popular 'stand-alone' computing machines. Microsoft DOS (disk operating system) was a very widely used operating system for desktops based on the Intel family of microprocessors. It was a single user mono programming system. Later, DOS ver. 7 was designed to be a single user multitasking operating system. Microsoft also developed a new technology operating system called 'Windows NT' which was a single user multitasking operating system.

In order to attract DOS users, Microsoft offered a series of Windows variants such as Windows 1.01, Windows for work groups 3.1, Windows 95, Windows 98, and Windows 2000 etc. Windows 1.01 and Windows for work groups were only graphical user interfaces (GUI), sitting on top of DOS operating system. Windows 95 and 98 were 32-bit operating systems with an option for the user to run 16-bit DOS applications through an 'MS Dos prompt' available on the Windows interface. From Windows 2000 onwards the 16-bit support for DOS applications was withdrawn.

DOS 7 offered cooperative multitasking whereas Windows NT supported pre-emptive multitasking. Similarly, MAC system 5 was a single user cooperative multitasking operating system. MAC OS X is a pre-emptive multitasking operating system.

Note: In cooperative multitasking the various tasks cooperate with each other, in the sense that a task voluntarily surrenders the CPU to other tasks. On the other hand, in pre-emptive multitasking, the operating system is in full control of the tasks. It may pre-empt the CPU from a currently running task and allocate the same to another task.

7.2.4 Batch Processing Systems

A batch processing system is generally a non-interactive environment. The users submit their jobs to the operator. Thereafter, the operator sorts the jobs into batches of similar types. For example, all the jobs that require a printer may form a batch. Similarly, all jobs that require a COBOL compiler may form another batch. Thus, a **batch** is a collection of jobs which require similar types of resources. The various jobs, belonging to a batch, are placed in a queue. The required resources are made available to the currently executing job. As soon as the current job is finished, the resources are allocated by the operating system to the next job waiting in the queue.

Bank transactions are generally processed as a batch. Similarly, billing activity of a company is often done in batches.

A job control language (JCL) is used by the operator to create, monitor, and run a batch of jobs. JCL commands are used to specify the sequence of execution of jobs. It also specifies the input and output requirements of the jobs of the batch being processed.

In old mainframe systems, card readers and tape drives were very popular I/O devices. Therefore, the packs of cards, belonging to different users, were batched together. Alternatively, a collection of jobs stored on a magnetic tape were submitted as a batch to the system.

Example: The operating systems such as VME/B and VME/K on ICL 2900 mainframes supported batch processing.

The advantages of batch processing are:

1. Enhanced speed of processing
2. Better management of resources

The **disadvantages** of batch processing on old mainframes were:

1. Punched cards and magnetic tapes were serial devices and were extremely slow.
2. After the completion of the current program, the loading of new program from a magnetic tape involved a much slower I/O operation. During the I/O operation the CPU remained idle.
3. Computer systems were non-interactive. The user would receive the results a day later, after submitting his bunch of cards. Obviously, an error in a single punched card would result in a delay of 24 hours.

By and by, the card readers and tape devices were replaced by much faster devices like hard disks, optical disks etc. Owing to its various advantages, batch processing was carried out and is still in vogue in the form of online transaction processing. For instance, modern mainframe operating systems like IBM Z/Os allow interactive on-line batch processing. In this type of system, the transactions are periodically processed, as in the case of reports etc.

7.3 MULTIPROCESSOR OPERATING SYSTEMS

Multiprocessor computer systems are non- Von Neumann computer architectures. They support more than one CPU, organized in varied configurations. The operating systems designed for such systems are called multiprocessor operating systems. Depending upon the load, the operating system schedules multiple programs/tasks on different CPUs. This activity of concurrent execution of multiple programs on multiple CPUs is called **multiprocessing**. Multiprocessing can be divided into two types: *asymmetric* multiprocessing and *symmetric* multiprocessing.

In **asymmetric** multiprocessing (ASMP), the operating system sits on one CPU or processor and the other processors run user program/tasks, as shown in Fig. 7.9(a).

Example: 'OS/VS2' for IBM 370 was an asymmetric multiprocessor operating system.

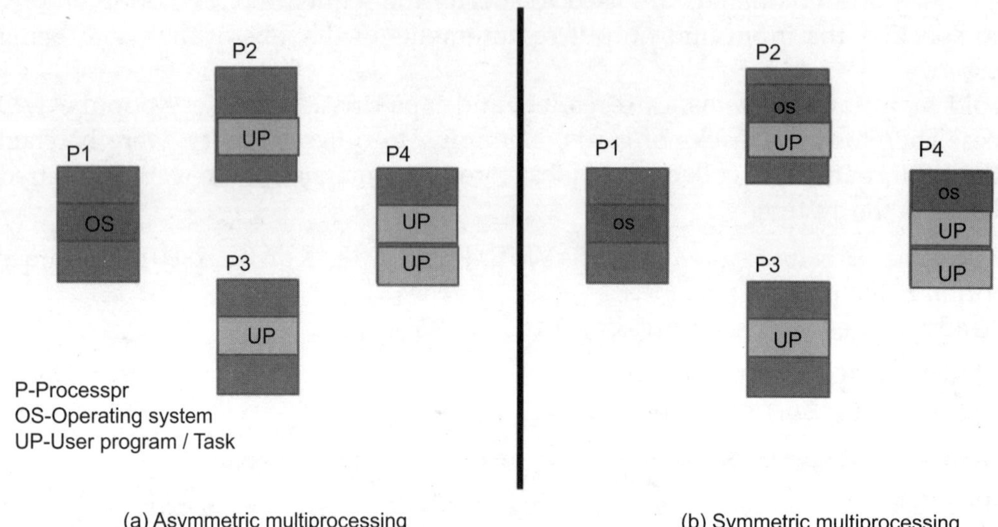

(a) Asymmetric multiprocessing

(b) Symmetric multiprocessing

Fig. 7.9 Types of multiprocessing

On the other hand, a **symmetric** operating system runs on any available processor or on all processors simultaneously along with the user programs/tasks (See Fig. 7.9(b)) .

Example: Windows NT is a symmetric multiprocessing operating system. Since it is a multitasking operating system, it maps the user tasks on different processors. It is able to run on any available processor and on multiple processors at the same time.

7.3.1 Parallel Processing

There are some algorithms which are inherently parallel in nature. For example, algorithms like quicksort and merge sort divide the data into partitions which can be processed independently of each other, provided a sufficient number of processors are available in the computer system.

With the availability of multiprocessor computer systems, it becomes possible to map independent portions of a program on different processors, as shown in Fig. 7. 10.

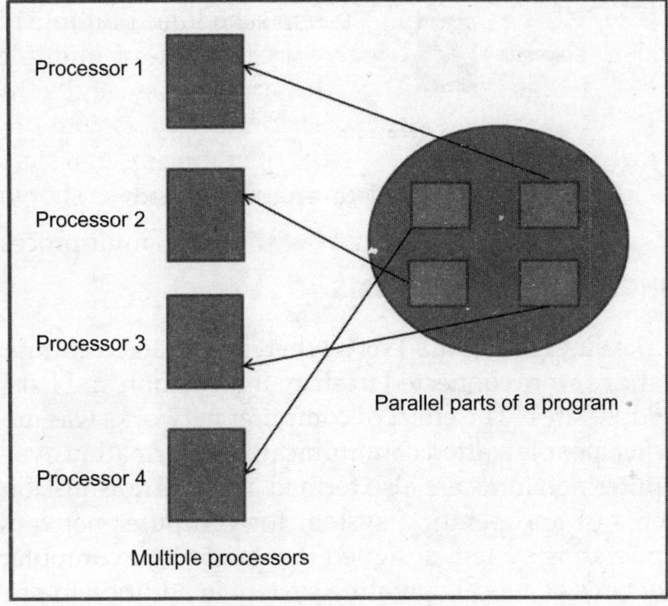

Fig. 7.10 Parallel processing

The ability of an operating system to execute different parallel parts of the same program on multiple processors is called **parallel processing.**

Example: Windows 2000 and UNIX are used for parallel processing on multiprocessor computer systems installed at 'Digital' and 'CRAY Research' organizations.

On some environments, the various parallel tasks of a program are called threads.. A thread can be precisely defined as: A separate path of execution through the code of a program is called a **thread**. The operating system that can handle multiple threads of a program is called a **multithreading operating system.** Example: Windows, OS X of Apple, UNIX etc. are multithreading operating systems.

If the computer system is uniprocessor, then one thread executes at a time. In case of multiple processors, the operating system maps various threads of a program on different processors, as shown in Fig. 7.11.

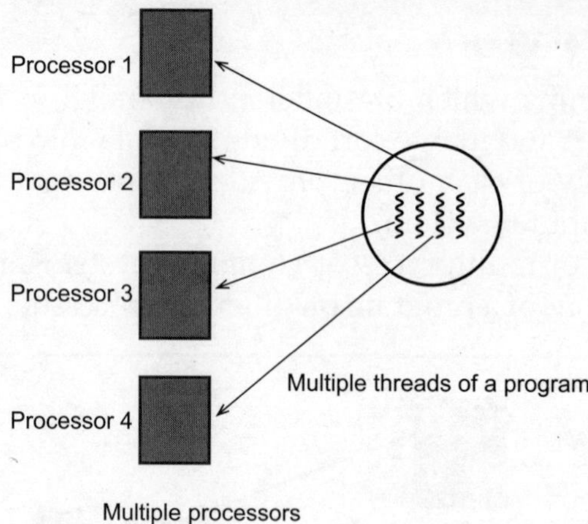

Fig. 7.11 Parallel execution of threads

7.4 NETWORKING OPERATING SYSTEMS

Computer networks emerged in the 1960s wherein various computers belonging to different organizations were connected to share information and hardware resources available at individual sites. The effect of computer networks was more prominently felt in the 1990s when people started communicating information over long distances. That is why computer networks are also termed as data-transmission networks.

The requirements of an operating system for computer networks are different from those of an operating system designed for stand-alone computers. In fact, it has to perform all functions of a local operating system in addition to providing support for communicating with other computers connected on the network.

Thus, a **network operating system** (NOS) can be precisely defined as: *It is an operating system that manages resources distributed over a computer network and enables communication across the network as well.*

Example: Novell NetWare 2.5, Windows NT Server, Mac OS AppleShare etc., are network operating systems.

7.5 SYSTEM VULNERABILITIES AND APPLICATION SECURITY

Since an operating system provides application programs with an environment to execute and access resources, the operating system becomes vulnerable to attacks on its security. An attack may be intended or unintended. For instance, an unanticipated error in a program may cause damage to the system or a programmer may by design, write code that accesses the system.

Information is a very costly resource. Nowadays, some attackers pose as trusted entities and try to extract information from users or institutions such as banks, military agencies etc. **Phishing** is a glaring example wherein the attacker poses as a known friend or organization and sends an email to an unsuspecting receiver who in his simplicity parts with confidential information. Another example is **pretexting** wherein the attacker impersonates a co-worker or an officer on the phone and asks for confidential information from an unsuspecting receiver. In the context of information security, such acts of gathering information by unfair means are termed **social engineering**.

In fact, it becomes imperative that the operating system be so designed that not only does it find the attack on the security but also prevents an application program from gaining unsupervised unbridled and complete access to the computer resources.

A brief discussion in following sections throws light on the types of malicious application programs and the kind of threat posed by them.

7.5.1 Malicious Codes

The old Indian saying is "Jis chhez ka sukh hai – usi ka dukh hai" i.e., "The same object is capable of giving you pleasure and pain". For example, a person builds a house and provides a door for entering it. A thief also uses the same door to enter that house. Similarly, in a computer system, software intentionally written with a design to attack the security, may enter into the system like any other application program. Such software is called malware or subversive code. Generally malware (malicious software) compromises the security of the system for following purposes:

Data collection: The malicious software may extract confidential information from files and databases of the system. It may collect the information by sniffing into the communication taking place between various nodes of a network.

Covert communication: This is an act of social engineering with a view to collect information from an unsuspecting individual, using unfair means such as pretexting, phishing etc.

Command and control: The purpose may be to control the activities of the system and deny its resources and services to its legitimate users. In extreme case, the malware may destroy the resources of the system. For instance, some malware corrupts the boot sector of the hard disk after which the hard disk becomes non available for use.

Stealth: The malicious code hides itself in order to dodge the protection mechanism of the operating system.

It may be noted from the above that the major goal of malicious code is to intrude a system by exploiting a security flaw in the system. Having intruded, it spreads itself into the connected systems and subsystems with a view to controlling them for variety of objectives. Malicious codes or subversive codes are of many types. Some of these are discussed below:

1. **Computer Virus**

   The computer virus is so called because it behaves exactly like a biological virus which passes from person to person. The computer virus is a program code. It infects a computer system by replicating itself on a visited computer system or device. In fact, it has been written with a view to enter a computer system and execute itself. Thus it has two phases: *Insertion* and *Execution*. Depending upon the mode of insertion, the virus is categorized into two types: file and boot sector virus.

   File virus: This virus attaches itself with a file called the carrier file. If it attaches itself to the end of the carrier file, then it is called an *appending file virus.* On the other hand, if the virus attaches itself at the beginning of the carrier file then it is called a *pre-pending file virus.* Generally, the carrier file is executable in nature. The structure of an executable file in the DOS environment is given in Fig. 7.12. It has two parts: a data part and an instruction part. The first location of the data part contains the instruction 'jump xxxx'. This instruction transfers the program control to the address 'xxxx', from where the instruction part of the program starts. Thereafter the execution of the program starts. In fact this arrangement does not let the control of execution enter into the data part, which is non executable in nature.

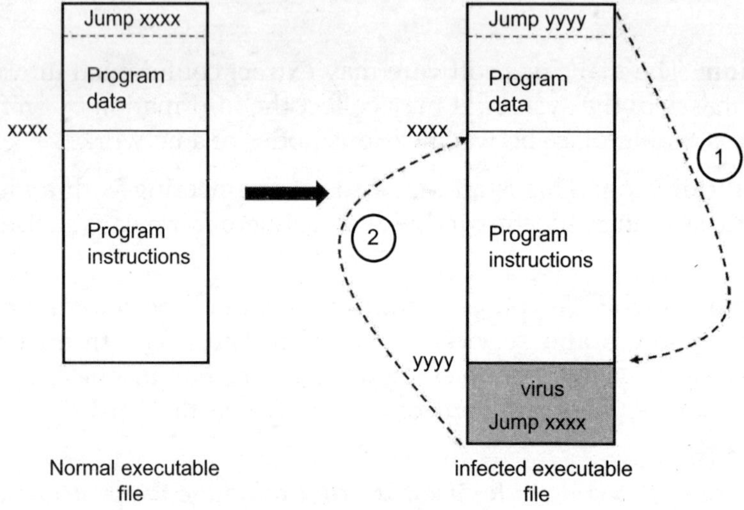

Fig.7.12 Attack of a file virus

A file virus makes use of the 'jump xxxx' statement of the executable program as an entry point to the system. It infects the executable files by the following steps:

1. The virus attaches itself at the end of the executable file and notes its address (say 'yyyy').
2. It modifies the 'jump xxxx' instruction at the beginning of the program to 'jump yyyy' so that the program control moves to the virus code.
3. It inserts the 'jump xxxx' instruction as the last statement of the virus code. This jump instruction takes the control to the executable part of the program.

It may be noted that when the infected executable program executes, the control first goes to virus code. The virus becomes active and starts monitoring the activities of the system. Thereafter the control is passed to the executable part of the program by the 'jump xxxx' instruction, inserted at the end of the virus code. Now the infected file starts executing normally whereas the user and the operating system remain unaware of the presence of the virus in the main memory. A typical example of this type of appending virus is **Vienna** virus. **Polimer.512.** A is an example of a prepending file virus.

Example: Chernobyl and Jerusalem are popular file viruses.

The **Chernobyl (CIH)** virus infects the executable files on Windows 95, 98, and ME systems. When such an infected file executes, CIH becomes resident in the main memory. While it is dormant, it infects other executable file on the system. On April 26, it gets activated and starts overwriting the hard disk with random data. It starts from sector 0 and keeps writing till the hard disk becomes useless i.e., it cannot be booted from. In addition to this, it also tries to corrupt the data present in the flash ROM.

The **Jerusalem** virus infects the executable files in much the same manner as CIH. On every Friday the 13th, it gets activated and deletes every program that was executed on that day. Otherwise on normal days, it creates a black window on the screen with coordinates (5, 5) – (16,16).

Some text files such as Microsoft word files are also used as carrier files by a computer virus to enter into the computer system. In fact, the virus attaches itself with the macros of the Word file because the macros are executed at the time of their expansion in the word document. Accordingly, these file viruses are called macro viruses. For instance, **Melissa** was a popular macro virus.

Boot sector virus: The boot sector virus displaces the code of the boot sector of a disk to some other sector and marks it as bad. It copies itself onto the boot sector and redirects the control to the sector that now contains the boot record as shown in Fig.7.13. At the time of booting, the virus gets loaded into the main memory much ahead of the operating system. The loaded virus then passes the control to the boot record so that the OS also gets loaded. However, the user and the OS remain unaware of the presence of the virus in the main memory.

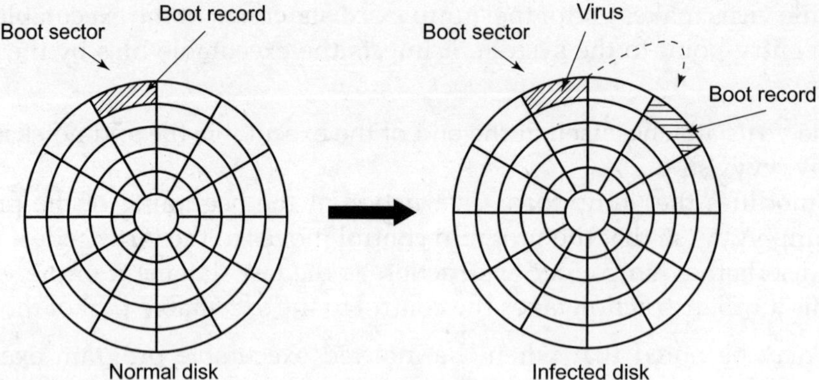

Fig.7.13 Boot sector virus displaces the boot sector

Having loaded itself into the main memory, the virus starts monitoring the computer system. Whenever a new disk is inserted into the system, the virus infects the disk by copying itself onto its boot sector and the infection spreads further.

As and when the infected disk is taken to a new system, the virus gets loaded into the main memory of the system and infects the hard disk of the system.

It may be noted that the computer virus's capability to replicate itself is the most dangerous tool because it helps the virus in spreading itself to other uninfected computer systems or devices that come into its contact.

Example: Brain virus was a popular boot sector virus.

Normally a computer virus remains hidden, and keeps infecting the objects that come into its contact. Meanwhile, it does not show its presence in the system. In fact it waits for an event such as a date of birth, or a special keypress by the user etc. As soon as the desired event happens, the virus becomes active and performs actions as per the goal set by the designer of the virus. A generalized algorithm of a virus program is given below.

Algorithm virus()

```
{
  While(1)
{
  If ( new object not infected)
       Then infect the object by copying itself on the
       object;
  If (the desired event occurred)
       Then perform actions to achieve the goals of the
       virus writer;
  }
}
```

Thus, a virus is of parasitic nature in the sense that it attaches to a carrier object. The object can be an executable program, a new disk, or a new MS-Word file etc. Generally, the virus has two main components: **replication** module and **payload** module.

Replication module: This module searches for potential carrier objects and infects them. Generally, it resides in the memory and monitors the activities of the system. As and when a new carrier object is detected, it infects the object. The virus may use any of the following infection methods:

1. **Append:** The virus code appends itself to an unaffected program.
2. **Replace:** In this method the virus code replaces the original executable program code partially.
3. **Insert:** The virus code inserts itself in the body of the executable program
4. **Delete:** The virus deletes some part of the code from the body of the executable program.
5. **Redirect:** The normal flow of control within the executable program is so directed that some other code appended at the beginning or end of the program gets executed.

Payload module: This module is a function that acts as per the goal of the virus writer. It may delete files, modify data, steal confidential data and reveal it to its creator. It may also show nuisance data or pictures on the screen to irritate the user. Sometimes it plays music. In extreme cases, the payload may harm or damage the hardware. For instance, the 'W32/CIH' virus erases the flash BIOS chip of the computer system on 26th April of every year. Since the system boots with the help of the BIOS, it becomes unusable in the absence of BIOS because it cannot be booted. It is more damaging in the case of laptops because In laptops, the flash BIOS is soldered to the motherboards, hence the chip cannot be removed and reprogrammed.

A **multipartite** virus has the traits of both file and boot sector viruses. When an infected program executes, the multipartite virus not only infects the other executable files in the system but also infects the boot sector of the hard disk. In fact, it also infects the floppy disks which are used in the system.

2. Trojan Horse

The term 'Trojan Horse' has its origin in the Greek legend of the Trojan War wherein the Greeks gave a big wooden horse as a gift to the Trojans and apparently left the shores of Troy. The horse had a large number of Greek soldiers hidden in its belly. The Trojans dragged the horse into their city. In the night, Greek soldiers sneaked out of the horse's belly and captured the city of Troy.

Similarly, a Trojan horse is malicious software. It is self-standing, non-replicating code. It has a mischievous goal disguised behind an 'attractive stated goal'. Generally, the Trojan horses are sent as attachments with e-mails or are embedded into games.

Example: Computers and servers in the lower house of Japan's parliament became infected by a Trojan horse virus after one politician opened an email attachment titled:

"According to a report from Channel News Asia".

Similarly, a mail circulated around Albion had as subject the following text:

"Tony Blair's e-mail account has been hacked by BBC news".

Thereafter, whosoever clicked on the above link got a Trojan installed on his/her computer.

Thus, the Trojan horse has two purposes: Overt and covert where the overt purpose is known to the user of the system whereas the covert purpose remains unknown to the user until the time of the attack. We can precisely define a Trojan horse as:

Trojan horse: A program that hides itself in a host program and contains unexpected additional functionality.

Depending upon the ulterior motive behind its creation, a Trojan horse can be categorized as follows:

1. Destructive Trojan: This type of Trojan deletes files from the system.
2. Proxy Trojan: It steals important data such as passwords, credit card information etc. for its creator.
3. Remote Access Trojan: It takes control of the system on behalf of a remote hacker.
4. Denial of service (DOS) Trojan: It makes the resources unavailable on the computer system or the computer network. For instance, it may flood the network with useless tasks.

3. Worm

A computer worm is a malicious program that searches for a security hole in a network. Thereafter, it replicates itself and spreads through the hole to other computers over a network. It replicates itself at such a fast rate that it not only disrupts the network bandwidth but also consumes heavily the memory of the computer systems. For instance, in January 2004, 'mydoom' worm infected around 2–3 lakh computers in a single day.

Mail worm: A mail worm uses an email message as a carrier. It attaches itself to the e-mail message. When the user opens the attachment, the worm gets activated. After activation, the worm searches the address book of the host and uses it to automatically send the messages to persons listed in the address book.

4. Logical bomb

A logical bomb is a latent program that executes when a specific condition occurs. It acts as daemon and wakes up on a trigger like change in a file property, pressing of a series of keystrokes, a specific date or time. Many a times it has been found that a frustrated employee established a logical bomb that wreaked havoc in the company after the employee left the job.

7.5.2 Virus Detection and Prevention

The virus detection system can be categorized into two types: **signature detection and anomaly detection**.

Signature detection systems use pre-generated signatures to check the integrity of files or disks. For instance, the file virus detector may keep the checksum of a file as its signature. After regular intervals the detector computes the checksum of the file and matches it with its original signature. If the match is correct then it is business as usual but a mismatch definitely indicates that the file is infected.

The anomaly detection system checks for abnormal behavior of an executing program. For example, a program may try to write on the boot sector of a disk, which is an anomaly. Similarly, a program may try to modify an interrupt vector or write on system files, both actions being considered anomalous.

Some other abnormal behaviors of virus infected system are:

1. Asking to open an executable file for both reading and writing operations.
2. Trying to read the header of an executable file.
3. Appending or prepending into a file.
4. Writing into the header of an executable file.

All the above listed actions are suspicious in nature. The detection system monitors the currently running programs for such suspicious actions. For instance, when a host tries to send requests to many unique IP addresses, the anomaly detection system takes a note of this because that indicates the behavior of a worm, which tries to contact a large number of devices connected on a network. If the TCP RST packets received by the host are found to be more than a threshold value, the host is considered to be an infected one. Similarly, if a large number of identical packets containing the same data are sent by a host, the detection system checks for the possibility of a new worm spreading itself across the network.

If the detection system is stationed on a host then it can detect the activation of a virus or worm by monitoring the system calls or buffer overflows. Having detected suspicious activity from a program, the host-based system prevents the suspicious operations of the infected program by blocking the operations or in extreme cases by terminating the infected program. On the other hand, a network-based detection system will come to know about the virus or worm activation only when the virus or worm has already been activated.

Some systems use the concepts of **honeypots**. In a network, some nodes are defined as honeypots indicating that these nodes will not have incoming traffic. Now, when some host sends packets to a honeypot, the detection system comes into play. It checks whether the traffic seems to be a mistake or is deliberate and if the traffic is deliberate then the host is scanned for possible infection.

Similarly, sandboxing is also used to prevent virus attacks in a system. In this method, the operating system provides a **sandbox** which acts like a confined secured area. It is a simulated virtual environment that can emulate the operating system. The untested and untrusted programs are executed in the sandbox and their output is observed. The objects accessed by the program are also scrutinized. Any malicious activity by the program thereof is not only caught but also prevented from causing the targeted damage. However, malicious codes such as logic bombs are difficult to catch by sandboxing because the logic bombs get activated on a particular time, remaining dormant otherwise.

Nevertheless, detection systems suffer from following drawbacks:

1. A virus detection system can detect only a known virus.
2. The detection activity is a very slow process because it takes considerable time to scan the computer system or a network.
3. In order to remain relevant, a detection system must keep itself continuously updated with the signatures of newer viruses.

A computer user can also observe the computer system for the following symptoms of a virus attack:

1. System takes longer time to boot.
2. Changed size of a file.
3. Programs and utilities take a longer time to be invoked.
4. System performance becomes slow.
5. Abnormal system behavior such as unforced system shutdown or restart.
6. The disk or RAM space gets consumed quickly.

7.6 FUNCTIONS OF OPERATING SYSTEMS

From the above discussion it is clear that an operating system provides a variety of services such as access to and execution of application programs, access to files and I/O systems, protection from unauthorized access to system resources etc. A resource is a component of the computer system for which processes can compete. Therefore, the operating system has to perform housekeeping for the various resources of the system as well as allocate them to users or programs which are currently active in the system. As a resource manager of the system, it performs the following functions:

1. Process management
2. Memory management
3. Processor management
4. Input/ Output and files management
5. Security

Note: The following sections provide a brief discussion on the architectures of popular operating systems.

7.7 UNIX KERNEL ARCHITECTURE

The UNIX operating system was developed at Bell laboratories in 1970. In 1973, Dennis Ritchie and Ken Thompson rewrote UNIX in C making it a more portable and understandable operating system. UNIX has now been implemented on a wide variety of computer systems from super computers to personal computers. AT & T's 'System V' and Berkley '4.2 BSD' system are two very popular versions of UNIX.

The UNIX operating system considers files and processes as most important entities. The file occupies space and the process lives a life time. Based on this central concept, UNIX is designed as a layered architecture consisting of three levels: user, kernel and hardware, as shown in Fig. 7.14.

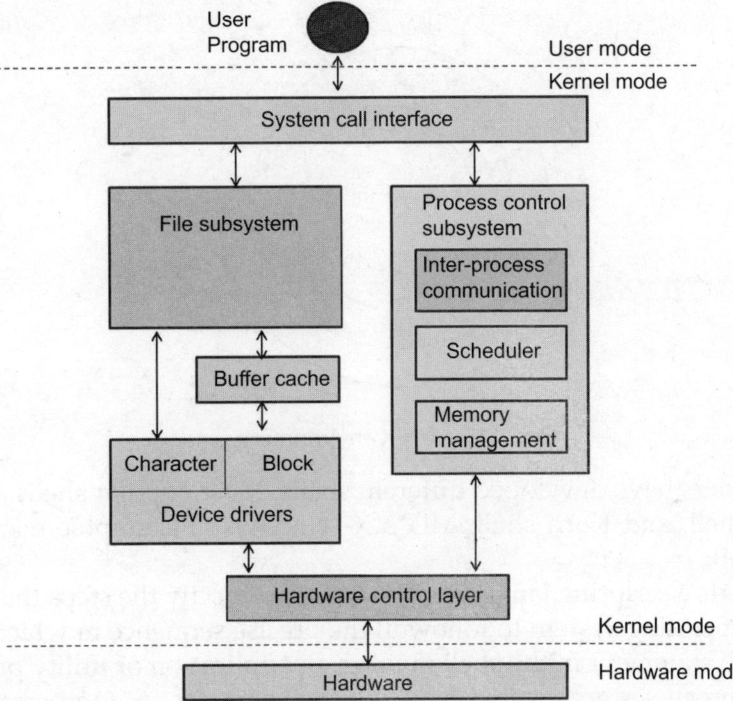

Fig. 7.14 UNIX kernel system architecture

The user programs call the system services through system calls. Depending upon the type of service needed by the user, the system call interface maps it to the file subsystems or the process control subsystem. The file system interacts with the device driver of the target device. The exchange of data between the device and the file subsystem takes place through a buffer cache. For instance, during an output operation, the file subsystem would fill the buffer cache and send a signal to the device driver to pick up the data from the buffer. Similarly, during an input operation, it is the device driver that fills the buffer cache and sends the signal to the file system to pick up the data from the buffer cache. The process control subsystem creates an environment for inter-process communication. It also manages the scheduler and the memory supported by the system.

It may be noted that the kernel architecture is a layer based model of the computer system. The hardware related code has been placed in a separate layer called the 'hardware control layer'. This layer interacts with the underlying hardware leading to an easily portable operating system.

From a user point of view, UNIX offers a shell that acts as a command interpreter between the user/ AS (application software) and the kernel (see Fig. 7.15). A relevant part of the kernel is permanently loaded into the memory whereas the shell is swapped in as and when needed by the system.

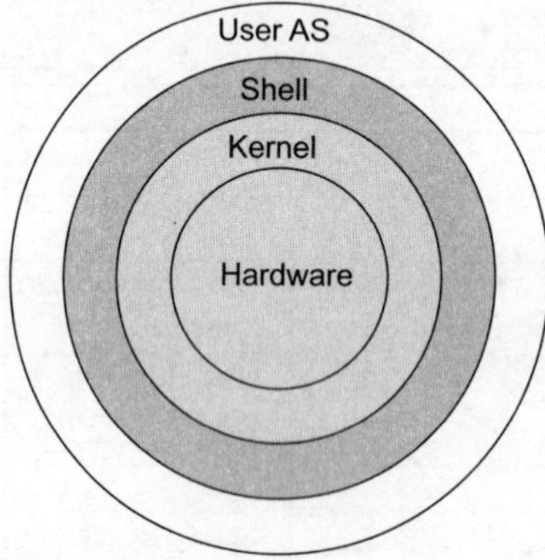

Fig. 7.15 UNIX environment

Different venders have developed different shells. Most popular shells are Bourne shell, Berkley shell, and Korn shell. MIT's X-Windows is a graphic user interface (GUI) based shell.

A shell supports a scripting language. The user can specify the steps that he or she wishes for the operating system to follow in the precise sequence in which the steps are written. Each statement in the shell invokes an application or utility program.

Background processes are created by using the character '&' (ampersand) at the end of a command at the shell level. As and when a command followed by '&' is issued, the shell does not wait for the command to finish the execution; rather, it offers a new prompt to the user for a new command. Thus, the user can have multiple tasks. He/she may interact with a task in for foreground while other tasks execute in the background. This is a classic case of multitasking.

7.8 LINUX KERNEL ARCHITECTURE

Linux was created by Linus Torvalds as a free operating system kernel in 1991. Later on it was augmented with GNU towards creating a UNIX-like operating system. In fact, the modern day Linux operating system is called the GNU/Linux operating system. The Linux kernel is a monolithic architecture (see Fig. 7.16). It consists of the following five components:

1. Process scheduler
2. Memory manager
3. File system
4. Inter process communication
5. Network interface

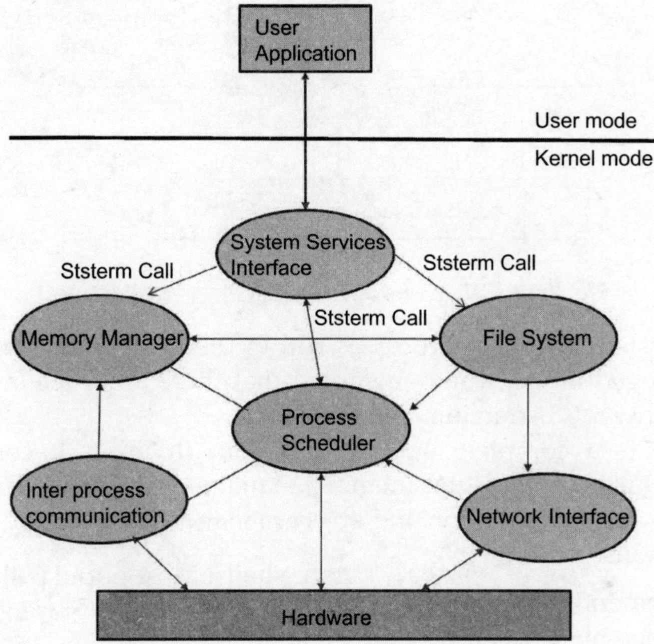

Fig. 7.16 Linux architecture

It may be noted that the process scheduler is at the heart of the operating system. Almost all the modules interact with each other. The user applications interact with the Linux kernel through system calls. A large number of modules interact with the hardware. Therefore, it is comparatively difficult to port Linux to new platforms and machines. Similar to UNIX, Linux also provides a shell command line interface. The name of the shell is bash shell. It is primarily based on the Bourne shell of UNIX.

7.9 WINDOWS ARCHITECTURE

The Windows operating system is primarily a 'client-server' operating system architecture. It is a hybrid between layered and microkernel architectures, as shown in Fig. 7.17.

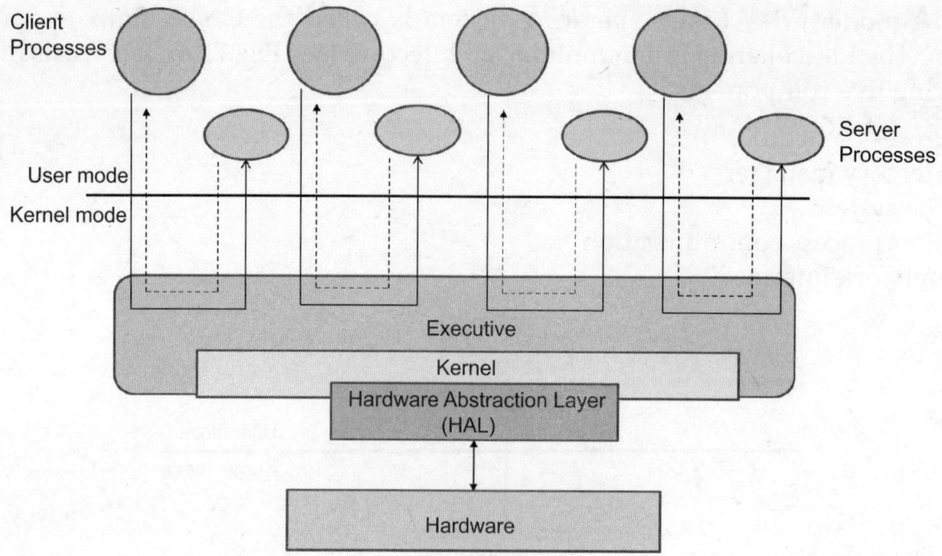

Fig. 7.17 Windows operating system architecture

Most of the system and user processes run in the user mode. This mode is also called the privileged mode. It may be noted that there are three layers: Executive, Kernel, and Hardware Abstraction Layer (HAL).

The executive is a complete operating system in itself. It consists of many components: I/O manager, virtual memory manager, local procedure call module, process manager, security monitor, and object manager. Accordingly, it performs the following operations:

1. I/O management
2. Object management
3. Security
4. Process management
5. Virtual memory management

In a food chain, the kernel is the bottommost componer Similarly, the kernel forms the lowest layer in an operating system. In Windov performs following operations:

1. Thread scheduling
2. Thread dispatching
3. Interrupt handling
4. Multiprocessor synchronization

The HAL contains modules that are hardware specific. HAL needs to be modified only when Windows is ported to a new platform. Therefore, Windows is an easily portable operating system.

7.10 MACH SYSTEM ARCHITECTURE

This is a microkernel architecture consisting of three layers: user processes, server processes and the kernel, as shown in Fig. 7.18.

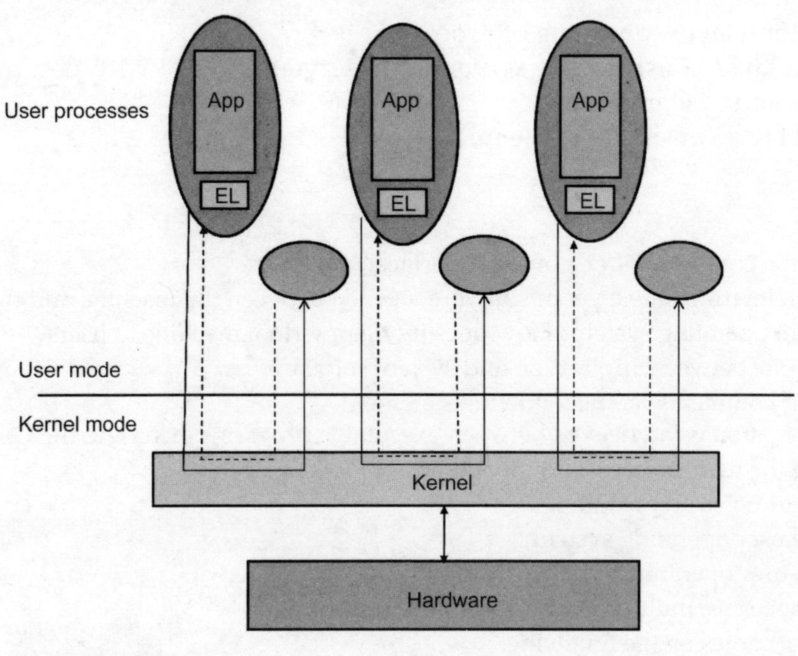

Fig. 7.18 Mach system architecture

The kernel performs the basic minimum functions as listed below:

1. Task and thread management: Tasks and threads are scheduled by the Mach kernel.
2. Inter-process communication: Inter-process communication is facilitated through ports.
3. Memory object management: The address space of a Mach task is represented as a memory object. Therefore, physical memory is considered as a store of memory objects.
4. System call redirection: In user mode, Mach allows binary emulation of other operating systems such as Unix. The system calls generated by the application programs are redirected by the kernel to their appropriate severs.
5. Device support: The kernel provides low-level support for the devices attached to the system.
6. Multiprocessing: Supports multiprocessing.
7. Multicomputer support: It supports multiple computers i.e., multiprocessors whose processors do not share physical memory.

Each process is represented as a task. A task contains two parts: application program and emulation library. The emulation library handles the system calls generated by the application programs. The system calls are redirected to the appropriate server by the kernel. The servers also run in the user mode. Thus, there are three layers:

1. Simulation layer consisting of processes
2. Service layer consisting of servers. The servers are of two types: application servers and system servers.
3. Kernel layer consisting of the micro kernel.

Exercises

1. Why does a computer offer a binary interface?
2. Why is an intermediate layer of software needed between the machine and the user?
3. What is an operating system? How does it offer a virtual machine to users?
4. Differentiate between application and system software.
5. Give your comments on the following statement:
   "CPU execution is interleaved between executable programs including the OS"
6. What are the basic objectives of an operating system?
7. Write short notes on the following:
   a. Single user operating system
   b. Multi-user operating system
8. Define the terms: multiprogramming and multitasking.
9. Write short notes on the following:
   a. Single user multitasking operating system
   b. Batch processing systems
10. Discuss multiprocessor operating systems.
11. Differentiate between symmetric and asymmetric multiprocessing.
12. Discuss parallel processing in brief.
13. What is a thread? Name a multithreading operating system.
14. Differentiate between networking and distributed operating systems.
15. Define the terms: phishing, pretexting, and social engineering.
16. What is a malicious code? What are its purposes?
17. What is a computer virus?
18. Discuss the working of a file virus.
19. Discuss the working of a boot sector virus.
20. What are the two main components of a virus? Discuss them in brief.
21. What is a multipartite virus?
22. What is a Trojan Horse? Discuss the categories of Trojan horse?
23. Define the terms: worm and logical bomb.
24. Differentiate between signature detection and anomaly detection.
25. Differentiate between a 'honeypot' and a 'sandbox'.
26. List the functions of an operating system.
27. Discuss UNIX kernel architecture.
28. Discuss Linux kernel architecture.
29. Discuss Windows architecture.
30. Discuss Mach system architecture.

CHAPTER

8 Computer Networks and Internet

8.1 INTRODUCTION

In large and wide spread organizations, better efficiency can be achieved by linking its various computerized departments and plants. Instead of each department having its own set of standalone computers, most organizations prefer to connect the computers as a network to provide valuable data and information to every department.

"A **Computer Network** is a group of computers and devices that are linked for sharing resources, transport files, and allow electronic communication".

However, any discussion about networks has to be preceded by the history of **data communication**. The term data communication simply means sending data economically over long distances and ensuring that the data is received properly.

8.1.1 Need for Data Transmission

Data communication or transmission is basically needed for the following reasons:

1. The data consisting of text, graphics, sound, motion pictures etc. can be communicated at extremely fast rate through networks.
2. The data becomes available online. For instance, a user can browse through university results or railway reservations through the Internet.
3. The productivity and effectiveness of the people and organizations is increased because of increased transfer rate of data transmission.
4. The user gets better services such as email, e-commerce, Internet shopping, cloud services etc.

This chapter briefly discusses the basic concepts of data communication related to computer networks and their applications.

8.2 DATA COMMUNICATION

The basic purpose of data communication is to transport data from one agent to another. The agent can be a computer, a device, or even a person. A model of a data communication system is shown in Fig. 8.1.

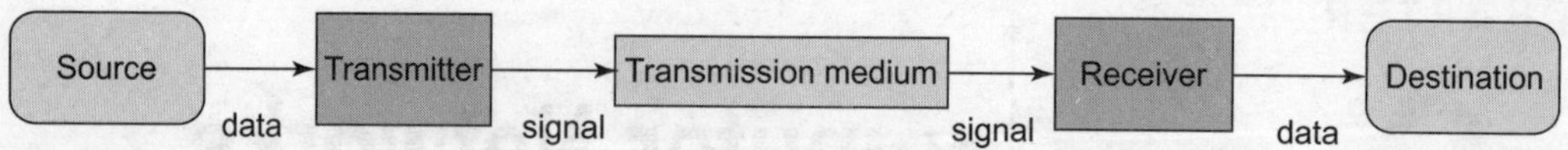

Fig. 8.1 Data communication model

The data is transmitted from a source to a destination through a transmission medium, in the form of electromagnetic waves. The transmission media can either be a physical connection (wires, cables etc.) or simply air. The wired media is known as guided media and the wireless as unguided media. The guided media provides a direct link between the two communicating devices and therefore, it is also known as point-to-point communication. However, multipoint guided transmission is also possible wherein several communicating devices share the same transmission media.

A closer look at Fig. 8.1 reveals that a data communication system consists of five basic components:

1. The source agent which has some data to send. The data can be a file, a video, or simply sound.
2. A data communication device, called transmitter, which converts the data into electromagnetic signals that can be transmitted.
3. A transmission medium or communication channel that transports the signals from one point to another.
4. A data communication device, called receiver, which converts electromagnetic signals to the original data form.
5. The destination agent that finally receives the data.

For example, in a telephone conversation, the speaker (source) sends a message in the form of sound data to a telephone (communicating device). The telephone converts the sound waves into electrical signals and transmits them over telephone lines (transmission media). The lines carry the electrical signals to another telephone (communicating device) which converts the signals back into sound waves. The listener (destination) receives the sound data from the telephone.

Let us now define and explain the various terms associated with data communication and networking.

1. **Amplitude**: It is the value of a signal at any point on its wave (see Fig. 8.2). From Fig. 8.2, it may be observed that amplitude is the vertical distance from the horizontal axis to the given point on the wave.

2. **Time period and frequency**: A full pattern on a wave is called a cycle, as shown in Fig. 8.3. A period T is the time taken by a wave to complete one cycle. It is expressed in seconds.

   The following table shows the variations of time measurements used by the electronics industry.

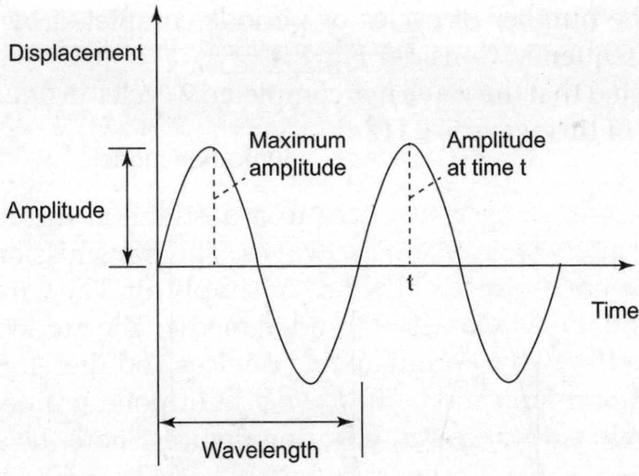

Fig. 8.2 Amplitude

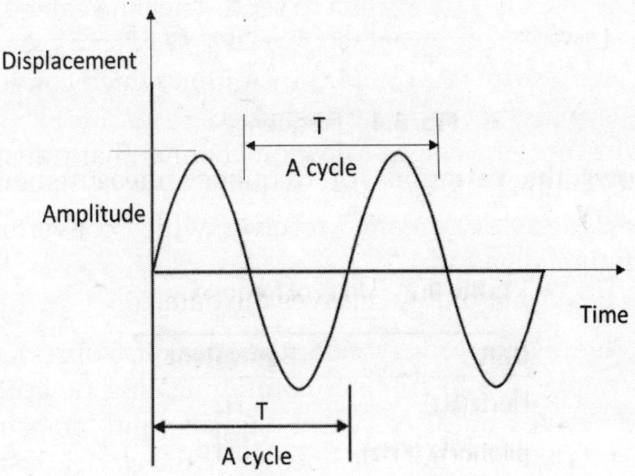

Fig. 8.3 Time period

Table 8.1 Units of time period

Unit	Equivalent
Seconds	s
Milliseconds (ms)	10^{-3} s
Microseconds (μs)	10^{-6} s
Nanoseconds (ns)	10^{-9} s
Picoseconds (ps)	10^{-12} s

3. **Frequency**: The number of cycles or periods completed by a wave per sec is known as its frequency. Consider Fig. 8.4.

It may be noted that the wave has completed 2 cycles in one second. Therefore, the frequency of this wave is 2 Hz.

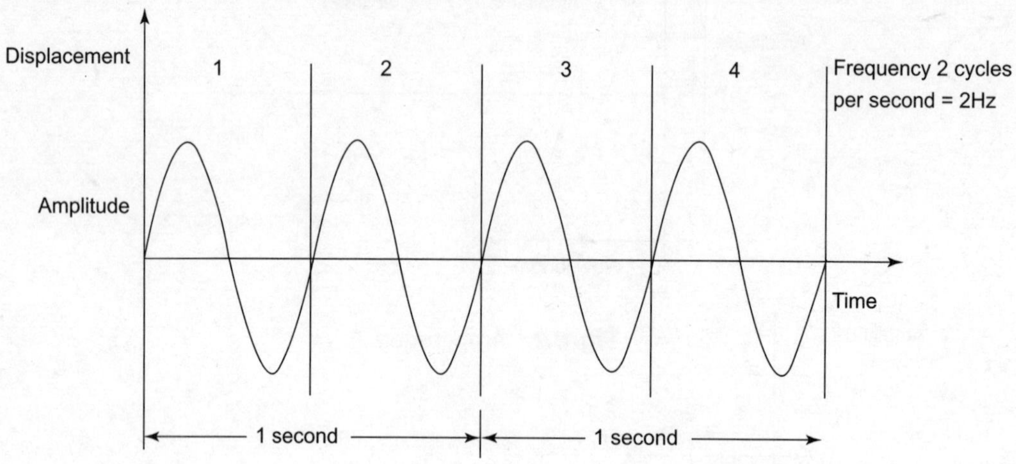

Fig. 8.4 Frequency

Table 8.2 shows the variations of frequency measurements used by the electronics industry

Table 8.2 Units of frequency

Unit	Equivalent
Hertz(Hz)	Hz
Kilohertz (KHz)	10^3 Hz
Megahertz (MHz)	10^6 Hz
Gigahertz (GHz)	10^9 Hz
Terahertz (THz)	10^{12} Hz

Frequency (*F*) and time period (*T*) are related by the following expression

$$F = 1 / T \tag{8.1}$$

Note: The information carried by a wave can be changed by changing any one of the attributes of the wave i.e., the amplitude or frequency, as shown in Fig. 8.5.

4. **Bandwidth (B)**: Every material can allow waves of certain frequencies to pass through the medium. For example, a telephone line may allow waves of 300 to 3400 Hz to travel through its medium.

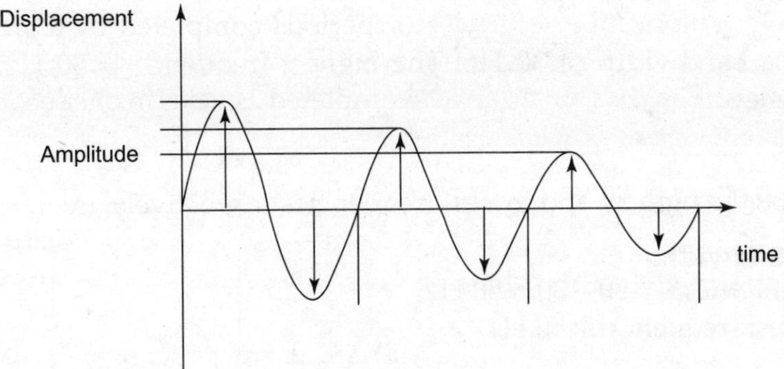

Fig. 8.5 (a) Decreasing amplitude

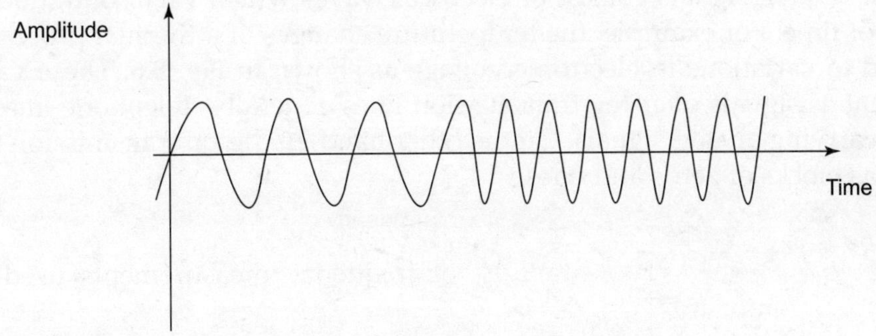

Fig. 8.5 (b) Increasing frequency with time

The difference between the highest and the lowest frequencies allowed on a transmission media is called its bandwidth. Thus, the bandwidth (B) measures the information-carrying capacity of a line or a network.

$$\rightarrow \quad B = F_h - F_l$$

where F_h and F_l are the highest and lowest frequencies respectively.

Example 1

A sine wave completes one cycle in 50µs. What is its frequency?

Solution:

Let T be the time period and f be the frequency of the given wave. From Equation (8.1), we have:

Given $T = 50\mu s$.

$= 50 * 10^{-6}$ s

$\rightarrow F = 1 / T = 1/ (50 \times 10^{-6}) = 20000\text{Hz} = 20$ KHz

The frequency of the wave = 20 KHz

Example 2

A signal has a bandwidth of 30 Hz. The highest frequency is 80 Hz. What is the lowest frequency?

Solution

Let fh and fl be the highest and lowest frequencies respectively, then,

$\rightarrow F_h - F_l = \text{bandwidth}$
$\rightarrow F_l = F_h - \text{bandwidth} = 80 - 30 = 50 \text{ Hz}$
Thus the lowest frequency is 50 Hz.

8.2.1 Digital and Analog Transmission

On a communication channel, the data can be transmitted in two forms: analog or digital. Analog signals consist of electrical waves which vary continuously as a function of time. For example, the temperature changes of a thermal process can be converted to variations in electronic voltage as shown in Fig. 8.6. These variations can be sent as signals over the transmission lines generally. Telephone lines can be used for carrying analog signals. On the other hand, in digital transmission the data is coded as blocks of zeros and ones.

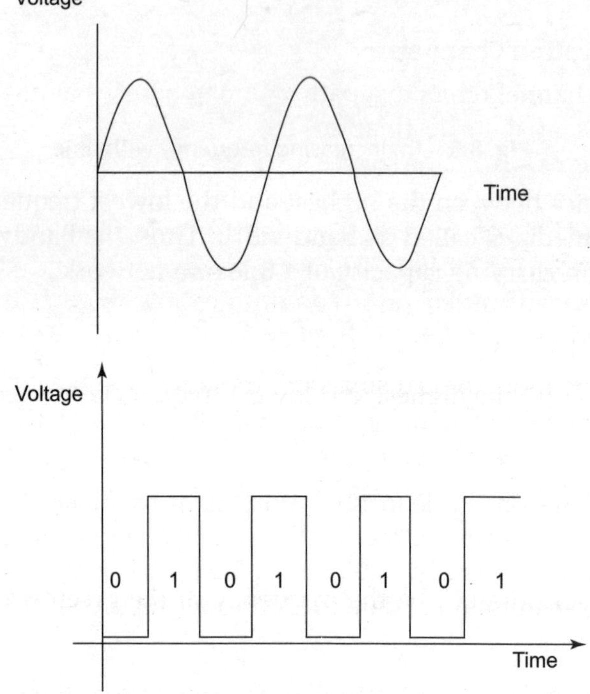

Fig. 8.6 Analog and digital communication

In simple words, we can say that the information is transmitted as discrete electrical quantities i.e., as signals representing zeros and ones, rather than as a continuum of voltages (see Fig. 8.6). The analog signals can be converted to digital signals by A-D converters. Similarly, digital signals are converted to analog signals by D-A convertors.

The advantages of digital transmission over analog transmission are:

1. Digital transmission has a very low error rate.
2. Voice, data, music, television, facsimile, video telephone etc. can all be multiplexed through digital transmission.
3. A comparatively higher data rate is possible in digital communication.

The following sections describe the various communication channels (transmission media) and communication devices that can be used in a data communication system.

8.2.2 Data Communication Technologies

Data communication is an important activity in an organization. The technologies that generate, process, store, and transport data have been changing at a fast rate. A brief discussion on the critical concepts of some of the important data communication technologies is given the following sections.

8.2.2.1 Communication Channels

A communication channel refers to a path, a line or a link that interconnects a source from which data is sent, to its destination. Thus, the channel is a data highway which carries the data or signals from the source to destination. The data transmission rate of a communication channel is often expressed in its baud rating. One baud essentially corresponds to one bit per second. The data transmission in microcomputers is generally to the tune of 1200, 2400, 7200, 9600 baud etc.

The data can be transmitted on a communication channel through one of the following three modes:

1. **Simplex**. In this mode of transmission, the data or signal is always sent in one direction, as shown in Fig. 8.7. For example, a keyboard attached to a computer can only send data to the computer. Thus, for two-way transmission of data, two such lines will be needed, one transmitting in each direction.

2. **Half-duplex**. A half-duplex mode allows transmission in either direction at a time but not simultaneously. This mode is also known as two-way alternate. For example, the transmission of data to and from a hard disk is done in half-duplex mode.

3. **Full-duplex**. This mode allows transmission in both directions simultaneously. Special purpose telephone lines provide this capability. This mode is also called a two-way simultaneous mode.

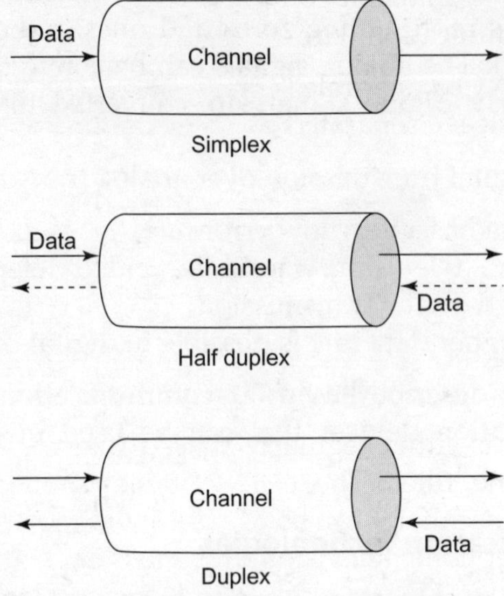

Fig. 8.7 Modes of transmission

8.2.2.2 Popular Communication Channels

A list of popular communication channels is given below:

1. Twisted pair wires
2. Coaxial cables
3. Fiber optic cables
4. Microwave transmission.
5. Radio Transmission or Radio Frequency (RF) Transmission
6. Infrared Transmission.
7. Satellite Communication.

1. **Twisted Pair Wires and Cables**. A twisted pair is an inexpensive transmission media. It consists of two insulated copper wires twisted in a spiral pattern. One pair acts as a single communication link. A bunch of hundreds of such pairs is packed into a cable that carries signals over longer distances (see Fig.8.8).

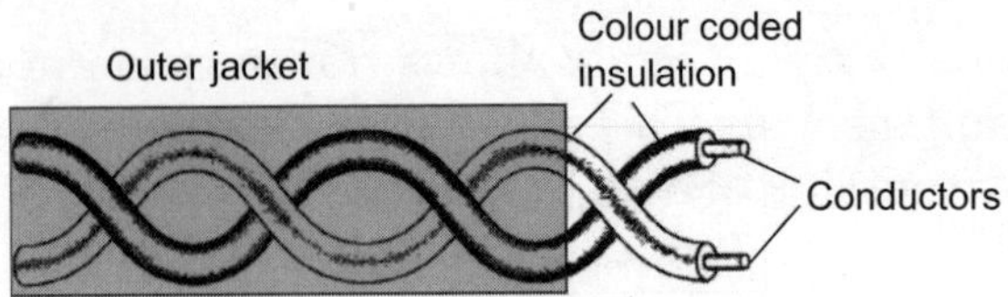

Fig. 8.8 Twisted pair cable

Twisted-pair wires are used extensively in telephone systems in the form of two- and four-wire pairs, each wrapped in a plastic coating. Some modems allow these lines to transmit computer data, thereby saving the cost of laying down new communication wires.

2. **Coaxial Cables**. A Coaxial cable is made up of a central copper wire surrounded by a conductive sleeve separated by an insulation, as shown in Fig. 8.9.

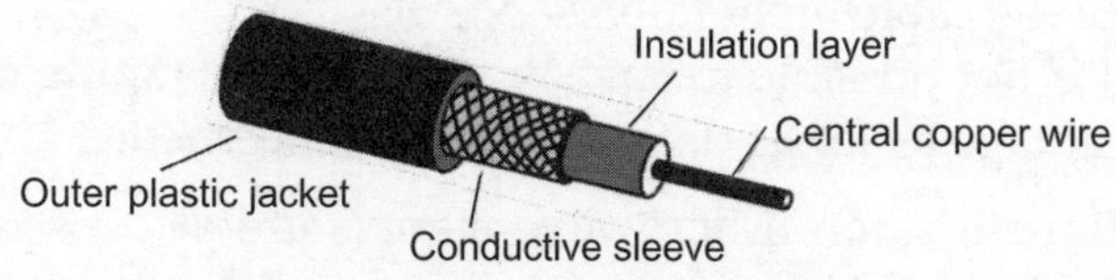

Fig. 8.9 Coaxial cable

The insulation is either regularly spaced rings or a solid dielectric material such as polythene filler. The coaxial cable is an all-purpose transmission medium in the sense that it can be used in a wide variety of applications such as long distance telephone, television, transmission, cable networks etc. It is very widely used in cable TVs.

There are two types of coaxial cables: base band and broad band. A base band cable can transmit voice, data, or video on a single channel at very high speeds. Many users can share the channel in a time-shared manner.. However, the distance over which the signals can be transmitted on a base band cable is limited to few hundred meters.

The broadband cable, on the other hand, can carry multiple signals at a time. For example, it can be used in a TV network, where as many as 60 to 100 channels are available in metropolitan cities. Therefore, a broad band cable is complex in construction as compared to base band cable.

3. **Optical Fiber**. An optical fiber is a thin strand of light conducting glass or plastic fiber. The fiber is a flexible cylinder of size 2 to 125 μm that acts as the transmission medium for pulses of light carrying data. The optical fiber cable has three sections: core, cladding, and the jacket. (Fig. 8.10). Generally, multiple strands are bundled together in a cable.

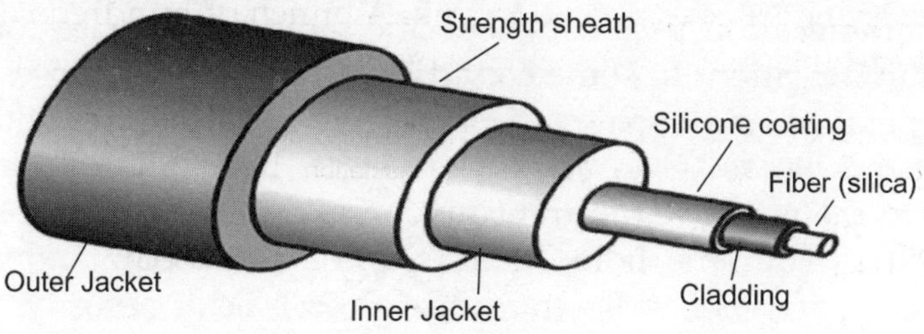

Fig. 8.10 Optical fiber cable

The cladding is provided to refract travelling light pulses back into the glass. The jacket or sheath gives the necessary cable strength. Optical fiber has the capacity to carry voice, video and data at extremely high speeds in the range of several million bits per second. It offers low bit error rates, zero electrical interference and complete electrical isolation. The isolation from electrical currents is a major advantage of optical fiber systems. The disadvantage of optical fiber is that a limited number of direct connections can be made on a given length of the cable (generally 24 or so).

However, it is not possible to have branch lines by taping off a fiber, which is an added advantage as far as data security is concerned.

4. **Microwave Transmission**. Microwave signals are also used to transmit data and voice over long distances through the air, without any wire or cable. The signals are transmitted through directional parabolic antennas placed on tops of buildings, towers, or hills so that the terrain does not block the line of sight, as shown in Fig. 8.11. In fact, it is a line-of-sight method of communication.

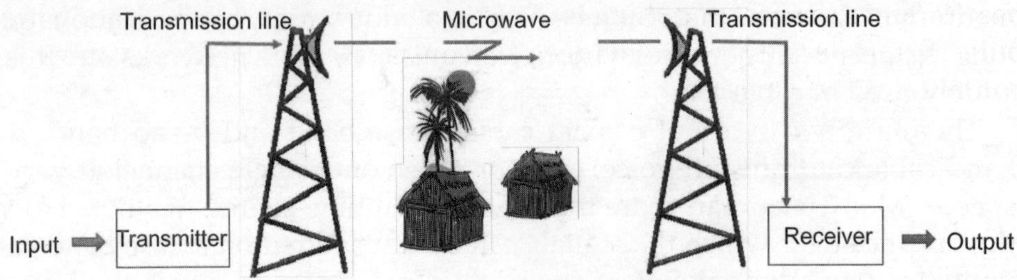

Fig. 8.11 Microwave transmission

Repeater stations at every 35 to 40 km are installed for the purpose of sending and receiving signals along line-of-sight paths. Microwave communication is used when it is not possible to communicate through ground methods due to the following two main reasons :

- due to fading of signals that cannot be amplified without noise.
- Rugged terrain such as desert, sea, hills etc.

5. **Radio Transmission or Radio Frequency (RF) Transmission**. This method of wireless communication uses some specific radio frequencies for direct data or voice communication. In some countries such as USA, licenses are granted to taxicab operators and business people. They communicate with each other through Citizen Bands (CB) radio. The citizen band allows about 40 radio frequencies to the users. Radio transmission is extremely useful for customer services such as couriers, home deliveries, on-site repair and maintenance etc. The disadvantage of radio transmission is lack of security. Moreover, it is not suitable for transfer of large files or data bases because it has very low transmission speeds.

6. **Infrared Transmission**. Similar to microwave transmission, infrared transmission also discards wiring altogether. There are point-to-point infrared links that are used to replace cables between adjacent buildings.

   Infrared waves refer to energy in the region of the electromagnetic radiation spectrum having wavelengths longer than that of visible light and shorter than that of radio waves.

   A high-intensity modulated infrared beam is bounced off the ceiling of an office which scatters the waves around the room. The infra-red wave can be received by a data communicating device using a simple solid-state detector. This device can also bounce its own data against the ceiling through a solid-state infrared emitter and broadcast it to all other devices in the office (see Fig. 8.12). In this way, sufficient area can be covered with little power consumption.

   The infrared transmission allows an entire office to be tied together by infrared beams. Thus, the cost of cabling is avoided which is an important factor in some buildings, especially where changes are constantly made to the position of data communicating devices.

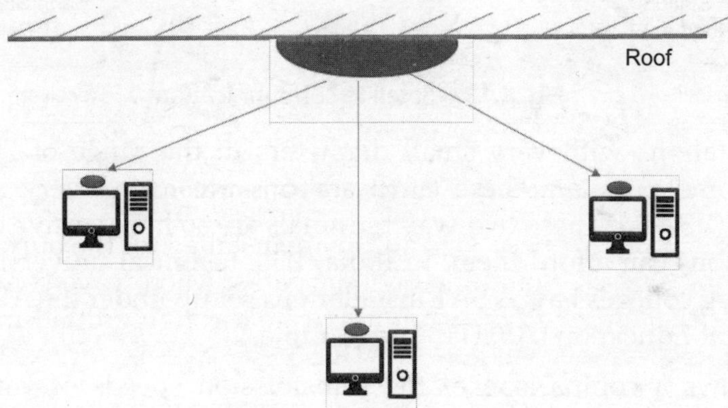

Fig. 8.12 Infrared transmission

   The main advantage of this transmission is that the data communicating devices do not require exact positioning. However, the infrared signals are highly susceptible to high intensity light and the data can be overheard by the neighbours also. This poses a serious threat to data security.

7. **Satellite Communication**. Similar to microwave and radio transmissions, this is also a wireless communication channel. When the distance between sites is extremely large or there are obstructions in the way, satellite communication is used. The satellite revolves round the earth at the height of approximately 35200 km, as shown in Fig. 8.13.

The satellite receives signals from an earth station, amplifies and sends them to another earth station. In fact, it acts as a relay between the two earth stations. In order to avoid interference of signals, the frequency of the transmitting frequency of a satellite is kept different from the receiving frequency.

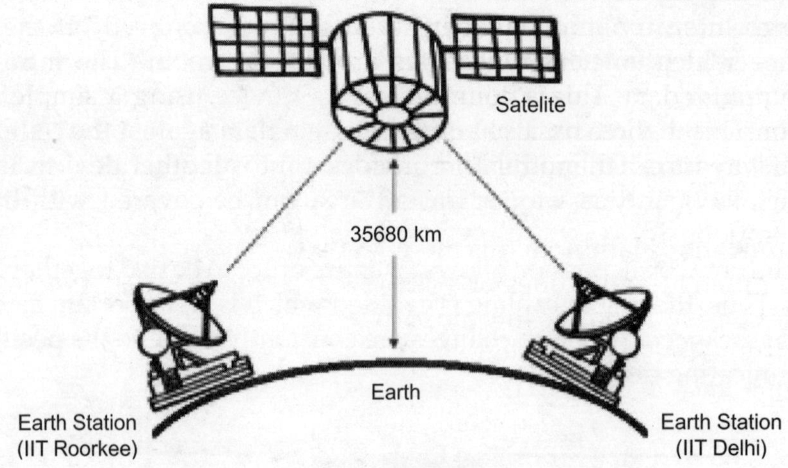

Fig. 8.13 Satellite communication

Earth stations with very small diameters in the range of 75 cm to 1.2 m have become popular. These earth stations are called very small aperture terminals (VSATs). These two-way terminals are so inexpensive that even small organizations can afford them. In India, IITs, technical universities and major engineering colleges have VSAT installations set up under the All India Council of Technical Education (AICITE) programme.

Table 8.3shows a comparison of the transmission speeds of various channels discussed in this section.

Table 8.3 Transmission speed of channels

Communication Channel	Transmission Speed
Twisted pair	100 Mbps
Coaxial cable	140 Mbps
Fiber optics	2 Gbps
Microwave	275 Mbps
Radio	2 Mbps
Infrared	275 Mbps
Satellite	275 Mbps

8.3 MODULATION

Telephone lines are still the most commonly used transmission media. However, these lines are not suitable for the transmission of digital or computer data because these were designed primarily for voice communication, which can be done through continuous analog signals i.e., electrical wave forms. A wave form is characterized by three characteristics, amplitude, frequency and phase. Since, a pure sine wave can be transmitted over telephone lines without much distortion, it can also be used to carry digital or computer data. This is done by encoding the digital data on the sine wave by varying one of the three basic characteristics of the wave. The process of sending the data on a wave is called modulation and the wave is termed as a carrier. Thus we can have the following types of modulation techniques:

1. **Amplitude modulation**. In this modulation the binary 0 and 1 are represented by two different amplitudes or voltage levels (Fig. 8.14). The high amplitude indicates binary 1 and the low amplitude binary 0. The transmission rate on telephone lines is up to 1200 baud. This type of modulation is also used in the transmission of data over optical fibers.
2. **Frequency modulation**. In frequency modulation the binary 0 and 1 are represented by two different frequencies of the carrier wave (see Fig. 8.14). Compared to amplitude modulation, this technique is less error prone. The transmission rate in telephone lines is up to 1200 baud. This modulation technique is also used for high frequency radio transmission.
3. **Phase modulation**. In this modulation, the phase of the carrier wave is shifted 20 degrees to represent data switches. A binary 1 is assumed unless there is a phase shift. The phase shift represents a binary 0 (see Fig. 8.14). Thus, the phase shift is with reference to the previous bit transmitted. The transmission rate on telephone lines is 9600 baud.

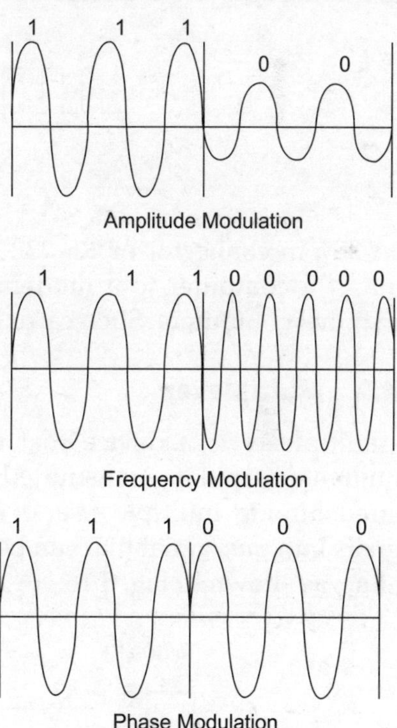

Fig. 8.14 Signal modulation

8.4 NETWORK DEVICES

A data communication device is used to provide an interconnection between the computer and the communication channel. The various communication devices are:

modems, communication control units, data service units, multiplexers, concentrators etc. A brief discussion on some of the devices is given in the following sections.

8.4.1 Modem (Modulator/Demodulator)

A modem is a device used as an interface between a computer and a communication channel or line. It modulates digital signals from the input/output devices into analog signals for transmission. At the receiving terminal, another modem demodulates the transmitted signal back into digital. Thus the modem can act both as a modulator and a demodulator.

Modems are also useful in situations when an input signal is not powerful enough to travel the required distance over a transmission line. It amplifies the signals before the transmission. Fiber optic modems convert digital signals into pulses of light for the transmission over the glass fiber. Generally, for long distance computer communication, the preferred communication channel is telephone lines.

Fig. 8.15 Modem

A 25 pin connector or RS-232 C interface is a common standard that is used to connect a computer to a modem. Modems are also available as add-on cards for personnel computers. Such cards do not require an external connector.

8.4.2 Multiplexer

A multiplexer is a device that allows a single communication channel to carry simultaneously data transmitted from many terminals. Thus, the channel can be shared among multiple users. The multiplexer combines two or more separate signals into one signal that can be transmitted over a single communication channel or line, as shown in Fig. 8.16.

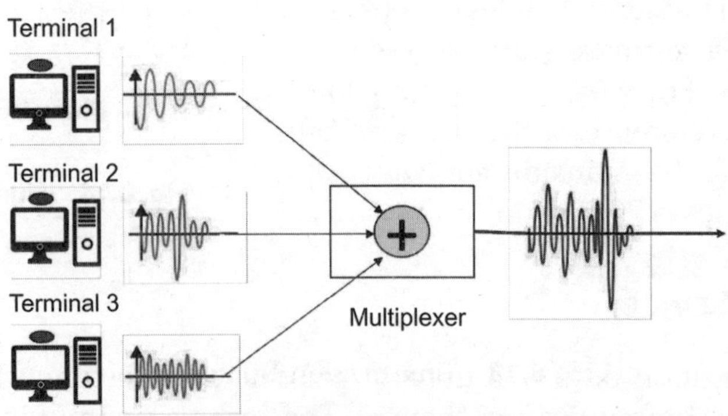

Fig. 8.16 Multiplexer

The multiplexing can be done by two methods: Frequency division multiplexing (FDM) and time division multiplexing (TDM).

1. **Frequency Division Multiplexing**. FDM divides the available transmission band into separate frequencies to establish multiple channels within the transmission medium. Each frequency belongs to a separate terminal that is used to transmit data of that terminal as shown in Fig. 8.17.

   For example, in broadband systems such as radio transmission, each radio station is assigned a separate frequency range. The radio receiver gets signals from all the stations. However, the tuner in the home radio set isolates the required signal for the listener.

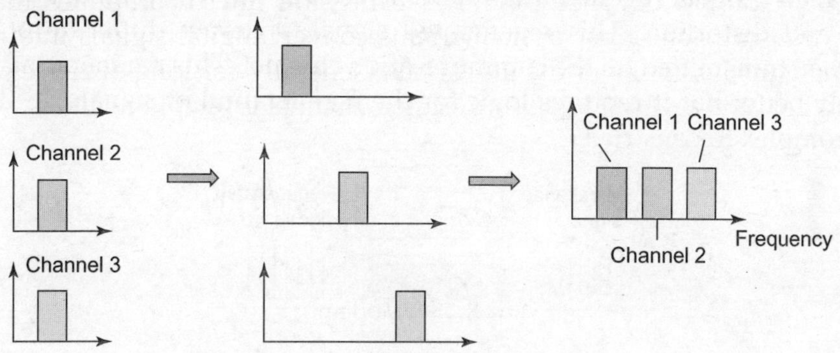

Fig. 8.17 Frequency division multiplexing

2. **Time Division Multiplexing**. TDM divides the channel into short time slots of fixed intervals. The various terminals time-share the channel. The total transmission time is divided into time slots and each terminal transmits the data during its allotted slot (Fig. 8.18).

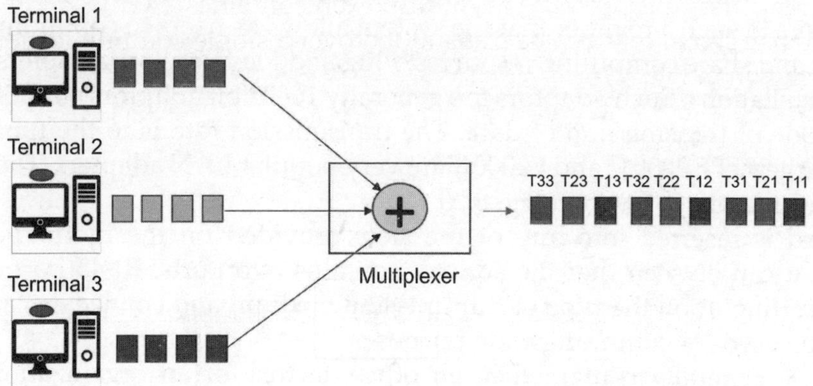

Fig 8.18 Time division multiplexing

It may be noted here that the time slots are always of fixed duration and are assigned in the same order to the terminals. TDM is extensively used in base band systems which can only support one signal at a time. A device having the capabilities of a multiplexer and some built-in intelligence to perform routing functions is known as a concentrator. It also acts as a data buffer for incoming signals.

8.4.3 Repeater

A repeater is a simple device that amplifies all incoming electromagnetic signals on a communication channel and transmits the amplified signals on the communication channel. This device is helpful in a situation where the signal becomes weaker over the transmission medium after a certain distance (Fig. 8.19). However, the noise or distortion in the signal also gets amplified in a simple repeater. Another type of repeater called a signal regenerating repeater receives the weak signal and discards the noise and distortion. This regenerated signal, an exact duplicate of original signal, is then transmitted on the communication channel. This regenerating repeater is definitely better but it requires logic for the regeneration of signals. It, therefore, becomes complex to construct.

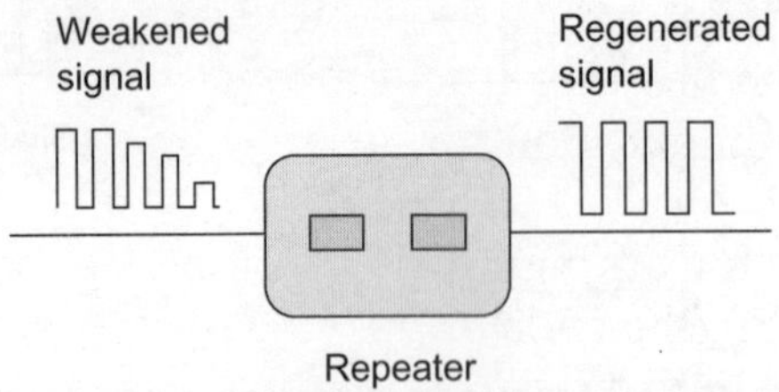

Fig. 8.19 Repeater

8.5 LOCAL AREA NETWORKS

A LAN is a network of closely located computers connected by transmission media and adaptors in such a manner that the system allows its users to communicate with each other and share computing resources. Plug and Play network adopters are used in LAN installations. Such adaptors are generally 16–32 bit adaptors supporting full-duplex mode of transmission of data. The transmission rate is to the tune of 10 to 20 Mbps. Ethernet E 2000 C and E2000 T are very popular LAN adapters. The diagram of a general adaptor is given in Fig. 8.20.

This card is inserted into any of the slots provided on the motherboard of a computer. It can be seen that the adapter contains two ports: RJ-45 port and BNC port. Depending upon the type of transmission medium and connecters, any one of them can be used for communication purposes.

A LAN is generally contained in an office, factory or an organization housed in a building. It is confined to a small sized geographical area. The rate of data communication ranges from moderate to high depending upon the type of transmission media being used.

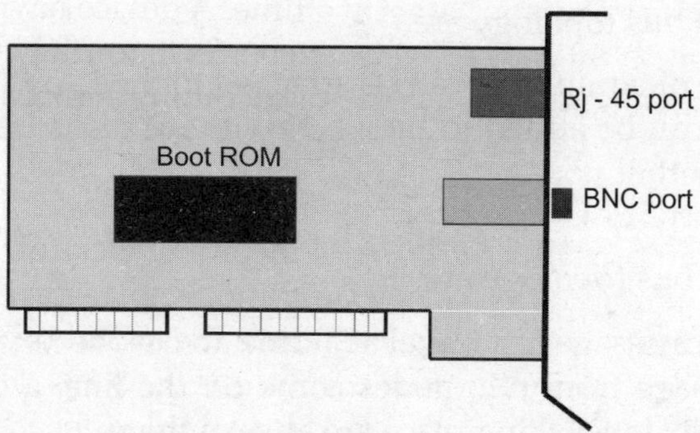

Fig. 8.20 A general LAN adaptor

The design of a LAN involves the selection of a topology and an architecture that guides the interconnection of components.

8.5.1 Network Topologies

The term topology is defined as the structure consisting of paths and devices that provide the necessary communication interconnections among the components of the network.

There are many choices for arranging the components. We can link everything together in a line; we can join the ends of this line to form a ring; we can radiate all our links out from a central hub; or we connect all the components on point to point basis. Respectively, these topologies are discussed below:

1. **Linear Bus Topology (Multi-drop topology)**. A bus structure usually uses a main trunk called a backbone. It is a long twisted-pair or coaxial cable into which the peripherals and PCs are connected (Fig. 8.21) with the help of short cables called drop cables. A peripheral or PC connected to the backbone or bus is commonly known as a node. The two ends of the backbone cable are terminated at both ends by absorbers. These absorbers absorb the signals from the cable after it has passed all the devices. Each node has a network interface card (NIC) to recognize its address from the information being transmitted by other nodes.

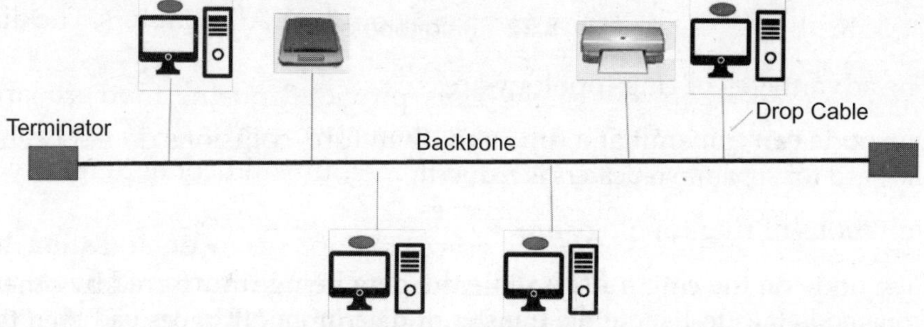

Fig. 8.21 Linear bus topology

The advantages of bus topology are:

- A wide range of equipment can be attached to the LAN without a problem.
- A new node can be added to the LAN without disturbing or disrupting the network and other nodes.
- Low cabling cost.

The limitations of bus topology are:

- Only a single message can travel at a time across the network.
- When a message from two nodes come on the line, a collision occurs. The chances of collisions taking place are always there.
- It has low reliability in the sense that a break or short circuit in the cable can halt the whole network.

Example. Ethernet is a very widely used bus topology LAN.

2. **Ring Topology (Loop Network)**. A ring, also known as a daisy chain, is a large circular cable (see Fig. 8.22). The ring can be twisted pair, coaxial cables, or optical fiber. All nodes are connected together in the ring and all data and information passes through each node in the system.

The NIC at each node regenerates each input signal that travels around the ring. Thus, separate repeaters are not required in this topology.

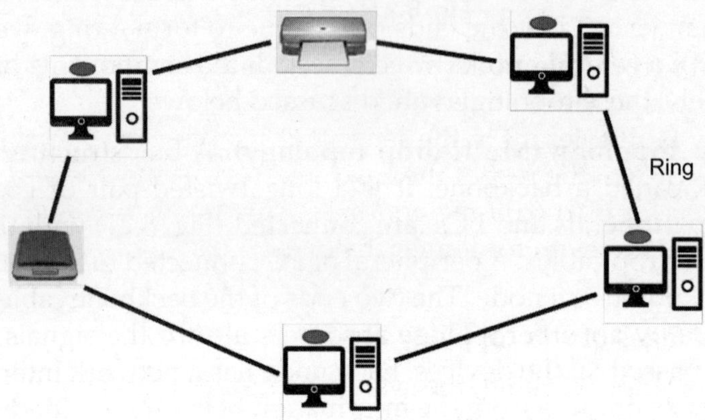

Fig. 8.22 Ring topology

The advantages of ring topology are:

- One node can transmit at a time and, therefore, collisions do not occur.
- The need for separate repeaters is reduced.

The limitations of ring topology are:

- Each node on the ring must handle the data being transferred by other nodes.
- If one node fails to handle the transfer of data or an NIC goes bad then the whole network fails.

Example. MITRENET uses a ring topology LAN. Token ring is another example of this topology.

3. **Star Topology**. In a star topology, the various nodes are directly wired to a central, dedicated computer called the hub of the star. The drop cables extend in all directions and each device is connected to the hub via these cables, as shown in Fig. 8.23.

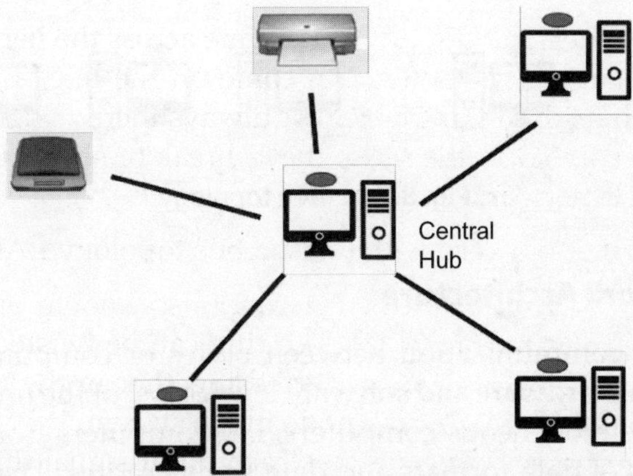

Fig. 8.23 Star topology

The data from one node travels over the drop cable to the hub and from hub, it travels to the destined node via another drop cable. The star topology is inherently fault tolerant in the sense that if a break in the cable occurs or some node goes down, the rest of the LAN keeps working without any disturbance. For distances up to 6.00 meters or so, star LANs are connected by twisted-pair cables. However, for longer distances, coaxial cable or optical fiber can be used.

The advantages of star topology are:

- If a node stops working, the system continues uninterrupted.
- Networking management is easy.

The limitations of star topology are:

- If the hub crashes, the whole network fails.
- More cabling is needed as compared to bus or ring topologies.

Example. ARCNET can be configured as star topology LAN. Common landline telephone connections follow star topology.

4. **Tree Network**. In this type of network, passive branches are added to groups or individual nodes in the sense that the original bus splits into a number of separate branches. The structure of a tree network is shown in Fig. 8.24.

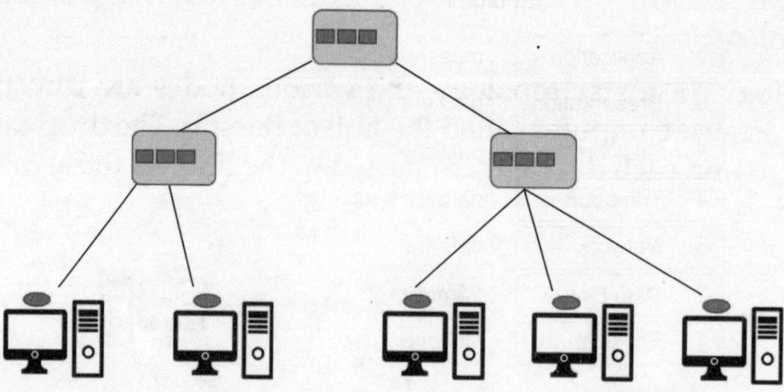

Fig. 8.24 Tree topology

8.5.2 Basic Network Architecture

In order to support communication between nodes or computers, some functions must be performed at hardware and software level. Most of the time it so happens that a LAN consists of heterogeneous computers, i.e., computers from different vendors having different sets of data formats and data transfer rates. These dissimilarities in heterogeneous computers create problems when connected to a LAN. For example, two persons knowing different languages cannot communicate with each other. The solution for this problem is that the computer vendors adopt and implement a common convention and set of rules for communication. The set of rules that allow different devices to communicate with each other is known as a **protocol**.

A protocol tries to give answers to the following questions.

1. What is the transmission media?
2. How is the data transmitted on the media?
3. How a node on the network is known as and when and how to transfer data?
4. How do the different nodes on the network contact each other.
5. What is the communication language, i.e., data format, rate of transfer, mode of transfer etc.?
6. What is the guarantee that the data reaches its destination?

However, the task is too large and complex to be handled as a unit. Therefore, before the standards and conventions are formulated, one must establish the structure or architecture of the communication task.

In 1977, the International Standard Organization (ISO) divided the task into seven subtasks called ISO layers. Each layer performs a specific task required for communication with other system. It depends upon its lower layer to perform the basic functions and provides service to its next higher layer. These layers were standardized and documented in the form of the OSI (Open System Interconnect) model (Fig. 8.25). This model serves as a guideline for network designers.

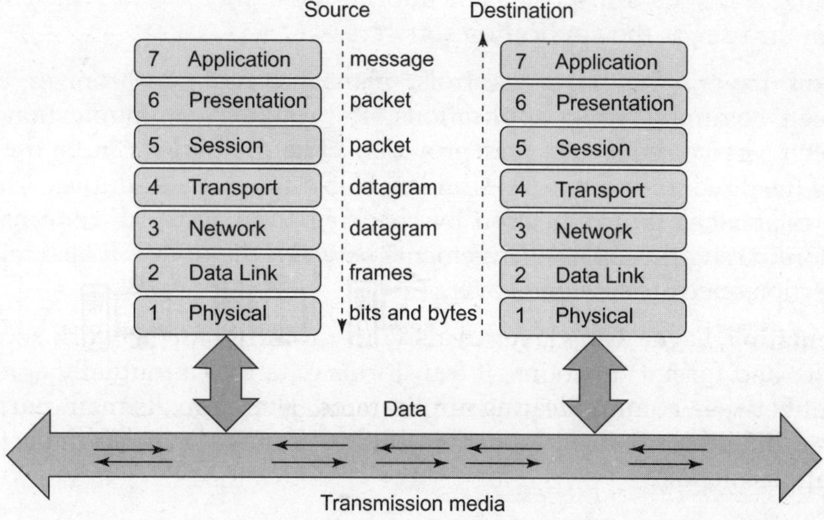

Fig. 8.25 OSI model

1. **Physical Layer**. This layer defines the electrical, mechanical and functional specifications of the network transmission media. It establishes protocols for voltage, data transfer rate, timing and rules for handshaking between the communicating nodes. It also activates the transmission media to transmit data in the form of bits in either direction. This is the only layer that is concerned with hardware whereas the rest of the higher layers focus on software.
2. **Data Link Layer**. This layer organizes the data received from the physical layer, into frames or packets. It defines protocols for governing data packetizing and transmission into and out of each node. Error detection and error control is also the responsibility of this layer. Thus, with a fully functional data link layer, the next higher layer (Network layer) may assume virtually error free transmission over the link.
3. **Network Layer**. This layer establishes protocols for data routing, in the sense that it is responsible for establishing, maintaining and terminating connections between various nodes in the network. This layer moves information across the network by examining the destination network layer address and sends the packet to the destined node.
4. **Transport Layer**. This layer ensures reliable data delivery, in the sense that error free data units are delivered in the proper sequence, with no losses or duplications. The size and complexity of this layer depends upon the type of service it can get from its lower layer, i.e., the Network layer. If the network layer is unreliable then this layer compensates it by including protocols for extensive error detection control. If the data is not delivered correctly to the

receiving node, the transport layers informs the higher layers, which eventually inform the user or the application software.

5. **Session Layer**. This layer controls, manages and synchronizes dialogues between communicating applications. It provides communication sessions between service requesters and providers. The dialogues can be delivered in one of the three control modes: simplex, half-duplex or full-duplex. The session layer establishes the connection by checking the password, code names and by coordinating the acknowledgements between the nodes. It also releases the connection once the session is over.

6. **Presentation Layer**. This layer deals with protocols for network security, file transfer and format functions. It transforms data into a mutually agreed upon format between communicating applications. Therefore, its main purpose is to resolve differences in format and data entities. It may also perform the following operations on data:
   - data compression and expansion
   - data encryption and decryption

7. **Application Layer**. This layer is the communication interface between the user and the OSI environment. It is the top layer of the OSI model and provides network services to the user application processes that lie outside the seven-layer architecture. Examples of application processes are: file server programs, E-mail etc.

8.6 WIDE AREA NETWORK (WAN)

A wide area network is a computer network that spreads across a region, country or whole of the world. WANs interconnect LANs located in any part of the world. The LANs are connected with the help of WAN back bones. Generally, WANs use satellites as the primary transmission media and, therefore, the transmission is comparatively costly. Where the LAN market has grown at a very fast rate, WAN growth has been relatively slow. The popular WAN protocols are: X.25, Frame Relay, and ATM (asynchronous transmission mode).

X-25 Protocol. This protocol is a low bandwidth transmission protocol with 56 kbps to 2 Mbps data transfer rate. It was earlier used by most of the WANs.

Frame Relay. The frame relay is a high bandwidth protocol with 1.54 Mbps(T1 line) to 45 Mbps (T3 Line) data transfer rate. In fact, this is a streamlined version of the X.25 protocol that assumes reliable communication links. It is a very cost effective transmission protocol and is very popular within networking companies.

ATM. This is an extremely fast transmission protocol with bandwidth as high as 9953 Mbps using optical carriers. It is also designed to handle integrated data, voice, and video transmission. This protocol is gaining popularity worldwide because it can handle both video and multimedia applications.

Example. DHLNET uses both X.25 and Frame relay technology to connect the various LANs of its offices world over.

8.7 SWITCHING TECHNIQUES

The data can be transmitted on a network by using either of the following services offered by a network.

1. Connection-oriented (CO) service
2. Connectionless (CL) service.

The connection-oriented transmission of data is also called **circuit switching** whereas the connectionless transmission is known as **packet switching.**

Circuit Switching: This type of data transfer is similar to a telephone system. In a telephone system, the connection must be established between the two participants i.e., the caller and the receiver. The circuit or route is established between the sender and receiver before the start of the transfer of data. The following steps are followed to establish the connection.

1. A request signal is sent by the source node over the network to set up the connection with the destination node.
2. All intermediate nodes are identified. These nodes are also called switching nodes (see Fig. 8.26).
3. If the destination node is available to receive data, it sends back acceptance signals.
4. The data transfer starts.

It may be noted here that some amount of time is spent in Steps 1 and 3 which causes delay in sending the data the first time. However, once the connection is established, almost no delay occurs in the switching nodes.

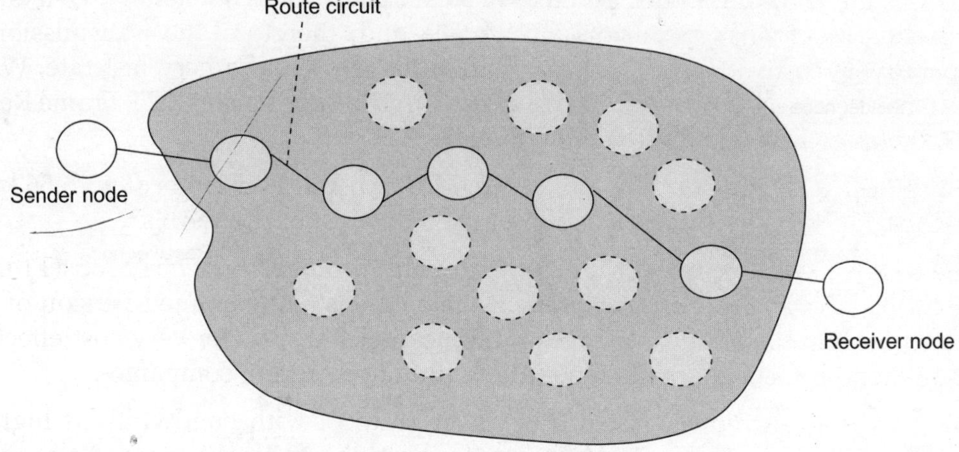

Fig. 8.26 Circuit switching

In fact, a full duplex transmission line is set up between the sender node and the receiver node. This connection remains available through the communication session.

Packet Switching: The packet switching mode of sending data over the network is similar to post office operations. In the case of a post office, the sender writes the destination address on the letter and drops it into the post office mailbox. The post office personnel send the letter to the destination post office through the route available. Finally the postman delivers the letter to the destination.

This type of network divides the data into small blocks of data called packets. The size of such a packet is generally 128 bytes or 512 bytes. Such a packet has a format as shown in Fig. 8.27.

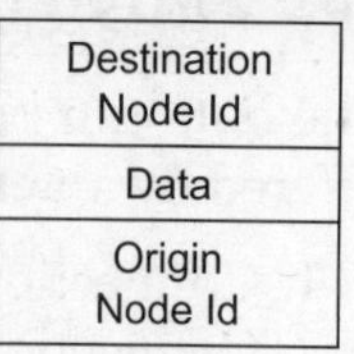

Fig. 8.27 Format of a packet

The following steps are used for sending data over the network.

1. The origin node locates an intermediate node.
2. The origin node sends the packets one by one to the intermediate node.
3. The intermediate node checks the destination ID of the packet.
4. If the ID of the node does not match with the destination ID of the packet, it sends the packet to the next available node.
5. Repeat Steps 3 and 4 till the packet reaches its destination.
6. Repeat Steps 2 to 5 till all the data packets are sent and delivered.

The action taken by intermediate nodes (Steps 3 and 4) is known as the **store and forward** method of packet transfer. Since there is no connection or circuit to be established between the sender and destination node, the path followed by each packet from the sender to receiver can be different. Therefore, due to different paths and the propagation delays at intermediate nodes, the packet may arrive at the destination node in a disordered fashion, as shown in Fig. 8.28.

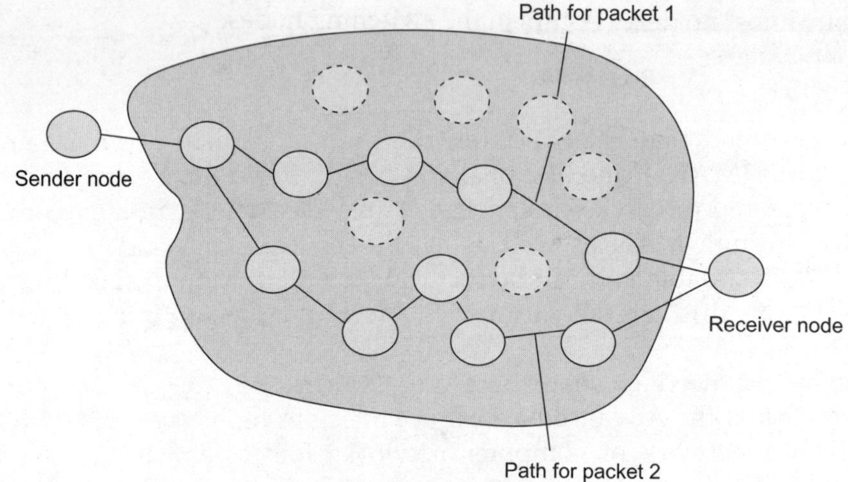

Fig. 8.28 Packet switching

A comparison between the two switched networks is given in Table 8.4.

Table 8.4

	Circuit switching	Packet switching
1.	Fast	Slow
	Constant data rate across the network	Involves a delay at each node data path because of a store and forward policy
2.	Requires a dedicated path	Can use dynamic paths
3.	If the path is overloaded than the call is blocked and the communication is delayed.	In case of an overloaded path, the packets are sent through other available (different) paths.

8.8 INDIAN NETWORKS

The popular Wide Area Networks of India are Nicnet, I-Net. Calibnet, Coalnet, Ernet, Sail net and Star net. The salient features of ERNET (Education and Research Network) are given below:

1. This network is primarily meant for promotion of information exchange among the various educational and research institutes such as IITs, IISc, DOE etc.
2. The number of institutes connected with this network is around 350 or so.
3. It provides network services across India to many research organizations. The common services provided by this network are:
   - file transfer
   - data bases access
   - remote login
   - conferencing
   - E-mail

It may be noted that ERNET interconnects the various LANs, Metropolitan Area Networks (MANs), and National and International Data Networks (NIDNs). Thus, teachers and research scholars can share their ideas with their counterparts in the city through MAN as well as across the nation through satellite WAN. The network is scalable and can be further expanded by connecting more LANs, MANs or WANs through the various ES (End System) shown in the architecture of ERNET.

Driven by the need to share data and information, the defence ministry of U.S.A. established the Advanced Research Projects Administration Network (1969) (ARPANET), a network of computer networks for researchers involved in the development of software tools and communication equipment for the military. In order to connect LANs of different types, a powerful communication architecture based on the TCP/IP set of protocols was also evolved as part of ARPANET. With the passage of time, around 1986, this network of networks called Internet was opened for educational and commercial institutes.

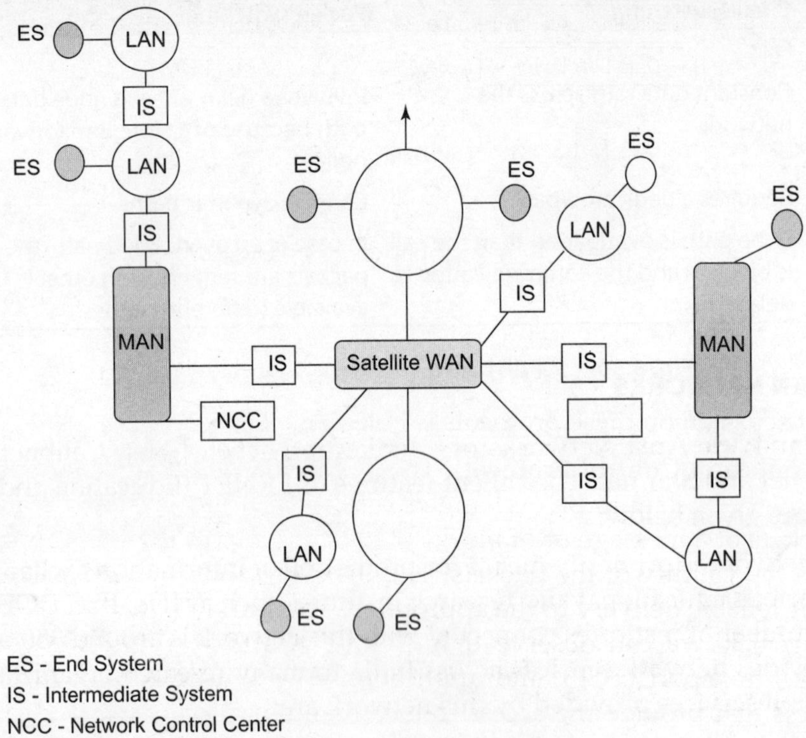

Fig. 8.29 ERNET architecture

8.9 INTERNET AND PROTOCOLS

The Internet is a network of networks consisting of thousands of networks spanning the entire globe. It uses TCP/IP based communication architecture to interconnect different types of LANs, as shown in Fig. 8.30. The TCP/IP architecture consists of five core protocols. This family of protocols is known as the "Internet protocol suite". TCP and IP are the two most common protocols of this suite.

IP (Internet Protocol): This is a protocol used by the Internet for transferring messages from one machine to another. The messages are sent in the form of packets. Each packet consists of 1500, or fewer bytes. Thus, IP uses packet switching to connect multiple LANs within the same building or at different sites.

This protocol identifies each network and each computer by a unique fixed address (32 bit). This address is used by IP to determine the source and destination of a packet.

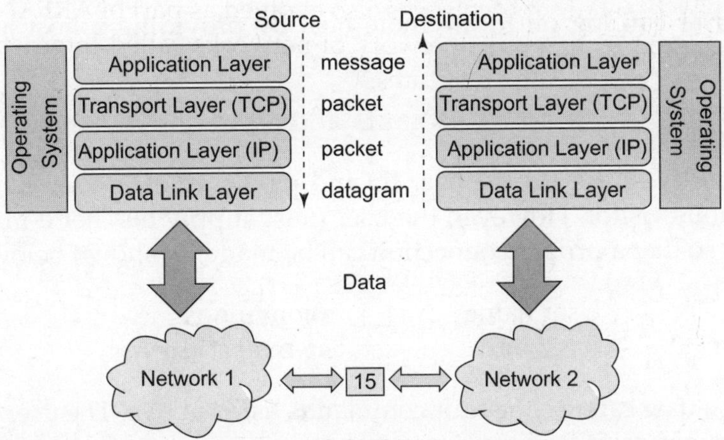

Fig. 8.30 TCP/IP based communication architecture

A brief discussion on these protocols is given below:

TCP (Transmission Control Protocol): The TCP provides the logic for ensuring the reliable delivery of data to be exchanged between the host systems. It collects the related packets of a message or of blocks of data and places them in proper order. It also checks the validity of the packets. Thus, it keeps track of the blocks of data to ensure their reliable delivery to the appropriate application.

From Fig. 8.30 we can observe that TCP/IP has four layers: Network access, internet (IP), transport (TCP), and application. The network access layer contains the protocols that provide the access to the communication network such as LAN. The internet layer consists of internet protocol (IP). The transport layer consists of transport control protocol (TCP). The application layer consists of protocols for specific user applications.

The Application Layer Protocols: The application layer of TCP/IP communication architecture consists of protocols for specific user applications. There are four such protocols: FTP, TELNET, SMTP and PPP. These protocols are discussed below:

A. **FTP (File Transfer Protocol):** This protocol helps in transferring files from one network to another network. FTP, generally known as anonymous FTP, takes care of different character codes used by the different systems connected to the internet. It also accommodates text and binary files and provides features of controlling user access. When logged on to the internet-enabled system, the user can give commands on anonymous FTP. Some of the popular commands are given below:

cd	change directory
ls	display contents of a directory
get	transfer a file from a remote host
mget	multiple file transfers

The user can log on to a remote host by providing a host address at the system prompt as shown below:

➢ `ftp <host address> <symbol>`

The host will ask for the user ID and password. The user can log in as an anonymous visitor. However, the user must supply his/her e-mail address to the host so that a proper connection can be made, as shown below:

User name	:	anonymous
Password	:	<e-mail address>

Now a user can use the four commands listed above. The user can leave the host by typing *quit* at the system prompt

➢ quit

In addition to the above commands, FTP also supports a large number of commands. A list of FTP commands is given in Appendix D.

B. Remote Login TELNET (The Network Terminal Protocol): Telnet helps a user to log in at a remote computer and function as if he or she were connected locally to that computer. It is a form of dial up connection between the two computers for the exchange of data. The user starts a remote session by providing the host address at the system prompt as shown below :

➢ `telnet <host address>`

Normally, the telnet session requires a valid user login and password to be given by the user. However, some internet sites such as LOCIS can be reached without a username or password. Once a connection is established, anything typed by the user is directly sent to the remote computer. The user can terminate the session by typing LOGOFF or LOGOUT on the system prompt

➢ LOGOFF <symbol>

The user returns to the primary operating environment after logging off the remote system. The telnet also supports a command mode which can be used for a variety of purposes such as dial up service, using programs residing on another computer, changing account password, using client-server applications etc. A list of telnet commands is given in Appendix E.

C. SMTP (Simple Mail Transfer Protocol). SMTP helps a user to send mail to other networks or computers. The incoming mail is also received by the user through this protocol. SMTP does not provide facilities to create messages. Therefore, a user can create a message through a local editor. Once the message is created, SMTP takes it and uses TCP to send it to an SMTP lying on another host. The target SMTP uses local e-mail services to store the incoming message in the corresponding mail box. The various features of SMTP include mailing lists, returns receipts, and forwarding.

D. **PPP (Point-to-Point Protocol).** Generally, internet is accessed through dedicated leased lines. Point-to-Point Protocol (PPP) can be used to connect telephone dialup lines to the internet. The communication takes place through a high speed modem. The user needs to install PPP drivers at the time of creating a dial up connection. This protocol allows a temporary IP address to be assigned by the Internet to the computer and the communication takes place.

The following steps are required to connect to the Internet:

Step

1. Double click on the Dialup icon.
2. Dial the number of the IP provider.
3. Enter login and password.
4. If the password is verified, open a browser like Netscape, Internet Explorer, Firefox etc.

After the browser home page is displayed, the user can surf the internet. Serial Line Internet Protocol (SLIP) can also be used for connecting the Internet through a Dialup connection, but PPP being the latest, is better. PPP retransmits the garbled packets automatically whereas SLIP does not. PPP also provides error detection and compression.

8.10 BACKBONE NETWORK

The internet uses a central high-speed network, called the **backbone** to connect smaller independent networks. For example, NSFNet is a backbone used in USA for internet connections. In India **GIAS** (Gateway Internet Access Services) is being employed for the same. India Backbone Implementation Network (IBIN) is designed to be the next generation backbone network. INet is being used for high speed connectivity to Internet and E-mail. The INet is India's X.25 based packet switched public data network. The packet switching technique allows almost error free transmission between components running at different speeds and protocols. INet offers the following types of connections to the users:

1. **X.25 connection:** With the help of X.25 compatible software and hardware, the user can send or receive several simultaneous calls. The speed of connection can be 2400, 4800, 9600, 19600, or 64000 bps.
2. **X.32 connection:** It enables the X.25 users to have a backup access to INet. It uses the dialup mode for communication at speeds of 2400, 4800, or 9600 bps.

3. **X.28 connection:** A user of x.28 can use any computer with a suitable communication software such as Procomm, Xtalk etc. The calls can be sent or received through dialup at speeds of 300, 1200, 2400, 4800 or 9600 bpts.
4. **Frame Relay:** The users of this connection can have PVCs (Permanent Virtual Circuits). It provides high speed connectivity between LANs situated 100 kms apart.

8.11 NETWORK CONNECTING DEVICES

We know that the Internet is a network of networks. This means that at the physical level, the participating networks are joined together by network connectors and not by one cable, but thousands of them. There are four different network connectors with broadly similar functions: repeaters, bridges, routers, and gateways. A brief discussion on these connectors is given below:

1. **Repeater (Physical Relay)**: An introduction to repeaters is given in Section 8.4.3. A LAN repeater is used to regenerate data and voice signals. These devices are dealt with only at the physical layer of the OSI model, as shown in Fig. 8.31.

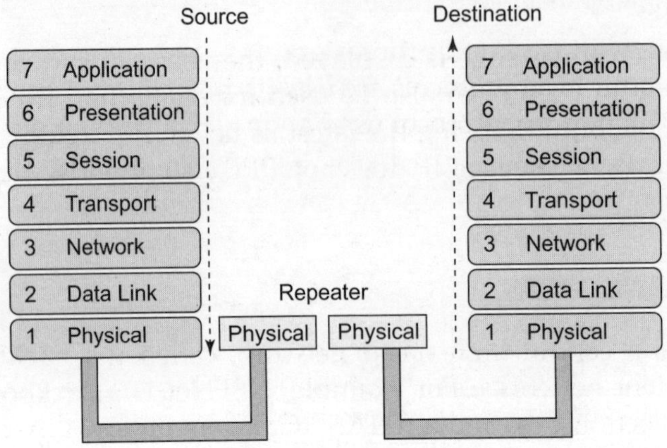

Fig. 8.31 Repeater

An incoming packet from a network segment is read by the repeater. The packet is amplified and transmitted to another segment of the network. Thus, repeaters work purely at bit level. Therefore, the limitation of a repeater is that it can link to segments of one single LAN. The term single LAN means that the LAN is physically as well as logically same.

2. **Bridges (Data Link Relay):** A bridge connects two LANs of the same type, such that the LANs are logically same but physically separate. Once a bridge is connected between two LANs of the same type, the devices on each side of the bridge simply address packets to each other as if they were on the same LAN. Bridges operate at the level of the data link layer of the OSI model, as shown in Fig. 8.32.

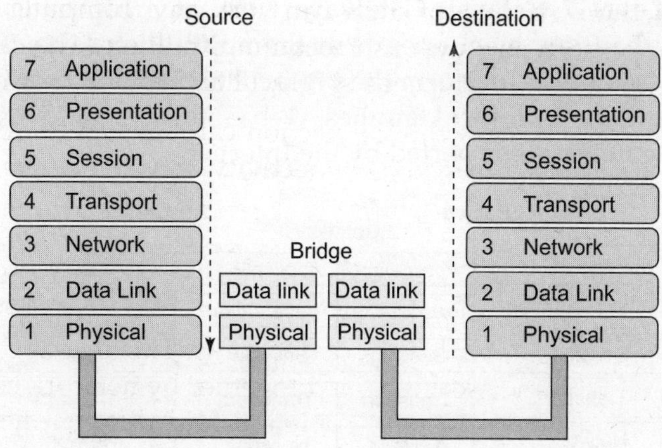

Fig. 8.32 A bridge

The main difference between a repeater and a bridge is that a bridge filters and drops the packets sent for a local site. However, it regenerates the packets sent to a remote site, i.e., on the other side of the bridge. Moreover, a bridge handles data at packet level rather than at bit level.

3. **Routers (Network Relay)**: A router operates at the Network layer level, in the sense that at this level protocols are used to interconnect complex networks (see Fig. 8.33). The popular protocol used at this level is IP (Internet protocol).

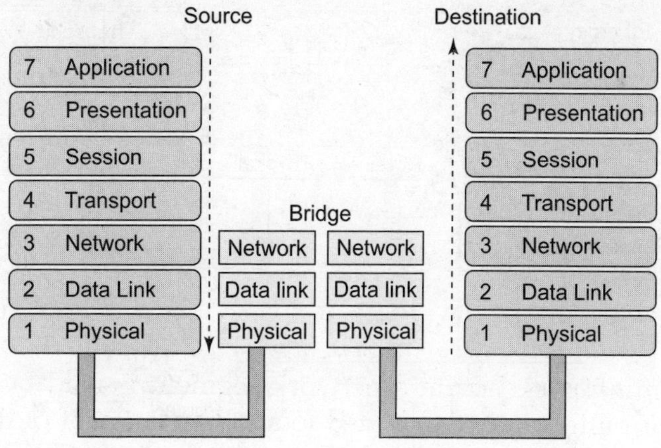

Fig. 8.33 Router

Routers are intelligent devices because they can route the packets over multiple communication paths belonging to LANs which are physically and logically separate.

For example, Netware V3.11 provides an internal router that allows a Netware server to connect up to 16 different networks, making them appear as one logical network. Cisco 1600 R is another example of a router for WAN connectivity.

4. **Gateways (Level 7 Relays):** Gateways work at a higher level than routers, in the sense that they even operate at the application layer level as shown in Fig. 8.34. These devices perform the protocol conversion between the networks which have different protocol families. Web Gateways and Finger Gateways are examples of gateways supported by the Internet.

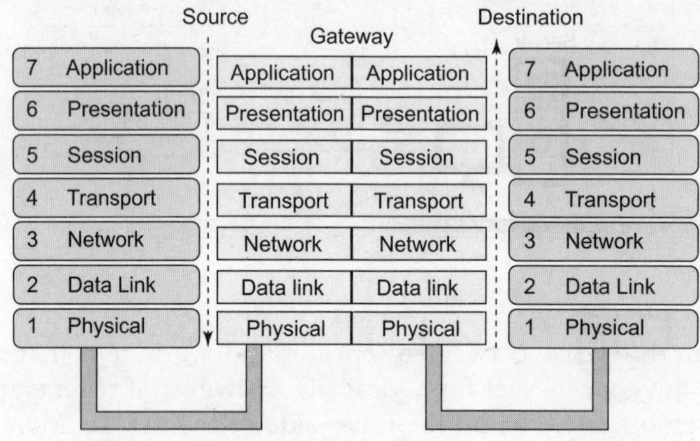

Fig. 8.34 Gateway

Fig. 8.35 illustrates the usage and placement of the above discussed connectors in a framework of different network topologies.

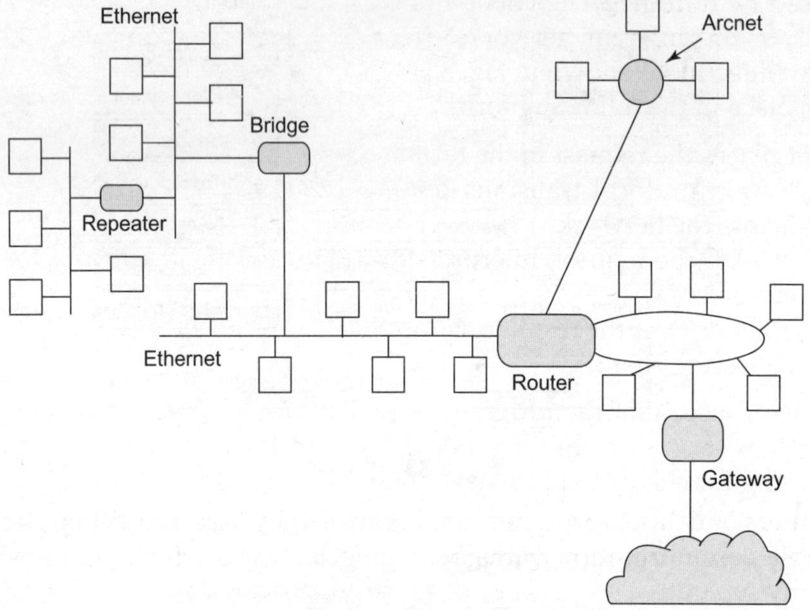

Fig. 8.35 Placement of network connecting devices

8.12 CLIENT SERVER MODEL

The client server model of computing is based on distributed network computing. In this model, an application is executed cooperatively by two computers. The computer called the client is a front end computer and the computer called the server, is a back end computer. Most of the Internet applications have been developed on this model.

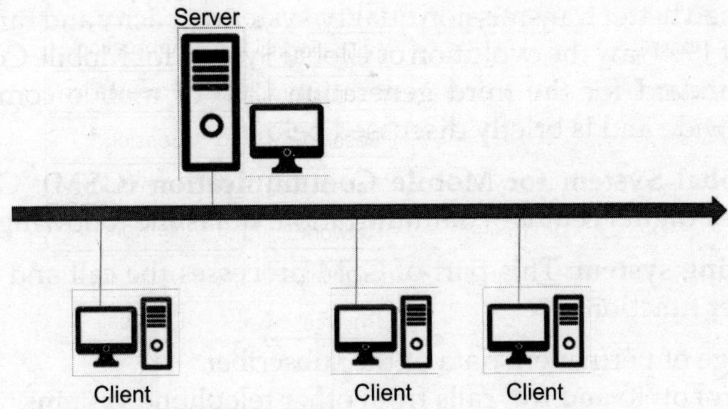

Fig. 8.36 Client server architecture

Applications are distributed across the network. Both client and server communicate with each other through application protocols. Thus, it is possible to use data anonymously, in the sense that the user need not know the source of the data being used by him/her. The client and server nodes can be computers on the same network or on different networks even thousands of kilometres apart. The client server architecture is shown in Fig. 8.36. The conversation between a client and a server takes place in the following form:

1. The client places the request in the format required by the application protocol.
2. The application protocol transmits the request to the server in the form of a message across the network.
3. The server takes the request, interprets it, and locates the required information or resource.
4. The server hands over the result to the application protocol which in turn passes it to the requesting client.

It may be noted here that the program on a client node runs as long as the user needs resources or services from the server. However, the server runs continuously and keeps waiting for clients to place new requests.

8.13 MOBILE PHONE COMMUNICATION

The nineteenth century saw the discovery of electromagnetic waves paving the way for wireless communication. In a span of a few decades, that is, in 1950 the first mobile telephone services were introduced. The service was extremely poor because of its low capacity, interference and poor speech quality.

With the advent of microprocessors in the 1970s and 1980s, mobile systems became smaller, light weight and sophisticated. These were called the first generation (1G) mobile phones, capable of transmitting analog signals.

With advances in semiconductor technology and microwave devices, digital transmission became possible with mobile phones. Such second generation (2G) mobile phones had better transmission quality, system capacity and range of coverage.

The decade of 1990 saw the evolution of Global System for Mobile Communications (GSM). This standard for the third generation (3G) of mobile communications is accepted worldwide and is briefly discussed below:

1. **GSM (Global System for Mobile Communication (GSM)**: GSM is a world standard for digital cellular communication. It has the following three systems:

   A. **Switching system**: This part of GSM processes the call and user functions. The user functions are:

   - Storage of permanent data of the subscriber.
   - Control of 'to and fro' calls from other telephone systems.
   - Allow roaming to mobile phones users.
   - Provides authentication of the user's identity.
   - Prevents calls from stolen, unauthorized or defective mobile stations.

   B. **Base station system**: This part of GSM provides radio-related functions, as listed below:

   - Call handover
   - Cell configuration data
   - Control of radio frequency

   C. **Operation and Support system**

   This part of GSM helps in monitoring and controlling the network. It offers the following two functions:

   - Provide network overview.
   - Support the maintenance activities of different operations.

   The arrangement of the functional units of GSM is shown in Fig. 8.37. The GSM is made up of cells. Each cell is a geographic area. It identifies each cell by a CGI (Cell Global Identity). The CGI is a number that is assigned to each cell. A group of cells is provided a location area (LA), as shown in Fig. 8.38.

   GSM provides an 1850–1990 MHz frequency band with a duplex distance of 80 MHz. Duplex distance means the difference between the uplink and downlink frequencies of the communication system. The transfer rate of this mode of communication is 270 kbps.

GSM provides the following services.

- Dual tone multi-frequency
- Facsimile Group III
- Short message services
- Cell broadcast
- Voice mail
- Fax mail
- Call forwarding, cell hold, call waiting
- Closed user groups etc

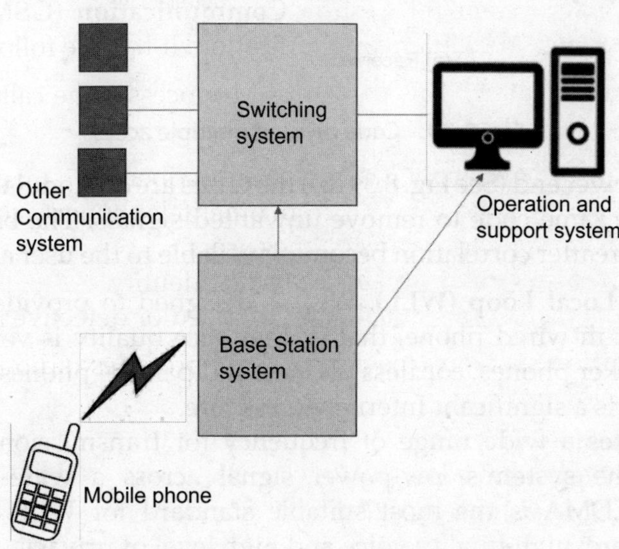

Fig. 8.37 The functional units of GSM

2. **CDMA (Code Division Multiple Access):** Code Division Multiple Access (CDMA) scheme allows the division of the transmission medium into different channels so that the transmissions from different stations are separated from each other. The separation is achieved by assigning different codes (G chip) to different transmitters. The receivers use these codes to recover the signal from the desired station.

   At the transmitter end (See Fig. 8.39(a)) the user bits are multiplied by the G chip values (i.e., code) and G bits are obtained. The G bits are then modulated and transmitted.

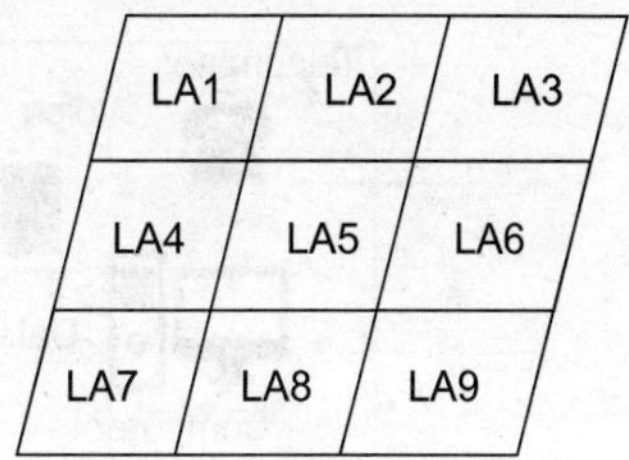

Fig 8.38 Location area (LA) of group cells

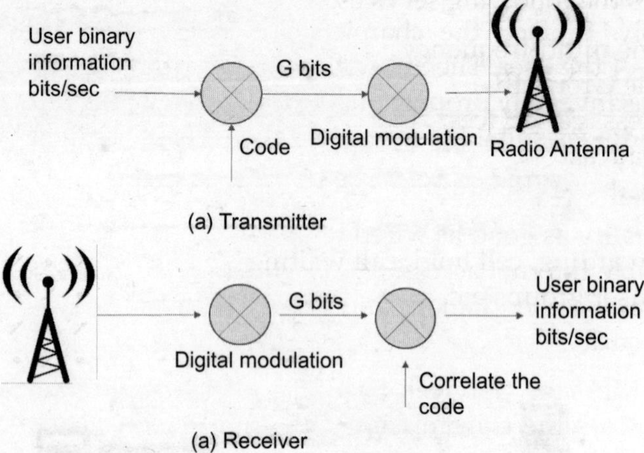

Fig. 8.39 Code division multiple access

At the receiver end (See Fig. 8.39 (b)) the G bits are demodulated and correlated by using the same code to remove unwanted signals. The binary information obtained thereafter correlation becomes available to the user at the receiver end.

3. **Wireless in Local Loop (WLL).** WLL is designed to provide voice quality as good as that in wired phone, that is, the voice quality is very high. The user can use speaker phones, cordless phones, and parallel phones etc. Additionally, WLL supports a significant Internet access rate.

   CDMA uses a wide range of frequency for transmission. It also helps in spreading the system's low-power signal across a wide-frequency range. Therefore, CDMA is the most suitable standard for WLL applications. The advantages are: high-quality voice and high level of privacy.

   The frequency spectrum as used by WLL is most suitable for packet switching mode of data transfer of internet. The Access Units (AU) can assign a channel to a subscriber only when the user desires to transmit a packet. The arrangement is shown in Fig. 8.40.

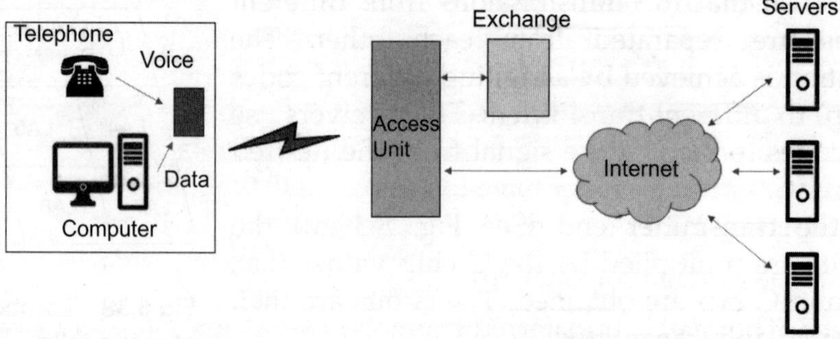

Fig. 8.40 WLL connection to the internet

It may be noted that telephone and the Internet connections are not used simultaneously. In fact, the channels are assigned by the AU as per the requirements of the user. The Subscriber density (SD) (the number of users per Km^2) in WLL is inversely proportional to the square of the cell radius. Therefore, a small cell radius is suitable for a reasonable subscriber density.

The Advantages of WLL are

- Voice quality as good as wired telephones
- Reasonable Internet access.
- Free from weather damage and external threats.
- More security.

4. **SMS (Short Message Service).** SMS is a service provided by mobile phone systems. It allows the transmission of a small piece of text from one mobile phone to another. The piece of text is termed as a short message. The mobile user can compose the message by using the keypad of the phone and then send it to another mobile user, as shown in Fig. 8.41.

   The sender sends an SMS request to the central system wherein the home location register (HLR) is used to locate the receiver. Once the receiver is identified, the short message is sent there.

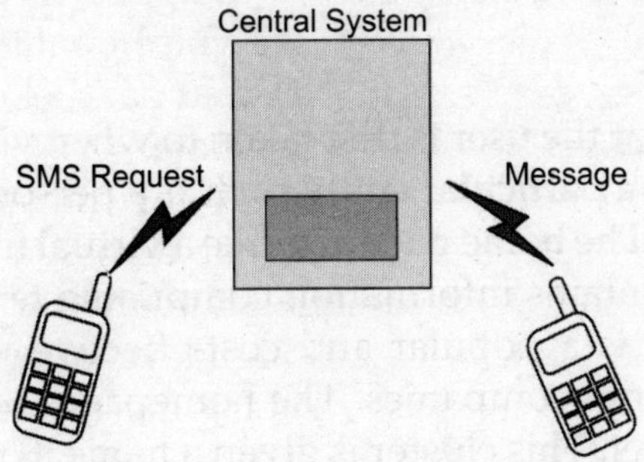

Fig. 8.41 Short message service

5. **e-Mail (Electronic mail).** The Internet Service Provider (ISP) allows the subscribers to communicate with each other through electronic text or letters. This service is termed electronic mail. This is a connectionless service that uses the TCP/IP protocol suite to transmit the mail from one user to another. Obviously a packet switching mode of transfer of data is used. However, both the receiver and the sender have to have an e-mail id., that is, an account with their respective ISPs.

   The main advantages of email are:

   a) Speed: The mail is transferred from one user to another at an extremely fast rate, which is, within a few minutes on the same ISP.

b) Low cost: There is practically no cost involved in e-mail. The only cost involved is that of internet usage and one local telephone call.
c) Paperless environment: E-mail helps in having a paperless office.

Disadvantages

a) High hardware cost: At least a computer, a modem, and a telephone connection are required. Nevertheless, one can easily use an internet cafe to send an e-mail at a very nominal rate.
b) Insecure transfer: Sometimes crackers (intruders) crack the password of a user and then misuse it.
c) Junk mail: Unnecessary mail is sometimes sent to users, which may carry unnecessary information or at times even viruses.

6. CHAT program (Online textual talk): This is a better version of communication than e-mail in the sense that the sender and receiver exchange text with each other online. Both interact with each other in half duplex mode. Mr A types the data and presses Enter. The data is displayed to Mr B's screen. Mr. B types the reply and presses Enter and so on.

   Windows Live Messenger, AOL Internet Messenger, MSN Messenger etc. are some of the popular chat programs.

8.14 HOME PAGE

A home page is the page that the user is first taken to when visiting any website. This page contains details about a particular entity such as a person, a company, a group of people, or an organization. The home page acts like a virtual front door for a company. This door when opened contains information comprising text graphs, pictures, and even animation. In fact, it is a popular and cost-effective way of broadcasting or advertising information about companies. The homepages belonging to a group are hyperlinked to form a cluster. This cluster is given a name. For example, we can have "YWCA pages", "India pages" etc.

A hypertext document can be created with the help of HTML (Hypertext Markup Language). It helps in embedding the text in the document wherein some words have links to other sources of information. The user has to simply write the HTML commands in an ASCII file.

8.14.1 Hypertext Documents

Ted Nelson developed a program called Xanadu which included the first use of the word *hypertext*. In this work, he proposed a nonlinear way of storage of text. In 1980, Tim Burner Lee wrote a program called "Enquire" for keeping track of the software with which he was involved. It allowed storage of snippets of information. The related snippets were connected to each other via links. To find information, one browsed via the links from one sheet to another. The snippets emulated his personnel record of programmers and the modules being developed by them. In fact, Lee's model ultimately led to the creation of the World Wide Web.

Since Standard Generalized Mark-up Language (SGML) was an internationally recognized standard for text information processing. It was used by Lee to describe the Hypertext Mark-up Language (HTML).

HTML offered a platform-independent means of marking data for interchange. The concept was that servers would store and supply data and clients would retrieve and display it.

The Structure of an HTML Document

Like other languages used with computers, HTML has its own rules of grammar. It uses conventional punctuation symbols in unusual ways and uses free format input. The motivation behind this format is that HTML does not specify how to display the output on the screen. However, for a given computer screen, the browser has the freedom to choose a form that is appropriate to display the information as per the specifications of the screen.

To separate HTML instructions from text to be displayed, each instruction consists of characters surrounded by less than (<) and greater than (>) symbols. The resultant group of characters is known as a Tag. For example, some valid tags are given below:

<HTML>
<HEAD>
<BODY>

Each HTML document is divided into two main parts, a head and a body, as shown in Fig. 8.42.

The head contains information to identify the page, while the body contains the actual information to be displayed.

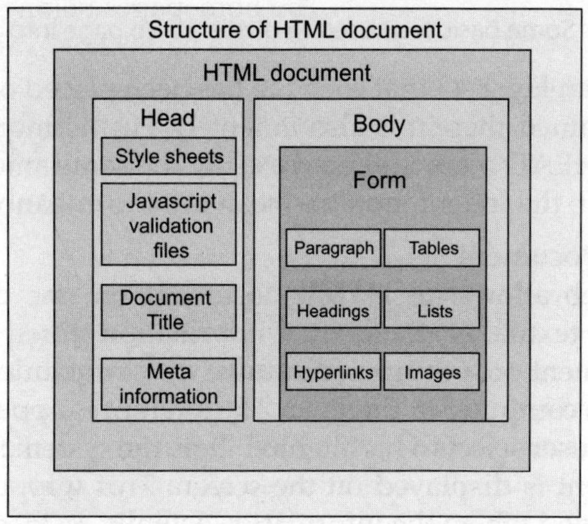

Fig. 8.42 Structure of HTML document

An author uses tags to tell the browser which part of the page corresponds to the heading and which part corresponds to the body. As discussed earlier, the tag uses less than (<) and greater than (>) characters to bracket the name of the tag in pairs, with one of the pair being used to start the section and another being used to close it. Both tags in a pair have the same name except that the closing tag includes a slash(/) before the name. For example, the following pair of tags bracket the heading.

<HEAD> and </HEAD>

Similarly the following pair of tags bracket the body.

<BODY> and </BODY>

Another example of paired tags appears inside a heading, where the pair of tag <TITLE> and </TITLE> bracket the document title.

Fig. 8.43 illustrates the arrangement of paired tags in a typical web page. Of course, the browser does not display the tags. In fact the tags are browser directives to control the display of information on the screen.

```
<HTML>
      <HEAD>
      Format document title goes here...
             <TITLE>
             Additional heading information, if needed
             </TITLE>
      </HEAD>
<BODY>
      Actual information to be displayed on the page
</BODY>
```

Fig. 8.43 Some basic tags used to divide a web page into a heading.

It may be noted from Fig. 8.43 that each tag has been placed on a separate line and the information contained therein is also indented. Furthermore, pairs of tags such as <HEAD> and </HEAD> are indented exactly the same amount. Though HTML uses free format input, the indentation has been used to enhance readability.

Links in an HTML Document

The World Wide Web allows an HTML document on one computer to include hyperlinks to refer to textual or non-textual information stored on other computers. For example, a document on a computer in India may contain a reference to another document stored on a computer in England. The references appear highlighted in the document. When the user selects a highlighted item, the system follows the reference. The referred document is displayed on the screen. This way, the user browses the WWW without knowing where the information actually resides.

In fact, to make it possible for an individual to record the location of a document, the World Wide Web assigns each page of information a unique identifier called a

Uniform Resource Locator (URL). A URL can be precisely defined as: A uniform resource locator consists of a short character string that identifies a particular multimedia document or resource. Given a valid URL, a browser can go directly to the referred page. For example the following URL refers to the home page of rediffmail, the popular free email server.

www.rediffmail.com

Each URL contains the following information:

1. Name of the protocol for accessing the server that contains the required document.
2. Domain name of the remote computer on which the server is running.
3. Name of the document/resource being requested from the server.

Fig. 8.44 illustrates how the URL encodes the information.

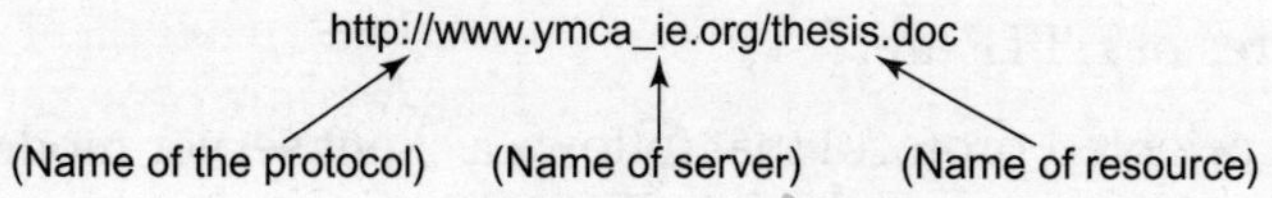

Fig. 8.44 URL format

The first part of the URL specifies an access protocol that tells the browser how to contact the remote server. The domain name of the computer on which the server runs follows the colon after two slashes. Finally a slash is used to separate the computer name from the suffix that identifies a specific item.

It may be noted that that the URL mechanism contains an identifier for a service as well as the name of a computer on which the service operates. For instance, a URL that begins with the string 'http' refers to the www service that clients use when they retrieve a standard web document. Similarly, a URL that begins with the string 'ftp' refers to a file accessible through FTP service.

When a user enters a URL in the interface, the browser extracts the prefix of the URL that specifies the service and accordingly chooses the appropriate client to get the service. The client is thereafter invoked to obtain the specified item (see Fig. 8.45) and displays the result for the user.

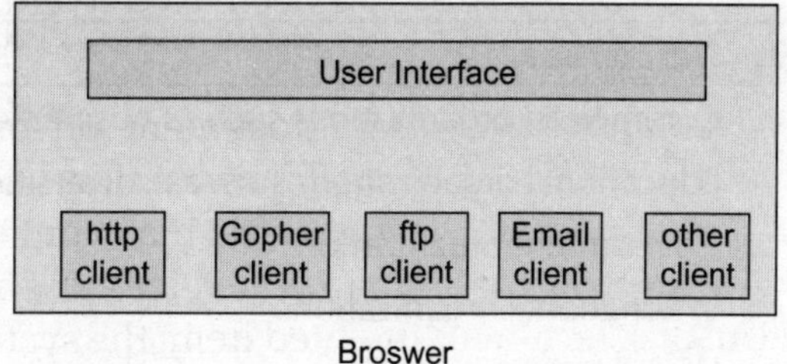

Fig. 8.45 Conceptual organization of a browser

For instance when a URL specifies that a file can be obtained via FTP, the browser uses the FTP client to retrieve the file.

8.14.2 Hypertext Transfer Protocol (HTTP)

This protocol is used to transfer hypertext documents across the internet. A client makes a request for a particular document. The URL of the document is sent to the Web server. The web server uses HTTP (Hypertext Transfer Protocol) to serve web documents to the requesting HTTP client as shown in Fig. 8.46.

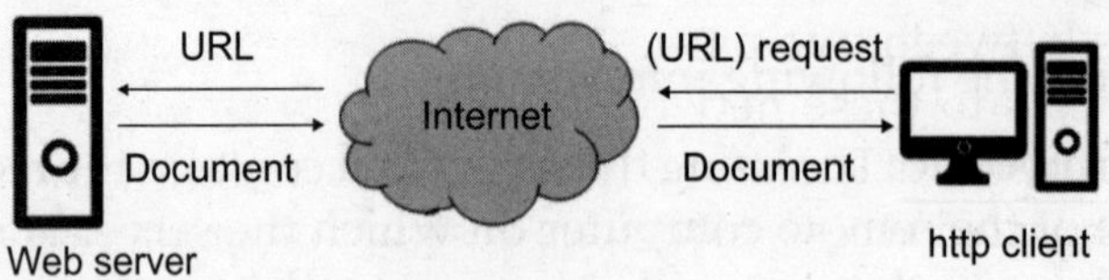

Fig. 8.46 Client server model

The main features of HTTP are:

- It is an object oriented protocol that follows a client server model of the Internet.
- It works within the framework of the TCP/IP protocol suite
- It is a stateless protocol i.e., each HTTP request/response is an independent activity. No session information is retained.
- It is a request-response protocol.
- It uses port number 80.

8.14.3 Domain Names

The internet is a huge repository of resources such as computers, servers, networks, network services, hypertext documents, multimedia objects. For the purpose of identification, each internet resource is provided a domain name.

These resources are generally housed on organizational servers. Based on their field of activity, organizations are grouped into separate groups such as commercial or educational organizations. Each group is assigned a three-character domain label such as 'com', 'edu' and 'gov', as listed in Table 8.5.

Table 8.5 The three-character organization domains

Domain	Description
com	Commercial organizations such as businesses
edu	Educational organizations such as universities
gov	Government organizations
int	International organizations
mil	US military organizations
net	A network that doesn't fit in any category
org	An organization that does not fit in any category

8.15 NETWORK SECURITY

The internet allows users to access large amounts of information on a single click. Internet shopping, trading, chatting, mailing etc. has long prevailed, yet users feel insecure over the network. They feel that there is a higher chance of being cheated over the network as the person on the other side, mostly being anonymous, may be someone with malicious intentions.

As an email travels between two parties, it crosses many networks. Anyone with sufficient skill and access to these networks can read these messages and may use them for fraudulent purposes. Therefore, transactions across the internet need to be protected from unauthorized access, malicious destruction or alteration etc. Similarly, it is vital to protect the individual users and organizations from unauthorized intruders in the system.

8.15.1 Network Security Concepts

The various important concepts regarding network security are discussed below:

8.15.1.1 Firewalls

A firewall is a software or hardware that protects a computer network or individual computers connected to the Internet. The firewall filters the information coming from the Internet to the network or a computer.

The network administrator can frame certain security rules to protect the network. The firewall implements those rules. Consider the following rule

"Do not allow Telnet service to a group of users: G4"

The firewall can use the above rule to deny G4 group the Telnet service on the system. A firewall can use any of the following methods to filter the information:

- **Packet filtering**: It analyses the data stored in the incoming and outgoing packets.
- **Proxy service**: The information is received in firewall and sent to the proxy server. The information is not directly sent to the requester.
- **IP address blocking**: The data from a particular IP address or domain name can be very easily blocked by a firewall.
- **Protocol blocking**: The firewall can be set to disallow a particular protocol service to a particular user or a group of users.
- **Port blocking:** Generally, HTTP and FTP services are available through Port 80 and Port 21 respectively. The firewall can be used to block a particular port.

In addition to the above, the firewall can be used to block specific words and phrases through its packet filtering service. This is useful for blocking unwanted sites.

A firewall can also be used to protect a user from the following:

1. Remote login by others
2. Application backdoors
3. SMTP session hijacking
4. e-mail bombs
5. Viruses and macros
6. Spam i.e., junk mail etc.

Examples of Firewalls available in the market are: Comodofirewall, Ashampoo firewall, CISCO Firewall 501, NetGear FV5318, DLink DFL 300 etc.

8.15.1.2 Cookies

A cookie is a piece of text that a website stores on a user's hard disk. The information is stored in the form of a name value pair. On a Windows platform, the cookies are generally stored in the directory called C:\Windows\Cookies. Most websites store a user id in their cookies file whereas some web sites store an id for each session of user interaction with the website. The state information of the session is used later in the website.

A cookie works in the following fashion:

1. When a user types a URL of a web site (say www.hotmail.com) on the web browser, the browser contacts the DNS server to get the IP address. The browser looks for the cookies in the hard disk.
2. The IP address is used to contact the corresponding server along with cookies data.
3. If no cookies data is supplied, then the website comes to know that the user is visiting the site first time. The server creates an Id of the user and stores it as a cookie on the hard disk of the user.

The state information stored by the website is used to get the following information:

- How many visitors have visited the site.
- How many are new visitors.
- How many are repeated visitors.
- What the frequency of a particular visitor is.
- What the preference of a particular visitor is, so that the site can customize its interface as per the user's choice. In fact, e-commerce sites use cookies information to take the user to a particular shop or a shopping item. However, some sites use cookies to collect data about the users and sell it to other websites, which is illegal.

Note: The browsers can be set to disable cookies.

8.15.1.3 Hackers and Crackers

A hacker is a computer programmer who is enthusiastic to build something. In fact, hackers have built the Internet, the present day LINUX and UNIX operating systems, USENET etc. Even USENET is being run by hackers. Hackers solve problems and build things and offer multi-net help to each other. They solve problems of their peers and give solutions so that the information could be shared with other hackers. HTML, XHTML, Python etc. are good programming languages for hackers.

A cracker on the other hand is a programmer who wants to break things such as

- crack the password of somebody
- break into/read/monitor someone else's email
- steal channel privileges.

8.15.2 Principles of Data Security

The principles of data security are discussed in the following text.

1. **The data must be protected throughout its life cycle:** If some data is very important than it should be provided protection from unauthorized users. Generally, many layers of security are formed around sensitive data, as shown in Fig. 8.47.

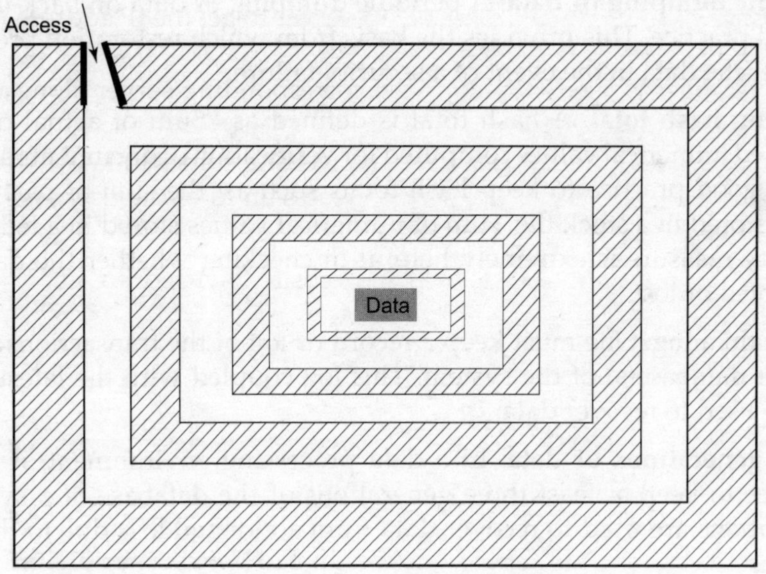

Fig. 8.47 Onion-like security layers

2. **The cost of data security must be less than the cost of data:** The value of the data decides the type of security it needs. For example, if the data is of national

importance then it is placed inside the innermost layer of security else it may be placed in appropriate upper layers.

3. **The system should be guarded against natural disasters**: The computer system should be guarded against floods, earthquakes etc. For example, if the computer centre is near a river then it must not be situated on the ground floor.

4. **Recovery procedures as part of the security**: In the event of a mishap, there must be some plan or procedure to recover the data. For example, the system must have elaborate procedures to allow recovery from lost passwords. Similarly, a RAID (Redundant Array of Independent Disks) installation can provide the desired data recovery mechanism in the event of a hard disk failure.

8.15.3 Preventive Maintenance and Trouble Shooting

Absolute security is unattainable. Very high degrees of software and hardware security tools are commercially available. When evaluating various approaches, consider how much security you really need. In many cases, a simple power-on password may be sufficient. Besides the password control, the system must use the following maintenance procedures.

1. **Periodic dumping of data**: A periodic dumping of data on back-up devices is a good practice. This provides the basis from which restoration procedures can recover the data in the event of a security failure.

2. **Keeping hash total**: A hash total is defined as "Sum of actual or arbitrarily assigned numerical values computed for verification of documents and records." It is a good practice to keep hash totals such as: the sum of part numbers of items stored in a stock file, sum of numerical values stored in a ledger etc. This security measure is extremely helpful in checking whether the data has been corrupted or lost.

3. **Maintain a log**: One must keep a record or log of the transactions made in the files or database(s) of the system. This log coupled with the latest data dump can be used to recover data.

4. **Keep generations of data:** In a data processing environment, it is a general practice to keep at least three generations of the database of a system. These generations are used to recover data from accidental loss due to the following reasons:
   - Data crashes during transaction processing
   - Anomalies caused by concurrent access to the database
   - Violation of some assumptions caused by a logical error.

Troubleshooting is an activity that comes into play when some data loss has occurred. It involves the following actions:

- Consult the procedure laid down for such an eventuality.
- Contact the designated person and bring the event to his/her notice.
- The authorized person should activate the recovery process.

8.15.4 Concept of Security and Related Terms

Before a system is made secure, it is important to evaluate the risk. If the risk is mainly from outsiders, then physical-access control may be most useful. If it is from insiders, then **user trails** can be a powerful tool. The basic security model for a computer system resembles an onion (see Fig. 8.49). Layers of security surround the data that needs to be secured. Each layer insulates the data and makes it more difficult to access in any way other than those planned for. Physical security is the outermost layer. It prevents access to the hardware. The inner layers of security are concerned with logical security or the methods that cover control of access to the system resources and services. Some of the important terms related to system security are discussed below:

1. **Secrecy**: Hiding some relevant information from unauthorized users is called Secrecy. This can be achieved by cryptography which is defined as the art of devising ciphers. A cipher is a coded form of plain text. In fact the cipher text is transferred over networks.
2. **Privacy**: Sensitive data kept in a system not for general or public use is called private data.
3. **Authentication**: This activity deals with determining the identity of the user before sensitive data is revealed to the him/her. In a network, authentication is the technique by which a process verifies that its communication partner is a valid user. Verifying the identity of a remote user is a difficult task especially as the network may be subject to various kinds of malicious attacks.
4. **Authorization**: It is an act of giving authority to an authenticated user of the system. The authorized user becomes a legal user of the system resources for the use of which he has permission.
5. **Password protection**: A password protected system allows access to resources based upon a secret word entered by the user. However, most of the advanced operating systems allow access to resources based upon user identity or group membership, rather than requiring a password. Such operating systems control access to every type of resource.
6. **File permissions**: We know that an advanced operating systems can control access to every type of resource. Since a file is one of the most important resources on a system, the operating system provides access control to each and every file present in the system. Each file has an access control list attribute that describes which authenticated user or group accounts have what type of access to the file, as shown in Fig. 8.48.

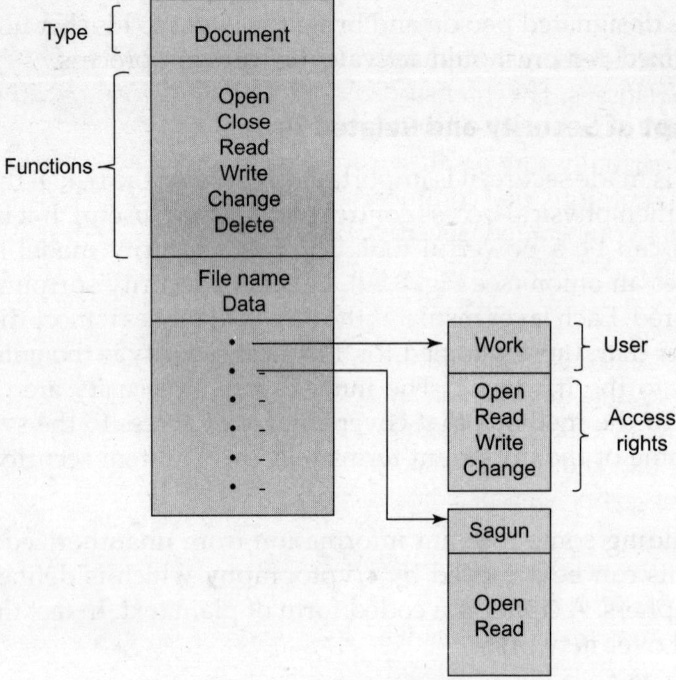

Fig. 8.48 Access control entries for a file

8.15.4.1 Cyber Law

The laws that govern cyber space are known as Cyber law. Cyber space encompasses the following entities:

a) Computers
b) Computer Networks
c) Internet
d) Data
e) Software

Cyber law further consists of the following laws

a) Electronic and Digital Signature Law
b) Computer Crime Law
c) Intellectual property law (Copyright law, Trademark law, Patent law etc.)
d) Data protection and privacy law.
e) Telecommunication laws.

The idea of data security is not new. In fact, security is a pervasive concern. In our day-to-day life, we provide an ignition lock to our car, a dead bolt on the door, and present an ATM card on a bank's automatic teller machine. These are all nothing but access control measures.

Data security is provided in a system against loss of any nature including accidental as well as intentional losses. The intensity with which you choose to protect your data may depend on what you perceive its value to be. Today, when access to computer data is simple and virtually universal, sensitive information may be as easy to steal as copying a disk. Therefore, use common sense and as many preventive measures as you can to protect your valued, sensitive data.

EXERCISES

1. What is the purpose of data communication devices and how is data transmitted?
2. Explain the various data transmission modes used in data communication.
3. Differentiate between guided and unguided transmission media.
4. Explain the three data transmission modes in brief.
5. What are the basic components of a data communication system?
6. What is data highway?
7. Write an explanatory note on communication channels.
8. What is meant by baud rating?
9. Why are modems used in data communication systems?
10. What is meant by modulation? Explain the various types of modulation techniques used in data communication.
11. What are the popular multiplexing techniques?
12. What is meant by multiplexing? Differentiate between a multiplexer and a repeater.
13. What is a computer network?
14. Write an explanatory note on network topology.
15. Define the term network topology.
16. What are the advantages and limitations of a linear bus topology?
17. What are the advantages and limitations of a ring topology?
18. What is an OSI model? Explain its seven layers in brief.
19. How is WAN different from LAN? Explain ERNET with the help of a diagram.
20. Write an explanatory note on distributed systems.
21. Define the term internetworking.
22. What is meant by Internet? How it is related to ARPANet?
23. What is the purpose of Internet protocol in the context of internetworking?
24. What is the purpose of TCP in the context of internetworking?
25. Explain TCP/IP communication architecture in detail with the help of a suitable diagram.
26. What is meant by a Backbone Network? Explain in brief.
27. What is a bridge?
28. What is a router?
29. What is a gateway?

30. List the various connectors used in the interconnection of networks. Explain each connector in brief.
31. Write a note on the client-server model of computing.
32. Explain the following terms:
    a) FTP
    b) TELNET
    c) NFS
33. What is meant by a Home page? Write few lines about the utility of a Home page.
34. Draw a conceptual organization of a browser.
35. What is an HTML document? Draw the structure of such a document.
36. Define the terms: fire wall, hacker, cookie, DNS.
37. Differentiate between authorization and authentication.
38. Differentiate between the terms: privacy and secrecy.
39. Explain the terms: Preventive maintenance and troubleshooting.
40. Write short notes on the following:
    - SM
    - WLL
    - CDMA
    - SMS
    - e-mail
    - Chat.

Part II

Programming in C

CHAPTER

9 Introduction to C

9.1 THE HISTORY

For the development of UNIX, a large and complex operating system, Dennis Ritchie of Bell laboratories developed in 1971-72, a language called 'C'. Later, American National Standard Institute (ANSI) standardized the C language in 1989 and termed it 'ANSI C'. Therefore, some programmers also refer to standard C as 'C89'. Though other standards such as 'C90', 'C99' with more powerful features are also available, ANCI C is more widely used because ANSI C programs are portable.

C is a high-level language that not only supports the basic data types and data structures needed by a normal programmer but can also be used to access the computer hardware through specially designed declarations and functions. It is popular because of the following characteristics:

1. Small size
2. Wide use of functions and function calls
3. Loose typing
4. Bitwise low-level programming support
5. Structured language
6. Wide use of pointers to access data structures and physical memory of the system.

Besides the above characteristics, C programs are small and efficient. A C program can be compiled on a variety of computers. Generally, the C compiler is an integrated development environment (IDE) having the following components:

1. User-configured editor
2. Project-oriented Make process
3. A fast linker
4. An extremely fast C compiler

C also supports the development of Interrupt Service Routines (IRS) and memory resident programs. It is an excellent programming environment for **system**

programming and no wonder that it is used to write system programs such as compilers, interpreters, operating systems etc. In fact some of the compilers of C are also written in C.

It may be noted that since C has both high level and low level features, it is often called a *middle-level* language.

Before we take up detailed discussions on C, let us have a look at its fundamentals, in the following sections.

9.2 CHARACTERS USED IN C

The set of characters allowed in C consists of alphabets, digits, and special characters, as listed below:

(i) Letters: Both uppercase and lowercase letters of English:
A, B, C, ... X, Y, and Z
a, b, c, ... x, y, and z

(ii) Decimal Digits:
0, 1, 2, ... 7, 8, 9

(iii) Special characters:
! * + \ " <
(= ! { >
%) ; " /
^_[: , ?
& -] ' . blank

9.3 DATA TYPES

The world is passing through an important phase in the use of Information technology (IT). ***IT** is an umbrella term comprising technologies related to computers, communication, and problem-solving. Computers generate, store, and process data. Communication technologies transport the data. Experts use these technologies and the know-how to solve the problems at hand.* So data is an important part of the world in general and the IT industry in particular.

A worthwhile program specifies a set of operations to be performed on some data in a particular sequence. However, the data can be of many types such as a numbers, characters, floating points etc. C supports the following simple data types:

9.3.1 Integer Data Type

An integer is an integral whole number without a decimal point. These numbers are used for counting. Examples of integers are: 536, 5, and 12983 etc.

C allows the following four types of representations of integers: integer, long integer, short integer, and unsigned integer.

Integer: An integer is referred to as *int*. It is stored in one word of the memory.

Long integer: A long integer is referred to as *long int* or simply *long*. It is stored in 32 bits and does not depend upon the word size of the memory.

Short integer: A short integer is referred to as *short int* or simple *short*. It is stored in 16 bits and does not depend upon the size of the memory.

Unsigned integers: C supports two types of unsigned integers: the *unsigned int* and the *unsigned short*. The unsigned int is stored in one word of the memory whereas the unsigned short is stored in 16 bits and does not depend upon the word size of the memory.

Examples of invalid integers are:

Invalid integer	Remarks
12,786	illegal-comma used
8,94	illegal decimal point used
67 89	blank used

9.3.2 The Character Data Type (char)

It is a non-numeric data type consisting of single alphanumeric character enclosed between a pair of apostrophes or single quotation marks.

Examples of valid character data type are:

'S'
'n'
'*'
'8'

It may be noted that the character '8' is different from the numeric value 8. In fact, the former is of type char and the latter of type int. Each character has a numeric code called the ASCII code. For instance the ASCII code for the character 'A' is 65 and that for '*' is 42. A table of ASCII codes is given in Table 4.11.

A character data type is referred to as *char*. It is stored in one byte of the memory. However, the representation varies from computer to computer. For instance, some computers support signed as well as unsigned characters. Signed characters can store integer values from -128 to +127 whereas unsigned characters can store ASCII codes from 0 to 255.

9.3.3 The Floating Point (float) Data Type

A floating point number is a real number which can be represented in two forms: decimal and exponent forms. Floating point numbers are generally used for measuring quantities.

Decimal Form

The floating point number in this form has a decimal point. Even if it is an integral value, it must include the decimal point.

Examples of valid 'decimal form' numbers are:

973.24
849.
73.0
82349.24
9.0004

Exponent Form

The exponent form of a floating point number consists of the following parts:

<integer>.<fraction> e <exponent>

Examples of valid floating point numbers are:

243.034
0.249 e-6
456.004 e12

It may be noted that the exponent form is a scientific notation wherein the number is broken into two parts: *mantissa* and an *exponent*. The mantissa is a floating point number of decimal form. The exponent part starts with a letter 'e' followed by an integer (signed or unsigned).

For example, the number 324.5 can be written as 3.245×10^2. In exponential form the number is represented as: 3.245 e2. It may be noted that the base 10 has been replaced by the character e (or E).

The utility of the exponential form is that very small numbers can be represented easily by this notation of floating points.

For example, the number 0.00001297 can be written as 0.1297 e-4 or as 12.97 e-6 or as 129.7 e-7. C allows the following two data types for floating points.

1. **float**:These numbers are stored in 32 bits of memory.
2. **double**: These numbers are stored in 64 bits of memory.

A summary of the C basic data types is given the Table 9.1. From this table, it may be observed that character and integer type data can also be declared as unsigned. Such data types are called unsigned data types. In this representation, the data is always a positive number with a range starting from 0 to a maximum value. Thus, a number twice as big as a signed number can be represented through unsigned data types.

Table 9.1 'C' basic data types

C Data Type	Size	Lower bound	Upper bound	Represents
Char	1	−128	127	Character
Unsigned Char	1	0	255	Character
Short (int)	2	−32768	+32767	Whole number
Unsigned Short int	2	0	65535	Whole number
Long int	4	2,147,438,648	2,141,438,647	Whole number
float	4	−3.4x10 ±38	+3.4x10 ±38	Real number
double	8	−1.7x10 ±308	+1.7x10 ±308	Real number

9.4 C TOKENS

A token is a group of characters that logically belong together. A programmer can write a program by using tokens. C supports the following types of tokens:

- Identifiers
- Keywords
- Constants
- Variables

9.4.1 Identifiers

Identifiers are symbolic names used for defining data items in a program. For example, if a programmer desires to store a value 27, then he can choose any symbolic name (say `ROLL`) and use it as given below:

`ROLL` = 27;

where `ROLL` is a memory location and the symbol '=' is an assignment operator.

The significance of the above statement is that `ROLL` is an identifier for a memory location where the value 27 is being stored.

An identifier is a sequence of characters taken from the C character set. The number of characters in an identifier is not fixed, though most C compilers allow 31 characters. The rules for the formation of an identifier are:

1. An identifier can consist of alphabets, digits and and/or underscores.
2. It must not start with a digit.
3. C is case sensitive, i.e., uppercase and lowercase letters are considered different from each other.

4. An identifier can start with an underscore character, although this is discouraged since some special C names begin with the underscore.
5. Special characters such as blank space, comma, semicolon, colon, period, slash etc. are not allowed.
6. The name of an identifier should be so chosen that its usage and meaning becomes clear. For example, `total`, `salary`, `rollno` etc. are self explanatory identifiers.

Examples of acceptable identifiers are:

```
TOTAL
Sum
Net_sal
P123
a_b_c
total
_sysreg
```

Example of unacceptable identifiers are: `Ba sic` (blank not allowed)
`H, rent` (special character ',' included)
It may be noted here that `TOTAL` and `total` are two different identifier names.

9.4.2 Keywords

A keyword is a reserved word of C. This cannot be used as an identifier by the user in a program. The set of C keywords is given in Table 9.2.

Table 9.2 Standard Keywords

auto	double	int	struct
break	else	long	switch
case	enum	register	typedef
char	extern	return	union
const	float	short	unsigned
continue	for	signed	void
default	goto	sizeof	volatile
do	if	static	while

9.4.3 Variables

A variable is the most fundamental element of any computer language. It is a location in the computer memory which can store data and is given a symbolic name for easy reference. Variables can be used to hold different values at different times during a program run. To understand this concept, let us have a look at the following set of statements:

```
Total  = 500.25;                ...(i)
Net    = Total - 100.00;        ...(ii)
```

In statement (i), a value 500.25 has been stored in a memory location called `Total`. The variable `Total` is being used in statement (ii) for the calculation of another variable `Net`. The point worth noting is that the variable `Total` is used in statement (ii) by its name not by its value.

Before a variable is used in a program, it has to be defined. This activity enables the compiler to make available the appropriate amount of space and location in the memory. The definition of a variable consists of its type followed by the name of the variable. For example, a variable called Total of type float can be declared as shown below:

```
float Total;
```

Similarly the variable `Net` of type int can also be defined as shown below:

```
int Net;
```

Examples of valid variable declarations are:

```
(i)    int count;
(ii)   int i, j. k;
(iii)  char ch, first;
(iv)   float Total, Net;
(iv)   long int sal;
(v)    double salary;
```

Let us now look at a variable declaration from a different perspective. Whenever a variable (say `int val`) is declared, a memory location called val is made available by the compiler as shown in Fig. 9.1.

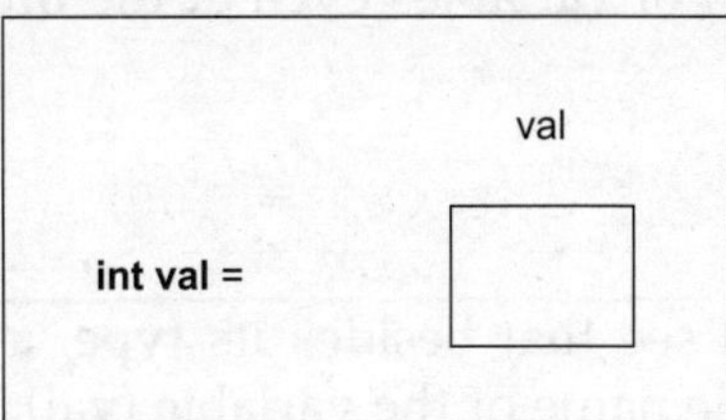

Fig. 9.1 Memory allocated to variable val

Thus, `val` is the name associated by the compiler with a location in the memory of the computer. Let us assume that at the time of execution, the physical address of this memory location (called `val`) is 4715 as shown in Fig. 9.2:

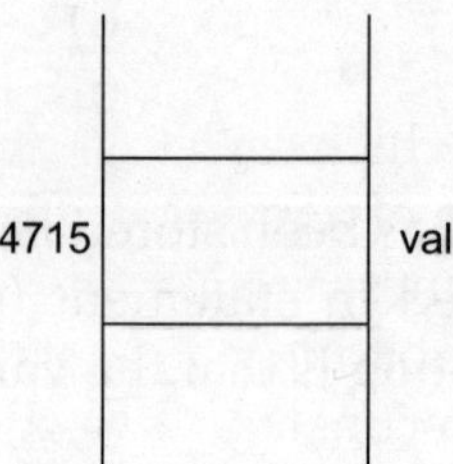

Fig. 9.2 The physical address of `val`

Now, a point worth noting is that this memory location is viewed by the programmer as a variable called `val` and by the computer system as an address 4715. The programmer can store a value in this location with the help of an assignment operator i.e., '='. For example, if the programmer desires to store a value 100 into the variable val, he can do so by the following statement:

```
val = 100;
```

Once the above statement is obeyed, the memory location called `val` gets the value 100 as shown in Fig. 9.3.

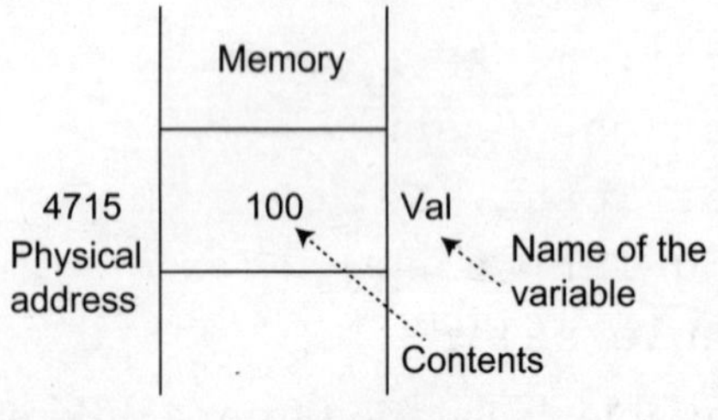

Fig. 9.3

C allows the initialization of variables even at the time of declaration, as shown below:

```
int val = 100;
```

From Figure 9.3, we can see that besides its type, a variable has three entities associated with it, that is, the name of the variable (val), its physical address (4715), and its contents (100). The contents of a variable are also called as its *rvalue* whereas the physical address of the variable is called as its *lvalue*. Thus, lvalue and rvalue of variable val are 4715 and 100 respectively. The lvalue is of greater importance because it is an expression that should appear on the left hand side of assignment operator because it refers to the variable or object.

9.4.4 Constants

A constant is a memory location which can store data in such a manner that its value does not change during execution of a program. Any attempt to change the value of a constant will result in an error message. A constant in C can be of any of the basic data types, i.e., integer constant, floating point constant, and character constant. The const qualifier is used to declare a constant as shown below:

const <type> <name> = <val>;

where

const : is a reserved word of C
<type> : is any of the basic data types
<name> : is the identifier name
<val> : is the value to be assigned to the constant.

Integer constant: This is a constant which can be assigned integer values only. For example, if we desire to have a constant called rate of type integer containing a fixed value 50, then the following declaration can be used:

```
const int rate = 50;
```

The above declaration means that *rate* is a constant of type integer having a fixed value 50. Consider the following declaration:

```
const int rate;
    rate = 50;
```

The above initialization of constant rate is illegal. This is because a constant cannot be initialized for a value at a place other than where it is declared. It may be further noted that if a program does not change or mutate to a constant or constant object then the program is called **const correct**.

Floating point constant: It is a constant which can be assigned values of real or floating point type. For example, if it is desired to have a constant called `Pi` containing value 3.1415, then the following declaration can be used.

```
const float Pi = 3.1415;
```

The above declaration means that `Pi` is a constant of type float having a fixed value 3.1415. It may be noted here, that by default a floating point constant is of type double.

Character constant: A character constant can contain a single character of information. Thus, data such as 'Y' or 'N' is known as a character constant. Let us assume that a constant called `Akshar` is needed, containing the character 'Q'. The following declaration can be used to obtain such a constant.

```
const char Akshar = 'Q';
```

The above declaration means that `Akshar` is a constant of type char having a fixed value `Q'.

A sequence of characters enclosed within quotes is known as a string literal. For example, the character sequence: "computer" is a string literal. When a string literal is assigned to an identifier declared as a constant then it is known as a *string constant*. In fact, a string is an array of characters.

9.5 STRUCTURE OF A C PROGRAM

A simple program in C can be written as a module. More complex programs can be broken into sub-modules. In C all modules or subprograms are referred to as functions.

The structure of a typical C program is given below:

```
main ()
{
    ....;
    ....;
    ....;
}
```

Note:

(i) C is a case sensitive language, i.e., it distinguishes between uppercase and lowercase characters. Thus `main()` is different from `Main()`. In fact, most of the characters used in C are lowercase. Hence, it is safest to type everything in lowercase except when a programmer needs to capitalize some text.

(ii) Every C program has a function called main followed by parentheses. It is from here that program execution begins. A function is basically a subprogram and is complete in itself.

(iii) The task to be performed by a function is enclosed in curly braces called its body i.e. {}. These braces are equivalent to `BEGIN` and `END` keywords used in some other languages like Pascal. The body of a function contains a set of statements and each statement must end with a semicolon.

9.5.1 Our First Program

Let us break the myth that C is a difficult language to start with. Without going into the details, the beginner can quickly start writing the program such as given on the next page.

```
# include <stdio.h>
main()
{
  puts ("This is my first program");
}
```

The above program displays the following text on the screen:

```
This is my first program.
```

The program has five lines. The explanation of each line is given below.

Line 1 `#include < stdio.h>`: This statement has been placed at the top of the program. It directs the complier to include a header file called `stdio.h`. The file `studio.h` is needed for input/output requirements of the program. A detailed discussion on header files is given later in the book.

2. `main ():` This statement defines main () as the first function to be executed in any C program.

3. `{ :` The beginning of the body of the main () function.

4. `puts("This is my first program"):` A function called *puts()* has been used to display the string "`This is my first program`" on the screen. In fact any text written within quotes is displayed by `puts()` on the screen. For instance change the text to "I Love India" and run the program. As expected the following text is displayed on the screen.

```
I Love India.
```

It may be noted that this is an executable statement. The `;' at the end of the statement is called the **statement terminator**. It indicates the end of a statement.

5. }: Marks the end of the body of the function.

It may be noted that a function called *puts()* was used to display the message: "`This is my first program`", a piece of text, on the screen. Let us now use another useful function called `getchar()`, that reads a character input by the user through the keyboard. However, the character read by this function has to be stored in a variable of type char (say `ch`) as shown below:

```
char ch;          ...(i)
ch = getchar (); ...(ii)
```

Statement (i) defines a variable ch of type char whereas the statement (ii) reads a character from the keyboard and stores it into ch. Similar to getchar(), there is another function called putchar() that can be used to display a character on the screen, as shown below:

```
char ch
ch = `X';
putchar (ch);
```

The above set of statements defines a variable ch of type character, stores the character 'X' into ch, and displays the character on the screen.

Example 1

Write a program that reads a character input by a user from the keyboard and displays it on the screen.

Solution:

The puts(), getchar(), and putchar() functions will be used to do the required task. The required program is given below:

```
# include <stdio.h>
main()
  { char ch;
    puts("Enter a Character");
    ch = gatchar();
    puts ("The char typed by you is : ");
    putchar (ch);
  }
```

It may noted that the above program has been designed as interactive in the sense that it displays appropriate messages to the user. The user can read the messages and input the data accordingly. This type of design of a program is called a user-centric design.

The input-output functions discussed above can read and display data of char type only. The general functions that can read and display any type of data are discussed in the next section.

9.6 THE printf() AND scanf() FUNCTIONS

C uses printf() and scanf() functions to write and read respectively, from I/O devices. These functions have been declared in the header file called stdio.h.

Let us use the printf() function to rewrite our first program. The modified program is given below:

```
# include <stdio.h>
main()
   {
     printf ("This is my first program");
   }
```

This program displays the following message on the screen:

```
This is my first program.
```

In fact, any text written within the pair of quotes (" ") is displayed as such by the printf() function, on the screen. However, this functions is much more powerful than puts() in the sense that it can display all types of data on the screen as explained in the following text.

9.6.1 How to Display Data Using printf()

An integer stored in a variable can be displayed on the screen by including a format specifier (% d) within a pair of quotes as shown below:

```
# include  <stdio.h>
void main ()
{
   int age = 25;
   printf (" %d", age);
}
```

The above program does the following:

1. declare a variable age of type int
2. initialize age to 25, an integer value,
3. specify %d, a format specifier indicating that an integer is to be displayed by printf(). The data is stored in the variable called age.
4. It may be noted that printf () has two arguments separated by a comma i.e., a format specifier written within quotes and the variable, age. It may further be noted that both messages and format specifiers can be included within the pair of quotes as shown below:

```
printf (" The age of student = %d", age);
```

The above statement would display the following message and data on the screen.

```
The age of student = 25
```

Thus, the text between the quotes has been displayed as such, but for %d, the data stored in the variable age has been displayed.

A float can be displayed on the screen by including a format specifier (%f) within a pair of quotes, as shown below:

```
float rate = 9.5;
printf ("The rate of provident fund = %f", rate);
```

The above of statements would produce the following display.

```
The rate of provident fund = 9.5
```

A char can be displayed by including a format specifier (%c) within the pair of quotes, as shown below:

```
char ch = 'A'
printf ("The first alphabet is : %c", ch);
```

Obviously the output of the above set of statements would be:

```
The first alphabet is : A.
```

The other specifiers which can be used in the `printf ()` function are given in Appendix A

9.6.2 How to Read Data from the Keyboard Using `scanf ()`

Similar to the `printf ()` function, the `scanf ()` function also uses the %d, %f, %c, and other format specifiers to specify the kind of data to be read from the keyboard. However, it expects the programmer to prefix the address operator '&' to every variable written in the argument list as shown below:

```
int roll;
scanf ("%d", &roll);
```

The above set of statements declares a variable called `roll` of type int, and reads the value for `roll` from the keyboard. It may be noted that the address operator ('&') has been prefixed to the variable `roll`. The reason for specifying `&' would be discussed later in the book.

Example 2

Write an interactive program that reads the marks secured by a student for four subjects Sub1, Sub2, Sub3, and Sub4, the maximum marks for a subject being 100. The program shall compute the percentage of marks obtained by the student.

Solution:

The `scanf ()` and `prinf ()` functions would be used to do the required task. The required program is given below:

```
# include <stdio.h>
main()
  {
   int sub1, sub2, sub3, sub4;
   float percent;
   printf ("Enter the marks for four subjects:");
   scanf ("%d %d %d %d",&sub1, &sub2, &sub3, &sub4);
   percent = (sub1+ sub2 + sub3 + sub4)/ 400.00* 100;
   printf("The percentage = %f", percent);
  }
```

For input data: 45 56 76 90, the above program computes the percentage and displays the following output.

```
The percentage = 66.750000
```

Though the output is correct, it has unnecessarily displayed four trailing zeros. This can be controlled by using field width specifiers, discussed later in the book.

9.7 COMMENTS

A comment can be added to the program by enclosing the text between the pair: `/* .. */`. Where the character pair `/*` indicates the beginning of the comment and the pair `*/` marks the end of it. It is also known as multiple line comment. For example, the following line is a comment:

```
/* This is my first program */
```

Everything written within '/*' and '* /' is ignored by the compiler. A comment written in this fashion can overflow to multiple lines, as shown below:

```
/*This is an illustration of a multiple line comment.
The C compiler ignores these lines. A programmer
```

```
can use comment lines for documentation of his/her
programs */
```

In fact, a comment is a non executable statement in the program. To start with, let us now write a trivial program:

Example 3

Write a C program that displays the message 'Enter an integer value on the screen'. It reads the value in a variable called `val` and displays it on the screen with the message

`The value entered by you =` .

Solution:

Suitable string constants would be used to display the messages. The integer value would be read into the variable `val` by the `scanf` statement and the output displayed by the `printf` statement. The required program is given below:

```
/* This program demonstrates the usage of comments as
  a documentation tool */

# include <stdio.h>
main()
 {
 int val; /* declaration of a variable val */

 printf("Enter an integer value: ");
 scanf ("%d", &val);
 printf ("The value entered by you =%d", val);

 }        /* End of program */
```

Example 4

Write a C program that reads two values `A` and `B`, exchanges their contents and prints the output.

Solution:

Let us assume that `A` and `B` are of type int. In order to properly exchange the contents of these variables, we will use a third variable called `temp` of type int as a temporary location. The program is given below:

```
/* This program exchanges the contents of two variables */
# include <stdio.h>
```

```
main()
   {
     int A, B; /* the two variables */
     int temp; /* the temporary variable */

     printf ("Enter the values of A & B");
     scanf ("%d %d", &A, &B);

                  /*  exchange the contents of A & B  */
     temp = A;
     A = B;
     B = temp;
                  /* display the exchanged contents */
     printf (" The exchanged contents are %d & %d", A, B);

   }
```

Sample Input : `Enter the values of A & B  -    35 & 18`
Sample Output: `The exchanged contents are -    18 & 35`

9.8 ESCAPE SEQUENCE (BACKSLASH CHARACTER CONSTANTS)

C has some special character constants called backslash character constants. These are unprintable ASCII characters which can perform special functions in the output statements. A backslash character constant is a backslash ('\') character followed by another character.

For example, "\n" can be used in a `printf ()` statement to send the next output to the beginning of the next line.

Consider the following program:

```
# include <stdio.h>
main()
   {
    printf(" A backslash character constant");
    printf(" prints the output on the next line");
   }
```

The output of this program would be:

```
A backslash character constant prints the output on the next
line.
```

It may be noted that though two separate printf () statements were written in the above program, the output has been displayed on the same line. In order to display the text in two lines, the "\n" character constant should be placed either at the end of the text in the first printf () statement or at the beginning of the text in the second printf () statement.

Consider the following modified program:

```
# include  <  stdio.h>
main()
{
      printf(" A backslash character constant");
      printf(" \n prints the output on the next line");
}
```

The character constant "\n" has been placed at the beginning of the text of the second printf () statement and therefore the output of the program would be:

```
A back slash character constant
prints the output on the next line.
```

Some other important backslash constants are listed below:

Meaning	Backslash character constant
tab	\t
backspace	\b
bell (alert)	\a
newline character	\n

Note: The backslash characters are also known as escape sequences. Such characters can be used within apostrophes or within double quotes.

A brief discussion on these backslash characters follows:

1. '\t' (tab)

This character is called a tab character. Whenever it is inserted in an output statement, the display moves over to the next present tab stop. Generally a tab is of 8 blank spaces on the screen. An example of the usage of character '\t' is given below:

```
# include <stdio.h>
main()
{
printf("\n hello \t Comp-Boy");

}
```

The output of the above statement would be on a new line with spacing as shown below:

```
hello                    Comp-Boy
```

2. '\b' (Backspace)

This character is also called the backspace character. It is equivalent to the backspace key available on the computer or typewriter. It moves one column backward and positions the cursor on the character displayed on that column. An example of the usage of character '\b' is given below:

```
# include <stdio.h>
main()
  {
  printf("\n ASHOKA\b?");

  }
```

The output of the above statement would be :

```
ASHOK?
```

We can see that the trailing letter 'A' has been overwritten by the character '?' at the end of the string constant `ASHOKA`, the reason being:

- '\b' moved the curser one column backward, i.e., at 'A'
- `printf()` printed the character '?' on that column position.

3. '\a' (Alert)

This character is also called an alert or bell character. Whenever it is inserted in an output statement, it sounds a bell which can be heard by the user sitting at the computer terminal. It can be used in a situation where the programmer wants to catch the attention of the user of the program. An example of the usage of '\a' character is given below:

```
# include <stdio.h>
main()
 {
 printf("\n Error in data \a");

 }
```

The output of the above statement would be the following message on the screen and the sounding of a bell on the system speaker.

```
Error in data
```

4. '\n' (new line)

As discussed earlier, this character is called the newline character. Wherever it appears in the output statement, the immediate next output is taken to the beginning of the next new line on the screen.

Consider the statement given below:

```
# include <stdio.h>
main()
 {
  printf("\n This is \n a test");

 }
```

The output of this statement would be:

```
This is
a test
```

Note: A table of the complete set of escape sequences is given in Appendix H.

9.10 USE OF AN EDITOR

A C program can be created on DOS by using any of the available editors such as: NE, Wordstar etc. The Turbo C compiler is an integrated program development environment (IDE). It contains an editor, compiler, and linker. In a Unix environment, vi editor can be used, whereas in a Windows environment, Notepad, can be used to write a program. If you are using Turbo C then the program can be created by using its own editor.

FREQUENTLY ASKED QUESTIONS

1. Differentiate between an identifier and a keyword.
   Solution: An identifier is a sequence of letters and digits with a restriction that the first character has to be a letter or an underscore. It is a user defined name required for the purpose of assigning names to various data used by a programmer in a program. Thus, every identifier in a program must have a type. However, some identifiers called keywords are reserved for the C language. These keywords cannot be used by a programmer as identifiers in a program. Thus, every keyword is inherently an identifier.
2. Differentiate between a character constant and a string literal or constant.
   Solution: A single letter enclosed within apostrophes is known as a character constant. On the other hand, a character or a sequence of characters (string) enclosed within double quotes is known as a string constant or literal. For example : 'I' is a character constant and "I" is a string constant.
3. Can we consider char as an integer data type? If yes, why?

Solution: Yes, char can be treated as an integer data type in the sense that at memory level it is stored as one byte which is the same size as short integer data type. Interestingly both are interchangeable for all practical purposes. Consider the following set of statements:

```
char ch = 'A';
char ch = 65;
```

Both the statements are equivalent because the ASCII equivalent of character constant 'A' is 65 (see Appendix G).

4. What do the file extensions `.c`, `.obj` and `.exe` stand for and when are they created?
   Solution:
   (a) `.c` is a C source file created by the programmer. It contains the instructions in source language (C) and is created using a text editor.
   (b) `.obj` is an object file created after the process of compilation is over. It contains the instructions in machine language.
   (c) `.exe` is an executable file which is created from the `.obj` file after linking it to the required C libraries or other object files. Now the file is ready for execution.
5. Write the shortest possible C program.
   Solution: The shortest possible C program is given below, though it does not produce any output.

```
main () {}
```

6. What are compile-time errors? Give two examples.
   Solution: During the process of compilation, the program is checked for correctness and if any errors are identified at this stage they are known as compile time errors. Syntax errors and semantic errors are examples of compile time errors.
   For example,

```
Sum = a + b
```

is a syntax error because the statement is not terminated by a semicolon.

```
char a;
float b;
a = b;
```

The above statement (`a = b`) is semantically incorrect because the contents of float type are being loaded in a variable of type `char`.

7. Define the term const correctness.
   Solution: If a program does not change or mutate a constant or constant object then the program is called const correct.

Test Your Skills

1. Point out the errors in the following program

```
# include < stdio.h>
void main ()
  {
  const float pi;
  pi=3.1415;
  printf ( "%f", pi);
  }
```

Solution: The constant pi cannot be initialized by a value at a place other than where it is declared. The correct declaration is given below:

```
const float pi = 3.1415;
```

2. What will be the output of the following program?

```
# include  <stdio.h>
main()
 { printf("Compu");
   printf ("ter");
 }
```

Solution: The output will be : `Computer`

3. What will be the output of the following program?

```
# include  < stdio.h>
main()
 { printf("Compu\buter");
 }
```

Solution: The output will be : `Computer.`

4. Will the following program compile?

```
void main ()
       {
        # include  <  stdio.h>
       }
```

Solution: No

5. What will the output of the following program be?

```
# include  < stdio.h>
void main ()
       {
        char ch ="text";
        printf ("\n%c", ch);
       }
```

Solution: This will give a compilation error, because the variable `ch` can store only one character, not a string such as text.

6. What will the output of the following program be?

```
# include  <  iostream.h>
void main ()
       {
        int k=20;
   /*
              printf ("k = %d," k);
   */
   printf ("value of k, %d",k );
 }
```

Solution: The output statement within the pair `/*' and `*/' will be ignored because it is treated as a comment. Therefore, the output would be : `value of k , 20.`

7. What will the output of the following program be?

```
# include  < stdio.h>
void main ()
    {
       /* float x = 2.371;*
       int y;
       printf  ("\n Enter a value");
       scanf  (" %d", &y);
       printf  ("\n x = % f and y=% d", x,y);
    }
```

Solution: The program will result in compilation error because the definition of variable x has been placed within a comment. The compiler will ignore this line and therefore, it will display error in the output statement indicating that a variable cannot be used without definition.

8. What will the output of the following program be?

```
# include <stdio.h>
void main()
  {
  unsigned val;
  char ch;
  val = 65537;
  ch = 'A';
  ch= ch + val;
  printf ("%c", ch);
  }
```

Solution: B – (Hint : `val` is of type unsigned int with range 0 to 65535 and the next number 65536 is equal to 0;

Exercises

1. Define the terms : token, keyword, identifier, variable, and constant.
2. Differentiate between the following:
   (i) identifier and keyword
   (ii) constant and variable
   (iii) `printf ()` and `scanf ()`
   (iv) '`\n`' and '`\t`'.
3. Write a C program that displays the following text on the screen.
   C is an easy language
4. What is meant by basic data types? Explain in brief.
5. What is meant by a character constant? What is common between char and short data types?
6. What would be the appropriate data type to store the following:

(i) length of a cloth
(ii) Age of a student
(iii) An exclamation mark (!)

7. Explain as to how an identifier is named.
8. Which of the following are invalid identifiers in C?
   (i) `Mydat` (ii) `text` (iii) `19 set` (iv) `cout` (v) `net-sal` (vi) `Tot.al` (vii) `S12-97`
9. Differentiate between lvalue and rvalue of a variable.
10. What is meant by backslash characters? What is their utility in a program?
11. How can comments be added to a C program?
12. Comment on the statement 'A variable must be declared before it is used in a program.'
13. Which of the following are invalid character constants?
    (i) 'k' (ii) '6' (iii) `!' (iv) 'k51' (v) '\n' (vi) '*' (vii) 'o' (viii) '$' (ix) '/n' (x) ' '
14. Which of the following are invalid string literals?
    (i) This is a test (ii) .... (iii) .... do .... (iv) `Hello' (v) $Temp #
15. Give suitable complete declarations for the following:
    (i) Height of a student of type float
    (ii) Integer variables : I = 0, J = 1, K
    (iii) Character variable `ch` initialized with the value `P'
    (iv) Double precision variables : `fract = 1.792 <$Etimes> 10 6, tot = 22.9 107`
    (v) Long integer variables : `large = 79253871`
16. Given the declarations:

```
char ch;
int i, j, k;
const char c = `A';
float val;
```

which of the following assignments are illegal?
(i) `ch = c;` (ii) `c = ch;` (iii) `val = 23.27;` (iv) `k = val;` (v) `i = j = 25;`

17. What is the output of this program?

```
# include  < stdio.h>
  main ()
  {
   int k;
   printf ("k = %d", k)
  }
```

(i) An error (ii) unpredictable (iii) 56721 (iv) 0

18. Are there any errors in the following program?

```
# include  < stdio.h>
  main ()
  {
    int i;
    i = 50;
    printf ("i = %d", i);
  }
```

19. A real number by default is considered as:
    (i) float (ii) double
    (iii) long double (iv) Any one of the above depending upon the model.

20. What will the output of the following program be?

```
# include  <stdio.h>
main ( )
{
print ("Bre\nak");
}
```

21. Will the following program compile?

```
# include  <  stdio.h>
main ()
{
   int _int = 20;
   printf (" %d", _int);
}
```

22. Explain in brief the process of creation and execution of a C program in the Turbo C integrated development environment.

CHAPTER

10 Operators and Expressions

10.1 OPERATORS

An operator is a symbol or letter used to indicate a specific operation on variables in a program. For example, the symbol `+' is an add operator that adds two data items called operands.

Expressions. An expression is a combination of operands (i.e., constants, variables, numbers) connected by operators and parentheses. For example, in the expression given below, A and B are operands and `+' is an operator.

$$A + B$$

C supports many types of operators such as arithmetic, relational, logical etc. An expression that involves arithmetic operators is known as an arithmetic expression. The computed result of an arithmetic expression is always a numerical value. An expression which involves relational and/or logical operators is called a boolean expression or logical expression. The computed result of such an expression is a logical value, i.e., either 1 (True) or 0 (False).

The rules of formation of an expression are:

1. A signed or unsigned constant or variable is an expression.
2. An expression connected by an operator to a variable or a constant is an expression.
3. Two expressions connected by an operator also form an expression.
4. Two operators should not occur in continuation.

10.2 ARITHMETIC OPERATORS

The valid arithmetic operators supported by C are given in Table 10.1.

Arithmetic operators can further be classified as unary operators and binary operators.

Table 10.1 Arithmetic operators

Symbol	Stands for	Example
+	Addition	X + Y
–	Subtraction, negation	X – Y, –X
*	Multiplication	X * Y
/	Division	X / Y
%	Modulus or remainder	X % Y
– –	Decrement	– –X, X– –
++	Increment	++X, X++

10.2.1 Binary Arithmetic Operators

The binary arithmetic operators supported by C are addition, subtraction, multiplication, division, and modulus or remainder. They are called binary operators because they require two operands to work with.

Similar to other languages, the precedence of multiply and divide operators are evaluated before add and subtract operators, as specified by the precedence rules. The evaluations of binary operators is left associative, in the sense that in an expression, operators of the same level are evaluated from left to right. Consider the following set of statements:

```
int x;
x = 7 + 3 * 5;
```

Since multiplication is performed before addition, the contents of x would be 22. In case the addition is to be performed before multiplication then we must modify the expression as shown below:

```
int x ;
x = (7 + 3)  * 5;
```

Now the contents of x would be: 50. The remainder operator (%) has the same priority as the multiply and divide operators. Consider the following set of statements.

```
int y ;
y = 10 % 4 * 3;
```

The contents of y would be: 6. On the other hand, after the execution of the following statement, the contents of y would be: 2

```
int y = 3 * 10 % 4;
```

The difference in output is because evaluation takes place from left to right for operators having equal priority.

Examples of invalid arithmetic expressions are:

(i) {a * + b} : invalid because two binary operators cannot be used in succession.
(ii) {a (b * c)}: invalid because there is no operator between a and (.

10.2.2 Unary Arithmetic Operators

A unary operator requires only one operand or data item. The unary arithmetic operators supported by C are, unary minus ('–'), increment ('++'), and decrement ('--').Compared to binary operators, the unary operators are right associative in the sense that they evaluate from right to left.

The unary minus operator is written before a numerical value, variable or an expression. Examples of usage of unary minus operator are:

(i) – 57 (ii) – 2.923 (iii) – x (iv) – (a * b) (v) 8 * (– (a + b))

It may be noted here that the result of application of a unary minus on an operand is the negation of its operand.

The operators '++' and '--' are unique to C. These are called increment and decrement operators respectively. The increment operator ++ adds 1 to its operand. Therefore we can say that the following expressions are equivalent.

i = i +1 ; ≡ ++i

For example, if the initial value of i is 10 then the expression ++i will increment the contents of i to 11.

Similarly, the decrement operator -- subtracts 1 from its operand. We can say that the following expressions are equivalent:

j = j – 1; ≡ --j;

For example, if the initial value of j is 5, then the expression --j will decrement the contents of j to 4.

The increment and decrement operators can be used both as a prefix and postfix to a variable, as shown below:

++ x or x++
– –y or y– –

As long as the increment or decrement operator is not used as part of an expression, the prefix and postfix forms of these operators do not make any difference. For example, ++x and x++ would produce the same result. However, if such an operator is part of an expression then the prefix and postfix forms would produce entirely different results.

In the prefix form the operand is incremented or decremented before the operand is used in the program.

Let us consider the following program segment:

```
i = 10;
net = ++ i * 5;
printf (" i = % d\n",i);
printf ("net = %d", net);
```

The output of this program segment would be:

```
i = 11
net = 55
```

In the postfix form, the operand is incremented or decremented after the operand is used in the program. Let us consider the following program segment.

```
:
i = 10;
net =  i++ * 5;
printf ("i = %d\n" , i);
printf ("net = %d", net);
:
```

The output of this program segment will be:

```
i = 11
net = 50
```

Thus, the following two statements are different from each other

```
sum = x++ ;                ... (i)
sum = ++ x;                ... (ii)
```

The statement (i) is equivalent to:

```
sum = x;
x = x + 1;
```

Whereas the statement (ii) is equivalent to:

```
x = x + 1;
sum = x;
```

Note: The stored value of a variable or an object can be modified only once during evaluation of an expression between two sequence points.

Thus, the following expression is illegal:

K = val++ * val++;

The reason being that the variable `val` is being modified twice in the above expression. However, it is possible in a logical expression. For example, the expression: K = val ++ && val ++; is perfectly valid, the reason being that the logical operator breaks the expression into two arithmetic expressions.

10.2.3 Arithmetic with Characters

A peculiar aspect of C is that arithmetic operations can also be performed with characters as shown in the following program segment:

```
:
char ch;
ch = `A';
ch = ch + 1;
printf ("ch = % c", ch);
:
```

The output of this program segment would be:

```
ch = B
```

Consider the following program segment also

```
:
int i;          /*...declare integer i */
i = 10;         /*...set i to 10*/
i = i + `A'; /*...add character `A' to integer i */
printf ("i = % d", i);
:
```

The output of this program segment would be:

```
i = 75
```

It may be noted here that while performing the operation `i` + 'A', the character 'A' has been converted to its equivalent ASCII value (i.e., 65). Therefore, the final value of `i` is the sum of its previous contents (i.e., 10) and ASCII of 'A' (i.e., 65).

10.2.4 Type Combination and Promotion

Different data types can be mixed together in arithmetic expressions. For instance, `int` and `float` can be combined in an expression as shown below:

```
int x = 10;
```

```
float y = 9.2;
y = y + x;          ...(i)
```

In fact, whenever the complier encounters such expressions, it promotes the smaller sized operand to the same size as that of the larger size operand. Thus, in the above expression (i), `x` (int) is promoted to a float and then it is added to `y`.

Similarly in the expression (ii) given below:

```
char ch = 'A'
int x = 10;
x = x + ch;         ...(ii)
```

The smaller operand `ch` (char) would be promoted to the size of the larger operand `x` (int) and then the expression would be evaluated. The benefit of such promotions is that the information of operands is not lost.

10.2.4.1 Truncation

In a promotion, the values of the smaller type are moved by the assignment operator to a bigger type. However, in the opposite case, truncation takes place, i.e., when values from a bigger type are moved by the assignment operator to a smaller type; consider the following program segment:

```
char ch;
int val = 329;
ch = val;
printf ("\n % c, %d," ch, ch);
```

The output of the above segment would be: `I, 73.`

It may noted that while moving the value contained in `val` (i.e. 329) to `ch`, the assignment operator has dropped upper bits of `val`. The lower bits of `val` (329) represent 329 – 256 = 73. The ASCII equivalent of 73 is 'I'.

Similarly, the output of the segment given below:

```
:
float val1 = 7.92345
int val2;
val2 = val1;
printf ("\n %d", val2);
```

would be = `7`

Thus, the fractional part has been truncated by the assignment operator while moving `val1` to `val2`.

Note:

1. The division of an integer by another integer always results in an integer value. For example, the result of 5/2 is 2 (the decimal portion of the result is dropped).

2. If both or one of the operands in a division operation is a floating point, the result is always a floating point. For example, the result of 15/2.0 is 7.5.
3. The remainder operator % produces the remainder of an integer division. For example, the result of 5% 2 is 1. This operator cannot be used with floating point numbers.

10.3 RELATIONAL AND LOGICAL OPERATORS

A relational operator is used to compare two values and the result of such an operation is always logical, i.e. either true or false. The valid relational operators supported by C are given in Table 10.2.

Table 10.2 Relational operators

Symbol	Stands for	Example
>	Greater than	X > Y
>=	Greater than equal to	X >= Y
<	Less than	X < Y
<=	Less than equal to	X <= Y
==	Equal to	X == Y
!=	Not equal to	X != Y

Example 1

Take two variables x and y with initial values 10 and 15 respectively. Demonstrate the usage of relational operators by using x and y as operands.

Solution

The usage of relational operators is illustrated below with the help of a table:

x = 10, y = 15

Expression	Result
x > y	0 (False)
x + 5 >= y	1 (True)
x < y	1 (True)
x +10 <= y	0 (False)
x == y	0 (False)
x + 5 == y	1 (True)
x != y	0 (False)

A logical operator is used to connect two relational expressions or logical expressions. The result of such an operation is always logical, i.e. either True (1) or False (0). The valid logical operators supported by C are given in Table 10.3.

Table 10.3 Logical operators

Symbol	Stands for	Example
&&	Logical AND	x && y
||	Logical OR	x || y
!	Logical NOT	!x

Rules of logical operators

1. The output of a logical AND operation is true if both its operands are true. For all other combinations the result is false.
2. The output of a logical OR operation is false if both of its operands are false. For all other combinations the result is true.
3. The logical NOT is a unary operator. It negates the value of the operand.

For the initial value of `x = 5` and `y = 7`, consider the following expression

```
(x < 6) && (y > 6)
```

The operand: `x < 6` is true and the operand: `y > 6` is also true. Thus, the result of the logical expression given above is also true. However, the result of following expression is false because one of the operands is false:

```
(x < 6) && (y > 7)
```

Similarly, consider the following expression:

```
(x < 6) || (y > 7)
```

The operand: $x < 6$ is true whereas the operand $y > 7$ is false. Since these operands are connected by a logical OR, the result of this expression is true (Rule 2). However, the result of following expression becomes false because both the operands are false.

```
!(x < 6) || (y > 7)
```

Note: The expression on the right hands side of the logical operators && and || does not get evaluated in case the left hand side determines the outcome.

Consider the expression given below:

x && y

If x evaluates to false (zero) then the outcome of the above expression is bound to be false, irrespective of y evaluating to any logical value. Therefore, there is no need to evaluate the term y in the above expression.

Similarly, in the following expression, if x evaluates to True (non zero) then the outcome is bound to be True. Thus, y will not be evaluated.

x | | y

Example 2

Take two variables x and y with initial values 10 and 15 respectively. Demonstrate the usage of logical operators by using x and y as operands.

Solution

The usage of logical operators is illustrated below with the help of a table:

x = 10, y = 15

Expression	Result
(x>=10) && (y < 15)	0 (False)
(x>=10) && (y <=15)	1 (True)
(x==10) && (y >= 20)	0 (False)
(x==10) || (y > 20)	1 (True)
!(x==10)|| (y == 15)	1 (True)
(x==10) && (!(y<20))	0 (False)

10.3.1 Conditional Operator

C provides a conditional operator (? :) which can help the programmers in performing simple conditional operations. It is represented by the symbols '?' and ':'. For example, if one desires to assign the bigger of two variables `x` and `y` to a third variable `z`, the condition operator is an excellent tool. The general form of this operation is:

E1 ? E2 : E3

where E1, E2 and E3 are expressions.

In the conditional operation, the expression E1 is tested; if E1 is true then E2 is evaluated otherwise the expression E3 is evaluated, as shown in Fig. 10.1

Consider the following conditional expression:

```
z = (x > y) ? x : y ;
```

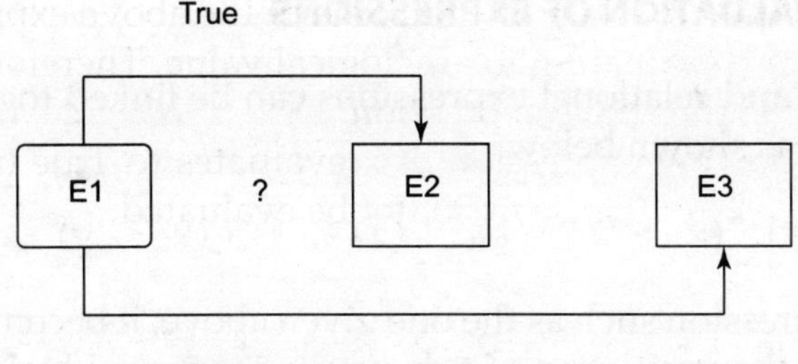

Fig. 10.1 Conditional operator

The expression x > y is evaluated. If x is greater than y, then z is assigned x otherwise z gets assigned y.

Examples of valid conditional expressions are:

```
(i) y = (x >= 10) ? 0 : 10;
(ii) Res = (i < j) ? sum + i : sum + j;
(iii) q = (a = = 0) ? 0 : (x/y);
```

It may be noted here that the conditional operator (? :) is also known as a ternary operator because it operates on three values.

Example 3

Write a program that reads two integers x and y. It prints 'x is greater' if x > y and 'y is greater' otherwise?

Solution

We will use conditional expression in this program.

```
/* This program uses conditional expressions to determine
the bigger of two numbers */
#include <stdio.h>
main()
 {
 int x,y;
 char ch;
 printf("\n Enter Two integers x and y;");
 scanf("%d%d", &x,&y);
                      /*Check greater using ternary operator*/
 ch = (x>y) ? 'x':'y';
 printf ("\n%c is greater",ch);
 }
```

10.4 ORDER OF EVALUATION OF EXPRESSIONS

A number of logical and relational expressions can be linked together with the help of logical operators, as shown below:

```
(x < y) || (x > 20) && !(z) || ((x < y) && (z > 5))
```

For a complex expression such as the one given above, it becomes difficult to make out as to what order the evaluation of sub expressions would take place in.

In C, the order of evaluation of an expression is according to the operator precedence given in Table 10.4.

Table 10.4 Operator precedence

Operators	Priority	Associativity
- ++ -- !	Highest	Right to Left
* / %		Left to Right
+ –		-do-
< <= > >=		-do-
== !=		-do-
&&		-do-
||	Lowest	-do-

It may be noted here that in C, false is represented as zero and true as any non-zero value. Thus, expressions that use relational and logical operators return either 0 (false) or 1 (true).

For example, the following statements:

```
int x = 10;>
printf ("\n % d", x > 5);
```

will give the output as `1` because the expression is true, whereas the statement

```
printf ("\n % d", x < 5);
```

will give the output as `0` because the expression is false.

The following points should be kept in mind when working with relational and logical operators:

1. Relational operators have lower precedence as compared to arithmetic operators. Therefore, the expression

$$5 > 10 + 1$$

is evaluated as if it were written as

5 > (10 + 1)

and not as (5 > 10) + 1

2. One very common error that C programmers make is that they use the assignment operator (=) in place of the equality operator (==). The distinction between the two is worth mentioning.

   For example, the statement

```
val = 5;
```

   assigns a value 5 to variable `val`, whereas the statement

```
(val == 5)
```

   checks whether `val` is equal to 5 or not. If the expression is true, the result is 1 otherwise it is 0.

   It may be noted here that using the operator `=' in place of `==' is not a syntax error but a logical error.

3. Equality and inequality comparisons using floating point numbers should be avoided because floating point arithmetic is not as exact as integer arithmetic.

4. Relational operators are grouped left to right i.e `a < b < c` implies

```
(a < b ) < c
```

   and not

```
a < ( b < c )
```

5. The relational operators have higher precedence over the logical operators (&& and !!). In the following expression

   a. `((a == 5) && ( b == 10))`

   the inner parentheses are not required because they will automatically be evaluated first. However, the logical NOT operator (!) has even higher precedence than relational or arithmetic operators.

6. Evaluation of a logical expression is also from left to right and the evaluation stops as soon as the final outcome can be determined.

The following points regarding conditional operators are worth considering:

1. The conditional operator has a lower precedence as compared to all other operators that we have discussed i.e., arithmetic, relational and logical.
2. The conditional expressions could be nested i.e., expression 2 and expression 3 instead of being values, could be expressions using conditional operators. For example, suppose you wish to assign a variable Z the largest of the 3 values out

of a, b and c. The following conditional expression would achieve the desired result.

```
Z = (a > b) ? (( a > c) a : c) :( b > c) ? b : c)
```

The first condition to be tested is (a > b). If this condition is true, the true part of the expression is evaluated, which itself is another condition. Now, if a is greater than c then Z is assigned the value contained in 'a' otherwise it is assigned the value contained in c. Otherwise if the condition {a > b} > is false, the false part of the expression is evaluated, which itself is another condition and checks if b is greater than c. If this condition is true, Z is assigned the contents of b otherwise the contents of c.

3. The order of evaluation of the ?: operator depends upon the outcome of the leftmost operand which is evaluated first. If it is true, the middle operand is evaluated and the last one ignored. If it is false, the last operand is evaluated and the middle one ignored.

It may be noted here that the operator precedence can be overruled by the usage of parentheses. Thus, in an expression the parenthesized sub expression will be evaluated first. Another point worth noting is that the operators of same priority like `*'` /', and `%' are evaluated from left to right. However, the unary operators like unary - , ++ etc. are evaluated from right to left.

Example 4

For given values of x, y, and z, evaluate the following expression
x < y && x > z > (y + 5 > z – 2)

(i) x = 9, y = 5, z = 3
(ii) x = 19, y = 5, z =18

Solution

(i) Given values are x = 9, y = 5, z = 3. For these values:
The term x < y is false
The term x > z is true
The term y + 5 > z -2 is true
Substituting the above terms in the given expression, we get
false && true | | true
false | | true
true - Ans

(ii) Given values are x = 19, y = 5, z = 18. For these values:
The term x < y is false
The term x > z is true
The term y + 5 > z -2 is false

Substituting above terms in the given expression, we get
false && true | | false
false | | false
false - Ans

Example 5

Determine the order of evaluation of the following expression:

A + B − C * D

Solution

The order of evaluation is given in Fig. 10.2.

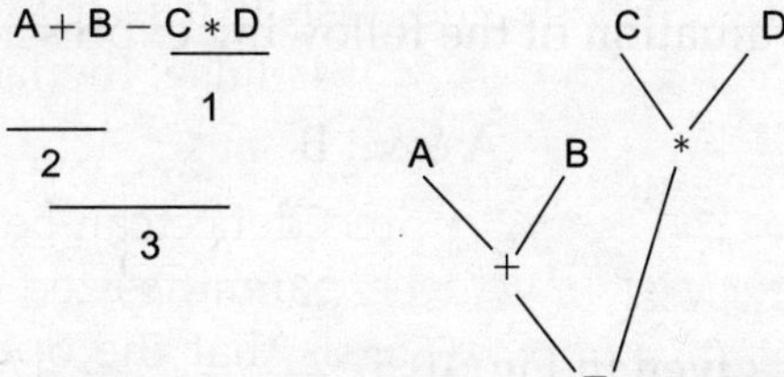

Fig. 10.2

Example 6

Determine the order of evaluation of the following expression

A | | B && C

Solution

The order to evaluation is given in Fig. 10.3.

A || B && C
1
2
B C
A &&
||

Fig. 10.3

Example 7

Determine the order of evaluation of the following expression.

A < B && C | | D > A

Solution

The order of evaluation is given in Fig. 10.4.

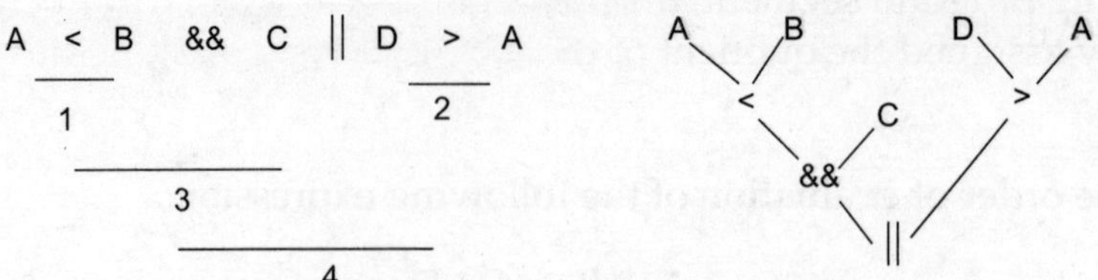

Fig. 10.4

Example 8

Determine the order of evaluation of the following expression

A && ! B

Solution

The order of evaluation is given in Fig. 10.5

A && 1B
1
2
B
A
|
&&

Fig. 10.5

It may be noted that the logical NOT (i.e.,!) is a unary operator and it requires only one operand. It is suggested that parentheses should be used to enhance the readability of the expression. For example, the expression A && ! B can be written as shown below:

A && (! B)

10.4.1 Type Conversion in Expressions

C provides type casting facility i.e., to convert an expression to be of a specific type. It is useful in a situation where the expression on the right hand side of an assignment operator is of a different type compared to the type of the variable on the left hand side of the assignment operator. Mixed mode expressions can also be handled by this feature of C. The format of a cast is:

`(type)` expression

where `type` : is a valid C data type.

It may be noted that the name of the data type (cast) is enclosed within parentheses and placed to the left of the value to be converted to (cast) the data type. For example, in the following program segment, the fractional part of the division is truncated and z is effectively assigned the quotient of the integer division x/y.

```
:
        int x, y;
        double z;
        z = x/y;
:
```

However, the integer expression x/y can be converted to a double expression as shown below:

```
z = (double) x/y;        /* x type cast into double */
```

Now the above expression will be evaluated to type double. It may be noted here that the type casting can only be done on the right hand side of the assignment statement.

Examples of valid type casts are:

(i)
```
int x = 5;
float y;
y = (float) x + 3.9;
```

(ii)
```
int z;
z = (int) 3.1415;
```

(iii)
```
double x;
x = (double) (9 * 5/2);
```

10.4.2 Handling Complex Expressions

Often the programmer is confronted with mathematical expressions which are complex in nature. For example, the following expression cannot be expressed easily in a 'C' language expression:

$$\frac{x^2+y^2}{x+\dfrac{x-y^2}{z^2}}$$

The solution to such complex mathematical expressions is to suitably parenthesize the sub expressions appearing within the complex expression at hand. Thereafter, write the parenthesized sub-expressions in a 'C' expression in left to right and top to bottom fashion. The above expression can be rewritten as shown below:

$$\frac{x^2+y^2}{x+\dfrac{x-y^2}{z^2}} = \frac{(x^2+y^2)}{\left(x+\left(\dfrac{(x-y^2)}{z^2}\right)\right)} = (x^2+y^2)\,/\,(x+((x-y^2)\,/\,z^2)$$

$$= (x * x + y * y) / (x + (x - (y * y)) / (z * z))$$

Example 9

Write the following complex mathematical expressions as 'C' expressions.

1. $\dfrac{x+y}{x-y}$ 2. $\dfrac{ab+c}{a-cd}$ 3. $x + \dfrac{1}{y + \dfrac{1}{z}}$

Solution

1. $(x+y)/(x-y)$ 2. $(a*b+c)/(a-c*d)$ 3. $x+1(1/(y+(z)))$

10.5 SOME SPECIAL OPERATORS

There are many other operators in C. In this section, two frequently used operators: **sizeof** and **comma** operators have been discussed.

10.5.1 Size of Operator

C provides a compile time unary operator called **sizeof**, that when applied on an operand, returns the number of bytes the operand occupies in the main memory. The operand could be a variable, a constant or a data type. For example, the following expressions:

```
int sum;
a    =    sizeof (sum);
b    =    sizeof (char);
c    =    sizeof (123L);
```

would return the sizes occupied by variable `sum`, data type `char` and constant '`123L`' in a program.

It may be noted that

1. The parentheses used with sizeof are required when the operand is a data type. However, with variables or constants, the parentheses are not necessary.
2. The sizeof operator has the same precedence as prefix increment/decrement operators.

10.5.2 Comma Operator

The `comma` operator is used to string together a number of expressions which are performed in a sequence from left to right. For example, the following statement

```
a = (x = 5,  x + 2);
```

executes in the following order

(i) a value 5 is assigned to variable `x`.

(ii) `x` is incremented by 2.
(iii) the value of expression `x + 2` (i.e. 7) is assigned to the variable `a`.

The following points may be noted regarding `comma` operators.

1. A list of expressions, separated by comma, is always evaluated from left to right.
2. The final value and type of a comma separated list of expressions is always the same as the type and value of the rightmost expression in the list.
3. The `comma` operator has the lowest precedence among all C operators.

10.6 ASSIGNMENT STATEMENT

Statements are the smallest executable units of a C program and each statement is terminated with a semicolon. An assignment statement assigns the value of the expression on the right hand side to a variable on the left hand side of the assignment operator (=). Its general form is given below:

```
< variable name > = < expression >
```

The expression on the right hand side could be a constant, a variable or arithmetic, relational, or logical expression. Some examples of assignment statements are given below:

```
a = 10;
a = b;
a = b * c;
```

The assignment operator is a kind of a store statement i.e., the value of the expression on the right hand side is stored in the variable appearing on the left side of the assignment operator. The variable on the left side of the assignment operator is also called lvalue and is an accessible address in the memory. Expressions and constants on the right side of the assignment operator are called rvalues.

The assignment statement overwrites the original value contained in the variable on the left hand side with the new value of the right hand side.

Also, the same variable name can appear on both sides of the assignment operator as shown below:

```
count = count +1;
```

Multiple assignments in a single statement can be used, especially when the same value is to be assigned to a number of variables.

```
a = b = c = 30;
```

These multiple assignment statements work from right to left and at the end all variables have the same value. The above statement assigns the value (i.e., 30) to all variables `c, b,` and `a`. However, the variables must be of the same type.

A point worth nothing is that C converts the type of the value on the right hand side to the data type on the left.

10.6.1 Variable Initialization

You can initialize a variable at the time of declaration or in a separate statement after it is declared. For example, if a variable Z is to be initialized with a value 10, we can use any of the following ways

(a)
```
int Z;
Z = 10;
```
(b)
```
int Z = 10;
```

C also allows you to assign the same value to many variables in a single statement using multiple assignments.

```
int a, b, c;
a = b = c = 0;
```

If more than one variable is to be initialized with different values, we can provide a comma separated list as follows:

```
int a = 5, b = 10, c = 15;
```

10.6.2 Compound Assignment Operator (Expression Shorthands)

In addition to the standard assignment operator ('='), C also supports compound assignment operators as listed below:

+ =
– =
* =
/ =
% =

The general form of a compound assignment expression is:

```
<var> op = E;
```

where < var> : is a variable
op : is a compound assignment operator
E : is a valid arithmetic expression.

Consider the expression given below :

```
x = x + 5;
```

The purpose of above statement is to add a value 5 to the old value of x and store the result in x as a new value. The above statement can be replaced by the following shorthand expression.

```
x    +=    5;
```

Similarly we can replace;

```
total = total * Rate;
```

with

```
total    *=    Rate;
```

This type of assignment is useful in a situation where the variable names are exceptionally long. Consider the following assignment expression:

```
total_sal_of_emp = total_sal_of_emp * 1.5;
```

This expression can be simplified as shown below:

```
total_sal_of_emp *= 1.5;
```

Thus, much of typing work can be saved by using compound assignment operators.

Examples of valid compound assignment expression are :

(i) `amount_to_pay += 100;`
(ii) `next_rem %= 10;`
(iii) `x_tex *= 0.2;`
(iv) `term /= N;`

10.7 BITWISE OPERATORS

C is a system programming language because it supports bitwise operators. These operators are used for the manipulation of integer data items at bit level. A table of bitwise operators supported by C are given in Table 10.5

Table 10.5 Bitwise operators

Operator	Stands for
<<	Left shift
>>	Right shift
&	Bitwise AND
|	Bitwise OR
^	Bitwise XOR
~	1's Complement

A brief discussion on these operators is given in the following sections.

10.7.1 Bitwise Shift Operators

C supports special bitwise shift operators: shift left (< <) and shift right (> >) operators. Such data at machine level is represented in the binary form; it can be shifted to the left or right by these special operators. However, the number of bits to be shifted is specified by an integer written next to the operator, as shown below:

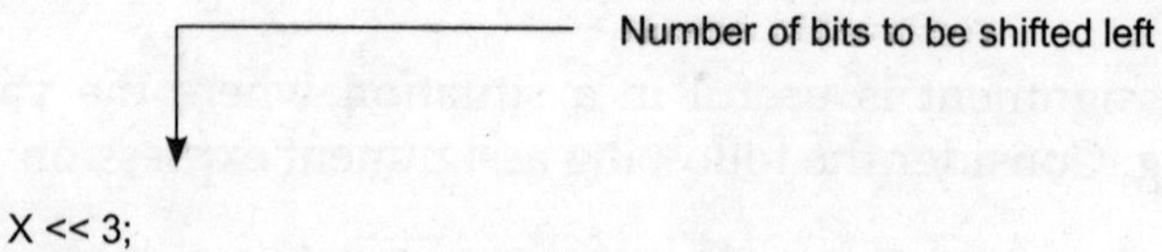

The statement means that the value contained in x is shifted to the left by 3 bits. Thus, the leftmost 3 bits of X will be lost and the resultant rightmost 3 vacant bits will be filled by zeros, as shown in below:

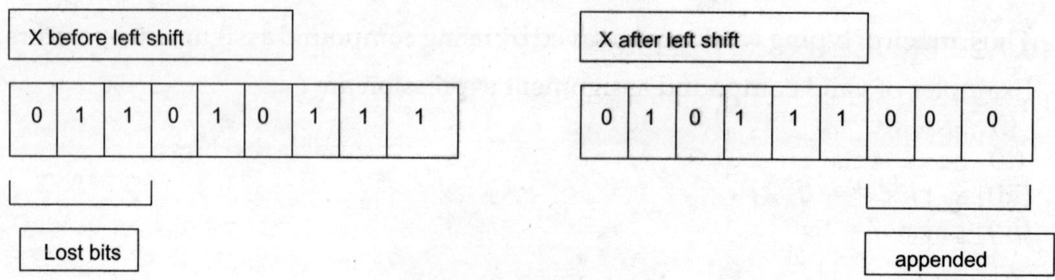

Fig. 10.6 Left shift operator

Similarly, the following expression would shift the contents of y to the right by two bits

y >> 2

In this case the rightmost two bits would be lost and the resultant leftmost 2 vacant bits would be filled by zeros, as shown below:

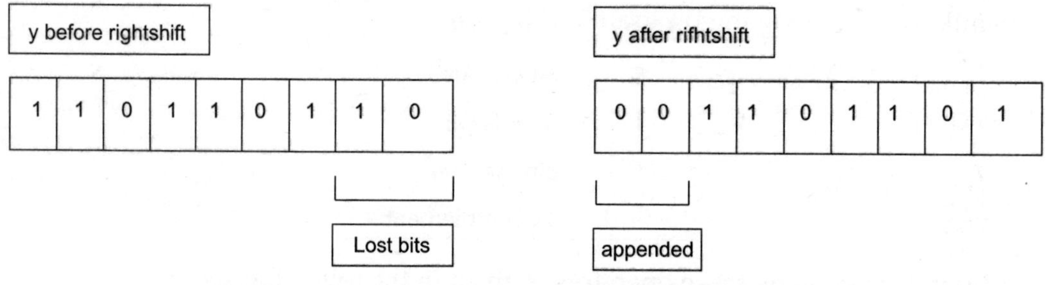

Fig. 10.7 Right shift operator

It may be noted that the shift operations are carried out in temporary locations whereas the original contents of the variables remain intact.

For instance, consider the following program:

```
# include <stdio.h>
main()
 {
  int x = 8;
  printf("\n %d %d", x>>1, x);
  }
```

The output of above program is: `4 8`.

The first output 4 indicates that the contents of x have been shifted by one bit to the right but the operation has been done in a temporary location. The second output 8 indicates that the contents of the variable x have remained intact.

10.7.2 Bitwise Logical Operators

The `bitwise AND (&)` operator takes two operands and produces a bitwise logical `AND` with them. For example, consider the following program:

```
# include<stdio.h>
main()
 {
 int x = 5;
 int y = 7;
 int z;
 z = x & y;
 printf {"\nz=%d" z};
 }
```

The binary representation of x (5) is '101' and that of y (7) is '111'. The logical bitwise `AND` of x and y will produce '101' which is 5. Therefore, the output of above program is : `z = 5`.

Similarly, the following program

```
# include<stdio.h>
main()
 {
 int x = 13;
 int y = 10;
 int z;
 z = x & y;
 printf {"\nz=%d" z};
 }
```

would give the following output:

```
z = 8;          (1101 AND 1010 = 1000)
```

The bitwise OR (|) operator takes two operands and produces their bitwise logical OR. For example, consider the following program:

```
# include <stdio.h>
main()
 {
 int x=5;
 int y=7;
 int z;
 z= x | y;
 printf ("\nz=%d",z);
 }
```

The binary representation of x (5) is '101' and that of y (7) is '111'. The logical bitwise OR of x and y will produce '111' which is 7. Therefore, the output of above program is : z = 7.

Similarly, the following program

```
# include <stdio.h>
main()
 {
 int x=13;
 int y=10;
 int z;
 z = x & y;
 printf ("\nz=%d",z);
 }
```

would give the following output:

```
z = 15;          (1101 OR 1010 = 1111)
```

The **bitwise XOR (^)** operator takes two operands and produces their bitwise logical XOR. For example, consider the following program:

```
# include <stdio.h>
main()
 {
 int x=5;
 int y=7;
 int z;
```

```
 z = x ^ y;
 printf ("\nz=%d",z);
 }
```

The binary representation of x (5) is '101' and that of y (7) is '111'. The logical bitwise XOR of x and y will produce '010' which is 2. Therefore, the output of above program is : `z = 2`.

Similarly, the following program

```
# include<stdio.h>
main()
 {
 int x = 13;
 int y = 10;
 int z;
 z = x ^ y;
 printf {"\nz=%d" z};
 }
```

would give the following output:

```
z = 7;                          (1101 XOR 1010 = 0111)
```

10.7.3 Bitwise Assignment Operators

There are two more variations of assignment operators called 'Bitwise right shift assignment operator (>>=)' and 'Bitwise left shift assignment operator (<<=)'. A brief discussion on both is given in the following text.

Bitwise left shift assignment operator (<<=):

This operator is a combination of the left shift operator and an assignment operator. Consider the following expression:

```
val <<= 2;
```

The above expression left shifts the contents of variable `val` by 2 bits and stores the new contents back into `val` itself.

Bitwise Right shift assignment operator (>>=):

This operator is a combination of the right shift operator and an assignment operator. Consider the following expression:

```
num >>= 3;
```

The above expression right shifts the contents of the variable `num` by 3 bits and stores the new contents back into `num` itself.

10.7.4 One's (1's) Complement Operator (~)

From our knowledge of binary arithmetic, we know that subtraction (x - y) is carried out by adding the 2's complement of the second operand (i.e., y) to the first operand (i.e., x). The 2's complement is obtained by ORing 1 to the 1's complement of y.

The 1's complement can be obtained by using the '~' operator of C . For example, the following statement will produce 1's complement of 'y', an integer variable.

```
int y =5;
y = ~ y;
```

The following statement would give the 2's complement of y.

```
y = y + 1;
```

Therefore the following program would print `y = -5`, that is, the 2's complement of `y` or the negation of variable `y`.

```
# include<stdio.h>
main()
 {
 int x = 5;
 y = ~y;        /* produce 1's complement of y*/
 y = y + 1;           /* produce 1's complement of y*/
 printf ("\ny=%d",y)
 }
```

Example 10

What would be the output of the following program:

```
# include<stdio.h>
main()
 {
 int x = 4;
 int y = 6;
 x << = 1;
 y >> = 1;
 printf (" \n %d %d",x,y);
 }
```

Solution:

The output would be: `8 3`

Note: The first output (i.e. 8) establishes the fact that one bit left shift is equivalent to multiplication of the variable by 2.
The second output (i.e. 3) establishes the fact that one bit right shift is equivalent of division of the variable by 2.

Example 11

What would be the output of the following program

```
# include<stdio.h>
main()
 {
 int val = 4;
 (val <<1>10)? printf("\n True"):printf("\n false");
 }
```

Solution:

The output would be: false, the reason being that the sub expression (`val <<1`) evaluates to 8 and 8 > 10 is false.

Example 12

What would be the output of the following program

```
# include<stdio.h>
main()
 {int x = 5;
  int y = ~2;
 y = y+1;
 z = x+y;
 printf{"\nz=%d", z};
 }
```

Solution:

```
z = 3;
```

FREQUENTLY ASKED QUESTIONS

1. Write four equivalent C statements that subtract 1 from a variable called `val`.

   Solution: The required statements are:
   a) `val = val -1;`
   b) `val--;`
   c) `val - =1;`
   d) `--val;`

2. Are the following statements equal?
   e) `Num = 8 %3*3`
   f) `Num = 8 * 3 % 3`

   Solution: The above statements are not equal. The outputs of first and second statements are `Num =6`, and `Num = 0` respectively.

3. The increment (++) and decrement (--) operators can either be used as prefix or postfix. Will they always yield the same result?

   Solution: They will yield the same result only when they operate on standalone variables. For example, given `val =5;`

   (i) `val++ ;`
   `printf ("%d", val);`
   will display 6

   (ii) `++val ;`
   `printf ("%d", val);`
   will display 6

   However, when they operate on variables appearing in expressions, the results are different in different situations. For, example, given `val =5,`

   (iii) `printf ("%d", ++val);`
   will display 6

   (iv) `printf ("%d", val++);`
   will display 5

4. Using the comma operator, write a single statement that exchanges the value of a and b using a temporary variable t.

   Solution: The required statement is: `t=a, a=b, b=t;`

5. Write the following expressions without using relational operators.
   (i) `if (a == 0)`
   (ii) `if (a != 0)`

   Solution: Since 1 represents true and 0 represents false in C, the following statements can be used instead of those given above:
   (i) `if (!a)`
   (ii) `if (a)`

6. Write a single statement that increments the value of a variable `val` by one and then adds it to a variable called `num`

   Solution: The required statement is: `num += ++ val;`

Test Your Skills

1. What will be the output of the following statements:
   (i) `ch = 'A' + 10;`
   `printf ("%d", ch);`

```
(ii) int a = 5;
     printf ("%d", a < 10);
```

Solution: The output would be : (i) K, (ii) 1

2. Identity the errors in the following program

```
# include <stdio.h>
main()
 {
 x= 50;
 printf("x=%d",x);
 }
```

Solution: The variable x has been used without proper definition.

3. Identify the errors in the following program segment:

```
    x = y + 20/A * k +++++ i;
```

Solution: There should be a blank between the increment operators. The modified expression is shown below:

```
    x = y + 20/A * k ++ + ++ i;
```

4. What would be the output of the following program

```
# include <stdio.h>
main()
 {
 int a,b,c;
 a=0;
 b=4;
 c=5;
 a=+c+ ++b/c;
 printf("\n a=%d",a);
}
```

Solution: the output would be: a = 6

5. Are the following statements same?

```
(x < 15) ? i = 10 : j = 10;
(x < 15) ? i  : j = 10;
```

Solution: No.

6. What would be the output of the following program

```
# include <stdio.h>
main()
 {
 int k = 20;
 int i = 20, j;
   j = i/++k;
```

```
printf("\n j=%d",j);
}
```

Solution: the output would be: `j = 0`

7. What would be the contents of variable `val`?

```
float val;
val = 7/3;
```

Solution: `2.000000`

8. What would be the output of the following

```
# include <stdio.h>
main()
 {
 float val;
 val = 2 + (float)7/(int)2.0;
 printf("\n %f",val);
}
```

Solution: The output would be : `5.500000`

9. What would be the output of the following

```
# include <stdio.h>
main()
 {
 printf("\n %d",7 > 10);
}
```

Solution: The output would be : `0`

10. What would be the output of the following

```
# include <stdio.h>
main()
  {
   int i = 10;
   i = i == 10;
printf("%d",i);
}
```

Solution: The output would be : `1`

11. What would be the output of the following

```
# include <stdio.h>
main()
{
int k = 20;
 (k !=(k = --k))? puts("true"):puts("false");
printf("%d",i);
}
```

Solution: The output would be : `false`

12. What would be the output of the following

```
# include <stdio.h>
main()
{
int i = 205;
i%=100;
printf("\n i=%d",i);
}
```

Solution: The output would be : `i = 5`

13. What would be the output of the following

```
# include <stdio.h>
main()
{
printf("\n %d",7 && 4);
}
```

Solution: The output would be : 1

14. What would be the output of the following

```
# include <stdio.h>
main()
{
printf("\n %d",7 && 0);
}
```

Solution: The output would be : 0

15. What would be the output of the following

```
# include <stdio.h>
main()
{
printf("\n %d",7 || 0);
}
```

Solution: The output would be: 1

16. What would be the output of the following?

```
# include <stdio.h>
main()
{
printf("\n %d",7 | 4);
}
```

Solution: The output would be : 7

17. What would be the output of the following?

```
# include <stdio.h>
main()
{
printf("\n %d",7 & 4);
}
```

Solution: The output would be : 4

18. What would be the output of the following?

```
# include <stdio.h>
main()
{
int val = 45;
val = ! val == 0;
printf("\n %d",val);
}
```

Solution: The output would be : 1 (Hint – the '!' operator has precedence over the '==' operator)

Exercises

1. Identify the errors in the following program:

```
main()
 {
 int i = 10;
 k = 10 * i ++-5* ++;
 printf("\n", k);
 }
```

2. Identify the errors in the following program segment:

```
int i = 50;
k = * 100;
int temp =k/i;
```

3. Write a program that reads a temperature in degrees Celsius and converts into degrees Fahrenheit.
4. Define the terms: operator, operand, expression, conditional operator.
5. Write a program that demonstrates the usage of the various arithmetic operators of C.
6. Write a program that demonstrates the usage of the various relational operators of C.
7. Write a program that demonstrates the usage of the various logical operators of C.
8. Given the values of a, b, and c, evaluate the following expression:

   (a >= b) | | (!(c ==b) && (c < a))

   (i) a = 10, b = 5, c = 11
   (ii) a = 10, b = 10, c = 10
   (iii) a = 9, b = 10, c = 2
9. Differentiate between unary, binary, and ternary operators.

10. Would the following program compile?

```
# include <stdio. h>
main()
 {
 int i = 10;
 printf("\n%d%d",++i++,i);
 }
```

11. What would the output of the following be

```
# include <stdio. h>
main()
 {
 int i;
 i = 7/3;
 printf("\n%d",i);
 }
```

12. What would the output of the following be

```
# include <stdio. h>
main()
 {
 int i;
 i = 7/3;
 printf("\n%d",i);
 }
```

13. What would the output of the following be

```
# include <stdio. h>
main()
 {
 int k = 10;
 k = ++k == 11;
 printf("\n%d",k);
 }
```

14. What would the output of the following be

```
# include <stdio. h>
main()
 {
 printf("\n %d",8 & 3);
 }
```

15. What would the output of the following be

```
# include <stdio. h>
main()
 {
 printf("\n %d", 8|4);
 }
```

CHAPTER

11 Flow of Control

11.1 INTRODUCTION

A statement is the smallest executable unit of a C program. It is terminated with a semicolon. It is an instruction given to the computer to perform a particular task like reading input, displaying output or evaluating an expression etc.

A single statement is also called as a simple statement. Some examples of simple statements are given below:

(i) `int a = 100;`
(ii) `S = S + a;`
(iii) `count ++;`

A statement can also be an empty or null statement as shown below:

```
;
```

High level languages such as Pascal, ADA,C etc. are called imperative languages because they are imperative to Von-Neumann architecture. This is the basic architecture of a desktop computer. Since this architecture supports only sequential processing, the normal flow of execution of statements in a high level language program is also sequential i.e., each statement is executed in the order of its appearance in the program. For example, in the following C program segment, the order of execution is sequential from top to bottom

```
:
x = 10;
y = 20;        Order of execution
z = x + y;
.
```

The first statement to be executed is `x = 10`, and the second statement executed is `y = 20`. The execution of the statement `z = x + y`, will take place only after the execution of the statement `y = 20`. Thus, the processing is strictly sequential. Moreover, every statement is executed once and only once.

Depending upon requirements of a problem, it is often required to alter the normal sequence of execution in the program. This means that we may desire to selectively and/or repetitively execute a program segment. A number of C control structures are available for controlling the flow of processing. These structures are discussed in the following sections.

11.2 THE COMPOUND STATEMENT

A compound statement is a group of statements separated from each other by a semicolon. This group of statements, also called a **block of code**, is enclosed between a pair of curly braces i.e., '{' and '}'. The significance of a block is that the sequence of statements enclosed in it are treated as a single unit. For example, the following group of statements is a block.

```
/* a block of code*/
{
    scanf ("%d %d", & a, & b);
    c =c a + b;
    printf ("\n %d", c);
}
```

One compound statement can be embedded in another as shown below:

```
{
  :
   {
          :
   }
  :
}
```

In fact, the function of the curly braces '{' and '}' in a C program is the same as the function of *Begin* and *End*, the reserved words in Pascal. C calls these braces delimiters.

11.3 SELECTIVE EXECUTION (CONDITIONAL STATEMENTS)

In some cases, it is desired that a selected segment of a program be executed on the basis of a test, i.e., depending upon the state of a particular condition being true or false. In C, an `if` statement is used for selective execution of a program segment.

11.3.1 The `if` Statement

This statement helps us in the selection of one out of two alternative courses of action. The general form of the `if` statement is given on the next page.

```
if (expression)
{
 statement sequence
}
```

where `if` : is a reserved word

`expression`: is a Boolean expression enclosed within a set of parentheses These parentheses are necessary even if there is a single variable in the expression.

`statement sequence`: is either a simple statement or a block. However, it cannot be a declaration.

An equivalent flowchart for the `if` statement is given in Fig. 11.1.

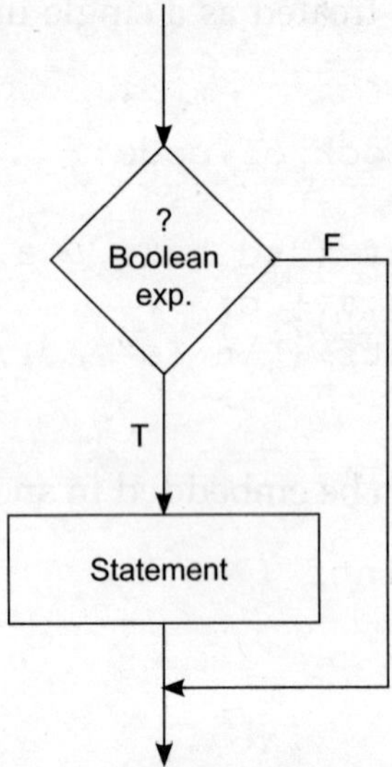

Fig. 11.1 An equivalent flowchart for an `if` construct

From Fig. 11.1, it may be observed that the course of action taken depends upon the result of the Boolean expression. If the result is true then the statement sequence is executed, otherwise the statement is bypassed and the control moves to the rest of the program.

Examples of acceptable `if` statements are:

(i) `if (A > B) A = B;`

(ii)
```
if (total < 100) {
        total = total + val;
        count = count + 1;
        }
```

(iii)
```
if ((Net > 7000) && (incomeTax == 500)) {
                                :
                        }
```

In order to illustrate the usage of `if` statements, let us take a very small problem and write a program for the same.

Example 1

Write a program that reads two numbers A, B and prints the bigger of the two. Assume that A and B are not equal.

Solution

We will use an `if` statement in this program to perform the test : A > B. The required program is given below:

```
/* This program reads two integer numbers and determines the
bigger of the two*/
  # include <stdio.h>
  main()
  (
    int A, B;
    printf ("\n Enter two integer values A & B:")
    scanf ("%d %d", &A, &B);
                                   /* Determine the Bigger */
    if (A > B)
                        printf ("\n A is Bigger");
    if (B > A)
                        printf ("\n B is Bigger");
    }
```

Example 2

Write a program that reads the units of consumption of electricity by a consumer during a month. The charges per unit of electricity consumed are 90 paise. The minimum payable amount is Rs 30. The program prints the net payable charges.

Solution

The required program is given below:

```
/* This program computes the electricity charges payable by a
consumer */
  # include <stdio.h>
  main()
  (
   int units;
   float charges;
   printf ("\n Enter Number of units consumed;")
```

```
 scanf ("%d", &units);
 charges = (float) units * 0.9;
 if (charges <30.0)
                  charges = 30.0;
 printf ("\n charges = %f", charges);
}
```

Example 3

Write a program that reads three sides of a triangle and determines whether a triangle can be formed using the given data.

Solution

The property of a triangle "that the sum of two sides cannot be less than the third side", would be used in this program. The required program for this problem is given below:

```
/* This program determines whether a triangle
      can be formed using three sides input by the user */

# include <stdio.h>
main()
(
 int side1, side2, side3;
 int flag;        /* a variable to keep track of
                          the results of the if condition */
 printf ("\n Enterthree(non zero) sides of the triangle");
 scanf ("%d%d%d", &side1, &side2, &side3);

 flag = 1;   /*Assume the triangle exists*/

 if(((side1+side2)<side3) || ((side1+side3)<side2)
                          || ((side3+side2)<side1))flag = 0;
 if(flag==0) printf("\n The triangle does not exist");
 if(flag==1) printf("\n The triangle exist");
}
```

11.3.2 The `if-else` Statement

It can be observed from the above programs that the simple if statement does nothing when the expression is false. An if-else statement takes care of this aspect. The general form of this construct is given on the next page.

```
if (expression)
{
        statement sequence1
}
        else
        {
        statement sequence2
        }
```

where **if**: is a reserved word
expression: is a boolean expression, written within parentheses
statement sequence1: can be a simple or a compound statement
else: is a reserved word
statement sequence2: can be a simple or a compound statement

An equivalent flowchart for the `if-else` statement is given in Fig. 11.2.

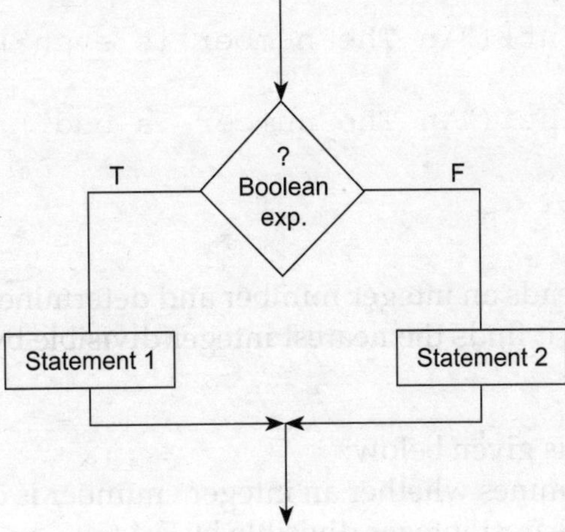

Fig. 11.2 Equivalent flowchart for the `if-else` statement

From Fig. 11.2, it can be observed that the Boolean expression is tested and depending upon whether the test expression is true or false, one of the two statements is executed.

Examples of `if-else` statements are:

(i)
```
if (A > B) C = A;
        else C = B;
```

(ii)
```
if (x == 100)
        printf ("\n Equal to 100");
    else
        printf ("\n Not Equal to 100");
```

It may be noted here that both the `if` and `else` parts are terminated by semicolons.

Example 4

Write a program that reads a number and determines whether it is odd or even.

Solution

The required program is given below:

```
/* This program determines whether a integer number is odd or
even */
# include <stdio.h>
main()
(
 int Num;
 printf ("\n Enter an integer");
 scanf ("%d", &Num);
                    /*Check if the number it is odd or even*/
 if((Num%2)==0)
            printf("\n The number is even");
 else
            printf("\n The number is odd");
}
```

Example 5

Write a program that reads an integer number and determines whether it is divisible by 7 or not. If not, then it finds the nearest integer divisible by 7.

Solution

The required program is given below:
/* This program determines whether an integer number is divisible by 7 or not if not then displays the nearest integer divisible by 7 */

```
/* This program determines whether a integer number is
divisible by 7 or not if not then displays the nearest integer
divisibleby 7 */

# include <stdio.h>
main()
(
 int num, rem, newnum;
 printf ("\n Enter the number:");
 scanf ("%d", &num);
 rem =  (num % 7);
 if (rem == 0)
```

```
printf("\n yes the number is divisible by 7");
else
{
 if(rem>3)
        newnum = num-rem+7;
 else
        newnum = num-rem;
 printf("\n No, the nearest number is: %d", newnum);
 }
}
```

Example 6

Write a program that reads a year and determines whether it is a leap year or not.

Solution

We know that a year is leap if it is evenly divisible by 4 or 400. However, a century year such as 1900 is not a leap year. Thus, it should not be divisible by 100. The program for this problem is given below:

```
/* This program determines whether a year is leap year
   or not */

# include <stdio.h>
main()
(
 int leapyear;
 printf ("\n Enter the year");
 scanf ("%d", &leapyear);

      /* Check if the year is divisible by 4 and not divisible
                                   by 100 or divisible by 400 */
 if ((leapyear %4 == 0)&&((leapyear %100) !=0)  ||  (leapyear
                                                   %400 == 0))
      printf("\n The year %d is leapyear");
 else
      printf("\n The year %d is not a leapyear");
}
```

11.3.3 Nested if Statements (`if-else-if` Ladder)

The statement sequence of the `if` or `else` part may contain another `if` statement i.e., the `if-else` statements can be nested within one another, as shown on the next page.

```
if (exp1)
    if (exp2)
    {
    :
    }
    else
        if (exp3)
        {
        :
        }
        else
            {
            :
            }
```

It may be noted here that sometimes the nesting may become complex in the sense that it becomes difficult to decide "which `if` does the `else` match". This is called a "dangling `else` problem". The C compiler follows the following rule in this regard:

Rule: *Each `else` matches up with its nearest unmatched preceding if.*

Consider the following nested if :

```
if (x < 50) if (y > 5) Net = x + y; else Net = x - y;
```

In the above statement, the `else` part matches the second `if` (i.e. `if (y > 5)`) because it is the nearest preceding `if`. It is suggested that the nested `ifs` should be written with proper indentation. The `elses` should be lined up with their matching `ifs`. Nested `ifs` written in this fashion are also called an `if-else if` **ladder.** For example, the nested `if` given above should be written as :

```
if (x < 50)
    if (y > 5)
        Net = x + y;
    else
        Net = x - y;
```

However, if one desires to match the `else` with the first `if`, then the braces should be used as shown below:

```
if (x << 50) {
    if ( y > 5)
    Net = x + y;
    }
else
    Net = x - y;
```

The evaluation of an `if-else-if` ladder is carried out from top to bottom. Each conditional expression is tested and only if found true will its corresponding statement be executed. The remaining ladder is, therefore, bypassed. In a situation where none of the nested conditions are found true, the final else part is executed.

Example 7

Write a program that reads a number and determines if the number is zero, positive or negative.

Solution

The required program is given below:

```
/* This program determines if the number is negative, zero,
or positive*/

# include <stdio.h>
main()
(
 int Num;
 printf ("\n Enter the Number:");
 scanf ("%d", &Num);
                                        /* if else ladder */
 if (Num == 0)
                 printf("\n The Number is zero");
 else
          if (Num == 0)
                 printf("\n The Number is Positive");
          else
                 printf("\n The Number is negative");
                                        /*end of ladder*/
 }
```

Example 8

Write a program that reads three numbers A, B, and C and prints the largest.

Solution

We will use an `if-else` ladder to decide the largest among the given three numbers. The program is given below:

```
/* This program displays the largest of three Numbers */

 # include <stdio.h>
 main()
  {
  int A, B, C;
  printf ("\n Enter the Numbers A, B, C :
```

```
scanf ("%d %d %d", &A, &B, &C);
                                          /* if else ladder */
if (A>B)
            if (A>C)
                 printf ("\n A is largest");
            else
                 printf ("\n C is largest");
else
            if (B>C)
                 printf ("\n B is largest");
            else
                 printf ("\n C is largest");
                                          /* end of ladder */
```

Note: We should not compare floating point numbers by using `==' or `!=' operators. The reason for this caution is that two seemingly identical floating point numbers may differ very slightly at the representation level. For example the result of the expression `1/3*3' will be stored in the computer as 0.999999 and not as `1.0'. In such cases, we can check whether the two variables or quantities are very close to each other or not. For example, two variables `f1` and `f2` of type float can be tested as shown below:

```
if (fabs (f1-f2) < 0.00001)
     printf ("\n The numbers are almost equal    );
```

where `fabs` is a function that provides the absolute value of a floating point number.

11.3.4 Switch Statement (Selection of One of Many Alternatives)

If the selection of one of several different courses of action is required in a program, then the switch statement of C can be used. In fact, it is a multi branch selection statement that makes the control jump to one of the several statements based on the value of an `int` variable or expression. The general form of this statement is given below:

```
switch (expression)
{
     case constant 1:
          statement;
          break;
     case constant 2:
          statement;
          break;
                                   :
     default :
          statement;
}
```

where `switch`: is a reserved word
`expression`: it must evaluate to an integer or character value
`case`: is a reserved word
`constant`: it must be an `int` or `char` compatible value
`statement`: a simple or compound statement
`default`: is a reserved word and is an optional entry
`break`: is a reserved word that stops the execution within the switch and control is passed on to the statement immediately after the switch block

The switch statement works according to following rules:

1. The value of the expression is matched with the random case constants of the switch construct.
2. If a match is found then its corresponding statements are executed and when `break` is encountered, the flow of control jumps out of the switch statement. If a `break` statement is not encountered then the control continues across other statements. In fact, switch is among those statements in C which can be error prone if not used carefully. This is because there can be situations where the program enters a particular case and then continues to run through all remaining cases. Omitting a break statement results in this common error. This phenomenon is called ***fall-through***.
3. If no match is found and if a default label is present then the statement corresponding to the default is executed.
4. The values of the various case constants must be unique.
5. There can be only one default statement in a switch statement. It can be placed anywhere in the switch statement.

The equivalent flowchart for the switch statement is given in Fig. 11.3
Examples of acceptable switch statements are:

(i)
```
switch (BP)
      {
      case 1 : total + = 100;
      break;
      case 2 : total + = 150;
      break;
      case 3 : total + = 250;
      }
```

(ii)
```
switch (code)
      {
      case 101 : Rate = 50; break;
      case 102 : Rate = 70; break;
```

```
case 103 : Rate = 100; break;
default  : Rate = 95;
}
```

In statement (ii) it can be observed that depending on the value of the code, one out of the four instructions is selected and obeyed. For example, if the code is 103, the third instruction (i.e. `Rate = 100;`) is selected. Similarly if the code evaluates to 101 then the first instruction (i.e. `Rate = 50`) is selected.

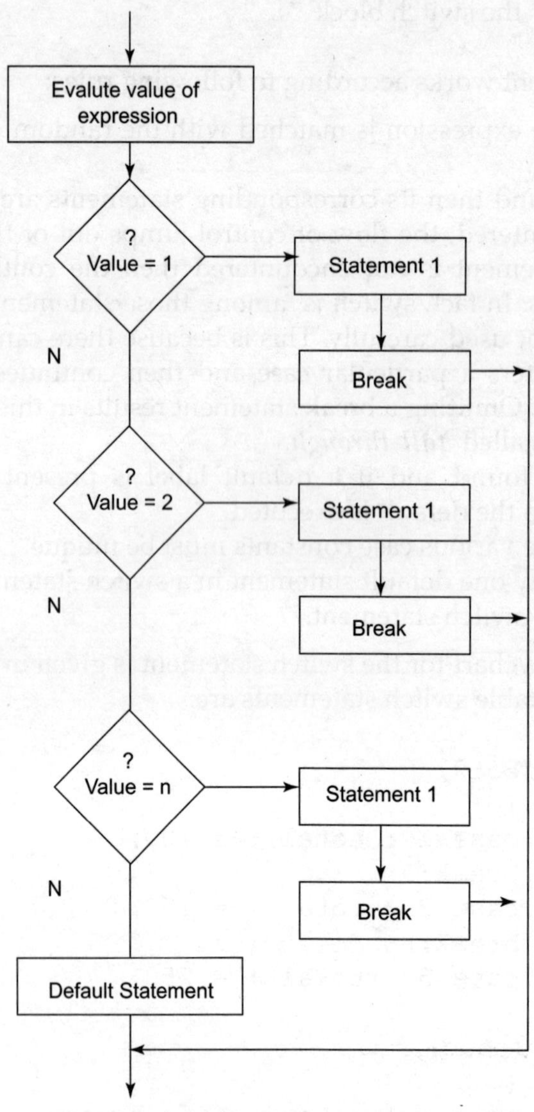

Fig. 11.3 Equivalent flowchart of the switch statement

Example 9

Write a program which computes the roots of a quadratic equation

$$\mathbf{ax^2 + bx + c = 0}$$

Solution

The roots of the quadratic equation can be computed by the following formulas.

$$x_1 = \frac{-b + \sqrt{b^2 - 4ac}}{2a} \tag{3.1}$$

$$x_2 = \frac{-b - \sqrt{b^2 - 4ac}}{2a} \tag{3.2}$$

The roots x_1 and x_2 are:

(i) Real and equal for $b^2 - 4\,ac = 0$
(ii) Real and unequal for $b^2 - 4\,ac > 0$
(iii) Imaginary for $b^2 - 4\,ac < 0$

The program is given below:

```
/* This program computes the roots of a quadratic equation.
It also illustrates the usage of a switch statement for the
purpose of choosing alternative paths*/

# include <stdio.h>
# include <math.h>
main()
(
 float root1, root2;
 float term, temp;
 float a, b, c; /*The coefficients"/
 int select;

 printf ("\n Enter the coefficients");
 scanf ("%f%f%f", &a, &b, &c);
                                    /* compute term */

 term=b*b-4*a*c;
 term=2*a

 if (term == 0)
                              select = 0;
```

```
else
 {
 if (term > 0)
                         select = 1;
 else
                         select = 2;
 }
                              /* compute roots    */
   switch (select)
    {
    case 0:    root1 = -1 * b / temp;
               root2 = root1;
               printf ("\n The roots are real and equal :");
               printf ("\n Root1 = %f and Root2 = %f", root1,
                      root2);
               break;
    case 1:    term = sqrt (term);
               root1 = (-1 * b + term) / temp;
               root2 = (-1 * b - term) / temp;
               printf ("\n The roots are real and unequal :");
               printf ("\n Root1 = %f and Root2 = %f", root1,
                      root2);
               break;
    case 2:    printf ("\n The roots are imaginary");
    }
}
```

It may be noted in the above program that a function `sqrt( )` has been used to compute the square root of the term. This function is part of a header file called `math.h`. Therefore, this file was included at the beginning of the program.

Example 10

Write a program which reads two integer values `val1` and `val2`. If `val1` is less than `val2`, display the message `up`. If `val2` is less than `val1`, display the message `down`. If both are equal, display the message `equal`.

Solution

We know that a conditional expression evaluates to 1 if the condition is true else it evaluates to 0. Therefore, the following expression:

```
(val1 > val2)   -   (val1 = = val2)
```

would evaluate to

```
0 : if val1 < val2
```

```
1: if val1 > val2
-1 : if val1 = = val2
```

We would use the above expression to obtain the case constant (say flag) of a switch statement so that the appropriate message can be displayed. The required program is given below:

```
#include <stdio.h>
main()
 {
  int val1, val2;
  int flag;
  printf ("\n Enter two integers");
  scanf ("%d %d", &val1,&val2);

     flag = (val1 > val2) - (val1 == val2);
                            /* Display message */
     switch (flag)
       {
               case 0: printf ("\n down");break;
               case 1: printf ("\n up");break;
               case -1 :printf ("\n Equal");break;
       }
 }
```

Example 11

Write a program that determines in which quadrant an angle lies.

Solution

The program for this problem is given below :

```
/* This program determines the quadrant for a given angle */

# include <stdio.h>
main()
 {
  int angle;
  int term;
  printf ("\n Enter the angle in degrees 0-360 : ");
  scanf ("%d", &angle);
  if (angle > 0 && angle <=360)
           {
           term = angle / 90;
           switch (term)
```

```
            {
            case 0 : printf ("\n Ist quadrant");
                     break;
            case 1 : printf ("\n 2nd quadrant");
                     break;
            case 2 : printf ("\n 3rd quadrant");
                     break;
            case 3 : printf ("\n 4th quadrant");
                     break;
            }
         }
       else
         printf ("\n Error in data");
  }
```

Example 12

Write a program which reads three integers representing a date (for example: 14, 6, 05) and prints the date in full as: 14th June 2005. Note that the day should be followed by an appropriate suffix: 'st', 'nd', 'rd' or 'th'.

Solution

We will use the switch statement in this program to print the date in the desired format. The required program is given below:

```
/* This program reads a date in three integers: Day, Month,
and Year, and prints the date in a suitable format */

  # include <stdio.h>
  main()
    {
      int Day, Month, Year;
      printf ("\n Enter the date: dd mm yy");
      scanf ("%d %d %d", &Day, &Month, &Year);


  if ((Day > 0 && Day <=31) && (Month > 0 && Month <=12)
        && (Year > 0 && Year <= 99))
        {
         printf ("\n The Date is .. ");
                       /* Check and print the Day */
         switch (Day)
         {
               case 1:
               case 21:
               case 31: printf ("%dst", Day); break;
```

```
        case 2:
        case 22: printf ("%dnd", Day); break;
        case 3:
        case 23: printf ("%drd", Day); break;
        default: printf ("%dth", Day);
       }
                            /* Check and print the month */
       switch (Month)
       {
        case 1: printf (" Jan");break;
        case 2: printf (" Feb");break;
        case 3: printf (" Mar");break;
        case 4: printf (" Apr");break;
        case 5: printf (" May");break;
        case 6: printf (" Jun");break;
        case 7: printf (" Jul");break;
        case 8: printf (" Aug");break;
        case 9: printf (" Sep");break;
        case 10: printf (" Oct");break;
        case 11: printf (" Nov");break;
        case 12: printf (" Dec");break;
        }
                            /* Print the Year */
        printf (" %d", 2000 + Year);
   }
  else
    printf ("\n Error in data");

 }
```

Example 13

Write a program that reads a character in uppercase and prints out whether it is a vowel or not.

Solution

The required program is given below:

```
/* This program determines whether a character is vowel or not */

 # include <stdio.h>
 main()
  {
  char ch;
```

```
printf ("\n Enter an Uppercase alphabet : ");
ch = getchar();
switch (ch)
        {
        case 'A':
        case 'E':
        case 'I':
        case 'O':
        case 'U': printf ("\n It is a vowel");
                  break;
        default : printf ("\n It is not a vowel");
        }
}
```

A switch statement can also be nested within another switch statement as shown below:

```
switch (expression)
{
case constant : switch (expression)
                {
                     case constant
                          :
                }
                break;
case constant : statement
default : statement
}
```

11.4 REPETITIVE EXECUTION (ITERATIVE STATEMENTS)

Some problems require that a set of statements be executed a number of times, each time changing the values of one or more variables so that every new execution is different from the previous one. This kind of repetitive execution of a set of statements in a program is known as **iteration** or a **loop**.

We can categorize loop structures into two categories: *non-deterministic* loops and *deterministic* loops. When the number of times the loop is to be executed is not known, then the loop is called a non deterministic loop, otherwise it is called a deterministic loop.

C supports `while`, `do while`, and `for` loop constructs to help repetitive execution of a compound statement in a program. The `while' and `do while' loops are non deterministic loops and the `for' loop is a deterministic loop.

11.4.1 The `while` Loop

It is the fundamental conditional repetitive control structure in C. The general form of this construct is given below:

`while` <<cond>> statement;
where `while` is a reserved word of C
<cond>: is a boolean expression
statement: can be a simple or compound statement.

The sequence of operation in a `while` loop is as follows:

1. Test the condition.
2. If the condition is true then execute the statement and repeat step 1.
3. If the condition is false, leave the loop and proceed with the rest of the program.

An equivalent flowchart for a `while` loop is given in Fig. 11.4. It may be noted that the loop is repeated as long as the condition remains true. As soon as the condition becomes false, the control leaves the loop and goes to the next immediate statement after the `while` loop.

It may be noted here that the variables used in the <cond> or boolean expression must be initialized somewhere before the while statement is encountered.

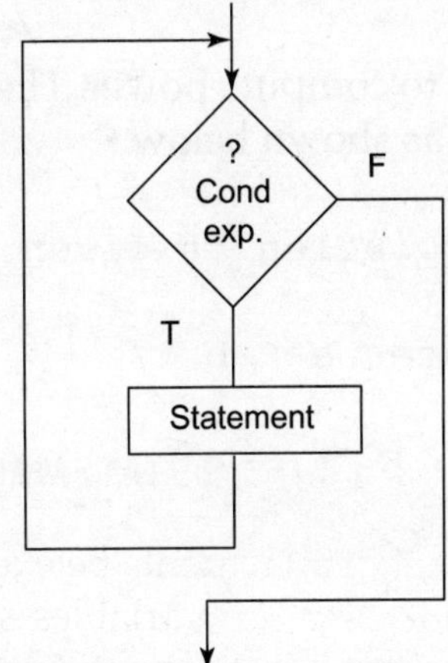

Fig. 11.4 Control flow in a while loop

Example 14

Write a program that generates and prints all even numbers from 2 to 20. It also prints their sum.

Solution

We will use a `while` loop to perform the given task. The required program is given on the next page.

```
/* This program generates and prints even numbers from 2 to 20
  and their sum */
  main()
  {
   int even = 2;
   int even_sum=0;
   printf ("\n The even numbers : ");
    while ( even <= 20)
          {
          printf ("%d ", even);
          even_sum += even;
          even += 2;
          }
   printf ("\n The Sum of even numbers = %d ", even_sum);
   }
```

Example 15

Write a C program which computes a^b, where a and b are of type `real` and `integer` respectively.

Wherea ^{b} = a* a* a* ---------* a (b times)

Solution

C does not provide an operator to compute power. Therefore, a ^{b} can be computed by multiplying a to itself b times, as shown below :
For example: $5^3 = 5 * 5 * 5$.
The program for this solution is given below:

```
 /* This program computes a ^ b */
 #linclude<stdio,h>
 void main{)
 {
 float a;
 int b;
 float pow;     /* The result is accumulated in pow */
 printf ("\n Enter the values of a and b");
 scanf ("%f %d", &a, &b);
 pow = 1.0;
                             /* Set up the while loop for b times */
 while {b >= 1)
 {
  pow = pow * a;
  b--;
 }
 printf ("\n a^b = %5.2f", pow);
 )
```

A very important point about the `while` loop is that the condition is tested before the loop is entered into. This means if the condition is initially false, the loop will never be executed. Therefore this loop is also called a **pre-test** loop. Let us consider the program given in Example 15. If the value of b read from the keyboard is already zero then the condition in the while loop will become false and therefore, the body of the `while` statement will be skipped, the control flow of execution will jump to the `printf` statement and the following output will be displayed :

```
A^B = 1.0
```

11.4.2 The `do-while` Loop

This is another conditional repetitive control structure provided by C. The syntax of this construct is given below:

```
do
{
        statement;
}
while  <cond> ;
```

where do	: is a reserved word.
statement	: can be a simple or a compound statement.
while	: is a reserved word.
<cond>	: is a boolean expression.

The sequence of operations in a `do-while` loop is as follows:

1. Execute the statement.
2. Test the condition.
3. If the condition is true then repeat step 1 to 2.
4. If the condition is false, leave the loop and go on with the rest of the program.

Thus, it performs a **post-test** in the sense that the condition is not tested until the body of the loop is executed at least once. An equivalent flowchart for a `do-while` loop is given in Fig. 11.5. It may be noted that the loop is repeated as long as the *loop condition* remains true. As soon as the condition becomes false, the control leaves the loop and goes to the next immediate statement after the `while` reserved word.

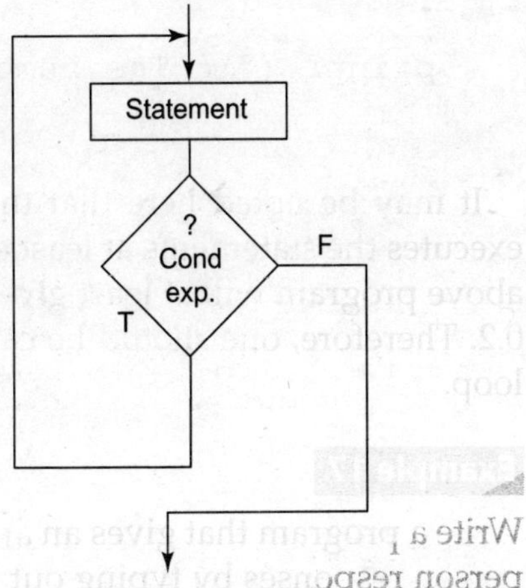

Fig. 11.5 Control flow in a `do while` loop

Example 16

Write a program which counts the number of bounces a ball makes before it stops and comes to a rest on the ground. Assume that with each bounce, it reaches 0.8 its previous bounce. The ball is considered to be at rest if the height is less than 0.2 cm. Read the initial height as input from the keyboard.

Solution

The program for this problem is given below:

```
/* This program counts the number of bounces a ball makes
before it comes to rest */

 # include <stdio.h>
 main()
  {
  int count;
  float ball_height;
  printf ("\n Enter the height of the ball: ");
  scanf ("%f", &ball_height);

  count = 0;
                        /* set up the do-while */
  do
   {
   ball_height =ball_height * 0.8;
   count++;
   }
   while (ball_height > 0.2);

   printf ("\n The number of bounces =%d ", count );
  }
```

It may be noted here that there is a drawback with the `do-while` loop i.e., it executes the statements at least once before performing any test. This means that the above program will at least give count = 1 even if the initial value of hgt is less than 0.2. Therefore, one should be careful in this regard while constructing a `do-while` loop.

Example 17

Write a program that gives an arithmetic test to a person sitting at the keyboard. The person responses by typing out his answer on the keyboard. The program keeps on asking the user to try again as long as the answer is wrong. Suitable messages are displayed during the run of the program.

Solution

We will use `do-while` loops in the program to check the responses of the user at the keyboard. The program is given below:

```
/* This program gives an arithmatic test to the user and waits
for the user response. As long as the answer is wrong, it asks
the user to enter again */


  # include<stdio.h>
  main()
   {
   int a = 20, b = 10, c = 25, result;
   int flag = 1;

   printf ("\n This is an Arithmatic test");
   printf ("\n Enter your responses in front of the questions");

   do
   {
         printf ("\n Enter your response");
         printf ("\n %d + %d * %d = ", a, b, c);
         scanf ("%d", &result);
         if (result == a + b * c)
          {
                    printf ("\n Well Done");
                    flag = 0;
          }
        else
                    printf ("\n try again");
   }
   while (flag);
   do
   {
         printf ("\n Enter your response");
         printf ("\n %d * %d / %d = ", a, b, c);
         scanf ("%d", &result);
         if (result == a * b / c)
          {
                    printf ("\n Well Done");
```

```
                    flag = 0;
          }
        else
                    printf ("\n try again");
    }
    while (flag);
    do
    {
        printf ("\n Enter your response");
        printf ("\n %d * %d + %d = ", a, b, c);
        scanf ("%d", &result);
        if (result == a * b + c)
          {
                    printf ("\n Well Done");
                    flag = 0;
          }
        else
                    printf ("\n try again");
    }
    while (flag);
  }
```

Example 18

Write a program which computes the factorial of a given positive integer N.

Solution

The factorial N can be computed by the formula given below :

$$N! = N * (N-1) * 4 * 3 * 2 * 1$$

The program is given below:

```
# include <stdio.h>
main()
 {
 int num;
 int  fact;
 printf ("\n Enter a number :");
 scanf ("%d", &num);

 fact = 1;
  do
```

```
    {
     fact = fact * num;
     num--;
     }
    while (num > 1);
   printf ("\n The factorial= %d", fact);
   }
```

A comparison between `while` and `do-while` constructs is given in Table 11.1.

Table 11.1 Comparison of `while` and `do-while` constructs

`while`	`Do-while`
It performs a loop pre-test	It performs a loop post test
The statement may not be executed at all	The loop is executed at least once

11.4.3 The `for` Loop

It is a count controlled loop in the sense that the program knows in advance how many times the loop is to be executed. The general form of this construct is given below:

```
for (initialization; expression; increment)
{
statement
}
```

where `for`: is a reserved word

`initialization`: is usually an assignment expression wherein *a loop control variable* is initialized.

`expression`: is a conditional expression required to determine whether the loop should continue or be terminated

`increment`: it modifies the value of the loop control variable by a certain amount.

`statement`: can be a simple or a compound statement.

The loop is executed with the loop control variable at initial value, final value and the values in between. An equivalent flow chart of the `for` loop is given in Fig. 11.6.

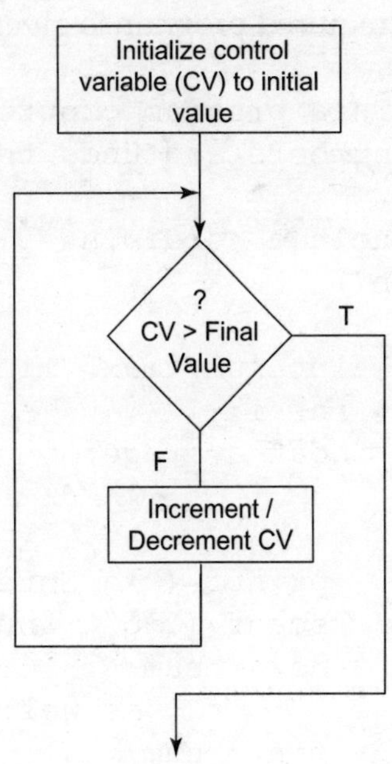

Fig. 11.6 Control flow in a `for` loop

Example 19

Write a program to generate and print all even numbers from 2 to 20.

Solution

The required program is given below:

```
# include <stdio.h>
main()
 {
   int even;
      printf("\n");
   for (even = 2; even <=  20; even +=2 )
   {
     printf ("%d ", even);
   }
 }
```

Example 20

Write a program which reads 10 numbers and compute the average, maximum and minimum values.

Solution

The required program is given below:

```
/* This program cmputes the average of 10
   numbers and finds the max and min values */

# include <stdio.h>
main()
     {
     int num, max, min, sum;
     int i;
     float average;


      printf ("\n Enter first Number");
      scanf ("%d", &num);
      max = num; /* Consider first number to be max
               as well as min           */
      min = num;

      sum = num;
```

```
    for ( i=2; i<=10; i++)
     {
     printf ("\n Enter Next Number");
     scanf ("%d", &num);
     sum = sum + num;
     if ( max < num ) max = num;
     if ( min > num ) min = num;
     }
  average = (float) sum/10;
  printf ("\n The  avarage = %f", average);
  printf ("\n The maximum value = %d", max);
  printf ("\n The minimum value = %d", min);
}
```

Note: If need be, we can leave out any of the three expressions of a `for` statement. However, in such a case, the delimiting semicolons must remain, as shown in the following example.

```
(i)  for (;;)
     {
                                                    :
     }
(ii) for (i = 2; i < 10;)
     {
                                                    :
     }
```

11.4.4 The Comma Operator

We can increase the power of a `for-loop` with the help of a comma operator. This operator allows the inclusion of more than one expression in place of a single expression in a `for` statement, as shown below:

```
for (exp1a, exp1b; exp2; exp3a, exp3b)
     {
     statement;
     }
```

Consider the following program segment :

```
                                       :
for (i = 1, j = 10; i < = 10; i ++, j--)
{
                   :
}
```

The variables `i` and `j` have been initialized to values 1 and 10 respectively. Please note that these initialization expressions are separated by a 'comma'. However, the required semicolon remains as such. During the execution of the loop, `i` increases from 1 to 10 whereas simultaneously, `j` decreases from 10 to 1. Similarly the increment and decrement operations have been separated by a 'comma' in the `for` statement.

Though the power of the loop can be increased by including more than one initialization and increment expressions separated with the comma operator, **there can be only one test expression** which could be simple or complex.

Example 21

Write a program that computes the sum of the first 10 natural numbers.

Solution

The required program is given below:

```
# include <<stdio.h>>
void main( )
{
  int i, s;
                          /* multiple initialization */
      for (i = 1, s = 0; i < = 10; i + +)
           {     s = s + i;
           }
    printf ("\n The sum = %.d", s)
}
```

Since multiple increment expressions can be included, the program given above can be optimized. The modified program is given below:

```
# include <<stdio.h>>
void main( )
{
  int i, s;
          for (i = 1, s = 0;  i <= 10; s = s + i, i ++)
          { ;
          }
  printf ("\n The sum = %d", s);
}
```

In fact the `for` loop can also be written as follows:

```
for ( i = 1, s = 0; i < = 10; s = s + i , i+ +);
```

11.4.4.1 Time Delay Loops

A loop which does not contain any statements in the body of the loop, and does no computation, is called a time delay loop. A delay loop that delays the execution of the rest of the program by a 1000 instruction execution time is given below:

```
for (i = 1; i < = 1000; i+ + );
```

These loops are also called **empty loops**. Such a loop just increments the value of the control variable by one till it reaches the terminating value and then comes out of the loop.

These loops are normally useful for delaying the execution of the next statement. For example, such loops can be used to display outputs on the screen for a longer time so that the user gets enough time to see them.

11.4.5 The `Break` and `Continue` Statements

The `break` statement can be used in a C loop to terminate execution of the loop. We have already seen that it is used to exit from a switch statement. In fact, whenever the break statement is encountered in a loop, the control is transferred out of the loop. This is used in a situation where some error is found in the program inside the loop or it becomes unnecessary to continue with the execution of the rest of the loop.

Consider the following program segment:

```
while (val != 0)
{
        scanf (" % d", &val);
        if (val < 0)      {
        printf ("\n Error in input");
        break;
        }
}
```

Whenever the value read in variable `val` is negative, the message: 'Error in input', would be displayed and because of the `break` statement, the loop will be terminated.

A `continue` statement can also be used in any C loop to bypass the rest of the code segment of the current iteration of the loop. The loop, however, is not terminated. In fact, the execution of the loop resumes with the next iteration. For example, the following loop computes the sum of positive numbers in a list of 50 numbers:

```
      :
sum = 0;
for (i = 0; i < 50; i ++)
{
        printf ("\n % d", val);
```

```
        if (val < = 0) continue;
        sum = sum + val;
    }
```

It may be noted here that the `continue` statement has no relevance as far as the `switch` statement is concerned. Therefore, it cannot be used in a `switch` statement. The actions of both `break` and `continue` statements are shown in Fig. 11.7.

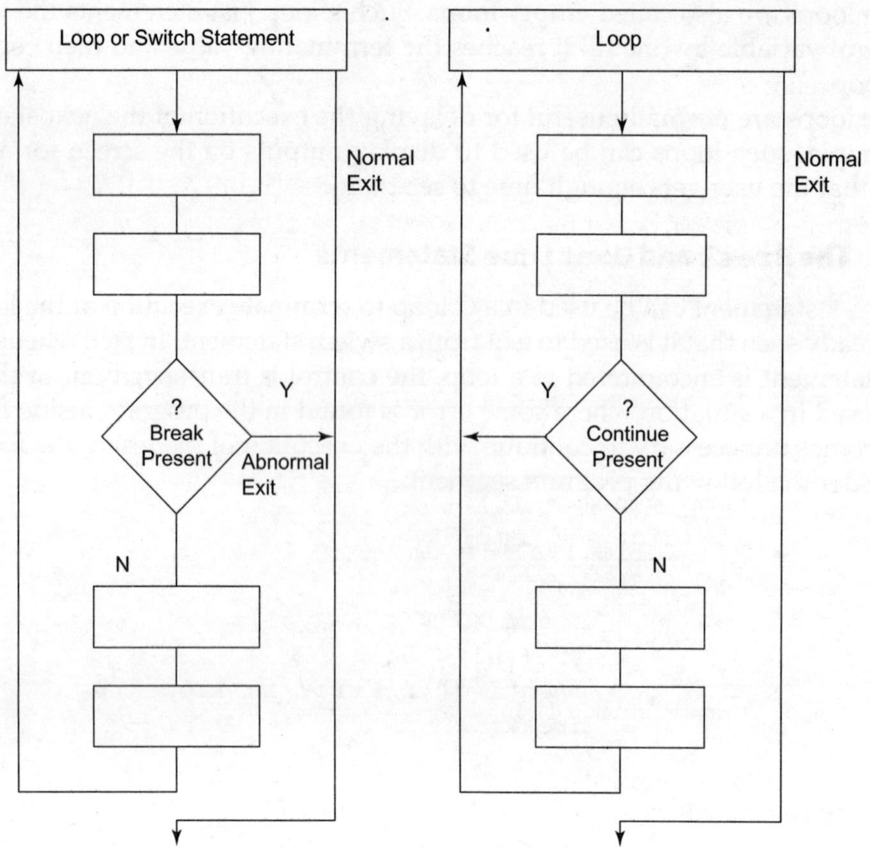

Fig. 11.7 `Break` and `Continue` statements

Example 22

Write a program that reads a number and a single digit. It determines whether the first number contains the digit or not.

Solution

In a loop, we will extract the digits one by one from the number by using the remainder operator '%'. Each digit extracted from the first number will be matched with the digit contained in the second number. A variable flag would be used to indicate whether the match was found or not. The program is given below:

```
/* this program detrmines whethera digit is present in a
number or not                  */

 # include <stdio.h>
 main()
  {
  int num;
  int digt, temp, flag;
  int x;

  printf ("\n Enter the number:");
  scanf ("%d", &num);
  printf ("\n Enter the digit");
  scanf("%d", &digt);

  flag = 0; /* assume that the digit is not present */
  do
       {
        temp = num % 10;
        if (digt == temp)
         {
          flag = 1;   /* digit is found */
          break;
         }
        num = num /10;
       }
      while (num !=0);
  if (flag == 1)
                      printf ("\n The digit is present");
  else
                      printf ("\n The digit is not present");
  }

}
```

11.4.5 The `exit( )` Function

In the event of encountering a fatal error, the programmer may desire to terminate the program itself. For such a situation, C supports a library function called `exit( )` which can be invoked by the programmer to exit from the program. This function can be called from anywhere inside the body of the program. For normal termination, the programmer can include an argument 0 while invoking this function, as shown below:

```
#include <<stdio.h>>
#include <<process.h>>
void main( )
{
          :
          if (error) exit (0);
          :
}
```

It may be noted here that the file `process.h` has to be included as header file because it contains the function prototype of the library function `exit( )`.

11.5 NESTED LOOPS

It is possible to nest one loop construct inside the body of another. The inner and outer loops need not be of the same construct, as shown below:

```
while <<cond>>
{
          do
          {

          } while <<cond>>;

          for (int, exp, ine)
          {



                    :

          }
}
```

The rules for the formation of nested loops are:

1. An outer `for` loop and an inner `for` loop cannot have the same control variable
2. The inner loop must be completely nested inside the body of the outer loop

Examples of valid nests are given in Fig. 11. 8.

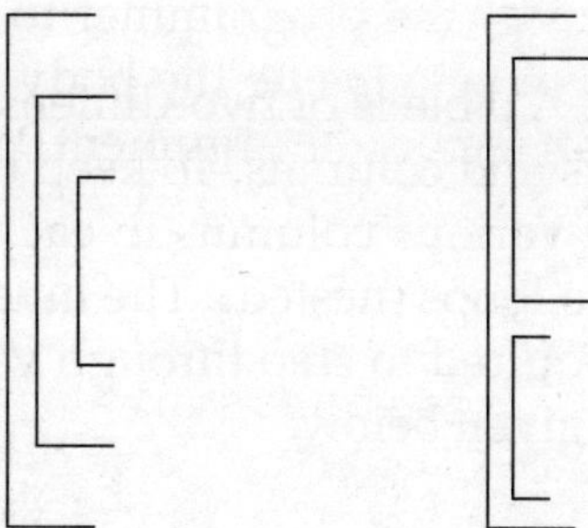

Fig. 11.8 Examples of valid loops

Example 23

Write a program to print out the following pattern on the screen.

```
1
1 2
1 2 3
1 2 3 4
1 2 3 4 5
```

Solution

The required program is given below:

```
/* This program displays a pattern on the screen */
# include <stdio.h>
 main()
  {
  int i,j;
  printf("\n");
  for (i = 1; i <= 5; i++)
    {
              for (j = 1; j <= i; j++)
                        printf ("%d ",j);

                    printf("\n");
    }
  }
```

Example 24

Write a program to print a multiplication table in the following form:

1	**2**	**3**	**4**	**5**	**6**	**7**	**8**	**9**	**10**
2	**4**	**6**	**8**	**10**	**12**	**14**	**16**	**18**	**20**
:	**:**	**:**	**:**	**:**	**:**	**:**	**:**	**:**	**:**
:	**:**	**:**	**:**	**:**	**:**	**:**	**:**	**:**	**:**
10	**20**	**30**	**40**	**50**	**60**	**70**	**80**	**90**	**100**

Solution

This problem involves a table. A table is of two-dimensional nature in the sense that it has a certain number of rows and columns. To keep track of rows, we need a loop. At the same time, to generate various columns in each row, we need another loop. Thus, the solution requires two loops (nested). The inner loop prints 10 columns of a row, while the outer loop is required to step through various rows. The program for the solution to the problem is given below:

```
/* This program prints a multiplication */

# include <stdio.h>

 main()
  {
  int row, col;
  int N;    /* Number of rows */
  printf ("\n Enter the number of rows");
  scanf ("%d", &N);
  printf ("\n The Multiplication Table...");
  for (row = 1; row <= N; row++)
       {
       printf ("\n");

       for (col = 1; col <= 10; col++)
           printf ("%d ", row * col);
       }
  }
```

The above program displays the required table. However, the various column of the table are not aligned and therefore, not pleasing to look at, as shown in Fig. 11.9

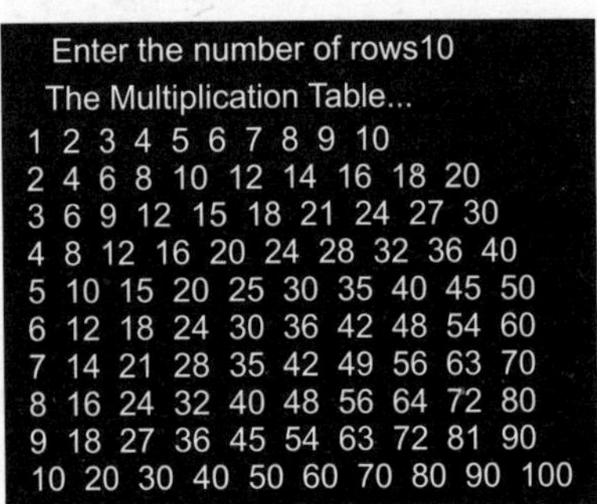

Fig. 11.9 The multiplication table

The display can be made better by displaying the information using a function called `goto (int, int) function`. This function takes two arguments X-co-ordinate and Y co-ordinate and locates the cursor on the point represented by the co-ordinates. The modified program is given below:

```
/* This program prints a multiplication table using gotoxy() */
# include <stdio.h>

 main()
  {
  int row, col;
  int N;   /* Number of rows */
  int x,y;
  clrscr();
  printf ("\n Enter the number of rows");
  scanf ("%d", &N);
  printf ("\n The Multiplication Table...");
  y=5;
  for (row = 1; row <= N; row++)
   { x=5;
   for (col = 1; col <= 10; col++)
          {
          gotoxy(x,y);
          printf ("%d", row * col);
          x= x+3;
          }
          y= y + 2;
  }
 }
```

The output of the above program is given in Fig. 11.10.

```
 Enter the number of rows10
 The Multiplication Table...
1  2  3  4  5  6  7  8  9  10
2  4  6  8  10 12 14 16 18 20
3  6  9  12 15 18 21 24 27 30
4  8  12 16 20 24 28 32 36 40
5  10 15 20 25 30 35 40 45 50
6  12 18 24 30 36 42 48 54 60
7  14 21 28 35 42 49 56 63 70
8  16 24 32 40 48 56 64 72 80
9  18 27 36 45 54 63 72 81 90
10 20 30 40 50 60 70 80 90 100
```

Fig. 11.10 The mathematical table using `gotoxy ()`

It may noted that another function called `clrscr()` has been used in this program. This function clears the display screen before displaying the table.

11.6 THE goto STATEMENT (UNCONDITIONAL BRANCHING)

Unconditional transfer of control means that the sequence of execution will be broken without performing any test and the control will be transferred to some statement other than the immediate next one. C supports the following statement for this purpose.

```
goto    <<statement label>>
```

where `goto` : is a reserved word

<statement label> : is an identifier used to label the target statement

The `goto` statement causes control to be transferred to a statement whose label is specified in the `goto` statement. Consider the following program segment

```
      —
      —
      —
      —
      goto rpara;
      —
      —
      —
rpara:
      —
      —
```

The `goto` statement will cause the control to be transferred to a statement whose label is `rpara`. The normal flow of execution will continue from this statement (i.e., having label `rpara`) onwards. Consider the following program segment:

```
       :
k = 50;
   back : I ++
            :
   sum = sum + k * z ;
   k-- ;
   goto back;
            :
```

From the above segment, it is clear that as and when the control reaches the `goto` statement it is transferred to the statement with the label `back`.

11.6.1 Statement Label

A statement label is an identifier which can be placed before any C statement followed by a colon (:), as shown below:

```
again : C = A + B;
```

Thus, `again` is a label attached to the statement `C = A + B` and the control of execution can be transferred to this statement by the following `goto` statement.

```
goto again;
```

It may be noted here that the transfer of control out of a control structure is allowed. However a `goto` branch into a control structure is not allowed (see Fig. 11.11).

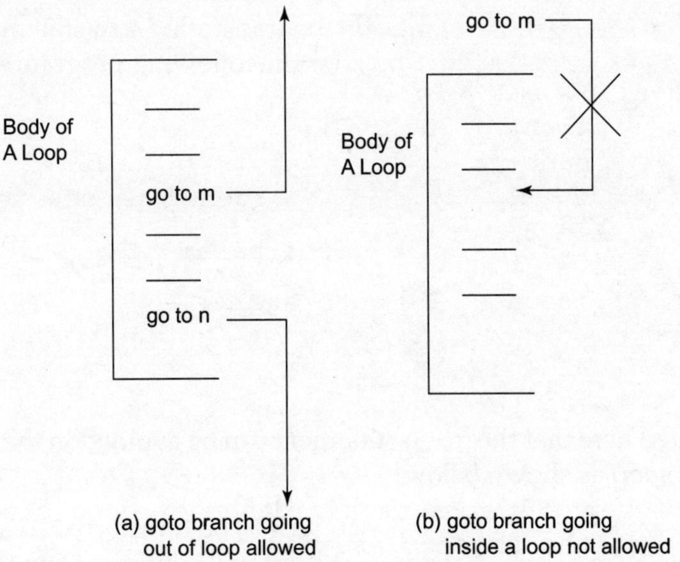

Fig. 11.11 `goto` branching

Example 25

Generate and print the first *n* terms of the Fibonacci series. The series is as given below :

1, 1, 2, 3, 5, 8

Solution

Each term (after the first two terms) is a sum of its two nearest predecessors in the sequence. The program for this problem is given on the next page.

```
/* This program illustrates the usage of goto statement
   It generates the fibonacci series */

   # include <stdio.h>
   main()
    {
     int N;
     int A, B, C, count;
      printf ("\n Enter the number of terms to be generated :");
     scanf("%d", &N);

     A=1;
     B=1;      /* initialize */

     printf ("\n %d %d ",A, B);
     count = 2;
          again:  C = A + B;
                  printf ("%d ", C);
                  count++;
                                        /* generate new terms */
                  A = B;
                  B = C;
               if (count < N) goto again;

     }
```

It may be noted here that the goto statement can be avoided in the above program by using a for loop as shown below:

```
/* This program illustrates avoidance of goto statement
   It generates the fibonacci series */

   # include <stdio.h>
   main()
    {
     int N;
     int A, B, C, count;
      printf ("\n Enter the number of terms to be generated :");
     scanf("%d", &N);

     A=1;
     B=1;       /* initialize */
```

```
    printf ("\n %d %d ",A, B);

    for (count = 2; count <= N; count ++)
            {
              C = A + B;
              printf ("%d ", C);

                         /* generate new terms */
              A = B;
              B = C;

            }
    }
```

The use of the goto statement is discouraged in structured languages such as Pascal and C because it is possible to write a program entirely without goto statements. Since C supports a rich set of control statements, a programmer rarely needs a goto statement for the transfer of control from one point to another.

The goto statement is controversial in the sense that for few situations goto offers excellent solutions but the over use of this statement makes a program difficult to understand. A comparison of the following program segments illustrates that the use of goto statements makes a program difficult to understand. (both the segments are equivalent)

```
:
:
```

```
:
:
while (total > = x)
          total = total-x;
printf (" %.d", total);

:
:
if A < = B
             small = A;
else
             small = B;
printf ("\n %d", small);
:
:
```

```
:
:
back : if (total << x )
                 goto ahead;
            total = total-x;
            goto back;
ahead: printf ("%d", total);
:
:
            if A > B
                 goto xpara;
            small = A;
            goto ypara;
xpara : small = B;
ypara : printf ("\n%d");
:
:
```

Note: The **break and continue statements are structured forms of the goto statement** because these statements allow control to be unconditionally transferred within or just outside a loop construct.

11.7 GRADED PROBLEMS

Problem 1. Write a program that reads a positive integer and does the following operations

1. If the number is even then divide by 2.
2. If the number is odd then multiply by 3 and add 1.
3. Repeat steps 1 and 2 until the number has value = 1.
4. Print out each value generated in step 1 and 2.
5. Print the total number of iterations performed in the program.

Solution: The required program is given below:

```
# include <stdio.h>
# include <conio.h>
main()
 {
 int num, count;
 clrscr();
 printf ("\n Enter the integer");
 scanf ("%d", &num);
 printf ("\n The number is...%d", num);
 count =0;
  while (num!=1)
  {
  if ( num % 2 == 0)
                    num = num / 2;
  else
                    num = num * 3 + 1;
  printf ("\n The next number is..%d", num);
  count = count +1;
  }
  printf ("\n The number of operations = %d", count);

}
```

For a given value 40, the output is shown in Fig. 11.12:

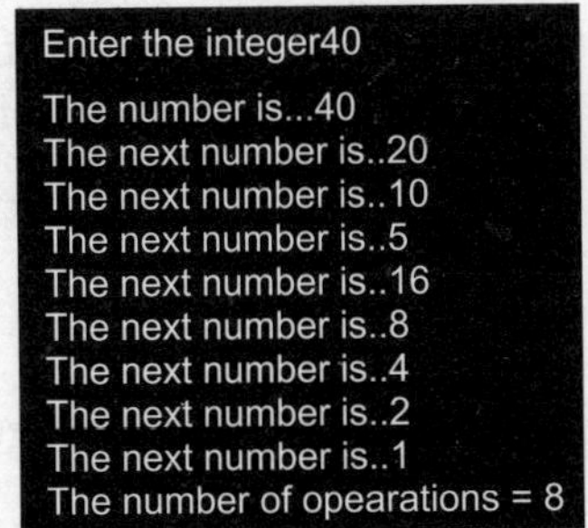
Enter the integer40
The number is...40
The next number is..20
The next number is..10
The next number is..5
The next number is..16
The next number is..8
The next number is..4
The next number is..2
The next number is..1
The number of opearations = 8

Fig. 11.12 The output for integer value:40

Problem 2. Write a program that prints all perfect numbers between 2 and 9999, both inclusive. A perfect number is a positive integer such that :

- The number is equal to the sum of its proper divisors.
- A proper divisor is any divisor whose value is less than the number.

For example, 6 is a perfect number because the sum of its proper divisors: 1, 2, 3 is equal to 6, the number itself.

Solution: The following facts have been considered while designing the program.
The remainder (%) operator would be used to find whether a number is a divisor of another number or not. The maximum value of a perfect divisor cannot be more than half the value of the number.

The required program is given below:

```
/* This program finds out all the perfect numbers between 2
   and 9999 both inclusive*/

# include <stdio.h>
void main()
{
   int num, divisor;
   int sum;
   char ch;
   for ( num = 2; num <= 9999; num++)
     {
        sum = 1; /* 1 is a proper divisor for all positive
integers*/
       for ( divisor = 2; divisor <= num/2; divisor ++)
       {
         if ( num % divisor ==0)
        sum = sum + divisor;
       }
```

```
  if (sum == num)
 printf ("\n %d is a perfect number",num);
 }
}
```

The output of the above program is given in Fig. 11.13:

```
6 is a perfect number
28 is a perfect number
496 is a perfect number
8120 is a perfect number
```

Fig. 11.13 Perfect numbers between 2 and 9999

The above program can be optimized by considering the following fact:

The divisors exist in pairs i.e., if 2 is a divisor of 6, then 3 (the quotient) is also a divisor. Thus 2 is the first divisor and 3 is the second divisor of 6. The first divisor of a number cannot exceed the square root of the number.

The modified program that uses the above facts is given below:

```
/* This program finds out all the perfect numbers
 between 2 and 9999 both inclusive */

 #include <stdio.h>
 #include <math.h>
 main()
  {
   int num, divisor1, divisor2;
   int sum;
   char ch;

   for (num= 2; num <= 9999; num++)
   {
   sum = 1;     /* 1 is proper divisor of all positive
                   integers */

  for (divisor1 = 2; divisor1 <= (int) sqrt (num); divisor1++)
         {
         if (num % divisor1 == 0)
                 {divisor2 = num/divisor1;
                   sum = sum + divisor1 + divisor2;
                 }
         }
         if ( sum == num )
```

```
            printf ("\n  %d is a perfect number", num);
        }
    }
```

Problem 3. Write a program to print all integers between 2 and 1000 (both inclusive) which are equal to the sum of the cubes of their digits.

Solution: The required program is given below:

```
# include <stdio.h>
  # include <math.h>
  main()
   {
    int num, digt, sum, temp;
    for (num = 2; num <= 1000; num ++)
       {
       sum = 0;
       temp = num;
        do
         {
         digt = temp % 10;
         sum = sum + pow(digt,3);
         temp = temp / 10;
         }
         while (temp > 0);
         if (num == sum)
         printf ("\n %d is equal to  sum  of  cubes  ofits
                                  digits", num);
       }
   }
```

Frequently Asked Questions

1. When two `if` statements are nested, what is the rule that determines which `else` clause matches with which `if`?
   Solution: Each `else` matches its nearest unmatched preceding `if`.
2. What is the major difference between a `while` and a `do-while` loop ?
   Solution: The `while` loop checks the conditions before the execution of the body of the loop whereas the `do-while` loop checks it after the body of the loop is executed.
3. What happens if the condition in the `while` loop is initially false ?
   Solution: Control will not be passed onto the body of the loop and it will be skipped.
4. What criteria would you apply in deciding which of the three forms of loops to use in a program ?
   Solution: When the number of iterations is already known, the `for-loop` is most suitable. The choice between a '`while`' and '`do-while`' loop depends on whether the loop is to be

executed '0 or more times' or to be executed at least once. However, the `do-while` loop is excellent for a menu selection part of a program whereas the `while` loop is most suitable for true iteration (i.e., the loop executes 0 or more times).

Test Your Skills

1. What would be the output of the following program ?

```
# include <stdio.h>
main( )
{
int x=5;
switch (x)
{
  default  : printf("\n At the strike of midnight on");
  case 1 : printf("\n 14 Aug'47, Pt. Jawaharlal Nehru" );
  case 2 : printf("\n made his famous speech wherein he" );
  case 3 : printf("\n refered to keeping his tryst with" );
  case 4 : printf("\n destiny  and awakening to life and freedom" );
};
}
```

Solution:
The output would be:

```
At the strike of midnight on
14 Aug'47, Pt. Jawaharlal Nehru
made his famous speech wherein he
refered to keeping his tryst with
destiny and awakening to life and freedom_
```

2. Point out the errors, if any, in the following while loop

```
:
int k = 10;
while( )
{
printf ("\n % d", k++);
if (k > 50);
break;
}
```

Solution: Since there is no condition in the `while` statement, therefore it will result in a compilation error.

3. Rewrite the following statement using an `if-else` construct.
   (x > 50)? (y = 20) : (z = 30);

Solution:
The required statement would be:

```
if (x > 50)
        y = 20;
else
        z = 30;
```

4. What is more efficient : an if-else ladder or a switch statement ?
Solution: There is practically no difference. However, the usage of switch is considered better from a program clarity and understanding point of view

5. What will the output of the following program be?

```
# include <stdio.h>
void main  ( )
{
int ind;
for (ind = 0; ind <=20; ind ++,   printf ("\n %d", ind));
}
```

Solution: The output would a list from 1 to 21, each number appearing on separate line..

6. How many times will the following program print Verbatim?

```
#include <stdio.h>
main( )
{
while (1)
{
printf    ("Verbatim");
}
}
```

Solution: Since the value of the expression in the while loop is constant at 1 i.e. true, it has becomes an infinite loop. Therefore, it will keep on printing Verbatim for ever unless ^C is pressed.

7. What will the output of the following program be?

```
#include <stdio.h>
main( )
{
goto there;
              printf ("\nThis");
              printf ("\n neglect");
back:         printf ("\n goto confuses"); goto last;
              printf ("\n That");
there:        goto back;
last:;
}
```

Solution: The output would be: goto confuses

8. What would the output of the following be:

```
#include <stdio.h>
main( )
{
int x, y =1;
if (y=x=0)
            printf ("\n This");
else
            printf ("\n That");
}
```

Solution: The output would be: That – the reason being that the expression in the if statement would evaluate to 0 i.e., false.

9. Will the following two programs produce same output?

Program 1

```
#include <stdio.h>
main( )
{
int x, y =1;
if ((x=y)!=0)
            printf ("%d %d",x,y);
}
```

Program 2

```
#include <stdio.h>
main( )
{
int x, y =1;
if ((x=y=1)==1)
            printf ("%d %d",x,y);
}
```

Solution: Yes both the programs would produce the same output : 1 1.

10. What will the output of the following program be?

```
#include <stdio.h>
main( )
{
 int x=10, count =0;
      while (x)
      { x--;
        if (x == 4)
            continue;
        count++;
      }
 printf ("\n %d", count);
}
```

Solution: The output would be : 9

11. What would the output of the following be?

```
#include <stdio.h>
main( )
{
  int i;
  for (i=0; i<=5;i++);
        printf ("\n Hello");
}
```

Solution: It will print the word Hello only once.

12. What would the output of the following be?

```
# include <stdio.h>
void main( )
{
int val=5;
            if (val++ == 6)
                  printf ("Six");
            else
                  if (--val == 5)
                        printf ("Five");
                  else
                        if (++ val == 5)
                        printf("Still Five");
}
```

Solution: The output would be: five

13. What would the output of the following be?

```
# include <stdio.h>
void main( )
{
  int x=1;
  do
  {  printf ("%d ",x);
  } while (x--);
}
```

Solution: The output would be: 1 0.

14. What is the output of the following ?

```
# include <stdio.h>
void main( )
{
 int x = 5;
 if ( x = x!=5)
    printf ("\n This");
 else
```

```
        printf ("\n That");
    }
```

Solution: The output would be : That.

15. What would the output of the following be?

```
# include <stdio.h>
void main( )
{
int k;
int x = 2;
      do
      {
      k=50;
      printf ("\n %d %d", x, k);
      x--;
      k--;
      }while (x);
}
```

Solution: The output would be: 2 50
1 50.

EXERCISES

1 What statement in C allows decisions to be taken depending upon a test being true or false?
2 What is the utility of the `else` clause in an `if` statement in C?
3. Comment on the following
"We should not compare floating point numbers by using `==' or `!=' operators."
4. What is meant by nested `if` statements ? Explain `if-else-if` ladder in brief.
5. Differentiate between `while` and `do while` constructs.
6. Give the advantages of a `for` loop.
7. Write a program which computes `a sup b` > where `a` and `b` are of real and integer types respectively.
8. Write a program to generate the following on the screen.

```
                1
            1   2   1
        1   2   3   2   1
    1   2   3   4   3   2   1
1   2   3   4   5   4   3   2   1
```

9. Identify the errors or logical mistakes in the following statements.
   (i) `GOTO 10 + 20`
   (ii) `if (x > y) x = y;`
   (iii) `GOTO 150;`
   (iv) `for (i = 1; i < = 15; i + +);`
        `x = x + 1;`
10. What will the following program segment do?

```
:
for (i = 1; i << 5; i ++)
{
for (j = 1; j << = i; j ++)
            printf ("*");
            printf (" \n );
}
```

11. Write a program which reads the integers K and L. If K is divisible by L, print 1 otherwise print 0.
12. Write a C program segment for the expression "If x is less than y, or z is greater than or equal to A, or both, then Add A to Total".
13. The following program segment uses `goto` needlessly. Rewrite the segment using a while statement.

```
:
again : if A < B goto next;
      A = A - B;
      goto again;
next : printf ("\n %d", A);
:
```

15. What is the purpose of the `break` statement in C?
16. How does the `continue` statement differ from the break statement ?
17. Where and why is the `exit( )` function used in a C program.
18. What is meant by nesting of loops?
19. Given the value of a positive integer N, write a program segment which determines how many decimal digits are needed to write down the value N (for example, 38 requires two digits, and 270 needs three digits).
20. Write a program which reverses and sums the digits of an integer number.
21. Write a program to accept a single integer and print a multiplication table for all the positive integers up to the one specified as input.
22. Point out the errors, if any, in the `for` loop given below:

```
:
int k =10;
for ( ; ; )
{
printf ("% d", k++);
if ( k >50 )
      break;
}
:
```

A. The two semicolons should not be used
B. Some condition should be used in the `for` loop
C. No errors

23. Point out the error, if any, in the following program segment:

```
:
int x =5,k=3;
:
```

```
switch (x)
{
case 1 : printf (" \n We should cease to think" );
case 2 : printf (" \n in terms of States or Provinces");
case k : printf (" \n instead we should think that");
          printf  (" \n We are Indians";
}
:
```

24. How many times is the following loop executed?

```
:
int k;
for (k = 0; k = 5 ; k++)
printf ("\n%d", k);
:
```

25. How many times will the following loop print `once` ?

```
:
do
{
printf ("\n once" );
}while (0);
```

26. How many times will the following loop print `Aloha` ?

```
:
unsigned int i;
for (i = - 5; i > = 5; i -- )
printf("\n Aloha");
:
```

27. What will the output of the following program be?

```
# include<stdio.h>
main()
{
int x, y=0;
if (y=x=1)
      printf ("\n This");
else
      printf ("\n That");
:
```

28. What would the output of the following be?

```
# include <<stdio.h>>
 main( )
{
unsigned int val = - 10;
if (val < 0)
printf ("\n %d", val ++);
}
```

[Hint : It will print nothing because val has been declared as an unsigned integer and therefore the `if` expression would evaluate to 0, i.e. false and there is no `else` part in the `if` statement.]

29. What would the output of the following be?

```
# include <stdio.h>
void main( )
{
int val=5;
      if (val++ == 6)
            printf ("Not Six");
      else
            if (val == 6)
                  printf ("Six");
            else
                  if (-- val == 5)
                  printf("Five");
}
```

30. What would the output of the following be?

```
# include <stdio.h>
void main( )
{
int x = 1;
      switch (x)
      {
      case 0: printf ("\n%d",        x);
      case 1: printf ("\n%d",        x);
      case 2: printf ("\n%d",        x);
      };
}
```

31. What would the output of the following be?

```
# include <stdio.h>
main( )
{
      int x = 1;
      while (x--   )
      printf ("\n%d",        x);
}
```

ANSWERS TO SELECTED EXERCISES

22. C 23. We cannot use variable *k* in place of constant 3. 24. infinite 25. 1
26. 0 27. This 28. Nothing 29. Six 30. 1 1 31. 0

CHAPTER

12 Input–Output Functions

12.1 INTRODUCTION

Like human beings, a program also needs to interact with its surroundings. Primarily, a program interacts with the user through a console to input data and to display messages, alerts and results. However, for large data it needs to interact with the peripheral storage devices such as hard-disks CD-ROMs , pen-RAMs etc.,

The programs read and write data through input/output devices such as screens, keyboards, printers, and disk devices etc. Obviously, the programmer must learn how to correctly perform I/O operations so that efficient interactive programs could be written. There are large numbers of I/O operations supported by C. We have already used two C functions, `printf()` and `scanf ()`, in the previous chapters. In the following sections we will discuss the following additional input output functions:

Function	Type	Description
1. `getchar ()`	stream	read a character from a stream
2. `putchar ()`	stream	write a character to a stream
3. `getc ()`	stream	read a character from a stream
4. `putc ()`	stream	write a character to a stream
5. `gets ()`	stream	read a string from a stream
6. `puts ()`	stream	write a string to a stream
7. `cgets ()`	console	read a string from the system console
8. `getche ()`	console	read a character from the system console
9. `putch ()`	console	write a character onto the system console
10. `cputs ()`	console	write a string onto the system console

In order to use the above functions, the programmer must include the **`stdio.h`** header file at the beginning of the program. The C environment assumes a keyboard as the standard input device and the LCD display as the standard output device. The display is also called a visual display unit (VDU). A console comprises both keyboard and the VDU.

Since the interacting devices (say printer and RAM) may differ in speed, the I/O between them is carried out through a buffer. Therefore, by default all stream I/Os are buffered. At this point, it is better that we understand the term buffered I/O before we proceed to discuss the stream I/O functions.

12.2 BUFFERED I/O

When data is read from the keyboard or from a file stored on a device, it is stored in a buffer called input buffer. The input stream, thereafter, reads from the buffer until the input buffer becomes empty (see Fig. 12.1). As soon as the buffer becomes empty, the next block of data is transferred into the buffer from the I/O device.

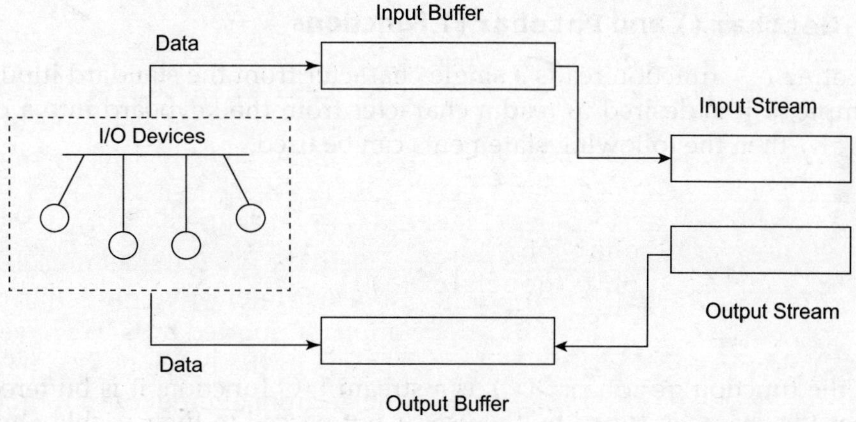

Fig. 12.1 Buffered I/O

Similarly, data written by an output stream is not directly written onto the device, but into an output buffer. As soon as the output buffer becomes full, a block of data is written on to the I/O device making the output buffer empty.

When the header file `stdio.h` is included in a program, the following standard stream pointers are automatically opened.

Name	Meaning
`stdin`	standard input
`stdout`	standard output
`stderr`	standard error
`stdaux`	auxiliary storage
`stdprn`	printer

In the computer, `stdin` and `stdout` refer to the user's console i.e., the standard input device as keyboard and the standard output device as VDU (screen). The stream pointers `stdprn` and `stdaux` refer to the printer and auxiliary storage respectively. The error messages generated by the stream are sent to standard error (stderr).

In order to clear the buffers, a function called fflush ( ) can be used. For example, the input buffer of the standard input device can be cleared by invoking the function: fflush (stdin).

12.3 SINGLE CHARACTER FUNCTIONS

C supports many character based input and output functions. These functions read or write one character at a time. C supports both stream and console I/O character based functions. These will be discussed in the following sections.

12.3.1 Getchar() and Putchar() Functions

The getchar( ) function reads a single character from the standard input device. For example, if it is desired to read a character from the keyboard into a character variable ch, then the following statements can be used.

```
    :
char ch;
ch = getchar ( );
    :
```

Since the function getchar ( ) is a stream I/O function, it is buffered, in the sense that the character typed by the user is not passed to the variable ch until the user hits the Enter or Return key i.e., the symbol ↵. The ASCII code of the Enter key is itself a character and it also gets stored in the buffer along with the character typed by the user. The entry of the 'enter key' character into the buffer creates problems in the normal functioning of the getchar() function. Therefore, it is suggested that after an input operation from the standard input device (i.e. keyboard), the input buffer should be cleared. This operation is necessary to avoid interference with subsequent input operations. The function call for this activity is: **fflush (stdin)**. The usage is shown below:

```
 :
char ch;
ch = getchar ( );
fflush (stdin);
   :
```

The function putchar ( ) is used to send a single character to the standard output device. The character to be displayed on the VDU screen is included as an argument to the putchar ( ) function, as shown on the next page.

```
:
ch = 'A';
putchar (ch);
:
```

Once the above program segment is executed, the character 'A' will be displayed on the screen. The `putchar ( )` function is also buffered. The function call for clearing the output buffer is : **`fflush (stdout)`**. However, when a new line character '\n' is used as an argument to `putchar ()`, the output buffer is cleared automatically.

Example 1

Write a program that demonstrates the usage of `getchar ( )` and `putchar ( )` functions.

Solution

The following program reads a character from the keyboard and displays it on the VDU screen. This process is repeated till the user types 'Q' or 'q'.

```
/* This program illustrates the usage of getchar() and
   putchar() functions */
# include <stdio.h>
main()
 {
  char ch;
  do
  {
   ch = getchar();
   fflush(stdin);
   putchar (ch);
   fflush(stdout);
   }
   while (ch !='Q' && ch !='q');
   }
```

Example 2

Write a program that reads an alphabet `ch` from the keyboard and prints it in the reverse case i.e., if input is in uppercase it is changed to lowercase and vice versa. Continue till the user wants.

Note: The ASCII codes for A–Z are : 65–90 and a–z are : 97–122.

Solution

The required program is given below:

```
# include <stdio.h>
void main ()
{
 char ch, ans;
 ans ='Y';
 while (ans == 'Y'|| ans == 'y')
 {
   printf ("\n Enter a character");
   ch = getchar ( );
   fflush (stdin);
   if (ch >= 65 && ch <= 90)
                     ch = ch + 32;
   else
    if (ch >= 97 && ch <= 122)
                     ch = ch-32;
      else
      {
                     printf ("n It is not an alphabet");
                     continue;
      }
         putchar (ch);
               printf ("\n Do you wish to continue (Y/N)");
   ans = getchar ();
   fflush (stdin);
   }
 }
```

Example 3

Write a program that prints the following output on the screen.

```
A
A B
A B C
A B C D
A B C D E
```

Solution

It may be noted that there are five rows to be printed on the screen. Each row contains columns equal to the row number i.e., in row number 3, there are 3 columns to be displayed. Therefore, this is a case of nested loops. We will initialize a variable (say ch) with the character 'A' at the beginning of each row and print it. Subsequent increments of variable ch will generate the next character (column) required in the row. At the end of each row, the character '\n' will be printed, to go to the next line. The required program is given below:

```
/* This program illustrates the usage of getchar ( ) and
   putchar ( ) functions */

# include <stdio.h>
main ( )
{
  char ch;
  int i, j;
  for (i = 1; i <= 5; i++)
  {
  ch = 'A';
  for (j= 1; j <= i; j++)
   {
         putchar (ch);
         putchar(' ');
         ch++;
   }
  putchar ('\n');
  fflush (stdout);
  }
}
```

12.3.2 getc ( ) and putc ( ) Functions

The getc ( ) and putc ( ) functions are also character based functions. They have basically been designed to work with files. However, these functions can also be used to read and write data from the standard input and output devices by specifying stdin and stdout as input and output files respectively.

For example, the function getc (stdin) is equivalent to the function getchar ( ). Both will get a character from the standard input device (keyboard). Where the function getchar ( ) by default reads from the keyboard, the argument stdin of the function getc (stdin) makes it read from a file represented by the standard input device, which is nothing but the keyboard.

Similarly, the function putc (ch, stdout) is equivalent to the function putchar (ch). Both the functions send the character ch to the standard output device i.e., the VDU screen.

Example 4

Write a program that reads a character from the keyboard and displays its successor on the screen. For example, if the character 'A' is typed by the user, then the program displays the character 'B' on the screen.

Solution

The required program is given below:

```
/* This program illustrates the usage of getc( ) and putc( )
   functions */
   # include <stdio.h>
   void main ( )
   {
         char ch;
         printf ("\n Enter a character :"   );
         ch = getc(stdin);
         fflush (stdin);
         ch++;    /*Incrementnt character */
         printf  ("\nThe next character in the order is ...");
         putc( ch, stdout);
   }
```

We have seen that `getc ( )`, `putc ( )` are equivalent to `getchar ( )`, `putchar ( )` respectively. Therefore, it is suggested that the functions `getchar ( )` and `putchar ( )` may be used because of their simplicity of usage as far as standard input/output devices are concerned.

12.3.3 getche ( ) and putch ( ) Functions

These two functions are character based versions of console I/O functions. Therefore, the header file **conio.h** has to be included. In fact, these functions act as an extension to the stream I/O functions. The console I/O functions read and write directly to and from the keyboard and the screen.

1. `getche ( )`: This function directly reads a character from the console as soon as it is typed, without waiting for the enter key (↵) to be pressed. There is another similar function `getch ( )` which also reads a character from the keyboard exactly in the same manner, but does not show it on the screen. This function is useful in menu selections where the programmer does not want to display the character typed by the user. In fact, the extra `e` in the `getche ( )` function stands for echo i.e., display the character.
   Examples of usage of these functions are:
   (i) `ch = getche ( );`
   (ii) `ch = getch ( );`

2. `putch ( )`: This function directly writes a character on the console. It takes character as an argument. Examples of the usage of this function are:
   (i) `putch ('\n');` /* It takes the cursor to the next line of the screen. */

(ii) `putch (ch);` /* It displays the character stored in the variable `ch` on the screen. */

(iii) `putch ('A');` /* It displays the character 'A' on the screen.*/

Note: These functions cannot read special keys from the keyboard, such as FUNCTION keys.

Example 5

Write a program that illustrates the usage of `getche ( )` and `putch ( )` functions.

Solution

The desired program is given below:

```
/* This program illustrates the usage of console I/O functions
  */
 # include <conio.h>
 void main( )
        {
          char ch;
          printf  ("\n Press a key (alphabet)");
          ch= getche();
          putch('\n');
          putch(ch);
        }
```

Example 6

Write a program that creates a menu with four options, the fourth being Quit. It uses the `getch ( )` function to read the key pressed by the user and displays a suitable message for the corresponding option associated with the key.

Solution

We will create a menu of the following type within a `do-while` loop. The key pressed in response to the message `'enter your choice'`, would be detected by a `switch` statement.

Menu
option 1 'A'
option 2 'B'
option 3 'C'
Quit 'Q'
Enter your choice:

The various cases of switch would be utilized to display appropriate messages.

The corresponding program is given below:

```
/* This program illustrates the usage of console I/O functions
   */
# include <conio.h>
void main( )
{
   char ch;
int flag = 1;
clrscr();
        do
         {
         printf  ("\n Menu");
         printf  ("\n");
         printf  ("\n Option1   'A'");
         printf  ("\n");
         printf  ("\n Option2   'B'");
         printf  ("\n");
         printf  ("\n Option3   'C'");
         printf  ("\n");
         printf  ("\n Quit      'Q'");
         printf  ("\n");
         printf  ("\n Enter Your Choice");
         ch = getch();
         switch (ch)
            {
               case 'A' : printf ("\nYou opted for Option1");
                    break;
               case 'B' : printf ("\nYou opted for Option2");
                    break;
               case 'C' : printf ("\nYou opted for Option3");
                    break;
               case 'Q' : printf ("\nYou opted to  Quit");
                    flag=0;
                    break;
               default  : printf("\ngive correct option"  );
            };
         }while (flag);
}
```

In case of menu-driven programs, it is a matter of choice whether a programmer wants to use the `getchar ()` or the `getch ()` function. Some programmers feel that buffered input gives the users time to decide their response or change it with a backspace, if need be, before the `Enter` key is pressed. However, the `getch ()` function is useful where the user has to switch frequently between menus and sub-menus.

12.4 STRING BASED FUNCTIONS

String based functions read or write a string of characters at a time. C supports both stream and console I/O string based functions.

12.4.1 gets ( ) and puts () Functions

These functions are string-based input–output functions. The function gets ( ) reads a string from the standard input device (keyboard). It is also buffered and therefore the Return or Enter key has to be typed to terminate the input. The fflush ( ) function should also be used after each gets ( ) to avoid input of unnecessary characters. For example, the program segment given below reads a string in a variable name from keyboard.

```
:
fflush (stdin);
name = gets ( ) ;
:
```

Similarly the function puts ( ) is used to send a string to the standard output device. The string to be displayed on the VDU screen is included as an argument to the puts function, as shown below:

```
:
  city =  "  New Delhi " ;
puts (city);
  fflush (stdout);

:
```

Once this program segment is executed, the following message will be displayed on the screen:

```
New Delhi
```

Example 7

Write a program that reads a character from the keyboard and determines if it is uppercase or lowercase.

Solution

In this program, we will use the puts ( ) function to print the messages and the getchar ( ) function to read the character from the keyboard. However, a nested if-else construct will be employed to check the case of the input character. The required program is given below:

```
/* This program determines whether a character is uppercase,
   lowercase or otherwise */
# include <stdio.h>
main ( )
{
   char ch;
   puts ("\n Enter the character");  /* read character */
   ch = getchar ( );
   fflush (stdin);                    /* clear buffer */

  if (ch >= 'A')
   {
   if (ch <= 'Z')
         puts  ("\nThe input character is Upper Case");
   else
         if (ch >= 'a')
         {
          if (ch <= 'z')
            puts ("\n The input character is lower case");
          else
            puts ("\n The character is > z");
         }
        else
              puts ("\n The Character is < a but  > Z");
    }
    else
            puts ("\nthe Character is < A");
}
```

Example 8

Write a program that accepts a character from the keyboard and determines if it is a vowel. If yes, then it prints the vowel, otherwise gives the message:

"It is not a vowel."

Solution

In this program we will use the `puts ( )` function to print the messages and the `getchar ( )` function to read the character from the keyboard. However a `switch` construct will be employed to check if the input character is a vowel. The required program is given on the next page.

```
/* This program determines if an input character is a vowel*/
# include <stdio.h>
main ()
{
  char ch;
 /*read character*/
   puts  ("\n Enter a lower case character");
   ch = getchar();
   fflush(stdin); /*clear input buffer*/
   switch (ch)
             {
             case 'a' : puts ("\n The vowel is a"  );
                          break;
             case 'e' : puts ("\n The vowel is e"  );
                          break;
             case 'i' : puts ("\n The vowel is i"  );
                          break;
             case 'o' : puts ("\n The vowel is o"  );
                          break;
             case 'u' : puts ("\n The vowel is u"  );
                          break;
             default  : puts ("\n  It is not a vowel");
             }
  }
```

Example 9

Write an interactive program that illustrates the use of `gets ( )` and `puts ( )` functions.

Solution

We will write a program wherein the name of the user is read and displayed with appropriate messages. Let us assume that the name of the user is not more than 20 characters.

```
/*An interactive program*/
# include <stdio.h>
main ( )
 {
   char name [20]; /*declaration of the string*/
   char ch;
   puts  ("\n  Enter your name");
   gets (name);
```

```
    fflush (stdin);
    puts   ("\n Hello");
    puts (name);
    puts (" I like your name" );
    puts (" Do you want to be my friend ?");
    puts ("\n Press Y/N"  );
          ch = getch ( );
          fflush (stdin);
                if ((ch == 'Y') || (ch == 'y'))
                    puts ("\n  Thank you we will meet again" );
          else
                    puts    ("\n  Any way, forget it"  );
  }
```

It may be noted in the above program that a character string called `name` has been declared as shown below:

```
char name [20].
```

The above declaration means that " It is desired to have a character string called `name` which can contain 20 characters.

Example 10

Rewrite the program given in Example 5 such that the Menu is created with the help of the `puts ( )` function.

Solution

We will create the Menu by including the various messages of the menu as arguments to the function `puts ( )`. The required program is given below:

```
/* This program illustrates the usage of console I/O functions */
          # include <conio.h>
          void main( )
          {
             char ch;
             int flag = 1;
             clrscr();
                do
                {
                  puts (" Menu");
                  puts ("\n");
                  puts (" Option1   'A'");
                  puts ("\n");
                  puts (" Option2   'B'");
```

```
            puts ("\n");
            puts (" Option3   'C'");
            puts ("\n");
            puts (" Quit      'Q'");
            puts ("\n");
            puts (" Enter Your Choice");
            ch = getch();
            switch (ch)
              {
                case 'A' : puts ("You opted for Option1");
                           break;
                case 'B' : puts ("You opted for Option2");
                           break;
                case 'C' : puts ("You opted for Option3");
                           break;
                case 'Q' : puts ("You opted to  Quit");
                           flag=0;
                           break;
                default : puts ("give correct option" );
              };
           }while (flag);
        }
```

Example 11

Write a program that displays a box of the following type on the screen having a maximum of 15 lines. It accepts the number of lines from the user in a variable num and displays the box accordingly.

```
------------------------------------------------------------------------------------------
|                                                                                        |
|                                                                                        |
|                                                                                        |
|                                                                                        |
|                                                                                        |
------------------------------------------------------------------------------------------
```

Solution

We will use the puts ( ) function to display the required program. The program is given below:

```
/* This program draws a box on the screen*/
 # include <stdio.h>
 void main( )
 {
```

```
      int num;
      int i;   /* No. of lines */
      puts("\n Enter the number of lines in the box :"   );
      scanf ("%d", &num);
      if (num >0)
       {
              puts   ("        Box");
              puts   ("  ________________________  ");
              puts   ("|                        |");
              for (i=1; i<=num; i++)
                     puts  ("|                   |");

              puts ("|                          |");
    puts ("  _______________________  "   );
       }
  }
```

12.5 MORE ON `scanf()` AND `printf()` FUNCTIONS

During data input and output operations, the data items can be properly composed and formatted by specifying the maximum field width (a number) for the variables. The field width can be specified by placing a number between the (%) sign and the format specifier.

For example, the following statement:

```
scanf ("%4d", & val);
```

indicates that the maximum number of input digits allowed for variable `val` is 4.

However, in `printf ()`, the field width for integer data cannot be less than the size of the data itself, otherwise some bits will be lost.

Example 12

What would be the assignment for the following statement?

```
scanf ("%4d %3d", & val1, & val2)
```

data input = (1) 5293 8275
(2) 529363

Solution

The assignment would be

(i) `val1 = 5293, val2 = 827`
(ii) `val1 = 5293, val2 = 63`

Example 13

What would be the assignment for the following statement?

```
scanf ("%3d %5f %2d", & val1, & val2, & val3);
```

data input = (i) 2374 8234.29 723
(ii) 632497.82985

Solution

The assignment would be

(i) `val1 = 237, val2 = 4.0, val3 = 82`

The reason for the (seemingly) unexpected behaviour is that `scanf ()` takes consecutive non-white space characters for all variables, starting from the leftmost bit of the input data.
Therefore, it has taken 3 digits (i.e. 237) for `val1` and next digit (i.e. 4) for `val2`. After the whites space, it has taken 2 digits (i.e. 82) for `val3`.

(ii) `val1 = 632, val2 = 497.8, val3 = 29`

It may be noted that it has counted, '.' as one of the digits.
Sometimes it becomes important for the programmer to find out whether the operation of `scanf ()` was successful or not. For this purpose, the programmer can use a special feature of the `scanf()` function, wherein this function returns an integer indicating how many input fields were read successfully. In fact `scanf()` scans the input values from left to right. As soon as it encounters an unexpected input value, it abandons the rest of the input values.

Example 14

Consider the example given below. We will use a variable called flag to test the outcome of the scan function.

```
/* This program illustrates the special feature of scanf()*/
 # include <stdio.h>
 # include <conio.h>
 void main( )
 {
   int num;
   float val;
   char ch;
   int flag;
   printf ("\n\n Enter- int float char: ");
   flag= scanf ("%d %f %c", &num, &val, &ch);
   printf ("\n The correct number of input values are:%d",
                                                        flag);
   printf ("\n int=%d float =%f char =%c", num,val,ch);
 }
```

Sample inputs/ outputs for the above program are given below:

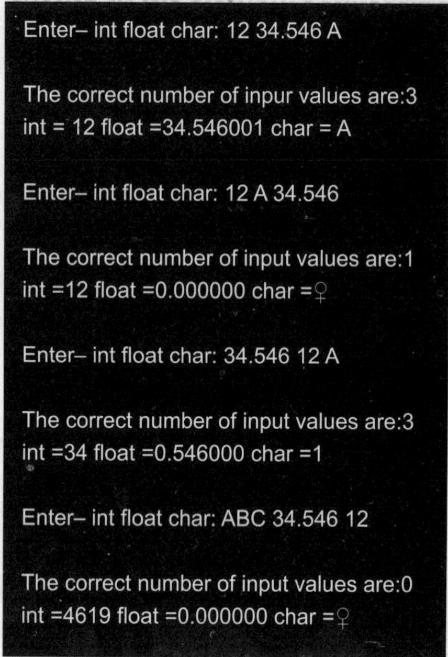

```
Enter– int float char: 12 34.546 A

The correct number of inpur values are:3
int = 12 float =34.546001 char = A

Enter– int float char: 12 A 34.546

The correct number of input values are:1
int =12 float =0.000000 char =♀

Enter– int float char: 34.546 12 A

The correct number of input values are:3
int =34 float =0.546000 char =1

Enter– int float char: ABC 34.546 12

The correct number of input values are:0
int =4619 float =0.000000 char =♀
```

It may be noted that in the last run of the program the first value itself was wrong. Therefore the `scanf()` returned 0 indicating that it could not scan even a single value correctly.

Example 15

What would be the output of the following program segments:

```
int val1 = 2934;
  float val2 = 295.673;
  printf ("%4d %5.2f", val1, val2);
```

Solution

The output would be: 2934 295.67

Example 16

What would be the output of the following program segement:

```
float val = 295.678
  printf ("% 5.1 f %12 e", val, val);
```

Solution

The output would be : 295.7 2.95678 e + 02

It may be noted that the `printf()` function rounds off the last digit of the output data:

The `printf()` function can also skip the first k characters of the string literal as shown below:

```
printf ( "nightwatch" + 5);
```

The above statement will skip the first k (5 in this case) characters of the string literal: `"nightwatch"` and will print the rest of the string i.e. `watch`.

12.5.1 Flags used in `printf ()`

The output produced by `printf ()` can be further controlled by using the flags listed in Table 12.1

Table 12.1 Some important flags used in `printf()`

Flag	Usage
–	When '-' is included in the Format specifier, the data is displayed left justified within the field width
+	When '+' is included in the Format specifier, the data item is displayed with its sign, i.e., the numerical data is displayed as a signed data item.
0	The data item is displayed as right justified with leading zeros instead of the leading blanks

Example 17

The output of the following program:

```
# include <stdio.h>
 main()
 {int val  = 2;
   printf ("\n %-4d %04d", val, val);
 }
```

would be: `2 БББ  0002` (Б means a blank)

Example 18

The output of the following program:

```
# include <stdio.h>
 main()
 {float val1  = 25.26;
```

```
   float val2  =-29.34;
   printf ("\n %+4.2f %+4.2f", val1, val2);
  }
```

would be: + 25   26   29.34

TEST YOUR SKILLS

1. What would be the output of the following program ?

```
# include <stdio.h>
main()
  {
   int val = 400;
   printf ("\n %5.2f", val);
   getch();
   }
```

Solution: 400.00

2. What would be the output of the following program ?

```
# include <stdio.h>
main()
 {
   char ch1 ='A';
   char ch2 ='B';
   putchar (ch1,ch2);
 }
```

Solution: Wrong number of arguments to putchar()– only one argument is allowed.

3. What would be the output of the following program ?

```
# include <stdio.h>
main()
 {
   char ch1 ='A';
   printf ("\n %f", ch1);
 }
```

Solution: Run time error – mismatch of formats

4. What would be the output of the following program ?

```
# include <stdio.h>
main()
 { float val =5.3421;
   printf ("\n val = %f", val);
   printf ("\n val = %5.1f", val);
   printf ("\n val = %5.0f", val);
 }
```

Solution: `val = 5.34210`
`val = 5.3`
`val = 5`

5. **What would be the output of the following statement ?**
`printf ("%v", 15);`
Solution: `%v`

6. **What would be the output of the following statement?**
`printf ("Misfortune" +3);`
Solution: fortune.

7. **What would be the output of the following statement?**
`printf (3+"Misfortune");`
Solution: It will have the same effect i.e., the `printf()` function will skip the first 3 characters and print the rest of the string: fortune.

EXERCISES

1. Differentiate between the following
   (i) `getchar ( )` and `gets ( )`
   (ii) `putchar ( )` and `puts ( )`
2. Explain the term buffered I/O in brief.
3. "`getchar()` function is buffered" – give your comments.
   Explain the function `fflush(stdin)` in brief.
4. Write a program that inputs a character from the keyboard and displays it on the screen.
5. Write a program that prompts for and accepts a name with a maximum of 25 characters. It displays the following message:
   `<name>, I like your name.`
6. Write a program that prints the following output on the screen:

```
A
B  B
C  C  C
D  D  D  D
E  E  E  E  E
```

7. Explain the functions `getc( )` with the help of suitable examples.
8. Explain the functions `getche ( )` and `putch ( )` with the help of suitable examples.
9. Write a program that reads two characters from the keyboard and displays them one after the other, using the functions `getc ( )` and `putc ( )`.
10. Write a program that uses the `putchar ( )` function to display the following word on the screen
    `'MOGLI'`
11. Write a program that uses the `puts ( )` function to display the following on the screen.

```
" OBJECT : C"
"The C compiler is a fatherly old chap"
" Who doesn't nag you with small little details"
```

12. Write a program that reads a character from the keyboard and determines whether it is an uppercase alphabet or not?
13. Write a program that reads a character from the keyboard and does the following
    (i) if the character is not alphabetic, do nothing
    (ii) if the character is alphabetic, print the next successive character. For example successive character of 'p' is 'q'.
14. Write a program that implements a menu of the following type

```
Menu
option 1      'a'
option 2      'b'
option 3      'c'
option 4      'q'
Enter your option:
```

In response to the user's selection, it prints the following messages

(i) option 1 — 'one is alone'
(ii) option 2 — 'two is company'
(iii) option 3 — 'three is a crowd'
(iv) option 4 — 'Quitting'

If the option is invalid, it gives the message "wrong option" .

15. How would you output the string "\n" on the screen?
16. What will be the output of the following

```
main ( )
  {
   puts     "  \n H\ne\n\ll\no  );
  }
```

17. Write a program that accepts N number of characters and at the end displays the smallest and largest of all characters.
18. Print the following pattern on the screen using the `printf()` function

```
  *
 ***
*****
```

20. Write a program that allows the user to enter a character until he inputs the character 'q'. Each time a character is entered, the program displays whether it is an alphabet or not.

CHAPTER

13 Arrays

13.1 INTRODUCTION

An *array* is a data structure with the help of which a programmer can refer to and perform operations on a collection of similar data types such as simple *lists* or *tables* of information. For example, a list of names of 'N' number of students of a class can be grouped under a common name (say `studList`). This list can be represented easily by an array called `studList` for 'N= 45' students, as shown in Fig. 13.1

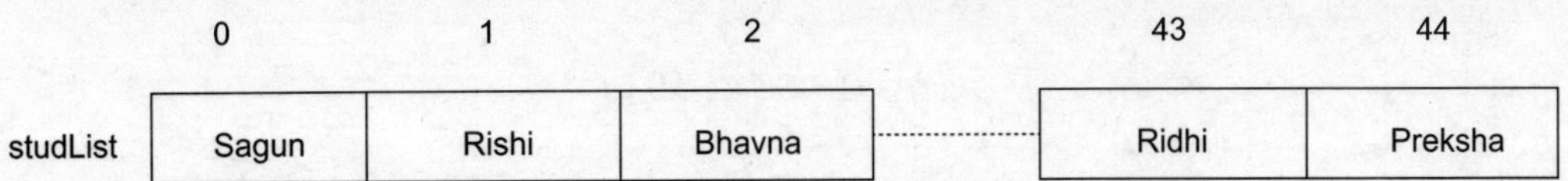

Fig. 13.1 Schematic representation of an array

In fact, the `studList` shown in Fig. 13.1 can be looked upon by the following two points of view:

1. It is a linear list of 45 names stored in contiguous locations – an abstract view of a list having a finite number of homogeneous elements (i.e., 45 names) .
2. It is a set of 0 to 44 memory locations sharing a common name called `studList`. It is an array data structure in which 45 names have been stored.

It may be noted that all the elements in the array are of same type i.e. *string of char* in this case. The individual elements within the array can be designated by an index. The individual elements are randomly accessible by integers, called the index.

For instance, the 0th element (Sagun) in the list can be referred to as `studList[0]` and the 45rd element (Ridhi) as `studList[45]`, where 0 and 45 are the indices and an index has to be of type integer.

An index is also called a subscript. Therefore, individual elements of an array are called subscripted variables. For instance, `studList [0]` and `studList [45]` are subscripted variables.

From the above discussion, we can arrive at the following definition:

Array: A finite ordered collection of items of the same type. It is a set of *index, value* pairs.

An array is a built-in data structure in every programming language. It is designed to have a fixed size. Some languages provide 0-based indexing whereas other languages provide 1-based indexing. C is an example of a *0-based indexing* language because the index of its arrays starts from 0. Pascal is the example of *1-based indexing* because the index of its arrays starts from 1.

An array whose elements are specified by a single subscript is known as a *one-dimensional array.* The array whose elements are specified by two or more than two subscripts is called a multidimensional array.

13.2 ONE-DIMENSIONAL ARRAYS

One-dimensional arrays are suitable for processing lists of items of identical types. An array can be declared in C just like any other variable. The definition consists of the type, array name, and size. The squared brackets are used to delimit the array size. The array size has to be a positive integer constant. For example, an array called LIST of 50 locations of integer type can be declared as shown below:

```
int LIST [50];
```

The above declaration means that LIST is an array of 50 memory locations, each of which is of integer type. Once this declaration is enforced, we get a group of 50 locations of integer type in the memory of the computer, as shown below:

	0	1	2		48	49
LIST				....		

It may be noted here that in C, the first array element has the subscript 0. Thus, we have access to the 50 elements in the range of 0 to 49 subscripts. In fact, the element LIST [50] does not exist.

The programmer should not use a subscript outside the specified range of the array. For example, access to an element such as LIST[60] will produce unpredictable results. However, the compiler of C, being flexible and robust, may not give any errors in this connection.

Examples of valid array declarations are:

(i) int series [100] ;
(ii) char names [20] ;
(iii) float sal [50] ;

Generally, arrays are manipulated in a fashion of component-by-component processing. In simple words we can say that similar operations are performed on some or all the components of the array. In order to help beginners or novices to learn the idea behind array processing, some C statements involving array elements are given in Table 13.1.

Table 13.1 Examples of array processing

Statement	Meaning
`scanf ("%d", &LIST[5]);`	Read an integer from the keyboard and store it in the 5th location of `LIST`
`printf ("%d", LIST [i];`	Print the ith element of `LIST` onto the screen.
`LIST [i] = LIST [j];`	Assign the contents of the jth element of `LIST` to its ith element.
`LIST [k]++;`	Increment the contents of the kth element of `LIST`
`net = gross - LIST [5];`	Subtract the contents of the 5th element of `LIST` from variable `gross` and store into variable `net`.
`for( i = 0; i< 10; i++)` `scanf("%d", & LIST [i];`	Read integers one by one from the keyboard and store them one by one in `LIST [0]` to `LIST [9]`.

From Table 13.1 it can be observed that an individual element of an array behaves like a normal variable whereas the array as such represents a list of items of a certain data type. The items are internally stored in continuous memory locations.

One-dimensional arrays are very useful for problems that require the same operation to be performed on a group of data items. Consider the following example.

Example 1

The examination committee of the university has decided to give 5 grace marks to every student of a class. Assume that the number of students in the class is 50 and their marks are stored in a list called `marksList`. Write a program that adds the grace marks to every entry in the `marksList`.

Solution

As the problem deals with a list of marks, we can select a one-dimensional array called `marksList` to represent the list. The grace marks are to be added to all elements of the list, for which we must use the `For` loop. The required program is given on the next page.

```
/* This program adds grace marks to all elements of a list of
   marks */
#include <stdio.h>
void main()
 {
    int marksList[50];
    int i;
    int grace = 5;          /*grace marks */
                            /* Read the marksList */

    printf( "\n Enter the list of marks one by one");
      for (i=0; i< 50; i++)
        {
          scanf ("%d", &marksList[i]);
          marksList[i] = marksList[i] + grace;
        }
                            /* Print the Final list */
    printf ("\n The final List is ...");
    printf ("\n S.No.\t Marks");
      for (i=0; i < 50; i++)
          printf ("\n %d\t%d", i, marksList[i]);
 }
```

It may be noted that in the above program, *a component by component processing* has been done on the all elements of the array called `marksList`.

The following operations are defined on the array data structure:

- **Traversal**: An array can be traveled by visiting its elements starting from the 0th element to the last in the list.
- **Selection**: An array allows selection of an element for a given (random) *index.*
- **Searching**: The array can be searched for a particular value.
- **Insertion**: An element can be inserted in an array at a particular location.
- **Deletion**: An element can be deleted from a particular location of an array
- **Sorting**: The elements of an array can be manipulated to obtain a sorted list .

A discussion on the above mentioned operations on arrays is given in the following sections:

13.2.1 Traversal

Traversal is an operation in which each element of a list, stored in an array, is visited. The travel proceeds from the 0th element to the last element of the list. Processing of the visited element can be done as per the requirement of the problem.

Example 2

Write an algorithm called `listTravel` that travels a list stored in an array called `List` of size N. Each visited element is operated upon by an operator called *OP*.

Solution

The `For` loop can be employed to visit and apply the operator OP on every element of the array. The required algorithm is given below:

```
Algorithm listTravel()
  {
     Step
     1. For ( i = 0; i < N, i++)
          {
            1.1  List[i] = OP(List[i]);
          }
  }
```

Example 3

A list of N integer numbers is given. Write a program that travels the list and determines how many of the elements of the list are *less than zero, zero,* and *greater than zero* numbers present in the list.

Solution

In this program, three counters called `numNeg`, `numZero` and `numPos`, would be used to keep track of the number of *less than zero, zero,* and *greater than zero* present in the list. The required program is given below:

```
/* This program determines the number of less than zero,
zero, and greater than zero numbers present in a list */

# include <stdio.h>
void main()
  {
    int List [50];
    int N;
    int i,numNeg, numZero,numPos;

    printf ("\n Enter the size of the list");
    scanf("%d", &N);
    printf("Enter the elements one by on");
                                             /* Read the List*/
         for (i=0; i < N; i++)
```

```
            {
              printf("\n Enter Number:");
              scanf  ("%d", &List[i]);
            }
    numNeg=0;                                   /* Initialize counters*/
    numZero=0;
    numPos=0;
                                                /* Travel the List*/
    for (i=0; i < N; i++)
     {
          if ( List[i] < 0)
               numNeg = numNeg+1;
          else
               if ( List[i] == 0)
                         numZero = numZero+1;
               else
                         numPos = numPos+1;
     }
 }
```

13.2.2 Selection

An array allows selection of an element for a given (random) *index*. Therefore, the array is also called a random access data structure. The selection operation is useful in a situation wherein the user wants to query on the contents of a list for a given position.

Example 4

Write a program that stores a merit list in an array called `Merit`. The index of the array denotes the merit position i.e., 1st, 2nd, 3rd, etc., whereas the contents of the various array locations represent the percentage of marks obtained by the candidates. On demand by the user, the program displays the percentage of marks obtained for a given position in the merit list, as per the following format:

Position : 4
Percentage : 95.25

Solution

An array called `Merit` would be used to store the given merit list. Two variables `pos` and `percentage` would be used to store the merit position and the percentage of a candidate respectively. A `do-while` loop would be used to iteratively interact with the user through the following menu displayed to the user.

```
Menu:
Query----1
Quit------ 2
Enter your choice
```

Note: As per the demand of the program, we will leave the 0th location unused and fill the array from index 1.

The required program is given below:

```
/* This program illustarates the random selection operation
   allowed by array data structures */

   # include<stdio.h>
   # include<conio.h>

   void main()
    {
     float Merit[50];
     int size;
     int i;
     int pos;
     float percentage;
     int choice;

     printf ("\n Enter the size of the list");
     scanf ("%d", &size);

     printf("\n Enter the merit list one by one");

         for (i=1; i<= size; i++)         /* Read Merit */
          {
           printf ("\n Enter data:" );
           scanf ("%f", &Merit[i]);
          }
                              /* display menu and start session */
          do
          {clrscr();
           printf ("\n Menu");
           printf ("\n Query--------1");
           printf ("\n Quit --------2");
           printf ("\n Enter your choce: ");
           scanf ("%d", & choice);
```

```
                 /* use switch statement fordeterminingthe
                                               choice*/
                switch (choice)
                 {
                 case 1 : printf("\n Enter Position");
                                scanf("%d", &pos);
                                percentage = Merit[pos]; /* the
                                     random selection */
                                printf ("\n position =%d", pos);
                                printf ("\n percentage = %4.2f",
                                          percentage);
                                break;
                     case 2 : printf ("\n Quitting");
                 }
            printf ("\n press a key to continue...");
            getch();
           }
           while (choice != 2);
    }
```

Searching and sorting are very important activities in a data processing environment and a detailed discussion on these operations is given in following sections.

13.2.3 Searching

There are many situations where we want to find out whether a particular item is present in a list or not. For instance, in a given voter list of a colony, a person may search for his name to ascertain whether he is a valid voter or not? For similar reasons, passengers look for their names in railway reservation lists.

Note: Systems programs extensively search symbols, literals, mnemonics, *compiler and assembler* directives etc.

In fact search is an operation in which a given list is searched for a particular value. The location of the searched element is returned. A precise definition of search is given below:

Search is an activity of looking for a value or item in a list.

A list can be searched *sequentially* wherein the search for the data item starts from the beginning till the end of the list. This simple method of search is also called a **linear search.** It may be noted that for a list of size 1000, the worst case would involve 1000 number of comparisons.

Let us consider a situation wherein we are interested in searching a list of numbers called `numList` for an element having a value equal to the contents of a variable called `val`. It is desired that the location of the element, if found, be displayed.

The list of numbers can be comfortably stored in an array called `numList` of type `int`. To find the element, the list would be traveled in such a manner that each visited element would be compared to the variable `val`. If the match is found then the location of the corresponding position would be stored in a variable called `Pos`. As the number of elements in the list is known, a `For` loop would be used to travel the array.

```
Algorithm searchList()
{
  step
    1. read numList
    2. read Val
    3. Pos = -1              'initialize Pos to a non existing position'
    4. for ( i = 0; i < N; i++)
       {
            4.1 if ( val == numList[i] )
                        Pos = i;
       }
    5. if ( Pos != –1)
            print Pos.
}
```

The C implementation of the above algorithm is given below:

```
/* This program searches a given value called Val  in a list
   called numLIst   */

   # include<stdio.h>
   void main()
    {
      int numList[20];
      int N;    /* Size of the list*/
      int Pos,val,i;

      printf("\n Enter the size of the List");
      scanf("%d", &N);
      printf ("\n Enter the elements on by one");

          for (i=0; i < N; i++)
           {
             scanf("%d", &numList[i]);
           }
```

```
        printf ("\n Enter the value to be searched");
        scanf("%d", &val);
            /* Seach the element and its position in the list*/
        Pos = -1;
            for (i=0; i< N; i++)
             {
              if ( val== numList[i])
                {
                Pos =i;
                break;
                  }  /* The element is found - come out of loop*/
             }
        if (Pos != -1)
            printf ("\n The element found at %d location", Pos);
        else
            printf ("\n Search Failed");
    }
```

Example 5

Write a program that finds the second largest element in a given list of N numbers.

Solution

The most basic solution for this problem is that if there are two elements in the list then the smaller of the two will be the second largest. In this case we would initialize the second largest number to '-9999', a value not possible in the list.

In given problem, the list will be searched linearly for the required second largest number. Two variables called `firstLarge` and `secLarge` would be employed to store the largest and second largest numbers respectively. The following algorithm will be used:

```
Algorithm secLarg()
 {
   step
     1. read num;
     2. firstLarge = num;
     3. secLarge = -9999;
     4. for (i = 2; i <= N; i++)
        {
              4.1 read num;
              4.2 if (firstLarge < num)
                          { secLarge = firstLarge;
                            firstLarge = num;
```

```
                    }
            else
                if (secLarge < num)
                        secLarge =num;
    }

    4. prompt "Second Large =";
    5. write secLarge;
}
```

The equivalent program is given below:

```
/* This program finds the 2nd Largest in a given list of
   numbers */

# include <stdio.h>

int Num, firstLarge, secLarge;

int N,i;
void main()
{
   printf ("\n Enter the size of the list");
   scanf ("%d", & N);

   printf ("\n Enter the list one by one");

   scanf ("%d", &Num);

   firstLarge = Num;
   secLarge =-9999;

   for (i = 2; i <= N; i++)
    {
             scanf ("%d", &Num);

             if (firstLarge <  Num)

                 {secLarge = firstLarge;
                   firstLarge = Num;
                 }
             else
             if (secLarge < Num)
```

```
                    secLarge = Num;
    }

    printf( "\n Second Large = %d", secLarge);
}
```

The above discussed search through a list, stored in an array, has the following characteristics:

- The search is linear
- The search starts from the first element and continues in a sequential fashion from element to element till the desired entry is found.
- In the worst case a total number of N steps need to be taken for a list of size N.

Thus, the linear search is slow and to some extent inefficient. In special circumstances, faster searches can be applied.

For instance, *binary search* is a faster method as compared to linear search. It mimics the process of searching a name in a directory, wherein one opens a page in the middle of the directory and examines the page for the required name. If it is found, the search stops, otherwise the search is applied either to the first half of the directory or to the second half. A detailed discussion on binary search is given in next section.

13.2.3.1 Binary Search

If a list is already *sorted* then the search for an entry (say `Val`) in the list can be made faster by using a *divide and conquer* technique. The list is divided into two halves separated by the middle element, as shown in Fig. 13.2

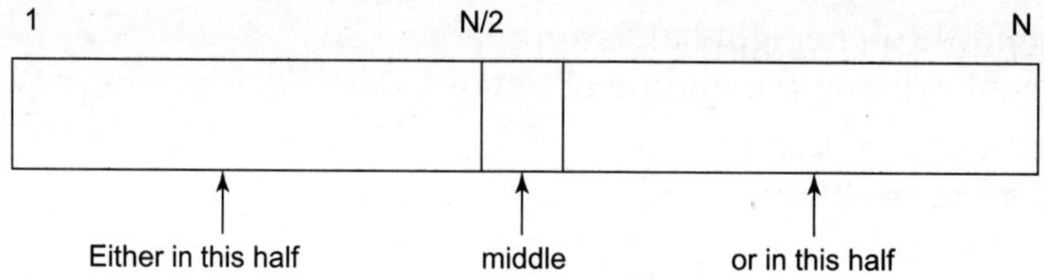

Fig. 13.2 Binary search

The binary search follows the following steps:

1. The middle element is tested for the required entry. If found then its position is reported else the following test is made:
2. If (`Val` < `Middle`) search the left half of the list else search the right half of the list
3. Repeat steps 1 and 2 on the selected half until the entry is found, otherwise report failure.

This search is called binary because in every iteration the given list is divided into two (i.e., binary) parts. Therefore, in the next iteration, the search becomes limited to half the size of the list to be searched. For instance, in the first iteration the size of the list is N which reduces to almost *N*/2 in the second iteration, and so on.

Let us consider a sorted list stored in an array called `Series`, given in Fig. 13.3 :

	0	1	2	3	4	5	6	7	8
Series	3	4	5	7	11	13	14	17	21

Fig. 13.3 `Series` containing 9 elements

Suppose we desire to search `Series` for a value (say 14) and its position in `Series`. Binary search begins by looking at the middle value in `Series`. The middle index of the array is approximated by averaging the first and last indices and truncating the result i.e., (0+8)/2 = 4. Now the contents of the 4th location in `Series` happen to be '11', as shown in Fig. 13.4. Since the value we are looking for (i.e., 14) is greater than 11 (the middle value), it may be present in the right half (`Series[5]` to `Series[8]`).

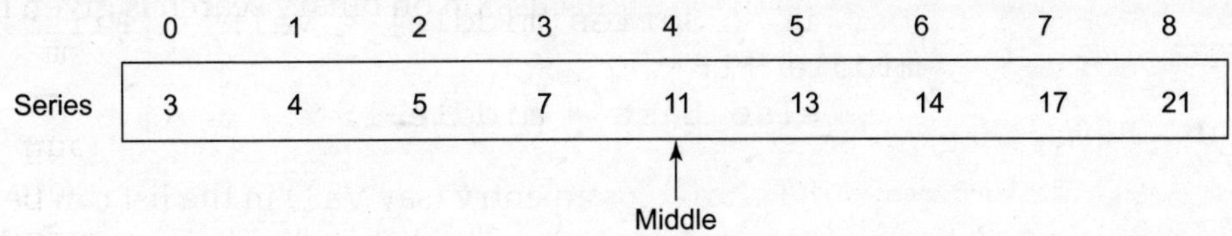

Fig. 13.4 The middle value in `Series` (1st Step).

Now the middle of the right half is approximated i.e., (5+8)/2 = 6. We find that the desired element exists at the middle of the right half i.e. Series [6] = 14, as shown in Fig. 13.5.

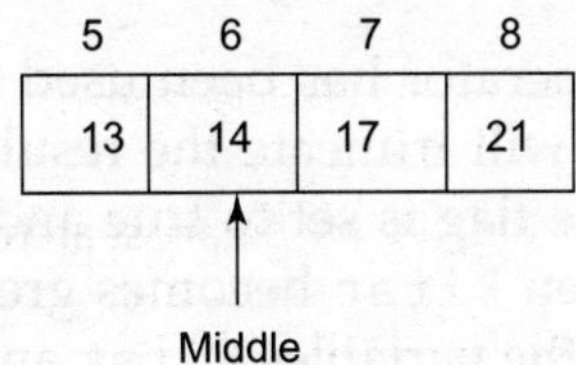

Fig. 13.5 The middle value in `Series` (2nd Step).

It may be noted that the desired element has been found in only two steps. Thus, it is a much faster method than linear search. For instance, a list of 1000 sorted elements would require 10 comparisons to search the entire list. An algorithm for this method is given on the next page.

In this algorithm, we will employ a Boolean variable called `Flag`, which will indicate the presence or absence of the element being searched.

```
Algorithm binSearch ()
{
  Step
  1. First = 0;
  2. Last = N-1;
  3. Pos =-1;
  4. Flag = false;
  5. While (First <= Last and Flag == false)
  {
        5.1 Middle =  (first + last) div 2
              If ( Series [middle] == Val)
                 { Pos= middle;
                   flag = true;
                   break from the loop;
                 }
              else
                    if ( Series[middle] < Val)     First
              =middle +1;
                    else Last = middle-1;
        }

  6. if (flag == true)
        prompt "The value found at";
        write Val;
     else   prompt "The value not found";

 }
```

It may be noted that `div` operator has been used to indicate that it is an integer division. The integer division will truncate the results to the nearest integer. If the desired value is found then the flag is set to true and the `while loop` terminates. Otherwise, a stage arrives when `First` becomes greater than the `Last`, indicating the failure of the search. Thus, the variables `First` and `Last` keep track of the lower and upper bounds of the array.

Example 6

Write a program that uses binary search to search a given value called `Val` in a list of N numbers called `Series`.

Solution

The above given `Algorithm binSearch ()` is being used to write the required program.

```
/* This program uses binary search to find a given value called
   val in a list of N numbers */

# include <stdio.h>
# define true 1
# define false 0

void main()
  {

int First;
int Last;
int Middle;
int Series[20];        /*The list of N sorted numbers*/
int Val;
int flag;              /*The value to be searched */
int N, Pos,i;

printf ("\n Enter the size of the list");
scanf ("%d", & N);

printf ("\n Enter the sorted list one by one");

for (i=0;i< N; i++)
  {
   scanf( "%d", &Series[i]);
  }

printf ("\n Enter the number to be searched");
scanf ("%d", & Val);
                       /* BIN SEARCH begins */

Pos =-1;      /* Non Existing position */

flag = false;          /* Assume search failure */

First = 0;
```

```
Last = N-1;

        while ((First <= Last) && (flag == false))
        {
                 Middle = (First + Last) / 2;
                 if ( Series [Middle] == Val)
                          { Pos= Middle;
                          flag = true;
                          break;
                          }
                 else
                          if ( Series[Middle] < Val)
                                   First =Middle +1;
                          else
                                   Last = Middle-1;
        }

if (flag == true)
        printf( "\n The value found at %d", Pos);

 else
        printf ("\n The value not found");
}
```

Binary search through a list stored in an array has the following characteristics:

- The list must be sorted i.e., ordered.
- It is a fast search method as compared to linear search.
- A list with a large number of elements would increase the total execution time. The reason being that the list must first be ordered, which requires extra effort.
- Thus, binary search shall be applied only to already sorted data.

13.2.4 Insertion and Deletion

13.2.4.1 Insertion

Insertion is an operation in which a new element is added at a particular place in a list. When the list is represented using an array, the element can be added very easily at the end of the list, provided the space is available. However, insertion of an element at a particular location within the list is a difficult operation. For instance, if it is desired to insert an element at the *i*th location of a list then an empty space will have to be created at the ith location of the list. In fact, all the elements from the *i*th location onwards are shifted by one place to the right to accommodate the new element.

Consider a list of characters represented using an array called `charList,` as shown in Fig. 13.6. Suppose it is desired to insert a character 'D' at its proper place in `charList` i.e., at the 3rdth location.

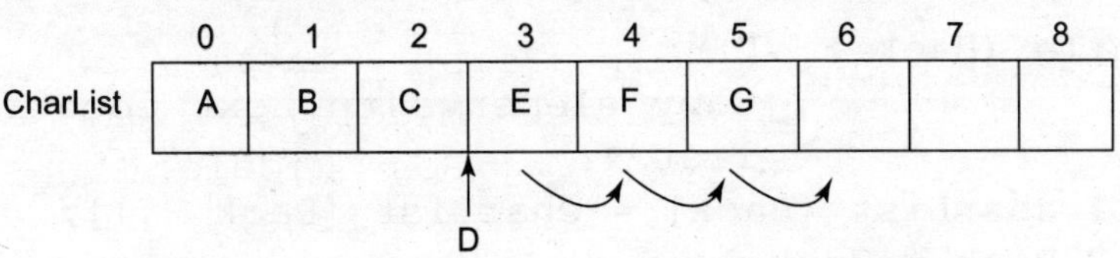

Fig. 13.6 The list `charList` before insertion

Now to accommodate the character 'D', the characters 'G', 'F', and 'E' will have to be shifted one step to the right to the 6th, 5th, and 4th locations respectively as per the operations shown below:

```
charList [6] = charList[5];
charList [5] = charList[4];
charList [4] = charList[5];
```

Once the above copying operation is over, `charList [3]` becomes available for the storage of incoming character 'D', as shown below:

```
charList [3] = 'D';
```

The array `charList` after the insertion operation is shown in Fig. 13.7.

	0	1	2	3	4	5	6	7	8
CharList	A	B	C	D	E	F	G		

Fig. 13.7 The array `charList` after insertion

An algorithm for insertion of an element called `val` at the *i*th location in an array called `charList` of size N, is given below. Let us assume that the last element in the array is at the Mth location. For instance, N=8 and M=5 in the case of `charList` shown in Fig. 13.6. A variable called `Back` is being used to point to the last empty location:

```
Algorithm insertArray ()
 {
    Step
                        /* point to the last vacant position */
```

```
1. if ( M < N ) then Back = M+1;
   else
           STOP;

2. while (Back >  I );
   {                    /*Copy elements to next location in the
                          list */
      2.1 charList [Back] = charList [Back - 1];
      2.2 Back = Back-1;
   }
                        /*Insert the element at Ith location */
3. charList [I] = val;              4. M=M+1;
}
```

Example 7

Write a program that inserts an element called `key` at a location called `loc` in a list called `List`, with M numbers.

Solution

The algorithm `insertArray ()` is being used to implement the required program.

```
/* This program inserts an element called Key into a list of
   numbers */

 # include <stdio.h>

 # define N 20

 void main()
 {
         int List[N];
         int Key;
         int Loc;
         int i, M;
         int back;

         printf ("\n Enter the size of the list (< 20)");
         scanf ("%d", &M);

         printf ("\n Enter the list one by one");
         for (i=0; i< M; i++)
            {
```

```
        scanf ("%d", &List[i]);
      }
    printf ("\n Enter the key and location relative to
    0 index");
    scanf("%d %d", &Key, &Loc);

                /* Insert the 'key' at 'Loc' in 'List' */
    if ( Loc > M+1)
         printf ("\n Insertion not possible");
    else
      {
      back = M +1;
                /* Shift elements one step right */
      while (back > Loc)
        {
            List[back] = List [back-1];
            back--;
        }
                /* Insert Key*/
      List[back] = Key;
      M=M+1;

                /* Display the final list */
      printf ("\n The Final List is ......");

      for (i=0; i < M; i++)
      {
            printf ("%d ", List[i]);
      }
      }
}
```

13.2.4.2 Deletion

Deletion is the operation that removes an element from a given location of a list. When the list is represented using an array, the element can be deleted very easily from the end of the list. However, if it is desired to delete an element from the *i*th location of the list, then all elements on the right of the (*i* +1)th location will have to be shifted one step towards the left to preserve contiguous locations in the array.

For instance, if it is desired to remove an element from the 4th location of the list given in Fig. 13.8 then all elements on the right of the 4th location would have to be shifted one step towards the left.

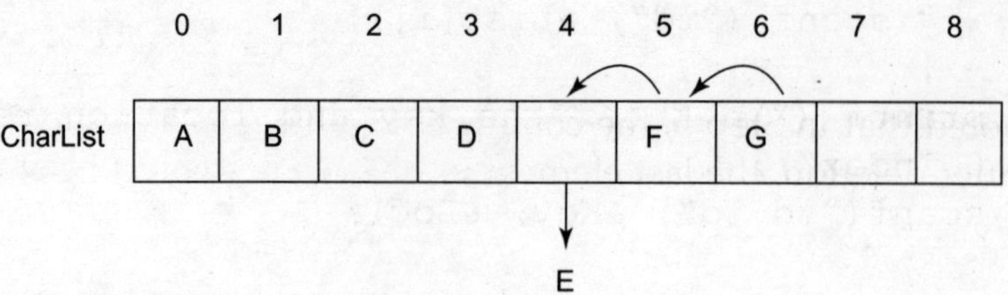

Fig. 13.8 Delete an element from the 4th location

Now to delete the character 'E', the characters 'F', and 'G' will have to be shifted one step towards the left to locations 4 and 5 respectively, as per the operations shown below:

```
charList [4] = charList[5];
charList [5] = charList[6];
```

It may be noted that the contents of `charList[5]` (i.e., 'F') overwrites the contents of `charList[4]` (i.e. E). The array `charList` after the Deletion operation is shown in Fig. 13.9.

	0	1	2	3	4	5	6	7	8
CharList	A	B	C	D	F	G			

Fig. 13.9 The array `charList` after deletion

An algorithm for deletion of an element from the *i*th location in an array called `charList` of size N, is given below. Let us assume that the last element in the array is at the Mth location. For instance, N = 8 and M = 6 in case of `charList` shown in Fig. 13.8. A variable called `Back` is being used to point to the last empty location:

```
Algorithm delElement()
{
 Step
    1. Back = I;          /* point to the location from where deletion is desired */
    2. while (Back < M)
    {
       2.1 charList[Back] = charList[Back+1];      /* Shift elements one step left*/
       2.2 Back = Back + 1;
    }

    3. M=M-1;
```

4. Stop

}

It may be noted that in Step 5, the contents of M have been decremented by 1 to indicate that after deletion, the last element in `charList` would be at the (M – 1)th location.

Example 8

Write a program that deletes an element from a location called `loc` in a list of M numbers, called `List`.'

Solution

The algorithm `delElement()` is being used to implement the required program.

```
/*This program deletes an element from list of numbers */

   # include <stdio.h>
   # define N 20
   void main()
   {
        int List[N];
        int Loc;
        int i, M;
        int back;

        printf ("\n Enter the size of the list (< 20)");
        scanf ("%d", &M);

        printf ("\n Enter the list one by one");
        for (i=0; i< M; i++)
           {
             scanf ("%d", &List[i]);
           }
        printf ("\n Enter location from where the deletion
        is required");
        scanf("%d", &Loc);
                       /* Insert the 'key' at 'Loc' in 'List' */
        if ( Loc > M)
              printf ("\n Deletion not possible");
        else
           {
             back = Loc;
                            /* Shift elements one step left */
```

```
        while (back < M)
         {
              List[back] = List [back+1];
              back++;
         }
         M=M-1;
                               /* Display the final list */
        printf ("\n The Final List is ......");

        for (i=0; i < M; i++)
         {
              printf ("%d ", List[i]);
         }
      }
}
```

It may be noted that arrays are not suitable data structures for problems requiring insertions and deletions in a list. The reason is that we need to shift elements to the right or left for insertion and deletion operations respectively. The problem gets aggravated when the size of the list is very large, as an equally large number of shift operations would be required to insert and delete the elements. **Thus, insertion and deletion are very slow operations as far as arrays are concerned.**

13.2.5 Sorting

It is an operation in which all the elements of a list are arranged in a predetermined order. The elements can be arranged in a sequence from smallest to largest such that every element is less than or equal to the succeeding element in the list. Such an arrangement is called an *ascending order*. Assuming an array called `List` containing N elements, the ascending order can be defined by the following relation:

```
List[i] <= List [i+1] ,   0 < i < N-1
```

Similarly, in descending order, the elements are arranged in a sequence from largest to smallest such that every element is greater than or equal to the succeeding element in the list. The descending order can be defined by the following relation:

```
List[i] >= List [i+1] ,   0 < i < N-1
```

It has been estimated that in a data processing environment, 25% of the time is consumed in sorting of data. Many sorting algorithms have been developed. Some of the most popular sorting algorithms that can be applied to arrays are *In-Place* sort algorithms. An *In-Place* algorithm is generally a *comparison based* algorithm that stores the sorted elements of the list in the same array as occupied by the original one. A detailed discussion on sorting algorithms is given in the following sections.

13.2.5.1 Selection Sort

This is a very simple and natural way of sorting a list. The smallest element in the list is located and exchanged with the element present at the head of the list, as shown in Fig. 13.10.

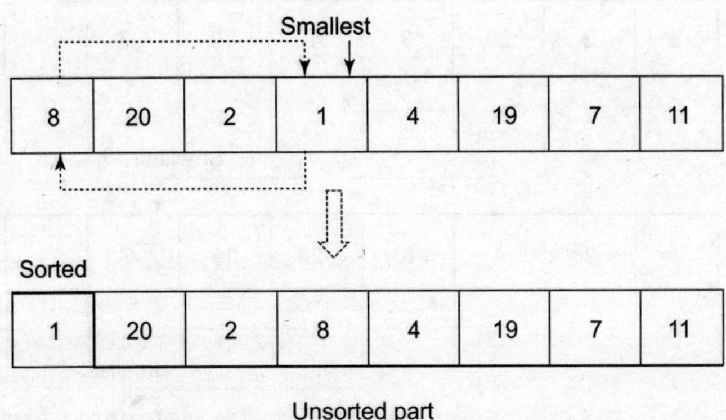

Fig. 13.10 Selection sort (first pass)

It may be noted from Fig. 13.10 that initially the whole list was unsorted. After the exchange of the smallest element with the element at the head of the list, the list is divided into two parts: sorted and unsorted.

Now the smallest is searched in the unsorted part of the list i.e., '2' and exchanged with the element at the head of the unsorted part i.e., '20', as shown in Fig. 13.11.

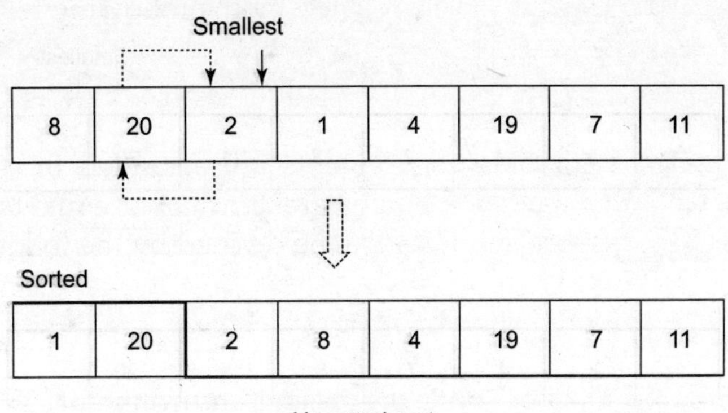

Fig 13.11 Selection sort (Second pass)

This process of selection and exchange (i.e., a pass) continues in this fashion until all the elements in the list are sorted (see Fig. 13.12). Thus, in selection sort, two steps are important: *selection* and *exchange*.

From Fig. 13.11 and 13.12, it may be observed it is a case of nested loops. The outer loop is required for passes over the list and the inner loop for searching smallest element within the unsorted part of the list. In fact, for N number of elements, N-1 passes are made.

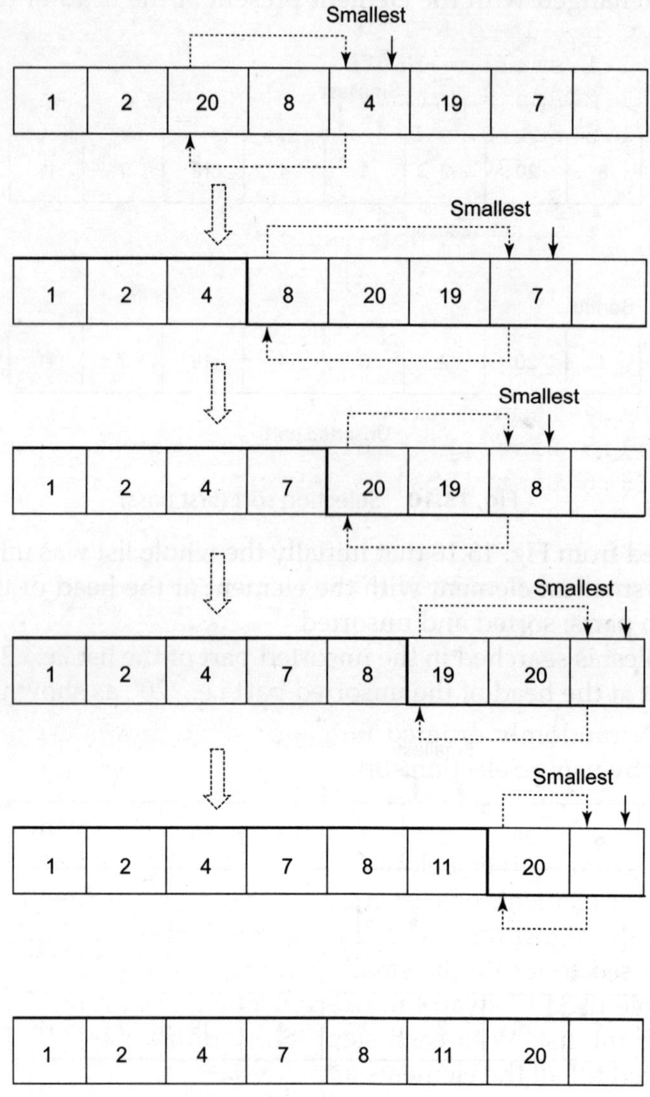

Fig. 13.12 Selection sort

An algorithm for selection sort is given below. In this algorithm, the elements of a list stored in an array called `LIST[N]` are sorted in ascending order. Two variables called `small` and `pos` are being used to locate the smallest element in the unsorted part of the list. `Temp` is the variable being used to interchange the selected element with the first element of the unsorted part of the list.

```
Algorithm SelSort()
    {Step
      1. For I = 1 to N-1                    /* Outer Loop */
         { 1.1 small = List [I];
           1.2 Pos = I;
           1.3 For J = I+1 to N              /* Inner Loop */
           {     1.3.1  if (List [J] < small)
                        {     small = List[J];
                        /* Note the position of the smallest*/
                                 Pos    = J;
           }
         }
                        /*Exchange smallest with the Head  */
           1.4 Temp = List [I];
           1.5 List [I] = List [Pos];
           1.6 List [Pos] = Temp;
         }

      2. Print the sorted list
    }
```

Example 9

Given a list of N randomly ordered numbers, write program that sorts the list in ascending order by using Selection sort.

Solution

The required program is given below:
In this program, the elements of a list are stored in an array called `List`. The elements are sorted using the algorithm `selSort()` given earlier. Two variables `small` and `pos` have been used to locate the smallest element in the unsorted part of the list. `Temp` is a variable used to swap the selected element with the first element of the unsorted part of the list. With each step, the unsorted part becomes smaller. The process is repeated till all the elements are sorted.

```
/* This program sorts a list by using selection sort */
  # include <stdio.h>
```

```
main()
{
 int list [10];
 int small, pos, N, i,j, temp;

 printf ("\n Enter the size of the list :");
 scanf ("%d", & N);

 printf ("\n Enter the list : ");
      for ( i = 0; i < N; i++)
       {
        printf ("\n Enter Number :");
        scanf ("%d", &list[i]);
       }
                              /* Sort the list   */

      for (i = 0; i < N -1; i++)
       {
        small = list[i];
        pos = i;
           /* Find the smallest of the unsorted list */
         for ( j = i+1; j < N; j++)
          {
           if ( small > list [j])
                 {
                  small = list [j];
                  pos = j;
                 }
          }          /* Exchange the small with the
                      first element of unsorted list */
                 temp = list [i];
                 list [i] = list [pos];
                 list [pos] = temp;
       }
      printf ("\n The sorted list ...");
      for ( i = 0; i < N; i++)
        printf ("%d ", list[i]);
}
```

13.2.5.2 Bubble Sort

This is another very simple sorting algorithm. It proceeds by looking at the list from left to right. Each adjacent pair of elements is compared to see that the larger number is to the right of the smaller one. Whenever a pair is found not to be in order, the elements are exchanged. Therefore after the first pass, the largest element bubbles up to the right end of the list. A trace of the first pass on a list of numbers is shown in Fig. 13.13

It may be noted that after the pass is over, the largest element in the list (i.e., 20) has bubbled up to the end of the list and 6 exchanges were made. Now the same process can be repeated for the list for the second pass, as shown in Fig. 13.14.

We observe that after the second pass is over, the list has become sorted and only two exchanges were made. Now a point worth noting is as to how and when it will be decided that the list has become sorted? The simple criteria would be to check whether or not any exchange(s) has been made during the current pass. If 'yes' then the list is not yet sorted, otherwise if 'no, then it can be assumed that the list has just become sorted.

An algorithm for bubble sort is given below.

In this algorithm, the elements of a list stored in an array called `List[N]` are sorted in ascending order. The algorithm uses two loops: the outer `while` loop and an inner `For` loop. The inner `For` loop makes a pass of the list. If during the pass, any exchange(s) is made, then it is recorded in a variable called `Flag` i.e., `Flag` is set to False. The outer `while` loop keeps track of `Flag`. As soon as the `Flag` indicates that no exchange(s) took place during the current pass indicating that the list is now sorted, the algorithm stops processing.

```
Algorithm bubbleSort()
{
  Step
      1. Flag = false;
      2. While (Flag == false)
          {
            2.1 Flag = true;
            2.2 For j = 0 to N-2
            {
                        2.2.1 if (List [J] > List [J+1] )
                  {
                        temp = List[J];
                        List[J] = List [J+1];
                        List [J+1] = temp;
                        Flag=false;
                  }
                  }
          }
      3. print the sorted list
      4. Stop
}
```

It may be noted that the algorithm stops as soon as the list becomes sorted. Thus, Bubble sort is a very useful algorithm when the list is almost sorted i.e., only a very small percentage of elements are out of order.

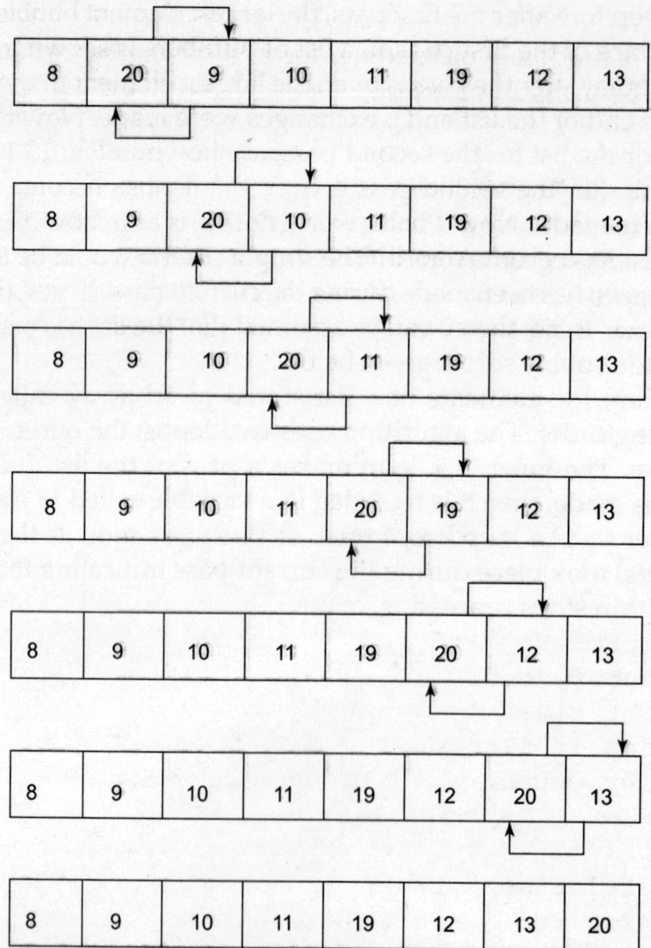

Fig. 13.13 First pass of bubble sort on a list of numbers

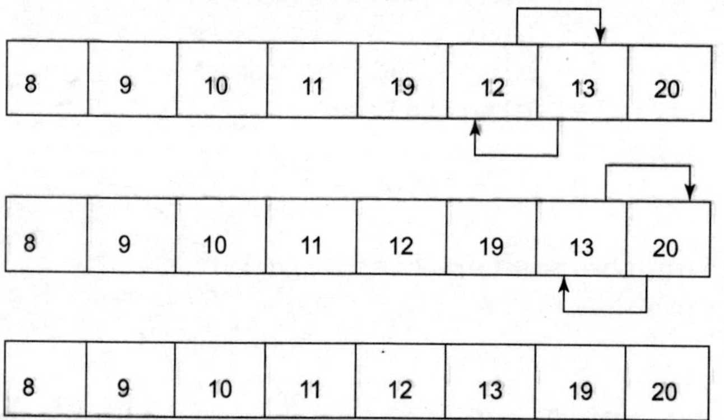

Fig. 13.14 Second pass of bubble sort

Example 10

Given is a list of N randomly ordered numbers. Write a program that sorts the list in ascending order by using Bubble sort.

Solution

The required program is given below:
In this program, the elements of a list are stored in an array called `List`. The elements are sorted using above given Algorithm `bubbleSort()`.

```
/*This program sorts a given list of numbers in ascending
order, using Bubble sort */

   # include <stdio.h>
   # define N 20
   # define true 1
   # define false 0

   void main()
    {
         int List[N];
         int flag;
         int size;
         int i, j,temp;
         int count;        /* counts the number of passes*/

         printf ("\n Enter the size of the list (< 20)");
         scanf ("%d", &size);

         printf ("\n Enter the list one by one");
         for (i=0; i< size; i++)
           {
            scanf ("%d", &List[i]);
           }
                           /* Sort the list by bubble sort */
         flag = false;
         count =0;
         while (flag == false)
          {
            flag = true;     /* Assume no exchange takes place*/
            count++;
             for (j =0; j< size-1; j++)
             {
               if (List[j] > List[j+1])
                    {            /* Exchange the contents */
```

```
                    temp = List[j];
                    List[j] = List[j+1];
                    List[j+1] = temp;
                    flag = false;/* Record the exchange
                                        operation*/
                    }
            }
        }
                                /* Print thesorted list*/
        printf ("\n The sorted list is ....");
        for (i=0; i< size; i++)
                printf ("%d ", List[i]);
        printf ("\n The number of passes made = %d",count);
    }
```

It may be noted that the above program has used a variable called `count` that counts the number of passes made while sorting the list. Test runs conducted on the program have established that the program is very efficient in the case of an almost sorted list of elements. In fact, it takes only one scan to establish that the supplied list is already sorted.

Note: Bubble sort is also called a *Sinking Sort*, meaning that the elements sink down in the list, to their proper position.

13.2.5.3 Insertion sort

This algorithm mimics the process of arranging a pack of playing cards. In the pack of cards, the first two cards are put in the correct relative order. The third card is inserted at the correct place relative to the first two. The fourth card is inserted at the correct place relative to the first three, and so on.

Given a list of numbers, it divides the list into two parts: a sorted part and an unsorted part. The first element becomes the sorted part and the rest of the list becomes the unsorted part, as shown in Fig. 13.15. It picks up one element from the front of the unsorted part and inserts it at its proper position in the sorted part of the list. This insertion action is repeated till the unsorted part is exhausted.

It may be noted that the insertion operation requires following steps:

1. Scan the sorted part to find the place where the element from unsorted part can be inserted. While scanning, shift the elements towards the right, to create space.
2. Insert the element from unsorted part into the created space

The algorithm for the Insertion Sort is given below:

In this algorithm, the elements of a list stored in an array called `List[N]`, are sorted in ascending order. The algorithm uses two loops: an outer `For` loop and an inner `While` loop. The inner `while` loop shifts the elements of the sorted part by one step to the right so that a proper place is created for the incoming element. The outer `For` loop inserts the element from the unsorted part into the place created, and moves to the next element of the unsorted part.

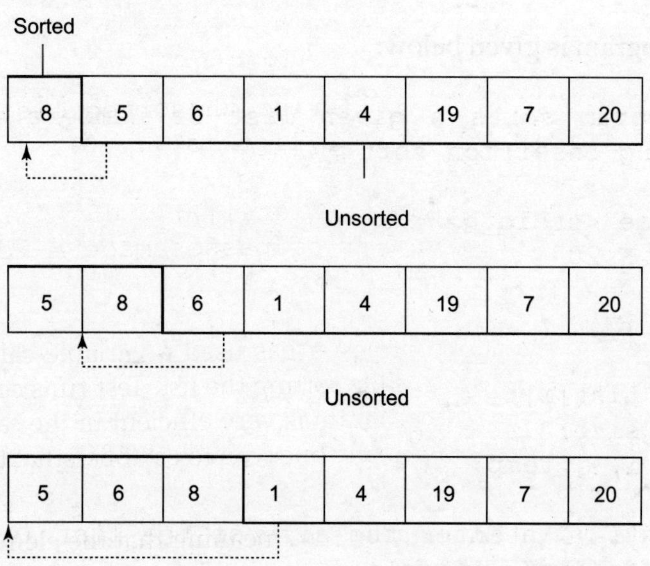

Fig. 13.15 Insertion sort

```
Algorithm insertSort()
 {
    Step
    1. For I = 2 to N                  /* The first element becomes the sorted part */
     {
        1.1 Temp = List [I];     /* Save the element from unsorted part into
                                                                        temp */
        1.2 J=I-1;
        1.3 While (Temp < = List [J] AND J > = 0)
              {
                    List[J+1] = List[J];    /* Shift elements towards right */
                    J = J-1;
              }
        1.4 List [J+1] = Temp;
     }
    2. Print the list
    5. Stop
 }
```

Example 11

Given a list of N randomly ordered numbers, write a program that sorts the list in ascending order by using Insertion sort.

Solution

The required program is given below:

```
/*This program sorts a given list of numbers in ascending
order, using Insertion sort */

   # include <stdio.h>
   # define N 20

   void main()
   {
       int List[N];
       int size;
       int i, j,temp;

       printf ("\n Enter the size of the list (< 20)");
       scanf ("%d", &size);

       printf ("\n Enter the list one by one");
       for (i=0; i< size; i++)
        {
         scanf ("%d", &List[i]);
        }
                         /* Sort the list by Insertion sort */
        for (i=1; i<size; i++)
        {
         temp = List[i];       /* Pick and save the first
                                  element of the unsorted part*/

        j= i-1;
                                  /* Scan for proper place */
       while ((temp < List[j])&& (j>=0))
       {
         List[j+1] = List[j];
         j = j-1;
       }

       List[j+1] = temp;  /* Insert the element at the
                             proper place */
       }
```

```
                /* Print the sorted list*/
   printf ("\n The sorted list is ....");
   for (i=0; i< size; i++)
   {
   printf ("%d ", List[i]);
   }
 }
```

13.3 STRINGS

A string is a group of characters of any length. The string enclosed within double quotation marks is known as a literal. For example, "Hello" is a literal. We have already used such strings in our programs to display various kinds of messages on the screen. In C, strings can be stored and manipulated as arrays of characters. The last character in a string is always '\0', a null character. For example, the string "COMPUTER" can be stored in an array (say `item`) as shown below:

	0	1	2	3	4	5	6	7	8
Item	C	O	M	P	U	T	U	R	\0

Fig. 13.16 A string of 8 characters

The string requires in total 9 locations of an array called `item` : eight for the alphabets in the string COMPUTER and one for the null character. The array `item` can be declared as:

```
char item [9];
```

Strings can be read or written in C in many ways. We will use either `scanf` and `printf` or `gets( )` and `puts ( )` functions for this purpose.
Consider the following declaration:

```
char text [20];
```

The array text can be read or written in one of the following ways:

(i) **Component by Component Method**
In this method, the array of characters is read as a normal array inside a `for` loop as shown below:

```
:
char text[20];

for (i = 0; i < 19; i++)
```

```
        scanf ("%d", &text [i]);

    text[19]= '\0';
    :
```

It may be noted that it is the responsibility of the programmer to place the null character '\0' in the last location of the array as has been done in the last statement of the above program segment.

(ii) **String Method**

In this method, the array of characters is considered as one unit i.e. a string. The string is read by the name of the array as shown below:

```
        char text [20];
        scanf ("%s", text);
        :
```

Once the above statement is executed, the string of characters typed by the user is read into the array called `text`. It may be noted here that the name of the array is enough to read the whole of the array. It may be further noted that the address operator (`&`) is not required as the name of every array itself contains the address of the array.

Similarly, a string can also be read by the function `gets ( )` as shown below:

```
        :
        char text [20];
        gets (text);
        :
```

We can use the `printf ( )` or `puts ( )` functions to display a string on the screen. The string method is definitely a better way of reading and displaying strings because of its simplicity. Moreover, the programmer's job becomes easy because the compiler, places the null character `\0' at the end of the string, on its own.

Example 12

Write a program that reads a string and checks if the string is a palindrome or not.

Solution

A palindrome is a word that spells the same both ways i.e., forward and backwards. MADAM, MALAYALAM, RADAR etc. are examples of palindrome.

The algorithm is given below:

Algorithm palindrome()

{

Step 1. Read the string in an array called text.

2. Find the length (Lenth) of the string.

3. Initialize beg = 0 and back = Lenth -1.

4. Compare text [beg] and text [back].

5. If match is found set flag = 1 else, set flag = 0.

6. Increment beg, decrement back.

7. Repeat steps 4 to 6 till beg < = back and flag == 1.

8. Depending upon the value of flag, give appropriate message.

9. Stop.

}

The program is given below:

```
/* This program checks the existence of a palindrome */

# include <stdio.h>
main()
  { char text [30];
  int beg, back, i, flag;

   printf ("\n Enter the string : ");
   scanf("%s",text);

                        /* find the length of the string */
   i=0;
   while (text[i] != '\0') i++;

    flag = 1;           /* assume that the palindrome exists */
    beg =0;
    back =i-1;
    while (beg <= back && flag)
     {
     if (text[beg] != text[back])
          flag =0;      /* The palindrome does not exist */
          beg++;
          back--;
     }
     if (flag)
          printf ("\n Yes it is a palindrome ");
     else
```

```
            printf ("\n No it is not a palindrome ");
    }
```

It may be noted here that the scanf ( ) statement has a limitation, in the sense that it considers a space to be a terminating character. Therefore, only a single word can be read by the scanf( ) function. However, the function gets ( ) can read a string containing blanks as well.

Example 13

Write a program that reads a string and counts the number of vowels, words and white spaces present in the string.

Solution

In this program, the string is read in an array called text with the help of the gets() function. Three variables vcount, wrcount and whcount are used to count vowels, words, and white spaces respectively.

```
/* This program counts vowels , words, and white spaces in a
string*/
# include <stdio.h>
main()
  {
   char text [80];
   char ch;
   int vcount, wrcount, whcount;
   int i;

   printf ("\n Enter the line of text");
   gets(text);
   fflush(stdin);

   i=0;
   vcount = wrcount = whcount = 0;
   while ( (ch = text[i]) != '\0')
    {
         if (ch == 'a' || ch == 'e' || ch == 'i'|| ch == 'o'||
         ch == 'u')
              vcount ++;
         else
          if (ch == ' ')
           {
            whcount++;
            wrcount++;
           }
```

```
        i++;
    }
    wrcount ++;        /* counts the last word */
    printf ("\n The Total number of");
    printf ("\n Vowels= %d", vcount);
    printf ("\n whitespaces= %d", whcount);
    printf ("\n words= %d", wrcount);
}
```

Note: A string can also be initialized with a piece of text enclosed in pair of double quotes as shown below:

```
char country [] = "India";
```

The compiler, on its own, computes the length of the text and stores the text into the string (i.e., `country` in this case) and also inserts the `NULL` character at the end.

13.3.1 Copying of strings

The assignment operator of C does not allow copying of one string to another. For example, let us consider the following statements.

```
string1[] = "WELCOME";
stringÿ2 =   string1
```

The above assignment/copying operation is invalid. If we wish to copy `string1` to `string2` we can do so either by copying it character by character or by using the `strcpy()` function, available in the header file called `string.h`.

The usage of `strcpy ( )` is given below:

```
strcpy (string 2, string 1);
```

The above statement copies the contents of `string1` to `string1`.

This discussion on copying of strings has been included with a view to highlight the following points:

1. C has minimal support for character strings.
2. Generally, strings operate as ordinary arrays of characters.
3. The programmer is responsible for allocating array space for the storage of the string i.e., the programmer has to provide a large enough space for the string to be stored.
4. C includes a standard library (`string.h`) of functions which perform common string operations such as: string copy, string comparison, string concatenation etc.

13.4 MULTIDIMENSIONAL ARRAYS

An array having more than one subscript is called a multidimensional array. C supports arrays of arbitrary dimensions. However, we will restrict ourselves to two dimensions only. A two dimensional array has two subscripts. It represents two dimensional entities such as tables, matrices etc. Therefore, sometimes the two dimensional arrays are also called *matrix arrays*. For example, consider the matrix A given in Fig.13.17:

$$A = \begin{pmatrix} 5 & 9 & 7 & 4 \\ 2 & 8 & 3 & 5 \\ 6 & 1 & 0 & 12 \end{pmatrix}_{3 \times 4}$$

Fig. 13.17 The matrix 'A'

The matrix A has 3 rows and 4 columns. It contains 12 elements. Such a matrix can be represented by a 2-dimensional array, capable of storing 12 elements in a row-column fashion. Let `MAT_A [3][4]` be the required array with two subscripts. The first subscript denotes the rows of the matrix varying from 0 to 2 whereas the second subscript denotes the columns varying from 0 to 3.

Now the matrix A of Fig. 13.17 can be comfortably stored in the array called `MAT_A[3][4]` as shown in Fig. 13.18.

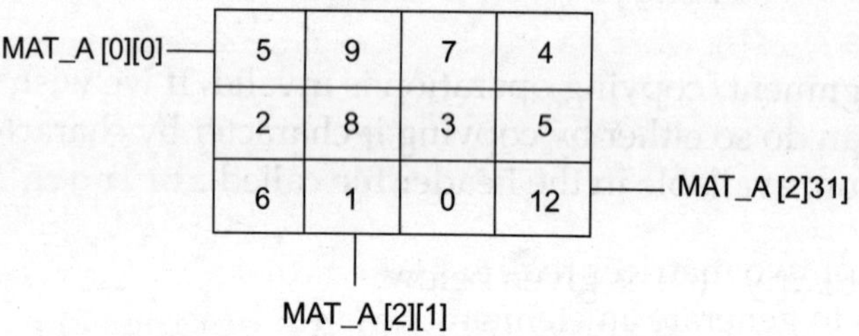

Fig. 13.18 Two-dimensional array representing the matrix 'A'

Let us consider a situation where it is desired that a value '5' may be added to all elements of the matrix 'A', stored in an array called `MAT_A`. This operation can be done by picking the element `MAT_A[0][0]` (i.e., 0th row and 0th column) and adding the required value '5' to its contents as shown below:

```
MAT_A[0][0] = MAT_A[0][0] + 5;
```

Now to complete the rest of the operations, there is a choice i.e., either move along the 0th row (`MAT_A[0][1], MAT[0][2]`...) and add '5' to each visited element or to move along the 0th col (`MAT_A[1][0], MAT[2][0]...`) and add '5' to each visited element. Once a row or column is over, we can move to the next row or column in the order and continue to travel in the same fashion.

Thus, a 2-dimensional array can be traversed *row-by-row* or *column-by-column*. The former method is called a **row major order** and the latter a **column major order.**

An algorithm for the row major order of travel of the array `MAT_A` is given below:

This algorithm visits every element of the array `MAT_A` and adds the value '5' to the contents of the visited element.

```
Algorithm rowMajor()
{
  Step
    1. For row = 0 to 2
    2. For col = 0 to 3
           MAT_A[row][col] = MAT_A[row][col] + 5;
    3. Stop
}
```

In the above algorithm, nested loops have been used. The outer loop has been employed to travel the rows and the inner to travel the columns within a given row.

Example 14

Given two matrices `A[ ]m x r and B[ ]r x n`, compute the product of two matrices such that :

`C[ ]m x n = A [ ] m x r * B [ ] r x n`

Solution

The multiplication of two matrices requires that a row of matrix A be multiplied to a column of matrix B to generate an element of matrix C, as shown in Fig. 13.19.

$$\begin{pmatrix} 5 & 4 \\ 3 & 2 \end{pmatrix} * \begin{pmatrix} 1 & 7 \\ 2 & 9 \end{pmatrix} = \begin{pmatrix} 5*1 + 4*2 & 5*7 + 4*9 \\ 3*1 + 2*2 & 3*7 + 2*9 \end{pmatrix}$$

Fig 13. 19 The matrix multiplication operation

A close observation of the computation shown in Fig. 13.19 gives the following relation for an element of matrix C:

`C[I][J] = A[I][K] + B[K][J]; for k varying from 0 to r-1`

We would use the above relation to compute the various elements of the matrix C. The required program is given below:

```
/* This program multiplies two matrices A & B and stores the
resultant matrix in C */

# include <stdio.h>
main()
 {
  int   A[10][10], B[10][10], C[10][10];
  int i,j,k;                   /* The array indices */
  int m,n,r;                   /* Order of matrices */

  printf ("\n Enter the order of the matrices m,r,n :");
  scanf ("%d %d %d", &m,&r,&n);

  printf ("\n Enter The elements of Matrix A :");
   for ( i = 0; i < m; i++)
        for (j = 0; j < r; j++)
         {
          printf ("\n Enter an element : ");
          scanf ("%d", &A[i][j]);
         }
  printf ("\n Enter The elements of Matrix B :");
   for ( i = 0; i < r; i++)
        for (j = 0; j < n; j++)
         {
          printf ("\n Enter an element : ");
          scanf ("%d", &B[i][j]);
         }
                                /* Multiply the matrices */
   for (i = 0; i < m; i++)
         {
          for (j = 0; j < n;  j++)
           {
                  C[i][j] = 0;
                  for ( k = 0; k < r; k++ )
                  {
                  C[i][j] = C[i][j] + A[i][k] * B[k][j];
                  }

           }
         }
```

```
    printf ("\n The resultant matrix is ...\n");
  for ( i = 0; i < m; i++)
   {
        for (j = 0; j < n; j++)
         {
           printf ("%d ", C[i][j]);
         }
         printf ("\n");
   }
}
```

Example 15

A *nasty* number is defined as a number which has at least two pairs of integer factors such that the difference of one pair equals to sum of the other pair. For instance, the factors of '6' are 1, 2, 3, 6.
Now the difference of factor pair (6, 1) is equal to the sum of factor pair (2, 3) i.e., 6 – 1 = 2 + 3 Therefore, '6' is a nasty number.
Choose appropriate data structures and write a program that displays all the nasty numbers present in a list of numbers.

Solution

The following data structures would be used to store the list of numbers and the list of factor-pairs.

1. A 1-dimensional array called `List` to store the list of numbers.
2. A 2-dimensional array called `pair_of_factors` to store the list of pair-factors of a given number.

For example, the list of pair factors of '24' would be stored as shown below:

1	24
2	12
5	8
4	6

Finally, using a nested loop, the difference of pair factors would be compared with the sum of all pair of factors for equality. The required program is given below:

```
/* This program finds all the Nasty numbers from a given list
of integer numbers */
```

```
# include <stdio.h>
# include <math.h>
main()
 {
  int LIST [20];
  int pair_of_factors[50][2];
  int i, j, k, size, num, diff,sum, count;

  printf ("\n Enter the size of the list : ");
  scanf ("%d", &size);

   printf ("\n Enter the list : ");
   for (i = 0; i < size; i++)
    scanf ("%d", &LIST[i]);

   for (i=0; i<size; i++)
    {
         num = LIST[i];
         count = 0;
                              /* Compute the factors */
         pair_of_factors[0][0] = 1;
         pair_of_factors[0][1] = num;

         for (j = 2 ; j <= sqrt(num); j++)
          {
            if ( num % j == 0)
                  {
                   count++;
                  pair_of_factors[count][0] = j;
                  pair_of_factors[count][1] = num/j;
                  }
          }
                              /* Check for nastiness  */
         for (j = 0; j <= count; j++)
          {
           diff = pair_of_factors[j][1] - pair_of_
           factors[j][0];
             for ( k = 0; k <=  count; k++)
                 {
                 sum = pair_of_factors[k][1] + pair_of_
                 factors[k][0];
                 if (diff == sum )
                  {
```

```
                printf ("\n %d is a Nasty number", num);
                break;
              }
            }          /* End of k loop   */
        }           /* End of j loop   */
    }            /* End of i loop   */
  }              /* End of program */
```

13.5 ARRAY OF STRINGS

A two dimensional array of characters can be considered as an array of strings. The *row* subscript decides how many strings can be stored in the array and the *col* subscript gives the size of each string. For example, an array **dir** of 10 strings of 30 characters each can be declared as given below:

```
char dir [10][30];
```

The compiler provides a group of 10 memory locations of string type, as shown below:

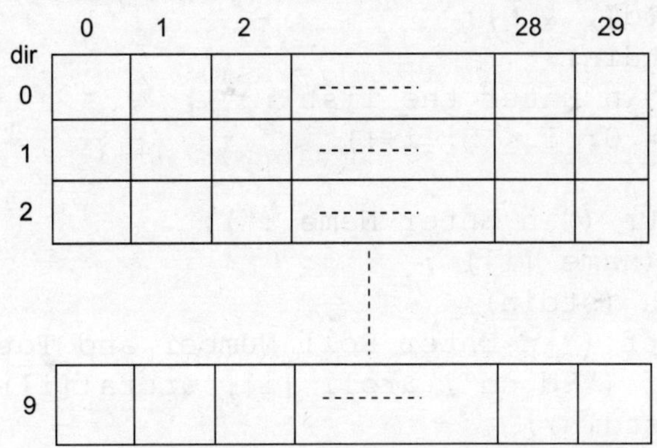

Fig 13.20 An array of strings

A string in such an array can be accessed by the row subscript with the help of the `gets()` function. For example, the second string in array `dir` can be read by the following statement:

```
gets (dir [2]);
```

Example 16

Write a program that reads the name, roll number and total marks of all the students in a class. Generate the merit list of the class.

Solution

The program is given below:
/* In this program the data of a student is read in three parallel arrays: name, roll, total. The array total is sorted in descending order by using the algorithm given for Example 9 */

```
/* This program prints the merit list of students */

  # include <stdio.h>
  # include <string.h>
  main()
   {
    char name [25][20];
    int roll [20];
    int total [20];
    char tname[20];      /* temp variable to store a name */
    int large, pos, N, i,j, temp;

    printf ("\n Enter the number of students :");
    scanf ("%d", & N);
    fflush (stdin);
    printf ("\n Enter the list : ");
    for ( i = 0; i < N; i++)
     {
        printf ("\n Enter Name :");
        gets(name [i]) ;
        fflush (stdin);
        printf ("\n Enter Roll Number and Total marks :");
        scanf ("%d %d", &roll [i], &total[i]);
     fflush (stdin);
        }
             /* Sort the student data in ascending order */

    for (i = 0; i < N -1; i++)
        {
        large = total[i];
        pos = i;
                          /* Find the largest total */
        for ( j = i+1; j < N; j++)
         {
         if ( large < total [j])
             {
```

```
                large = total [j];
                pos = j;
            }
        }
                      /* Exchange the data of students */

        strcpy(tname, name [i]);
        strcpy (name [i], name [pos]);
        strcpy (name[pos], tname);

        temp = roll[i];
        roll[i] = roll[pos];
        roll[pos]= temp;

        temp = total[i];
        total[i] = total[pos];
        total[pos] = temp;
      }
      printf ("\n The merit list is ...\n" );
      for ( i = 0; i < N; i ++)
        printf ("\n %s %d %d", name[i], roll[i], total[i]);
  }
```

It may be noted that the function `strcpy()` (i.e., string copy) has been used for the purpose of copying strings. This function is part of the `string.h` header file. Therefore this header file has been included at the beginning of the program.

13.6 ARRAY INITIALIZATION

An array can be initialized even during its declaration. This is done by specifying the values of all or some of its elements. For example, the string "SCHOOL" can be initialized in an array called texts in following two ways:

```
char texts [7] = {"SCHOOL"};
char texts [7] = {'S','C', 'H','O', 'O', 'L', '\0'};
```

In the first case the string "SCHOOL" has been moved to the array called `text` of size 7 characters, because 6 locations are required for the characters in the string and the 7th for the null character '\0'. The null character '\0' gets automatically attached in this case. However, in the second case the string "SCHOOL" is being moved character by character. Therefore, it is necessary for the programmer to provide the null character '\0' at the end of the string.

When an array is initialized at the time of declaration, one need not specify the size of the array, as shown on the next page.

```
int rol [ ] = {101, 105, 210, 319, 570};
```

The C compiler automatically calculates the size (s) of the initialized arrays. The above declaration initializes `rol [0]` with 101, `rol [1]` with 105, and so on. It may be noted that the various values are separated by comma. This type of unsized array initialization is also possible for strings in C. For example, the following array initialization is a valid initialization:

```
char text [ ] = {"SCHOOL"};
```

In this case also, the C compiler automatically computes the size of the array.

It may be noted here that if the number of elements being initialized is less than the specified size of an array, then the remaining locations are loaded with 0's or blanks. Consider the following declaration:

```
int B[5] = {3, 9};
```

After initialization, the contents of B would be as shown below:

	0	1	2	3	4
B	3	9	0	0	0

Fig. 13.21 The effect of array initialization

Multidimensional arrays can be initialized in a similar fashion. Consider the matrix of order 4 * 3 given below:

$$A = \begin{pmatrix} 5 & 2 & 7 \\ 3 & 2 & 9 \\ 8 & 2 & 5 \\ 1 & 2 & 6 \end{pmatrix}_{4 \times 3}$$

This matrix can be initialized in a two dimensional array as shown below:

```
int A [4] [3] =
{
    5, 2, 7,
    3, 2, 9,
    8, 2, 5,
    1, 2, 6
};
```

Similarly, a two-dimensional array of character or an array of strings can also be initialized as shown below:

```
char stud list [5] [10] = {
                            "Rohit",
                           "Harish",
                           "Rakesh",
                           "Seema",
                           "Rita"
                           };
```

Note: The initialization of arrays at the time of declaration is possible only outside a function. Inside the function the initialized array has to be declared as `static`.

Example 17

Write a program that uses two parallel arrays, `country` and `capital`, to store the names of countries and their corresponding capitals of this world. It interacts with the user in such a way that for a given country, it gives the name of its capital. Use the array initialization concept to store the names of states and capitals in the arrays.

Solution

For the sake of simplicity, we will store only ten countries and their capitals. The required program is given below:

```
/* This program illustrates the usage of array initialization.
It stores the names of countries and their capitals in two
parallel arrays and manipulates them */

# include <stdio.h>
main()
 {
  static char country [10][20] = {
                 "India          ",
                 "Bangla Desh    ",
                 "Bhutan         ",
                 "Nepal          ",
                 "Great Britain",
                 "Germany        ",
                 "Sri Lanka      ",
                 "Pakistan       ",
                 "France         ",
```

```
                     "Italy          "
                     };
    static char  capital [10][20] = {
                     "New Delhi      ",
                     "Dhaka          ",
                     "Thimpu         ",
                     "Kathmandu      ",
                     "London         ",
                     "Berlin         ",
                     "Colombo        ",
                     "Islamabad      ",
                     "Paris          ",
                     "Rome           "
                     };
     int Num, i;
     char choice;
      do
       {
         printf ("\n The World Database contains the following");
         printf ("\n list of countries...");

         printf ("\n Country\t\tNumber");
          for (i=0; i<10; i++)
            printf ("\n%s\t\t%d", country[i], i);
         printf("\n Enter the number of the country to see its
         capital:");
         scanf ("%d", &Num);
         printf ("\n The capital is ..: %s", capital[Num]);
         printf ("\n Want to countinue Y/N");
         fflush(stdin);
         choice = getchar();
       }
      while (choice == 'Y' || choice =='y');
    }
```

13.7 REPRESENTATION OF ARRAYS IN PHYSICAL MEMORY

A programmer looks upon one-dimensional and two-dimensional arrays as 'lists' and 'tables' (or matrices) respectively. This is a logical view of the programmer regarding arrays as data structures, capable of storing lists or tables. However, at the physical level, the main memory is RAM, which is just a linear memory. The relationship between the logical and physical views of arrays is shown in Fig. 13.22.

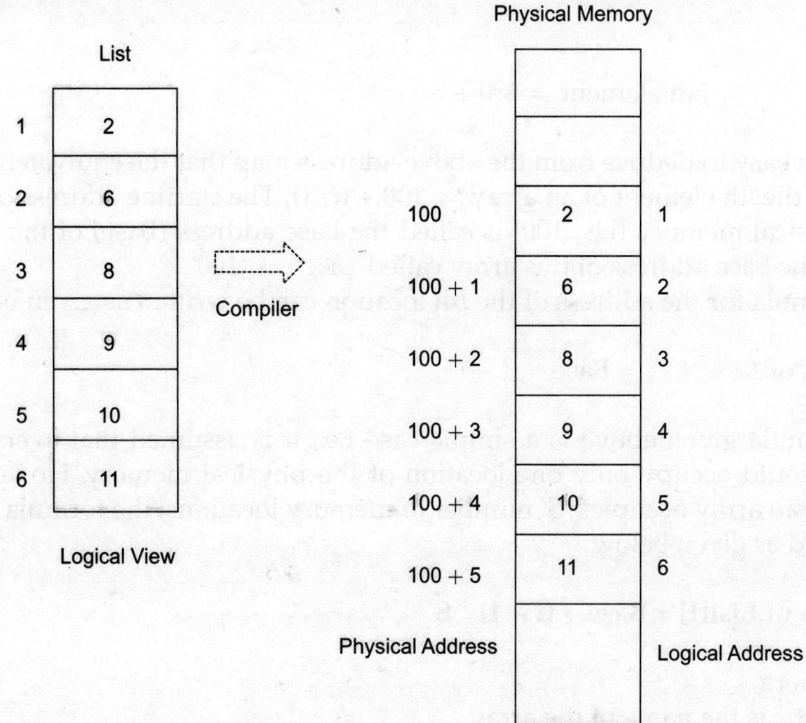

Fig. 13.22 Address mapping by compiler from logical to physical memory.

Thus the compiler has to map the various locations of arrays to locations of the physical memory. In fact, for a given array index, the compiler computes its physical load-time address of physical memory location. For example `List[5]` would be loaded at physical address = 104, in the physical memory (see Fig. 13.22).

Since physical memory is linear by construction, the address mapping is quite a simple exercise. The compiler needs to know only the starting address of the first element in the physical memory. The rest of the addresses can be generated by a trivial formula. A brief discussion on address computation is given in following sections.

13.7.1 Physical address computation of elements of one-dimensional arrays

Let us reconsider the array (`LIST[N]`) shown in Fig. 13.22. The array called `LIST` has 6 elements. It has been stored in physical memory at a starting address '100'. The address map is given on the next page.

The address of the 1st element = 100
2nd element = 100 + 1
3rd element = 100 + 2
–
–
6th element = 100 + 5

It is very easy to deduce from the above address map that the equivalent physical address of the *i*th element of an array = **100 + (*i* -1).** The starting address of an array at the physical memory (i.e., 100) is called the base address (Base) of the array. For example, the base address of this array called `LIST` is '100'.

The formula for the address of the *I*th location can be written as given below:

Address of `List[I]` = Base + (I – 1) (13.1)

The formula given above is a simple case i.e., it is assumed that every element of `List` would occupy only one location of the physical memory. However, if an element of an array occupies 'S' number of memory locations, the formula (13.1) can be modified as given below:

Address of List[I] = Base + (I – 1) * S (13.2)

Where
List : is the name of the array
Base : is the starting or base address of the array
I : is the index of the element
S : is the number of locations occupied by an element of the array

13.7.2 Physical address computation of the elements of two-dimensional arrays

Let us reconsider the two-dimensional array called **TAB[2][5]** as shown in Fig. 13.23

The array called `TAB` has 2 rows and 3 columns. It has been stored in physical memory at a stating address '100'. The address map is given below:

The address of the 1st row, 1st col. = 100
1st row, 2nd col = 100 + 1
1st row, 3rd col = 100 + 2
–
–
2nd row , 3rd col = 100 + 5

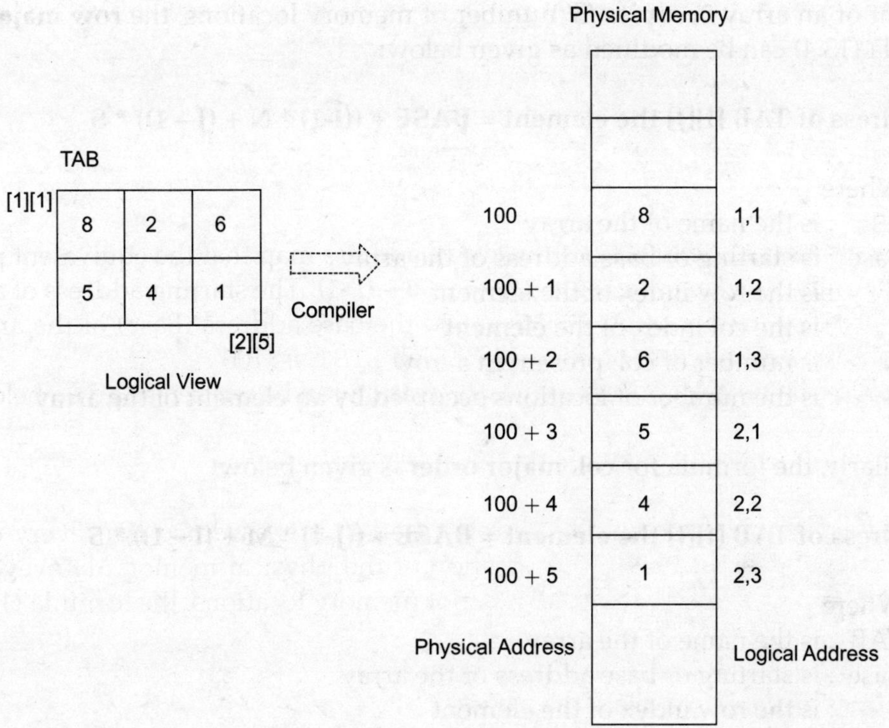

Fig. 13.23 Address mapping by the compiler from logical to physical memory.

We know that in the 2-dimensional array called `TAB`, for every row, there are 3 columns. Thus, for an element of the Ith row, the starting address becomes : Base + (I – 1) * 3 and if the element in row is at the Jth col., the complete address becomes :
Address of `List[I][J]` = Base + (I –1)* 3 + J – 1 (13.3)

To test the above row major order formula, let us calculate the address of an element represented by TAB[2][1] with Base = 100.
Given I = 2, J = 1, Base = 100. Substituting these values in Eq. 13.3, we get,

Address = 100 + (2-1) *3 + 1-1 = 100 + 3 + 0 = 103.

From Fig. 13.23, we find that the address value is correct.
Now we can generalize the formula of Eq. 13.3 for an array of size `[M]{N]` in the following form

Address of [I][J] the element = BASE + (I – 1) * N + (J – 1) (13.4)

The formula given above is a simple case i.e., it is assumed that every element of `List` would occupy only one location of the physical memory. However if an element of an array occupies 'S' number of memory locations, the **row major order** formula (13.4) can be modified as given below:

Address of TAB [I][J] the element = BASE + ((I-1) * N + (J – 1)) * S (13.5)

Where
`AB` : is the name of the array
Base : is starting or base address of the array
I : is the row index of the element
J : is the col index of the element
N : is number of col. present in a row
S : is the number of locations occupied by an element of the array

Similarly, the formula for **col. major order** is given below:

Address of TAB [I][J] the element = BASE + ((J-1) * M + (I – 1)) * S (13.6)

Where
TAB : is the name of the array
Base : is starting or base address of the array
I : is the row index of the element
J : is the col index of the element
M : is number of rows present in a col.
S : is the number of locations occupied by an element of the array

Example 18

`TAB` is a two-dimensional array with 5 rows and 5 columns. Each element occupies 1 memory location. If `TAB[1][1]` begins at address 500, find the location of `TAB[4][2]` for a row major order of storage.

Solution

Given base = 500, I = 4, J = 2, M = 5, N = 5. Applying the formula 13.5, we get:

Address = Base + ((I-1) * N + (J – 1)) * S
= 500 + ((4 – 1) * 5 + (2 – 1)) * 1
= 500 + (9 + 1)
= 510 Ans.

Example 19

`MAT` is a two-dimensional array with 10 rows and 5 columns. Each element is stored in2 memory locations. If `MAT[1][1]` begins at address 200, find the location of `MAT[5][4]` for a row major order of storage.

Solution

Given base = 200, I = 5, J = 4, M = 10, N = 5. Applying formula 13.5, we get:

Address = Base + ((I-1) * N + (J-1)) * S
= 200 + ((5 – 1) * 5 + (4 - 1)) * 2
= 200 + (10 + 5) *2
= 226 Ans.

Example 20

An array `A[10][20]` is stored in the memory with each element requiring 2 memory locations. If the base address of the array in the memory is 400, determine the location of array element `A[8][5]` when the array is stored as column major order.

Solution

Given base = 400, I = 8, J = 5, M = 10, N = 20. Applying formula 13.6, we get:

Address = Base + ((J-1) * M + (I-1)) * S
= 400 + ((5 – 1) * 10 + (8 - 1)) * 2
= 400 + (20 + 9) *2
= 458 Ans.

13.8 APPLICATIONS OF ARRAYS

Arrays data structures find wide use in numerous applications. Some of the popular applications are discussed below:

13.8.1 Polynomial representation and operations

An expression of the form $f(x) = a_n x^n + a_{n-1} x^{n-1} + a_{n-2} x^{n-2} + ...+ a_0$ is called a polynomial

where $a_n \neq 0$.

$a_n x^n , a_{n-1} x^{n-1},.... a_1 x^1 , a_0$ are called terms.

$a_n , a_{n-1} ,.... a_1, a_0$ are called coefficients.

x^n , x^{n-1} , x^{n-2} are called exponents

Now, a polynomial can be considered as a list comprising coefficients and exponents, as shown below:

$$f(x) = \{ a_{n,} x^n , a_{n-1,} x^{n-1},.... a_{1,} x^1 , a_0 , x^0 \}$$

For example, the polynomial : $6\ x^5 + 8\ x^2 + 5$ can be represented as the list shown below:

```
Polynomial = {6, 5, 8, 2, 5, 0}
```

The above list can very easily be implemented using a one-dimensional array say `Pol []`, as shown in Fig. 13.24,

	coef	exp	coef	exp	coef	exp
Pol	6	5	8	2	5	0

Fig. 13.24 Array representation of a polynomial

where every alternate location contains the coefficient and exponent of a polynomial term. The above representation can be modified to incorporate the number of terms present in a polynomial by reserving the first location of the array for this purpose. The modified representation is shown in Fig. 13.25

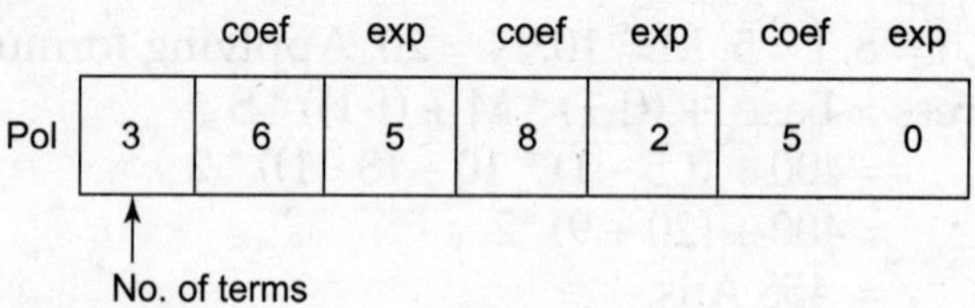

Fig. 13.25 Array representation of a polynomial

It may be noted from above discussion that a general polynomial can be represented in an array, with descending order of its degree of terms. Therefore the operations such as addition, multiplication, division on polynomials can be done easily.

Example 21

Write a program that reads two polynomials pol1 and pol2, adds them and gives a third polynomial pol5, such that pol5 = pol1 + pol2.

Solution

A close look at the array representation of polynomials indicates that two polynomials can be added by merging them. When the exponents from both the polynomials are same, then the coefficients of both the terms would be added.

The required program is given below:

```
/* This program adds two polynomials Pol1 and Pol2 to give
third polynomial called pol5.  It merges the two polynomials
with the help of  Algorithm merge() with minor modifications * /

    # include <stdio.h>

    void readPol( int pol[], int terms);
    void dispPol( int pol[]);
```

```
void main()
  {
     int pol1[11];
     int pol2[11];
     int pol5[21];
     int i,j,k;
     int terms;
     int m,n;              /* size of polinomials */

     printf( "\n Enter the number of terms in Pol1");
     scanf("%d", &terms);
     m = terms * 2 +1;

     readPol(pol1,terms);

     printf( "\n Enter the number of terms in Pol2");
     scanf("%d", &terms);
     n = terms * 2 +1;

     readPol(pol2,terms);

           /* Add the polynimoials by merging their terms */
     i= j = k = 2;

     while (i < m && j < n)
        {
        if (pol1[i] > pol2[j])
           {
           pol5[k] = pol1[i];
           pol5[k-1] = pol1[i-1];
           i=i+2;
           k= k+2;
           }
  else
        if (pol2[j] > pol1[i])
          {
          pol5[k] = pol2[j];
          pol5[k-1] = pol2[j-1];
          j= j+2;
          k = k+2;
          }
        else
        {
```

```
        pol5[k-1] = pol1[i-1] + pol2[j-1];
        pol5[k] = pol1[i];
        i=i+2;
        j= j+2;
        k= k+2;
       }
      }
                                /* copy the remaining Pol1 */
      while (i < m )
       {
        pol5[k] = pol1[i];
        pol5[k-1] = pol1[i-1];
        i=i+2;
        k= k+2;
       }
                                /* copy the remaining Pol2 */
      while (j < n)
       {
        pol5[k] = pol2[j];
        pol5[k-1] = pol2[j-1];
        j= j+2;
        k = k+2;
       }

      pol5[0] = (k-1)/2;

                                /* Display the final polynomial */
      printf ("\n Final Pol =");
      dispPol(pol5);
      printf ("\b ");
}

void readPol( int pol[], int terms)
  {
  int i;
  pol[0] = terms;
  i=1;
  printf ("\n Enter the terms (coef exp) in decreasing
  order of degree");
```

```
while (terms > 0)
        {
        scanf ("%d %d", &pol[i], &pol[i+1]);
        i= i+2;
        terms--;
        }
  }
void dispPol( int pol[])
       {
        int size;
        int i;
        size = pol[0] * 2 +1;
        printf("\n");
        for (i = 1; i < size ;i+=2)
        {
         printf ("%d * x ^ %d +", pol[i],pol[i+1]);
        }
       }
```

We can also choose other data structures to represent polynomials. For instance, a **term** can be represented by using the *'struct'* construct of C as shown below:

```
struct term
       {
           int coef;
           int exp;
       };
```

and the polynomial called `pol` of ten terms can be represented by an array of structures of type `term` as given below:

```
struct  term  pol1[10];
```

Now the algorithm `merge` can be applied to add two such polynomials with the data structures chosen above. It is left as an exercise for the readers to write the program for the same.

13.9 GRADED PROBLEMS

Problem 1. In 1897, Charles L.. Dodgson gave the following algorithm for divisibility by 11.

STEP 1. Read the number

2. If the number has more than 2 digits then
    2.1 delete the units digit to form a new number
    2.2 subtract the deleted digit from the new number
3. Repeat step 2 until the number is reduced to 2 digits
4. If the reduced 2 digit number is divisible by 11 then the original number was also divisible by 11

For example, consider the number 50248 and apply the above algorithm

50248 → 5024 - 8 = 5016
5016 → 501 - 6 = 495
495 → 49 - 5 = 44
Now, 44 is divisible by 11.
Therefore 50248 is divisible by 11

Write a program that implements this algorithm.

Solution: The required program is given below:

```
/* This program implements Charles L. Dodgson algorithm for
   divisiblity by 11 */

# include <stdio.h>
main()
  {
   unsigned num, newnum;
   int length;
   int i;
   printf ("\n Enter the Number");
   scanf ("%u", &num);
   length =0;
                          /* Determine the length of the number  */
   newnum = num;
   while (newnum > 0)
   {
    newnum = newnum/10;
    length++;
   }
                          /* Find the divisibility by 11 */
    newnum = num;
    printf ("\nOutput \n%-u", num);
    while (length > 2)
     {
         newnum = (newnum/10)  - (newnum % 10);
         printf ("\n%-u", newnum);
```

```
        length --;
    }
    if ((newnum % 11 ) == 0)
        printf ("\n %u is divisible by 11", num);
    else
        printf ("\n %u is not divisible by 11", num);
  }
```

Problem 2. The rules of construction of Roman numbers are:

1. The symbols used for Roman numbers are given below:

Symbol	Value
I	1
V	5
X	10
L	50
C	100
D	500
M	1000

2. The numbers are written from left to right. The symbols are chosen for the largest possible value.
3. The symbols M, C, X or I may be used at the most three times in succession. If this rule is violated, then the following sub rules apply:
   3.1 When a single I immediately precedes a 'V' or 'X', it is subtracted.
   3.2 When a single 'X' immediately precedes a 'L' or 'C', it is subtracted.
   3.3 When a single 'C' immediately precedes a D or M, it is subtracted.

Write a program that takes two Roman numbers, adds them and displays the total in the Roman format. However, if the total is more than 1000, it displays the message: "**The sum of Roman numbers is not printable**".

Solution:

```
/* This program reads two Roman numbers and displays their
   sum */

# include <stdio.h>
# include <string.h>
main()
  {
    char Roman1[15], Roman2[15], temp[15];
    int Num1, Num2, num;
    int Total, flag;
```

```
int i;
                                        /* Read the Roman Numbers */
printf ("\n Enter first Roman number - Use Capital letters
:");
scanf ("%s", Roman1);
printf  ("\n  Enter  Second  Roman  number  --  Use  Capital
letters :");
scanf ("%s", Roman2);

flag = 0;

strcpy(temp,Roman1);
while (1)
{
    num=0;
    i=0;
    while (temp[i] != '\0')
      {
        switch (temp[i])
         {
          case 'M' : num = num + 1000; break;
          case 'D' : num = num + 500; break;
          case 'C' : if (temp[i+1] == 'M')
                            {
                             num = num + 1000 - 100;
                             i++;
                            }
                        else
                          if (temp [i+1] == 'D')
                            {
                                 num = num + 500 - 100;
                                 i++;
                            }
                        else
                              num = num + 100;
                 break;
      case 'L' : num = num + 50; break;
      case 'X' : if (temp[i+1] == 'C')
                {
                 num = num + 100 - 10;
                 i++;
                 }
```

```
                else
                  if (temp [i+1] == 'L')
                    {
                   num = num + 50 - 10;
                   i++;
                    }
                 else
                    num = num + 10;

    if (flag == 0)   /* only Roman1 has been computed */
                 {
                  flag = 1;
                  Num1 = num;
                  num =0;
                  strcpy (temp, Roman2);
                 }
                else     /* Both numbers have been computed */
                 {
                  Num2 = num;
                  break;             /* exit the loop */
                 }

      }
      Total = Num1 + Num2;
      if (Total > 1000)
        printf("\n The Sum of Romans is not printable");
      else
        printf ("\n The Sum = ");
       while (Total > 0)
        {
        if ( Total == 1000 )
                 { printf ("%c", 'M');
                   Total = Total - 1000;
                 }
        else
                 if (Total >= 900)
                   { printf ("%s", "CM");
                     Total = Total - 1000 + 100;
                   }
                 else
                   if ( Total >= 500 )
                    { printf ("%c",'D');
```

```
                          Total = Total - 500;
                      }
                    else
                      if (Total >= 400)
                      { printf ("%s","CD");
                           Total = Total - 500 + 100;
                      }
                      else
                        if (Total >=100)
                          { printf ("%c", 'C');
                            Total = Total - 100;
                          }
                          else
                            if (Total >= 90)
                                 {
                                   printf ("%s", "XC");
                                   Total = Total - 100 + 10;
                                 }
                                else
                                 if (Total >= 50 )
                                   { printf ("%c", 'L');
                                       Total = Total - 50;
                                   }
else
                       if (Total >= 40)
                        {
                         printf ("%s", "XL");
                         Total = Total - 50 + 10;
                        }
                       else
                        if (Total >= 10)
                          {
                           printf ("%c", 'X');
                           Total = Total - 10;
                          }
                         else
                          if (Total >= 9)
                           {
                            printf ("%s","IX");
                            Total = Total - 10 + 1;
                           }
                           else
```

```
            if (Total >= 5)
                {
                 printf ("%c", 'V');
                 Total = Total - 5;
                }
            else
                if (Total >=4)
                {
                 printf ("%s", "IV");
                 Total = Total - 5 +1;
                }
                else
                  {
                   printf ("%c",'I');
                   Total = Total -1;
                  }

    }
  }
```

Problem 3. Write a program that reads list of subjects, list of verbs, and a list of objects and produces all possible sentences from them

A sentence = subject + verb + object

Example Input = **Subject** **Verb** **Sub**
He liked him
The lion saw the goat

Output: He liked him
He liked the goat
He saw the goat
The lion liked him
The lion saw the goat

Solution: The list of subjects, verbs and objects would be stored in three parallel arrays of strings. The sentences would be displayed with the help of three nested loops. The required program is given below

```
/* This program constructs the sentences */

# include <stdio.h>
main()
  {
```

```
char subject[5][20], verbs[5][20], objects[5][20];
int i,j,k;
int m,n,r;     /* Number of subject,verbs, and objects */

printf ("\n  Enter The number of subjects, verbs, and
objects :");
scanf ("%d %d %d", &m, &n, &r);
            /* Read Data */
printf ("\n Enter list of %d subjects\n", m);
for (i=0; i < m; i++)
         {
          printf ("\n Enter subject :");
          fflush(stdin);
          gets(subject[i]);
         }
printf ("\n Enter list of %d verbs", n);
for (i=0; i < m; i++)
         {
          printf ("\n Enter verb :");
          fflush(stdin);
          gets(verbs[i]);
         }
printf ("\n Enter list of %d objects", r);
for (i=0; i < m; i++)
         {
          printf ("\n Enter object :");
          fflush(stdin);
          gets(objects[i]);
         }

printf ("\n The possible sentences are");
 for (i=0; i < m; i++)
   for (j=0; j <n; j++)
         for (k =0; k < r; k++)
          printf  ("\n%s %s %s", subject[i], verbs[j],
          objects[k]);

 }
```

Frequently Asked Questions

1. Why is an array called a derived data type?
   Solution: **It is made from a combination of other already known types.** Now, we know that an array is a data type which represents a set of elements. All elements of the array are

of a particular type, such as integer, float etc. Thus, the array is not a basic data type but it derives its type from its elements. Let us consider the following declaration:

```
int series [50];
```

This declaration means that **series is of type array of 50 locations of integer type.**

2. Can an array be assigned to another of the same size and type? For example if two arrays `A [5]` and `B [5]` are available of the same type, what would be the effect of the following statement?
   A = B;
   Solution: No, an array cannot be assigned to another. Arrays are designed to work in a **component by component** fashion. The assignment statement given above would result in a syntax error.

3. Is it necessary to use all locations of an array of specified size?
   Solution : No it is not necessary; any number of locations can be used within the specified range. However, if not even a single location is used then the compiler may give a warning in this regard.

4. What would be the contents of the following array after initialization?
   int A [5] = {5, 3, 7};
   Solution: In this array initialization, the number of elements being initialized is less than the specified size i.e., 5. The elements are loaded from the 0th location, in the order of their appearance, and the remaining locations are loaded with zeros, as shown below:

5. Is it necessary to read or display the elements of an array in the order of its subscripts?
   Solution: No, this is not necessary.

	0	1	2	3	4
A	5	3	7	0	0

6. For arrays, what is the maximum number of dimensions followed in C?
   Solution: C allows an arbitrary number of dimensions i.e., there is no specified limit on the number of dimensions.

TEST YOUR SKILLS

1. What would be the contents of the following array after initialization?
   ```
   int B [5] = {5, 3, 7, 9, 0, 2, 11};
   ```
   Solution: It will result in a syntax error because the number of elements being iniatialized is more than the specified size of the array.

2. What would be the output of the following:

```
# include <stdio.h>
void main ()
{
int x[10];
x[ 5]=10;
x[7] =30;
prinf ("\n %d", x[- 5]);
}
```

Solution: The results will be unpredictable because the index, –5, is not defined.

3. Would the following program generate an error?

```
#include <stdio.h>
void main ()
{
float list [5] = {10.2,30.7,8.0,6.0,2.21};
list++;
printf (" %d ",list [3]);
}
```

Solution: The name of an array (`list` in this case) is always a pointer constant and therefore it cannot be incremented. An L-value error will be generated.

4. What would be the output of the following code?

```
#include <stdio.h>
void main ()
{
char ch[];
ch[0]=65;
printf ("% c", ch);
}
```

Solution: The above program would result in a compilation error because the size of the array `ch` is unknown at the time of declaration. However, the second statement is perfectly valid.

5. What would be the output of the following?

```
#include <stdio.h>
void main ()
{
char ch[5] = {`C', `+' `+', `:', `\0'};
printf ("% c", ch);
}
```

Solution: The output would be: `C++:`

6. What would be the output of the following?

```
#include <stdio.h>
void main ()
{
```

```
char ch [10*1/2] = {`T',`e',`s',`t',`\0'};
printf ("%c %c %c," ch[2], ch[1], ch[3]);
}
```

Solution: The output would be `set`

7. What would be the output of the following?

```
#include <stdio.h>
void main ()
{
   char list [4][3] = {
              ``Rat'',
              ``Sat'',
             ``Bat'',
             ``Pat''
           };
   printf ("% c", list [3] [0]);
}
```

Solution: The output would be `P`

8. What would be the output of the following?

```
#include <stdio.h>
void main ()
{
  char list [3][2] = {`i',`t',`i',`s',`a',`n'};
  printf ("% c", list [2]);
}
```

Solution: The output would be: `an`

9. What would be the output of the following program?

```
main ( )
{
   char text [ ] = ``Test''
   char word [ ] = ``Test''
   if (text = = word)
   printf (`\n Yes'');
   else
   printf (`\n No'');
}
```

Solution: The output would be `No`. The reason being that strings cannot be compared by the "==" operator.

10. Identify the error in the following statement

```
int xyz = {5, 9, 2, 3, 6};
```

Solution: `xyz` has been declared as a variable of type integer. Therefore, it cannot be initialized with more than one value. The correct statement would be:

```
int xyz [ ] = {5, 9, 2, 3, 6};
```

11. Would the following statements compile?

```
:
char xyz [4];
xyz = { ''abc''};
:
```

Solution: No, these statements will not compile. The reason being, that *we cannot assign a string literal in this fashion to a character array after it has been declared.*

EXERCISES

1. Define the terms: arrays, subscript, subscripted variables, and strings.
2. Write suitable array declarations for the following:
   (i) 100 items of integer type
   (ii) A string of 25 characters
   (iii) A matrix of order 5 times 4
3. Can an array be initialized? If yes, how?
4. What is the purpose of initializing an array?
5. Can an array be initialized at the time of declaration?
6. How can a string be stored in an array?
7. Write a program that finds the largest and smallest elements in an array.
8. Write a program that removes duplicates from a list.
9. Write a program that removes an element from an array.
10. Write a program that searches an array `SOME` of `float` type for a value less than *x*. The program should give an appropriate messages depending upon the outcome of the search.
11. Write a program which searches an ordered array `sal` of `integer` type for a value *x*. *If* such a value is found then it prints the message "The value found", otherwise it inserts Xat the proper place.
12. Write a program that gives the sum of positive elements of an array `LIST` of `integer` type.
13. Write a program that reads two matrices `A` and `B` of the order m × n and computes the following:
$$C = A + B$$
14. Write a program that computes the sum of diagonal elements of a square matrix.
15. What happens to an array, at the time of initialization , if it is assigned with less number of elements than its size?
16. Identify the errors in the following statements.
   (i) `int list = {9, 5, 7, 2, 0, 20};`
   (ii) `char ch {5};`
   `ch [ ] = {'A', 'B', 'C', 'D'};`
   (iii) `int series [5] = {3, 9, 2, 4, 7, 6, 8};`
17. What would be the contents of the following array after initialization?
   `int Rate [4] = {30, 20, 10}`
18. What would be the output if the following program?

```
main ()
   {char ch [5];
```

```
    ch [0] = 'A'
    ch [-4] = 'T'
    ch [3] = 'S'
  prinft (" %c %c %c", ch[10], ch[3], ch[- 4]),
  }
```

19. What would be the output of the following program?

```
main ()
  {
  char ch [6] = {'E', 'N', 'D', '\0', 'S'}
  printf ("\n %s", ch);
  }
```

20. What would be the output of the following program?

```
main ()
  {
  char part_list [3][5] = { "TC",
  "TC12",
  "TP31"
  };
  printf ("\n %c", part_list [2][1];);
  }
```

ANSWERS TO SELECTED EXERCISES

18. unpredictable **19.** END **20.** P.

CHAPTER

14 Structures

14.1 INTRODUCTION

Arrays are very useful data structures for list and table processing. However, the elements of an array must be of the same data type. In certain situation, we observe that some objects are made up of components of different types. For example, a date is composed of three parts: day, month, and year, as shown in Fig. 14.1.

	Day	Month	Year
Date	07	01	2012

Fig. 14.1 Date

Similarly, the information on students of a college may be composed of many components such as : Name, Age, Roll No., and Class; each belonging to a different data type.

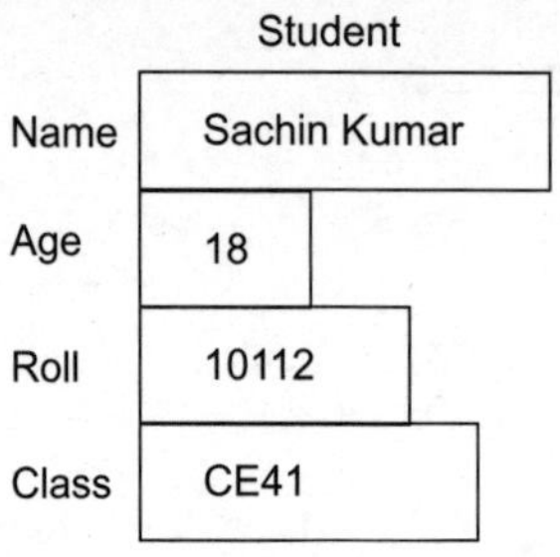

Fig. 14.2 Student

Therefore, we require a construct that can store data items of mixed data types. C supports **structures** for this purpose. The basic concept of a structure comes from day-to-day life. The collective information about a student, as shown in Fig. 14.2 is called a structure. It is similar to a record construct supported by other programming languages. Similarly, the date is also a structure. To define the term structure more precisely: **A group of related data items of arbitrary types is called a structure. Each member of a structure is, in fact, a variable that can be referred to through the name of the structure.**

14.2 DEFINING A STRUCTURE IN C

A structure can be defined in a C program by the keyword **struct** followed by its name and a body enclosed in curly braces. The body of the structure contains the definition of its members and each member must have a name. The declaration ends with a semicolon.

The general format of structure declaration in C is given below:

```
struct  <name>{
member 1
member 2
:
member n
};
```

where `struct`: is the keyword
<name> : is the name of the structure
`member 1, 2 ... n`: are the individual member declarations.

Let us now define the C structure to describe the information about the student, given in Fig. 14.2

```
struct student
{
        char Name [20];
        int age;
        int roll;
        char class[5];
};
```

The above declaration means that `student` is a structure consisting of data members called `name`, `age`, `roll` and `class`. A variable of this type can be declared as given below:

```
struct student x;
```

Once the above declaration is complied with, we get a variable x of type `student` in the computer memory, which can be visualized as shown in Fig. 14.3.

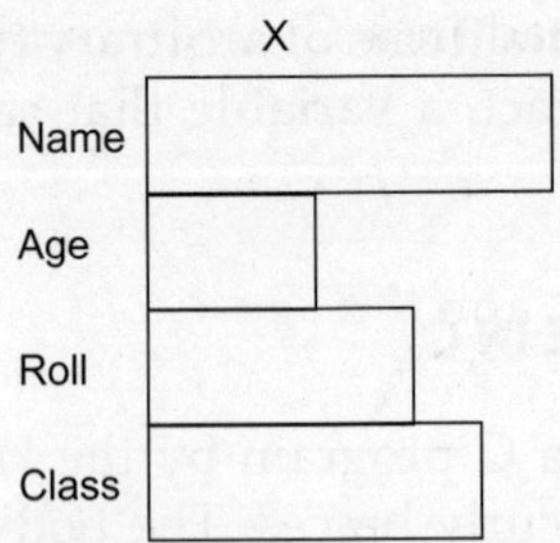

Fig. 14.3 Memory space allocated to variable x of type `student`

The programmer is also allowed to declare one or more variables of a `struct` type along with the `struct` declaration, as shown below :

```
struct student
          {
                    char name [20];
                    int age;
                    int roll;
                    char class [5];
                    }
     stud1, stud2;
```

In the above declaration, the structure declaration and the variable declaration of structure type have been clubbed, i.e. the structure declaration is followed by two variable names `stud1` and `stud2` followed by a semicolon.

14.2.1 Referencing Structure Elements

The structure variable `x` has four members; `name, age, roll,` and `class`. These members can be designated as: `x.name,x.age, x.roll,`and `x.class` respectively. In this notation, an individual member of the structure is designated or qualified by the structure variable name followed by a period and the member name. The period is called a structure member operator or simply a dot operator.

However, the information of a student (Fig. 14.2) can be stored in structure variable x in either of the following ways:

1. Initialize the elements of the structure

```
strcpy (x.name = "SACHIN KUMAR");
x.age = 18;
x.roll = 10112;
strcpy (x.class, "CE41");
```

2. The variable x can be read in a C program by the I/O statements as shown below:

```
gets(x.name);
fflush (stdin);
scanf ("% d %d", x.age, x.roll);
gets (x.class);
```

Example 1

Write a program which reads the record of a student and computes the total marks obtained by him. It also prints the grade according to the rules given below:

Marks	Grade
<200	D
>=200<240	C
>=240<320	B
>=320	A

The structure of a student record is given below:

Student

Name
Roll
Sub 1
Sub 2
Sub 3
Sub 4
Total

Solution

The solution to this problem is simple. The required program is given below:

```
/* This program determines the grade of a student  */
              # include  <stdio.h>
              # include  <string.h>
              main()
               {
                struct student
                   {
```

```
            char Name[20];
            int Age;
            int Roll;
             int sub1, sub2, sub3, sub4;
             int total;
             };
    struct student stud;
    printf ("\n Enter the record of the sudent");
    printf ("\n Name :");
    gets(stud.Name);
    fflush(stdin);
    printf ("\n Age :");
    scanf ("%d", &stud.Age);
    printf ("\n Roll :");
    scanf ("%d", &stud.Roll);
    printf ("\n Subject 1 :");
    scanf ("%d", &stud.sub1);
    printf ("\n Subject 2 :");
    scanf ("%d", &stud.sub2);
    printf ("\n Subject 3 :");
    scanf ("%d", &stud.sub3);
    printf ("\n Subject 4 :");
    scanf ("%d", &stud.sub4);
    stud.total = stud.sub1 + stud.sub2 +
    stud.sub3 + stud.sub4;
    printf ("\n %s( %d )", stud.Name, stud. Roll);
    if (stud.total  < 200 )
            printf ("got the %c grade", 'D');
    else
    if (stud.total  < 240 )
            printf ("got the %c grade", 'C');
    else
    if (stud.total  < 320 )
            printf ("got the %c grade", 'B');
    else
            printf ("got the %c grade", 'A');
   }
```

14.2.2 Array of Structures

An array of structures can be declared just like an ordinary array. However, the structure has to be defined before an array of its type is declared. For example, a 50-element array of type `student` called `stud_list` can be defined as shown on the next page.

```
struct student {
      char name [20];
      int roll;
      int sub1, sub2, sub3, sub4;
      int total;
      };
structstudent stud_list [50]; /* declaration of an
                                 array of structures*/
```

Example 2

Modify the program developed in Example1 so that the new program reads the record of N (say 30) number of students in a class. It prints the list of students in the following format:

List of Student

Name	Roll	Sub 1
–	–	–
–	–	–
–	–	–
–	–	–

Solution

In this problem we will use an array of structures called `stud_list` to read the records of the students. The array of size 30 can be declared as given below:

```
struct student stud_list [30];
```

The required program is given below:

```
/* This program determines the grade of all students of a
class. It illustrates the usage of an array of structure */

   # include <stdio.h>
   main()
    {
     struct student {
         char name[20];
         int age;
         int roll;
         int sub1, sub2, sub3, sub4;
```

```
int total;
};

struct student  stud [30]; /* array of structures */
int N, i;
printf  ("\n  Enter  the  number  of  students  in  the
class ");
scanf ("%d", &N);

printf ("\n Enter the records of the students ");
for (i = 0; i < N; i++)
 {
 fflush(stdin);
  printf ("\n Name :"); gets(stud[i].name);
  printf ("\n Roll :"); scanf ("%d", &stud[i].roll);
  printf ("\n Age :"); scanf ("%d", &stud[i].age);
  printf ("\n Subject1 :",i); scanf ("%d", &stud[i].
  sub1);
  printf ("\n Subject2 :",i); scanf ("%d", &stud[i].
  sub2);
  printf ("\n Subject3 :",i); scanf ("%d", &stud[i].
  sub3);
  printf ("\n Subject :",i); scanf ("%d", &stud[i].
  sub4);

 stud[i].total  =  stud[i].sub1  +  stud[i].sub2  +
 stud[i].sub3 + stud[i].sub4;
 }
 printf ("\n The Merit list is...");
 printf ("\n Name\t\t Roll \t Grade");
 for ( i = 0; i < N; i++)
  {
  printf  ("\n%s\t\t  %d\t",  stud[i].name,  stud[i].
  roll);
if (stud[i].total < 200)
     printf ("%c",'D');
else
        if (stud[i].total < 240 )
         printf ("%c", 'C');
     else
         if (stud[i].total < 320 )
         printf ("%c", 'B');
```

```
            else
            printf ("%c", 'A');
        }
}
```

14.3 INITIALIZING STRUCTURES

When a structure variable is declared, its data members are not initialized and therefore contain undefined values. Similar to arrays, the structure variables can also be initialized at the time of variable declaration. For instance, the structure shown in Fig.14.2 can be declared and initialized as follows:

```
struct student
{
char name[20];
int age;
int roll;
char class[5];
};
/* Initialize variable of type student*/

struct student stud1 = {SACHIN KUMAR,18,10112,"CE41"};
```

Please notice that the values are enclosed within curly braces. The values are assigned to the members of the structure in the order of their appearance, i.e., the first value is assigned to the first member, second to the second and so on.

14.4 ASSIGNMENT OF COMPLETE STRUCTURES

It has been appreciated that the individual fields of a structure are treated as simple variables. The main benefit of a structure, however, is that it can be also be treated as a single entity. For example, if two structure variables `stud1` and `stud2` have been declared as shown below:

```
student stud1, stud2;
```

then the following assignment statement is perfectly valid.

```
stud1 = stud2;
```

This statement will perform the necessary internal assignments. The concept of structure assignment can be better understood by the following program example.

In this program, a structure variable `stud1` is initialised with certain values and it is assigned to another structure variable `stud2`. The contents of the variable `stud2` are displayed.

```
/*This program illustrates copying of complete structures */

 # include <stdio.h>
 main()
  {
    struct student {
          char name[20];
          int roll;
          int age;
          char class[6];
  };

             /* initialize a variable of type student */
   struct student stud1 = {"Sachin Kumar", 101, 16, "CE_IV"};

   struct student stud2;

            /* assign stud1 to stud2 */
   stud2 = stud1;

            /* Display contents of stud2 */
    printf ("\n The copied contents are....");

    printf ("\n Name: %s", stud2.name);
    printf ("\n Roll: %d", stud2.roll);
    printf ("\n Age : %d" , stud2.age);
    printf ("\n class: %s", stud2.class);
  }
```

The reader is advised to run the above program to verify the assignment operation of the structures.

14.5 NESTED STRUCTURES

Nested structures are structures as members of another structure. For instance, the `date of birth (DOB)` is a structure within the structure of a `student` shown in Fig. 14.4. These types of structures are known as nested structures.

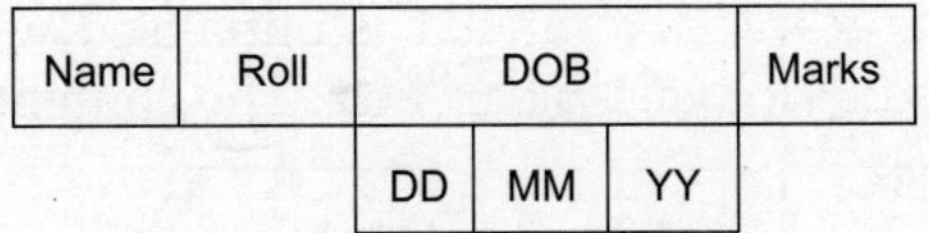

Fig. 14.4 Nested structures

The nested structure shown in Fig. 14.4 can be declared in a program as shown below:

```
/* Nested structures /*
struct date
{
    int dd;
    int mm;
    int yy;
};
struct student
{
    char name[20];
    int roll;
    struct date dob;
    int marks;
};
```

It may be noted here that the member of a nested structure is referenced from outermost to innermost with the help of dot operators. Let us declare a variable `stud` of type `student`:

```
struct student stud;
```

The following statement illustrates the assignment of value 10 to the member mm of this nested structure stud

```
stud.dob.mm = 10;
```

The above statement means : store a value 10 in `mm` member of a structure `dob` which itself is a member of the structure variable called `stud`.

Example 3

Write a nested C structure for the record given in Fig. 14.5. Use appropriate data types for various members.

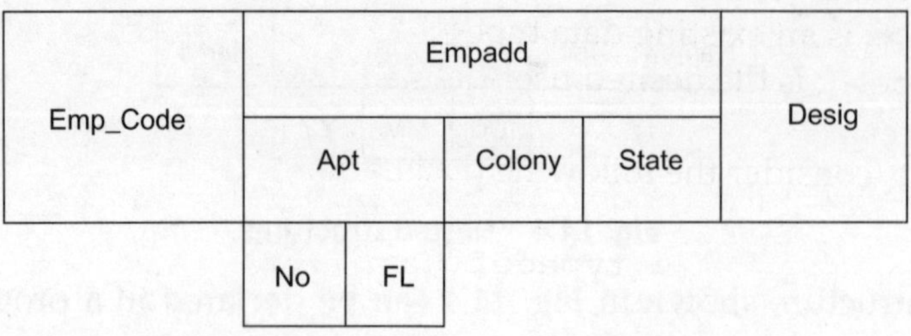

Fig. 14.5 Employee – A nested structure

Solution

This structure consists of three levels of hierarchy. The required C nested structures are given below:

```
/* Nested structure definition of employee */
struct apartment
     {
          int hno;
          char floor[2];
     };
struct address
     {
          struct apartment apt;
          char colony[10];
          char state[10];
     };
struct employee
{
int emp_code;
struct address empadd;
char desig[5];
};
```

In fact, the nesting of structures can be done to any depth.

14.6 USER DEFINED DATA TYPES

In addition to the simple data types such as `integer`, `float`, `char` etc., C allows the users to declare new data types called user defined data types. These data types can be declared with the help of a keyword called `typedef` whose general form is given below:

```
typedef  <type>  <new_type>
```

where typedef : is a reserved word
<type> : is an existing data type
<new_type> : is the desired user-defined data type.

For example, consider the following declaration

```
typedef float xyz;
```

In this declaration, an existing data type (float) has been redefined as xyz. Now, the user can use xyz as a synonym for the type float as a new type, as shown below.

```
xyz x1, x2;
```

In fact, the above declaration is equivalent to the following declaration:

```
float x1, x2;
```

Apparently it looks as if we have not achieved anything great because the user will have to remember xyz as a new type whereas its equivalent float type is already available. Nevertheless, the utility of typedef lies in a situation where the name of a particular type is very long. The user can also self document his code, as shown in the following declaration :

```
typedef float salary;
        •.
        •.
        •.
salary wages-of-month;
```

In the above declaration, the variable wages-of-month has been declared of type salary, where salary itself is of float type. Thus, we can see that the readability of a program can be enhanced by self documenting the variables and their data types with the help of typedef.

For example, the declaration:

```
typedef int age;
```

can be used to increase the clarity of code as shown below :

```
age boy, girl, child;
```

The above statement clearly suggests about what data the variables, boy, girl, and child are going to store.

Similarly, typedef can also be used to define arrays.

```
typedef float lists [20];
lists BP, SAL, GSAL;
```

These statements are equivalent to the following

```
float BP [20], SAL [20], GSAL [20]
```

typedef is also extremely useful for shortening the long and inconvenient declarations of structures. For instance, the structure struct can be declared as a typedef as shown below:

```
typedef struct {
    char name [20];
    int age;
    int roll;
    char class[6];
    } student;
```

Now the structure student has become the type and a variable of this type can be defined as shown

```
student stud1, stud2;
```

The above declaration means that stud1 and stud2 are variables of type student.

14.7 ENUMERATED DATA TYPES

A user can define a set of integer type identifiers in the form of new data types called enumerated datatypes. For instance, the user can create a new data type called color with the help of enum definition as shown below:

```
enum color {
      Blue,
      Yellow,
      White,
      Black
      };
```

Where enum is the keyword that defines an enumerated data type.

The enum declaration given above means that a new type color has been defined. This type contains the constant values : Blue, yellow, white, and black. Each of these symbols stand for an integer value. By default the value of first symbol (i.e. Blue) is 0, the value of second symbol is 1 and so on. Once the type `color` has been defined then variables of that type can be defined in the following manner;

```
enum color A, B;
```

Now, the variable `A` of type `color` can use the enumerations (Blue, yellow etc) in a program.

Thus, the following operations on variable `A` are valid.

```
A = red;
      :
if (A == red)
      x = x + 10;
else
x = x - 5;
```

The precise definition of enumerated data type is: **The ordered set of distinct constant values defined as a data type in a program**

Examples of some valid enumerated data types are:

(i)

```
enum furniture
 {
        chair,
        table,
        stool,
        desk
 };
```

(ii)

```
enum car
 {
        Maruti,
        Fiat,
        Contessa,
        Tata_Sierra
 }
```

It may be noted here that the ordering of elements in enumerated data type is specified by their position in the `enum` declaration. Thus for furniture type, the relations given in the table on the next page hold good.

Expression	Value
`chair < table`	`true`
`stool > desk`	`true`
`table = = desk`	`false`
`desk < chair`	`false`

The enumerated types can also be used in a switch construct. Consider the following program segment.

```
                        :
/* Enumerated type declaration */
        enum furniture
                 {
                        chair,
                        table,
                        stool,
                        desk
                 };
        main()
        {
/* Enumerated variable declaration */
        enum furniture item;
        float cost;
                :

switch item
 {
        case chair : cost = 250; break;
        case table : cost = 700; break;
        case stool : cost = 120; break;
        case desk : cost = 1500; break;
 }
                :
```

Similarly, enumerated data types can also be used as control variables in a `for` loop as shown below:

```
                                                :
for (item = chair; item  <= desk; item ++)
                {
                        :
                        :
                }
```

The enumerations are also called as symbolic constants because an enumeration has a name and an integer value assigned to it which cannot be changed in the program. Therefore, enumerated data types cannot be plainly used in input output statements. As a result, the statements `scanf`, `printf`, `gets`, `puts` etc cannot be directly applied to these data types because the results will not be as desired.

The following example would further help in understanding the concept.

Example 4

The attendance record of each student in a school is computed every week. Write a program using enumerated data types that reads the attendance for each day of the week and prints the weekly list of attendance.

Solution

Let us assume that there are a maximum of 30 students in the class. Since the attendance records are to be maintained for a week, we can choose an array of structures to store and manipulate the data. The record structure of a student chosen for this program is given below:

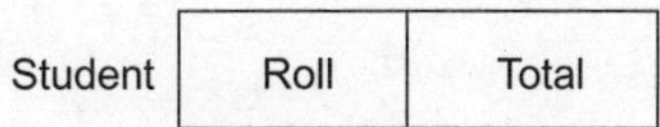

The program is given below:

```
/* This program uses enumerated data type for maintaining
the attendance record of students */
 # include <stdio.h>
   typedef struct  {
            int roll;
            int total;
            } student;
 enum day { mon, tue, wed, thur, fri, sat } ;

   main()
    {
      student studlist[30];

      enum day d; /* declare a variable of type day */
      int N, i, Attendance;
      printf ("\n Enter the number of students");
      scanf ("%d", &N);

      printf ("\n Enter the attendance record...");
```

```
for (i =0; i < N; i++)
    {
      printf ("\n Roll No.:");
      scanf ("%d", &studlist[i].roll);
      printf ("\n Attandance for ");
        studlist[i].total = 0;
       for (d = mon; d <= sat; d++)
         {
              switch(d)
              {
              case mon : printf ("Monday (0/1):");
                         scanf ("%d", &Attendance);
                         break;
              case tue : printf ("Tuesday(0/1):");
                         scanf ("%d", & Attendance);
                         break;
              case wed : printf ("Wednesday(0/1):");
                         scanf ("%d", & Attendance);
                         break;
              case thur : printf ("Thursday(0/1):");
                         scanf ("%d", & Attendance);
                         break;
              case fri : printf ("Friday(0/1):");
                         scanf ("%d", & Attendance);
                         break;
              case sat : printf ("Saturday(0/1):");
                         scanf ("%d", & Attendance);
              }

           studlist[i].total = studlist [i].total +
           Attendance;
         }
     }
     clrscr();
     printf ("\n ....The weekly Attendane....\n");
     printf ("Roll No.\t Attendance");
     for (i=0; i < N; i++)
     printf ("\n%d    \t\t    %d",    studlist[i].roll,
           studlist[i].total);
}
```

14.7.1 Changing Default Ordinal Values

From our previous discussions on enumerated data types, we know that an `enum` declaration assigns an integer value to each symbol contained in its definition. Consider the following declaration:

```
enum car
        {
                Maruti,
                Fiat,
                Contessa,
                Tata_Sierra
        };
```

By default, the integer values assigned to the various symbols of this definition are listed below:

Symbol	Value
Maruti	0
Fiat	1
Contessa	2
Tata_Sierra	3

If the need be, these default values can be changed by assigning the desired values explicitly in the definition itself. For example, if we desire to assign a value 5 to Contessa, it can be done by the following declaration:

```
enum car
    {
            Maruti,
            Fiat,
            Contessa = 5,
            Tata_Sierra,
    };
```

The new values of the enumeration constants will be as listed below:

Symbol	Value
Maruti	0
Fiat	1
Contessa	5
Tata_Sierra	2

It may be noted here that two enumerations belonging to two different enumerated data types, cannot be assigned to each other. For instance the assignment `car = chair;` is illegal.

14.8 UNIONS

Suppose in a fete, every visitor is assured to win any one of the items listed below:

1. wall clock
2. toaster
3. electric iron
4. DVD player

Obviously, a visitor to the fete must carry a bag large enough to carry the largest item so that any one of the items won by him can be held in that bag. With the same philosophy in mind, the designers of C introduced a special variable called `union` which may hold objects of different sizes and types, but one at a time. Though a `union` is a variable and can hold only one item at a time, it looks like a `structure`. The general format a `union` is given below:

```
union    <name> {
member 1
member 2
       :
member
};
```

where `union` : is a keyword

`<name>` : is the name of the union

`member 1, 2, ... n` : are the individual member declarations

It may be noted that in a `structure`, each member has its own memory location whereas in a `union`, only one memory location is allocated. The memory allocated is large enough to hold the largest member of the `union`.

Example 5

Write a program that uses a `union` to maintain the examination record of a student as per the following criteria.

> If the student has passed the examination: store the percentage of marks secured by the student else store 'C' for compartment, 'F' for fail, 'A' for absent.

Solution

The following union would be used to store the column status for a student.

```
union exam status {   float percentage;
                      char flop_status;
          };
```

The complete information of a student would be stored in the following structure:

```
struct student {
    char name [20];
    int roll;
    int outcome;
     union exam_status ES;
};
```

The required program that uses the above structure to maintain the examination status of N member of students is given below:

```
/* This program illustrates the usage of a UNION for the
maintenaince of exam status of students */

# include <stdio.h>
#include <math.h>

union exam_status {
        float percentage;
        char flop_status;
        };
typedef struct  {
        char name [20];
        int roll;
        int outcome;
        union exam_status ES;
    }student;

main()
 {
    student studlist [30];
    int N, i, outcome;
    float temp;
    printf ("\n Enter the number of students in the class");
    scanf ("%d", &N);
    printf ("\n Enter the exam data of the students");
```

```
for (i = 0 ; i < N; i++)
  {
      printf ("\n Name ?:"); fflush(stdin); gets(studlist[i].
      name);
      printf  ("\n  Roll  ?:");  scanf  ("%d",&studlist[i].
      roll);
      printf ("\n Pass\Fail?-(Enter 1/0)");
                         scanf ("%d", &studlist[i].outcome);


      if (studlist[i].outcome == 1)

      { printf ("\n percentage ?:");

        scanf ("%f", &temp);
        studlist[i].ES.percentage = temp;}
      else
      { fflush(stdin);
        printf ("\n Enter Flop status - F/C/A :");
            studlist[i].ES.flop_status=getchar();}
      }

   printf ("\n\t\tResult");
   printf ("\n-----------------------------------");
   printf ("\nNAME\t\tROLL\tExam_status");
   for (i=0; i < N; i++)
      {
        printf("\n%s", studlist[i].name);
        printf ("\t\t%d", studlist[i].roll);
        if (studlist[i].outcome == 1)

        printf ("\t%5.2f",studlist[i].ES.percentage);
        else
         printf ("\t%c",studlist[i].ES.flop_status);
        }

}
```

Note: There are few programming situations where `unions` are used. Hcwever, they are widely used in libraries of C code wherein `unions` are passed as parameters to function. Therefore, it is necessary for the readers to understand the concept so that serious programmers may understand C code that utilises such `unions`.

14.9 GRADED PROBLEMS

Problem 1. A positive integer is called "Nasty" if it has at least two pairs of positive integer factors such that the difference of one pair equals the sum of the other pair.

For example the number 6 is *nasty* as illustrated below:

$$1, 6 \text{ are factors of } 6 \rightarrow 6 - 1 = 5$$
$$2, 3 \text{ are factors of } 6 \rightarrow 2 + 3 = 5$$

Solution: This problems has already been discussed in Chapter 5 using parallel arrays. Now the structures would be suitably used to reduce the number of computations in terms of `sum` and `diff` of the pairs of factors. The following structure would be used to store a pair of factors, their difference, and its sum.

```
struct factorpair {
        int factor1;
        int factor2;
        int diff;
        int sum;
        };
```

All the factors of the number under examination would be stored in the array called fplist . With a nested loop, the difference of a pair of factors would be compared with the sum of the other pair of factors to determine if the number is nasty or not. The required program is given below:

```
/* This program determines whether a given Number is Nasty
or not */

# include <stdio.h>
# include <math.h>

                        /* Struct to store a pair of factors */
typedef struct  {
           int factor1;
           int factor2;
           int diff;
           int sum;
         } factorPair;
 enum nastynum { true, false };

main()
  { factorPair fplist[15];
    int Number;
    int i,j, count ;
```

```
    enum nastynum nasty;
    printf ("\n Enter the Number:");
    scanf ("%d", &Number);
                        /* Store the default pair of factors */
    fplist[0].factor1=1;
    fplist[0].factor2=Number;
    fplist[0].diff=Number-1;
    fplist[0].sum=Number+1;
                        /* Find and store pair of factors */
    count = 1;
    for ( i = 2; i <= sqrt (Number); i++)
     {
        if (Number % i == 0)
         {
          fplist[count].factor1=i;
          fplist[count].factor2=Number/i;
          fplist[count].diff=fplist[count].factor2 -
          fplist[count].factor1;
          fplist[count].sum=fplist[count].factor2 +
          fplist[count].factor1;
         }
        count++;
        }
                        /* Find the Nasty Number    */
     nasty = false;      /* Assume Number is not nasty     */
     i = 0;
     while ( i <= count && nasty == false)
        {
          for (j = 0; j <= count; j++)
         { if (fplist[i].diff == fplist[j].sum)
                  { nasty = true;
                   break;
                  }
          }
          i++;
         }

         if ( nasty == true)
            printf ("\n The Number : %d is Nasty ", Number);
         else
           printf  ("\n  The  Number  :  %d  is  not  Nasty  ",
           Number);

   }
```

Problem 2. A DNA sequence is represented as a string of characters from the set {A, C, G, T}. Write a program that reads two DNA sequences: DNA1 and DNA2 and finds all the portions of similarity in the two DNA sequences. The similar portions with the highest count are aligned by inserting the '_' characters into the sequences. Consider the following DNA sequences:

DNA1 : **ACCGTGT**
DNA2 : **TCGCGTA**

The program should produce the following output:

ACCGT--
-- CGTA

Solution: This is a problem of pattern matching. The two DNA sequences would be stored into character arrays: `Dna1 [20]` and `Dna2 [20]`. Using nested loops for every character appearing in `DNA2`, a match in `DNA1` would be searched for. If found, then their corresponding starting locations (i.e. indices) `Jplace` and `Iplace` would be noted. As long as further characters match, the number of matches would be counted. The `Jplace`, `Iplace` and `count` would be stored in a structure given below:

```
struct match {
     int iplace;
     int jplace;
     int  no_of_matches;
};
```

The required program is given below:

```
/* This program alignes two DNAs at the portions that are
similar */

# include <stdio.h>
main()
  {
    char Dna1[20];
    char Dna2[20];
    struct match {  /* Structure to store a pattern match */
      int iplace;
      int jplace;
      int no_of_matches;
```

```
  };
  struct match matchlist[20];
                          /* List to store all matches   */
  int count, Iplace, Jplace, i, j, m, n,temp;
  int next, max;
  fflush(stdin);
                          /* Read the DNAs */
  printf ("\n Enter DNA1:");
 fflush(stdin);
  scanf ("%s", Dna1);
  printf ("\n Enter DNA2:");
  fflush(stdin);
  scanf ("%s", Dna2);
                          /* Find the length of the DNAs */
  i=0;
  while (Dna1[i] != '\0')  i++; m=--i;

  i=0;
  while (Dna2[i] != '\0')  i++; n=--i;
  next = 0;
                          /* Find similar portions     */
  for (Jplace = 0; Jplace <= m; Jplace++)
    {
     Iplace = 0;
        while (Iplace <= n)
         {
          while (Dna1[Iplace] != Dna2 [Jplace] && (Iplace
          <= n))
                            Iplace++;
          if (Dna1[Iplace] == Dna2 [Jplace]) /* A portion
          is found */
          {
          i = Iplace + 1;
          j = Jplace + 1;
          count = 1;
          while (Dna1[i] == Dna2[j] && (i <= m) && (j <= n))
              {
              count ++;
              i++;
              j++;
              }        /* Store the info about the match */
          matchlist[next].iplace = Iplace;
```

```
        matchlist[next].jplace = Jplace;
        matchlist[next].no_of_matches = count-1;
        next++;
        }
        Iplace++;
       }
     }
           /* Find the similar portins with max count */
  max = matchlist[0].no_of_matches;
  Iplace=0;
  for (i=1; i< next; i++)
     {
      if ( max < matchlist[i].no_of_matches)
          { max = matchlist[i].no_of_matches;
                 Iplace = i;
          }
     }           /* Align and display  */
```

A list of all such pattern matches is stored in an array of structures called `matchlist [20]`. Finally, the pattern match with the largest number of matches is selected and accordingly the DNAs are aligned and displayed.
Some example Input/Output are given below:

```
Input:   DNA1 : ACCGTGT
         DNA2 : TCGCGTA
Output:        ACCGT--
              -- CGTA
Input:   DNA1 : AAATCGT
         DNA2 : AATCA
Output:        AAATC--
              -- AATCA
```

It may be noted that the program would work with any pattern matching situation, as indicated by the following sample input/output processed by the program

```
Input:   DNA1: AAABCHJ
         DNA2: XABCD
Output:        AAABC---
               -- ABCD
```

Problem 3. Write a program that produces a list which is the reverse (at all levels) of a given list. For example if the given list were.

[[4 7 8] 2 9 [1 9 6] 2 0 3]]

The reversed list would be

[3 2 0 [6 1 9] 9 2 [8 7 4]]

Solution: From the example, it may be observed that a list can contain a sublist. In this program an array of records can be employed to store such a nested list where each record can have the following entries.

```
struct sublist {
int no-of-elements;
int sub_list [10];
};
```

Nested loops would be employed. In the outer loop the structure containing the sublists would be so exchanged so that the list becomes reversed. In the inner loops, each sublist contained in the structure, would be reversed. A program that uses this strategy is given below:

```
# include <stdio.h>
struct sublist {
    int no_of_elements;
    int sub_list [10];
        };
main()
 {
  struct  sublist list[20], TEMP;
  int N,n, i,j,k,l,temp;

  printf ("\n Enter the number of sublists in the list");
  scanf ("%d", &N);

  printf ("\n Enter the sublists");
                                  /* Read the List */
  for (i=0; i < N; i++)
   {
         printf ("\n No_of_elements in %d sublist", i);
         scanf ("%d", &n);
         list[i].no_of_elements= n;
```

```
        printf ("\n Enter the elements");
                                /* Read sublist  */
        for (j=0; j < n; j++)
          scanf ("%d", &list[i].sub_list[j]);
    }
                                /* Reverse the list */
    i=0; j =N-1;
    while ( i < j)
     {
        if (list[i].no_of_elements > 1)
          {                     /* Reverese the sublist */
          k=0; l= list[i].no_of_elements-1;
           while ( k < l)
            {
              temp = list[i].sub_list[k];
              list[i].sub_list[k] = list[i].sub_list[l];
              list[i].sub_list[l] = temp;
              k++; l--;
            }
     }
   if (list[j].no_of_elements > 1)
          {                     /* Reverse the sublist */
           k=0; l= list[j].no_of_elements-1;
                 while ( k < l)
                  {             /* Exchange the elements */
                   temp = list[j].sub_list[k];
                  list[j].sub_list[k] = list[j].sub_
                                        list[l];
          list[j].sub_list[l] = temp;
          k++; l--;
                  }
          }
                                /* Exchange the sublists */
           TEMP = list[i];
           list[i] = list [j];
           list [j] = TEMP;
           i++; j--;
          }
                            /* Print the reversed list */
         printf ("\n The reversed list is ....");
         printf ("\n[ ");
```

```
        for (i=0; i < N; i++)
         {
          if (list[i].no_of_elements > 1)
          { printf ("[ ");
            for (j = 0; j < list[i].no_of_elements; j++)
                 printf ("%d ",list[i].sub_list[j]);
            printf (" ] ");
           }
           else
           printf ("%d ",list[i].sub_list[0]);
         }
}
```

Frequently Asked Questions

1. Differentiate between an array and a structure.
   Solution: Arrays are suitable for list and table processing and all the elements of an array must be of the same type. A structure, on the other hand, combines a group of related data items of arbitrary types. A structure is suitable for processing records of an entity.

2. Can structure elements be initialized during the declaration of the structure?
   Solution: No. A variable of structure type can be initialized at the time of its declaration

3. What is the limitation of enumerated data types?
   Solution: They cannot be used in input and output statements.

4. For what purpose the is keyword `typedef` used?
   Solution: It is used to define user defined data types.

5. For what purpose is the keyword `enum` used?
   Solution: It is used to define enumerated data type.

6. Is it necessary that all members of a structure should be of the same type?
   Solution: No, that is not necessary.

7. Can the names of two fields of two different structures be the same?
   Solution: Yes

Test Your Skills

1. Point out the errors in the following declaration:

```
struct xyz {
      int roll;
```

```
int age;
}
```

Solution: The structure must end with a semicolon.

2. Point out the errors in the following program.

```
# include <stdio.h>
void main()
{
    struct stud {
                    int roll;   int age;
        };
    struct stud s1, s2;
    s1 = { 101, 15 };
    s2 = s1;
    if ( s1 == s2)
          printf  ("\n The structures are equal);
    else
           printf ("\n  The structures are not equal);
}
```

Solution: The structures cannot be compared by ! = and = = operations. The programmer has to perform a component by component comparison of the structure elements for the purpose of comparison of two structures.

3. What will the output of the following code be?

```
#include  <stdio.h>
void main ( )
{
      struct roll
      {
      int roll;
      };
      struct roll roll;
      roll.roll =100;
      printf ("\n Roll = %d", roll.roll);
 }
```

Solution: Roll = 100

4. Which line will give an error in the following program segment.

```
            #include  <stdio.h>
Line 1      void main ()
Line 2        {
```

```
Line 3        struct xyz
Line 4                {
Line 5                int i;
Line 6                char ch;
Line 7                }
Line 8        char name [10];
Line 9        struct xyz rec;
Line 10               :
Line 11       }
```

Solution: Line No. 8 because line no. 7 requires a semicolon at the end of it.

5. Will the following program compile ?

```
# include  <stdio.h>
void main ()
  {
   struct some {
   int some;
    };
    some some;
    int some;
    some.some = 100;
    some = 100;
    printf ("\n %d %d", some, some.some);
  }
```

Solution: No, it will not compile and will generate the error Multiple declaration for `some' in the line : int some;

6. What would the output of the following program be.

```
enum furniture { Chair,
          Table,
          Bed,
          Almirah
          };
          # include  < stdio.h >
          main ( )
          {
          printf ("\n %d %d %d %d," Chair, Table, Bed, Almirah);
          }
```

Solution: The output would be: 0 1 2 3

7. Write a statement that declares an enumerated data type called boolean with values True and False.

Solution: In C, the value zero is considered logical False and a non-zero value as logical True. Therefore, we will use the following declaration so that the C rule and our declaration agree on their usage i.e.

```
enum boolean {false, true};
```

The above declaration assigns the values zero and one to false and true respectively.

8. How can enumeration values be displayed symbolically?
Solution: There is no direct method available with C. However, a programmer can map an enumeration to a string symbol with the help of a switch statement. The following program segment illustrates the concept.

```
:
enum car
{
      Indica;
      Maruti,
      Fiat,
      Contessa,
      Sierra,
      Sumo,
};
:
switch (car)
{
Case 0 : printf ("\n Indica");
break;
Case 1 : printf ("\ Maruti");
break;
Case 2 : printf  ("\ Fiat");
break;
Case 3 : printf  ("\ Contessa");
break;
Case 4 : printf ("\ Sierra");
break;
Case 5 : printf ("\ Sumo");
}
```

9. What will be the output of the following program?

```
# include <stdio.h>
main()
 {
  struct node {
  char name [20];
  int age;
  int roll;
  };
 struct node stud = {"Atul"};

 printf ("%d %d", stud.age, stud.roll);
 }
```

Solution: 0 0

EXERCISES

1. Define the terms: structure and member variables. Explain how an array differs from a structure.
2. Declare a structure in C that can store length of a cloth in metres, centimetres, and millimetres.
3. Differentiate between structures and structure variables.
4. Write structure definitions for statements containing the following:
   (i) member name, membership number, Date of joining, Amount of fee.
   (ii) first name, middle name, last name
   (iii) item code, item type, quantity. Choose appropriate names for the structures and data types for their corresponding members.
5. A date structure comprises day, month and year. Write a program that uses such a structure to read a date and checks for its validity.

Day		(2 digits)
Month		(2 digits)
Year		(2 digits)

6. Give appropriate statements to accept values into the members of the structure date and then print out the date as

   mm/dd/yyyy
7. Write a C structure for the record structure given below

Book

Title	Author Name	Publisher		Cost	Edition
		Name	Address		

8. Using the structure of Ex. 7 (above), write a program which maintains a list of computer books available in a library.
9. What is meant by enumerated data type ? Explain this concept with suitable examples.
10. What will the following declarations do ?
```
typedef char sentence [40];
sentence complex [10];
```
11. Give a suitable declaration that stores the data of 50 players. The record structure of a player is given below:

Player

Name			Age	Game	Address			
First Name	Middle Name	First Name			H No.	Street	City	State

12. Write a program that uses the declaration of Ex. 11 and perform the following tasks.
    (a) To read the name of a player and displays his game and address.
    (b) For a given game, it displays the list of players who play that game.
    (c) For a given city name, it displays the list of players who live in it.
13. Point out the errors in the following program.

```
# include   <stdio.h>
void main ()
     {
          struct twoval {
          int first;
          int second;
     } x, y;
          x = { 20, 70};
          y = x;
          if (y ! = x)
               printf (\n Not equal”);
          else
               printf (\n Equal”);
     }
```

14. Write a statement that declares an enumerated data type called gadgets consisting of values TV, VCR, Tel_phone, CD_player, AC and FAX. Assign values 3, 9, 11 to VCR, AC and FAX.
15. Write a program that compares two given dates `D1` and `D2` having the following structure The program should display the message for `D1` being earlier date than `D2`, same as `D2`, later date than `D2`, respectively.

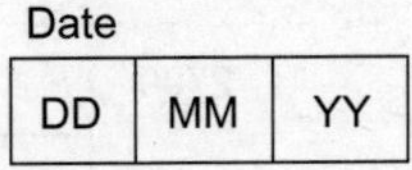

16. Use the structure of date given in Ex. 15 to write a program that adds a given number of days to a date and displays the new date.

CHAPTER

15 Pointers

15.1 INTRODUCTION

Pointers are amongst the most powerful features of C. Beginners in C find pointers hard to understand and manipulate. In an attempt to unveil the mystery behind this concept, the basics of pointers which generally remain in background are being discussed in the following sections.

15.1.1 The '&' Operator

When a variable x is declared in a program, a storage location in main memory is made available by the compiler. For example Fig. 15.1 shows the declaration of x as an integer variable and its storage location in main memory.

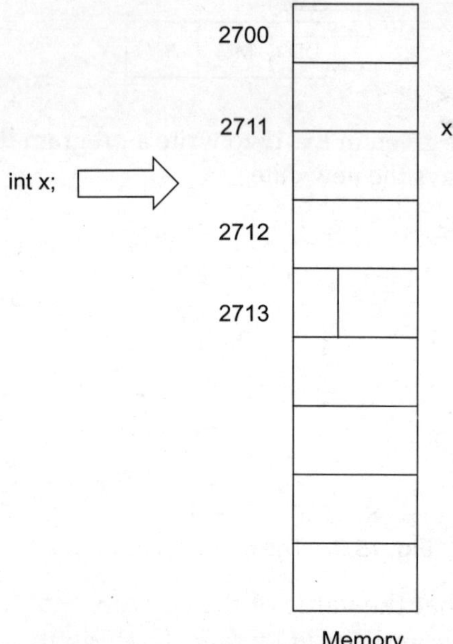

Fig. 15.1 The variable x and its equivalent representation in memory

From Fig. 15.1, it may be observed that x is the name associated by the compiler with a location in the memory of the computer. Let us assume that at the time of execution, the physical address of this memory location (called x) is 2712. Now, a point worth noting is that this memory location is viewed by the programmer as variable x and by the operating system as an address 2712. The address of variable x can be obtained by `&', an address of operator. This operator when applied to a variable gives the physical memory address of the variable. Thus, &x will provide the address 2712. Consider the following program segment:

```
x = 15;
printf ("\n Value of x = %d", x);
printf ("\n Address of x = %d", & x);
```

The output of the above program segment would be as shown below:

```
Value of x   = 15
Address of x = 2712                (assumed value)
```

The contents of variable x (memory location 2712) are shown in Fig. 15.2

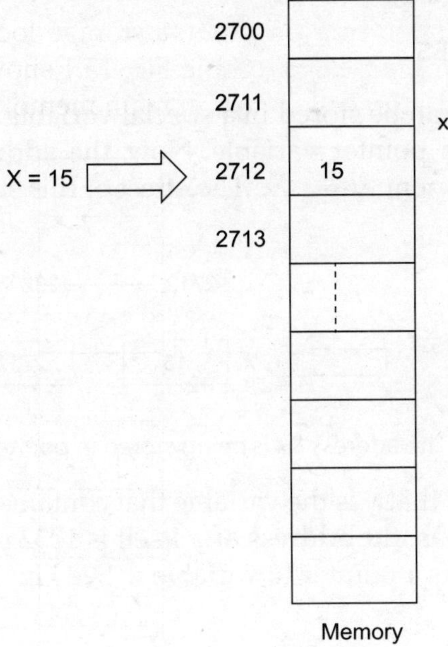

Fig. 15.2 The contents of variable x.

It may be noted here that the value of the address of x (i.e., 2712) is assumed and the actual value is *machine* and *execution time* dependent.

15.1.2 The '*' operator

The '*' is an indirection operator or 'value at address operator'. In simple words, we can say that if the address of a variable is known then the '*' operator provides the contents of the variable. Consider the following program segment:

```
# include <stdio.h>
main()
  {
    int x =15;
    printf ("\n Value of x =%d ", x);
    printf ("\n Address of x =%u ", &x);
    printf ("\n Value at address %d = %d", *(&x));
  }
```

The output of the above program segment would be as shown below:

```
Value of x = 15
Address of x = 2712
Value at address 2712 = 15
```

15.2 POINTER VARIABLES

An address of a variable can be stored in a special variable called a pointer variable. Let us assume that y is a pointer variable. Now, the address of variable x can be assigned to y by the statement: y = &x. The effect of this statement as shown in Fig. 15.3 is:

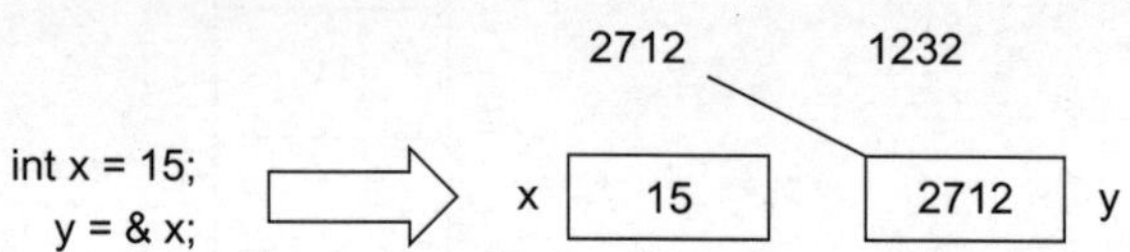

Fig. 15.3 The address &x is being stored in pointer variable y

From Fig.15.3, it is clear that y is the variable that contains the address (i.e., 2712) of another variable x, whereas, the address of y itself is 1232 (assumed value). In other words, we can say that y is a pointer to variable x. See Fig. 15.4.

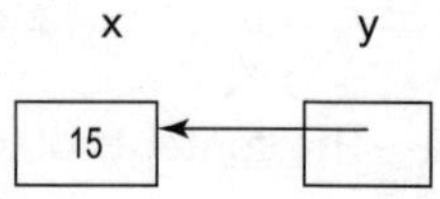

Fig. 15.4 y is a pointer to x

A pointer variable y can be declared in C as shown below:

```
int  *y;
```

The above declaration means that y is a pointer to a variable of type int. Similarly, consider the following declaration:

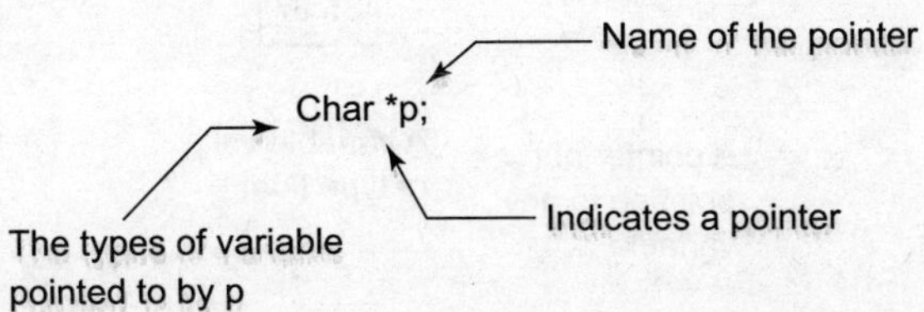

The above declaration means that p is a pointer to a variable of type char. A pointer can be precisely defined as: A pointer variable contains the address of another variable.

Consider the following program segment:

```
# include <stdio.h>
main()
  {
   int x =15;
   int *y;
   y = &x;
   printf ("\n Value of x =%d ", x);
   printf ("\n Address of x =%u ", &x);
   printf ("\n Value of x =%d ", *y);
   printf ("\n Address of x = %u", y);
   printf ("\n Address of y = %u", &y);
   }
```

The output of the above program segment would be as shown below:

```
Value of x = 15
Address of x = 2712
Value of x = 15
Address of x = 2712
Address of y = 1232
```

Let us, now, consider the following statements:

```
float val = 35.67;
   float *pt;
```

The first statement declares `val` to be a variable of type `float` and initializes it with a value 35.67. The second statement declares `pt` to be pointer to a variable of type `float`. Please note that `pt` can point to a variable of type `float` but it is currently not pointing to any variable, as shown in Fig. 15.5 :

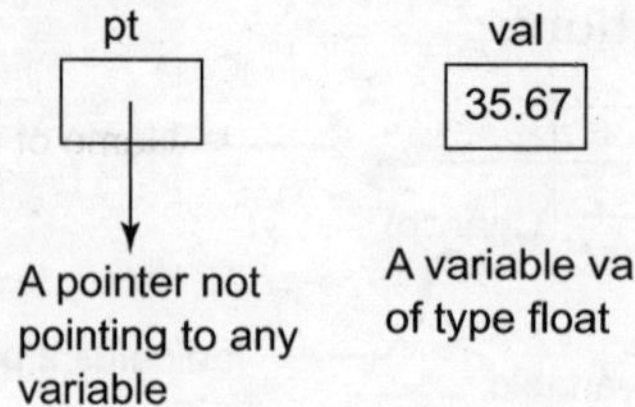

Fig. 15.5 The pointer `pt` is not pointing to any variable

The pointer `pt` can point to the variable `val` by assigning the address of `val` to `pt` as shown below:

```
pt = &val;
```

Once the above statement is executed, the pointer `pt` gets the address of `val` and we can say that logically `pt` points to the variable `val` as shown in Fig. 15.6.

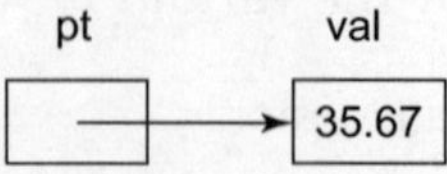

Fig. 15.6 The pointer `pt` pointing to variable `val`

However, one must keep in mind that the arrow is for illustration sake. Actually, the pointer `pt` contains the address of `val`. The address is an integer which is not a simple value but a reference to a location in the memory.

Examples of some valid pointer declarations are:

(i) `int *p;`
(ii) `char *i, *k;`
(iii) `float *pt;`
(iv) `int **ptr;`

The example (iv) means the `ptr` is a pointer to a location which itself is a pointer to a variable of type `integer`.

It may be noted here that a pointer can also be incremented to point to an immediately next location of its type. For example, if the contents of a pointer p of type `integer` are 5224 then the contents of p++ will be 5226 instead of 5225 (see Fig. 15.7). The reason being that an int is always of 2 bytes in size, and therefore stored in two memory locations, as shown in Fig. 15.7.

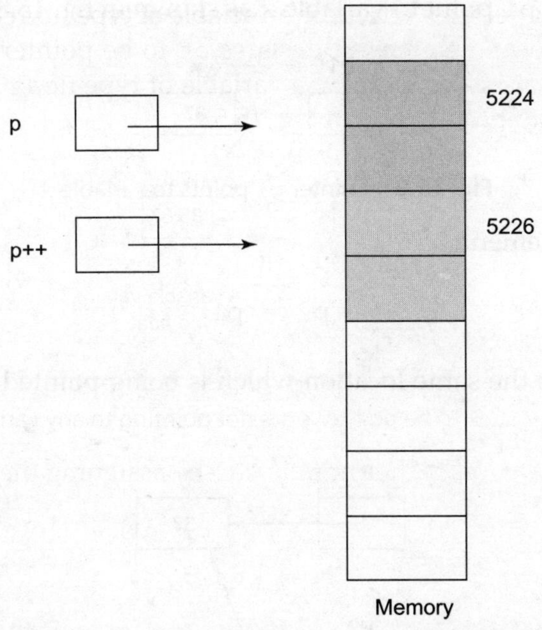

Fig. 15.7 The variable of type `int` occupies two bytes

The amount of storage taken by the various types of data is tabulated in Table 15.1

Table 15.1 Amount of storage taken by various data types

Data type	Amount of storage
character	1 byte
integer	2 byte
float	4 byte
long	4 byte
Double	8 byte

Thus, a pointer of `float` type will point to an address of 4 bytes and therefore an increment to this pointer will increment its contents by 4 locations. It may be further noted that more than one pointer can point to the same location. Consider the following program segment:

```
int x = 37
int * p1, * p2;
```

The following statement:

```
p1=& x;
```

makes the pointer `p1` point to variable `x` as shown in fig. 15.8

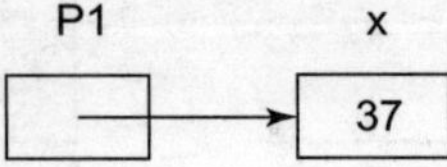

Fig. 15.8 Pointer `p1` points to variable `x`

The following statement:

```
p2 = p1
```

makes `p2` point to the same location which is being pointed to by `p1`, as shown in fig. 15.9

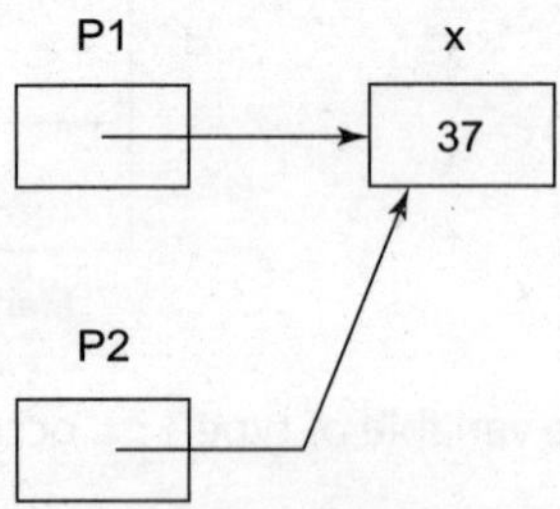

Fig. 15.9 Pointers `p1` and `p2` pointing to `x`

The contents of variable `x` are now reachable by both the pointers `p1` and `p2`. Thus, two or more entities can cooperatively share a single memory structure with the help of pointers. In fact, this technique can be used to provide efficient communication between different parts of a program.

The pointers can be used for a variety of purposes in a program. Some of them are:

1. To pass addresses of variables from one function to another
2. To return more than one value from a function to the calling function
3. For the creation of linked structures such as linked lists and trees.

Example 1

Write a program that reads from the keyboard, two variables `x` and `y` of type `integer`. It prints the exchanged contents of these variables with the help of pointers, without altering the variables.

Solution

We will use two pointers `p1` and `p2` for variables `x` and `y`. A third pointer `p3` will be used as a temporary pointer for the exchange of pointers `p1` and `p2`. The scheme is shown in Fig. 15.8.

The program is given below:

```
/* This program illustrates the usage of pointers to exchange
   the contents of two variables */

   # include <stdio.h>
   main()
     {
       int x,y;
       int *p1, *p2, *p3; /* pointers to integers  */
       printf("\n Enter two integer values");
       scanf ("%d %d", &x, &y);
             /* Assign the addresses x and y to P1 and p2 */
       p1 = &x;
       p2 = &y;
             /* Exchange the pointers */
       p3 = p1;
       p1 = p2;
       p2 = p3;

           /* Print the contents through exchanged contents */
       printf( "\n The exchanged contents are ");
       printf (" %d & %d", *p1, *p2);
     }
```

Note: The output would show the exchanged values because of the exchange of pointers (see Fig.15.10), whereas the contents of x and y have remained unaltered.

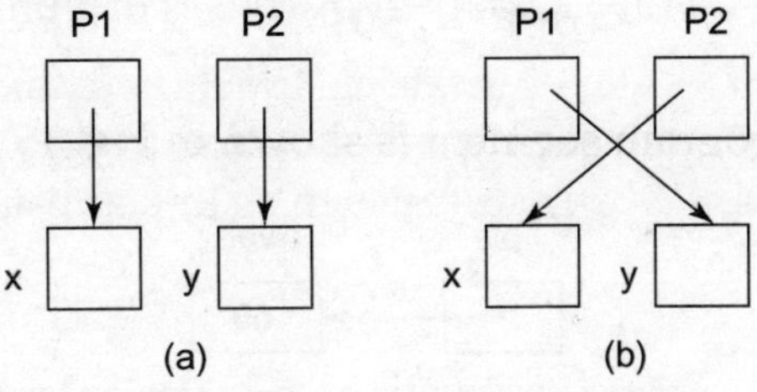

Fig. 15.10 Exchange of contents of variables by exchanging pointers

15.2.1 Dangling Pointers

A dangling pointer is that pointer which has been allocated but does not point to any entity. Such an un-initialized pointer is dangerous in the sense that a dereference operation on it will result in an unpredictable operation or may give a runtime error.

Consider the following code

```
int * ptr;
*ptr = 50;
```

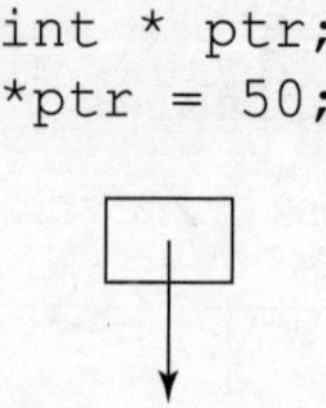

Fig. 15.11 The dangling pointer

The first statement allocates the pointer called `ptr` as shown in Fig. 15.11. it may be noted that currently `ptr` is a dangling pointer. The second statement is trying to load a value (i.e., 50) to a location which is pointed to by `ptr`. Obviously, this is a dangerous situation because the results will be unpredictable. The C compiler does not consider it as an error. Some compilers though, may give a warning.

Therefore, if pointers are being used, the following steps must be followed
Step

1. Allocate the pointer.
2. Allocate the variable or entity to which the pointer is to be pointed.
3. Point the pointer to the entity.

Let us assume that it is desired that the pointer `ptr` should point to a variable `val` of type `int`. The correct code in that case would be as given below:

```
int * ptr;
int val;
ptr = &val;
* ptr = 50;
```

The result of above program segment is shown in Fig. 15. 12

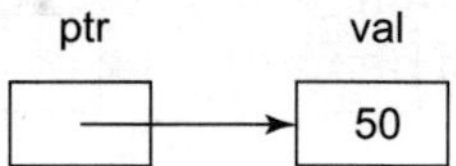

Fig. 15. 12 The correct assignment

15.3 POINTERS AND ARRAYS

Pointers and arrays are very closely related to each other. In C, the name of an array is a pointer that contains the base address of the array. In fact, it is a pointer to the first element of the array. Consider the array declaration given on the next page.

```
int list[] = { 20, 30, 35, 36, 39 };
```

This array will be stored in contiguous locations of the main memory with a starting address equal to 1001(assumed value), as shown in Fig. 15.13. Since the array list is of **integer** type, each element of this array occupies two bytes. The name of the array contains the starting address of the array i.e., 1001

List	20	30	35	36	39
	1001	1003	1005	1007	1009

Fig. 15.13 The contiguous storage allocation with starting address = 1001

Consider the following program segment:

```
printf ("\n Address of zeroth element of array list",  list);
printf ("\n value of zeroth element of array list", *list);
```

Once the above program segment is executed, the output would be as shown below:

```
Address of zeroth element of array list = 1001
Value of zeroth element of array list = 20
```

We could have achieved the same output by the following program segment:

```
printf ("\n Address of zeroth element of list", &list [0]);
printf ("\n value of zeroth element of list", list [0]);
```

Both the approaches given above are equivalent because of the following equivalence relations:

`list  ≡ &list [0]` - both denote address of zeroth element of the array list
`*list ≡ list[0]` - both denote value of zeroth element of the array list

The left side approach is known as the pointer method and the right side as the array indexing method. Let us now write a program that prints out a list by the array indexing method:

```
/* Array indexing method    */

# include <stdio.h>
```

```
main()
{
 static int list [] = { 20,30,35,36,39 };
 int i;
 printf ("\n The list is ...");
 for ( i = 0; i < 5; i++)
printf ("\n %d   %d ---element", list[i], i);
}
```

The output of this program would be:

```
The list is...
           20
           30
           35
           36
           39
```

The above program can also be written by the pointer method as shown below:

```
/* pointer method of processing an array  */

# include <stdio.h>
main()
 {
   static int list [] = { 20,30,35,36,39 };
   int i;
   printf ("\n The list is ...");
   for ( i = 0; i < 5; i++)
     printf ("\n %d    %d ---element", *(list +i), i);
 }
```

It may be noted that in the above program we have used the term : `*(list + i)` to print an ith element of the array. Let us analyze this term. Since `list` designates the address of the zeroth element of the array, we can access its value through the 'value at the address operator' i.e., '*' operator.

In fact, the following terms are equivalent:

→ `*list ≡ *(list + 0) ≡ list [0]`
→ `*(list + 1) ≡ list [1]` and so on

Thus, we can refer to the ith element of an array list by either of the following ways :

`*(list + i)` or `*(i + list)` or `list [i]`

So far we have used the name of an array to get its base address and manipulate it. However, there is a small difference between an ordinary pointer and the name of an array. The difference is that the array name is a **pointer constant** and its contents cannot be changed. Thus, the following operations on `list` are illegal because they try to change the contents of `list`, a pointer constant.

```
List = NULL;        /* Not allowed */
List = & Val;       /* Not allowed */
list++              /* Not allowed */
list--                  /* Not allowed */
```

Consider the following program:

```
# include <stdio.h>
main()
 {
  char text[6] ="Helpme";
  char *p ="Helpme";
  printf ("\n %c", text[3]);
  printf ("\n %c", p[3]);
  }
```

The output of above program would be:

```
p
p
```

From the above program, it looks as if the following declarations are equivalent as `text [3]` and `p[3]` behave in identical manner.

```
char text [6];
char *p;
```

It may be noted that the above declarations are not at all equivalent though the behaviour may be the same. In fact, the array declaration '`text [6]`', asks from the complier for 6 locations of `char` type whereas the pointer declaration `char *p` asks for a pointer that can point to any variable of the following type:

(i) `char` - a character
(ii) `string` - a string of a characters
(iii) `Null` - nowhere

Consider the following declarations:

```
int list = {20, 30, 35, 36, 39};
int *p;      /* pointer variable p */
p = list;    /* assign the starting address of array list to pointer p*/
```

Since p is a pointer variable and has been assigned the starting address of the array list, the following operations become perfectly valid on this pointer:

p++, p-- etc.

Let us now write a 3rd version of the program that prints out the array. We will use pointer variable p in this program.

```
/* pointer variable method of processing an array  */

# include <stdio.h>
main()
 {
   static int list [] = { 20,30,35,36,39 };
   int *p;
   int i =0;
   p = list;    /* Assign the starting address of the list */

   printf ("\n The list is ...");
     while ( i < 5)
     {
           printf ("\n %d   %d ---element", *p, i);
           i++;
           p++;          /* increment pointer */
     }
   }
```

the output of above program would be as shown below:

```
20
30
35
36
39
```

}

From our discussion on arrays, we know that strings are stored and manipulated as arrays of characters with the last character being a null character (i.e., '\0'). For example, the string ENGINEERING can be stored in an array (say text) as shown in Fig. 15.14:

	0	1	2	3	4	5	6	7	8	9	10	11
Test	E	N	G	I	N	E	E	R	I	N	G	\0

Fig. 15.14 The array called `Text`

We can declare this string as a normal array by the following array declaration:

```
char Text [11];
```

Consider the following declarations:

```
char *p;
p=Text;
```

In the above set of statements, we have declared a pointer `p` that can point to a character or string of characters. The next statement assigns the starting address of character string `Text` to the variable pointer `p` (see Fig.15.15).

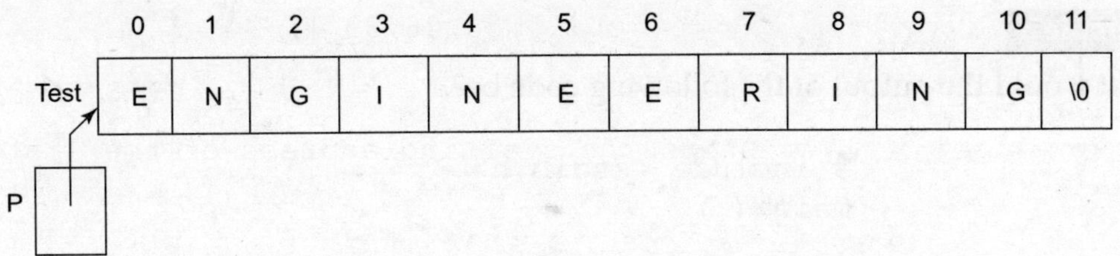

Fig.15.15 Pointer `p` points to the array called `Text`

Since text is a pointer constant, its contents cannot be changed. On the contrary `p` is a pointer variable and can be manipulated like any other pointer, as shown in the program given below:

```
/* This program illustrates the usage of pointer to a string */

# include <stdio.h>
main()
 {
    char text[] = "ENGINEERING"; /* The string    */
    char *p;                     /* The pointer   */

             /* Assign the starting address of string to p */
    p = text;
    printf ("\n The string..");   /* Print the string */
```

```
while ( *p != '\0')
{   printf ("%c", *p);
    p++ ; }

}
```

Example 2

What would the output of the following code be?

```
# include <stdio.h>
{
        char *ptr;
        ptr = "Nice";
        printf ("\n % c", * &ptr [1]);
}
```

Solution

The output would be: i

Example 3

What would the output of the following code be?

```
# include <stdio.h>
main ( )
{
        int list [5] ={ 2, 5, 6, 0, 9};
        3[list] = 4[list] + 6;
        printf ("%d", * (list + 3));
}
```

Solution

The output would be 15

15.4 ARRAY OF POINTERS

Like any other array, we can also have an array of pointers. Each element of such an array can point to a data item such as a variable, array etc. For example, consider the declaration given below:

```
float *x [20];
```

This declaration means that x is an array of 20 elements and each element is a pointer to a variable of type float. Let us now construct an array of pointers to strings:

```
char *item [ ]{ Chair,
               Table,
               Stool,
               Desk,
               };
```

The above declaration gives an array of pointers called item. Each element of item points to a string as shown in Fig. 15.16.

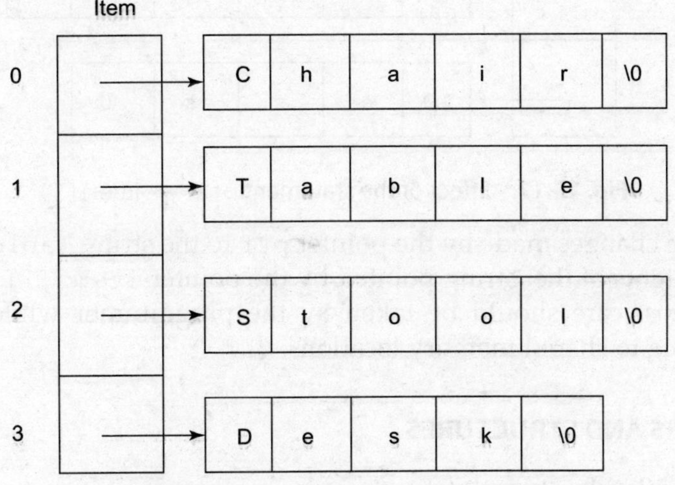

Fig. 15.16 Array of pointers to strings

The advantage of having an array of pointer to strings is that manipulation of strings becomes convenient. For example, the string containing Table can be copied into a pointer ptr without using strcpy( ) function, by the following set of statements:

```
char *ptr; // declare a pointer to a string
ptr = item [1]; // assign the appropriate pointer to ptr
```

It may be noted that once the above set of statements are executed, both the pointers, item[1] and ptr, will point to the same string: Table as shown in Fig. 15.17.

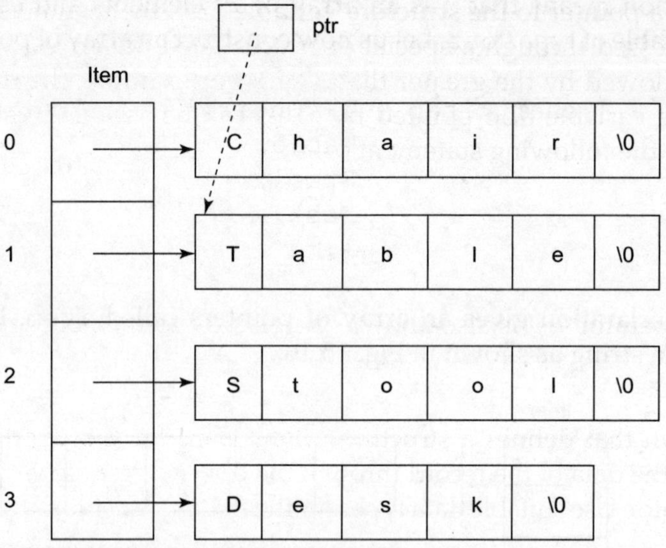

Fig. 15.17 Effect of the statement `ptr = item[1]`

However, the changes made by the pointer `ptr` to the string `Table` will definitely disturb the contents of the string pointed by the pointer `item [1]` and vice versa. Therefore, utmost care should be taken by the programmer while manipulating pointers pointing to shared memory locations.

15.5 POINTERS AND STRUCTURES

As is the case with other types of pointers, we can have a pointer to a structure, i.e., we can also point a pointer to a structure. A pointer to a structure variable can be declared by prefixing the variable name by a '*'. Consider the following declaration:

```
struct xyz {     /* structure declaration */
         int a;
         float y;
         };
struct xyz abc; /* declare a variable of type xyz */
struct xyz *ptr; /* declare a pointer ptr to a variable
                    of type xyz */
```

Once the above declarations are made, we can assign the address of the structure variable `abc` to the structure pointer `ptr` by the following statement:

```
ptr = &abc;
```

Since `ptr` is a pointer to the structure variable `abc`, the members of the structure can also be accessed through a special operator called the arrow operator i.e., '→' (minus sign followed by the greater than sign). For example, the members `a` and `y` of the structure variable `abc` pointed by `ptr` can be assigned values 30 and 50.9 respectively by the following statement:

```
ptr→a = 30;
ptr→y = 50.9 ;
```

The arrow operator '→' is also known as a pointer-to-member operator.

Example 4

Write a program that defines a structure called `item` for the record structure given below. It reads the data of the record through the dot operator and prints the record by the arrow operator. Use suitable data types for the members of the structure called `item`.

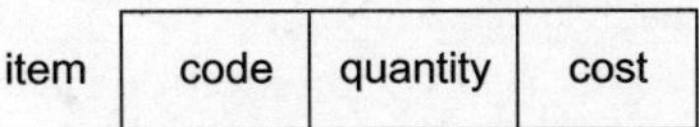

Solution

We will use a pointer `ptr` to point to the structure called `item`. The required program is given below:

```
/* This program demonstrates the usage of an arrow operator */
# include <stdio.h>
main()
 {
    struct item {
           char code[5];
           int Qty;
           float cost;
    };
    struct item item_rec; /* define a variable of struct type */
    struct item *ptr;     /* define a pointer of type struct */
                       /* Read data through dot operator */
    printf ("\n Enter the data for an item");
    printf ("\nCode:"); scanf ("%s", &item_rec.code);
    printf ("\nQty :"); scanf ("%d", &item_rec.Qty);
    printf ("\nCost :"); scanf ("%f", &item_rec.cost);
                       /* Assign the address of item_rec */
    ptr = &item_rec;
```

```
                         /* print data through arrow operator   */
    printf ("\n The data for the item...");
    printf ("\nCode:%s", ptr->code);
    printf ("\nQty :%d", ptr->Qty);
    printf ("\nCost :%5.2f", ptr->cost);
  }
```

From the above program, we can see that the members of a static structure can be accessed by both dot and arrow operators. However, dot operator is used for simple variables whereas the arrow operator is used for pointer variables.

Example 5

What is the output of the following program.

```
#include <stdio.h>
 main()
  {
    struct point
     {
                    int x,y;
     } polygon[]= { {1,2},{1,4},{2,4},{2,2}};

     struct point *ptr;
     ptr = polygon;

     ptr++;
     ptr->x++;
     printf ("\n %d", ptr->x);
  }
```

Solution

From the above program it can be observed that `ptr` is a pointer to an array of structures called `polygon`. The statement `ptr++` moves the pointer from the zeroth location (i.e {1, 2}) to the first location (i.e. {1, 4}). Now, the statement `x++` has incremented the field `x` of the structure by one (i.e., 1 has been incremented to 2). The output would be: 2

15.6 DYNAMIC ALLOCATION

We know that in a program when a variable `x` is declared, a storage location is made available to the program as shown in Fig. 15.18.

int x; ≡ x

Fig. 15.18 Memory allocation to variable x

This memory location remains available to the program as long as the program is being executed even if it is not needed. Therefore, the variable x is known as a **static variable**. Dynamic variables, on the other hand can be allocated from or returned to the system according to the needs of a running program. However, a dynamic variable does not have a name. It can only be accessed through its address and therefore can be referenced only through a pointer.

Consider the declaration given below:

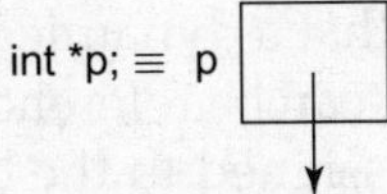

Fig. 15.19 The dangling pointer p

The above declaration gives us a dangling pointer p that points to nowhere (see Fig. 15.19). Now, we can connect this dangling pointer either to a static variable or a dynamic variable. In our previous discussion on pointers, we have always used pointers with static variables. Let us now see how the pointer can be connected to a dynamic variable.

In C, dynamic memory can be allocated by a function called malloc (). The format of this function is given below:

```
(<type> *) (malloc (<size>))
```

where <type>: is the type of variable, which is required at run time
malloc: is a reserved word indicating that memory allocation is to be done.
<size>: is the size of memory to be allocated. In fact the size of any variable can be obtained by the sizeof () operator.

Consider the following declaration

```
int * p;
int Sz;
Sz = sizeof (int);
P = (int *) malloc (Sz);
```

The above set of statements is executed in the following manner:

1. The pointer p is created. It is dangling i.e., not connected anywhere (see Fig. 15.20 (a))

2. A variable called `Sz` is declared to store the size of the dynamic variable.
3. The size of the dynamic variable (`int` in this case) is stored in the variable called `Sz`.
4. A dynamic variable of type `integer` is taken through the `malloc` function and the dangling pointer `p` is connected to the variable (see Fig. 15.20 (b))

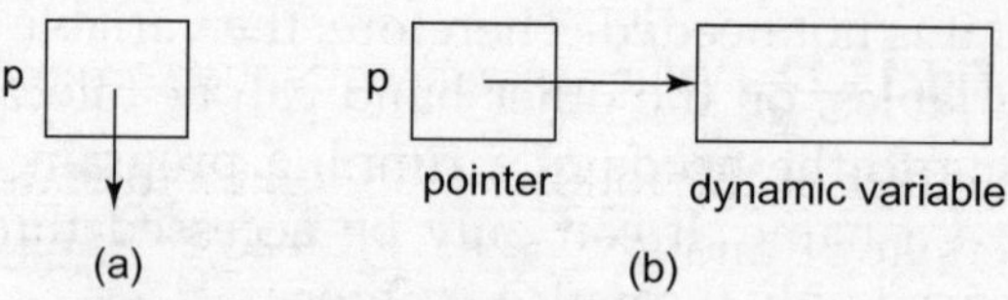

Fig. 15.20 The effect of `malloc` function

It may noted from Fig. 15.20 (b) that a dynamic variable is anonymous in the sense that it has no name and therefore it can be referenced only through the pointer `p`. For example, a value (say 50) can be assigned to the dynamic variable by the following statement:

```
*p = 50;
```

The above statement means that it is desired to store a value 50 in a memory location pointed to by the pointer `p`. The effect of this statement is shown in Fig.15.21.

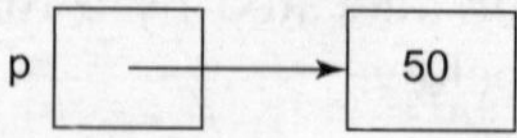

Fig. 15.21 The effect of the assignment `*p = 50`

It may observed that `p` is simply a pointer or an address and `*p` gives the access to the memory location or the variable it is pointing to. It is very important to learn the difference between the pointer and its associated dynamic variable. Let us consider the following program segment:

```
int *Aptr, *Bptr;                    /* declare pointers */
Apt = (int *) malloc (sizeof int));   /* allocate
                                     dynamic memory */
Bptr = (int *) malloc (sizeof (int));
*Aptr = 15;
*Bptr = 70;
```

The outcome of the above program segment would be as shown in Fig.15.22.

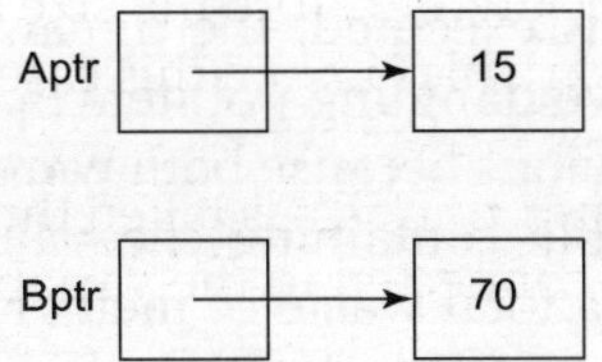

Fig. 15.22 Value assignment through pointers

Let us now see the effect of the following assignment statement on the memory allocated to the pointers `Aptr` and `Bptr`.

```
Aptr = Bptr;
```

The above assignment makes `Aptr` point to the same location or variable which is already being pointed to by `Bptr`, as shown in Fig. 15.23. Thus, both `Aptr` and `Bptr` are now pointing to the same memory location.

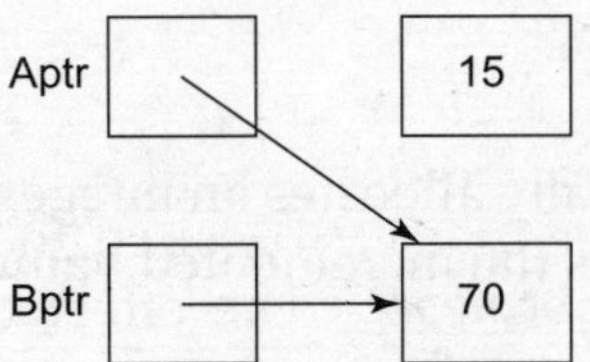

Fig. 15.23 Both pointers pointing to the same location

A close observation would reveal that the dynamic variable containing the value 15 is now lost, in the sense that neither is it available to `Aptr` anymore nor is it available to the system. The reason being the system assigned it to the pointer `Aptr` and now `Aptr` is pointing to some other location. This dynamic variable being anonymous (i.e. without a name), is no longer accessible. Even if we want to reverse the process, we simply cannot do it. This phenomenon of losing dynamic variables is known as *memory bleeding*. Thus, utmost care should be taken while manipulating dynamic variables. It is better to return a dynamic variable whenever it is not required in the program.

A dynamic variable can be returned to the system by a function called `free ()`. The general form of usage of this function is given below:

```
free (p_var);
```

where `free`: is a reserved word

`p_var`: is the pointer to the dynamic variable to be returned to the system.

Let us consider the pointers shown in Fig. 15.23. If it is desired that the dynamic variable pointed to by the pointer `Bptr` has to be returned to the system, we can do so by means of the following statement :

```
free (Bptr);
```

Once the above statement is executed, the dynamic variable is returned to the system and we are left with two dangling pointers `Bptr` and `Aptr` as shown in Fig. 15.24. The reason for this is obvious because both were pointing to the same location. However, the dynamic variable containing the value 15 is anonymous and not available anymore and hence a total waste of memory. This phenomenon is known as **memory leak** wherein an application dynamically allocates memory, and does not return (free) that memory after using it.

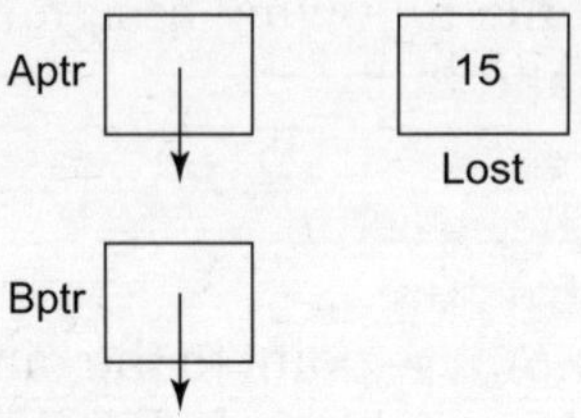

Fig. 15.24 The two dangling pointers and a lost memory variable

Example 6

Write a program that dynamically allocates an integer. It initializes the integer with a value, increments it, and prints the incremented value.

Solution

The required program is given below:

```
# include <stdio.h>
# include <alloc.h>
main()
{
  int *p;                    /* A pointer to an int  */
  int Sz;
                             /* Compute the size of the int */
  Sz = sizeof (int);
                         /* allocate a dynamic int pointed by p */
  p = (int *) malloc (Sz);
  printf ("\n Enter a value :");
  scanf ("%d", p);
  *p = *p +1;
                                /* print the incremented value  */
  printf ("\n The Value = %d", *p);
  free(p);
}
```

Example 7

Write a program that dynamically allocates a structure whose structure diagram is given below. It reads the various members of the structure and prints them.

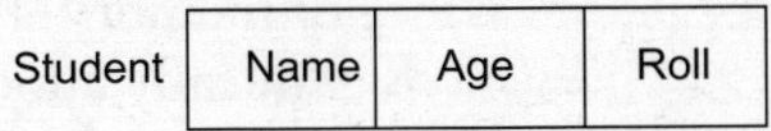

Solution

We will use the following steps to write the required program

1. Declare a structure called `student`.
2. Declare a pointer `ptr` to the structure student.
3. Compute the size of the structure.
4. Ask for dynamic memory of type `student` pointed to by the pointer `ptr`.
5. Read the data of the various elements using the arrow operator.
6. Print the data.
7. Return the dynamic memory pointed to by `ptr`.

The required program is given below:

```
# include <stdio.h>
# include <alloc.h>
main()
{
  struct student {                    /* Declare the structure  */
    char name[15];
    int age;
    int roll;
    };
  struct student *ptr;
  int Sz;
                              /* Compute the size of struct */
  Sz = sizeof(struct student);
                         /* Ask for dynamic memory of type student*/
  ptr = (struct student *) malloc (Sz);

  printf ("\n Enter the data of the student");

  printf ("\nName :"); /*fflush(stdin);*/ gets(ptr->name);
  printf ("\nAge :"); scanf ("%d",&ptr->age);
  printf ("\nRoll :"); scanf ("%d",&ptr->roll);

  printf ("\n The data is...");
```

```
    printf ("\nName :"); puts(ptr->name);
    printf ("\nAge :%d",ptr->age);
    printf ("\nRoll :%d",ptr->roll);
    free (ptr);
}
```

An array can also be dynamically allocated as demonstrated in the following example program.

Example 8

Write a program that dynamically allocates an array of integers. A list of integers is read from the keyboard and stored in the array. The program determines the smallest in the list and prints its location in the list.

Solution

The solution to this problem is simple and the required program is given below:

```
/* This program illustrates the usage of dynamically allocated
   array */

# include <stdio.h>
main()
 {
  int i,min, pos;
  int *list;
  int Sz,N;
  printf ("\n Enter the size of the list :");
  scanf ("%d", &N);
  Sz= sizeof(int) * N ;   /* Compute the size of the list */

                          /* Allocate dynamic array size N */
  list = (int *) malloc (Sz);
  printf ("\n Enter the list");
                    /* Read the list                */
  for (i = 0; i < N; i++)
    {
                      printf ("\n Enter Number :");
                      scanf ("%d", (list + i));
    }

  pos = 0;          /* Assume that the zeroth element is min */
  min = *(list + 0);
```

```
                        /* Find the minimum        */
for ( i = 1; i < N; i++)
  {
        if ( min > *(list + i))
                 {  min = *(list + i);
                 pos = i;
                 }
  }              /* print the minimum and its location */
printf ("\n The minimum is = %d at position = %d ", min,
pos);
free (list);
}
```

From the above example, it can be observed that the size of a dynamically allocated array can be specified even at the run time and the required amount of memory is allocated. This is in sharp contrast to static arrays for which the size has to be declared at compile time.

FREQUENTLY ASKED QUESTIONS

1. What is meant by a pointer?
   Solution: It is a variable which can only store the address of another variable.

2. Are the expressions `(*p)++` and `++*p` equivalent ?
   Solution: Yes

3. What happens if a programmer removes a pointer from a dynamic variable X and assigns it another variable Y .
   Solution: The dynamic variable X will be lost i.e., it becomes inaccessible to the program as well as to the operating system.

4. What is meant by memory leak?
   Solution: The lost dynamic variables lead to memory leak which is the gradual loss of available memory in the system

5. Pointers always contain Integers. Comment.
   Solution: We know that a pointer contains the address of other variables. Since an address can only be a whole number or integer, pointers contain only integers.

6. What does the term `**j` mean?
   Solution: The term `**j` means that j is a pointer to a pointer.

7. Are the expressions `*p++` and `++*p` equivalent?
   Solution: No. The expression `*p++` returns the contents of the variable pointed by `p` and then increments the pointer, on the other hand, the expression `++*p` returns the incremented contents of the variable pointed by `p`.

8. Differentiate between an un-initialized pointer and a NULL pointer.
   Solution: An un-initialized pointer is a dangling pointer which may contain any erroneous address. A NULL pointer does not point to any address location.

TEST YOUR SKILLS

1. Give the output of the following program

```
# include <stdio.h>
main()
  { int i, j;
   char *str = "CALIFORNIA";
   for ( i = 0; str[i]; i++)
    {
          for ( j = 0; j <= i; j++)
          printf ("%c", str[j]);
          printf ("\n");
    }
  }
```

   Solution: The output would be

```
C
CA
CAL
CALI
CALIF
CALIFO
CALIFOR
CALIFORN
CALIFORNI
CALIFORNIA
```

2. What would the output of the following be?

```
# include <stdio.h>
main()
 {
  int a;
  *& a = 50;
  printf ("%d", a);
 }
```

   Solution: The output would be `50`

3. What would be the output of the following?

```
# include <stdio.h>
main()
 {int i = 50;
  int *j = &i;
```

```
  printf ("\n %d", ++ *(j));
}
```

Solution: The output would be 51

4. What would be the output of the following ?

```
# include <stdio.h>
main()
 {char *ptr = "abcd";
  char ch = ++ *ptr ++;
  printf ("\n %c", ch);
  }
```

Solution: The output would be b

5. What would be the output of the following? Assume that the array starts at location 5714 in the memory?

```
# include <stdio.h>
main()
 {
  int tab [3][4] = { 5,6,7,8,
                     1,2,3,4,
                     9,10,0,11 };
  printf ("\n %d  %d", *tab[0] + 1, *(tab[0] + 1));
  printf ("\n %d", *(* (tab + 0) + 1));
  }
```

Solution: The output would be

```
6 6
6
```

6. What would be the output of the following?

```
# include <stdio.h>
main()
 {
  struct val {
             int Net;
             };
          struct val x;
          struct val *p;

          p = &x;
          p->Net = 50;
          printf ("\n %d", (x.Net)++);
}
```

Solution: The output would be 50

7. What would be the output of the following?

```
# include <stdio.h>
main()
 {
  struct val {
           int Net;
           };
        struct val x;
        struct val *p;

        p = &x;
        p->Net = 50;
        printf ("\n %d", (x.Net)++);
 }
```

Solution: The output would be 21

EXERCISES

1. Explain the '&' and '*' operators in detail, with suitable examples.

2. Find the errors in the following program segments

(a)

```
int val=10
int * p;
p=val;
```

(b)

```
char list [10];
char p;
list=p;
```

3. (i) What will be the output of the following program:

```
# include <stdio.h>
main()
  {
  int val=10;
  int *p, **k;
  p=&val;
  k=&p;
  printf ("\n %d %d %d %d", p, *p, *k, **k);
  }
```

(ii)

```
# include <stdio.h>
      main()
        {
         char ch;
```

```
        char *p;
        ch ='A';
        p=&ch;
        printf ("\n %c %c", ch, (*p)++);
       }
```

4. What will be the output of the following :

```
# include <stdio.h>
main()
  {
   int list[5], i;
   *list =5;
   for (i=1; i < 5; i++)
      *(list + i) =*(list + i-1)*i;
   printf ("\n");
   for (i=0; i < 5; i++)
      printf ("%d ",*(list + i)) ;
   }
```

5. Find the errors in the following program segment.

```
struct xyz {
   char *A;
   char *B;
   int val;
   };
   xyz s;
   A = "First text";
   B = "Second text";
```

6. What will be the output of the following program segment?

```
# include <stdio.h>
main()
  {
    struct Myrec {
           char ch;
           struct Myrec *link;
           };
     struct Myrec x,y,z, *p;
     x.ch='x';
     y.ch='y';
     z.ch ='z';
     x.link=&z;
     y.link =&x;
     z.link=NULL;
```

```
        p=&y;
         while (p!= NULL)
          {
        printf ("%c ",p->ch);
        p=p->link;
          }
    }
```

7. What will be the output of the following program?

```
# include <stdio.h>
main()
  {
   float cost []={ 35.2, 37.2, 35.42, 36.3 };
   float *ptr[4];
   int i;
   for ( i=0; i < 4; i++)
      *(ptr +i)=cost + i;
   for ( i=0; i < 4; i++)
      printf ("%f ",*(*(ptr +i)));
   }
```

Assume the base address of the array `cost` to be 2025.

8. What will be the output of the following program?

```
# include <stdio.h>
main()
  {
    char item[]="COMPUTER";
    int i;
    for (i=7; i >=0 ; i--)
    printf ("%c", *(item + i));
   }
```

ANSWERS TO SELECTED EXERCISES

4. 5 5 10 3 0 120 **6.** y x z **7.** 35.2 37.2 35.42 36.29 **8.** RETUPMOC

CHAPTER

16 Functions

16.1 INTRODUCTION

If an operation has to be performed at many different places in a program, the programmer writes the same set of instructions in the program as many times as is required. For example, in a program that computes the area of a triangle in different parts of a program, it would be a waste of the programmer's time and effort to code the sequence of instructions every time this is required, as shown below:

```
.
.
.
scanf ( "%d %d", &base, &height);
area = ½  * base * height;
.
.
.
scanf ( "%d %d", &base, &height);
area = ½  * base * height;
.
.
.
scanf ( "%d %d", &base, & height);
area = ½  * base * height;
.
.
.
```

The same set of statements has been written in the above program segment at three different places. This increases not only the size of the program, but also the chances of making typographical mistakes.

A better way to achieve the same effect, however, would be to use subprograms. A subprogram is a name given to a set of instructions that can be called by another program or a subprogram. Whenever the task to be done, control is transferred to the subprogram and after the job is over, control is transferred back to the normal program flow, as shown in Fig. 16.1. This technique simplifies the programming process because a single set of instructions in the form of a subprogram call is used for all instances of computational requirements with only the data changing. However, the communication between the calling program and the subprogram is done through arguments.

In C, the sub programs are called functions. Even the main program is written as a function called `main()`.

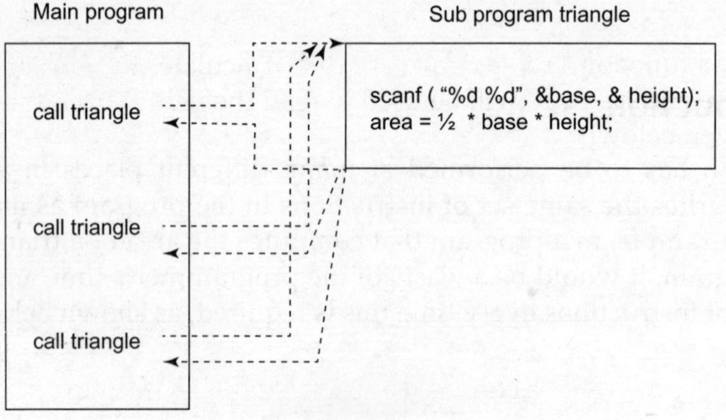

Fig. 16.1 Calling a subprogram called triangle

16.2 FUNCTION DECLARATION

A function is a subprogram that can be defined by the user in his program. It is a complete program in itself, in the sense that its structure is similar to the function `main ()` except that the name `main` is replaced by the name of the function. The general form of a function is given below:

```
<type> <name> (arguments)
      {
            ____
            ____
            ____
      }
```

where `<type>` : is the type of value to be returned by the function. If no value is returned then the keyword `void` should be used.
`<name>` : is a user defined name of the function. The function can be called from another function by this name.

arguments : is a list of parameters. This list can be omitted by leaving the parameters empty.

The program segment enclosed within the opening brace and closing brace is known as the function body. For Example the main function in C is written as shown below:

```
main ( )
    {
        ———
        ———
        ———
    }
```

Let us write a function Tri_area ( ) which calculates the area of a triangle. Two variables, base and height will be used to read the values from the keyboard. The function is given below:

```
float tri_area()
  {
    float base, height, area;
    printf ("\n Enter Base and Height");
    scanf ("%f %f", &base, &height);
    area = (0.5) * base * height;
    return (area);
  }
```

It may be noted here that the function tri_area() has defined its own variables. These are known as local variables. The advantage of their usage is that once the execution of the function is over, these variables are disposed off by the system, freeing the memory for other things.

Let us write another function clear ( ) which clears the screen of the VDU.

```
/* This function clears the screen
by writing blank lines on the screen */
void clear()
  {
   int i;
   for (i=0; i<=30; i++)
   printf ("\n");
  }
```

Similarly, let us write a function add which receives two parameters x and y of type integer from the calling function and returns the sum of x and y.

```
int add (int x, int y)
{
int temp;
temp = x + y;
return temp;
}
```

In the above function, we have used a local variable `temp` to obtain the sum of `x` and `y`. The value contained in temp is returned through the return statement. In fact, variable `temp` has been used to enhance the readability of the function only, otherwise it is unnecessary. The function can be optimised as shown below:

```
ind add (int x, int y)
  {
          return (x + y);
  }
```

Thus, a function has the following four elements:

1. A name
2. A body
3. A return type
4. An argument list

The name of the function has to be unique so that compiler can identify it. The body of the function contains the C statements which define the task performed by the function. The return type is the type of value that the function is able to return to the calling function. The argument or parameter list contains the list of values of variables from outside required by the function to perform the given task. For example, the function given above has a name `add`. It has a body enclosed between the curly braces. It can return a value of type `int`. The argument list is `x`, `y`.

16.3 FUNCTION PROTOTYPES

Similar to variables, all functions must be declared before they are used in a program. C allows the declaration of a function in the calling program with the help of a function prototype. The general form of a function prototype in the calling program is given below:

```
<type> <name> (arguments);
```

where `<type>` : is the type of value to be returned by the function
`<name>` : is a user defined name of the function
argument : is a list of parameters.
; : the semicolon is necessary.

For example, the prototype declarations for the functions `tri-area()`, `clear()`, and `add()` can be written as shown on the next page.

```
void tri_area ( );
void clear ( );
intadd(int x, int y);
```

It may be noted that a function prototype ends with a semicolon. In fact, a function prototype is required for those functions which are intended to be called before they are defined. In the absence of a prototype, the compiler will stop at the function call because it cannot do the type checking of the arguments being sent to the function. Therefore, the main purpose of a function prototype is to help the compiler in static type checking of the data requirement of the function.

16.4 CALLING A FUNCTION

A function can be called or invoked from another function by using its name. The function name must be followed by a set of actual parameters, enclosed in parentheses separated by commas. A function call to function `tri_area` from the main program can be written as:

```
tri_area ( );
```

This statement will transfer the control to function `tri_area`. Since this function does not require any parameter, the argument list is empty. Similarly, in order to call the function `clear`, the following statement will be sufficient.

```
clear ( );
```

A complete C program involving the two functions `tri_area` and `clear` is given below:

```
# include <stdio.h>
           /* Function ptototypes */
float tri_area();
void clear();

main()
  {
   char ch;
   int flag;
   float Area;
   clear();        /* Clear the screen    */
   flag = 0;
   while (flag == 0)
    {
     Area = tri_area(); /* call tri_area to compute area */
```

```
        printf ("\n Area of Triangle = %5.2f", Area);

        printf ("\n Want to calculate again -Enter Y/N");
        fflush(stdin);
        ch = getchar();
        if (ch == 'N' || ch == 'n')
            flag = 1;
        clear();
        }
        }

  float tri_area()
    {
     float base, height, area;
     printf ("\n Enter Base and Height");
     scanf ("%f %f", &base, &height);
     area = (0.5) * base * height;
     return (area);
    }

   /* This function clears the screen
      by writing blank lines on the screen */
      void clear()
        {
         int i;
         for (i=0; i<=30; i++)
         printf ("\n");  /* write a blank line */
         }
```

It may be noted here that when this program is executed, the first statement to be executed is the first executable statement of the function `main` of the program (i.e. `clear( );` in this case). A function will only be executed after it is called from some other function or itself.

The variables `base`, `height`, and `area` are local to function `tri_area()` and they are not available in the `main ( )` function. Similarly the variable `flag` declared in function `main` is also not available to functions `tri_area ( )` and `clear ( )`.

However, the variables declared outside any function can be accessed by all the functions. Such variables are called global variables.

Let us consider the following program which declares the variables `flag` and `area` outside the `main` function instead of declaring them inside the functions `main ( )` and `tri_area ( )` respectively.

```
# include <stdio.h>
            /* Function ptototypes */
void tri_area();
void clear();
            /* Global Variables    */
int flag;
float area;
main()
  {
   char ch;      /* Local Variable      */
   clear();      /* Clear the screen    */
   flag = 0;
   while (flag == 0)
     {
     tri_area();   /* call tri_area to compute area */
     printf ("\n Area of Triangle = %5.2f", area);

     printf ("\n Want to calculate again -Enter Y/N");
     fflush(stdin);
     ch = getchar();
     if (ch == 'N' || ch == 'n')
        flag = 1;
     clear();
     }
     }
                       /* Function Definitions    */
void tri_area()
  {
    float base, height;
    printf ("\n Enter Base and Height");
    scanf ("%f %f", &base, &height);
    area = (0.5) * base * height;
  }

/* This function clears the screen
   by writing blank lines on the screen */
   void clear()
     {
      int i;
      for (i=0; i<=30; i++)
      printf ("\n");
      }
```

It may be noted in the above program that the variable area is available to both the functions `tri_area()` and `main ( )`. On the other hand the local variables `base`, `height` are available to the function `tri_area` only. They are neither available to the function `main ( )` nor to the function `clear ( )`. Similarly variable `i` is also local to function `clear ( )`.

In our previous programs, we have used our own function `clear ( )` to clear the screen. C also provides a function called `clrscr ( )` that clears the screen. From now onwards we will use this function. However, in order to use `clrscr ( )` in a program, we will have to include `conio.h`, a header file, at the beginning of the program.

16.5 PARAMETER PASSING IN FUNCTIONS

We have seen that two way communication between functions can be achieved through global variables. This technique has its own limitations and drawbacks. Let us now see how this communication between the calling function and the called function can be improved and made more fruitful.

The two way communication between the various functions can be achieved through parameters and return statements as done in Example 1. The set of parameters defined in a function are called formal or dummy parameters whereas the set of corresponding parameters sent by the calling function are called actual parameters. For instance the variables `x` and `y` in the argument list of the function add( ) are formal parameters. The parameters included in the function call i.e. `val1` and `val2` of `main ()` are actual parameters.

The function that receives parameters can be called in one of the following two ways:

1. Call by value.
2. Call by reference.

16.5.1 Call by Value

For a better understanding of the concept of parameter passing, let us consider the function `big ()` given below. It receives two values as dummy arguments `x` and `y` and returns the bigger of the two through a return statement.

```
/* This function compares two variables and
   returns the bigger of the two           */
 int big (int x, int y)
   {
     if (x > y)
      return x;
       else
      return y;
   }
```

The function big ( ) can be called from the function main ( ) by including the variables a and b as the actual arguments of the function call, as shown below.

```
main()
  {
   int a = 30;
   int b = 45;
   int c;
   c = big (a,b);
   printf ("\n The bigger = %d ", c);
   }
```

The output of the above program would be:

The bigger = 45

Let us now write a program which reads the values of two variables a and b. The values of a and b are sent as parameters to a function exchange ( ). The function exchanges the contents of the parameters with the help of a variable temp. The changed values of a and b are printed.

```
# include <stdio.h>
# include <conio.h>
void exchange( int x, int y);

main()
 {
  int a, b;
  clrscr();        /* clear screen   */

  printf ("\n Enter two values");
  scanf ("%d %d", &a, &b);
  exchange(a,b);

        /* print the exchanged contents */
  printf ("\n The exachanged contents are : %d and %d", a, b);
 }
 void exchange (int x, int y)
   {
    int temp;
    temp =  x;
    x = y;
    y = temp;
   }
```

The above program seems to be wonderful but it fails badly because variables a and b do not get any values back from the function exchange(). The reason being that although all values of actual parameters (i.e., a, b) have been passed on to formal parameters (i.e., x, y) correctly, the changes done to the values in the formal parameters are not reflected back into the calling function.

Once the above program is executed for input value (say 30 and 45), the following output is produced.

```
The exchanged contents are : 30 and 45
```

The reason for this behaviour is that at the time of the function call, the values of the actual parameters a and b get copied into the memory locations of the formal parameters x and y of the function exchange ( ). (See Fig. 16.2).

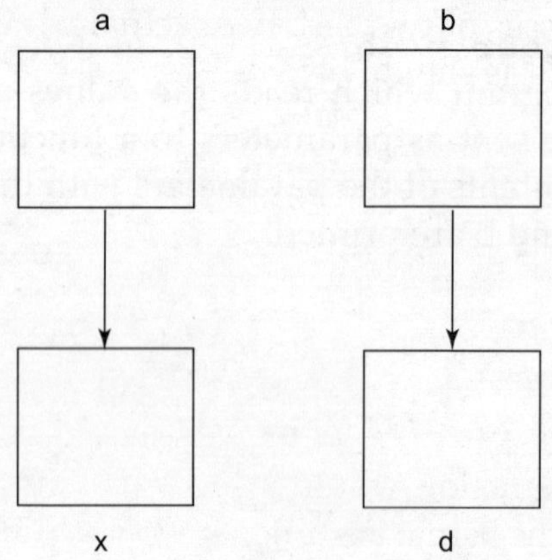

Fig. 16.2 Pass by copy

From Fig. 16.2, it is clear that the variables x and y have entirely different memory locations from variables aand b. Therefore any changes made to the contents of x and y are not reflected back to the variables a and b. Thus, the original data remains unaltered. In fact, this type of behaviour is desirable from a pure function.

Since in this type of parameter passing, only the values are passed from the calling function to the called function, the technique is called call by value.

16.5.2 Call by Reference

If the programmer desires that the changes made to the formal parameters be reflected back to their corresponding actual parameters then he/she should use the call by reference method of parameter passing. This technique passes the addresses or references of the actual parameters to the called function. Let us rewrite the function exchange( ).

In fact, in the called function, the formal arguments receive the addresses of the actual arguments by using pointers to them.

For instance, in order to receive the addresses of actual parameters of `int` type, the function `exchange ()` can be rewritten as shown below:

```
void exchange (int *val1, int *val2 )
   {
    int temp;
    temp =  *val1;
    *val1 = *val2;
    *val2 = temp;
   }
```

It may be noted that the above function has used two pointers called `val1` and `val2` to receive the addresses of two `int` type actual parameters. However, initially these are dangling pointers as shown below:

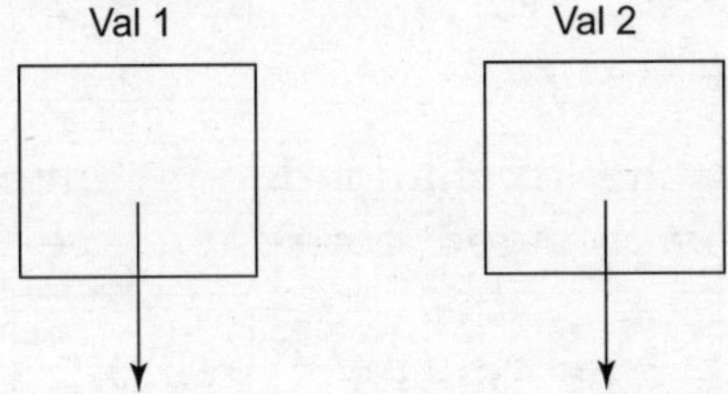

The `exchange ( )` function would be called from the `main ()` function by sending the addresses of the actual arguments as shown below:

```
exchange (& a, & b);
```

After the `exchange ()` function is called by the above statement, the addresses of the actual parameters `a` and `b` would be assigned to pointers `val1` and `val2` respectively as shown below:

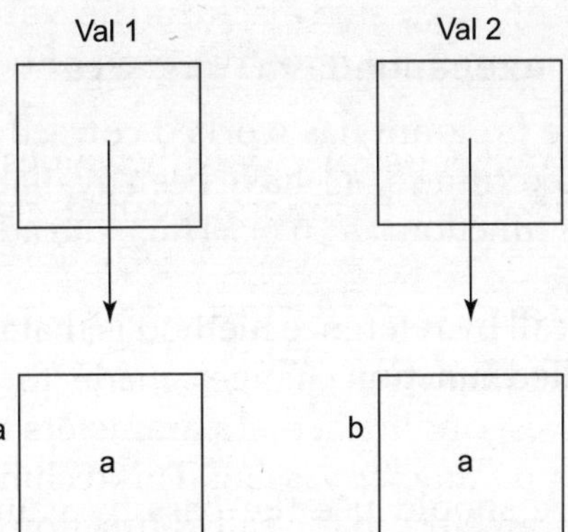

Since the function exchanges the contents of variables being pointed to by the pointers `val1` and `val2`, the contents of variables `a` and `b` get exchanged, which is the goal of this exercise.

The complete program is given below:

```
# include <stdio.h>
# include <conio.h>
void exchange( int *val1, int *val2);

main()
 {
  int a, b;
  clrscr();           /* clear screen     */

  printf ("\n Enter two values");
  scanf ("%d %d", &a, &b);
  exchange(&a,&b);

           /* print the exchanged contents */
  printf ("\n The exachanged contents are : %d and %d", a, b);
 }
 void exchange (int *val1, int *val2 )
   {
    int temp;
    temp =  *val1;
    *val1 = *val2;
    *val2 = temp;
   }
```

After the above program is executed for input values (say 30 and 45), the following output is produced.

`The exchanged values are : 45 30`

Now we can see that the program has worked correctly in the sense that changes made inside the function `exchange ()` have been available to corresponding actual parameters `a` and `b` in the function `main()`. Thus, the address operator `&` has done the required task.

The main advantage of call by reference method is that more than one value can be received back from the called function.

Note:

1. As far as possible, we should use the pass by value technique of parameter passing. If some value is to be received back from the function, it should be done through a return statement of the function.

2. A function call can use both the methods i.e., call by value and call by reference simultaneously. For example the following is a valid function prototype.

```
void calc (int a, float *b, float *c);
```

3. When, actual parameters are passed from the calling function to the called function by call by value, the names of the corresponding dummy parameters could be the same or different. However, it is suggested that they may be named as different in order to make the program more elegant.

Example 1

Write a program that reads two integer values in the `main` function and computes their sum in a subfunction called `add ()`. Print out the sum in the `main` function.

Solution

A function called `add ()` has been developed in section 16.2. It would be used in this program to do the required task. The program is given below:

```
# include <stdio.h>
        /* Function ptototype */
int add (int x, int y);
main()
  {
    int val1, val2, Sum;
    printf ("\n Enter two integers: ");
    scanf("%d %d", &val1, & val2);
    Sum = add (val1, val2);
    printf ("\n The sum = %d", Sum);
  }
        /* Function Definition  */
 int add (int x, int y)
  {
    int temp;         /* Local Variable  */
    temp = x + y;
    return temp;
  }
```

Example 2

Write a program which computes least common divisor of two integers M and N.

Solution

The least common divisor will be computed through a function called `lcd()`. The program is given on the next page.

```
/* This program computes LCD of two integers M and N */
# include <stdio.h>
# include <conio.h>
int lcd( int x, int y);

main()
 {
  int M, N, result;
  printf ("\n Enter the two integers");
  scanf ("%d %d", &M, &N);
  result = lcd (M, N);
  printf ("\n The least common divisor is: %d ", result);
 }
 int lcd (int x, int y )
   {
    int small, res;
    int found;
         /* store smaller in small  */
    if ( x > y )
      small = y;
    else
      small = x;
    res = 2;    /* assume lcd to be 2   */
    found = 0;
    while (( found == 0) && (res <= small))
     {
      if ((x % res == 0 ) && ( y % res == 0))
    found = 1;
    else res++;
      }
    if (found)
    return (res);
    else
    return (1);
  }
```

Note: When a function is called by reference then we cannot pass constants and expressions as parameters.

Example 3

Write a function which receives the length of a cloth in inches and returns the length in feet and inches to the calling function.

Solution

We will use the pass-by-reference method to pass the length of the cloth through the address of a variable called `inches`. The length in feet and inches will be received back through the variables `feet` and `inches` respectively. Let us name the function as `convert ( )`. The function `convert ( )` receives the address of the variables `feet` and `inches` in two pointers called `ftptr`, and `incptr`. The function is given below:

```
/* This function demonstrates the usage of
   pass by ref. technique of parameter passing    */

 /* The function converts inches into equivqlent
    feet and inches                               */

  void convert (int *incptr, int *ftptr)
   {
    *ftptr = *incptr /12;
    *incptr = *incptr % 12;
   }
```

Example 4

Write a program that reads the length of a cloth in inches and uses the function `convert` of Example 3 to convert it into feet and inches.

Solution

The required program is given below:

```
 # include <stdio.h>
void convert (int *incptr, int *ftptr);
main()
  {
    int Inches, Feet;
    printf ("\n Enter the length of the cloth in inches : ");
   scanf ("%d", &Inches);

    convert (&Inches, &Feet);
    printf ("\n The length of the cloth is :");
    printf ("Feet = %d, Inches = %d", Feet, Inches);
  }
```

```
/* This function converts the length in inches to
   feet and inches                                 */
void convert (int *incptr, int *ftptr)
 {
  *ftptr = *incptr /12;
  *incptr = *incptr % 12;
 }
```

Example 5

Write a function `fact` which generates the factorial of a number.

Solution

The factorial for a number N can be generated by the following formula:

N! = 1 * 2 * 3 * ... (N -1) * N

A function to generate the factorial using this formula, is given below:

```
/* This function computes N factorial */
      int fact (int N)
        {
    int j;
    int Fact = 1;
    for (j = 1; j <= N; j++)
      Fact = Fact * j;
    return Fact;
        }
```

Example 6

Write a program to find the sum of the following series taking only the first 5 terms.

$$Sum = \frac{x^3}{3!} + \frac{x^5}{5!} + \frac{x^7}{7!} + \ldots$$

Solution

The solution involves two functions **`power ()`** and **`fact()`**. The function `power()` computes the term x^y and the function `fact()` computes the term N!. The program is given on the next page.

```
/* This program computes the sum of a given series */

# include <stdio.h>
# include <conio.h>
              /* Prototypes  */
int power (int x, int y);
int fact (int n);

main()
  {
    float sum;
    int term1, term2, x, count;
    clrscr();
    sum = 0.0;

    printf ("\n Enter the value of x : ");
    scanf("%d", &x);
    clrscr();
    sum = 0.0;
    count = 3;
    while ( count <= 11)
     {
      term1 = power (x, count);
      term2 = fact(count);
      sum = sum + (float) term1/term2;
      count = count + 2;
      }
     printf ("\n The sum of series is : %6.2f", sum);
    }
              /* This function computes x^y    */
   int power(int x, int y)
     {
      int i; /* Local variables  */
      int pow=1;
      for (i=1; i<=y; i++)
     pow = pow * x;
     return pow;
      }
              /* This function computes N factorial */
   int fact (int N)
      {
    int j;
```

```
    int Fact = 1;
    for (j = 1; j <= N; j++)
      Fact = Fact * j;
    return Fact;
     }
```

Example 7

Write a function called `MIRROR()` which generates the mirror image of a given number i.e., for a given number 52374 the functions returns 47325.

Solution

The function for the above problem is given below:

```
long Mirror (long N)
  {
    long Rem_num;      /* stores remainder  */
    long mirror = 0;
    while (N != 0)
      {
       Rem_num = N % 10;
       N = N / 10;
       mirror = mirror * 10 + Rem_num;
       printf ("\n %d", mirror);
       }
      return mirror;
  }
```

16.5.3 Array Parameters

Arrays can also be passed as parameters to functions. This is always done through the call by reference method. In C, the name of the array represents the address of the first element of the array and therefore, during the function call, only the name of the array is passed from the calling function. For example, if an array `xyz` of size 100 is to be passed to a function `some ( )` then the function call will be as given below:

`some (xyz);`

The formal parameters can be declared in the called function in three ways. The different ways are illustrated with the help of a function `some( )` that receives an array `xyz` of size 100 of `integer` type.

Ist Method. In this method the array is declared without a subscript i.e., of an unknown size as shown on the next page.

```
void some (int xyz [ ])
    {
        ___
        ___
        ___
    }
```

The C compiler automatically computes the size of the array.

IInd Method. In this method an array of a given size and type is declared, as shown below:

```
void some (int xyz [100])
    {
        ___
        ___
        ___
    }
```

IIIrd Method. In this method the operator * is applied on the name of the array indicating that it is a pointer.

```
void some (int *xyz)
    {
        ___
        ___
        ___
    }
```

All the three methods are equivalent and the function some ( ) can be called by the following statement.

```
some (xyz);
```

Note:

1. The arrays are never passed by value and cannot be used as the return type of a function.
2. In C, the name of the array represents the address of the first element or the zeroth element of the array. So when an array is used as an argument to a function, only the address of the array gets passed and not a copy of the entire array. Hence, any changes made to the array inside the function are automatically reflected in the main function. You do not have to use ampersand (&) with the array name even though it is a call by reference method. The (&) is implied in the case of arrays.

Example 8

Write a program that reads a list of N numbers of `integer` type in an array called list. It sends the array to a function `mult ( )` that multiplies 10 to every element of the array. The modified list is displayed.

Solution

The program is given below:

```
  /* This program uses a function to multiply 10 to every
elements of a list */

  # include <stdio.h>
  # include <conio.h>
  void mult (int list [], int N);
  main()
    {
     int list [20];
     int i, N;
     clrscr();
     printf ("\n Enter the size of the list ");
     scanf ("%d", &N);
     printf ("\n Enter the list ");
     for (i = 0; i < N; i++)
        scanf ("%d", &list[i]);
              /* Call the function */
     mult (list, N);
     printf ("\n The modified list is ...");
     for (i = 0; i < N; i++)
        printf ("%d ", list[i]);
    }           /* The Function     */
    void mult (int list [], int N)
      {
        int j;
        for (j = 0; j < N; j++)
        list [j] = list [j] * 10;
      }
```

Example 9

Write a function in C that checks for matching braces in a parenthesised algebraic expression. The function returns a value one (1) if the match is successful and zero (0) otherwise. For example, `( ( a + b ) * c)` is a valid parenthesized expression. The expression `((a + b) *  c` is an invalid expression.

Solution

We name the required function `match`. An array of characters containing the parenthesised algebraic expression is passed to the function `match`. Two variables `open-brace` and `closebrace` are used to keep track of the matching braces. A variable `flag` is used to check the discrepancy in the expression. For example, if at any moment the number of opening braces is more than the closing braces than an error condition occurs.

The required function is given below:

```
/* This function  checks for matching braces in a
     paenthesised algebraic expression  */
int match (char AlgExp[], int N)
  {
   int openbrace = 0;
   int closebrace = 0; /* Variables to keep track of braces
*/

   int i = 0;
   int flag;            /* Variable to check matching braces  */

   flag = 1;            /* Assume that the braces match      */

   while ((AlgExp[i] != '\0') && (i < N))
      {
       if (AlgExp[i] == '(')
           openbrace++;
       else
       if (AlgExp[i] == ')')
           closebrace++;
       else
      if (openbrace < closebrace)
         {
           flag = 0;
           break;
         }
        i++;
       }
       if (flag)
     {
      if (openbrace == closebrace)
          return (1);
          else
            return (0);
       }
     else
       {
        printf ("\n Incorrect placement of braces");
```

```
        return (0);
      }

    }
```

Example 10

Write a program that reads a fully parenthesized algebraic expression and checks for matching parenthesis through the function `match` developed in Example 9.

Solution

The required program is given below:

```
/* This program checks for matching braces in a
   fully paenthesised algebraic expression  */
#include <stdio.h>
int match (char AlgExp[], int N);
main()
  {
   char AlgExp[30];
   int N;
   int res;
   printf ("\n Enter the length of the expression ");
   scanf ("%d", &N);
   printf ("\n Enter the expression");
   fflush(stdin);
   gets(AlgExp);
   res = match (AlgExp, N);
   if (res == 1)
     printf ("\n Correct matching braces ");
   else
     printf ("\n Incorrecting matching braces ");
   }
   /* This function  checks for matching braces in a
    paenthesised algebraic expression  */
int match (char AlgExp[], int N)
  {
   int openbrace = 0;
   int closebrace = 0; /* Variables to keep track of braces */

   int i = 0;
   int flag;        /* Variable to check matching braces  */
```

```
flag = 1;              /* Assume that the braces match    */
while ((AlgExp[i] != '\0') && (i < N))
  {
   if (AlgExp[i] == '(')
       openbrace++;
   else
   if (AlgExp[i] == ')')
       closebrace++;
   else
  if (openbrace < closebrace)
     {
       flag = 0;
       break;
     }
    i++;
   }
   if (flag)
 {
  if (openbrace == closebrace)
      return (1);
      else
         return (0);
  }
 else
   {
    printf ("\n Incorrect placement of braces");
    return (0);
   }
    }
```

16.6 RETURNING VALUES FROM FUNCTIONS

Earlier in this chapter we have used functions which either return no value or return integer values. The functions that return no value are declared as void. We have been prefixing `int` to functions which return integer values. This is valid but unnecessary because the default return value of a function in C is of type `int`. Thus, the following two declarations are equivalent in the sense that we do not need to prefix `int` to a function which returns an integer value.

```
int add (int a, int b);
add (int a, int b);
```

On the other hand, whenever a function returns non integer values, the function must be prefixed with the appropriate type. For example, a function xyz that returns a value of type float must be declared as shown below:

```
float xyz (.....)
   {     float a;
         :
         return a
   }
```

Similarly, a function ABC that returns a value of type char should be declared as shown below:

```
char ABC ( ..... )
   {     char ch;
               :
         return ch;
   }
```

16.7 PASSING STRUCTURES TO FUNCTIONS

As with variables, structures can also be passed to other functions as arguments both by value and by reference.

16.7.1 Call by Value

In this method of passing structures to functions, a copy of the actual argument is passed to the function. Therefore, the changes made to the contents of the structures inside the called function are not reflected back to the calling function.

The following program uses a structure variable called stud of type student and passes the structure variable by value to a function called print_data (). The function print_data () displays the contents of the various members of the structure variables.

```
/* This program illustrates the passing of the structures
      by value to a function  */
 # include <stdio.h>
   struct student
     {
       char name [20];
       int age;
       int roll;
       char class [5];
     };
```

```
/* Prototype of the function   */
    void print_data (struct student Sob);
    main()
      {
    struct student stud;
    printf ("\n Enter the student data");
    printf ("\nName:"); fflush(stdin);
    gets (stud.name);
    printf ("\nAge:");scanf("%d",&stud.age);
    printf ("\nRoll:");scanf("%d",&stud.roll);
    printf ("\nClass:"); fflush(stdin);
    gets (stud.class);
         /*The structure is being passed by value*/
    print_data(stud);
    }

    void print_data (struct student Sob)
    {
    printf ("\n The student data..");
    printf ("\nName:"); fflush(stdout);
    puts (Sob.name);
    printf ("Age: %d",Sob.age);
    printf ("\nRoll: %d",Sob.roll);
    printf ("\nClass:"); fflush(stdout);
    puts (Sob.class);
    }
```

16.7.2 Call by Reference

In this method for passing structures to functions, the address of the structure variable is passed. The address of the structure variable is obtained with the help of the address operator '&'. Thus, the changes made to the contents of such a variable inside the function are reflected to the calling function. The program given below illustrates the usage of the call by reference method.

This program reads the data of a student (Fig. 16.2) and prints the data through the function `print_data )`.

```
/* This program illustrates the passing of the structures
   by reference to a function                               */
   # include <stdio.h>
    struct student
     {
       char name [20];
```

```
    int age;
    int roll;
    char class [5];
  };
            /* Prototype of the function  */
  void print_data (struct student *Sob);
  main()
   {
 struct student stud;
 printf ("\n Enter the student data");
 printf ("\nName:"); fflush(stdin);
 gets (stud.name);
 printf ("\nAge:");scanf("%d",&stud.age);
 printf ("\nRoll:");scanf("%d",&stud.roll);
 printf ("\nClass:"); fflush(stdin);
 gets (stud.class);
 print_data(&stud);  /*The structure is being passed by
 reference*/
 }
 void print_data (struct student *sob)
 {
  struct student *ptr;
  ptr = sob;
  printf ("\n The student data..");
  printf ("\nName:"); fflush(stdout);
  puts (ptr->name);
  printf ("Age: %d",ptr->age);
  printf ("\nRoll: %d",ptr->roll);
  printf ("\nClass:"); fflush(stdout);
  puts (ptr->class);
 }
```

It may be noted here that structures are usually passed by reference in order to prevent the overheads associated with the technique of passing structures by value. The overheads are: extra memory space and CPU time used to pass bigger structures.

16.7.3 Returning Structures from Functions

It is possible to send a structure as a return value of a function. This can be done by specifying the structure as the return type of the function. This feature of C is helpful in a situation where a structure has been passed by value to a function and the changes done to the contents of the structure are needed by the calling function without disturbing the original contents. This concept is illustrated in the example given below:

Example 11

Write a program that reads the data of a student with the structure given below.

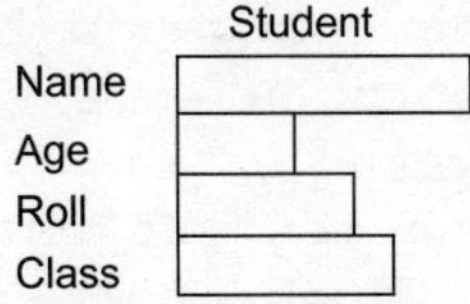

The structure is then passed by value to a function called `change-data ()` where the name of the student is changed to capital letters. The changed contents of the student data are returned by the function to the function `main ()`.

Solution

We will use the string function `toupper ()` in this program to change the characters of the name of the student to uppercase. The changes are done in a function called `change-data ()`. The required program is given below:

```
/* This program illustrates the process of returning a
structure
    from a function                                      */
   # include <stdio.h>
   # include <ctype.h>
    struct student
     {
       char name [20];
       int age;
       int roll;
       char class [5];
      };
                /* Prototypes of  functions  */
     void print_data (struct student sob);
     struct student change_data (struct student Sob);
     main()
       {
         struct student stud, newstud;
         printf ("\n Enter the student data");
         printf ("\nName:"); fflush(stdin);
         gets (stud.name);
```

```
        printf ("\nAge:");scanf("%d",&stud.age);
        printf ("\nRoll:");scanf("%d",&stud.roll);
        printf ("\nClass:"); fflush(stdin);
        gets (stud.class);
              /* call function to change data */
        newstud = change_data(stud);
        printf ("\n The changed data ..");
              /*The structure is being passed by value*/
        print_data(newstud);
}
   /* This function changes the data  of a student  */
struct student change_data (struct student Sob)
{
int i=0;
 while (Sob.name[i] != '\0')
      {                          /* Capitalize the letters */
      Sob.name[i] = toupper (Sob.name[i]);
      i++;
      }
 return (Sob);
 }
void print_data (struct student sob)
{
 printf ("\n The student data..");
 printf ("\nName:"); fflush(stdout);
 puts (sob.name);
 printf ("Age: %d",sob.age);
 printf ("\nRoll: %d",sob.roll);
 printf ("\nClass:"); fflush(stdout);
 puts (sob.class);
}
```

16.8 SCOPE RULES OF VARIABLES

The range of code in a program over which a variable has a meaning is called the scope of the variable. In simple words, the scope of a variable decides how it can be accessed by the different parts of the program.

In fact, there are three types of scopes in C

1. Local scope
2. Function scope
3. File scope

16.8.1 Local Scope

We know that a block in C is surrounded by a pair of curly braces i.e., '{' and '}'. We can declare variables inside the block. Such variables, called local variables, can be referenced only within the body of the block. These variables come into existence when the control of program execution reaches the opening brace, and get destroyed as soon as the control leaves the block through the closing brace. It may be noted that the variables are available to all the blocks enclosed by the block in which they have been declared. Consider the following declaration:

```
while (flag)
  {
       int x;
       if (i > x)
         {
              int j

         }
  }
```

The scope of variable `x` is the `while` block and that of variable `j` is `if` block. Now the variable `x` can also be referenced in the `if` block because this block is completely enclosed in the `while`block. On the other hand, the scope of variable `j` is only the `if` block.

Consider the following program:

```
# include <stdio.h>
main()
  {
   int i =50;
      while ( i > 0)
       {
  int j;
  j =i;
      if ( j > 40)
         printf ("%d ", j);
  i--;
  }
      printf ("\n %d", j);
  }
```

It may be noted that the `printf ()` statement, shown in bold, is out of the scope of the `while` loop. Therefore, the compiler will give the error : " Undefined symbol 'j' in function main()".

Since a function is a block in itself, all the variables declared in it have the local scope.

The formal parameters declared in a function have the local scope.

16.8.2 The File Scope

Since global variables are declared outside all blocks and functions, they are available to all the blocks and functions. Thus, the scope of a global variable encompasses the entire program file. This type of scope is known as file scope. For example, the global variables `some` and `rate` of Fig. 16.3 have a file scope.

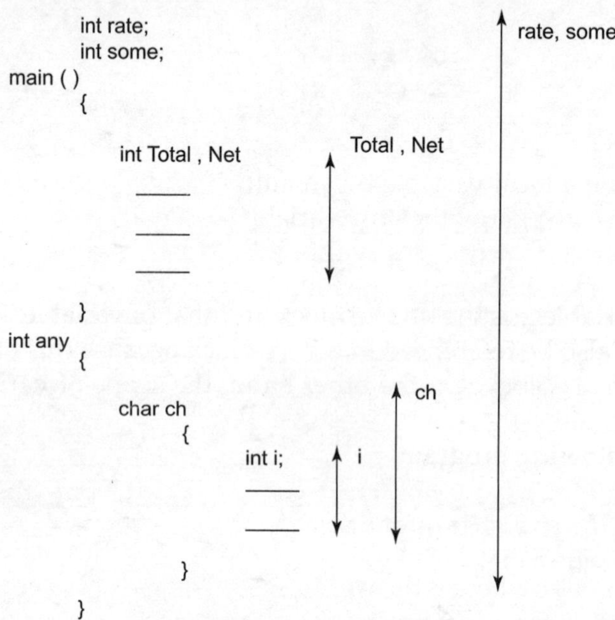

Fig. 16.3 Scope of variables

16.8.3 The Function Scope

The function scope pertains to the variables declared in a function in the sense that a variable can be used anywhere in the function in which it is declared. Thus, we can use different variables with the same names in different functions.

The scope rules can be summarized as:

1. A local variable can be accessed only within the block in which it is declared. The local variable declared in a function exists only during the execution of the function. Therefore, these variables are also called automatic variables because they are automatically created and destroyed.

2. Since global variables are not declared in a particular function, they are available to all the functions. Thus, the scope of a global variable encompasses the entire program.
3. The scope of a formal parameter is local to the function in which it is defined.

16.9 STORAGE CLASS SPECIFIERS

The storage class of a variable defines as to how it should be stored and what its scope is. 'C' characterizes the variable according to their *storage class*. There are four storage classes specified by the following specifiers:

(i) auto
(ii) extern
(iii) static
(iv) register

Auto. We can define a local variable by an auto specifier. However, this specifier is seldom used because we know that any variable declared within a block or function is a local variable and its scope lies within that block. Thus, a local variable is by default auto or automatic. Consider the following function:

```
void some ( )
    {
            int loc;
            auto int xyz;

    }
```

The function contains two variables `loc` and `xyz`. Now the variable `loc` is local and by default automatic whereas the variable `xyz` has been explicitly defined as auto. Both are equivalent as far as scope and storage class is concerned. Therefore, there is no use of the auto specifier except that it removes confusion in certain situations.

Static. If one desires that the local variable should retain its value even after the execution of the function in which it is declared, then the variable must be declared as `static`. The value of a static variable is not destroyed when the function terminates. On the contrary, the value is retained and is available to the user even if the control returns to the function.

Consider the following program.

```
# include <stdio.h>
# include <conio.h>
main ( )
  {
        int i, r;
```

```
        for (i = 1; i <= 5; i++)
             {
                   r = tot (i);
        printf ("\n the total is = % d", r);
             }
   }
   int tot (int x)
   {
        static s = 0;
        s = s + x;
        return (s);
   }
```

The function main( ) calls the function tot () five times, each time sending the value of i varying from 1 to 5. In the function the value is added to s and the accumulated result is returned. The output of the program is given below.

```
the total is = 1
the total is = 3
the total is = 6
the total is = 10
the total is = 15
```

It may be noted that the contents of the static variable called s have been retained in each function call.

Note:

1. The lifetime of a static local variable is the same as that of a global variable. However, static local variables have a function scope whereas global variables have a file scope.
2. Static variables are not known outside the function in which they are declared but retain their values between function calls. Also static local variables are created when the function is called for the first time whereas global variables are created when program execution begins.
3. The static specifier can be used with both local as well as global variables. Static local variables have a function scope whereas static global variables have a file scope. They are not available to any other file except where they are defined. However, both of them retain their values between subsequent calls.

Extern. When the size of the program becomes very large then it has to be divided into parts and each part is stored in a separate file. Now the global variables which should be available to all the functions of the program can be made known to the participating component files with the help of the extern specifier. A global variable declared in one file can be accessed in other file by extern declaration as shown below:

```
File 1                              File 2
int rate;                           extern int rate;
main ( )                            int compu ( )
{                                   {
  ___                               int tot, net;
  ___                               ___
  ___                               net = tot * rate;
                                    }
}
void any ( )                        void some ( )
{                                   {
  ___                               ___
  ___                               ___
  ___                               ___
}                                   }
```

It can be noted from the above that the global variable rate has been defined in File 1. The same variable is being accessed in File 2 by declaring it as extern.

Register. We know that a variable is a memory location in the main memory of the computer and the CPU has to access the main memory to manipulate the variable. This activity slows down the execution of the program because main memory is about 10 times slower than the CPU. Since a number of registers are available in the CPU itself and all of them are not used all the time, a few of them can be used to store some frequently used variables so that the execution becomes faster. Therefore, C allows some variables to be declared as register variables.

However, the number of such variables that can be used by the programmer varies from compiler to compiler. The reserved word `register` can be prefixed to an ordinary variable declaration for the purpose of declaring a register variable. For example, a variable count of `integer` type can be declared of type `register` by the following statement.

```
register int count ;
```

If a program asks for more than the allowed number of registers, then the extra variables are treated as automatic.

Note:

1. We cannot apply the operator '&' on a register variable.
2. We cannot declare an array or structure of type `register` i.e., it has to be a scalar type.

The various storage class specifiers are summarized in Table 16.1

Table 16.1 Storage Class Specifiers

Storage type	Created	Initialized	Scope	Purpose
auto	Each time the function is called First time when the function is called	Can be initialized at the time of declaration	Within the block or function	As a variable within a block
static	First time when the function is called	Initialized at the time of declaration	Within the block or function	As variables which retain their value even after the termination of a function
register	Same as auto	Same as auto	Same as auto	As most frequently used variables
extern	Created in the file in which it is created	Also initialized in the file where it has been declared as global	Both the files where declared as global and extern	As variables used by multiple files

Note: Functions can also be declared as static or extern. The keyword static provides the file scope for the function whereas the keyword extern makes the function available in multiple files. More discussion on this issue is beyond the scope of this book.

16.10 RECURSION

We have already discussed iteration through various loop structures discussed in Chapter 11. In an iterative structure, the computations are performed each time by the same method and the result of computation utilized as the source of data for the next repetition of the loop. For example, the factorial of an integer N can be computed by the following iterative loop :

```
fact = 1;
for (i = 1; i <= N; i++)
fact  = fact * i;
cout << "\nThe factorial of" << N << "=" << fact;
```

We can also use an alternative approach wherein we make use of the property that the factorial of N is simply a product of N and the factorial of N-1.

N! = N * (N-1) !

Thus, factorial of N has been defined in terms of factorial of N-1. This type of definition is known as a recursive definition in the sense that it refers to the concept being defined within the definition itself.

Now, by the same definition, the factorial of (N-1) can be defined as given below:

(N-1) ! = (N-1)! * (N-2) !

We can continue this process till we end up with 0! which is equal to 1. Thus the algorithm for computing the factorial N is expressed in terms of an algorithm for calculating the factorial N-1 and so on.

The process described above can be implemented by using a function `fact` which is defined in terms of itself, as shown below:

$$\text{fact(N)} = \begin{cases} 1 \text{ if } N=0 \\ N^{*}\text{fact}(N-1)\text{if } N>0 \end{cases}$$

The function `fact` has been defined recursively. In C, such recursive functions can be implemented by making the function call itself. For example, we can have a function `fact` which calls itself as shown below :

```
/* Function that computes the factorial */
long fact (int N)
{
if ( N = = 0 )
return (1);
else
return ( N * fact (N-1));
}
```

It may be further noted that the function `fact` is being called by itself but with the parameter N being replaced by N-1. ***This ability of a function to call itself is known as recursion.*** A complete program to compute the factorial of a number using recursion is given below.

```
/* This program computes N factorial
   where N is an integer                    */

# include <stdio.h>
# include <conio.h>

long fact (int N);

main()
  {
```

```
   int num;
   clrscr();
   printf ("\n Enter an Integer");
   scanf ("%d", &num);
  printf ("\n The factorial of %d is = %d", num, fact(num));
  }
                /* Function that computes the factorial */
 long fact (int N)
  {
   if ( N == 0 )
   return (1);
   else
   return ( N * fact (N-1));
  }
```

Recursion can be used to write simple, short, and elegant programs. However, a recursive algorithm requires a condition that must end the recursive calls. The absence of this condition would result in an infinite loop. For example, in the function `fact`, the condition "`N = = 0`" is the required terminating condition.

Since recursion involves overheads such as CPU time and memory storage, it is suggested that recursion should be used with care.

Example 12

Write a function that computes x^y by using recursion.

Solution

We can use the property that x^y is simply a product of x and x^{y-1}. For example, $5^4 = 5*$ 5^3 The recursive definition of x^y can be represented as shown below :

$$\text{power}(x, y) = \begin{cases} 1 \text{ if } y = 0 \\ x * \text{power}(x, y - i) \text{ if } y > 0 \end{cases}$$

The required function is given below :

```
/* Function that computes x^y */
 long power (int x, int y)
   {
    if ( y == 0 )
   return (1);
    else
   return ( x * power (x,y-1));
   }
```

Example 13

Write a program that computes x^y with the help of the recursive function power developed in Example 12.

Solution

The required program is given below:

```
/* This program computes the x to the power y using
recursion */
# include <stdio.h>
long power (int x, int y);

main()
 {
   int val1, val2, res;
   printf ("\n Enter two integers");
   scanf ("%d %d", &val1, &val2);
   res = power (val1, val2);

   printf ("\n %d ^ %d = %d", val1, val2, res);
 }

           /* Function that computes x^y */
long power (int x, int y)
 {
  if ( y == 0 )
  return (1);
  else
  return ( x * power (x,y-1));
 }
```

Example 14

Write a program that computes GCD (greatest common divisor) of two given numbers.

Solution

The recursive definition of given below:

$$GCD(M,N) = \begin{cases} GCD(N,M) \text{ if } M<N \\ M \text{ if } N=0 \\ \text{else } GCD(N, M \% N) \end{cases}$$

The above definition can be used to develop a recursive function called GCD which takes two arguments x and y of integer type and returns the required greatest common divisor.

```
/* This function computes greatest common divisor */

  int GCD (int M, int N)
    {
   if ( N == 0 ) return M;
    else
      return  GCD (N, M % N);
    }
```

The required program that uses the function GCD() is given below :

```
/* This program computes greatest common divisor  */

# include <stdio.h>
int GCD (int M, int N);
main()
  {
    int NUM1, NUM2;
    int gcd;
    printf ("\n Enter the two integers :");
    scanf ("%d %d", &NUM1, &NUM2);
    if ( NUM1 >= NUM2) gcd = GCD( NUM1, NUM2 );
      else gcd = GCD( NUM2, NUM1 );
    printf ("\n The highest common factor : %d" , gcd);
  }
  int GCD (int M, int N)
    {
   if ( N == 0 ) return M;
    else
      return  GCD (N, M % N);
    }
```

Example 15

Use the function GCD ( ) of Example 14 to compute the LCM (Least common multiple) where GCD (M, N) * LCM (M, N) = M * N.

Solution

The GCD () of Example 14 would be used to compute the desired LCM and the program that does the required task is given on the next page.

```
/* This program computes  LCM of two numbers  by using GCD()
function    */

 # include <stdio.h>
 int GCD (int M, int N);
 int LCM (int M, int N);
 main()
   {
     int NUM1, NUM2;
     int lcm;
     printf ("\n Enter the two integers :");
     scanf ("%d %d", &NUM1, &NUM2);
     lcm = LCM ( NUM1, NUM2);

     printf ("\n The least common multiple : %d" , lcm);
    }
   int LCM (int M, int N)
     {
       int gcd;
       if ( M >= N) gcd = GCD( M, N );
       else gcd = GCD( N, M );
       return (M*N/gcd); /* compute LCM  */
     }
   int GCD (int M, int N)
     {
     if ( N == 0 ) return M;
      else
        return  GCD (N, M % N);
      }
```

Example 16

Write a program that generates the first n terms of a Fibonacci sequence by recursion. The sequence is given below:

0, 1, 1, 2, 3, 5, 8, ...

Solution

In a fibonacci series, each term (except the first two) can be obtained by the sum of its two immediate predecessors. The recursive definition of this sequence is given below :

$$\text{fib}(n) = \begin{cases} 0 \text{ if } n = 2 \\ 1 \text{ if } n = 2 \\ \text{else fib}(n-1) + \text{fib}(n-2) \end{cases}$$

Let us now write a program that uses a function fib () to compute the first n terms of the series.

```
/* This program generates first n terms of a fibonacci series */

# include <stdio.h>
int fib (int N);
main()
 {
   int N;
   int i, term;
   printf ("\n Enter the number of terms to be generated");
   scanf ("%d", &N);
   printf("\n The series...: ");
   for (i = 1; i <= N; i++)
      { term = fib(i);
    printf (" %d", term);
      }
  }
/* This function computes a Fibonacci term */
 int fib ( int N)
   {
    if (N == 1) return 0;
    else
     if ( N == 2 )
         return 1;
     else
    return (fib(N-1) + fib (N-2));
    }
```

16.11 LIBRARIES

A library is a collection of programs or functions which can be used by other programs. Like all other high level languages, C provides function libraries containing built-in functions. These standard functions are extremely useful to the programmers, in the sense that if some of the available functions are called in a program then they are combined with the program code by the linker at the time of linking. The advantages of library functions are listed below:

1. Reusability of code. Program development requires three major activities: coding, testing, and debugging. If a function, developed previously by oneself or by somebody else, is available as a standard library function then the effort of redevelopment can be avoided.

2. Faster development. Since many useful functions are available to the programmer, covering a host of commonly performed tasks, productivity increases and the program development process becomes faster.
3. Easier software maintenance. Since a function available in the library is shared by other users, the changes or modifications in the function can be done at library level, thus making it easier to maintain the software.

In addition tothis, a lot of disk space is also saved because only one copy of the function is stored on the disk. There are two types of libraries provided by C: Standard C libraries and User libraries.

16.11.1 Standard C Libraries

The declarations of various library functions are maintained by C in the form of header files. In simple words, we can say that each function library has a corresponding header file with the extension h. For instance, `stdio.h` is a header file.

The required header files are included in the program with the help of angle brackets '<' and '>'. In fact, the angle brackets make the C compiler look for the header file in its `include` directory.

16.11.2 Standard Library Functions

C supports a rich library of standard functions. The access to a function is allowed by including its corresponding header file at the beginning of the program. We have already used functions such as: `getchar ( )`, `putchar ( )`, `gets ( )`, `puts ( )`, `strcpy ( )`, `fflush ( )` etc. Some more useful functions are given below:

1. **`isalnum ( )`**. This function has a prototype in the `ctype.h` header file. The argument to this function is a character represented as an `int`. It performs a test: *Is the character alphanumeric?* An alphanumeric character is a letter of either case or a digit. This function returns a non-zero value if the character is alphanumeric and zero otherwise. An example of the usage of this function is given below:

```
*This program uses isalnum(), a library funcion to
test a character for alphanumeric type or otherwise  */
# include <stdio.h>
# include <ctype.h>
main()
 {
  char ch;
 printf("\n Enter a Character: ");
 ch = getchar();
 fflush(stdin);
 if (isalnum(ch))
```

```
printf ("\n%c is alphanumeric", ch);
else
printf ("\n%c is not alphanumeric", ch);
}
```

It may be noted here that the character read from the keyboard is passed as an argument to the function `isalnum ( )`. The value returned by the function is used by the `if-else` statement to print the appropriate message.

2. **`isdigit ( )`**. This function has a prototype in the `ctype.h` header file. The argument to this function is also a character represented as `int`. It performs the test: *Is the character a digit?* The function returns a non-zero value if the character is a digit and zero otherwise. An example of the usage of this function is given below:

```
/*This program uses isdigit(), a library funcion to
  test a character for digit type or otherwise  */
  # include <stdio.h>
  # include <ctype.h>
  main()
   {
    char ch;
    printf("\n Enter a digit: ");
    ch = getchar();
    fflush(stdin);
    if (isdigit(ch))
  printf ("\n%c is digit", ch);
  else
  printf ("\n%c is not digit", ch);
   }
```

3. **`isalpha ( )`**. This function is very similar to the function `isdigit ( )`, in the sense that it performs the test: *Is the character alphabetic?* It returns a non-zero value if the character is a letter of either case and zero otherwise. An example of the usage of this function is given below:

```
/*This program uses isalpha(), a library funcion to
  test a character for alphabet  or otherwise  */
  # include <stdio.h>
  # include <ctype.h>
  main()
   {
    char ch;
    printf("\n Enter a charecter: ");
    ch = getchar();
```

```
    fflush(stdin);
    if (isalpha(ch))
  printf ("\n%c is an alphabet", ch);
  else
  printf ("\n%c is not an alphabet", ch);
   }
```

4. **islower ( ).** This function is also similar to the functions explained above. It performs the test: *Is the character a lowercase letter?* It returns a non-zero value for the outcome of the test being true and zero for false. An example of the usage for this function is given below:

```
/*This program uses islower(), a library funcion to
   test a character for lowercase  or otherwise  */
   # include <stdio.h>
   # include <ctype.h>
   main()
    {
     char ch;
     printf("\n Enter a charecter: ");
     ch = getchar();
     fflush(stdin);
     if (islower(ch))
   printf ("\n%c is a lowercase alphabet", ch);
   else
   printf ("\n%c is not a lowercase alphabet", ch);
    }
```

5. **isupper ( ).** The action of this function is exactly the same as `islower` except that it performs the test *Is the character an uppercase letter?* An example of the usage of this function is given below:

```
/*This program uses isupper(), a library funcion to
test a character for uppercase  or otherwise  */
# include <stdio.h>
# include <ctype.h> main()
 {
  char ch;
  printf("\n Enter a charecter: ");
  ch = getchar();
  fflush(stdin);
  if (isupper(ch))
  printf ("\n%c is an uppercase alphabet", ch);
  else
  printf ("\n%c is not an uppercase alphabet", ch);
```

```
}
```

6. **`tolower ( )`**. This is a case conversion function, in the sense that it converts a character to its corresponding lowercase value. If the character is an upper case letter (A to Z) then it is converted to its lowercase value (a to z). All others are left unchanged. The prototype of this function is also contained in the `ctype.h` header file. An example of the usage of this function is given below:

```
/*This program uses tolower(), a library funcion that
  converts an  uppercase alphabet to a lowercase one */
  # include <stdio.h>
  # include <ctype.h>
  main()
   {
    char ch;
    printf("\n Enter a charecter: ");
   ch = getchar();
    fflush(stdin);
    if (isalpha(ch))
  if (isupper(ch))
  { ch = tolower(ch);
  printf ("\nThe equivalent lower case is : %c",ch);
  }
  else
  printf ("\n%c is not an uppercase alphabet", ch);
     else
  printf ("\n%c is not an  alphabet", ch);
   }
```

7. **`toupper ( )`**. This is also a case conversion function. It converts a character to its uppercase value. The action is very similar to the function `tolower ( )`. An example of the usage is given below:

```
/*This program uses toupper(), a library funcion that
converts an  uppercase alphabet to a lowercase one  */
# include <stdio.h>
# include <ctype.h>
main()
 {
    char ch;
    printf("\n Enter a charecter: ");
    ch = getchar();
    fflush(stdin);
    if (isalpha(ch))
  if (islower(ch))
```

```
{ ch = toupper(ch);
printf ("\nThe equivalent upper case is : %c",ch);
}
else
printf ("\n%c is not a lowercase alphabet", ch);
  else
printf ("\n%c is not an  alphabet", ch);
 }
```

8. **strcpy ( )**. This function copies one string to another. The function prototype for this function is contained in the `string.h` header file. The general form of this function call is:

   strcpy (dest, source)

   This function copies the source string to the destination string. The copying action stops after the null character '/0' has been moved from source to destination. An example of the usage is given below:

```
/*This program uses strcpy(), a library funcion to copy a
string   */
 # include <stdio.h>
 # include <string.h>
 main()
  {
   char Dest_string[20], Source_string[20];
   puts("Enter a string");
   gets(Source_string);
   strcpy(Dest_string, Source_string);
   printf ("\n The input string is : %s", Source_string);
   printf ("\n The copied string is : %s", Dest_string);
  }
```

   In the above program, a string is read in a string variable `Source_string` and is copied to another variable `Dest_string`. Both the strings are displayed.

9. **strcat ( )**. The prototype for this function is also contained in the header file `string.h`. It appends a source string to the end of the destination string so that the length of the resulting string is equal to the total of both the strings. An example of the usage of this function is given below:

```
/*This program uses strcat(), a library funcion to append
a string to the end of another string  */
 # include <stdio.h>
 # include <string.h>
 main()
  {
```

```
    char result[35]="";
    char blank[] = " ";
    char S1[] = "Bharat";
    char S2[] = "is a";
    char S3[] ="Great Nation";
    strcat(result,S1);
    strcat(result,blank);
    strcat(result,S2);
  strcat(result,blank);
  strcat(result,S3);
  printf ("\n The resultant string is ...: %s", result);
 }
```

In the above program, three strings `Bharat` , `is a` and `Great Nation` have been concatenated to a string called result. The output of this program would be :

`Bharat is a Great Nation`

10. **`strlen ( )`**. This is also a `string.h` related function. The argument to this function is a string. It calculates the length of that string, that is, it returns the number of characters present in the string, other than the null character '\0'

    An example of the usage of this function is:

```
       /*This program uses strlen(), a library funcion to
    compute the length of a string  */
    # include <stdio.h>
    # include <string.h>
    main()
      {
       char vachan[] = "Yan na Bharati Than na Bhartam";
       char Arth [] = "What is not Indian is not Knowledge";
        printf ("\n A saying is : %s", vachan);
           printf ("\n The length is : %d characters",
           strlen(vachan));
       printf ("\n The meaning is : %s", Arth);
       printf ("\n The length is : %d characters",
       strlen(Arth));
      }
```

11. **`strcmp ( )`**. This is also a `string.h` function. It compares two strings `s1` and `s2`. The comparison begins with the first character of each string and continues with subsequent characters until the end of the strings is reached or the corresponding characters differ. `strcmp ( )` returns a value less than zero

if s1 < s2 or zero if s1 = s2. It returns a value more than zero if s1 > s2. An example of the usage of strcmp ( ) is given below:

```
/*This program uses strcmp(), a library funcion to
  compare two strings for equality or otherwise */
  # include <stdio.h>
  # include <string.h>
  main()
   {
    char S1[20], S2[20];
    puts("\n Enter the first string");
    gets(S1);
    fflush(stdin);
    puts("\n Enter the second string");
    gets(S2);
    if (strcmp(S1,S2) == 0 )
  puts("\n The strings are equal");
   else
        puts("\n The strings are not equal");
  }
```

It may be noted that the strcmp ( ) function is case sensitive. However the function stricmp( ) does the comparison without case sensitivity.

12. **abs ( )**. This function has a prototype in the math.h header file. The argument to this function is an integer. It calculates the absolute value of the integer. An example of the usage of this function is given below:

```
int val =   -2395;
int absval;
absval = abs (val);
```

Once the above program segment is executed, the variable absval gets the value 2395.

13. **fabs ( )**. This is also a math.h function. The argument to this function is a number of type float or double. It returns the absolute value of the argument. An example of the usage of this function is given below:

```
double val =   -99.23457;
double absval = fabs (val);
```

Once the above program segment is executed, the variable absval gets the value 99.23457.

14. **frexp ( )**. This is a math.h function. The argument to this function is a double. It splits the number into the mantissa and exponent. An example of the usage of this function is given below:

```
double m, N;
int e;
N = 30.9;
m = frexp (N, & e);
printf ("The number is : %d", N);
printf ("\n The mantissa = %d", m);
printf ( \n The exponent is %d", e);
```

In the above program segment, the variable m gets the mantissa and the variable e gets the exponent.

15. **fmod ( )**. This is a math.h function. It returns the floating point remainder of x/y i.e., the portion to the right of the decimal part of the result of the division operation. The x and y are of type double and the value returned is also of type double. However the sign of the returned value is the same as that of x. An example of the usage of this function is given below:

```
double r, x, y;
x = 10.3;
y = 5.7;
r = fmod (x, y)
printf ("\n The remainder is %d", r);
```

16. **log ( )**. This is a function that takes an argument of type double and returns the natural logarithm of the argument. This is also a math.h function. An example of its usage is given below:

```
double x, r;
x = 70.293;
r = log (x);
printf ("\n The log to base e is : %g", r);
```

17. **log10 ( )**. This function (math.h) takes an argument of type double and returns the logarithm to the base 10 of the argument. An example of its usage is given below:

```
double x, r;
x = 70.293;
r = log10 (x);
printf ("\n The log to base 10 is: %g", r);
```

18. **modf ( ).** This function (`math.h`) takes arguments `N` and `m` of type `double` and splits `N` into an integer part and a fractional part. The integer part is loaded in `m` and the fractional part is returned. An example of its usage is given below:

```
double m, N;
double r;
N = 30.9;
r = modf (N, & m)
```

19. **pow ( ).** This function (`math.h`) takes two arguments `a` and `b` of type `double` and returns a^b. An example of its usage is given below:

```
double a, b, c;
a = 10.5;
b = 2.3;
c = pow (a, b);
```

20. **sqrt ( ).** This function (`math.h`) takes one argument of type `double` and returns a non negative square root of the argument. An example of its usage is given below:

```
double x, y;

x = 20.34;
y = sqrt (x);
```

21. **sin ( ).** This function (`math.h`) takes an angle as argument of type `double` and returns the sine of the angle. An example of its usage is given below:

```
double angle, val;
printf ("\n Enter the angle")   ;
scanf ("%g",angle);
val = sin (angle);
printf ("\n The sum of the angle is .." %g", val);
```

Note: The angle must be specified in radians.

22. cos ( ). This function (`math.h`) takes an angle as argument of type `double` and returns the cosine of the angle. An example of its usage is given below:

```
double angle, val;
printf ("\n Enter the angle")   ;
```

```
scanf ("%g",angle);
value = cos (angle);
printf ("\n  The cos of the angle is ...: %g", val);
```

Note: The angle must be specified in radians.

Example 17

Write a program that reads a list of names and copies the list into another empty list. The new list is sorted in ascending order.

Solution:

In this program, we will use the functions : `strcpy( )` and `strcmp( )`. Since these functions are `string.h` functions, we will include this file in our program. The required program is given below :

```
/* This program reads a list of names in an array
   and copies it in another array. The copied list
   is sorted in ascending order   */
   # include <stdio.h>
   # include <string.h>
   # include <conio.h>
   sort (char list[30][20], int N);
   main()
     {
      char List[30][20], NewList[30][20];
      int i, N;
      while(1)
      {
      printf ("\n Enter the size of the list ( < 30)");
      scanf("%d", &N);
      if (N>30)
    printf ("\n Reduce size ");
   else
    break;
    }            /* Read the list    */
   printf ("\n Enter the list");
   for (i=0; i < N; i++)
    { printf ("\nEnter Name: ");
        fflush(stdin);
      gets(List[i]);
     }
             /*Copy the List       */
    for (i=0; i < N; i++)
```

```
    strcpy(NewList[i], List[i]);
                /* Sort the new list  */
    sort (NewList, N);
                /* Print the sorted list */
    printf ("\n The sorted list is....");
    for (i=0; i < N; i++)
     printf ("\n%s", NewList[i]);
 }
 sort (char list[30][20],int N)
   { char temp[20];
   int i;
   int j;
   for (i = 0; i < N-1; i++)
     {
       for (j = i+1; j < N; j++)
            {
             if (strcmp (list[i], list[j]) > 0)
            {
                   strcpy(temp, list[i]);
                  strcpy(list[i], list[j]);
                  strcpy(list[j], temp);
             }
            }
         }
     }
```

Example 18

Write a program that evaluates the following expression.

$$x^4 + y^3 + z^2$$

The values of x, y and z are input from the keyboard.

Solution

We will use the function `pow( )` of header file `math.h`. The required program is given below:

```
/* This program evaluates an expression using pow() function */
# include <stdio.h>
# include <math.h>
main()
  {
   int x, y, z;
   int Ans;
   printf ("\n Enter three integers : ");
```

```
scanf("%%d %d %d", &x, &y, &z);
Ans = pow(x,4) + pow(y,3) + pow(z,2);
printf ("\n The value of the expression= %d", Ans);
}
```

Example 19

Write a program that generates a list of real numbers representing a table of values of `sin(x)` for values of x at intervals of 0.1 for `0 < = x < = 3.5`

Solution

We will use the `sin( )` function of the header file `math.h`. The required program is given below :

```
/* This program computes a table of values of sin(x) */
# include <stdio.h>
# include <math.h>
main()
  {
   float x;
   printf ("\n\t\t Table of Sin(x)");
   printf ("\n");
   printf ("\n\t X \t\t\tSin(X)");
   for (x = 0; x<= 3.5; x+=0.5)
   printf ("\n\t%3.2f \t\t\t %8.7f", x, sin(x));
   }
```

16.12 GRADED PROBLEMS

Problem 1. Write a program that reads N strings of 50 characters each. It prints the frequency table of all the alphabetical characters appearing in the strings. The format of the table is given below:

Alphabet	**Frequency count**
A	.
B	.
C	.
:	

Note: The lower case and upper case characters should be considered as same.

Solution: In this program, we will read the strings in an array called `list`. The `toupper()` function would be used to convert the lowercase letters to uppercase. The frequency count of each alphabet appearing in the text would be kept in an integer array called `count`. Since the ASCII value of alphabets starts from 65, the count of an alphabet would be stared at index = ch-65.

The required program is given below:

```
/* This program computes the frequency count of alphbets
   appearing in N strings of 50 characters each  */
   # include <stdio.h>
   # include <string.h>
   # include <conio.h>
   main()
     {
      char List[30][50], ch;
      int count[26];          /* The array to keep frequency
      count*/
      int i,j, N;
      while(1)
      {
      printf ("\n Enter the size of the list ( < 30)");
      scanf("%d", &N);
      if (N>30)
    printf ("\n Reduce size ");
      else
    break;
       }              /* Read the list    */
      clrscr();
      printf ("\n Enter the list");
      for (i=0; i < N; i++)
    { printf ("\nEnter string: ");
          fflush(stdin);
     gets(List[i]);
     }                  /* initialize the frequency count
    */
       for (i=0; i< 26; i++) count[i] =0;
                 /* compute frequency count    */
       for (i =0; i< N; i++)
    {
     j=0;
     while (List [i][j] != '\0')
       {  ch = toupper(List [i][j]);
           count [ch -65] = count [ch-65] + 1; /* increment
    count */
          j++;
       }
     }
```

```
    clrscr();
                            /* Display frequency count            */
    printf ("\n\t\t Frequency count   ");
    printf ("\n\tAlphabet\t\tCount");
    for (i=0; i < 26; i++)
        if  (count[i]  >  0)  printf("\n\t%c\t\t\t%d", i+65,
count[i]);
  }
```

Problem 2. Write a program that displays the sine curve on the screen in the following format :

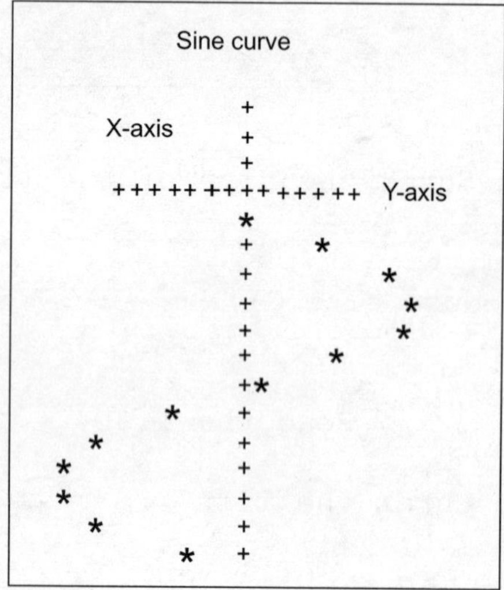

Where the distance of the character : '*' from the left represents the value of the function `sin(x)` and the position of the character : '+' represents the x-axis.

Solution: We will use the `sin( )` function of the `math.h` header file to compute the value of sin(x) for value of `x` varying from 0 to 2 π radians in steps of 0.5. The x-axis would be shown at column no. 20 from the left hand edge as a vertical line of characters: '+'. The sine curve would be displayed line by line. The required program is given below :

```
/* This program displays a sine curve */
# include <stdio.h>
# include <math.h>
# include <conio.h>
main()
  {
   const pi =3.1415;
   float x;
```

```
    float val;
    int i,j;
    clrscr();
    printf ("\n\t    Sine Curve");
    printf ("\n");
    printf ("\n\t  X-axis\n");
                        /* Display X- Axis   */
    for (j = 1; j <= 3; j++)
     {
      for (i = 1; i < 20; i++)
          printf (" ");
      printf ("+\n");
     }
     printf ("                ++++++++++++++ Y- Axis");
     printf ("\n");
     for (x =0; x <= 2*pi; x+=0.5)
        {
  val = sin(x) *10 +20; /* compute sin(x) and scale it by 10 */
  j = (int) val;        /* Take equivalent integer value    */
  if (j==20)          /* print value of sin(x) lying on x-axis*/
    {
     for (j =1; j<20; j++)
       printf (" ");
       printf ("*\n");
    }
   else
    if (j > 20)
     {
       for  (i= 1; i < j; i++)
         {
          if (i ==20) printf ("+");
              else
             printf (" ");
              }
              printf ("*\n");
          }
      else
      {
       for (i = 1; i < 20; i++)
         {
          if (i==j) printf ("*");
          else
            printf (" ");
```

```
            }
          printf ("+\n");
        }
      }
    }
```

Problem 3. Dynamic dictionary coding is a common data compression technique. In this method, the input text is scanned from the first word in such a manner that:

- The words are inserted into an empty dictionary in a search/insert fashion i.e., the word is searched in the dictionary; if not found it is inserted in the dictionary and also written on the output.
- If the word is found in the dictionary then its position from the dictionary is written on the output instead of the word.

Example: Input Text: "When you are on the left – you are on the right and when you are on the right– you are on the wrong".

The dynamic dictionary obtained from above input text is given below:

The dynamic dictionary

Word	Position
When	1
you	2
are	3
on	4
the	5
left	6
right	7
and	8

Output text: When you are on the left -2 3 4 5 right and 1 2 3 4 5 6 7 2 3 4 5 wrong.
Write a program that reads text into an array of strings and compresses the data using the dynamic dictionary coding technique.

Solution: An array of strings to store 50 words of 20 characters each would be used to represent the text. The required program is given below:

```
/* This program implements Dynamic Dictionary Decoding  */
# include <stdio.h>
main()
  {
    char text[50][20];
    char Dictionary[30][20];
```

```
    int i,j, flag, wordCount, DictCount;
    i=-1;
    printf ("\n Enter the text terminated by a ### : \n") ;
    do
     {
      i++;
      scanf ("%s", text[i]);
     }
     while (strcmp (text [i], "###"));
     wordCount = --i;
     strcpy (Dictionary[0], text[0]);
    DictCount =0;       /* The Dictionary gets the first word */
     printf ("\n The Text is : %s ",text[0]); /* print the
first word  */
     for (i = 1;i <= wordCount; i++)
        {
      flag= 0;
      for ( j = 0; j <= DictCount; j++)
  {
   if (!strcmp (text[i], Dictionary[j]))
     { printf ("%d ", j+1);
            flag = 1 ;
            break;
          }
        }                          /* End of j Loop */
     if (flag == 0)
        {
         DictCount ++;
         strcpy (Dictionary[DictCount], text[i]);
         printf ("%s ", text[i]);
        }
    }                      /* End i Loop    */
 }
```

Problem 4. An integer N can be partitioned into a collection of positive integers whose sum is N itself. For example, partition of 5 can be written as:

```
5
4 1
3 2
3 1 1
2 2 1
2 1 1 1
1 1 1 1 1
```

Write a program that uses a recursive function to print the partitions of a user defined positive integer N.

Note: This problem seems to be easy. The students are advised to first try on their own and later take the help of the solution given below:

Solution: The required program is given below:

```
/* This program prints the partitions of an integer N
   where a partiton ia a set of positive numbers whose
   sum is equal to N*/
# include <stdio.h>
# include <conio.h>
int set[30];
void generate_set(int N);
void printset();
int val;
main()
  {
   printf ("\n Enter the number N");
   scanf("%d", &val);
   clrscr();
   printf("\n%d", val);
   generate_set(val-1);
  }
void generate_set(int N)
 { char ch;
  int i, sum,t,j,k;
  if (N < 1) return;
  i=-1;
  sum = N;
  while (sum < val)
    { i++;
     set [i] = N;
     sum = sum + N;
    }
    if( val -(sum-N) >0) { i = i+1; set [i] = val -(sum-N); }
    set [i+1] = -1;
    t=i+1;
    if (N>1) { if (set[i] == 1) i--;
    printset();}
    else {printset();return;}
    /*while (i<=1) i++;*/
    while (i>0)
     {
```

```
   j=t;
  do
  {set[j+1]=set[j]; j--;}
  while (j>i);
  ch = getch();j++;
   set[j]=1;
   set[j-1] =set[j-1]-1;
   printset();
   ch = getch();
   if (set[i] == 1) i--;
   t++;
  }
 generate_set(N-1);
}
void printset()
 { char ch;
   int i;
   i=0;
   printf("\n");
   while (set[i] >=1)
   {printf("%d+",set[i++]);
ch = getch();
}
   printf("\b ");
 }
```

Problem 5. The Hamming distance between two bit patterns is the number of bit positions in which they differ. For example, the Hamming distance between the following two bit patterns is 2.

0101
1111

Write a program that reads two non-negative integers from the user, converts them into their binary representations, and computes the Hamming distance between the two.

Solution: A `while` loop would be constructed wherein binary bits from each number would be extracted and compared. If the bits do not match, a count would be incremented. The loop would terminate after both numbers became zero. Following is a program that uses the `while` loop for computing the Hamming distance:

```
/* This program computes hamming distance between two
bit patterns                                        */
# include <stdio.h>
                        /*Fn to compute hamming distance*/
int get_hamm_dist(int N1,int N2);
```

```
main()
  {
   int num1, num2;
   int ham_dist;
   printf ("\n Enter first number");
   scanf("%d", &num1);
    printf ("\n Enter 2nd number");
   scanf("%d", &num2);
   ham_dist = get_hamm_dist(num1,num2);
   printf ("\n The hamming distance = %d", ham_dist);
   }

   int get_hamm_dist(int n1,int n2)
   { int bit_n1, bit_n2;
     int  count=0;            /* extract bits and compare  */
     while (n1 !=0 || n2!=0)
     { bit_n1= n1 % 2;
       bit_n2= n2 % 2;
       if (bit_n1 != bit_n2)
          count++;
       n1 = n1 /2;
       n2 = n2 /2;
     }

    return count;
   }
```

Problem 6. Write a program that, for every even integer between 4 and 100, attempts to find a pair of prime numbers P1 and P2 such that

even = P1 + P2

The above relationship "every even number greater than 2 can be expressed as the sum of two prime numbers" is also called Goldback's conjecture.

Solution: We would use a function called `ifprime ()` to test whether an integer is prime or not. The rest of the solution is easy. The required program is given below:

```
# include <stdio.h>
# include <math.h>
int ifprime (int N);
main()
 { int even, j;
   char ch;
   for (even = 4; even <=100; even = even +2)
```

```
    {
     for (j =2; j<even; j++)
   {
    if(ifprime(j) && ifprime(even-j))
      {
        printf ("\n Even = %d, Prime1=%d, Prime2 = %d", even,
        j, even-j);
        break;
      }
     ch = getch();
    }
      }
  }
int ifprime(int N)
  {
   int i;
     for (i = 2; i <= (int)sqrt(N); i++)
     {
      if ((N % i)==0)  return 0;
     }
     return 1;
}
```

Problem 7. A text encoding scheme is given below: For a given keyword of 5 characters and a letter (not to be coded), a square of 5 × 5 is constructed. For example, for keyword sagun and letter K, the following square is obtained:

s a g u n
b c d e f
h i j l m
o p q r t
v w x y z

It may be noted that the keyword becomes the first row and rest of the letters are stored in the subsequent rows. However, the letter (K in this case) does not appear in the square because it is not to be coded.

The square is used to encode a piece of text by using the following steps.

1. Take a pair of successive alphabets from the text. If the alphabet is the letter, do not code, print the pair, and repeat step 1.
2. Code the pair by replacing each alphabet by the letter from the square appearing in the same row but in the column of the other. For example the text "no" will be coded as "st".

3. Repeat steps 1 and 2 till whole of the text is coded.
4. The last unpaired alphabet is left uncoded.

   Sample Input: Keyword = sagun
   letter = k
   Input text: musicforlife
   Output text: lnahfcroilef
   Write a program that implements this encoding technique.

Solution: The following data structure would be employed.

1. `char key[5]` to store the keyword.
2. `char letter` to store the letter which is to be left unaltered..
3. `char square [5][5]` to store the square.
4. `char text [50]` and `new [50]` to store the pieces of input and output texts.

The following functions would be coded:

1. `generate_sq ( )`: This function would generate the required square.
2. `display ( )`: This function would display the square
3. `code ( )`: This function would use the square and letter to encode the input text into the output text.

The required program is given below:

```
/* this program implements a text encoding technique */

# include <stdio.h>

void genrate_sq (char square[5][5], char key[5], char letter);
void code (char text[50], char square[5][5], char coded[50],
char ch);
void display(char t[5][5]);

main()
  {
   char text[50],new[50], square[5][5];
   char key[5];
   char letter;

   printf ("\nEnter key(5 charecters)");
   scanf ("%s", key);
   printf ("\n Enter the letter");
  fflush(stdin);
  letter = getchar();
  genrate_sq(square,key,letter);
  display(square);
```

```
printf ( "\n Enter the text to be coded");
fflush(stdin);
gets(text);
code(text,square,new, letter);
 clrscr();
 printf ("\n The original text:%s",text);
 printf ("\n The coded text   :%s",new);
 }
 void genrate_sq (char square[5][5], char key[5], char
 letter)
   {
     int i,j,k,flag;
     char ch;
        /*initialize the first row with key */
     i=0;
     for (j =0; j<5; j++)
        square[i][j] = key[j];
        /* complete the rest of the square */
     i=1;
     j=0;
     for (ch='a'; ch<='z';ch++)
   {                       /* keep letter out of square  */
     if (ch == tolower(letter)) continue;

       k=0;
        flag=0;
                       /* chech if the charecter
                          is part of the first row */
      while (!flag && k <5 )
         {
           if (ch == square[0][k])
              { flag=1;
             break;
              }
           k++;
         }        /* end of while  */
          if (!flag)
            {square[i][j] = ch;
            j++;
            if(j >4 ) {j =0;i++;}
            }
```

```
 }              /* end of for  */

   }


void code (char text[50], char square[5][5], char coded[50],
char letter)
   {
    char ch1, ch2;
    int i,j,k,l, pos1row,pos1col, pos2row, pos2col;
  i=0, j=1;
   ch1= text[i];
   ch2 = text[j];
  while (ch1 != '\0' && ch2 != '\0')
    {                     /* keep the letter unaltered    */
    if (ch1 == letter) { coded[i]= ch1; ch1 =ch2;
                  ch2= text[j+1]; i++;j++; continue; }
    if (ch2 == letter) { coded[i]= ch1;coded [j] = ch2;
    continue; }
   for (k =0; k<5; k++)
    {
      for (l=0; l< 5; l++)
        {
         if (ch1 == square[k][l]) {pos1row=k; pos1col=l; }
         if (ch2 == square[k][l]) {pos2row=k; pos2col=l; }
         }
    }                                  /* CODE THE TEXT   */
    coded[i] = square[pos1row][pos2col];
    coded[j] =square [pos2row][pos1col];
    i = i+2;
    j= j+2;
        ch1= text[i];
    ch2 = text[j];
      }
      if (ch1=='\0')  coded[i]='\0';
      else { coded[i] =text[i]; coded[j]='\0';  }

  }
  void display( char t[5][5])
    {
      int i,j;
      char ch;
      clrscr();
```

```
    for (i=0; i<5; i++)
     {
      for (j=0; j<5; j++)
         printf ("%c ", t[i][j]);
      printf ("\n");
      }
}
```

FREQUENTLY ASKED QUESTIONS

1. What happens when a function has more than one return statement?
Solution: A function can have more than one return statement but they should be logically placed. However, two return statements should never appear in succession.

2. What happens to the two parameters used by the following function
```
void xyz (int &x, int y);
```
Solution: The parameter `x` is passed by reference and the parameter `y` by value. Thus, the changes made to `x` inside the function `xyz` will be reflected back to the actual variable. The parameter `y`, on the other hand, contains the copy of the actual parameter.

3. What is the purpose of a function prototype?
Solution: The purpose of a function prototype is to help the compiler in static type checking, so that the compiler becomes aware of the data requirements of the function which has been defined somewhere else.

4. What is the advantage of a register variable?
Solution: Since registers are memory locations inside the CPU, the operations on registers are faster than those on the variables residing in main memory.

5. Why are global variables sometimes declared as static ?
Solution: A static global variable cannot be accessed outside the program file in which it is declared. Thus, such a variable is not a global variable for the whole program.

6. What is the advantage of the function scope?
Solution: We know that only labels have function scope. Therefore, we can use different labels with the same name in multiple functions without any confusion.

TEST YOUR SKILLS

1. Identity the errors in the following program.
```
 # include <stdio.h>
xyz ( int m, int n)
{
 int m = 20;
```

```
  n = m * 10;
  return n;
}
```

Solution: There is one error in the program i.e., the variable `m` has been redefined in the function.

2. Identify the errors in the following program

```
# include <stdio.h>
void xyz();
void main()
 {
   int val = 0;
   val = xyz();
   printf ("%d", val);
 }
void xyz()
 {
   printf ( \n VOID  );
 }
```

Solution: The assignment statement: `val = xyz ( )` is wrong because `xyz ()` cannot return a value as it has been declared as void.

3. What would be the output of the following function?

```
# include <stdio.h>
first(int ,int);
second ( int);
void main()
 {
   int x =10, y = 5, z;
z = first( x, y);
printf ("\n z = %d", z);
   }
first (int x, int y)
{
 return (x + second(y));
}
second ( int y)
{
 return ( ++y);
}
```

Solution: The output would be: `z = 16.`

4. What would be the output of the following program?

```
# include <stdio.h>
```

```
get_val ();
void main()
{
 int x;
 x = get_val();
 printf ( \n % d", x);
 x = get_val();
 printf ("% d", x);
}
get_val()
 {
   static int i = 10;
   return (i++);
 }
```

Solution: The output would be: `10 11`

5. What would be the output of the following program?

```
# include <stdio.h>
int val = 10;
divide (int);
void  main ()
 {
   int val = 8;
   val = divide (val);
   printf ( \n %d", val);
 }
divide ( int val)
 {
   return (val/2);
 }
```

Solution: The output would be : 4

6. What would be the output of the following program?

```
# include <stdio.h>
int val = 10;
divide (int);
void  main ()
 {
   int val = 8;
   val = divide (val);
   printf ( \n  %d", val);
 }
divide ( int x)
 {
```

```
    return (val/x);
  }
```

Solution: The output would be : `1`

7. Identify the errors in the following program:

```
# include <stdio.h>
int val = 10;
divide (int);
void  main ()
  {
    void increment ( int * x);
int val = 8;
val = divide (&val);
    printf ( \n %d   , val);
  }
divide ( int val)
  {
    increment (val);
    return (val/2);
  }
void increment (int * x)
  {
    *x++;
  }
```

Solution: The function prototype for the function `increment ()` has been placed inside the function `main()` and therefore, it becomes local to it. Now the function `divide()` is trying to call function `increment()`, which is not possible because it is not available to it. Thus, the function prototype of `increment()` should be placed outside the function `main()` in the form of a global function. This will solve the problem. However, if this prototype is brought inside the function divide, it becomes local to function `increment()` and also solves the problem.

8. What would be the output of the following program?

```
# include <stdio.h>
int val = 10;
divide (int);
void  main ()
  {
    int val = 5;
    val = divide ( val = val/5 );
    printf ( \n %d  , val);
 }
divide ( int x)
  {
```

```
    return (x/val);
}
```

Solution: The expression `val = val/5` is evaluated and `val` gets the value 2. Thus, value 2 is passed to function `divide`. Now the expression 2/10 evaluates to 0 and therefore, the output would be 0.

9. What would be the output of the following program?

```
# include <stdioh>
divide (int);
void  main ()
 {
   int i = 20;
   int val = divide (500) == 50;
   printf ("\n %d, val);
}
divide ( int i)
 {
   return (i/10);
 }
```

Solution: The actual parameter passed to the function divide is 500. Obviously, the local variable `i` of function divide gets a value 500. The value returned by the function is 50. Now, the expression divide (500) = = 50 evaluates to true i.e., 1. Therefore `val` gets value 1. The output would be 1.

10. What will be the output of the following program.

```
# include <iostream.h>
register  int val = 50;
main ()
 {
   int y = 20;
   printf ("%d", val + y);
 }
```

Solution:: It will result in error because a register variable cannot be declared as global.

11. What would be the output of the following program?

```
# include <stdio.h>
static int val = 50;
void display ();
void main ()
{
 static int val = 70;
 printf ( \n  %d  , val);
 display();
}
```

```
void display ()
{
 printf ("%d", val);
}
```

Solution: The output would be : `70 50`

12. What would be the output of the following program.

```
# include <stdio.h>
int temp ( int );
main ()
 {
   int x = temp (25);
   printf ( \n x= %d",      -<196>x);
 }
temp ( int x)
 {
   return x++;
 }
```

Solution: The output would be : `x = 24`

13. What would be the output of the following program?

```
first ( int );
second (int);
void main()
 {
   int val = 50;
   val = first (second(val *= val / val));
   printf ( \n   % d", val);
}
first (int x)
{
 return x++;
 }
second ( int y)
 {
 return y++;
 }
```

Solution: The expression `val = val/val` will evaluate to 50. Therefore, the output would be 50.

14. What would be the output of following program?

```
# include <iostream.h>
set_val ( int, int);
```

```
void main()
 {
   int a = 20, b=10;
set_val ( a++, b++);
printf ( \n     % d % d", a .b);
}
set_val( int x, int y)
 {
   x = x + y;
   y = y - x;
   x = x - y;
 }
```

Solution: The output would be = 11 21

EXERCISES

1. Define the terms subprogram, function, formal parameters, actual parameters, extern variables.
2. Write the various elements of a function.
3. What is meant by a function prototype and why it is needed?
4. Write a function to compute the following function for a given value of x

$$\sin(x) = x - \frac{x^3}{3!} + \frac{x^5}{5!}$$

5. Write a program that computes the trace of a given matrix `Mat` with the help of a function `trace( )`. The trace of a matrix can be defined as the sum of diagonal elements of the matrix.
6. Write a function `sort ( )` which sorts an array in descending order with the help of the selection sort algorithm.
7. Write short notes on the following:
   (i) Local and global variables
   (ii) Static and extern variable
   (iii) Call by value
   (iv) Call by reference
   (v) Array parameters
8. Explain in brief local scope.
9. Explain in brief file scope.
10. What is meant by a register variable? What is the utility of such a variable?
11. Explain in brief the functions that return a value.
12. Are there any errors in the following function?

```
void some ()
{
        static int a;
        a=50;
```

```
                printf ("\m a=%d", a);
        }
```

13. What would be the output of the following?

```
# include <stdio.h>
val();
void main()
        {
                int a;
                a= val();
                printf ( \n a= % d  , a);
a = val();
printf (  , %d", a);
}
val()
        {
                return (50);
        }
```

14. What would be the output of the following?

```
# include <stdio.h>
static int get_val ( );
void main()
        {
                int x;
                x = get_val ();
                printf ("\n      % d", x);
                x = get_val ();
                printf ("\n % d", x);
        }
static int  get_val( )
        {
                int i = 10;
                return (i++);
        }
```

15. Identify errors, if any, in the following program

```
# include <stdio.h>
void display();
void main()
        {
                display();
        }
void display()
        {
                return 0
        }
```

16. What would be the output of the following program.

```
#include <stdio.h>
```

```
temp(int);
void main()
        {
                int x = temp (25);
                printf ( \n x= % d  ,++x);
        }
temp (int x)
        {
                return   -<196>x;
        }
```

17. What is meant by a library in the context of programing languages?
18. What are advantages of having library functions?
19. What is the purpose of the usage of angled brackets '<' and '>' in the context of header files?
20. Explain `string.h` header file in brief.
21. Explain the usage of the following functions with the help of suitable examples.
    (i) `isalnum( )`
    (ii) `isdigit( )`
    (iii) `isalpha( )`
    (iv) `islower( )`
    (v) `isupper( )`
22. Explain the usage of the following case conversion functions with the help of suitable examples:
    (i) `tolower( )`
    (ii) `toupper( )`
23. Explain the usage of the following string functions with the help of suitable examples:
    (i) `strcpy( )`
    (ii) `strcat( )`
    (iii) `strlen( )`
    (iv) `strcmp( )`
24. Explain the usage of the following functions with the help of suitable examples:
    (i) `abs( )`
    (ii) `tabs( )`
    (iii) `log( )`
    (iv) `modf( )`
    (v) `pow( )`
25. Explain the usage of the following trigonometric functions with the help of suitable examples:
    (i) `sin( )`
    (ii) `cos( )`
26. Identify the errors to the following statements:
    (i) `#include < math.h`
    (ii) `isalnum (ch);`
    (iii) `strcat (xyz, 2.379);`
    (iv) `val = abs (-5.23);`
    (v) `sqrt (x, y).`

CHAPTER

17 Files

17.1 DATA AND INFORMATION

Ancient markings on rocks, writings on Ashoka pillars, the scriptures, and the caves of Ajanta and Ellora, all indicate that humans have a basic tendency to record information. The oldest records were made on clay tablets as long back as 3700 BC. Most of the Indian scriptures were written on the thin sheets of the bark of Bhojpatra, a tree found in the upper Himalayas. In the second century AD, paper was developed in China. This event brought a revolution and paper became a writing medium in whole of the world.

In any enterprise, whether it is a small corner shop, a school, or a large industry, it can be observed that each person uses lot of paper and a large amount of data and information exchange takes place. The workers deal with actual physical work and produce data whereas the managers deal with the information put down on paper.

Let us now delve upon the terms data and information especially in the context of files.

Data. The word data is a plural of datum, which means fact. Thus, data is a collection of facts and figures. It can be represented by symbols. For example, in a business house, data can be the name of an employee, salary, number of hours worked etc. Similarly in an educational institute, the data can be the marks of a student, roll number, percentage etc.

Information. This is the data arranged in an ordered and useful form. Thus, the data can be processed so that it becomes meaningful and understandable (see Fig. 17.1).

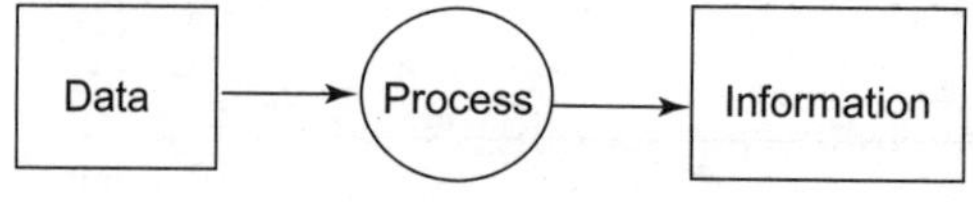

Fig. 17.1

For example, in Fig. 17.2 (a), the collection of characters and digits is meaningless by itself because it could refer to total marks and names of students, the house numbers and names of house owners etc. Once the data is arranged in an order, as shown in

Fig. 17.2 (b), it is clear that the data refers to names of persons and their corresponding ages. Therefore, this meaningful data can be called *information*.

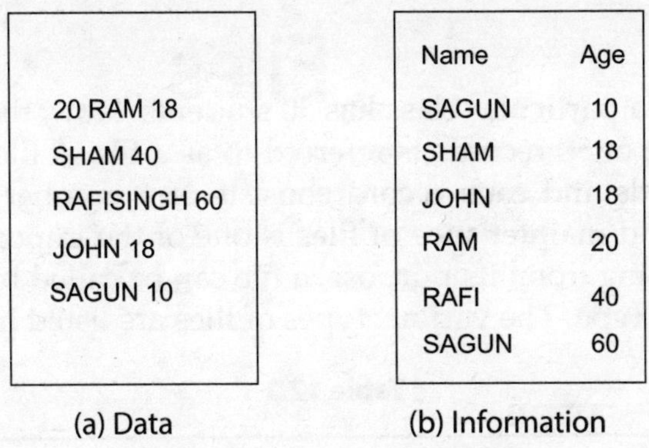

Fig. 17.2 Data and Information

17.2 FILE CONCEPTS

Let us consider the information recorded in Fig. 17.3. Each entry in the table shown in this figure is a set of three data items: Roll, Name, and Marks. The first entry states that the Roll number and total marks of a student named Ajay are 001 and 50 respectively. Similarly the second entry relates to a student named RAM whose Roll number is 002 and whose total marks equal to 70.

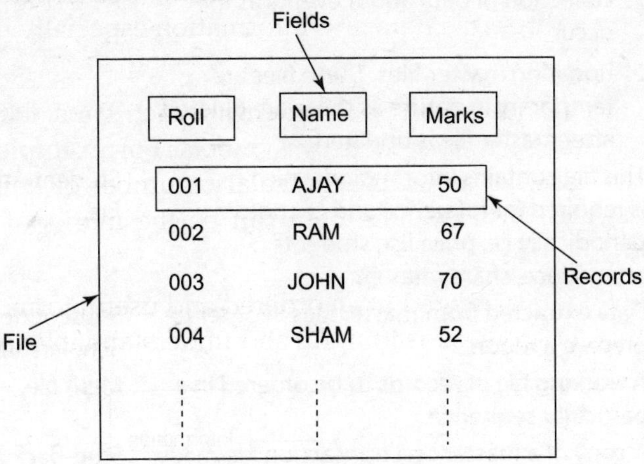

Fig. 17.3 File of records

Each entry in the table is also known as a record of a student. A set of related data items of a particular entity such as a person, machine, place, or operation etc is called a record. The individual data item within a record are known as fields.

Thus, the record of a student is made up of following three fields:

(i) Roll
(ii) Name
(iii) Marks

Let us assume that a particular class has 30 students. Now, the information of the entire class consisting of 30 records is referred to as a file. A file, therefore, consists of a number of records and each record consists of a number of items known as fields. The creation and maintenance of files is one of the important activities in an organization. Depending upon its purpose, a file can be called by a specific name or classified as a specific type. The various types of files are listed in Table 17.1.

Table 17.1

Type	Purpose	Examples
Master file	Collection of records about an important activity. Generally, it pertains to records of the main subject of the system whose data is being maintained. It may reflect the history of events or information which can be used as a source of reference. The master file is always kept up-to- date. These are fairly permanent files.	Student fee file, Personnel file, Inventory file, Stock file.
Transaction file	A temporary file with two purposes: 1. collection of data about events as they occur 2. updating master files. These files are temporary in nature as these are deleted after master file is updated.	Fee receipt file, Purchase file, Sales invoice file
Reference file	This file contains information which is required for reference and changes periodically i.e. price list, students attendance, share rates etc.	Student-attn. file, Share rates file.
Report file	Data extracted from master files in order to prepare a report.	Student detainee file, Scholarship file, Taxes file.
Sort file	A working file of records to be ordered in a particular sequence.	Merit file.
Backup files	A copy of a master or a transaction file made to ensure that a duplicate is available, if anything happens to the original.	Stud-backup file, Data backup file.
Archival files	Copies made for long-term storage of data maintained for future reference. The files are generally stored off-line i.e., away from the computer centre.	Security file, History file.

The arrangement of records in a file can be different for different situations. The file of records shown in Fig. 17.3 can be arranged according to Names instead of Roll numbers, i.e., in alphabetical order. The rearranged file is shown in Fig. 17.4.

Roll	Name	Marks
001	Ajay	50
003	John	70
002	Ram	67
004	Sham	52
⋮	⋮	⋮

Fig. 17.4 File in alphabetical order

It may be noted here that in the file shown in Fig. 17.3, the records were arranged according to the Roll field whereas in the file shown in Fig. 17.4, the records are arranged according to the Name field. However, a record in both the files can be identified by the field called Roll. Basically, a field which is used to identify a particular record within a file is called as a keyfield. It is the key field according to which all records within a file are generally arranged.

The records in a file can be arranged in the following three ways:

(i) Ascending/Descending order : The records in the file can be arranged in an ascending or descending order of a key field. For example, the records in the file of Fig. 17.3 are in ascending order of its Roll field.

(ii) Alphabetical order: If a field is of string or character type then this arrangement is used. For example, the records in the file of Fig. 17.4 are in alphabetical order.

(iii) Chronological order: In this type of order, the records are stored in the order of their occurrence i.e., arranged according to dates or events. If the key field is a date, i.e., date of birth, date of joining, etc. then this type of arrangement is used. For example, the records of a file shown in Fig. 17.5, are arranged according to the field DOB (Date of birth) .

Roll	Name	DOB
004	SHAM	09:02:79
003	JOHN	11:02:79
001	AJAY	15:03:79
002	RAM	23:11:79
⋮	⋮	⋮

Fig. 17.5 File in chronological order

17.3 FILE ORGANIZATION

In a non-computerised organization, the data and information is held on files kept in a paper filing system. If the company had a computer, the files would instead, be kept on computer storage. The former system is known as a Manual filing system and the latter is called an EDP filing system. The term EDP means Electronic Data Processing.

The characteristics of a Manual filing system are:

1. Records are stored as documents in files using papers.
2. Records are arranged using a system of indices.
3. The files are handled and maintained by people.

The characteristics of an EDP filing system are given below:

1. This is used in a computer environment.
2. Files are stored on computer storage.
3. Records are sorted and arranged according to a key field.
4. The files are handled and maintained by specific programmes written in a high level language such as PASCAL, C, software packages etc.

The manual filing system is suitable for small organizations where speed is not a very critical element and fast processing and storage of data is not required. In the EDP filing system, large amounts of data can be managed efficiently. Data storage and retrieval becomes very fast. It may be noted that in the manual filing system, the files are generally arranged in a meaningful sequence. The records are located manually by the person in charge of the files. However, when the files are stored on the computer, the files have to be kept in such a way that the records can be located, processed, and selected easily by the computer program. The handling of files depends on both input and output requirements, and the volume of data to be stored. How best can the files be arranged for ease of access? This necessity has led to the development of a number of file organization techniques, as given below:

(i) Sequential file organzation
(ii) Direct access file organization
(iii) Indexed sequential file organization.

17.4 FILES IN C

All the programs that we have seen in this book so far have extensively used input and output statements. The `scanf()` statement is used to input data from the keyboard and the `printf( )`statement to show the output or display data on the VDU screen. Thus, whenever some data is required in a program, it tries to read from the keyboard. The keyboard is an extremely slow device. For small volumes of data, this method of input works well. But what happens when huge data is needed by a program? For example, a program which generates the merit list of a joint entrance examination may require data to the tune of 10000 to 20000 records. It is not possible to sit down and type so much in one go. Another interesting situation is: what happens when the data or results produced by one program are required subsequently by another program? On the next day, the results may even be required by the program that produced them. Therefore, we need to have a mechanism such as files by virtue of which the program can read data from or write data onto magnetic storage medium.

When the data from a file is stored in the form of readable and printable characters then the file is known as a text file. On the other hand, if a file contains non-readable characters in binary code then the file is called a binary file. For instance, the program files created by an editor are stored as text files whereas the executable files generated by a compiler are stored as binary files.

The following sections give an introduction to the files supported by C.

17.5 FILES AND STREAMS

In C, a stream is a data flow from a source to a sink. The sources and sinks can be any of the input/output devices or files. For input and output, there are two different streams called input stream and output stream, as shown in Fig. 17.6

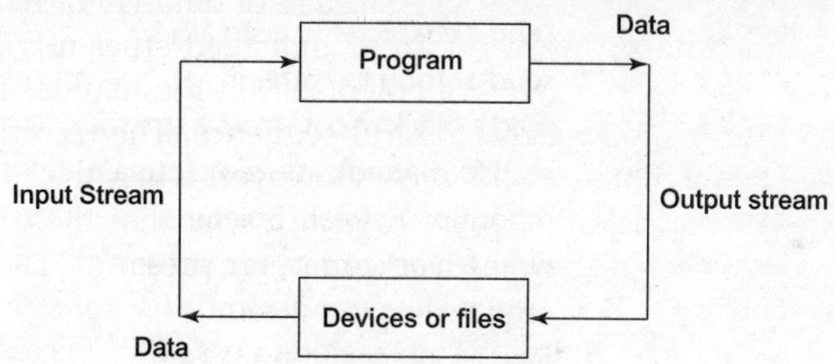

Fig. 17.6 Stream I/O

We have already used the following formatted stream I/O functions in our previous programs:

Stream	Description
`scanf`	standard input stream
`printf`	standard output stream

The standard source and sink are the keyboard and monitor screen respectively. These unformated streams are initialized whenever the header file `<stdio.h>` is included in a program.

In fact, C supports a very large number of I/O functions, capable of performing a wide variety of tasks. The I/O system of C is categorized into the following three categories:

1. The stream I/O system
2. The console I/O system
3. The low-level I/O system.

Some of the important stream I/O functions are listed in Table 17.2.

Table 17.2

Function	Purpose
`fclose`	close a stream
`feof`	test for end of file
`fflush`	flush a stream
`ftc`	read a character from a stream
`fgetchar`	read a character from a stream
`fgets`	read a string from a stream
`fopen`	open a stream
`fprintf`	send formatted data to a stream
`fputc`	send a character to a stream
`fputs`	send a string to a stream
`fread`	read a block of data from a stream
`fscanf`	read formatted data from a stream
`fseek`	reposition a stream pointer
`fwrite`	write a block of data to a stream
`fputs`	send a string to a stream
`getw`	read an integer from a stream
`putw`	send an integer to a stream

Some of the important console I/O functions are listed in Table 17.3.

Table 17.3

Function	Purpose
`cgets`	read a string from the console
`clrcsr`	clear text window
`cprintf`	write formatted data to the console
`getch`	read a character from the console
`getche`	read a character from the console and echo it
`gotoxy`	move the cursor to a specified location
`putch`	write a character to the console

Some of the low-level I/O functions are listed in Table 17.4.

Table 17.4

Function	Purpose
`chmode`	read a string from the console
`close`	clear text window
`eof`	write formatted data to the console
`filelength`	read a character from the console
`lseek`	read a character from the console and echo it
`open`	move the cursor to a specified location
`read`	write a character to the console
`setmode`	set mode of a file
`write`	write data to a file

17.6 WORKING WITH FILES USING STREAM I/O

An I/O stream is a sequence of characters flowing from a source to a sink. When the data is read by a program from a device, the device becomes the source which places the data on the stream (see Fig. 17.7). Obviously, the program becomes the sink that receives the data from the stream. While writing the data, the program and device reverse the roles.

A stream is accessed by a stream pointer, as shown in Fig. 17.7. The stream pointer points to the beginning of a stream.

A file is opened as a stream with the help of a pointer of type `FILE`. Having opened the file, it is accessed through a pointer in a fashion very similar to accessing an array of strings.

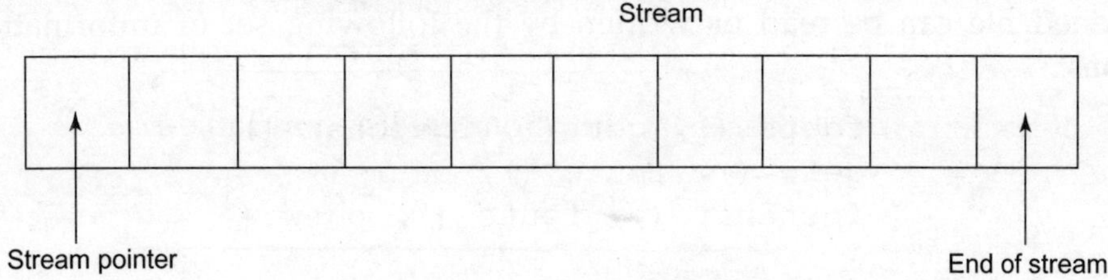

Fig. 17.7 Working of a stream

17.6.1 Opening of a File

A file can be opened in stream I/O by using function called `fopen()`. It takes two arguments: file name and type of operation (see Table 17.5). The `fopen ()` function returns a pointer of type `FILE`.

Thus, a file (say "Myfile") can be opened for reading by using the following steps.

STEP 1. Declare a pointer (say `ptr`) of type `FILE` symbol `FIle *ptr;`
STEP 2. Open the file using a stream I/O function called `fopen()`.

```
ptr = fopen ("Myfiles", "r");
```

The above statement requests the system to open a file called "myfile" in read mode and it assigns the pointer to `ptr`.

A file can be closed by a function called `fclose()` which takes one argument of type `FILE`.

Thus, the file ("Myfile") can be closed by the following statement.

```
fclose (prt);
```

Table 17.5 File opening modes

Mode	Purpose
"r"	Open a file for reading. If the file does not exist, NULL is returned.
"w"	Open a file for writing. It the file does not exist, a new file is created. If the file exists, the new contents overwrite the previous contents.
"r+"	Open the file for both reading and writing. If the file doesn't exist, NULL is returned.
"w+"	Open the file for both reading and writing. If the file does not exist, the previous contents are overwritten by the new one.
"a"	Open a file for appending. If the file exists, the new data is written at the end of the file else the new file is created.
"a+"	Open the file for reading and appending. If the file doesn't exist, a new file is created.

17.6.2 Unformatted File I/O Operations

An opened file can be read or written by the following set of unformatted I/O functions:

```
fgets (), get (), fgetchar ()
getw (), fputc (), putc ()
fputchar (), fputs (), putw ()
```

A brief description of each function has been provided in Table 17.2.

Let us consider a situation wherein we desire to create a file called "message.dat" containing the following text:

"when one apple fell, Newton was disturbed;
but when he found that all apples fell;
it was gravitation and he was satisfied".

The file "message.dat" would be opened with the help of the `fopen ()` function and the function `fputs ()` would be used to write a line in the file. The `fputs ()` function requires two arguments as shown below:

```
fputs (<string>, <file-pointer>)
```

where `<string>` : is string of characters to be written in the file
`<file-pointer>` : is the pointer to the file in which the text is to be written

The required program is given below:

```
# include <stdio.h>
main()
  {
   FILE *ptr;
   ptr = fopen("message.dat","w");

   if (!ptr)
     {
     printf ("\n The file cannot be opened");
     exit(1);
     }
   fputs( "when an apple fell, Newton was disturbed\n", ptr);
   fputs ("but when he found that all apples fell, \n", ptr);
   fputs ( "it was gravitation and he was satisfied",ptr);

   fclose (ptr);
  }
```

The above program is simple wherein the first statement of function `main ( )` declares a pointer to a FILE and in the second statement a file called "message.dat" is opened in write mode. The next compound statement checks whether the operation was successful or not. The rest of the statements write the text line by line in the file. The last statement closes the file.

A string from a file can be read by a function called `fgets ()`. This function requires three arguments as shown below:

```
fgets (<string>, n, <file-pointer>)
```

where `<string>` :is the character string i.e., an array of `char` in which a group of characters from the file would be read.

`n` : is the number of characters to be read from the file. The function reads a string of characters until the first new line ("\n") character is encountered or until the number of characters read is equal to n-1.

`<file-pointer>` :is the pointer to the file from which the text is to be read.

The end of a file can be detected by a function called `feof (<file.pointer>)`. This function can be used in a situation where a program needs to read the whole of the file. For example, the following program uses the `feof ()` and `fgets ()` functions to read the "message_data" file till the end of the file is encountered. The strings read from the file are displayed on the screen.

```
#include<stdio.h>
main()
{
char text[80];
FILE*ptr;
Ptr=fopen("message.dat","r");
if(!ptr)
{
printf("\n the file cannot be opened");
exit(1);
}
while(!feof(ptr))
{
fgets(text,80,ptr);
printf("\ %s",text);
}
fclose(ptr);
}
```

Similarly the functions `fgetc ()` and `fputc ()` functions can be used to read from or write a character to a file. The function `fputc ()` takes two arguments i.e., a character variable, and the file pointer whereas the function `fgetc ()` takes only one arguments i.e, the file pointer.

For example: **`ch= fgetc (ptr)`** - reads a character in `ch` from a file pointed to by the pointer called `ptr`.

`fputc(ch, ptr)` - writes a character stored in `ch` to a file pointed to by the pointer called `ptr`.

Example 1

Write a program that copies the file called "message.dat" to another file called "new. dat".

Solution

The above program can be written by using the steps given overleaf.

Step:

1. Open "message.dat" for reading.
2. Open "new.dat" for writing.
3. Read a character from "message.dat". If the character is "eof" then go to Step 5.
4. Write the character in "new.dat". Go to Step 3.
5. Close "message.dat" and "new.dat".

The required program is given below:

```
# include <stdio.h>
# include <conio.h>
main()
 {
  FILE *ptr1, *ptr2;
  char ch;
  ptr1 = fopen("message.dat","r");


  if (!ptr1)
    {
     printf ("\n The file %s cannot be opened", "message.
     dat");
    exit(1);
    }

  ptr2 = fopen("new.dat","w");
   if (!ptr2)
    {
     printf ("\n The file %s cannot be opened", "new.dat");
    exit(1);
    }
  clrscr();
  while (!feof(ptr1))
  {
   ch = fgetc (ptr1);
   fputc( ch, ptr2);
   }
  fclose (ptr1);
  fclose (ptr2);
  }
```

The efficacy of the above program can be verified by opening the file "new.dat" either in Notepad or in the Turbo-C editor.

It may be noted that till now we have used programs which are rigid in nature i.e., the programs work on particular files. For instance, the above program works on "message.dat" and "new.dat" files and will not work with other files. This situation can be easily handled by taking the name of the file from the user at run time. Consider the program segment given below:

```
.
.
.
char filename [20];
FILE *ptr;
printf("\n Enter the Name of the file to open for reading)";
scanf("%s",filename);
ptr=fopen(filename,"r");
.
.
.
```

The above program asks the user for the name of the file to be opened, giving the user freedom to opt for any of the available files or to provide an altogether new name for a file.

Example 2

Write a program that asks the user for the file to be opened and then displays the contents of the file.

Solution

The required program is given below:

```
# include <stdio.h>
# include <conio.h>
main()
   {
    char filename[20],ch;
    FILE *ptr;
    printf ("\n Enter the name of the file to be opened for
    reading:");
    scanf("%s",filename);
    ptr = fopen(filename,"r");
    if (!ptr)
       {
        printf ("\n The file %s cannot be opened", filename);
       exit(1);
```

```
    }
    clrscr();
  while ((ch=fgetc(ptr)) != EOF )
    printf ("%c",ch);
  fclose (ptr);
  }
```

Sample Input: `Enter the name of the file to be opened for reading: new.dat`

Output:

```
when an apple fell, Newton was disturbed ;
but when he found that all apples fell;
it was gravitation and he was satisfied.
```

It may be noted that in the above program, instead of `feof ()`, the keyword `EOF` has been used to detect the end of file. This is another method of doing the same thing. In fact, it is especially useful where a file has to be read character by character, as was the case in the above program.

Example 3

Write a program that reads a file of numbers and sorts the numbers in ascending order. The sorted numbers are stored in a new file.

Solution

Assume that the input file (say "datafile.dat" contains the numbers which need to be sorted. The `getw ()` function would be used to read the numbers from the file into an array of integers called `List`. The sorted list of numbers would be finally stored in an output file (say "sorted file.dat").The required program is given below:

```
/* This program reads a file of numbers, sorts them and
   writes the sorted list into a new file          */

   void sort (int List[100], int N);
   # include <stdio.h>
   main()
     {
       FILE  *infile, *outfile;
       int List[100];
       int i,j, Num;
       char input_file[20], output_file[20];
```

```
    printf ("\n Enter the name of Input file:");
    scanf("%s", input_file);
    printf ("\n Enter the name of output file:");
    scanf("%s", output_file);

    infile = fopen (input_file, "r");
    if (! infile)
   {
   printf ("\n The file %s cannot be opened", input_file);
   exit(1);
   }
    outfile = fopen (output_file, "w");
    if (! outfile)
   {
   printf ("\n The file %s cannot be opened", output_file);
   exit(1);
   }
                        /* read the input file         */
 i = -1;
 while (!feof(infile))
   { i++;
     Num = getw( infile);

                        /* Do not include EOF */
       if(! feof(infile)) List[i] = Num;
     }
                       /* Sort the list */
  sort(List, i);
                         /* write into the output file */
  for (j =0; j<=i; j++)
      putw(List[j],outfile);

  fclose(infile);
  fclose (outfile);
  }
   void sort (int List[100], int N)
  {
   int i, j,small, pos,temp;
     for (i = 0; i < N-1; i++)
       {
      small = List[i];
      pos = i;
        for (j = i+1; j< N; j++)
```

```
        {
          if (List [j] < small)
            {
             small = List[j];
             pos = j;
            }
        }
      temp = List[i];
      List[i] =List[pos];
      List[pos] = temp;
      }
    }
```

Note: The files created in the above program cannot be verified by opening in a text editor like Notepad. The reason is that the functions: `getw()` and `putw()`, read and write the numbers in a file in a format that is different from text format.

Therefore, a file consisting of numbers can be written and read by the `getw()` function. The following program can be used to create the datafile.dat.

```
# include <stdio.h>
main()
 {
  FILE *ptr;
  int val,i;
  ptr = fopen("datafile.dat", "w");
  do
   {
    printf ("\n Enter a value");
     scanf ("%d", &val);
     if (val != -9999) putw(val,ptr);
   }
   while (val != -9999);
  fclose(ptr);
 }
```

The numbers are written in the file as long as the system does not encounter - 9999, a number used to identify the end of the list.

Similarly, the following program can be used to see the contents of a file (say "sortedfile.dat").

```
# include <stdio.h>
main()
 {
  FILE *ptr;
  int val,i;
```

```
ptr = fopen("sortedfile.dat", "r");
printf ("\n");
while (!feof (ptr))
  {
   val =getw(ptr);
  if (!feof(ptr)) printf ("%d ",val); /*Do not print EOF*/
  }
 fclose(ptr);
}
```

It may be further noted that both the programs take care that the `EOF` (a number) does not get included into the list of numbers being manipulated by them.

17.6.3 Formatted file I/O Operations

C supports `fscanf ()` and `fprintf ()` functions to read to or write from files. The general format of these functions is given below:

```
fscanf (<file pointer>, <format string>, <argument list>);
fprintf (<file pointer>, <format string>, <argument list>);
```

where `<file pointer>`: is the pointer to the file in which I/O operations are to be done.

`<format string>`: is the list of format specifiers i.e.%d, %f, %s etc.

`<argument list>`: is the list of arguments.

Example 4

Write a program that takes a list of numbers from the user through a standard input device, i.e., keyboard. The number `-9999` marks the end of the list. The list is then written on a user defined file by using the `fprintf ()` function.

Solution

The required program is given below:

```
# include stdio.h
main()
{
   FILE *ptr;
   int val,i;
   char outfile[20];
   printf ("\n Enter the name of the file :");
   scanf("%s", outfile);
   ptr = fopen(outfile, "w");
  do
   {
   printf ("\n Enter a value");
```

```
scanf ("%d", &val);
if (val != -9999) fprintf (ptr, "%d ", val);
        }
            while (val != -9999);
             fclose(ptr);
        }
```

Example 5

Use the file created in Example 4. Read the list of numbers contained in the file using the `fscanf()` function. Print the largest number in the list.

Solution

The numbers from the file would be read one by one and compared for the largest. After `EOF`, the largest number would be displayed.

The required program is given below:

```
# include stdio.h
main()
  {
  FILE *ptr;
  int val,i, large;
  char infile[20];
  printf ("\n Enter the name of the
  file:");
            scanf ("%s", infile);
            ptr = fopen(infile, "r");
            printf ("\n The list is ...");
            large = -9999;
            while (1)
                {
                    fscanf(ptr,"%d", &val);
                    if (feof(ptr)) break;
                    printf ("%d ",val);
                    if (large  val ) large
                    = val;
                }
                printf ("\nThe largest is :
                %d", large);
                fclose(ptr);
            }
```

Sample output:

```
Enter the name of the file: Mydata.dat
The list is 12 34 56 78 32 41 21 13
The largest is = 78.
```

17.6.4 Reading or Writing Blocks of Data in Files

A block of data such as an array or a structure can be written to a file by using the `fwrite ()` function. Similarly the block of data can be read from the file using the `fread ()` function.

The general function of `fread ()` and `fwrite ()` functions is given below:

```
fread (<address of object>, <size of object>, <number of
items>, <file pointer>);
fwrite(<address of object>, <size of object>, <number of
items>, <file pointer>);
```

where `<address of object>` : is the address or pointer to the object from which the data is to be read/written on the file.

`<size of object>` : the size of the object is computed by the function `size of ()` and included in the argument list

`<number of items>` : the number of data items to be read or written. Generally it is set as 1.

`<file pointer>` : is the pointer to the file from which data is to beread or written.

Let us now try to write the following structure in to a file (say `test.dat`).

```
struct stud {
char name [20];
int roll;
};
```

The following statements can be used to do the required task.

```
File *ptr;
struct stud {
char name [20];
int roll;
};
struct stud ob = {"Ram", 101};
ptr = fopen ("test.dat", "w");
fwrite (& ob, size of (struct stud), 1, ptr);
fclose (ptr);
```

A similar code can be written to read the structure from a file.

A complete program that writes a structure into a file and then reads and displays it, is given below:

```
# include <stdio.h>
main()
 { FILE *ptr;
   struct stud {
     char name[20];
     int roll;
     };
    struct stud ob1;
    struct stud ob ={"ram",101};
    ptr = fopen("test.dat", "w");
    fwrite (&ob, sizeof (struct stud), 1, ptr);
    fclose(ptr);
    ptr = fopen("test.dat", "r");
    fread (&ob1, sizeof (struct stud), 1, ptr);
    fclose(ptr);
    printf ("\n %s", ob1.name);
    printf ("\n %d", ob1.roll);
 }
```

Example 6

Write a program that creates a file called "Marks.dat" and writes into it the records of all the students in the same class.

Solution

The required program is given below:

```
#include <stdio.h>
struct student {
    char name[20];
    int roll;
    int marks;
    };
main()
  { FILE * ptr;
    struct student studob;
    int t = sizeof (struct student);
    ptr = fopen ("marks.dat", "w");
    printf ("\n Enter the student data terminated by roll =
    -9999");
```

```
    while (1)
    {
      printf ("\nName :"); scanf("%s", studob.name);
      printf ("\nRoll :"); scanf("%d", &studob.roll);
      if (studob.roll == -9999) break;
      printf ("\nmarks :"); scanf("%d", &studob.marks);
      fwrite(&studob, t, 1, ptr);
      }

    fclose (ptr);
}
```

Example 7

A file called `Marks.dat` contains the records of students, having the following structure

```
struct student
      {
      char name [20]
      int roll;
      int marks

      };
```

Write a program that reads `Marks` and creates following two files.

1. "Pass.dat" should contains the roll numbers of students scoring more than or equal to pass marks stored in a variable called `pass_marks`.
2. "FAIL.dat" Should contain the roll numbers of students scoring below the pass marks.

Solution

The required program is given below:

```
#include <stdio.h>
struct student {
    char name[20];
    int roll;
    int marks;
    };
main()
 { FILE * ptr, *p, *f;
     struct student studob;
     int pass_marks;
     int t = sizeof (struct student);
```

```
    ptr = fopen ("marks.dat", "r");
    p = fopen("pass.dat", "w");
    f = fopen ("fail.dat", "w");
    printf ("\n Enter the passing parks :");
    scanf ("%d", &pass_marks);
    while (!feof(ptr))
      {
    fread(&studob,t,1,ptr);
    if (feof(ptr)) break;
        if( studob.marks >= pass_marks)
         fprintf (p, "%d ", studob.roll);
        else
         fprintf (f,"%d ", studob.roll);
    }
     fclose (ptr);
     fclose (p);
     fclose(f);
}
```

Example 8

Write a program that opens the `pass.dat` and `fail.dat` files created in the above program and displays two separate lists of roll numbers that have passed and failed in the examination.

Solution

The required program is given below:

```
#include <stdio.h>
main()
  {  int roll;
     FILE  *p, *f;
    p = fopen("pass.dat", "r");
    if (! p)
      {
    printf ("\n The file %s cannot be opened", "pass.dat");
    exit(1);
        }

    f = fopen ("fail.dat", "r");
    if (! f)
      {
    printf ("\n The file %s cannot be opened", "fail.dat");
```

```
exit(1);
   }
printf ("\n The list of pass students :");
while (! feof(p))
 {
fscanf(p,"%d", &roll);
if (!feof(p)) printf ("%d ", roll);
roll = getch();
   }
printf ("\n The list of fail students :");
while (! feof(f))
   {
fscanf(f,"%d", &roll);
if (!feof(f)) printf ("%d ", roll);
   }
 fclose (p);
 fclose(f);
}
   }
```

17.7 SEQUENTIAL FILE ORGANIZATION

This file organization is the simplest way to store and retrieve records in a file. In this kind of file, the records are stored in a meaningful order according to a keyfield. The first record in the order is placed at the beginning of the file. The second record is stored right after the first, the third after the second and so on. However, the records may be ordered in ascending or descending order by the key field, which can be numeric (such as student roll number) or alphabetic (such as student name). It may be noted that the order never changes afterwards. The arrangement of records in a sequential file is shown in Fig. 17.8.

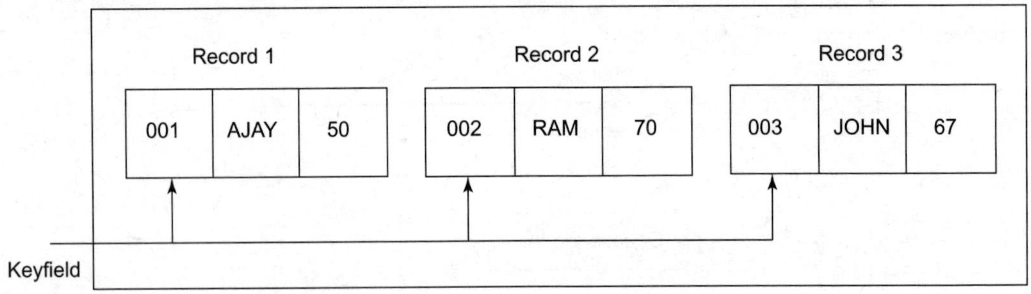

Fig. 17.8 Arrangement of records in a file

Since all records in the file are stored according to position, the records can be identified by the key field only.

17.7.1 Creating a Sequential File

A sequential file can be created on a storage device (magnetic tape or disk) by the following three steps:

1. A name is chosen for the file. The system is requested to open a file on the storage device with the chosen file-name.
2. The records for the file are input one by one into the computer which in turn stores them in the order of their arrival, on to the file.
3. After all the records are transferred into the file, the system is requested to close the file.

A flowchart given in Fig. 17.9 illustrates this process. The above listed steps are executed with the help of a program written in a high level language. All the high level languages such as BASIC, FORTRAN, PASCAL, C etc. support sequential files.

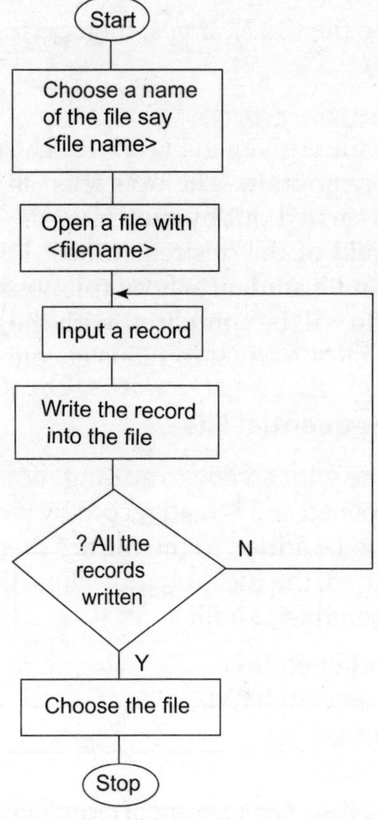

Fig. 17.9 Creating a sequential file

17.7.2 Reading and Searching a Sequential File

Let us say that student data of a school is maintained in a file (say `stud.data`). Let us assume that on a particular day, the principal of the school requires some information from the file called `stud.dat`. Now, the obvious step is to read the file to get the required information. The read operation for a sequential file is explained below.

To read a sequential file, the system always starts at the beginning of the file and the records are read one by one till the required record is reached or the end of the file is encountered. The end of the file (`EOF`) indicates that all the records in the file have been read. For instance, if the desired record happens to be the 50th one in a file, the system starts at the first record and reads ahead one record at a time until the 50th record is reached.

The reading of a file involves the following operations

1. Open the file.
2. Read a record.
3. Check if the record is the desired one. If yes, then display information and perform Step 6.
4. Check for the end of the file (`EOF`). If yes, then perform Step 6.
5. Go to step 2.
6. Close the file.

A flowchart for reading a file is given in Fig. 17.10. The process shown in Fig. 17.10 is done through a computer program. The operation in Step 3, i.e., to check if the record is the desired one, is carried out by matching the keyfield of the record read from the file with the keyfield of the desired record. For example, if the principal requires the information about a student whose roll no is 125 then the `ROLL` field of each record read from the file will be compared with the value 125. The process will be repeated till a record with `ROLL` equal to 125 is encountered.

17.7.3 Appending to a Sequential File

The append operation is done with a view to adding more records to an existing file. In this operation, the file is opened and is read record by record till `EOF` is encountered. The new records which are to be added to the file are then written into the file. Once all the records have been added, the file is closed. Thus, the following operations are done for the purpose of appending to a file

1. Open the file for append operation.
2. Read the file till EOF is encountered.
3. Read the record to be added.
4. Write the record on the file.
5. Close the file.

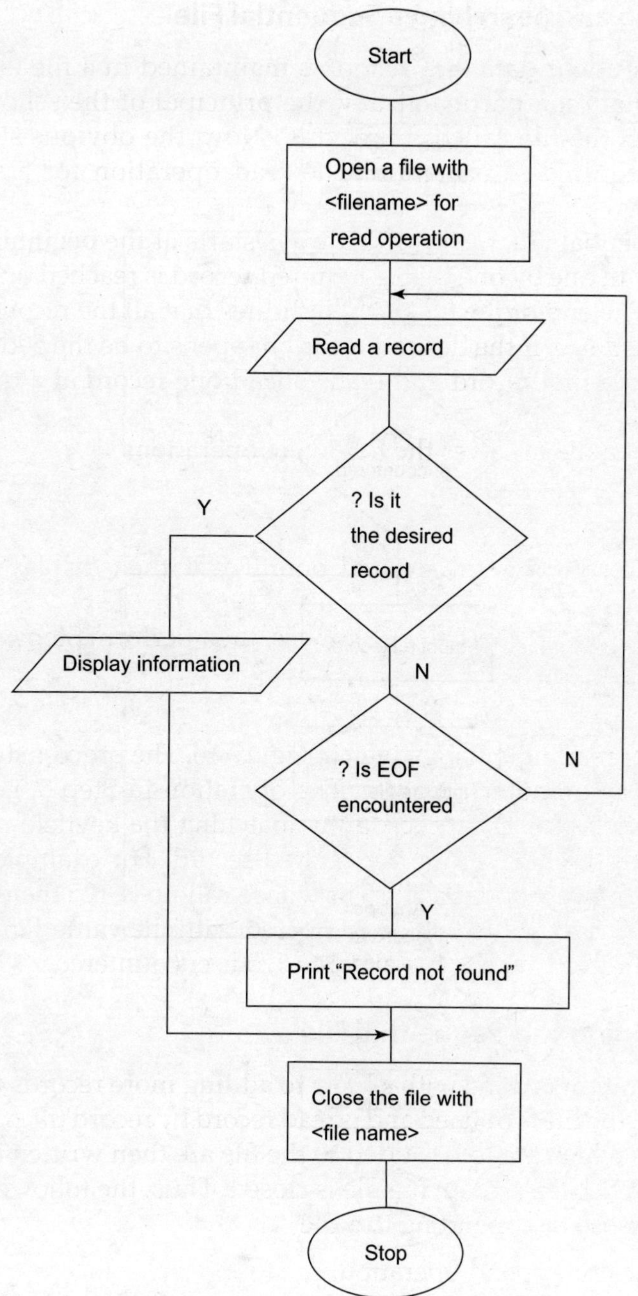

Fig. 7.10 Reading a sequential file

A flowchart for appending to a file is given in Fig. 17.11.

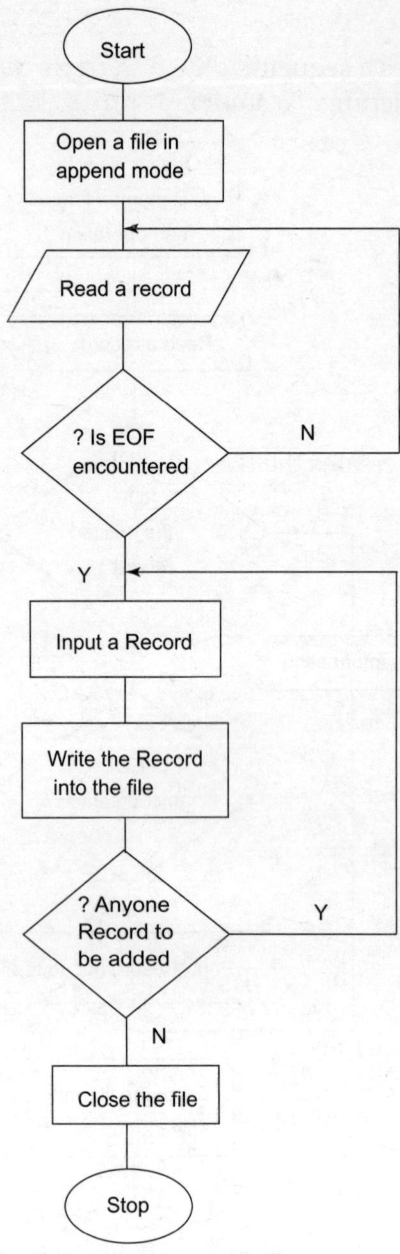

Fig. 17.11 Appending a sequential file

Example 9

Write a program that creates a sequential file of records of students who are players of different games. The structure of a student record is given below:

```
struct student
    {
    char name [20]
    int roll;
    char class [5];
    char game [15];
    };
```

Solution

The required program that creates the file (say "Play_Master.dat") is given below:

```
/* This program creates a sequential file */

# include <stdio.h>
struct student {
  char name[20];
  int roll;
  char class[5];
  char game[15];
  };
 main()
   {
    FILE *ptr;
  char myfile[15];
    int t = sizeof(struct student);
    struct student studrec;
    printf ("\nEnter the name of the file:");
    scanf("%s",myfile);
    ptr = fopen (myfile,"w");
   printf ("\nEnter the records of the students one by one");
    studrec.roll=0;
    while (studrec.roll !=-9999)
      {
    printf ("\nName:"); fflush(stdin); gets(studrec.name);
    printf ("\nRoll:"); scanf("%d",&studrec.roll);
    printf ("\nClass:"); fflush(stdin); gets(studrec.class);
    printf ("\nGame:"); fflush(stdin); gets(studrec.game);
    if (studrec.roll != -9999)
         fwrite(&studrec, t, 1, ptr);
      }
     fclose (ptr);
    }
```

Example 10

Write a program that uses "Play_Master.dat" created in Example 9. For a given game, it displays the data of all the students who play that game.

Solution

The required program is given below:

```
* This program searches a sequential file */

# include <stdio.h>
struct student {
  char name[20];
  int roll;
  char class[5];
  char game[15];
  };
 main()
   {
    FILE *ptr;
    char game[15], myfile[15];
    int t = sizeof(struct student);
    struct student studrec;
    printf ("\nEnter the name of the file to be opened");
    scanf("%s",myfile);
    ptr = fopen (myfile,"r");
    printf ("\n Enter the name of the game:");
  fflush(stdin);
    gets(game);

    fread(&studrec,t,1,ptr);
    while (!feof(ptr))
       {
    if (! strcmp( game, studrec.game))

      { printf ("\nName =%s", studrec.name);
        printf ("\nRoll =%d", studrec.roll);
        printf ("\nclass =%s", studrec.class);
        printf ("\nGame =%s", studrec.game);
      }
    fread(&studrec,t,1,ptr);
       }
     fclose(ptr);
   }
```

Example 11

Write a program that opens the `Play_Master` file and appends records in the file till roll = -9999 is not encountered.

Solution

The required program is given below:

```
/* This program appends records in  a sequential file */

# include <stdio.h>
struct student {
  char name[20];
  int roll;
  char class[5];
  char game[15];
  };
 main()
   {
    FILE *ptr;
    char myfile[15];
    int t = sizeof(struct student);
    struct student studrec;
    printf ("\nEnter the name of the file:");
    scanf("%s",myfile);
    ptr = fopen (myfile,"r+");
    printf ("\nEnter the records to be appended ");
    while (!feof (ptr))
      fread(&studrec,t,1,ptr);
    studrec.roll=0;

    while (studrec.roll !=-9999)
      {
    printf ("\nName:"); fflush(stdin); gets(studrec.name);
    printf ("\nRoll:"); scanf("%d",&studrec.roll);
    printf ("\nClass:"); fflush(stdin); gets(studrec.class);
    printf ("\nGame:"); fflush(stdin); gets(studrec.game);
    if (studrec.roll != -9999)
          fwrite(&studrec, t, 1, ptr);
      }
     fclose (ptr);
    }
```

It may be noted that in the above program, the file was opened in "r+" mode. In fact, the same job can be done by opening the file in "a" mode, that is, append mode. The following program uses this mode:

```
/* This program appends records in  a sequential file */

# include <stdio.h>
struct student {
  char name[20];
  int roll;
  char class[5];
  char game[15];
  };
 main()
   {
    FILE *ptr;
    char myfile[15];
    int t = sizeof(struct student);
    struct student studrec;
    printf ("\nEnter the name of the file:");
    scanf("%s",myfile);
    ptr = fopen (myfile,"a");
    printf ("\nEnter the records to be appended ");
    studrec.roll=0;
    while (studrec.roll !=-9999)
      {
    printf ("\nName:"); fflush(stdin); gets(studrec.name);
    printf ("\nRoll:"); scanf("%d",&studrec.roll);
    printf ("\nClass:"); fflush(stdin); gets(studrec.class);
    printf ("\nGame:"); fflush(stdin); gets(studrec.game);
    if (studrec.roll != -9999)
         fwrite(&studrec, t, 1, ptr);
      }
     fclose (ptr);
    }
```

Example 12

Modify the previous program so that it displays the contents of a file before and after the records are appended to the file.

Solution

A function called `show ()` will be used to display the contents of the file. The required program is given overleaf:

```
/* This program displays the contents before and after it
appends records in  a sequential file */

# include <stdio.h>
void show(FILE *p, char x[15]);
struct student {
  char name[20];
  int roll;
  char class[5];
  char game[15];
  };
 main()
   {
    FILE *ptr;
    char myfile[15];
    int t = sizeof(struct student);
    struct student studrec;
    printf ("\nEnter the name of the file:");
    scanf("%s",myfile);
    printf("\n The Records before append");
    show(ptr, myfile);
    ptr = fopen (myfile,"a");
    printf ("\nEnter the records to be appended ");
    studrec.roll=0;
    while (studrec.roll !=-9999)
      {
    printf ("\nName:"); fflush(stdin); gets(studrec.name);
    printf ("\nRoll:"); scanf("%d",&studrec.roll);
    printf ("\nClass:"); fflush(stdin); gets(studrec.class);
    printf ("\nGame:"); fflush(stdin); gets(studrec.game);
    if (studrec.roll != -9999)
         fwrite(&studrec, t, 1, ptr);
      }
     fclose (ptr);
     printf("\n The Records after append");
     show(ptr,myfile);
    }
   void show(FILE *p, char myfile[15])
    {
     struct student studrec;
     p=fopen(myfile,"r");
     fread(&studrec, sizeof(studrec),1,p);
```

```
   while (!feof(p))
     {
    printf ("\nName:"); fflush(stdout); puts(studrec.name);
  printf ("\nRoll:"); printf("%d",studrec.roll);
  printf ("\nClass:"); fflush(stdout); puts(studrec.class);
  printf ("\nGame:"); fflush(stdout); puts(studrec.game);
     fread(&studrec, sizeof(studrec),1,p);
     }
     fclose(p);
    }
```

17.7.4 Updating a Sequential File

The updation of a file means that the file is made up-to-date with the latest changes relating to it. The original file is known as a Master file or Old Master file and the temporary file which contains the changes or transactions is known as a Transaction file. Examples of transactions are: making purchases, payment for purchases, total sales in the day etc.

In order to update a sequential file, the transactions are sorted according to the same key as used for the old Master file, i.e., both the files are sorted in the same order on the same key. Thus the Master file and the Transaction file become co-sequential. A new file called New Master file is opened for writing. The Old Master file and the Transaction file are merged according to the following logic:

"The key of the record from the Transaction file is compared with key of the record from the Old Master file. If identical, the Transaction record is written on the New Master file. Otherwise the Master record is written on the New Master file".

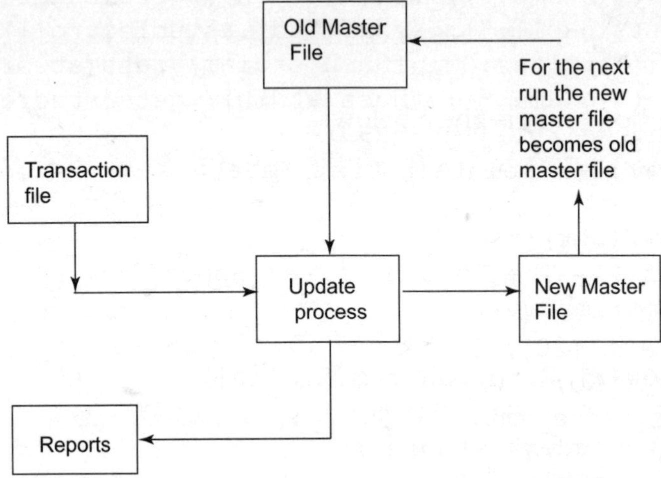

Fig. 17.12

Example 13

A file called `old master` of a bank contains the records of the Savings fund A/C of its customers in ascending order of A/C numbers. The format of the record is given below:

```
Name
ACNT-No
Balance-Amt
```

A file called `transaction file` contains the details of transactions done on the accounts on a particular day. It also contains the records in ascending order of A/C numbers. Each record of that file has following format:

```
ACNT-No
Trans-type
Trans-amt
```

The field `Trans-amt` contains the amount withdrawn from or deposited in the A/C depending upon the value of `Trans-type` being 0 or 1 respectively. Write a program that reads the two files and does the transaction processing giving a third file called `new master`.

Solution

In this program, the following Menu would be displayed so that the possible actions can be conveniently carried out by the user.

Menu	
Create old master file	0
Create transaction file	1
Generate New Master file	2
Show contents of a file	3
Quit	4

The required program is given below:

```
/* This program maintains the Saving A/C of a Bank   */

# include <stdio.h>
# include <conio.h>
struct Acnt_Rec {
   char name [20];
   int Acnt_No;
   float Balance_Amt;
   };
 struct Trans_Rec {
   int Acnt_No;
```

```
    int Trans_type;
    float Trans_Amt;
    };
 void creat_T(char Trans[15]);
 void creat_O(char O_master[15]);
  void  creat_N(char  O_master[15],char  Trans[15],  char  N_
  master[15]);
  void showfile(char fname[15],int f_type);
  main()
    {
     struct Acnt_Rec Acntob;
     struct Trans_Rec Transob;
     char O_master[15], N_master[15], Trans[15], fname[15];
     int choice, f_type;
                  /* Show Menu  */
    do
      { clrscr();
     printf("\nMenu");
     printf ("\n");
     printf ("\n Create Oldmaster   file          0");
     printf ("\n Create Transaction file          1");
     printf ("\n Create Newmaster   file          2");
     printf ("\n Show Contents of a file          3");
     printf ("\n Quit                              4");
     printf ("\nEnter your choice :"); scanf ("%d", &choice);

     switch (choice)
       {
       case 0 : clrscr();
             printf ("\n Enter the name of the file");
             fflush(stdin); gets(O_master); creat_O(O_master);
             break;
       case 1 : clrscr();
             printf ("\n Enter the name of the file");
 fflush(stdin); gets(Trans); creat_T(Trans);
             break;
       case 2 : clrscr();
             printf ("\n Enter the name of Oldmaster file");
             fflush(stdin); gets(O_master);
             printf ("\n Enter the name of Newmaster file");
             fflush(stdin); gets(N_master);
             printf ("\n Enter the name of Transaction file");
```

```
        fflush(stdin); gets(Trans);
        creat_N(O_master,Trans, N_master);
        break;
    case 3 : printf ("\nEnter the name of the file to be
    displayed");
       fflush(stdin); gets(fname);
        printf ("\n Enter 0/1 for Master/Transaction");
        scanf ("%d", &f_type); showfile(fname,f_type);
        break;
   }
   }
     while (choice != 4);
   }

void creat_O(char O_master[15])
   {
   FILE *ptr;
   struct Acnt_Rec Aob;
   int t = sizeof(Aob);
   ptr = fopen (O_master,"w");
   printf ("\nEnter the records one by one terminated by A/c
   = -9999");
   Aob.Acnt_No=0;

   while (Aob.Acnt_No != -9999)
     {
      printf ("\nName:"); fflush(stdin); gets(Aob.name);
       printf ("\nA/C No:"); scanf("\n%d", &Aob.Acnt_No);
       printf  ("\nBalance  Amount:");  scanf("\n%f",  &Aob.
       Balance_Amt);
       if (Aob.Acnt_No != -9999) fwrite (&Aob,t,1,ptr);
      }
      fclose(ptr);
   }

 void creat_T(char Trans[15])
 { FILE *ptr;
   struct Trans_Rec Aob;
   int t = sizeof(Aob);
   ptr = fopen (Trans,"w");
   printf ("\nEnter the records one by one terminated by A/c
   = -9999");
```

```
    Aob.Acnt_No=0;

    while (Aob.Acnt_No != -9999)
      {
        printf ("\nA/C No:"); scanf("\n%d", &Aob.Acnt_No);
        printf  ("\nTransaction  Type  (0/1):");  scanf("\n%d",
        &Aob.Trans_type);
    printf  ("\nTransaction  Amount:");  scanf("\n%f",  &Aob.
    Trans_Amt);
        if (Aob.Acnt_No != -9999) fwrite (&Aob,t,1,ptr);
      }
      fclose(ptr);
    }
void    creat_N(char  O_master[15],char  Tran[15],  char  N_
master[15])
    {
     FILE *Old, *New, *Trans;
     struct Acnt_Rec Oob;
     struct Trans_Rec Tob;
     int t1,t2;
     t1 = sizeof (struct Acnt_Rec);
     t2 = sizeof(struct Trans_Rec);
                 /* open files  */
     Old = fopen(O_master,"r");
     Trans = fopen (Tran,"r");
     New = fopen(N_master,"w");


                         /* perform Transaction processing */
     fread(&Oob,t1,1,Old);
   fread(&Tob,t2,1,Trans);
     while (!feof(Old) && !feof(Trans))
       {
        if (Oob.Acnt_No < Tob.Acnt_No)
        {fwrite (&Oob,t1,1,New);
         fread(&Oob,t1,1,Old);
        }
        else
         {
         while ((Oob.Acnt_No == Tob.Acnt_No ) && !feof(Trans))
          {
            if (Tob.Trans_type == 0)
```

```
            Oob.Balance_Amt =Oob.Balance_Amt - Tob.Trans_Amt;
           else
            Oob.Balance_Amt =Oob.Balance_Amt + Tob.Trans_Amt;
           fread(&Tob,t2,1,Trans);

         }
          fwrite (&Oob,t1,1,New);
          fread(&Oob,t1,1,Old);
        }
      }
                 /*Copy rest of the file*/
      while (!feof(Old))
    {
    fwrite (&Oob,t1,1,New);
     fread(&Oob,t1,1,Old);
     }
                 /*Close files */
       fclose(Old);
       fclose(New);
       fclose(Trans);

  }
void showfile(char fname[15],int f_type)
   { FILE *ptr;
    char ch;
      struct Acnt_Rec Aob;
   struct Trans_Rec Tob;
      int t1 = sizeof (Aob);
      int t2 = sizeof(Tob);
     if (f_type == 0)
    {
     ptr = fopen (fname, "r");
     fread (&Aob,t1,1,ptr);
     while(!feof(ptr))
       {
         printf ("\nName:"); fflush(stdout); puts(Aob.name);
         printf ("\nA/C No:"); printf("\n%d", Aob.Acnt_No);
         printf  ("\nBalance  Amount:");  printf("\n%f",  Aob.
         Balance_Amt);
         fread (&Aob,t1,1,ptr);
         ch = getch();
       }
```

```
    }
      else
    {ptr = fopen (fname, "r");
     fread (&Tob,t2,1,ptr);
     while(!feof(ptr))
       {
         printf ("\nA/C No:"); printf("\n%d", Tob.Acnt_No);
         printf ("\nTransaction Type :"); printf("\n%d", Tob.
         Trans_type);
         printf ("\nTransaction Amount:"); printf("\n%f", Tob.
         Trans_Amt);
         fread (&Tob,t2,1,ptr);
         ch = getch();
       }
    }
    fclose(ptr);
   }
```

17.8 DIRECT FILE ORGANIZATION

Direct files allow records to be read from or written onto a file without proceeding sequentially from the beginning. In this organization, the records are not stored in sequence. To read or write, an address is first calculated by applying a mathematical function to the key field of the record. The record is then stored at the generated address. The mathematical function is called a Hash function. However, a poor form of direct access can be obtained in C files by using the `fseek ()` function. With the help of this function, the stream file pointer can be positioned at a particular record. It takes three arguments as shown below:

```
fseek (<file pointer>, <offset>, <start-position>)
```

where `<file pointer>` : is the pointer to the file

`<start position` : is the start position of the file. It can have any of the following values.

Value	Meaning
0	The starting position is the beginning of the file.
1.	Use the current file pointer asthe starting position.
2.	The starting position is the end of the file.

`<Offset>` : is the offset i.e., how much the pointer should advance from the starting position.

From Fig. 17.13, it may be noted that the file pointer (`prt`) is positioned at the beginning of the file because the start position is equal to 0 (zero). The offset (i.e., 4) would move the file pointer to the fourth record.

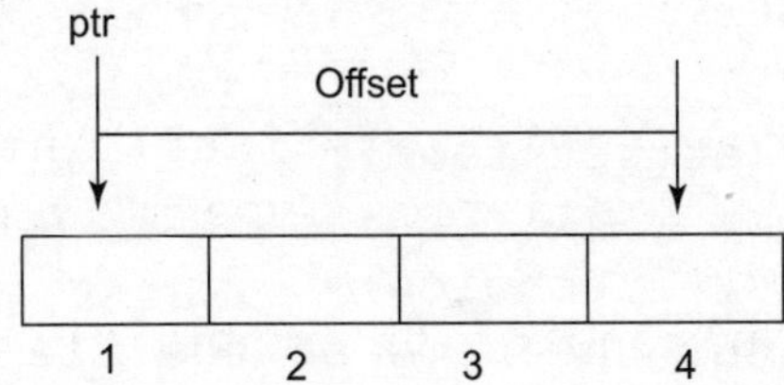

Fig. 17.13 The working of `fseek (ptr, 4, 0)` function

Similarly the `fseek (ptr, 9, 2)` suggests that from the end of the file, move back by 9 records.

Thus, it is a relative file organization wherein the records are accessed directly in relation with the start point, specified within the file. The offset is usually computed by the following formula:

offset = record number * size of a record

Example 14

Write a program that creates a file of room data of a hotel having, following structure. The rooms are numbered starting from 1.

```
struct room
        {
        int room_no;
        char room type;
        char status;
        };
```

where room type may take value S/D i.e., single bed or double bed. Similarly status may take value A/N i.e., available or not. Use `fseek ()` function to display the information about a particular room of the hotel.

Solution

The required program is given below:

```
/* This program uses fseek() function to search
   records in a file                              */

   # include <stdio.h>
   struct room {
    int room_no;
```

```
    char room_type;
    char room_status;
    };
  main()
    {  FILE *ptr;
    char filename[20];
    int t = sizeof(struct room);
    struct room rob;
    int no_of_rooms, i, choice;
    printf ("\n Enter the name of the file");
    fflush(stdin); gets(filename);

    printf("\nEnter the number of rooms");
    scanf("%d",&no_of_rooms);

                              /* create the file   */
    ptr = fopen(filename, "w");
    printf ("\nEnter the room data one by one");
    for  (i =1; i<=no_of_rooms; i++)
      {   rob.room_no=i;
        printf ("\nRoom No. %d :", i);
        printf("\nRoom Type (S/D):");
        fflush(stdin); scanf ("%c",&rob.room_type);
        rob.room_type=toupper(rob.room_type);
        printf("\nRoom_Status (A/N):");
        fflush(stdin); scanf ("%c",&rob.room_status);
        rob.room_status = toupper (rob.room_status);
        fwrite (&rob,t,1,ptr);
      }
      fclose(ptr);
      ptr = fopen(filename,"r");
                              /*search a record */
      do
       {
        printf ("\nMenu");
        printf("\n");
        printf("\nDisplay info                    1");
        printf("\nQuit                            2");
        printf ("\nEnter your choice");
        scanf("%d", &choice);
        if (choice == 1)
           {
          printf ("\n Enter the room no.");
```

```
            scanf("%d", &i);
            fseek(ptr, (i-1) * t, 0);
            fread(&rob, t, 1, ptr);
            clrscr();
            printf ("\nRoom No.= %d", rob.room_no);
            printf ("\nRoom Type = %c", rob.room_type);
            printf ("\nRoom Status= %c", rob.room_status);
            }
          else
            break;
      }
   while (1);
   fclose (ptr);
 }
```

17.9 GRADED PROBLEMS

Problem 1. A macro processor is a text substitution program where the macro consists of a macro name and its definition, as shown below:

Macro name	**Macro Definition (replacement text)**
YMCA	YMCA Institute of Engineering

The macro processor replaces all occurrences of macro name in a document by its corresponding definition. Write a program that takes a text in which the macros are defined at the beginning by the statements such as given below. The definitions end by the keyword "MEND".

```
# define       CE      Computer Engineering
# define       PC      Personal computer
MEND
<text of the Document>
```

The program implements the macro processor i.e., reads the macros and their definitions and does the text substitution for each macro call.

Solution: The following data structures would be employed to do the required task.

1. A structure to store a macro name and its definition.

```
struct macro
     {
     char Name [10];
     char Mdef [50];
     };
```

2. An array of structures of type macro to store all macro definitions

```
struct macro Mlist [15]
```

The program would require the following functions:

	Function		Description
1.	`get-taken ()`	:	to read a word from the input text document.
2.	`build-Mtable ()`	:	to build a table of macro names and definitions using the array of structure i.e., `Mlist[ ]`
3.	`writeout ()`	:	write the output to the output text file.

A complete program that does the required task is given below:

```
/* This program implements a macroprocessor, a text substitution
program     */

# include <stdio.h>
struct macro                          /* to store a macro   */
   {
     char Mname[10];
     char Mdef[50];
    };
 FILE *infile, *outfile;
                       /* A function to build Macro table */
 void build_Mtable(struct macro list[15], FILE *ptr);
                       /* function to read a word from input text
                       file */
void get_token (FILE *infile,char token[20], char *break_point
, int *flag);
 char inputfile[15], outputfile[15];
                       /* function to write a word to output text
                       file */
 void writeout(FILE *outfile,char token[20],char ch, struct
 macro Mlist[15]);
 main()
   {
   char token[20];
   char break_point;
   int flag, j;
   char ch;
    struct macro Mlist[15] ;
```

```
printf ("\n Enter the name of input file :");
fflush(stdin); gets(inputfile);
printf ("\n Enter the name of output file :");
fflush(stdin); gets(outputfile);

infile = fopen(inputfile,"r");
outfile = fopen(outputfile,"w");
build_Mtable(Mlist, infile);
flag = 0;
clrscr();
            /* flag == 3 indicates EOF encountered */
while (!feof(infile) && flag != 3)
  { flag=0;
token[0] ='\0';
ch= '';
   get_token(infile,token, &ch, &flag);
   writeout(outfile,token,ch,Mlist);
   }
   fclose(infile);
   fclose(outfile);
 }    /* end of main */

void  get_token(FILE * infile, char token[30], char *break_
pt, int *flag)
   {int i;
 char ch;
 i = -1;
  while (!(*flag))
   { ch = fgetc(infile); if (ch == EOF) { *flag = 3; return;
   }
     switch(ch)
      {                       /* break points for words or
      tokens */
       case '\n':
       case ' ' :
       case ',' :             /* flag == 1 indicates that a
       break point occured */
       case '.' :
       case ';' : *break_pt = ch; *flag = 1; token[++i] =
       '\0';
             break;
       default  : token[++i] = ch;
      }
```

```
        }
      }  /* end of get_token */

  void build_Mtable(struct macro list[15], FILE *ptr)
      {    char token[20], ch1, temp[2];
      int i;
      token[0]='\0';
      i =-1;
      while (strcmp(token,"MEND"))
        { int flag = 0;
          char ch ='';
          get_token(ptr,token, &ch, &flag);
          if (!strcmp(token, "define"))
  { i++;
           flag=0;
           ch='';
           get_token(ptr,token, &ch, &flag);
           strcpy (list[i].Mname, token);
           list[i].Mdef[0]='\0';
           while (ch != '\n')
           { flag=0;
             ch ='';
             get_token(ptr,token, &ch, &flag);
             strcat(list[i].Mdef , token);
             if (ch != '\n')
               {temp[0] = ch;
                temp [1] ='\0';
                strcat(list[i].Mdef , temp);
               }
            }
           }
        }
       i++;                  /* Marks the end of the macro list*/
       strcpy (list[i].Mname,"END");
     } /* end of build_Mtable  */

    void writeout(FILE *outfile,char token[20], char ch,struct
    macro Mlist[15])
      {
       int i = 0;
     while (strcmp(Mlist[i].Mname, "END"))
       {
                     /*  replace macro by its definition  */
```

```
        if (!strcmp(Mlist [i].Mname, token ))
          { fputs(Mlist[i].Mdef, outfile);
         fputc(ch,outfile);
         return;
           };
           i++;
       }
     fputs(token, outfile);
     fputc(ch,outfile);
     }
```

Sample Input:

```
# define ce Computer Engineering
# define ymca YMCA Institute of Engineering
# define aks A. K. Sharma
# define fbd Faridabad
# define MDU Maharishi Dayanand University Rohtak
MEND
```

ymca is an Institute situated in fbd. It is a Govt. of Haryana institute. It is affliated to MDU. The insitute is rated as the best engineeing college. in the state of Haryana. The ce department is the largest department of the institute. aks works in ce as a Professor.

Sample Output:

```
YMCA Institute of Engineering is an Institute situated in
Faridabad. It is a Govt. of Haryana institute. It is affliated
to Maharishi Dayanand University Rohtak. The institute is rated
as the best engineering college in the state of Haryana. The
Computer Engineering department is the largest department of
the institute. A.K. Sharma works in Computer Engineering as a
Professor.
```

Note: The program does not perform syntax checking, i.e., if the terms "define" and "MEND" are misspelled, the program will go haywire.

Problem 2. Statements in BASIC language are written in such a manner that each statement starts with an integer number, as shown below:

```
10 REM This is a sample statement
20 input A, B
30 goto 150
```

```
:
:
:
100 If (x y) goto 20
```

Write a program that reads a file of a BASIC program. For a given offset, it adds the offset to all the statement numbers. The arguments of the `goto` statements should also be modified to keep the program consistent. In fact, this type of activity is done by a loader when it loads a program into the main memory for execution, i.e., it adds the offset of the address of the main memory to all address modifiable parts of the program such as to the `goto` or `jump` statements etc.

Solution: The `get_token()` and `writeout ()` functions of the previous program would be used in this program to read a token and to write the tokens to a given file. The following functions of `stdlib.h` would be used to convert a string to integer and vice versa.

1. `<int> atoi (string)` : This function takes a string of Characters and converts it into an equivalent integer.
2. `void itoa (int, string, <radix>)` : This function converts an integer to an equivalent string; radix is the radix of the integer (such as 2, 10) depending upon the number being binary or decimal.

The required program is given below:

```
/* This program implements a relative loader */

# include <stdio.h>
# include <stdlib.h>
# include <ctype.h>
                  /* function to read a word from input text
                  file */
 void get_token (FILE *infile,char token[20], char *break_
 point , int *flag);
 char inputfile[15], outputfile[15];
                  /* function to write a word to output text
                  file */
 void writeout(FILE *outfile,char token[20],char ch);
 main()
```

```
{
FILE *infile, *outfile;
char token[20];
char last_token[20]="";
char break_point;
int flag, j, temp;
int offset;
char ch, ch1;
 printf ("\n Enter the name of input file :");
 fflush(stdin); gets(inputfile);
 printf ("\n Enter the name of output file :");
 fflush(stdin); gets(outputfile);
 printf ("\n Enter the value of offset (int) :");
 scanf("%d", &offset);

 infile = fopen(inputfile,"r");
 outfile = fopen(outputfile,"w");
 flag = 0;
 clrscr();
 ch1 = '\n';
           /* flag == 3 indicates EOF encountered */
 while (!feof(infile) && flag != 3)
   { flag=0;
 token[0] ='\0';
 ch= '';
    get_token(infile,token, &ch, &flag);

           /* Check if it is a number appearing at the
             beginning of a line or as argument of
              goto statement                          */

if ((isdigit (token [0]) && ch1 =='\n' ) || (isdigit (token
[0]) && (!strcmp(last_token, "goto"))) )
        { temp= atoi(token);
          temp = temp + offset;
          itoa(temp,token,10);
        }
      writeout(outfile,token,ch);
      ch1 = ch;
      strcpy(last_token ,token);
       }
      fclose(infile);
```

```
    fclose(outfile);
  }    /* end of main */

void get_token(FILE * infile, char token[30], char *break_
pt, int *flag)
     {int i;
  char ch;
  i = -1;
    while (!(*flag))
     { ch = fgetc(infile); if (ch == EOF) { *flag = 3; return;
     }
       switch(ch)
        {                         /* break points for words or
        tokens */
         case '\n':
         case ' ' :
         case ',' :     /* flag == 1 indicates that a break
         point occured */
         case '.' :
         case ';' : *break_pt = ch; *flag = 1; token[++i] =
         '\0';
                break;
  default  : token[++i] = ch;
        }
      }
    }  /* end of get_token  */

  void writeout(FILE *outfile,char token[20], char ch)
    {
     fputs(token,outfile);
    fputc(ch,outfile);
    }
```

Sample Input :

10 Rem this is a loader
20 Input A, B
30 If (A 20) goto 20
40 C = A + 5 * 20;
50 if (C 50) goto 100
60 C = C + B
70 go to 50
100 stop

Value of offset = 50

Sample input:

```
60 Rem this is a loader
70 Input A, B
80 If (A  20) goto 70
90 C = A + 5 * 20;
100 if ( C  50 ) goto 150
110 C = C + B
120 go to 50
150 stop
```

EXERCISES

1. What are the different methods of opening a file? Explain in brief.
2. Differentiate between `fwrite` and `fput` functions.
3. How can the end of file be detected? Explain in brief.
4. Write a program which counts the number of records in a given file.
5. Give suitable declarations for the following files:
   (i) A file containing components where each component contains the following information.

   ```
   Name  :    20 characters
   Code  :    integer type
   NET   :    float type
   ```

   (ii) A text file called `Book`.
7. Write a program which creates an exact copy of a given file called `Ofile` in the form of a new file called `Nfile`. Choose appropriate component types for this problem.
8. Write a program which counts the number of times a given alphabet stored in variable `ch` appears in a text file.
9. Write a program which searches a given file for a record equal to an input value of `emp-code`. The component record structure of the file is as given below

Emp code	
Total	

   Choose appropriate data types wherever necessary.
10. Write a program which reads a text file called `document` and generates a table of the frequency count of alphabets appearing in the text. The output should be displayed in the following form

Frequency count

Alphabet Count
A
B
C
.
.
Z

11. A student record is defined as given in Exercise 5. Write a program which reads a file of such records (say `class-file`) and prints the result in the following format.

S.No.	Condition	No. of Students
1	Marks < 50%	xx
2	Marks > 50% and < 60%	xx
3	Marks >= 60% and < 75%	xx
4	Marks >= 75% and < 90%	xx
5	Marks >= 90	xx

(Assume Max marks in each subject = 100),
12. What is `EOF`? Explain its utility.
13. Modify Exercise 11 such that it generates a list of students getting more than 80% marks.
14. Write an interactive menu-driven C program to create a text file and then display the file. Create another text file by converting each line of the newly created text file into a lowercase string. Display the newly created file. In case the number of lines exceeds 22, the file should be displayed one screen at a time.
15. Write an interactive menu-driven C program to create a text file and then display the file. Create another text file by reversing each line of the newly created text file. Display the newly created file. In case the number of lines exceeds 22, the file should be displayed one screen at a time.

CHAPTER

18 Preprocessor

18.1 INTRODUCTION

The concept of preprocessing has been inherited from systems programming. In systems programming it is popularly called known as macro-processing. The preprocessor is basically a **text substitution program.** It is needed by a programmer primarily for the following reasons:

1. Text substitution
2. Faster execution of programs
3. Writing elegant programs.

The C preprocessor is very powerful. It has many directives, and each directive begins with a hash (#) character. The various directives are discussed in the following sections.

18.2 THE # DEFINE DIRECTIVE

This directive is the most important tool for programmers. It performs the macro substitution wherein the user defines a macro consisting of a macro name and its definition. A simple format of this directive is given below:

```
# define <macro>  <substitute>
```

where `#`, `define` : are keywords
`<macro>` : is the name of the macro
`<substitute>` : is the definition of the macro.

Consider the following macro declaration:

```
# define ce Computer Engineering
```

It may be noted that in above declaration, the string 'ce' and 'Computer Engineering' are the *macro name* and *macro definition* respectively. Now the user can use this macro name (ce) in the program as shown below:

```
printf ("\n ce");
```

Now before compilation, the preprocessor will substitute the macro name (i.e., ce) by its definition (i.e.. Computer Engineering) as shown below:

```
printf ("\n Computer Engineering");
```

This activity of substituting the macro name with its definition is called macro expansion.

A macro name can also receive arguments, as depicted by the following macro declaration:

```
# include exchange (x, y)          temp = x; x = y; y = temp
```

Let us now write the following statement:

```
exchange ( val1, val2);
```

The preprocessor will expand the above statement to the following set of statements:

```
temp = vale1; vale1 = val2; vale2 = temp;
```

Example 1

Use the above macro declaration of exchange in a program to swap the contents of two variables val1 and val2 of integer type.

Solution

The required program is given below:

```
/* This program illustrates the activity of macro substitution
   */
# include <stdio.h>
                                        /* macro definition */
# define exchange (x, y)     temp = x; x = y; y = temp

main()
   {
    int val1 = 25;
```

```
int val2 = 35;
int temp;

printf ("\n The values are: %d  %d", val1, val2);

exchange ( val1, val2);      /* macro call */

printf ("\n The exchanged values are: %d %d", val1, val2);
}
```

The output of the program is given below:

```
The values are: 25  35
The exchanged values are: 35  25
```

Thus, we have achieved the following:

1. Instead of defining a small function called `exchange()`, we have used a macro to perform the same task.
2. The program will become a piece of running code as the preprocessor will substitute the macro definition in place of its macro name. Therefore, the program will run faster. Whereas in the case of a function, the program will become slower because of the following overheads involved at run time of the function. Each step in the process will consume following extra time:
   a. Match the function name in the function table.
   b. Store the return address on a stack.
   c. Pass the actual arguments to formal arguments.
   d. Execute the function.
   e. Pick the return address from the stack.
   f. Return control back to the calling program (`main()`) in this case.

The programs can be made more elegant with the help of macros. For instance, let us assume that a program needs to represent various departments of a college by integers, as shown below:

Dept.	No.
Computer Engineering	1
Electrical Engineering	2
Electronics Engineering	3
Mechanical Engineering	4

Consider the following code segment:

```
int  dept, no_of_seats;

if (dept == 1) no_of_seats = 120;
if (dept == 2) no_of_seats = 90;
if (dept == 3) no_of_seats = 120;
if (dept == 4) no_of_seats =100;
         .
         .
```

Now in the above code segment, it is difficult for the reader of the program to correlate the integers 1,2,3,4 with their corresponding departments. Even the programmer has to remember the correlation. Thus, the code segment is less readable.

As mentioned earlier, the programs can be made more elegant by using macros. In fact, the above code can be rewritten and made elegant by introducing suitable macros, as shown below:

```
# define Computer       1
# define Electrical     2
# define Electronics    3
# define Mechanical     4
# define equal           ==

int  dept, no_of_seats;

if (dept equal Computer)       no_of_seats = 120;
if (dept equal Electrical)     no_of_seats = 90;
if (dept equal Electronics)    no_of_seats = 120;
if (dept equal Mechanical)     no_of_seats =100;
```

It may be noted that the above program segment has become highly readable. There is no need to remember the correlation between the integers and the departments. However, the preprocessor will substitute the corresponding integers in place of their macro names before the compilation phase. Thus we have achieved the following:

1. The program at source code level has become highly readable
2. At execution level it is a shorter code because the text strings used for department names (Computer etc.) have been replaced by integers.
3. Even the operator '==' has been given an appropriate name ('`equal`').

Similarly the following macro definitions can be suitably used.

```
# define    GT    >
# define    GE    >=
```

```
# define    LT    <
# define    LE    <=
# define    OR    ||
# define    AND   &&
# define    NOT   !
```

Example 2

Write a program that finds the largest among three given numbers. Use a macro called `greater (x, y)` to determine the greater of the two arguments x and y.

Solution

The required program is given below:

```
/* This program uses a macro to find largest among given three
   numbers */

# include <stdio.h>

# define GT >                              /* macro definition */
# define great(x, y) x GT y ? x: y         /* nested macro */

main()
 {
  int val1, val2, val3, large;
  printf ("\n Enter three numbers");
  scanf ("%d %d %d", &val1, &val2, &val3);
  large = great(val1, val2);
  large = great(large, val3);

  printf ("\n The largest = %d", large);
 }
```

The sample output of the program is given below

```
Enter three numbers 25  78  37

The largest = 78
Enter three numbers 45  37  92

The largest = 92
```

It may be noted that in the above program, nested macros have been used, that is, the macro `great` is using the macro `GT`.

Another popular use of macro substitution is the declaration of the maximum size of arrays, as shown below:

```
# define maxSize  100
.
.
.
int  List [maxSize];
```

The above technique of defining macros for constants is one of the ways of self documentation style of programming. Some more examples of self documentation are given below:

```
1.  # define lineSize 80
    char  text [lineSize];
    getline(text, lineSize);
2.  # define maxSize 20
    int stack[maxSize];
3.  # define buffSize 512
    ptr = (char *)  malloc (buffSize);
```

18.2.1 Manipulating Strings by Macros

Often a programmer needs to convert a text or a parameter into a string constant. This can be done by enclosing the text/ parameter within double quotes as shown below:

Text	string constant
India	"India"
12345	"12345"
HNO234	"HNO234"
12FG67	"12FG67"

The above conversion can also be achieved by suitably using macros. In fact the preprocessor operator '#' can be used as a leading character to the parameter as shown below:

```
# define TS(x) #x
printf  (TS(Hello));
```

The above set of statements would be expanded by preprocessor to the following statement:

```
printf ("Hello");
```

It may be noted that the operator '#' has converted the parameter (Hello) to a string constant ("`Hello`");

Example 3

Write a program that uses a macro called **`textToString`** to print the following message on the screen:

The eyes are the window of the soul

Solution

The required program is given below:

```
# include <stdio.h>

# define textToString(x)   #x

main()
 {
   printf (textToString(The eyes are the window of the soul));
 }
```

The output of the program is:

```
The eyes are the window of the soul
```

Two strings can also be **concatenated** by the '##' operator of the preprocessor. This feature is usefully employed by a compiler for merging of tokens. The activity is called token concatenation or **token pasting**.

Example 4

Write a macro called `tokenPaste` to concatenate two tokens : `Jai` and `Hind` to display the following message:

JaiHind

Solution

The required program is given below:

```
# include <stdio.h>

# define tokenPaste(x,y)   #x ## #y
```

```
main()
 {
   printf (tokenPaste(Jai,Hind));
 }
```

It may be noted that the macro `tokenPaste` has first converted the tokens into strings and then concatenated them into one string as shown by the output of the program, given below:

```
JaiHind
```

18.3 CONDITIONAL COMPILATION

Conditional compilation is used by programmers to allow a section of the code to be compiled or by-passed depending upon a condition being true or false. For example, a programmer may divide the code into two parts – one relevant for an operating system (say Windows) and the second relevant for another operating system (say Linux), as shown in Fig. 18.1

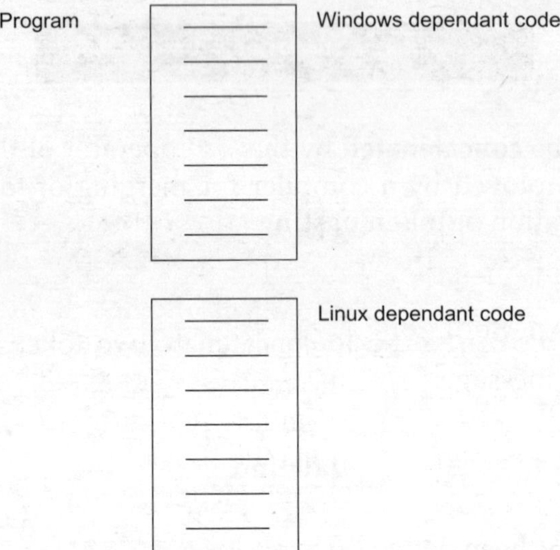

Fig. 18.1 Program containing sections relevant to different operating systems

The preprocessor supports the conditional directive **`Ifdef`** for the purpose of conditional compilation.

The format of conditional compilation is given below:

```
# define   <macName>
             .
             .
             .
#ifdef   <macName>
  Statement sequence1
#else
  Statement sequence2
#endif
```

Where: `<macName>` : is an identifier which would be tested during conditional compilation

`#ifdef` : is equivalent to an `if` construct. It checks whether `<macName>` is defined or not. If defined then the code following `#ifdef` is compiled.

`#else` : is equivalent to an `else` construct. If `<macName>` is not defined then the code followed by `#else` is compiled.

Consider the following program that has two sections after `#ifdef` and `#else`.

```
#include <stdio.h>

#define test

main()
 {
   #ifdef test
     printf ("\n Section 1");
   #else
     printf ("\n Section 2");
   #endif
 }
```

The macro `test` has been defined. Therefore, the code after the `#ifdef` directive would be compiled, as proven by the output given below:

```
Section 1
```

Let us now make the definition of `test`, the macro, a comment line. The modified program is given below. Now, in the absence of definition of test, the code under #else directive would be compiled.

```
#include <stdio.h>

/* #define test */    /* definition of macro commented */

main()
 {
  #ifdef test
    printf ("\n Section 1");
  #else
    printf ("\n Section 2");
  #endif
 }
```

The output of this program is as follows:

```
Section 2
```

Note: `#ifndef <macName>` directive is just an opposite of the `#ifdef <macName>` directive.

18.4 FILE INCLUSION

A header file contains declarations and macro definitions. The preprocessor also processes these header files included at the beginning of a C program. The header files are needed primarily for two reasons:

1. To create an interface for the host operating system.
2. To create interfaces between the various modules of the program.

We know that the input and output statements of a program are never compiled. They are converted into system calls for the operating system. The system header files are needed for invoking these system calls. Thus, system header files create the necessary interfaces with the host operating system.

The programmer can also include his/her own header files which may include declarations. These declarations help in creating interfaces among the various modules of the program.

The `#include` directive of C is used to include header files in a program, as discussed I the following text.

`#include <filename>`: When the header file name is included in angled brackets (<, >) then the header file is supposed to be a system file. This file is searched for in the corresponding standard system directory, that is, the default include directory.

Example:

- # include <stdio.h>
- # include <ctype.h>

`# include "filename"` : When the file name is included in a pair of double quotes (",") then the file is considered to be a user header file. It is searched for first in the current directory and if not found there, then in the system directories.

Example:

- # include "C:\interfaces\myfile.c"
- # include "C:\interfaces\definition.c"

Frequently Asked Questions

1. What is a preprocessor?
   Solution: It is a text substitution program. It modifies the source program as per directives provided by the programmer in the program.

2. Which symbol precedes preprocessor directives?
   Solution: The symbol '#' always precedes a preprocessor directive.

3. Why it is called a preprocessor?
   Solution: Since macro substitution is carried out before the compilation, it is called pre-compiler or preprocessor.

4. Can macros be nested?
   Solution: Yes macros can be nested.

5. Can macros create syntax or semantic errors?
   Solution: Yes carelessly written macros can generate series of syntax, semantic and logical errors.

6. What is the delimiter for macro arguments?
   Solution: Comma (',') is used to separate the arguments of a macro.

7. Where can a preprocessor directive be defined?
   Solution: A preprocessor directive be defined at the beginning of a program.

8. Which operator is used for string concatenation in macros?
   Solution: The '##' operator is used for concatenation of strings in macros.

9. What are the application areas of conditional compilation?
   Solution: These are:
   a. To compile different parts of a program for different operating systems.
   b. To compile a single source code into two different programs.

10. What is the directive for conditional compilation?
    Solution: The `#ifdef` directive is used for conditional compilation.

Test Your Skills

1. What is the output of the following program?

```
# include <stdio.h>
# define add(x)   x+10
main()
 {
  int val1,val2=5;

  val1 = add (++val2);
  printf ("\n %d", val1);
 }
```

Solution: 16

2. What is the output of the following program?

```
# include <stdio.h>

# define dec(x)    --x

main()
 {
  int val1,val2=5;

  val1 = dec (++val2);
  printf («\n %d», val1);
 }
```

Solution: 4

3. What is the output of the following program?

```
# include <stdio.h>

# define dec(x) --x

main()
 {
  int val1,val2=5;

  val1 = dec(val2++);
  printf ("\n %d", val1);
 }
```

Solution: This gives a compilation error because the macro will expand to `--val2++` as `--val2` gives `rvalue` and `(--val2)++` requires `lvalue`.

4. What is the output of the following program?

```
# include <stdio.h>
# define add(x) x+5
# define dec(x)   --x + add(x)

main()
 {
  int val1,val2=5;

  val1 = dec(val2);
  printf («\n %d», val1);
 }
```

Solution: 13

5. What is the output of the following program?

```
# include <stdio.h>
# define add(x) x+x

main()
 {
  int val1=5,val2;

  val2 = add(val1++);
  printf ("\n %d  %d", val1, val2);
 }
```

Solution: 7 10

6. What is the output of the following program?

```
# include <stdio.h>
# define add(x) x+x
main()
 {
  int val1=5,val2;
  #ifdef test
    val2 = add(val1);
  #else
    val2 = add(--val1);
  #endif
  printf («\n %d  %d», val1, val2);
 }
```

Solution: 3 6

7. What is the output of the following program?

```
# include <stdio.h>

# define mult(x, y)       x*y
```

```
main()
{
 int val1 = 5, val2 =10, val3;

 val3 = mult(val1+2, val2-3);
 printf ("\n Result =%d",val3);
}
```

Solution: 22

8. What is output of the following program?

```
# include <stdio.h>

#if var == 0
int val1 =111;
#endif
main()
  {
      int val2 = 5;
      printf ("\n %d %d", val1, val2);
  }
```

Solution: 111 5 (Hint: undeclared variables are treated by the preprocessor as having contents equal to 0).

INDEX

Symbols

0-based indexing 332
1-based indexing 332
1's complement 74, 250
2's complement 75
define directive 589

A

Absorptive laws 95
Accumulator 9
ACSL 118
Actual parameters 472
Address bus 8
Address decoder 29
Address of operator 435
Address pins 28
Algebra of logic 92
Alphabetical order 541
Alphanumeric keypad 42
Amplitude 150
Amplitude modulation 161
Analog signals 154
AND gate 104
Anomaly detection 141
Append operation 562
Application layer 170
Application software 125
Archival files 540
Arguments 547
Arithmetic operators 226
Arithmetic and logical unit 9
Arithmetic unit 4
ARPANET 173
Array 331
Array of pointers 448
Array of strings 373
Array of structures 404
Array parameters 482
Arrow operator 451
ASCII 79
Assembler 112
Assembly language 111
Assignment operator 205
Asymmetric multiprocessing 132
ATM 170
Authentication 195
Authorization 195
Auto specifier 495
AVA virtual machine 120

B

Backbone network 177
Backside bus 34
Backslash character constant 217
Backup files 540
Bandwidth 153
Base-2 system 59
Base band 157
Base station 182
Basic input/output system 39
Batch processing system 131
BCD 79
Binary instruction 111
Binary interface 124
Binary search 342
Bitwise operators 245
Bitwise shift operators 246
Block of code 259
Blue-ray disk 21
BNC port 164
Boolean algebra 92
 postulates of 94
 theorems of 95
Boolean expression 260
Boolean operator 93
Boot sector virus 137
`Break` statement 287
Bridges (data link relay) 178
Broad band 157
Bubble inkjet technology 51
Bubble sort 356
Buffer cache 143
Bus 7, 28
bus based computer architecture 7
Byte 6, 13

C

Cache 12, 16
Cache hierarchy 36
Call by reference 472
Call by value 472
Canonical term 97
Card readers 132
Case sensitive 205
Cathode ray tube 55
Cell global identity 182
Central processing unit 6
Chain printers 49
Character printers 49
Chipset 37
Chronological order 541
Circuit switching 171
Cladding 157
Client server model 181
Coaxial cable 157
COBOL 113
Code division multiple access 183
Collisions 166
Column major order 369
Command interpreter 144
Comma operator 242
Comment 215
Communication 135, 149
Communication channel 155
Compact disk 21
Compiler 113
Complement 75
Complex expressions 241
Complex instruction set computer 31
Compound assignment operators 244
Compound statement 259
Compute 4
Computer 4
Computer network 149
Computer virus 136
Computer worm 140
Concurrent programming languages 119

Conditional compilation 596
Conditional directive 596
Conditional operator 234
Console I/O 544
Constant 209
Const correct 209
`Continue` statement 287
Control bus 8
Control pins 28
Control unit 4, 8
Cookie 192
Co-processor 33
Core 157
Co-sequential 570
Count controlled loop 283
CPU clock 10
CPU cycle 11
Cracker 193
CSMP 118
Cursor 45
Cyber law 196
Cylinder 19, 20

D

Daisy wheel printer 50
Dangling `else` problem 266
Dangling pointer 441
Data 3
Data bus 8
Data cache 36
Data communication 149
Data link layer 169
Data pins 28
Data security 197
Data structures 201
Data types 201
- character data type 203
- floating point data type 203
- integer data type 202

Datum 3
Debugging 504
Declaration 208
Deduction method 95
Delay loop 287
Delimiter 259
Delimiter for macro 599
Demodulator 162
De Morgan's theorems 95
Deterministic loops 276
Device driver 143
Digital computer 24
Digital signal processor 45
Digital signals 155
Digital video disk 21
Digitizer 46
Direct access file 542
Direct access storage devices 20
Direct files 576
Directive 589
Dirty data 17
Divide and conquer 342
Dividend 89
Divisor 89
DNS server 192
Domain names 190
Dot matrix printers 49
Dot operator 402
`do-while` loop 279
Drop cable 167
Drum printers 49
Dual in-line memory modules 15
Duality principle 96
Dummy parameters 472
Dynamic allocation 452
Dynamic RAM 12
Dynamic variables 453

E

EBCDIC 79
ECAP 118
Eighth generation microprocessors 35
Electrically erasable programmable read-only memory 16
Electromagnetic signals 164
Electromagnetic waves 150
Electromechanical mouse 45
Electronic data processing 542
E-mail 185
Empty loops 287
Encapsulation 117
End of a file 548
`enum` definition 412
Enumerated data types 412
Enumeration constants 417
Erasable programmable read-only memory 15
ERNET 173
Escape sequence 217
Exclusive NOR gate 105
Expansion slot 39
Exponent 77, 204
Extern specifier 497

F

Fall-through 269
Fault tolerant 167
Fiber optic modem 162
Field 539
Field width specifiers 215
Fifth generation languages 121
File opening modes 546
File organization 542
File scope 494
File system 143
File transfer protocol 175
File virus 136
First generation languages 120
First generation microprocessors 32
Fixed point representation 74
Flash memory 23
Floating point number 203
Floppy disks 20
`For` loop 283
Format specifier 213
Formatted file I/O operations 554
FORTRAN 113
Fourth generation languages 121
Fourth generation microprocessors 33
Frame buffer 54
Frame relay 170
Frequency 150, 152
Frequency division multiplexing 163
Frequency modulation 161
Front side bus 38
Full-duplex 155
Function 201, 466
- function body 467
- function call 201, 469

function keys 42
function libraries 504
Function prototype 468
Function scope 494

G

Gateways (Level 7 relays) 180
G bits 183
Global system for mobile communication 182
Global variables 472
`goto` statement 294
GPSS 118
GSM 182
Guided media 150

H

Hacker 193
Half-duplex 155
Hard copy 48
Hardware 6
Hardware abstraction layer 146
Hash function 576
Hexadecimal number 70
Hierarchy of memory 12
High-level languages 113
Hit 16
Home page 186
Honeypots 141
Hub 167
Hyperlinks 188
Hypertext 186
Hypertext mark-up language 186
Hyper threading 34

I

Idempotent laws 95
Identifiers 205
`if-else` if ladder 266
`if-else` statement 262
`if` statement 259
Impact printer 48
Implementation 117
Increment and decrement operators 228
Indexed sequential file 542
Index hole 20
Indirection operator 436
Infix operators 93
Information 3, 538
Infrared transmission 159
Inheritance 117
Ink-jet printer 51
Input buffer 311
Input device 41
Input/output cycle 11
Insertion sort 360
Instruction cache 36
Instruction cycle 10
Instruction execution operation 11
Instruction fetch operation 10
Instruction register 9
Intel 4004 27
Intel 8085 27
Intelligent device electronics 39
Interface 117
Internet 149
Internet protocol 174
Internet protocol suite 174
Interpreter 114
I/O functions 544
I/O operations 310
ISCII 79
ISO layers 168
Iteration 276

J

Jacket 157
Job control language 131
Joystick 47

K

Kernel 143
Keyboard 41

L

L1 cache 17
L2 cache 17, 34
L3 cache 35
Laser 21
Laser printer 52
Layered architecture 143
Letter quality printers 49
Light emitting diode 45, 55
Linear bus topology 165
Linear search 338
Line printer 48
Linked list 440
Linker 504
Linux 144
Liquid crystal display 55
Literal 210, 338
Loader 584
Local area network (LAN) 164
Locality of reference 16
Local scope 493
Local variables 472
Logic 92
Logical bomb 140
Logical operators 58, 92, 226
Logical unit 4
Logic gate 104
Long integer 203
Look aside cache architecture 16
Loop 276
Loop control variable 283
Low-level I/O 544
Low-level languages 112
l value 208

M

Machine cycle 10
Machine instruction 111
Macro 589
macro definition 590, 591
macro expansion 590
macro name 590
macro processor 579
Magnetic disks 17
Magnetic ink character recognition 42
Magnetic tapes 17
Mainframe computers 25
Malware (malicious software) 135
Mantissa 78, 204
Manual filing system 542
Mark sensing 44
Master file 540
Maths processor 33
Maxterm 97
Memory address register 9
Memory bleeding 455

Memory cells 13
Memory cycle 11
Memory data register 9
Memory leak 456
MEND 579
Metal oxide semiconductor technology 27
Microcomputer 25
Microkernel architecture 147
Microprocessor 25, 27
Microwave transmission 158
Middle-level language 202
Mini-computers 25
Minterm 97
Minuend 86
Miss 16
Mnemonic 338
Mobile system 182
Modem 162
Modulation 161
Modulator 162
Module 210
Motherboard 37
Mouse 44
Multicore microprocessors 35
Multidimensional array 368
Multiplexer 162
Multiple zone recording 18
Multiplicand 88
Multiplier 88
Multiprocessing 132
Multiprocessor computer systems 132
Multiprogramming 129
Multitasking 35, 129
Multithreading 35
Multiuser systems 128

N

NAND gate 104
Nested structures 408
Network bandwidth 140
Network layer 169
Network operating system 134
New master file 570
Nibble 59
Non-deterministic loops 276
Non-impact printers 51
NOR gate 104
Normalized number 78
NOT gate 104
Numeric keypad 42

O

Object 117
Object oriented programming 117
OCR standard 43
Octal number 67
Old master file 570
On-chip cache 17
Op-code 10
Op-code table 112
Open system interconnect 168
Operands 10
Operating system 124
Operator precedence 238
Optical character recognition 43
Optical disks 17, 20
Optical fiber 157
Optical mark reader 43
Optical mouse 45
Ordinal values 417
OR gate 104
Output buffer 311
Output unit 7

P

Packet 172
Packet switching 171
Parallel processing 133
PARAM 25
Parameter list 468
Parity bit 81
PASCAL 117
Pen drive 22
Penrams 17
Pentium 33
Periodic dumping 194
Peripheral connect interface 39
Phase modulation 161
Phishing 135
Physical address 208
Physical layer 169
Physical relay 178
Piezoelectric inkjet technology 52
Pipelined processor 33
Pits and lands 21
Pixel 53
Pointer 201, 434
Pointer constant 445
Pointer-to-member operator 451
Pointer variable 436
Pointing device 44
Point-to-point communication 150
Point-to-point protocol 177
Polymorphism 117
Post-test 279
Power-on self-test 39
Preprocessor 589
Presentation layer 170
Pre-test loop 279
Pretexting 135
Primary memory 11
Printer 48
Privacy 195
Privileged mode 146
Problem-oriented language 118
Procedure-oriented language 116
Processor 5
Process scheduler 145
Product of sums 97
Product term 96
Program 5
Program counter 9
Programmable read-only memory 15
Programming language 110
Propositions 92
Protocol 168
Python 120

Q

Quotient 89
QWERTY keyboard 41

R

Radio frequency (RF) transmission 158
Random access memory (RAM) 6, 14
Random scan 54

Raster scan display 53
Read only memory (ROM) 6, 15
Record 539
Record construct 400
Recursion 498
Reduced instruction set computer 32
Reference file 540
Registers 9
Register variables 497
Relational operator 226
Relative file organization 577
Remainder 59, 68, 89, 227
Remote login TELNET 176
Repeater 158, 164
Report file 540
Resource manager 126
Resources 125
Return statement 472
Reusability of code 504
Reusable objects 117
Ring topology (loop network) 166
RJ-45 port 164
Routers (network relay) 179
Row major order 369
RS-232 C interface 162

S

Sandbox 142
Satellite communication 159
Scope of a variable 492
Scope rules 494
Scope rules of variables 492
Scroll wheel 46
Secondary memory 11
Second generation languages 121
Second generation microprocessors 33
Secrecy 195
Sectors 18
Selection sort 353
Self documentation 594
Sequential file 542
Server 25
Session layer 170
Seventh generation microprocessor 34
Short integer 203
Short message service (SMS) 185
Signature detection 141
Simple mail transfer protocol 176
Simplex 155
Single in-line memory modules 15
Single user mono programming system 127
Sinks 543
Sixth generation microprocessors 34
Size of operator 242
Snarf operation 17
Snoop operation 17
Social engineering 135
Socket 37
Socket 7 37
Socket 8 34
Software 6
Software maintenance 505
Sort file 540
Source code 113
Sources 543
Special characters 202
Stale data 17
Standard input device 310
Standard output device 310
Star topology 167
Statement label 295
Statement terminator 211
Static 495
Static RAM 12
Static variable 453, 496
Storage class 495
Storage class specifiers 495
Store and forward policy 173
Stored program computer 6
Stream 543
Stream I/O 544
String constant 210
Structures 400
Stylus 46
Subprogram 465
Subscript 482
Subtrahend 86
Subversive code 135
Sum of products 97
Sum term 96
Super computers 25
Switch statement 268
`Default` 269
Symbol 42, 58, 338
Symbol table 112
Symmetric multiprocessing 132
System bus 8
System software 125

T

Tablet 47
Target code 113
Task 129
TCP/IP 174
Text substitution program 589
Third generation languages 121
Third generation microprocessors 33
Thread 35, 133
Time division multiplexing 163
Time period 150
Token 205
Topology 165
Tracks 18
Transaction file 540, 570
Transcriptor 112
Transistor 58
Transmission control protocol 175
Transmission medium 150
Transport layer 169
Tree network 167
Trojan horse 139
Truncation 231
Truth table 92
TUSSI 80
Twisted-pair wires 156
Type casting 240
Type conversion 240
Typematic 42
Typematic rate 42

U

Unary operator 93, 228
Unconditional transfer of control 294

Unformatted file I/O functions 546
Unguided media 150
Unicode 80
Union 418
Uniprocessor 134
Universal serial bus 23
UNIX 143
Unsigned integer. 203
Updation of a file 570
USB port 39
User defined data types 410
User header file 599

V

Value at address operator 436
Variable 92, 206
Vector scan 54
Very small aperture terminals 160
Virtual machine 124
Visual display unit 48
Von neumann architecture 5
Von-neumann bottleneck 6

W

`while` loop 277
Wide area network 170
Wired media 150
Wireless in local loop 184
Wireless mouse 46
Word size 28
Write protect notch 20

X

X-25 protocol 170
XNOR gate 105
XOR gate 105

Z

Zero in force (ZIF) socket 37